Commentary on the Metaphysics of Aristotle

Library of Living Catholic Thought

VOLUME I

ST. THOMAS AQUINAS

Commentary on the Metaphysics of Aristotle

TRANSLATED BY

JOHN P. ROWAN

PROFESSOR OF PHILOSOPHY
DUQUESNE UNIVERSITY

Library of Living Catholic Thought

VOLUME I

HENRY REGNERY COMPANY
Chicago 1961

Nihil Obstat: R. W. Schmidt, S.J., *Censor Deputatus*

Imprimatur: Albert Cardinal Meyer, S.T.D., S.S.L.
Archiepiscopus Chicagiensis, March 29, 1961

© Henry Regnery Company 1961

Manufactured in the United States of America

Library of Congress Catalog Card Number 61-16878

CONTENTS

INTRODUCTION

I—THE TRANSLATION

The following translation of St. Thomas' *Commentary on the Metaphysics of Aristotle* includes a translation of the version of Aristotle's text that is found in the printed editions of the Commentary now in use and commonly thought to be the one employed by St. Thomas. The inclusion of a translation of this version appeared necessary from the very beginning for two reasons. First, since the Commentary is a detailed analysis and exposition of the text of Aristotle, it becomes fully intelligible only in relation to the text, to which it makes constant reference as its point of departure. Second, since the version frequently departs in some measure from the original, it would not have proved feasible to employ one of the modern English translations [1] based on the Greek.

The translation both of the Commentary and of the version of Aristotle is based on the edition of Raymund M. Spiazzi, O.P. This edition is fundamentally that of M. R. Cathala, O.P., with emendations.[2] Some assistance in clearing up obscurities, such as typographical errors and the like, was obtained by consulting the edition of Parma [3] and that of Vivès.[4] However, the usefulness of these editions in this regard proved to be limited inasmuch as both the edition of Vivès and that of Cathala use Parma as their basic text.[5]

Since the Cathala-Spiazzi edition is not a critical one, it was necessary in certain instances to alter the reading of the text. Where such alterations are made and are not obvious, they are indicated in a footnote, and the reason for making them is stated when such justification appears necessary. The more important variations between the Greek text as given in Bekker and the Latin version of Aristotle's text are also indicated in footnotes. If the reader wishes to make comparisons between the version, the Greek text, and the English translations, he will find the Bekker reference numbers given at the beginning of each lesson useful in locating the passages in which he is interested.

---

[1] For such translations see: MacMahon, John H., *The Metaphysics of Aristotle*, London: H. G. Bohn, 1857; G. Bell and Sons, 1889; 1896; 1912.—Ross, William D. (Oxford trans.), *Metaphysica*, in *The Works of Aristotle*, vol. VIII, Oxford: Clarendon Press, 1908; 2nd ed., 1928; and in *The Student's Oxford Aristotle*, vol. IV, London, New York: Oxford Univ. Press, 1942; and in *The Basic Works of Aristotle*, pp. 689-926, ed. by Richard McKeon, New York: Random House, 1941.—Taylor, Thomas, *The Metaphysics of Aristotle*, London: Davis, Wilks and Taylor, 1801.—Tredennik, Hugh, *The Metaphysics* (Greek text with Eng. trans.), 2 vols. (In Loeb Classical Library) London (W. Heinemann) and New York: G. P. Putman, 1933-1935, 2nd ed. revised, 2 vols., Cambridge, Mass.: Harvard Univ. Press, 1945.—Hope, Richard, *Aristotle's Metaphysics*, New York: Columbia Univ. Press, 1952.

[2] *In Duodecim Libros Metaphysicorum Aristotelis Expositio*, editio iam a M. R. Cathala, O.P., exarata retractatur cura et studio P. Fr. Raymundi M. Spiazzi, O.P.: Turin, 1950. This is referred to hereafter as the Cathala-Spiazzi edition. For a list of the emendations of Spiazzi (based on other editions and some manuscripts) see G. Ducoin, "St. Thomas commentateur d'Aristote," *Archives de Philosophie*, XX (1957), 84, n. 13.

[3] *Sancti Thomae Aquinatis Opera Omnia*, 25 vols., Parma: Fiaccadori, 1852-1873.

[4] *Doctoris Angelici Divi Thomae Aquinatis Opera Omnia*, vols. XXIV and XXV, edited by S. E. Fretté and P. Maré, Paris: Vivès, 1889.

[5] See A. Mansion, "Sur le texte de la version latine médiévale de la Métaphysique et de la Physique d'Aristote dans les éditions de Saint Thomas d'Aquin," in *Revue Néo-Scolastique de Philosophie*, XXXIV (1932), 67.

The translation does not pretend to be a transliteration of the original. Since strict adherence to this method very often results in the use of *latinisms* and word structures that are foreign to the English reader, it seemed advisable, if the thought of the original was to be presented in as accurate and readily understandable a form as possible, to render the Latin as idiomatically and meaningfully as current English usage permits. Where the English words and phrases used to translate technical Latin terms are not those commonly employed in presenting the thought of St. Thomas and of Aristotle, the reader will find this indicated either by a footnote or by giving the Latin in parenthesis after the word or phrase in question. Throughout the whole translation the aim has been to produce as faithful and accurate a rendition of St. Thomas' work as circumstances permit. The extent to which this has been achieved will be left for the critics to decide.

The reader will find that the form of the introductory statements customarily used by St. Thomas to designate the passages of Aristotle's text which he is about to explain, has been abbreviated. This has been done to avoid repetition and simplify the reading; for example, such statements as, "Then when Aristotle says, 'Animals by nature (2) . . . ,'" and, "Then when he says, 'Furthermore, it is necessary (126) . . . ,'" have been shortened to read, "Animals by nature (2)," and "Furthermore, it is necessary (126)."

The sections of the Commentary are indicated by numbers preceded by C, and are the same as those originally established by Cathala. Numbers not preceded by C designate the sections of the version of Aristotle, and are identical with those given by Spiazzi in his revision of the Cathala edition. The use of such numbers, singly or in combination, throughout the text, simplifies the matter of references and cross references where such are specified by the author, or where they would otherwise seem to be helpful. Thus in the case (267:C 489) the first number designates the section of the version of Aristotle, and the second, the section of St. Thomas' Commentary on this passage.

II—THE NATURE OF THE COMMENTARY

A commentary or exposition of the thought of some writer constituted one of the basic methods of teaching employed in medieval schools. Medieval writers inherited the commentary as a pedagogical instrument from two sources, the Fathers and Arabic writers, both of whom adopted it in turn from a common source—the literary and scientific writings of the last period of Greek thought. In the West the commentary took various forms. One type which appears as early as the sixth century is that employed by Boethius in certain of his writings, for example, his expositions of the *Categories* and the *De Interpretatione* of Aristotle. Here a portion of the original text in translation is given first, and then an explanation of its content in simpler form. Glosses upon a text constituted another form of commentary, and this became a popular form of exposition from the ninth to the twelfth century. During the twelfth and thirteenth centuries the West was introduced to the thought of antiquity by way of translations from the Greek and the Arabic. The latter were more numerous and presumably the first to appear,[6] and it was through them that Europe first came in contact with

[6] Whether translations were first made from the Greek or from the Arabic has been a matter of dispute among scholars. For a brief survey of the various opinions in this issue, and the probable source of translation of certain of Aristotle's works, see Maurice de Wulf, *History of Medieval Philosophy* (trans. from the 5th French edition by E. C. Messenger), London and New York: Longmans, Green & Co., 1926, vol. I, pp. 70-75; 237-246.

a large part of Aristotle's thought of which it had heretofore been ignorant. While there is ample evidence that these early translations extended to certain of Aristotle's works, and the *Metaphysics* was one of these,[7] the translations for the most part were of summaries or paraphrases of his writings, such as those composed by Alfarabi and Algazel, and especially the *Kitâb assifâ* of Avicenna, which is his principal work and a sort of philosophic encyclopedia covering the fields of logic, physics, metaphysics and mathematics. The method of paraphrasing was imitated by Latin writers since it provided a simple means of presenting and popularizing Aristotle's views. St. Albert the Great, for example, made an extensive use of it in his "adapting Aristotle for the use of the Latin races." [8]

In addition to the paraphrase the West was also introduced to a more technical form of commentary, a more systematic method of analysis and explanation, which came to be known as the *lectio,* and was so named because it consisted fundamentally of a number of *readings* or *lessons* (*lectiones*) of the text of an authority, accompanied by a literal explanation. This method of procedure, the literal commentary, eventually took precedence over the other forms of exposition and came to be widely used during the thirteenth and fourteenth centuries. Its originator is Averroes (The Commentator), who utilized it in what are called his "major commentaries." [9] In these the text of Aristotle is given paragraph by paragraph, and the views, intentions and expressions of the author exposed in detail.

Considering the importance of Aristotle for the West, and the need for a true understanding of his thought, it is not surprising that St. Thomas should have adopted the method of literally commenting upon his writings in preference to the procedure of paraphrasing, which had previously been used. He adopted it as "a new way of treating the text," as Ptolemy of Lucca points out,[10] because it provided him with the best critical instrument for keeping in contact with the original and interpreting it accurately. The influence of Averroes upon St. Thomas in his commentaries generally, and in his exposition of the *Metaphysics* in particular, cannot be denied; and many interesting comparisons can be drawn between the expositions of the two men; for example, even in the matter of the divisions of the text into lessons, St. Thomas is evidently following The Commentator.

While it is clear that St. Thomas' primary aim is to explain literally what Aristotle said, it should also be noted that, in keeping with his respect for authority, he does not hesitate to "interpret" Aristotle, when the occasion demands. Attention must be drawn also to the fact that, since St. Thomas is principally concerned with the advancement of truth, he sometimes proceeds to draw out what he feels is implicit in Aristotle's doctrines. In so doing he introduces his own personal views into his explanations inasmuch as he sees a fundamental agree-

[7] The decree of 1215 in the University of Paris prohibiting the use of certain works of Aristotle mentions specifically his books on natural philosophy and metaphysics, together with such commentaries or summaries of them as were used in explaining their content. See Denifle and Chatelain, *Chartularium Universitatis Parisiensis,* Paris, 1889-1891, vol. I, p. 78, n. 20.— Alfred of Sareshel (Alfredus Anglicus) cites the *Metaphysics* (*littera Boethii*) in his *De motu cordis* (1217).

[8] See Albert's *Physics,* lib. I, tr. 1, c. 1. In keeping with this guiding idea he made a complete paraphrase of Aristotle.

[9] For a brief description of the three methods of treating a text used by Averroes (the simple paraphrase, middle commentary and major commentary); his role as originator of the literal commentary, and his connection with St. Thomas, see Leon Gauthier, *Ibn Rochd* (*Averroes*): Presses Univ. de France, Paris, 1948, p. 16.

[10] "Quodam singulari et novo modo tradendi utebatur," in *Hist. Eccles.,* XXII, c. 24.

ment between them and those of the Philosopher. In the same spirit he sometimes finds it necessary to disagree with the interpretations of other commentators, chiefly those of Avicenna and of Averroes,[11] when he feels that they fail to grasp the thought of the master on some specific point of doctrine. But he can also use the opinions of those whom he has criticised in other respects,[12] when it is evident that their interpretations add something to the understanding of Aristotle's teachings.

In his role as commentator St. Thomas makes a masterful use, both of the many dialectical instruments which Aristotle puts at the disposal of his readers in his methodological treatises, as well as of those developed by medieval logicians.[13] In this respect alone the Commentary is an outstanding piece of work. Since Aristotle's text is fundamentally an inquiry or investigation into problems relevant to a specific subject matter, conducted along the lines recommended in the *Analytics* and *Topics,* it lends itself admirably to the kind of treatment to which St. Thomas subjects it. Aristotle's text might be described as an exercise in dialectic aimed at ascertaining truth in a certain sphere, and whose logical structure the reader is aware of only vaguely if at all. But in the treatment of the Commentary this structure is laid bare in order to better evaluate the conclusions to which it leads. For the medievals as for Aristotle a knowledge of method provided at once both the tools necessary for scientific research and the criteria, in large part at least, for judging the value of such research.

With this in mind St. Thomas proceeds from the very start to make evident with great precision both the content of Aristotle's thought and the process which he uses in formulating and presenting it. He divides and subdivides the text to reveal its essential structure, and within these divisions he follows step by step Aristotle's analyses of his predecessor's opinions and his evaluation of them; his examination of the various meanings of terms; the kind of arguments that are being used, and their demonstrative or probable character in the light of the premises from which they are derived.

The divisions of the text, which are given in the Commentary at the beginning of each lesson, serve to break up the passages to be commented upon into their constituent parts or members, thereby presenting the student with a schema that enables him to proceed in an orderly way to an understanding of the discussion contained therein. Sometimes the divisions given in one lesson will extend to subsequent lessons when the latter have an essential connection with it. There are also cases where the division extends to the work at large, indicating the issues dealt with in other books. Thus in Book III, after explaining the *aporiae* or difficulties which Aristotle raises, St. Thomas notes the respective books in which they will be solved; and again in Book XI, lesson 1, his division refers not only to certain issues that have yet to be treated, and where this will occur, but also designates topics that have already been discussed in previous books.

In his treatment of the text St. Thomas exhibits none of the critical and historical spirit that is so characteristic of our own era and began with the advances in philological studies and historical methodology made in the nineteenth cen-

[11] For example, in C 286, C 1467-8, C 2418, he considers Averroes to be in error; and in C 556-8, C 894, C 1981, C 2559, he criticises the views of Avicenna.

[12] In C 345, C 442, C 1442 f., he notes what Averroes adds to an understanding of the text; and in C 46, C 766-9, C 1165, C 1469, he makes use of certain views of Avicenna.

[13] For a general picture of the knowledge and use of Aristotle's logical works during the thirteenth century, and of the developments in medieval logic, see Philotheus Boehner, O.F.M., *Medieval Logic,* Univ. Chicago Press, 1952; and J. T. Clark, S.J., *Conventional Logic and Modern Logic,* Woodstock College Press: Woodstock, Maryland, 1952.

tury. This does not mean that he is lacking in historical sense or in critical ability (quite the reverse is true), but that he does not have at his disposal the variety of instruments in these fields that we now possess. His only method of ascertaining the true sense of Aristotle's text was to consult the various versions available to him. If he saw any development in Aristotle's thought, such as might be suggested by the text, and of the kind outlined in the works of modern scholars,[14] he gives no indication of it. Neither does he remark on the possibility of the various books which comprise the total work having been composed as distinct treatises at different times and combined into a whole by later hands. For him the work has the appearance of a single treatise whose parts have been skilfully knit together with the ultimate aim of exposing the nature of entity, its properties and causes.

III—RESEARCHES ON THE COMMENTARY

The most important issues with which scholars have been concerned in the matter of the Commentary are (1) the period of its composition and date of completion; (2) the version or versions upon which St. Thomas based his exegesis, and the exact status of the printed version now in use; (3) the history of certain of the books commented upon, and the possibility of an earlier and later writing. These issues have been investigated at length, and much progress has been made despite the obstacles that have had to be faced. However, the tentative character of many of the solutions proposed for them indicates that considerable work yet remains to be done.

One of the main obstacles in the way of attaining definitive answers is the state of the printed editions and the manuscripts of this work with which investigators have had to deal. Both are admittedly imperfect, containing errors of various kinds. It is quite possible too that the manuscripts representing the versions of Aristotle's text which St. Thomas used in his exposition are not yet completely known. There is also the matter of the interpretation which should be given to the passages in various works [15] which refer in some way to the Commentary or to the versions of Aristotle, and have been used as evidence by one or other investigator in support of his position regarding some phase of this work. These passages are often obscure, ambiguous and perhaps even inaccurate, and so have led in many instances to different and even contradictory hypotheses.

Although little if anything has been published on the errors to be found in the manuscripts, sufficient information is at hand regarding the kind of inaccuracies one can expect to meet in the printed editions, and the reasons for their occurrence. In this matter one can cite the brief article of A. Mansion, dealing with the Commentaries on the *Physics* and *Metaphysics*,[16] and the article of L. W. Keeler, S.J., which, while it deals specifically with one of the *Opuscula* of St. Thomas,[17] is nevertheless of importance for the *Commentary on the Metaphysics*.

Mansion draws attention to the role that simple negligence has played in falsifying the text of the Commentary, and uses as an example a passage at the

[14] For examples of philological and historical studies devoted to the *Metaphysics*, see Werner Jaeger's, *Enstehungsgeschichte der Metaphysik des Aristoteles*, Berlin, 1912; and *Aristoteles, Grundlegung einer Geschichte seiner Entwicklung*, Berlin, 1923 (trans. into English by Richard Robinson: Oxford, Clarendon Press, 2nd ed., 1948).

[15] Some of these passages are from other works of St. Thomas, and some are from the writings of his predecessors, contemporaries and successors.

[16] "Sur le texte . . . " *Rev. Néo-Scol.*, XXXIV (1932), 66-67.

[17] "Editions of the *De Unitate Intellectus*," *Gregorianum*, XVII (1936), 55-62.

beginning of Book I, corresponding to Bekker 980a 27-28, which, rendered into Latin, reads, "Animalia quidem igitur natura sensum habentia fiunt." The phrase, as he points out, is given in the editions of Venice 1519, Rome 1570, Venice 1603, and Antwerp 1612, but is omitted in the edition of Parma 1866, and therefore also in the edition of Vivès 1889 and in that of Cathala 1915 (although corrected in the 1926 and following editions), since both of the latter employ Parma as their basic text without any apparent revision. Mansion's conclusion is that in all probability there are many other such errors in the printed editions (which has been borne out by more recent studies), and that an examination of the manuscripts upon which these editions have been based will reveal inaccuracies of a similar kind.

Father Keeler's work reveals another and different kind of error in his descriptions of the procedures followed by the editors of the sixteenth century, whose editions have been employed in printings down to our own time. The outstanding weakness of early editors, he notes, consisted in their "undue readiness" to take all sorts of liberties with the text. Thus Paulus Soncinas did not hesitate to substitute certain passages from humanist translations of Aristotle's text for those in medieval Latin when the latter appeared obscure or were too strange or archaic to suit his taste. Thus in the case of St. Thomas' exposition of the *De Generatione Animalium* of Aristotle, Soncinas substituted passages of the *nova translatio* of this work for certain parts of the *media translatio,* which seems to have been the one that St. Thomas employed. The same kind of procedure is also characteristic of the work of Anthony Pizamanus, who, in his edition of the *De Unitate Intellectus,* is responsible for what Keeler calls the "scandal" connected with St. Thomas' supposed assertion that he had seen certain books of Aristotle, fourteen in number, which treat of separate substances but had not yet been translated into Latin (presumably the fourteen books of the *Metaphysics*). Keeler's researches reveal that there are no manuscripts that contain the reading *numero XIV,* but that all having a numerical reference read *numero X,* while one (St. Genevieve 238) omits the words in question altogether. Apparently Pizamanus, who was following an earlier edition of Soncinas, which omits any mention of the number of books, considered this a lacuna and supplied the reading *numero XIV* on the basis of a reading found in another edition of this work prepared by a certain Didascalus, which edition he was also following. The issue is significant for the history of the Commentary inasmuch as one thesis of D. Salman, O.P., an investigator in this field, depends on the assumption that the reading *numero XIV* is correct.

Difficulties of this kind will disappear only when critical editions have been made of all of St. Thomas' writings. In the meantime they will continue to make the undertaking of translation and historical investigation extremely difficult.

1. *The Date of the Commentary*

The extensive researches that have been made into the history and chronology of St. Thomas' writings would indicate that the commentaries on Aristotle were composed between the years 1266-1272.[18] Some were at least begun while St. Thomas resided in Italy, and some were completed at Paris after his return there to teach for the second time. The *Commentary on the Metaphysics* is generally considered to belong to this second group. However, while there seems to be

---

[18] See, for example, M. Grabmann, *Die Werke des hl. Thomas von Aquin,* 2nd ed., Münster, i. W., 1931, pp. 262 ff.; and A. Walz, O.P., *San Tommaso d'Aquino,* Rome, 1945, p. 117.

agreement as to the proximate date of its completion, both the time and place of its origin still remains a matter of dispute. One can appreciate the complexity of the problem and the tentative character of many of the solutions proposed for it only by surveying the studies that have been made.

One of the earliest dates given for the composition of the Commentary is that found in the account of St. Thomas' life and writings by Ptolemy of Lucca,[19] who ascribes it to the pontificate of Urban IV. According to Ptolemy, St. Thomas commented during this period upon the whole of philosophy, both moral and natural, and "especially upon the Ethics and Metaphysics." This would mean that the Commentary was written between 1261 and 1264. Ptolemy's authority in this matter has been questioned by M. Grabmann because of a discrepancy in the dates involved, inasmuch as St. Thomas resided at Rome from 1265 to 1267, whereas Urban IV reigned from 1261 to 1264.[20] However, P. Mandonnet has argued in favor of Ptolemy's statement on the grounds that, since one of these periods immediately succeeds the other, and since St. Thomas did teach at the court of Urban IV at Orvieto, which is adjacent to Rome, Ptolemy was very likely thinking of the whole period from 1261 to 1267.[21]

As early as 1921 Grabmann expressed the view that the Commentary could not have been completed before 1265, the date set earlier by Mandonnet,[22] but must have been in the process of composition during 1266. His opinion was based on a reference which St. Thomas makes in Book III, lesson 11 (C 468) to Simplicius' *Commentary on the Categories* of Aristotle, the translation of which was only completed by William of Moerbeke in March 1266, and was the one available to St. Thomas.[23]

In 1925 A. Mansion published his findings to the effect that the work could not have been completed before 1271, but must have reached its final state toward the end of that year or at the beginning of 1272. His decision was based on the date of the translation of Simplicius' *Commentary on the De Coelo* of Aristotle, which was completed by Moerbeke in June 1271. St. Thomas makes three references to this work in Book XII of the Commentary when he sets out to explain the use that Aristotle made of Eudoxus and Calippus in the formation of his astronomical system. Two of these references are paraphrases (C 2573; C 2582), and one is an exact citation (C 2578), and this would have been possible only if he had possessed the translation at the time of writing.[24]

In 1942 T. Deman published his researches on St. Thomas' opinion of Aristotle as an interpreter of Plato, and indicated in this article that the reference to Simplicius' *Commentary on the Categories*, given in Book III of St. Thomas' Commentary, appeared rather to be a reference to Simplicius' *Commentary on the De Coelo*.[25] This conclusion, contrary to that reached earlier by Grabmann, would necessitate putting the writing of Book III sometime after June 1271. But

[19] *Hist. Eccles.*, XXII, c. 24.
[20] "Die Aristoteleskommentare des hl. Thomas von Aquin," in *Mittelalterliches Geistesleben*, vol. I, Munich, 1926, pp. 272-273.
[21] "Saint Thomas d'Aquin, Lecteur à la Curie Romaine," in *Xenia Thomistica*, Rome, 1925, vol. III, pp. 9 ff.
[22] "Des Ecrits Authentiques de Saint Thomas d'Aquin," 2nd ed. Fribourg, 1910.—See his study of lists of works, and conclusion.
[23] *Die echten Schriften des hl. Thomas von Aquin*, in "Beiträge zur Geschichte der Philosophie des Mittelalters," XXII, 1-2: Münster, i. W., 1920, p. 60 (and subsequent editions).
[24] "Pour l'histoire du Commentaire de Saint Thomas sur la Métaphysique," in *Revue Néo-Scolastique de Philosophie*, Louvain, XXVII (1925), 274 ff.
[25] "Remarques critiques de Saint Thomas sur Aristote interprète de Platon," in *Les Sciences Philosophiques et Théologiques*, Paris, 1941-42, pp. 133-148.

granted that this were the case, it would follow that St. Thomas must have composed the whole of his exposition in a much shorter period than the many demands on his time as teacher, scholar and writer would reasonably allow. This has been the view expressed by D. Salman, and on the basis of this and what he considers to be internal evidence supplied by the Commentary and by other writings of St. Thomas, he argues in favor of an earlier writing composed in Italy between 1266 and 1268, and a revision of this made later at Paris between the end of 1270 and the beginning of 1272.[26] He also thinks that Ptolemy's account could simply refer to such a first writing, and that this might have taken the form of a simple *reportatio*.[27] In his opinion the argument for an earlier writing is not invalidated by the evidence summoned in support of a later period of composition, for example, the reference made to Simplicius in Book III, and the mentioning of Books XIII and XIV of Aristotle's work as early as the exposition of Book I, since these could have been added later at the time of revision.[28] In this matter Salman is in agreement with the view expressed earlier by Mansion,[29] and also with that of A. Dondaine, O.P.,[30] although the latter's argument for an earlier date of composition was based on the assumption that the *translatio media* constituted the basic text upon which the Commentary was made, and that the *translatio nova* was employed later when the work was revised.

The researches of F. Pelster, S.J., which have been aimed primarily at establishing the version or versions of Aristotle's text that were used by St. Thomas, deserves special attention in regard to the present problem. Pelster's findings agree with those of other scholars as to the proximate time of completion of the Commentary; and while he admits that the hypothesis of an earlier writing is not impossible, he thinks that such a hypothesis is unnecessary, since what is used as evidence in support of it can be explained in another way,[31] as will be noted later.

From such investigations, then, it appears probable that the Commentary was completed at Paris towards the end of 1271 or at the beginning of 1272, but that the time and place of its origin are still not definitely known. It seems possible that it could have been written in its entirety during St. Thomas' last period at Paris; or that it was begun during his stay in Italy and completed at Paris as a single writing; or that a first writing was composed in Italy, and this subsequently revised at Paris.

2. *The Versions on Which the Commentary Is Based*

In order to give an accurate exposition of the true thought of Aristotle, St. Thomas required a faithful version of the original texts as a basis for his commentaries. The various paraphrases then in vogue could, therefore, hardly serve his purpose. Being merely summaries they neither contained the actual text of Aristotle nor pretended to follow the original order of exposition, but employed

[26] "Saint Thomas et les traductions latines des Métaphysiques d'Aristote," in *Archives d'Histoire Doctrinale et Littéraire du Moyen Age*, VII (1932), 111; see also summary, p. 120.
[27] *Art. cit.*, pp. 110-111.
[28] *Art. cit.*, p. 118.
[29] "Pour l'histoire . . . ," *Rev. Néo-Scol.* (Cited n. 24 above), p. 284. See also "Date de quelques commentaires de St. Thomas sur Aristote," in *Studia Mediaevalia in honorem R. J. Martin, O.P.*, Brussels, 1948, pp. 283-287.
[30] "Saint Thomas et les traductions latines de la Métaphysique d'Aristote," *Bulletin Thomiste* III (1933), 201-204.
[31] F. Pelster, S.J., "Die Uebersetzungen der aristotelischen Metaphysik in den Werken des hl. Thomas von Aquin," *Gregorianum*, XVII (1936), 378.

instead a simpler and more systematic one established by the summarists them-selves. Moreover, they frequently incorporated the views of their composers, views that sometimes made the Philosopher the exponent of doctrines that were often difficult if not impossible to reconcile with the principles of Christian wis-dom. In view of the possibility that Aristotle himself might have something quite different to say, prudence dictated the exclusion of such paraphrases as the start-ing point for a satisfactory exposition.

The translation of certain of Aristotle's works made from the Arabic also proved to have serious defects, and therefore were useful only in a limited way as a point of departure for the exegetical work St. Thomas had in mind. This at least was true of the translation of the *Metaphysics,* which he reputedly knew from the very beginning of his literary career. For one thing it was clearly in-adequate inasmuch as it lacked Books XI, XIII and XIV, and contained only a garbled version of Books I (*A*) and II (α)—Book I being comprised of Book α and part of Book *A* (chapters 5 and 8), and Book II of the remainder of Book *A*. The possibility too of such translations misrepresenting the thought of Aristotle had already been recognized and indicated in the pronouncements prohibiting their use on the part of the Masters and students at the University of Paris, as set forth in the earlier decrees of 1210 and 1215, mentioned above, and in the later decree of 1263.[32] That these versions should be held suspect is not to be wondered at considering the fact that the original works had undergone suc-cessive translations from the Greek to the Syriac, from this to the Arabic, and from this again to the Latin through some vernacular language.[33]

Somewhat the same situation prevailed in the case of certain translations of the *Metaphysics* that were presumably based on the Greek and date from the end of the twelfth or the early years of the thirteenth century. The translation attrib-uted to Boethius (the *littera Boethii*) and another entitled the *translatio vetus* belong to this group. Both of these are incomplete, containing only a small part of the whole.

If the commentaries were to do justice to the real thought of Aristotle, it be-came evident that they would have to be based on complete and faithful trans-lations made from the original; and so it was, as William of Tocco tells us, that, when St. Thomas wrote his expositions on natural philosophy, moral philosophy and metaphysics, "he had these books newly translated so that the genuine thought of Aristotle should be more clearly expressed." [34] The translations of which Wil-liam of Tocco speaks are those of William of Moerbeke, made at the request of St. Thomas himself. For the role that Moerbeke played as Greek translator, and the invaluable assistance that he lent St. Thomas and others in their own work, one can profitably consult the work of M. Grabmann, *Guglielmo di Moerbeke, O.P., Il Traduttore delle Opere di Aristotele* (Rome, 1946). In the matter of the translations of Aristotle, Moerbeke made, in certain instances, a revision of al-ready existing versions, completing them where necessary, and also rendered into Latin certain texts that had not yet been translated. With such works in his possession St. Thomas was able to attain a knowledge of Aristotle superior to that of his predecessors and contemporaries, and give the first faithful ex-plication of his doctrines.

Granted that certain versions of the *Metaphysics* anteceded that of Moerbeke

[32] See F. Van Steenberghen, *Siger de Brabant d'après les oeuvres inédites*, II, 430-490.
[33] See G. Lucquet, "Herman le Dalmate," in *Revue de l'histoire des Religions*, XLIV (1901), 415.
[34] *Vita S. Thomae Aquinatis*, c. 17.

and were known to St. Thomas, the following questions have been raised by scholars in their investigations into the history of his Commentary on this work: Did St. Thomas base his exegesis solely upon the translation of Moerbeke, or did he also make use of these other versions? And if the latter, what versions were involved, and to what extent? Again, is the version of Aristotle now found in the printed editions of the Commentary to be identified with the translation of Moerbeke?

In regard to the version referred to in this last question, some clarification is necessary. As indicated earlier, the printed editions of the Commentary now in use are, for the most part, republications of editions dating from the sixteenth century. In some of these, for example the Parma, one finds at the beginning of each lesson two parallel versions. One is called the *versio antiqua,* and the other the *versio recens.* Since the latter is attributable to Cardinal Bessarion, a humanist of the Renaissance period, it has no bearing on St. Thomas' own work, and therefore is excluded from the present discussion. The *versio antiqua,* on the other hand, is presumably the version of William of Moerbeke, and therefore the one employed by St. Thomas.[35]

Although some of the studies devoted to finding solutions for these questions have not always been in agreement in terms of their results, it would nevertheless appear that we are now in a fair position to understand what actually occurred in the matter of the various versions.

In an article published in 1932, D. Salman outlines for us, by way of an introduction to the results of his own investigations, the discoveries of four scholars who have been chiefly responsible up to his own time for the progress made in the matter of the Latin translations used in the composition of the Commentary.[36] First, there is the work of Monsignor Grabmann, whose researches revealed two manuscripts containing two distinct versions of the *Metaphysics.* One of these, which came to be called the *translatio nova,* was complete, while the other, which was entitled the *metaphysica vetus* or *translatio vetus,* was not, but contained only the first three books and a part of Book IV (up to 1007a 30). The latter was considered to be the work of Boethius, and the former was identified as that of Moerbeke.[37]

In 1917 there appeared a work by B. Geyer which was devoted to a study of the citations from the *Metaphysics* as given in the works of St. Albert the Great and St. Thomas. By comparing the citations of St. Thomas drawn from a work which he referred to as the *littera Boethii* with the corresponding passages in the *vetus,* Geyer concluded that they were one and the same text. Moreover, since St. Thomas refers to the *littera Boethii* even for passages drawn from Books V and XII, Geyer also concluded that this translation, and therefore the *vetus,* which he identified with it, must go as far as Book XII rather than terminate with Book IV.[38] Additional researches, however, have not fulfilled his hope of discovering the whole text. In fact the studies of F. Pelster, published in 1923, revealed eight new manuscripts all terminating in Book IV, which would seem to indicate that the original version itself was incomplete and had under-

[35] This version is the one contained in the Cathala-Spiazzi edition.

[36] "Saint Thomas et les traductions latines des Métaphysiques d'Aristote," *Archives d'Histoire Doctrinale et Littéraire du Moyen Age,* Paris, VII (1932), 85-87.

[37] *Forschungen über die lateinischen Aristotelesübersetzungen des XIII Jahrhunderts* (Beiträge z. Gesch. d. Phil. des Mitt., Münster, XVII, 1916), pp. 105 ff.

[38] "Die Uebersetzungen der aristotelischen Metaphysik, bei Albertus Magnus und Thomas Von Aquin," *Philosophisches Jahrbuch,* XXX (1917), 392 ff.

gone a number of revisions.[39] But since this conclusion fails to account for St. Thomas' references to later books of the *littera Boethii,* Geyer's identification of this version with the *vetus* was considered to be untenable.

The main contribution to this issue made by Pelster in this early study consisted in the discovery of two manuscripts containing a heretofore unknown version in thirteen books (XI being excluded), which he named the *translatio media.* By comparing the citations from the *Metaphysics* in the *Summa Contra Gentiles* with the corresponding passages in the *media,* Pelster concluded that it was this version that St. Thomas had used, and that it must therefore have been known in 1260. This being so, it would have provided one source for the writing of the Commentary, and later investigations proved this to be true. Pelster also indicated that this text was the same as that known and used by St. Albert the Great in his paraphrase of the *Metaphysics,* which contains thirteen books, one corresponding to each of the books in question. Since comparisons also revealed that this version differed widely from the *vetus* but came very close to the *translatio nova,* identified as the work of Moerbeke, Pelster therefore decided that Moerbeke had employed the *media* in composing his own translation, retouching it where necessary in the light of the Greek text, and completing it by translating Book XI into Latin for the first time.

In a subsequent study, published in 1928, M. Birkenmajer added to the complexity of the problem by introducing still another version, whose existence he supported by three new manuscripts that he had discovered. This version, whose date he placed around the middle of the twelfth century, would be older than any of the others, and therefore was called by him the *vetustissima.* It resembled the *littera Boethii* and the *vetus* in being composed of the first three books and a part of the fourth. The *media* he dated earlier than Pelster, maintaining that it was in circulation as early as 1230 or even 1210, although he agreed with Pelster on the *nova* as the work of Moerbeke. The *vetus* he considered to be a reworking of the *vetustissima* in the light of the *media.*[40]

To the work of his predecessors Salman adds the results of his own researches to the effect that, if the facts were to be adequately accounted for, it would appear necessary to admit the existence of yet another translation, which would come between the *vetustissima* and the *media,* and would lack Books XI, XIII and XIV. In his opinion it would be upon this text rather than the *media* that St. Thomas relied in composing his first writing of the Commentary, since the *media* could not have been known as early as 1230 as Birkenmajer had claimed, or even as early as 1260 as Pelster had maintained.

Salman's argument for a later dating of the *media* is based upon certain passages in some of St. Thomas' works. According to him these passages indicate that St. Thomas came to know the last books of the *Metaphysics* only in the very last years of his career; and this being so, the *media* could not have been known or used by him, since it contained the books in question. The passages referred to are those in which St. Thomas speaks of a treatise of Aristotle on separate substances, belonging to the realm of metaphysics, and which Salman identifies, on the strength of the reading in the *De Unitate,* with Books XIII and XIV of the *Metaphysics.* In his opinion these books could not have reached St. Thomas before the later part of 1270. Indeed, according to the passage in

---

[39] *Die Griechisch-Lateinischen Metaphysikübersetzungen des Mittelalters* (Beitrage z. Gesch. d. Phil. des Mitt., Supplementband, II, Münster, 1923), pp. 89-118.

[40] Letter to Geyer in Ueberweg-Geyer, *Die Patristische und Scholastische Philosophie,* Berlin, 1928, p. 346 ff.

the *Commentary on the De Anima,* Book III, lesson 12 (n. 785), at the time of its composition (after 1266), St. Thomas was not even certain that such a treatise had ever been written; but he states categorically that it was still unknown in the West. The passages from the *Commentary on the De Sensu,* lesson 1 (n. 4) (dated after 1261), the *De Veritate,* q. 18, art. 5, obj. 8 and ans. (dated the beginning of 1258), and the *Quaestio Disputata de Anima,* art. 16 (dated the beginning of 1270), also bear witness to his ignorance of this treatise.[41] However, by the time of writing of the *De Unitate Intellectus* (dated 1270) St. Thomas knew that such a treatise actually existed, having seen the Greek text, and that it brought the total number of books up to fourteen, but that it had not yet been translated into Latin. The passage from the *De Unitate* to which Salman refers in support of his interpretation runs thus: "Hujusmodi autem quaestiones certissime colligi potest Aristotelem solvisse in his libros quos patet eum scripsisse de substantiis separatis, ex his quae dicit in principio XII Metaphysicae, quos etiam libros vidimus numero XIV, licet nondum translatos in linguam nostram."[42] Assuming, then, that St. Thomas did not know Books XIII and XIV until 1270, and that these books were presented for the first time in the *media,* he could not have employed this version in the first writing of the Commentary, which was composed, in Salman's opinion, during the period of his career in Italy. But neither could he have depended solely upon the *vetus* or *littera Boethii,* since these versions go only as far as Book IV, whereas the first writing must have covered all books with the exception of XI, XIII and XIV. Some other version therefore must have been available to him, and it would have to contain eleven books (I-X and XII).

According to Salman this version would be a combination of the *vetustissima* and an early translation based on the Arabic—one version making up for the deficiencies of the other. The existence of such a translation, he notes, is attested to by a document published by Lacombe, which describes three translations of the *Metaphysics* done at different times: a first or early version that was incomplete (which Salman identifies with the *vetustissima*); a second and later translation which is clearly identifiable with the Arabic by reason of its lacking Books XI, XIII and XIV, and the confusion of the first two books; and a third and still later translation containing thirteen books (which Salman presumably identifies as the *media*). Since this new version which Salman proposes as the foundation for St. Thomas' work would depend predominantly on the *second translation,* he named it the *metaphysica secunda.*[43]

However, Salman's argument appears to have lost most if not all of its force in the light of the investigations of Keeler and the extensive studies of Pelster. If the reading *numero XIV* of the *De Unitate Intellectus* cannot be substantiated by any documentary evidence other than the faulty edition of Pizamanus, as Keeler has apparently shown (since most manuscripts contain the reading *numero X,* while others make no specific mention of the number of books at all), it would seem reasonable to maintain, as Pelster has done, that the work to which St. Thomas alludes in the passages singled out by Salman, might be the *Theology of Aristotle* (an apocryphal work in ten parts) or some other work which Aris-

[41] For Salman's analyses of these texts and his conclusion see *art. cit.,* pp. 87-89.

[42] For the analysis of this passage in relation to the others see *art. cit.,* pp. 91-98. The passage of the *De Unitate* is taken from the Mandonnet edition, vol. I, p. 65.

[43] Salman, *art. cit.,* pp. 106-108. For the text published by Lacombe see p. 107 of Salman. See also "Medieval Latin Versions of the *Parva Naturalia,*" *The New-Scholasticism,* V (October 1931), 296.

totle is supposed to have written on separate substances.[44] This interpretation, however, does not appear to be confirmed by any positive evidence, and Salman himself has rejected it on the ground that, since the *Theology of Aristotle* is generally admitted to have been in circulation in the West as early as the beginning of the thirteenth century, and would thus be known to St. Thomas, it can hardly be the treatise to which he refers.[45]

The researches of Pelster, published in 1935 and 1936, are of special significance for the present problem.[46] His conclusions are based on an extensive study of the manuscripts of the various versions, and in this undertaking he has made great use of the collection of texts assembled earlier by Geyer. By comparing the citations from the *Metaphysics* that St. Thomas gives throughout his works at large, and the direct references that he makes to the text of Aristotle in his exposition of the *Metaphysics*, with the corresponding passages in the various versions, Pelster has been able to identify the translations that St. Thomas knew and used during his literary career. As a result of such studies he has concluded that St. Thomas knew the *metaphysica vetus* and the translation based on the Arabic from the very beginning of his career, and that, while he unquestionably employed the *vetus* in various works, he does not appear to have made any use of the translation from the Arabic (at least not in the Commentary); the *littera Boethii*, which for St. Thomas went beyond Book IV, is taken, not from the *metaphysica vetustissima*, but from the *translatio vetus*, so that the latter version and that of the *littera Boethii* are different; St. Thomas knew the *metaphysica nova* when he wrote the *De Unitate Intellectus* in 1270, and also when he composed the first part of the *Summa Theologiae*, shortly after 1265, since both of these works contain citations from this version; St. Thomas both knew and used the *translatio media* in the *De Unitate Intellectus* and in the *Summa Contra Gentiles*, composed about 1260, and probably also in the *De Veritate*, as some passages would seem to indicate.[47] There are of course some references which it is impossible or difficult to identify either with the *nova* or the *media*, since St. Thomas sometimes gives Aristotle's thought only in digested form.

It is in identifying the sources to which St. Thomas refers throughout the Commentary that the versions used in its composition become evident. According to Pelster's investigations these texts are evidently the *vetus, littera Boethii, media* and *nova*, and presumably another translation based on the Greek, that went beyond Book IV, unless the readings indicative of its existence are merely variants of the *media* and the *nova*, as could be the case. The undertaking has not been an easy one inasmuch as St. Thomas refers to the various versions which he is using simply as "this reading" (*haec littera*) when they constitute the basic text or first reading on which he is depending, and as "another reading" or "another translation" (*alia littera* or *alia translatio*) when they fill the role of a secondary text or alternate reading. It is only in the case of the text attributed to Boethius that his source is clearly designated.

Generally it can be said that it was by reason of the clarity of its presentation (and this established by comparison) that one of these versions was given

[44] Pelster, *Die Griechisch* . . . , p. 111; see also "Die Uebersetzungen . . . ," *Gregorianum*, XVI (1935), 330.

[45] Salman, *art. cit.*, p. 93.

[46] "Die Uebersetzungen der Aristotelischen Metaphysik in den Werken des hl. Thomas von Aquin," *Gregorianum*, XVI (1935), 325-348, 531-561; XVII (1936), 377-406. See also "Neuere Forschungen über die Aristotelesübersetzungen des XII und XIII Jahrhunderts," *Gregorianum*, XXX (1949), 46-77.

[47] *Art. cit., Gregorianum*, XVI (1935), 330-343.

precedence over the others as the basic reading to be followed; and since this varied from version to version in relation to the particular book or chapter that was being considered, it became necessary to change the basic reading. In this way a version that constituted a primary reading in some parts became a secondary or alternate reading in others, its place being taken by one that had previously been secondary.

Pelster's conclusions given in summary form amount to the following: from Books I to IV St. Thomas constantly used the *vetus* and the *media,* and often gave first place to the former, as in Book II, lesson 2, and Book IV, lesson 5. In Book V the *media* appears to be the basic text, and beginning with lesson 20 of this book the *nova* appears for the first time as "another reading," although sometimes the *vetus* can be understood in this role. It would seem too that St. Thomas knew the *nova* as early as the writing of Book I; but since the *vetus* and the *nova* have the same reading, it is difficult to decide in favor of the *nova.* While the *nova* cannot be shown to be the fundamental reading for the first five books, there is every indication that by the time of writing of Book VI St. Thomas began to make greater use of it as his point of departure, and often does this without taking the *media* into account at all. In the matter of the divisions that are given for the text of Aristotle, the *media* appears to have been used as an aid, and St. Thomas probably also derives from it the Greek words which are translated along with the *nova.* Sometimes, however, the *vetus* is preferred to the *media* in the establishing of these divisions. After Book IX St. Thomas appears to have relied solely upon the *nova,* since no alternate readings are given thereafter. The *versio antiqua* given in the printed editions is not simply the *nova* of Moerbeke, but a mixed form of the *nova* and *media.*[48]

Having established the foregoing, Pelster feels justified in dismissing Dondaine's opinion that the *media* constituted the basic text for St. Thomas' exposition, while the *nova* was used later only in a revisory capacity. Such a hypothesis is inadmissible in view of the position that the *nova* holds in the later books. Salman's assumption of a *metaphysica secunda* is similarly untenable inasmuch as St. Thomas was fully acquainted with the *media,* as numerous comparisons have shown.

3. *The Problem of the Last Books*

One of the central problems which scholars have had to face in their investigations into the history of the Commentary concerns the last books of the *Metaphysics,* specifically Books XI, XIII and XIV. Were they available or not to St. Thomas when he began his exposition? Some have felt that they were, while others have adopted the opposite position, maintaining that he came to know and use them only at a later date.

The doxology that St. Thomas gives at the end of Book XII seems to clearly indicate that he considered his work to be completed at this point. In this respect the *Commentary on the Metaphysics* is unique, as Mansion has pointed out, since other commentaries of Aquinas, as those on the *De Interpretatione,* the *De Coelo,* the *De Generatione et Corruptione,* the *Meteorologica* and the *Politica* remain unfinished, terminating either at the end of some book or at the end of some lesson.[49]

The supposition that St. Thomas did not comment upon the last two books —XIII and XIV—because he lacked a Latin translation of them, cannot be

---

[48] *Ibid.,* pp. 532-561.
[49] "Pour l'histoire . . . ," *Revue Néo-Scol.,* XXVII (1925), 278.

maintained. Mansion noted the untenableness of such a hypothesis as early as 1925,[50] using in support of his claim the earlier work of Pelster, mentioned above, which contains a collection of the various references to these books in certain works of St. Thomas and St. Albert the Great, which are evidently drawn from the *media*.[51] But the most direct evidence of St. Thomas' knowledge of the last books is to be found in the many references made to them in the Commentary itself, especially in the early part of the work. The majority of such references are given in Book III, which contains the fifteen *aporiae* or difficulties that Aristotle intends to consider in the development of subsequent books. In lessons 4-15 of this book St. Thomas examines these difficulties, and in each lesson designates the respective books in which they will be treated. In so doing he refers to Books XIII and XIV and describes the problems with which they actually deal.[52] In mentioning Book XIII he even cites the opening lines of chapter 1.[53] The objection that such references have been added later in a second writing would have to be dismissed in the light of Pelster's later researches.

It therefore could not have been the lack of a translation that prevented St. Thomas from commenting upon the books in question; and inasmuch as he gives no explanation for bringing his work to a close at the point at which he did, we are forced to look elsewhere for an answer. Here the suggestion of Mansion appears to be the most reasonable one.[54] He bases his opinion on a statement in Sylvester Maurus, who, in his synopsis immediately preceding Book XIII, says of the last two books that their teaching is most obscure and of little value, and that, in any event, since the subjects treated therein have already been dealt with in previous books, it would be pointless to dispute them any further.[55] Sylvester is referring to the fact that in these books Aristotle gives a systematic criticism of the theory of Ideas as interpreted by Plato's successors, Speusippus and Xenocrates, who identified the Ideas with numbers and extensions; and since this subject has nothing to do with the development of Aristotle's metaphysical views, properly speaking, and has already been exposed in great detail in earlier books, St. Thomas probably thought it unnecessary to deal with it again.

The problems regarding Book XI are not as easily solved. It is generally admitted that this book was the last one to have been introduced into the West, and its translation would without doubt be due to William of Moerbeke. However, the time at which St. Thomas first came to know of the existence of this book, and then received and used the translation of it in his exposition, is still an open question. Two different and opposite stands have been taken in this matter—one by Mansion and the other by Pelster—and both have something to be said in their favor.

Mansion's position, later accepted by Salman, is that St. Thomas was unaware of the existence of Book XI at the beginning of his exposition and even after his work was well under way. He grounds his argument on the fact that St. Thomas makes no mention of this book at the start of his Commentary, and even fails to take account of it as late as Book VII; for in the schematic division given at the beginning of this book, in which the issues to be dealt with in the

---

[50] *Ibid.*, p. 279.
[51] I.e., *Die Griechisch-lateinischen* . . . , p. 105.
[52] See C 422, C 501, C 514, C 518.
[53] See C 2488: "De sensibili quidem igitur substantia . . . "
[54] "Pour l'histoire . . . ," p. 279-280.
[55] *Aristotelis opera omnia quae extant brevi paraphrasi et litterae perpetuo inhaerente expositione illustrata* a Sylvestro Mauro, S.J., Rome 1669; re-ed. Paris, 1885-87 by F. Ehrle, S.J., and A. Bringmann, S.J., vol. IV, p. 569 (cited in Mansion, p. 280).

remaining books are outlined, no reference at all is made to Book XI. One large division covers Books VII to IX, and another covers Book X. But at the beginning of Book XI a new division is found, which, while not in absolute opposition to the previous one, is still not in complete agreement with it. Mansion concluded from this that, when St. Thomas composed his exposition of Book VII, he was either unaware of Book XI altogether, or at least had not yet received the translation of it, and so made no mention of it in his division. However, when this book came into his possession later on, he incorporated it into his work, and had therefore to make a new division which would account for it and also extend to the balance of his work. He would have received this new book just before he began his commentary of Book XII or after he had completed it; and assuming the later alternative to be true, it would then have been necessary for him to revise Book XII. Mansion feels that there is evidence to support such a second writing in a number of references given in early books, especially Book III, in which Book Λ is sometimes referred to as XI, following the numeration of the *media*.[56]

In Pelster's view the hypothesis of Mansion deserves attention, but it is not necessary to accept it.[57] That is to say, from the fact that St. Thomas in Book VII does not consider XI, it does not necessarily follow that he was unaware of it. He may have known it but simply found no occasion to use it. Since there is evidence that St. Thomas possessed the *nova* at the time he began his exposition, it is quite possible that he knew Book XI, which is found only in that version. He could have decided at first against using it and later changed his mind. This assumption is a reasonable one according to Pelster if certain facts are taken into consideration. St. Thomas in commenting upon Aristotle was interested primarily in explaining the development of his metaphysical views, and in this undertaking Book XI has no essential part to play, being neither a continuation of the thought of Book X nor an introduction in any necessary and proper sense to Book XII. This becomes evident when the contents of the book are examined, for they are merely a recapitulation of the main points developed in certain of the earlier books, to which extracts from the *Physics* have been added.[58] This book then could easily have been set aside without in any way affecting the development of Aristotle's main trend of thought. Pelster feels that, when St. Thomas came to treat Book XI he decided to introduce it into his exposition as an introduction to Book XII inasmuch as it can be used as a kind of preparation for the doctrine presented in this book. St. Thomas' change of mind can be accounted for, he thinks, in the light of the circumstances under which the Commentary was written. St. Thomas composed his commentaries for the use of teachers and students in the schools, and since the *vetus,* the *media* and the translation from the Arabic were all considered to be first class texts and the ones customarily employed, he would also have used them. But since these versions lacked Book XI, he would not have had to take this book into account. The *nova,* being new, would not be well enough known at first to use as a classroom text. However, when it did become better known and its superiority

---

[56] Mansion, *art. cit.,* pp. 280-284.

[57] For Pelster's argument see: *art. cit., Gregorianum,* XVII (1936), 376-380.

[58] The first eight chapters of Book XI (*K*) present in condensed form the doctrines of chapters 2-6 of Book III, chapters 1-8 of Book IV, and chapters 1, 2-4 of Book VI, while the last four chapters are made up of extracts from the *Physics:* chapters 5, 6 of Book II, chapters 1-7 of Book III, and chapters 1-3 of Book V.

was recognized, St. Thomas would have begun to employ it as his basic text, and so would have to consider Book XI which it contained.

Granted that this simpler hypothesis is acceptable, Pelster also thinks that it is unnecessary to admit a second writing or revision, in whole or in part, as others have proposed on the basis of the occasional appearances of the numeration of the *media* along with that of the *nova*. The designation of Book Λ sometimes as XI and sometimes as XII, and of Books *M* and *N* sometimes as XII and XIII, and sometimes as XIII and XIV, admits of a simpler explanation: since St. Thomas found himself in a transitional stage, he is sometimes thinking of the older numeration of the *media,* and sometimes of the newer numeration of the *nova*. His readers and custom would force him to use the older numeration, while his new findings would incline him to use the newer. If the degree of simplicity with which a hypothesis takes care of known facts determines its acceptableness, Pelster's hypothesis cannot be lightly dismissed.

The completing of this translation has been possible only as a result of the unfailing assistance I have received from several persons who have my most sincere thanks. I am quite unable to express my gratitude to Fathers Robert W. Schmidt and James J. Doyle, S.J., for their untiring patience in reading the greater part of the mansucript, for their criticisms and the innumerable valuable suggestions they have made in the matter of emendations. I am particularly indebted to Father Schmidt for his excellent supervision throughout the whole undertaking, and for locating a number of references, especially those to Avicenna. I also wish to acknowledge my indebtedness to Father Robert F. Harvanek, S.J., whose original interest in this work made its ultimate publication possible; and to Fathers George A. Curran, S.J. and Michael Montague, S.J. for their help in reading some parts of the manuscript.

J. P. R.

Commentary on the
Metaphysics of Aristotle

Library of Living Catholic Thought

VOLUME I

PROLOGUE

When several things are ordained to a single thing, one of them must rule or govern and the rest be ruled or governed, as the Philosopher [1] teaches in the *Politics*.[2] This indeed is evident in the union of soul and body, for the soul naturally commands and the body obeys. The same thing is also true of the soul's powers, for the concupiscible and irascible appetites are ruled in a natural order by reason. Now all the sciences and arts are ordained to a single thing, namely, to man's perfection, which is happiness. Hence one of these sciences and arts must be the mistress of all the others, and this one rightly lays claim to the name *wisdom;* for it is the office of the wise man to direct others.

We can discover which science this is and the sort of things with which it is concerned by carefully examining the qualities of a good ruler; for just as men of superior intelligence are naturally the rulers and masters of others, whereas those of great physical strength and little intelligence are naturally slaves, as the Philosopher says in the aforementioned book,[3] in a similar way that science which is intellectual in the highest degree should be naturally the ruler of the others. This science is the one which treats of the most intelligible objects.

Now the phrase "most intelligible objects" can be understood in three ways. First, from the viewpoint of the order of knowing; for those things from which the intellect derives certitude seem to be more intelligible. Therefore, since the certitude of science is acquired by the intellect knowing causes, a knowledge of causes seems to be intellectual in the highest degree. Hence that science which considers first causes also seems to be the ruler of the others in the highest degree.

Second, this phrase can be understood by comparing the intellect with the senses; for while sensory perception is a knowledge of particulars, the intellect seems to differ from sense by reason of the fact that it comprehends universals. Hence that science is pre-eminently intellectual which deals with the most universal principles. These principles are *being* and those things which naturally accompany being, such as *unity* and *plurality, potency* and *act.* Now such principles should not remain entirely undetermined, since without them a complete knowledge of the principles which are proper to any genus or species cannot be had. Nor again should they be dealt with in any one particular science; for, since a knowledge of each class of beings stands in need of these principles, they would with equal reason be investigated in every particular science. It follows, then, that such principles are treated by one common science, which, since it is intellectual in the highest degree, is the mistress of the others.

Third, this phrase can be understood from the viewpoint of the intellect's own knowledge. For since each thing has intellective power by virtue of being free from matter, those things must be intelligible in the highest degree which are altogether separate from matter. For the intelligible object and the intellect must be proportionate to each other and must belong to one and the same genus, since the intellect and the intelligible object are one in actuality. Now those things are separate from matter in the highest degree which abstract not only from desig-

---

[1] The title of "Philosopher" was the one which medieval writers reserved for Aristotle.
[2] *Politica,* I, 5 (1254a 20).
[3] *Ibid.,* I, 1 (1254a 31); 5 (1254b 29).

nated matter, "as the natural forms taken universally, of which the philosophy of nature (*scientia naturalis* [4]) treats," but from sensible matter altogether; and these are separate from matter not only in their intelligible constitution (*ratio*), as the objects of mathematics, but also in being, as God and the intelligences. Therefore the science which considers such things seems to be the most intellectual and the ruler or mistress of the others.

Now this threefold consideration should be assigned to one and the same science and not to different sciences. For the separate substances mentioned above are the universal and first causes of being. Moreover, it pertains to one and the same science to consider both the proper causes of some genus and the genus itself; for example, the philosophy of nature considers the principles of a natural body. Consequently it must be the office of one and the same science to consider separate substances and *being in general* (*ens commune*), which is the genus [5] of which the substances mentioned above are the common and universal causes.

From this it is evident that, although this science [i.e., metaphysics or first philosophy] studies the three classes of things mentioned above, [6] it does not investigate any one of them as its subject, but only being in general. For the subject of a science is the genus whose causes and properties we seek, and not the causes themselves of the particular genus studied, because a knowledge of the causes of some genus is the goal to which the investigation of a science attains. Now although the subject of this science is being in general, the whole of it is predicated of those things which are separate from matter both in their intelligible constitution and in being (*esse*). For it is not only those things which can never exist in matter which are said to be separate from matter in their intelligible constitution and in being, such as God and the intellectual substances, but also those things which can exist without matter, such as being in general. This could not be the case, however, if their being depended on matter.

Therefore in accordance with the three classes of objects mentioned above from which this science derives its perfection, three names arise. It is called *divine science* or *theology* inasmuch as it considers the aforementioned substances. It is called *metaphysics* inasmuch as it considers being and the attributes which naturally accompany being (for things which transcend the physical order are discovered by the process of analysis, as the more common are discovered after the less common). And it is called *first philosophy* inasmuch as it considers the first causes of things. Therefore it is evident what the subject of this science is, and how it is related to the other sciences, and by what names it is designated.

[4] In the works of Aristotle and St. Thomas the term *natural science* (*scientia naturalis*) is equivalent to the term *philosophy of nature* or *natural philosophy* (*philosophia naturalis*). The ancients drew no explicit distinction between a philosophic and what we call "scientific" study of nature.

[5] According to St. Thomas the term *being* or *being in general* is not a *genus* or generic term in the strict logical sense, for being is predicated of things analogically or proportionally and not univocally. Cf. *Metaphysics,* Book III, Lesson 8, C 433.

[6] I.e., God, the intellectual substances, and being in general.

2

BOOK I

Introduction to First Philosophy
History of Metaphysical Inquiry

CONTENTS

Book I

LESSON 1

The Dignity and Object of This Science

ARISTOTLE'S TEXT   Chapter 1: 980a 21-983a 3

1. All men naturally desire to know. A sign of this is the delight we take in the senses; for apart from their usefulness they are loved for themselves, and most of all the sense which operates through the eyes. For not only that we may act, but even when we intend to do nothing, we prefer sight, as we may say, to all the other senses. The reason is that of all the senses this most enables us to know and reveals many differences between things.

2. Animals by nature, then, are born with sensory power.

3. Now in some animals memory arises from the senses, but in others it does not; and for this reason the former are prudent and more capable of being taught than those which are unable to remember. Those which cannot hear sounds are prudent but unable to learn, as the bee and any other similar type of animal there may be. But any which have this sense together with memory are able to learn.

4. Thus other animals live by imagination and memory and share little in experience, whereas the human race lives by art and reasoning.

5. Now in men experience comes from memory, for many memories of the same thing produce the capacity of a single experience. And experience seems to be somewhat like science and art.

6. But in men science and art come from experience; for "Experience causes art, and inexperience, luck," as Polus rightly states.[1] Art comes into being when from many conceptions acquired by experience a single universal judgment is formed about similar things. For to judge that this [medicine] has been beneficial to Callias and Socrates and many other individuals who suffer from this disease, is a matter of experience; but to judge that it has been beneficial to all individuals of a particular kind, as the phlegmatic, the bilious, or the feverish, taken as a class, who suffer from this disease, is a matter of art.

7. In practical matters, then, experience seems to differ in no way from art. But we see that men of experience are more proficient than those who have theory without experience. The reason is that experience is a knowledge of singulars, whereas art is a knowledge of universals. But all actions and processes of generation are concerned with singulars. For the physician heals man only incidentally, but he heals Socrates or Callias, or some individual that can be named, to whom the nature *man* happens to belong. Therefore, if anyone has the theory without experience, and knows the universal but not the singulars contained in this, he will very often make mistakes; for it is rather the individual man who is able to be cured.

8. Yet we think that scientific knowledge and the ability to refute objections [2]

[1] See Plato, *Gorgias,* 448 C & 462 B.
[2] The Greek text says: "to understand." The Latin version reads *obviare.*

belong to art rather than to experience, and we are of the opinion that those who are proficient in art are wiser than men of experience, implying that it is more according to wisdom to know as one pursuing all things.[3]

9. Now this is because the former know the cause whereas the latter do not. For those who have experience know that something is so but do not know why, whereas the others know the why and the cause. For this reason, too, we think that the master planners in each art are to be held in greater esteem, and that they know more and are wiser than the manual laborers, because they understand the reasons for the things which are done. Indeed, we think that the latter resemble certain inanimate things, which act but do not know what they do, as fire burns. Therefore inanimate things perform each of their actions as a result of a certain natural disposition, whereas manual laborers perform theirs through habit, implying that some men are wiser not insofar as they are practical but insofar as they themselves have the theories and know the causes.

10. In general a sign of scientific knowledge is the ability to teach, and for this reason we think that art rather than experience is science. For those who have an art are able to teach, whereas the others are not.

11. Furthermore, we do not hold that any one of the senses is wisdom, since the cognition of singular things belongs especially to the senses. However, these do not tell us why a thing is so; for example, they do not tell us why fire is hot but only that it is so.

12. It is only fitting, then, that the one who discovered any art whatsoever that went beyond the common perceptions of men should be admired by men, not only because of some usefulness of his discoveries, but as one who is wise and as distinguishing [a thing] from others. And as more of the arts were discovered, some to supply the necessities of life, and others to introduce us [to the sciences],[4] those who discovered the latter were always considered to be wiser than those who discovered the former, because their sciences were not for the sake of utility. Hence, after all such arts had already been developed, those sciences were discovered which are pursued neither for the sake of pleasure nor necessity. This happened first in those places where men had leisure. Hence the mathematical arts originated in Egypt, for there the priestly class was permitted leisure. The difference between art and science and similar mental states has been stated in our work on morals.[5]

13. Now the reason for undertaking this investigation is that all men think that the science which is called wisdom deals with the primary causes and principles of things. Hence, as we have said before (8, 9), the man of experience is considered to be wiser than one who has any of the senses; the artist wiser than the man of experience; the master planner wiser than the manual laborer; and speculative knowledge wiser than practical knowledge. It is quite evident, then, that wisdom is a science of certain causes and principles.

[3] The Latin version reads: *Tamquam magis sit scire secundum sapientiam omnia sequentem.* The Greek text says: "inasmuch as wisdom belongs to all in proportion to their knowledge." None of the Latin versions to which St. Thomas refers in his commentary on this passage accord exactly with the Greek.

[4] This text differs from the Greek, which has: "and others with a view to recreation."

[5] *Ethica Nic.,* VI, 1-7 (1139b 14-1141b 8).

COMMENTARY

1. Aristotle first sets down an introduction to this science, in which he treats of two things. First (1:C 2),[1] he points out with what this science is concerned. Second (27:C 53), he explains what kind of science it is ("That this is not a practical science").

In regard to the first he does two things. First, he shows that the office of this science, which is called wisdom, is to consider the causes of things. Second (14:C 36), he explains with what causes or kinds of causes it is concerned ("But since we are in search").

In regard to the first he prefaces certain preliminary considerations from which he argues in support of his thesis. Second (13:C 35), he draws a conclusion from these considerations ("Now the reason for undertaking").

In regard to the first he does two things. First, he makes clear the dignity of scientific knowledge in general. Second (2:C 9), he explains the hierarchy in knowing ("Animals by nature").

Now he establishes the dignity of scientific knowledge from the fact that it is naturally desired as an end by all men. Hence, in regard to this he does two things. First, he states what he intends [to prove]. Second (1:C 1), he proves it ("A sign of this").

Accordingly, he says, first, that the desire to know belongs by nature to all men.

2. Three reasons can be given for this. The first is that each thing naturally desires its own perfection. Hence matter is also said to desire form as any imperfect thing desires its perfection. Therefore, since the intellect, by which man is what he is, considered in itself is all things potentially, and becomes them actually only through knowledge, because the intellect is none of the things that exist before it understands them, as is stated in Book III of The Soul;[2] so each man naturally desires knowledge just as matter desires form.

3. The second reason is that each thing has a natural inclination to perform its proper operation, as something hot is naturally inclined to heat, and something heavy to be moved downwards. Now the proper operation of man as man is to understand, for by reason of this he differs from all other things. Hence the desire of man is naturally inclined to understand, and therefore to possess scientific knowledge.

4. The third reason is that it is desirable for each thing to be united to its source, since it is in this that the perfection of each thing consists. This is also the reason why circular motion is the most perfect motion, as is proved in Book VIII of the Physics,[3] because its terminus is united to its starting-point. Now it is only by means of his intellect that man is united to the separate substances, which are the source of the human intellect and that to which the human intellect is related as something imperfect to something perfect. It is for this reason, too, that the ultimate happiness of man consists in this union. Therefore man naturally desires to know. The fact that some men do not

---

[1] In cross references given to this work the first number designates the Spiazzi divisions of Aristotle's text, and the second number, which is preceded by "C," designates the Cathala divisions of St. Thomas' Commentary.

[2] De Anima, III, 4 (429a 23).

[3] Physica, VIII, 7 (261a 12), 8 (263a 4).

devote any study to this science does not disprove this thesis; for those who desire some end are often prevented from pursuing it for some reason or other, either because of the difficulty of attaining it, or because of other occupations. And in this way, too, even though all men desire knowledge, still not all devote themselves to the pursuit of it because they are held back by other things, either by pleasures or the needs of the present life; or they may even avoid the effort that learning demands because they are lazy. Now Aristotle makes this statement in order to show that it is not pointless to search for a science that is not useful for anything else, as happens in the case of this science, since a natural desire cannot exist in vain.

5. Then he establishes his thesis by means of an example. Since our senses serve us in two respects: in knowing things and in meeting the needs of life, we love them for themselves inasmuch as they enable us to know and also assist us to live. This is evident from the fact that all men take the greatest delight in that sense which is most knowing, i.e., the sense of sight, which we value not merely in order to do something, but even when we are not required to act at all. The reason is that this sense—that of sight—is the most knowing of all our senses and makes us aware of many differences between things.

6. In this part it is clear that he gives two reasons why sight is superior to the other senses in knowing. The first is that it knows in a more perfect way; and this belongs to it because it is the most spiritual of all the senses. For the more immaterial a power is, the more perfectly it knows. And evidently sight is a more immaterial sense, if we consider the modification produced in it by its object. For all other sensible objects change both the organ and

medium of a sense by a material modification, for example, the object of touch by heating and cooling, the object of taste by affecting the organ of taste with some flavor through the medium of saliva, the object of hearing by means of motion in the body, and the object of smell by means of the evaporation of volatile elements. But the object of sight changes the organ and medium of sight only by a spiritual modification; because neither the pupil of the eye nor the air becomes colored, but these only receive the form of color in a spiritual mode of being. Therefore, because actual sensation consists in the actual modification of a sense by its object, it is evident that that sense which is changed in a more immaterial and spiritual way is more spiritual in its operation. Hence sight judges about sensible objects in a more certain and perfect way than the other senses do.

7. The other reason which he gives for the superiority of sight is that it gives us more information about things. This is attributable to the nature of its object, for touch and taste, and likewise smell and hearing, perceive those accidents by which lower bodies are distinguished from higher ones. But sight perceives those accidents which lower bodies have in common with higher ones. For a thing is actually visible by means of light, which is common both to lower and higher bodies, as is said in Book II of *The Soul*.[4] Hence the celestial bodies are perceptible only by means of sight.

8. There is also another reason. Sight informs us of many differences between things, for we seem to know sensible things best by means of sight and touch, but especially by means of sight. The reason for this can be drawn from the fact that the other three senses perceive those accidents which in a way flow from a sensible body and do

---

[4] *De Anima*, II, 7 (418b 5).

not remain in it. Thus sound comes from a sensible body inasmuch as it flows away from it and does not remain in it. The same thing is true of the evaporation of volatile elements, with which and by which odor is diffused. But sight and hearing perceive those accidents which remain in sensible bodies, such as color, warmth and coldness. Hence the judgment of sight and touch is extended to things themselves, whereas the judgment of hearing and smell is extended to those accidents which flow from things and not to things themselves. It is for this reason that figure and size and the like, by which a sensible being itself is disposed, are perceived more by sight and touch than by the other senses. And they are perceived more by sight than by touch, both because sight knows more efficaciously, as has been pointed out (C 6), and also because quantity and those [accidents] which naturally follow from it, which are seen to be the common sensibles, are more closely related to the object of sight than to that of touch. This is clear from the fact that the object of sight belongs in some degree to every body having some quantity, whereas the object of touch does not.

9. **Animals by nature, then** (2).

Here he considers the hierarchy in knowledge. He does this, first (2:C 9), with respect to brute animals; and, then (4:C 14), with respect to men ("Thus other animals").

With respect to brute animals he mentions first what all animals have in common; and second (3:C 10), that by which they differ and surpass one another ("Now in some animals").

Now all animals are alike in the respect that they possess by nature the power of sensation. For an animal is an animal by reason of the fact that it has a sentient soul, which is the nature of an animal in the sense in which the distinctive form of each thing is its nature. But even though all animals are naturally endowed with sensory power, not all animals have all the senses, but only perfect animals. All have the sense of touch, for this sense in a way is the basis of all the other senses. However, not all have the sense of sight, because this sense knows in a more perfect way than all the other senses. But touch is more necessary; for it perceives the elements of which an animal is composed, namely, the hot, cold, moist and dry. Hence, just as sight knows in a more perfect way than the other senses, in a similar way touch is more necessary inasmuch as it is the first to exist in the process of generation. For those things which are more perfect according to this process come later in the development of the individual which is moved from a state of imperfection to one of perfection.

10. **Now in some animals** (3).

Here he indicates the different kinds and three levels of knowing found among brute animals. For there are certain animals which have sensation, although they do not have memory which comes from sensation. For memory accompanies imagination, which is a movement caused by the senses in their act of sensing, as we find in Book II of *The Soul*.[5] But in some animals imagination does not accompany sensation, and therefore memory cannot exist in them. This is found verified in imperfect animals which are incapable of local motion, such as shellfish. For since sensory cognition enables animals to make provision for the necessities of life and to perform their characteristic operations, then those animals which move towards something at a distance by means of local motion must have memory. For if the anticipated goal by which they are induced to move did not remain

---

[5] *De Anima*, II, 3 (428b 10).

in them through memory, they could not continue to move toward the intended goal which they pursue. But in the case of immobile animals the reception of a present sensible quality is sufficient for them to perform their characteristic operations, since they do not move toward anything at a distance. Hence these animals have an indefinite movement as a result of confused [or indeterminate] imagination alone, as he points out in Book III of *The Soul*.[6]

11. Again, from the fact that some animals have memory and some do not, it follows that some are prudent and some not. For, since prudence makes provision for the future from memory of the past (and this is the reason why Tully in his *Rhetoric*, Book II,[7] makes memory, understanding and foresight parts of prudence), prudence cannot be had by those animals which lack memory. Now those animals which have memory can have some prudence, although prudence has one meaning in the case of brute animals and another in the case of man. Men are prudent inasmuch as they deliberate rationally about what they ought to do. Hence it is said in Book VI of the *Ethics*,[8] that prudence is a rationally regulated plan of things to be done. But the judgment about things to be done which is not a result of any rational deliberation but of some natural instinct is called prudence in other animals. Hence in other animals prudence is a natural estimate about the pursuit of what is fitting and the avoidance of what is harmful, as a lamb follows its mother and runs away from a wolf.

12. But among those animals which have memory some have hearing and some do not. And all those which cannot hear (as the bee or any other similar type of animal that may exist), even though they have prudence, are still incapable of being taught, i.e., in the sense that they can be habituated to the doing or avoiding of something through someone else's instruction, because such instruction is received chiefly by means of hearing. Hence in *The Senses and Their Objects*[9] it is stated that hearing is the sense by which we receive instruction. Furthermore, the statement that bees do not have hearing is not opposed in any way to the observation that they are frightened by certain sounds. For just as a very loud sound kills an animal and splits wood, as is evident in the case of thunder, not because of the sound but because of the violent motion of the air in which the sound is present, in a similar fashion those animals which lack hearing can be frightened by the sounding air even though they have no perception of sound. However, those animals which have both memory and hearing can be both prudent and teachable.

13. It is evident, then, that there are three levels of knowing in animals. The first level is that had by animals which have neither hearing nor memory, and which are therefore neither capable of being taught nor of being prudent. The second level is that of animals which have memory but are unable to hear, and which are therefore prudent but incapable of being taught. The third level is that of animals which have both of these faculties, and which are therefore prudent and capable of being taught. Moreover, there cannot be a fourth level, so that there would be an animal which had hearing but lacked memory. For those senses which perceive their sensible objects by means of an external medium—and hearing is one of these—

---

[6] *Ibid.*, III, 11 (434a 1).
[7] Cicero, *De Invent. Rhet.*, II, 53.
[8] *Eth. Nic.*, VI, 5 (1140b 5).
[9] *De Sen. et Sen.*, I, 1 (437a 12).

are found only in animals which have locomotion and which cannot do without memory, as has been pointed out (3:C 10).

14. **Thus other animals** (4).

Here he explains the levels of human knowing; and in regard to this he does two things. First (4:C 14), he explains how human knowing surpasses the knowing of the abovementioned animals. Second (5:C 17), he shows how human knowing is divided into different levels ("Now in men").

Accordingly, in the first part (4) he says that the life of animals is ruled by imagination and memory: by imagination in the case of imperfect animals, and by memory in the case of perfect animals. For even though the latter also have imagination, still each thing is said to be ruled by that [power] which holds the highest place within it. Now in this discussion life does not mean the being of a living thing, as it is understood in Book II of *The Soul*,[10] when he says that "for living things to live is to be"; for the life of an animal in this sense is not a result of memory or imagination but is prior to both of these. But life is taken to mean vital activity, just as we are also accustomed to speak of association as the life of men. But by the fact that he establishes the truth about the cognition of animals with reference to the management of life, we are given to understand that knowing belongs to these animals, not for the sake of knowing, but because of the need for action.

15. Now, as is stated below (6:C 18), in men the next thing above memory is experience, which some animals have only to a small degree. For an experience arises from the association of many singular [intentions] received in memory. And this kind of association is proper to man, and pertains to the cogitative power (also

[10] *De Anima*, II, 2 (413a 22).

called particular reason), which associates particular intentions just as universal reason associates universal ones. Now since animals are accustomed to pursue or avoid certain things as a result of many sensations and memory, for this reason they seem to share something of experience, even though it be slight. But above experience, which belongs to particular reason, men have as their chief power a universal reason by means of which they live.

16. And just as experience is related to particular reason [in men], and customary activity to memory in animals, in a similar way art is related to universal reason. Therefore, just as the life of animals is ruled in a perfect way by memory together with activity that has become habitual through training, or in any other way whatsoever, in a similar way man is ruled perfectly by reason perfected by art. Some men, however, are ruled by reason without art; but this rule is imperfect.

17. **Now in men** (5).

Here he explains the different levels of human knowing; and in regard to this he does two things. First (5:C 17), he compares art with experience; and, second (12:C 31), he compares speculative art with practical art ("It is only fitting").

He treats the first point in two ways. First, he explains how art and experience originate. Second (7:C 20), he explains how one is superior to the other ("In practical matters").

In regard to the first he does two things. First, he explains how each of the above originates. Second (6:C 18), he makes this clear by means of an example ("For to judge").

In regard to the first he does two things. First, he describes how experience originates, and second (6:C 18), how art originates ("But in men, science").

He says first (5), then, that in men

experience is caused by memory. The way in which it is caused is this: from several memories of a single thing a man acquires experience about some matter, and by means of this experience he is able to act easily and correctly. Therefore, because experience provides us with the ability to act easily and correctly, it seems to be almost the same as science and art. For they are alike inasmuch as in either case from many instances a single view of a thing is obtained. But they differ inasmuch as universals are grasped by art and singular things by experience, as is stated later (6:C 18).

18. **But in men science and art** (6).

Here he describes the way in which art arises. He says that in men science and art come from experience, and he proves this on the authority of Polus, who says that "Experience causes art and inexperience luck." For when an inexperienced person acts correctly, this happens by chance. Furthermore, the way in which art arises from experience is the same as the way spoken of above in which experience arises from memory. For just as one experiential cognition comes from many memories of a thing, so does one universal judgment about all similar things come from the apprehension of many experiences. Hence art has this [unified view] more than experience, because experience is concerned only with singulars, whereas art has to do with universals.

19. Thereupon he makes this clear by means of examples ("But in men [6]"). For when a man has learned that this medicine has been beneficial to Socrates and Plato, and to many other individuals who were suffering from some particular disease, whatever it may be, this is a matter of experience; but when a man learns that this particular treatment is beneficial to all men who have some particular kind of disease and some particular kind of physical constitution, as it has bene-

fited the feverish, both the phlegmatic and the bilious, this is now a matter of art.

20. **In practical matters** (7).

He compares art to experience from the viewpoint of pre-eminence; and in regard to this he does two things. First (7:C 20), he compares them from the viewpoint of action; and, second (8:C 23), from the viewpoint of knowledge ("Yet we think").

He says then that in practical matters experience seems to differ in no way from art; for when it comes to acting, the difference between experience and art, which is a difference between the universal and the singular, disappears, because art operates with reference to singulars just as experience does. Therefore the aforesaid difference pertains only to the way in which they come to know. But even though art and experience do not differ in the way in which they act, because both act on singular things, nevertheless they differ in the effectiveness of their action. For men of experience act more effectively than those who have the universal knowledge of an art but lack experience.

21. The reason is that actions have to do with singular things, and all processes of generation belong to singular things. For universals are generated or moved only by reason of something else, inasmuch as this belongs to singular things. For man is generated when this man is generated. Hence a physician heals man only incidentally, but properly he heals Plato or Socrates, or some man that can be individually named, to whom the nature man belongs, or rather to whom it is accidental inasmuch as he is the one healed. For even though the nature man belongs essentially to Socrates, still it belongs only accidentally to the one healed or cured; for the proposition "Socrates is a man" is an essential one, because, if Socrates were defined, man would be given in

his definition, as will be said below in Book IV.[11] But the proposition "What is healed or cured is man" is an accidental one.

22. Hence, since art has to do with universals and experience with singulars, if anyone has the theoretical knowledge of an art but lacks experience, he will be perfect insofar as he knows the universal; but since he does not know the singular, because he lacks experience, he will very often make mistakes in healing. For healing belongs to the realm of the singular rather than to that of the universal, because it belongs to the former essentially and to the latter accidentally.

23. **Yet we think** (8).

Here he compares art with experience from the viewpoint of knowing; and in regard to this he does two things. First (8:C 23), he states how art is superior to experience; and second (9:C 24), he proves this ("Now this is because").

He claims that art and science are superior to experience in three respects. First, they are superior from the viewpoint of scientific knowledge, which we think is attained by art rather than by experience. Second, they are superior from the viewpoint of meeting objections, which occurs in disputes. For in a dispute the one who has an art is able to meet the objections raised against that art, but one who has experience [alone] cannot do this. Third, they are superior from this point of view, that those who have an art come nearer to the goal of wisdom than men of experience, "Implying that it is," i.e., happens to be, "more truly to know if wisdom pursues all things," i.e., insofar as it pursues universals.[12] For one who has an art is judged wiser than one who has experience, by rea-

son of the fact that he considers universals. Or in another version: "Implying that it is more according to wisdom to know as one pursuing all things," i.e., universals. Another reading has: "As more conformable to knowing, since wisdom pursues all things," as if to say: "As more dependent upon knowing" than upon doing, "since wisdom pursues all things," i.e., it seeks to reach each single thing; so that those are rather called wise who are more knowing, not those who are more men of action. Hence another reading expresses this meaning more clearly, saying: "Implying that all pursue wisdom more with respect to knowing."

24. **Now this is** (9).

Then he proves the superiority of art and science mentioned above, and he does this by means of three arguments. The first runs thus: those who know the cause and reason why a thing is so are more knowing and wiser than those who merely know that it is so but do not know why. Now men of experience know that something is so but do not know the reason, whereas men who have an art know not merely that something is so but also know its cause and reason. Hence those who have an art are wiser and more knowing than those who have experience.

25. **For this reason too** (9).

Here he proves the first aspect of superiority, and this runs as follows. Those who know the cause and reason why a thing is so are compared to those who merely know that it is so as the architectonic arts are to the arts of manual laborers. But the architectonic arts are nobler. In a similar way, then, those who know the causes and reasons of things are more know-

[11] The example to which St. Thomas refers does not appear in Book IV, although he does note the distinction between essential and accidental propositions or predications in Lesson 7 (342:C 629-635). For the indefinable character of the singular see Book VII (627:C 1492-1497).

[12] The first reading which St. Thomas gives here is not that given in the Latin version of Aristotle's text. The statement of the text constitutes his second reading.

ing than those who merely know that things are so.

26. The first part of this proof becomes clear from the fact that architects, or master artists, know the causes of the things that are done. In order to understand this we must note that architect means chief artist, from ἀρχός meaning chief, and τέχνη meaning art. Now that art is said to be a chief art which performs a more important operation. Indeed, the operations of artists are distinguished in this way; for some operations are directed to disposing the material of the artifact. Carpenters, for example, by cutting and planing the wood, dispose matter for the form of a ship. Another operation is directed to introducing this form into the matter, for example, when someone builds a ship out of wood which has been disposed and prepared. A third operation is directed to the use of the finished product, and this is the highest operation. But the first operation is the lowest because it is directed to the second and the second to the third. Hence the shipbuilder is a superior artist compared with the one who prepares the wood; and the navigator, who uses the completed ship, is a superior artist compared with the shipbuilder.

27. Further, since matter exists for the sake of form, and ought to be such as to befit the form, the shipbuilder knows the reason why the wood should be shaped in some particular way; but those who prepare the wood do not know this. And in a similar way, since the completed ship exists in order to be used, the one who uses the ship knows why it should have some particular form; for the form should be one that befits its use. Thus it is evident that the reason for the operations which dispose the matter is taken from the design of the product in the artist's

mind, and the reason for the operations which produce the form of the artifact is taken from the use [to which the artifact is put].

28. It is evident, then, that the master artists know the causes of the things which are done. In fact we judge and speak about the others, i.e., the manual laborers, as we do about certain inanimate things. This is not because they do not [12a] perform artful operations, but because the things which they do they do without knowing the cause; for they know that something is to be done but not why it is, just as fire burns without knowing why. Hence there is a likeness between inanimate things and manual laborers from this point of view, that, just as inanimate things act without knowing the causes, inasmuch as they are directed to their proper end by a superior intellect, so also do manual laborers. But they differ in this respect, that inanimate things perform each of their operations as a result of their nature, whereas manual laborers perform theirs through habit. And while habit is practically the same as nature inasmuch as it is inclined to one definite effect, still habit differs from nature inasmuch as it is open to opposites by reason of human knowledge. For we do not habituate natural bodies, as is stated in Book II of the *Ethics;* [13] nor, indeed, is it possible to cause habits in things that lack knowledge. Now the statements that have been made, as is evident from the statements themselves, must be interpreted as meaning that some men are wiser, not insofar as they are "practical," i.e., men of action, as befits men of experience, but insofar as they have a plan for things to be done and know their causes, which are the basis of such a plan; and this befits master artists.

29. **In general a sign of scientific knowledge** (10).

[12a] Reading *non* not only before *ideo* but again before *faciunt.*
[13] *Eth. Nic.,* II, 1 (1103a 20).

Here he gives the second argument, which is as follows: a sign of knowledge is the ability to teach, and this is so because each thing is perfect in its activity when it can produce another thing similar to itself, as is said in Book IV of *Meteors*.[14] Therefore, just as the possession of heat is indicated by the fact that a thing can heat something else, in a similar way the possession of knowledge is indicated by the fact that one can teach, that is, cause knowledge in another. But men who have an art can teach, for since they know causes they can demonstrate from these; and demonstration is a syllogism which produces knowledge, as is said in Book I of the *Posterior Analytics*.[15] But men who have experience [only] cannot teach; for since they do not know the causes, they cannot cause knowledge in someone else. And if they do teach others the things which they know by experience, these things are not learned after the manner of scientific knowledge but after that of opinion or belief. Hence, it is clear that men who have an art are wiser and more knowing than those who have experience.

30. **Furthermore, we do not hold (11).**

Here he gives the third argument, which is as follows: knowing singular things is proper to the senses rather than to any other type of knowing [power], since our entire knowledge of singular things originates with the senses. Yet we do not hold that "any one of these," i.e., any one of the senses, is wisdom, because even though each sense knows that a thing is so, it does not know why it is so; for touch judges that fire is hot but does not know why it is hot. Therefore men of experience, who have a knowledge of singular things but do not know their causes, cannot be called wise men.

31. **It is only fitting (12).**

Here he compares practical art with

---

[14] *Meteorologica*, IV, 12 (390a 10).
[15] *Analytica Posteriora*, I, 1 (71b 18).

speculative art; and in regard to this he does three things. First (12:C 20), he shows that a speculative art is wisdom to a greater degree than a practical art. Second (*ibid*.), he answers an objection ("The difference").

He proves his first statement by this argument: in any of the sciences or arts we find that men with scientific knowledge are more admired and are held in higher esteem than all other men, because their knowledge is held to be nobler and more worthy of the name of wisdom. Now the discoverer of any art at all is admired because he perceives, judges and discerns a cause beyond the perceptions of other men, and not because of the usefulness of his discoveries. We admire him rather "as being wise, and as distinguishing [a thing] from others." As being wise, indeed, in the subtle way in which he investigates the causes of his discoveries, and as distinguishing [a thing] from others insofar as he investigates the ways in which one thing differs from another. Or, according to another interpretation, "as being distinct from the others" is to be read passively, as being distinguished in this respect from others. Hence another text has "one who is different." Some sciences, then, are more admirable and worthy of the name of wisdom because their observations are more outstanding, not because they are useful.

32. Therefore, since many useful arts have been discovered (some to provide the necessities of life, as the mechanical arts, and others to introduce us to the sciences, as the logical disciplines), those artists must be said to be wiser whose sciences were discovered not for the sake of utility but merely for the sake of knowing, that is to say, the speculative sciences.

33. That the speculative sciences were not discovered for the sake of utility is made clear by this fact, that

after all sciences of this kind "had already been developed," i.e., acquired or discovered, which can serve as introductions to the other sciences, or provide the necessities of life, or give pleasure (as those arts whose object is to delight man), the speculative sciences were discovered, not for this kind of end, but for their own sake. The fact that they were not discovered for the sake of utility becomes evident from the place in which they were discovered. For they originated in those places where men first applied themselves to such things. Another version reads, "And first in those places where men had leisure," i.e., they had time for study because they were released from other occupations as a result of the abundance of things necessary [for life]. Hence the mathematical arts, which are speculative in the highest degree, were first discovered in Egypt by the priests, who were given time for study, and whose expenses were defrayed by the community, as we also read in *Genesis* (47:22).

34. But because the names "wisdom," "science" and "art" have been used indifferently, lest someone should think that these terms are synonymous, he excludes this opinion and refers to his work on morals, i.e., to Book VI of the *Ethics*,[16] where he has explained the difference between art, wisdom, science, prudence, and understanding. And to give the distinction briefly—wisdom, science and understanding pertain to the speculative part of the soul, which he speaks of in that work as the scientific part of the soul. But they differ in that understanding is the habit of the first principles of demonstration, whereas science has to do with conclusions drawn from subordinate causes, and wisdom with first causes. This is the reason it is spoken of there

as the chief science. But prudence and art belong to the practical part of the soul, which reasons about our contingent courses of action. And these also differ; for prudence directs us in actions which do not pass over into some external matter but are perfections of the one acting (which is the reason why prudence is defined in that work as the reasoned plan of things to be done), but art directs us in those productive actions, such as building and cutting, which pass over into external matter (which is the reason why art is defined as the reasoned plan of things to be made).

35. **Now the reason for undertaking** (13).

From what has been said he proves his major thesis, that is to say, that wisdom deals with the causes of things. He says that the reason "for undertaking this investigation," i.e., the above piece of reasoning, is that the science which is called wisdom seems to be about first causes and principles. This is evident from the foregoing; for the more a man attains to a knowledge of the cause, the wiser he is. This is also evident from the foregoing; because the man of experience is wiser than one who has sensation alone without experience; and the artist is wiser than any man of experience; and among artists the architect is wiser than the manual laborer. And similarly among the arts and sciences the speculative are more scientific than the practical. All these things are clear from the foregoing remarks. It follows, then, that that science which is wisdom in an absolute sense is concerned with the causes of things. The method of arguing would be similar if we were to say that that which is hotter is more afire, and therefore that that which is afire in an absolute sense is hot in an absolute sense.

---

[16] *Eth. Nic.*, VI, 3-7 (1139b 15-1141b 23).

LESSON 2

Wisdom Considers Universal First Causes and First Principles

ARISTOTLE'S TEXT   Chapter 2: 982a 4-982b 11

14. But since we are in search of this science, it will therefore be necessary to consider with what kind of causes and principles wisdom or science deals. This will perhaps become evident if we take the opinions which we have about the wise man. First of all, then, we think that the wise man is one who knows all things in the highest degree, as becomes him,[1] without having a knowledge of them individually.

15. Next, we say that that man is wise who is capable of knowing things that are difficult and not easy for man to understand. For sensory perception is common to all, and is therefore easy and not a matter of wisdom.

16. Again, [we consider him wise who is] more certain.

17. And in every branch of science we say that he is wiser who is more capable of teaching us about the causes of things.

18. Again, among the sciences we think that that science which exists for itself and is desirable for the sake of knowledge is wisdom to a greater degree than one which is desirable for the sake of contingent effects.

19. And we think that a superior science which is rather the more basic comes nearer to wisdom than a subordinate science. For a wise man must not be directed but must direct, and he must not obey another but must be obeyed by one who is less wise. Such then and so many are the opinions which we have about the wise and about wisdom.

20. Now of these attributes, that of knowing all things necessarily belongs to him who has universal knowledge in the highest degree, because he knows in some respect all things which are subordinate.

21. But the things which are just about the most difficult for man to understand are also those which are most universal; for they are farthest removed from the senses.

22. Again, the most certain of the sciences are those which are most concerned with primary things. For sciences based on fewer principles are more certain than those which have additional principles, as arithmetic is more certain than geometry.

23. Moreover, that science which speculates about the causes of things is more instructive. For those who teach us are those who assign the causes of every single thing.

24. Again, understanding and scientific knowledge for their own sake are found in the highest degree in the science which has as its object what is most knowable. For one who desires scientific knowledge for itself will desire in the highest degree the science which is most truly science, and such a science has for its object what is most knowable. Now first principles and causes are most

[1] The Latin version reads *sicut decet*. The Greek text reads: "so far as possible."

knowable; for it is by reason of these and from these that other things are known, and not these from things which are subordinate to them.

25. But that science is highest and superior to subordinate sciences which knows the reason why each single thing must be done. This is the good of every single thing, and viewed universally it is the greatest good in the whole of nature.

26. In view of everything that has been said, then, the term which we are investigating evidently falls to the same science. For this science must speculate about first principles and causes, because the good, or that for the sake of which something is done, is also one of the causes.

COMMENTARY

36. Having shown that wisdom is a knowledge of causes, the Philosopher's aim here is to establish with what kinds of causes and what kinds of principles it is concerned. He shows that it is concerned with the most universal and primary causes, and he argues this from the definition of wisdom.

In regard to this he does three things. First (14:C 36), he formulates a definition of wisdom from the different opinions which men have about the wise man and about wisdom. Second (20:C 44), he shows that all of these are proper to that universal science which considers first and universal causes ("Now of these"). Third (26:C 51), he draws the conclusion at which he aims ("In view of everything").

In regard to the first he gives six common opinions which men have entertained about wisdom. He states the first (14) where he says "But since we are in search"; and this opinion is this: in general we all consider those especially to be wise who know all things, as the case demands, without having a knowledge of every singular thing. For this is impossible, since singular things are infinite in number, and an infinite number of things cannot be comprehended by the intellect.

37. Next, we say that (15).
Here he gives the second opinion, which is this: we hold that man to be

wise who is capable, by reason of his intellect, of knowing difficult things, and those which are not easy for ordinary men to understand. For sensory perception, i.e., the knowing of sensible things, is common to all men, and is therefore easy and so not a matter of wisdom. That is to say, it is neither a mark nor the office of a wise man. Thus it is clear that whatever pertains properly to wisdom is not easily known by all.

38. Again, [we consider] (16).
Here he gives the third opinion, namely, that we say that he is wise who, regarding what he knows, is more certain than other men generally are.

39. And in every branch (17).
Here he gives the fourth opinion, namely, that that man is said to be wiser in every science who can give the causes of anything that is brought into question, and can teach by means of this.

40. Again, among the sciences (18).
Here he gives the fifth opinion, which is this: among the many sciences that science which is more desirable and willed for its own sake, i.e., chosen for the sake of knowledge and for knowledge itself alone, is more of the nature of wisdom than one which is for the sake of any of the other contingent effects which can be caused by knowl-

edge, such as the necessities of life, pleasure, and so forth.

41. **And we think** (19).

Here he gives the sixth opinion, namely, that this wisdom, of which mention has been made, must be or is said to be "rather the more basic," i.e., nobler, than "a subordinate science." This can be understood from the foregoing. For in the field of the mechanical arts, subordinate artists are those who execute by manual operations the commands of superior artists, whom he referred to above as master artists and wise men.

42. That the notion of wisdom belongs to sciences which give orders rather than to those which take them, he proves by two arguments. The first is that subordinate sciences are directed to superior sciences. For subordinate arts are directed to the end of a superior art, as the art of horsemanship to the end of the military art. But in the opinion of all it is not fitting that a wise man should be directed by someone else, but that he should direct others. The second is that inferior artists are induced to act by superior artists inasmuch as they rely upon superior artists for the things which they must do or make. Thus the shipbuilder relies upon the instructions of the navigator for the kind of form which a ship ought to have. However, it does not befit a wise man that he should be induced to act by someone else, but that he should use his knowledge to induce others to act.

43. These, then, are the kind of opinions which men have of wisdom and the wise; and from all of these a description of wisdom can be formulated, so that the wise man is described as one who knows all, even difficult matters, with certitude and through their cause; who seeks this knowledge for its own sake; and who directs others and induces them to act. And in this way the major premise of the syllogism becomes evident. For every wise man must be such, and conversely whoever is such is wise.

44. **Now of these** (20).

Here he shows that all of the above attributes come together in the man who knows the first and universal causes of things; and he follows the same order as he did above. Thus he held first that knowledge of all things in the highest degree belongs to him who has universal knowledge. This was the first opinion, and it is made clear in this way: Whoever knows universals knows in some respect the things which are subordinate to universals, because he knows the universal in them.[1] But all things are subordinate to those which are most universal. Therefore the one who knows the most universal things, knows in a sense all things.

45. **But the things** (21).

Here he proves that the second attribute belongs to the same person, by the following argument. Those things which are farthest removed from the senses are difficult for men to know; for sensory perception is common to all men since all human knowledge originates with this. But those things which are most universal are farthest removed from sensible things, because the senses have to do with singular things. Hence universals are the most difficult for men to know. Thus it is clear that that science is the most difficult which is most concerned with universals.

46. But the statement which appears in Book I of the *Physics* [2] seems to contradict this. For it is said there that more universal things are known first by us; and those things which are known first are those which are easier. Yet it must be said that those things which are more universal according to simple apprehension are known first;

[1] Reading *in illis* for *in illa*.
[2] *Physica*, I, 1 (184a 24).

for being is the first thing that comes into the intellect, as Avicenna says,[3] and animal comes into the intellect before man does. For just as in the order of nature, which proceeds from potentiality to actuality, animal is prior to man, so too in the genesis of knowledge the intellect conceives animal before it conceives man. But with respect to the investigations of natural properties and causes, less universal things are known first, because we discover universal causes by means of the particular causes which belong to one genus or species. Now those things which are universal in causing are known subsequently by us (notwithstanding the fact that they are things which are primarily knowable according to their nature), although things which are universal by predication are known to us in some way before the less universal (notwithstanding the fact that they are not known prior to singular things). For in us sensory knowledge, which is cognitive of singular things, precedes intellective knowledge, which is about universals. And some importance must also be attached to the fact that he does not say that the most universal things are the most difficult absolutely, but "just about." For those things which are entirely separate from matter in being, as immaterial substances, are more difficult for us to know than universals. Therefore, even though this science which is called wisdom is the first in dignity, it is still the last to be learned.

47. **Again, the most certain** (22).

Here he shows that the third attribute belongs to the same science, by this argument: the more any sciences are prior by nature, the more certain they are. This is clear from the fact that those sciences which are said to originate as a result of adding something to the other sciences are less certain than those which take fewer things into consideration; for example, arithmetic is more certain than geometry because the objects considered in geometry are a result of adding to those considered in arithmetic. This becomes evident if we consider what these two sciences take as their first principle, namely, the point and the unit. For the point adds to the unit the notion of position, because undivided being constitutes the intelligible structure of the unit; and insofar as this has the function of a measure it becomes the principle of number. And the point adds to this the notion of position. However, particular sciences are subsequent in nature to universal sciences, because their subjects add something to the subjects of universal sciences. For example, it is evident that *mobile being,* with which the philosophy of nature deals, adds to *being* pure and simple, with which metaphysics is concerned, and to *quantified being,* with which mathematics is concerned. Hence that science which treats of being and the most universal things is the most certain. Moreover, the statement here that this science deals with fewer principles is not opposed to the one made above, that it knows all things; for the universal takes in fewer inferiors actually, but many potentially. And the more certain a science is, the fewer actual things it has to consider in investigating its subject-matter. Hence the practical sciences are the least certain, because they must consider the many circumstances attending individual effects.

48. **Moreover, that science** (23).

Here he proves that the fourth attribute belongs to the same science, by this argument: that science is more instructive, or better able to teach, which is concerned to a greater degree with causes. For only those teach who assign the causes of every single thing, because scientific knowledge comes about through some cause, and to teach is to

---

[3] *Metaphysica,* I, 6 (72rb, 73ra).

cause knowledge in another. But that science which considers universals considers the first of all the causes. Hence it is evidently the best fitted to teach.

49. **Again, understanding** (24).

Here he proves that the fifth attribute belongs to the same science, by this argument: it is the office of those sciences which deal with things that are most knowable most properly to know and understand for their own sake, i.e., for the sake of those sciences themselves and not for something else. But it is the sciences that deal with first causes which consider the most knowable things. Therefore those sciences are desired most for their own sake. He proves the first premise thus: One who most desires knowledge for the sake of knowledge most desires scientific knowledge. But the highest kind of knowledge is concerned with things that are most knowable. Therefore those sciences are desired most for their own sake which have to do with things that are most knowable. He proves the second premise thus: Those things from which and by reason of which other things are known are more knowable than the things which are known by means of them. But these other things are known through causes and principles, and not vice versa, etc.

50. **But that science** (25).

Here he proves that the sixth attribute belongs to the same science, by the following argument: that science which considers the final cause, or that for the sake of which particular things are done, is related to the other sciences as a chief or master science is to a subordinate or ancillary one, as is evident from the foregoing remarks. For the navigator, to whom the use, or end, of

the ship belongs, is a kind of master artist in relation to the shipbuilder who serves him. But the aforesaid science is concerned most with the final cause of all things. This is clear from the fact that that for the sake of which all particular things are done is the good of each, i.e., a particular good. But the end in any class of things is a good; and that which is the end of all things, i.e., of the universe itself, is the greatest good in the whole of nature. Now this belongs to the consideration of the science in question, and therefore it is the chief or architectonic science with reference to all the others.

51. **In view of everything** (26).

Here he draws from the foregoing arguments his intended conclusion, saying that it is clear from everything that has been said that the name wisdom which we are investigating belongs to the same science which considers or speculates about first principles and causes. This is evident from the six primary conditions which clearly pertain to the science that considers universal causes. But because the sixth condition touched on the consideration of the end, which was not clearly held to be a cause among the ancient philosophers, as will be said below (84:C 177), he therefore shows in a special way that this condition belongs to the same science, namely, the one which considers first causes. For the end, which is a good and that for the sake of which other things are done, is one of the many causes. Hence the science which considers first and universal causes must also be the one which considers the universal end of all things, which is the greatest good in the whole of nature.

LESSON 3

The Nature and Goal of Metaphysics

ARISTOTLE'S TEXT   Chapter 2: 982b 11-983a 23

27. That this is not a practical science is evident from those who first philoso-phized. For it is because of wonder that men both now and formerly began to philosophize, wondering at first about less important matters, and then progressing little by little, they raised questions about more important ones, such as the phases of the moon and the courses of the sun and the stars and the generation of the universe. But one who raises questions and wonders seems to be ignorant. Hence the philosopher is also to some extent a lover of myth, for myths are composed of wonders. If they philosophized, then, in order to escape from ignorance, they evidently pursued their studies for the sake of knowledge and not for any utility.

28. And what has happened bears witness to this; for when nearly all the things necessary for life, leisure and learning were acquired, this kind of prudence began to be sought. It is evident, then, that we do not seek this knowledge for the sake of any other necessity.

29. But just as we say that a man is free who exists for himself and not for another, in a similar fashion this is the only free science, because it alone exists for itself.

30. For this reason, too, it might rightly be thought that this science is not a human possession, since in many respects human nature is servile.

31. Hence, according to Simonides, "Only God has this honor," [1] and it is un-fitting that a man should not [2] seek a knowledge which befits him. Some poets accordingly say that the deity is naturally envious; and it is most likely that it should happen in this case, and that all those who are imperfect are unfortunate. But it is not fitting that the deity should be envious, for as the proverb says: "The poets tell many lies." [3]

32. Nor must we think that any other science is more honorable than this. For what is most divine is most honorable. But then it alone will be such, and in two ways. For of all knowledge that which God most properly has is divine; and if there is any such knowledge, it is concerned with divine matters. But this science alone has both of these characteristics; for God seems to be a cause and in some sense a principle according to all men; and such [knowledge as this] God either alone has, or has in the highest degree. Therefore, all the other sciences are more necessary, but none is more excellent.

33. But it is necessary in a sense to bring to a halt the progression of this science at the contrary of our original questions. Indeed, as we have said, all men begin by wondering whether things are as strange as chance occurrences appear to those who do not yet know the cause; or by wondering about the changes in

---

[1] Hiller, Frag. 3.
[2] Reading *non* before *quaerere* in keeping with St. Thomas' commentary (C 61).
[3] Hiller, Frag. 26 (Solon).

the course of the sun, or about the incommensurability of the diagonal [of a square]. For it would seem an object of wonder to all if something having the nature of number were immeasurable. But it is necessary to advance to the contrary view and, as the proverb says,[4] the worthier one, as also happens in a sense in these matters when men have learned them. For nothing would surprise a geometrician more than if the diagonal [of a square] should become commensurable [with a side]. It has been stated, then, what the nature is of the science which we are seeking, and what its goal is for which our search and whole method must be undertaken.

[4] Leutsch & Schneidewin, *Paroemiographi Graeci*, I, 371.

COMMENTARY

52. Having indicated the things with which this science deals, Aristotle now shows what kind of science it is. In regard to this he does two things. First (27:C 53), he reveals the dignity of this science; and second (33:C 66), the goal which it attempts to reach ("But it is necessary").

In regard to the first he does four things. First, he shows that this is not a practical science but a speculative one; second (29:C 58), that it is free in the highest degree ("But just as we say"); third (30:C 60), that it is not a human [possession] ("For this reason"); and fourth (32:C 64), that it is the most honorable science ("Nor must we think that").

He proves the first in two ways. First, by an argument, and second (28:C 57), by an example ("And what has happened").

53. First (27), he gives this argument. No science in which knowledge itself is sought for its own sake is a practical science, but a speculative one. But that science which is wisdom, or philosophy as it is called, exists for the sake of knowledge itself. Hence it is speculative and not practical. He proves the minor premise in this way. Whoever seeks as an end to escape from ignorance tends toward knowledge for itself. But those who philosophize seek

as an end to escape from ignorance. Therefore they tend towards knowledge for itself.

54. That they seek to escape from ignorance is made clear from the fact that those who first philosophized and who now philosophize did so from wonder about some cause, although they did this at first differently than now. For at first they wondered about less important problems, which were more obvious, in order that they might know their cause; but later on, progressing little by little from the knowledge of more evident matters to the investigation of obscure ones, they began to raise questions about more important and hidden matters, such as the changes undergone by the moon, namely, its eclipse, and its change of shape, which seems to vary inasmuch as it stands in different relations to the sun. And similarly they raised questions about the phenomena of the sun, such as its eclipse, its movement and size; and about the phenomena of the stars, such as their size, arrangement, and so forth; and about the origin of the whole universe, which some said was produced by chance, others by an intelligence, and others by love.

55. Further, he points out that perplexity and wonder arise from ignorance. For when we see certain obvious

effects whose cause we do not know, we wonder about their cause. And since wonder was the motive which led men to philosophy, it is evident that the philosopher is, in a sense, a philomyth, i.e., a lover of myth, as is characteristic of the poets. Hence the first men to deal with the principles of things in a mythical way, such as Perseus and certain others who were the seven sages, were called the theologizing poets. Now the reason why the philosopher is compared to the poet is that both are concerned with wonders. For the myths with which the poets deal are composed of wonders, and the philosophers themselves were moved to philosophize as a result of wonder. And since wonder stems from ignorance, they were obviously moved to philosophize in order to escape from ignorance. It is accordingly evident from this that "they pursued" knowledge, or diligently sought it, only for itself and not for any utility or usefulness.

56. Now we must note that, while this science was first designated by the name wisdom, this was later changed to the name philosophy, since they mean the same thing. For while the ancients who pursued the study of wisdom were called sophists, i.e., wise men, Pythagoras, when asked what he professed himself to be, refused to call himself a wise man as his predecessors had done, because he thought this was presumptuous, but called himself a philosopher, i.e., a lover of wisdom.[1] And from that time the name "wise man" was changed to "philosopher," and "wisdom" to "philosophy." This name also contributes something to the point under discussion, for that man seems to be a lover of wisdom who seeks wisdom, not for some other reason, but for itself alone. For he who seeks one thing on account of something else, has greater love for that on

whose account he seeks than for that which he seeks.

57. **And what has happened** (28).

Here he proves the same point by means of an example. The statement (he says) that wisdom or philosophy is not sought for any utility but for knowledge itself is proved by "what has happened," i.e., by what has occurred in the case of those who have pursued philosophy. For when nearly all those [arts] were discovered which are necessary for life, "leisure" (i.e., for the sort of pleasure which consists in a life of ease), and learning, such as the logical sciences, which are not sought for themselves but as introductions to the other arts, then man began for the first time to seek this kind of prudence, namely, wisdom. And from this it is clear that wisdom is not sought because of any necessity other than itself but for itself alone; for no one seeks something which he already possesses. Hence, because wisdom was sought after all other knowledge had been discovered, it is evident that it was not sought for some reason other than itself but for itself.

58. **But just as** (29).

Here he proves the second attribute, namely, that wisdom is free; and he uses the following argument: that man is properly said to be free who does not exist for someone else but for himself. For slaves exist for their masters, work for them, and acquire for them whatever they acquire. But free men exist for themselves inasmuch as they acquire things for themselves and work for themselves. But only this science exists for itself; and therefore among all the sciences only this science is free.

59. Now we must note that this can be understood in two ways. In one way, the expression "only this" may indicate every speculative science as a class. And then it is true that only this class of science is sought for itself. Hence, only those arts which are directed to know-

<hr/>

[1] See St. Augustine, *De Civitate Dei*, VIII, 2 (PL 41:225).

ing are called free [or liberal] arts, whereas those which are directed to some useful end attained by action are called mechanical or servile arts. Understood in another way, the expression may specifically indicate this philosophy or wisdom which deals with the highest causes; for the final cause is also one of the highest causes, as was stated above (26:C 51). Therefore this science must consider the highest and universal end of all things. And in this way all the other sciences are subordinated to it as an end. Hence only this science exists in the highest degree for itself.

60. **For this reason** (30).

Here he proves the third attribute, namely, that this science is not a human [possession]. In regard to this he does two things. First (30:C 60), he proves his thesis. Second (31:C 61), he criticizes an erroneous view held by certain men ("Hence, according to Simonides").

He proves his thesis by the following argument. A science which is free in the highest degree cannot be a possession of that nature which is servile and subordinate in many respects. But human nature is servile "in many respects," i.e., in many ways. Therefore this science is not a human possession. Now human nature is said to be servile insofar as it stands in need of many things. And on this account it happens that man sometimes neglects what should be sought for its own sake because of the things necessary for life. Thus it is said in Book III of the *Topics* [2] that it is better to philosophize than to become wealthy, although sometimes becoming wealthy is more desirable, that is, to one lacking life's necessities. From this it is clear that that wisdom is sought for itself alone which does not belong to man as his proper possession. For man has as his possession what he can have at his com-

mand and use freely. But that science which is sought for itself alone, man cannot use freely, since he is often kept from it because of the necessities of life. Nor again is it subject to man's command, because man cannot acquire it perfectly. Yet that very small part of it which he does have outweighs all the things known through the other sciences.

61. **Hence, according to Simonides** (31).

Here he rejects the error of a certain poet, Simonides, who said that it is proper to God alone to have the honor of desiring that knowledge which ought to be sought for its own sake and not for the sake of something else. But it is not fitting that man should not seek that knowledge which is in keeping with his own condition, namely, that which is directed to the necessities of life required by man.

62. Now Simonides' error came from that of certain poets who said that the Deity is envious, and that since He is envious He does not desire that the things which pertain to His honor should be shared by all. And if God is envious of men in other things, He is rightly more so in this case, i.e., in the case of the science which is sought for its own sake, which is the most honorable of all the sciences. And according to the opinion of these men it follows that all who are imperfect are unfortunate, for they said that men are fortunate as a result of the providence of the gods, who communicate their goods to men. Hence as a result of the envy of the gods, who are unwilling to communicate their goods, it follows that men, who remain outside the perfection of this science, are unfortunate.

63. But the basis of this opinion is most false, because it is not fitting that any divine being should be envious. This is evident from the fact that envy is sadness at someone else's prosperity.

[2] *Topica*, III, 2 (118a 10).

25

But this can occur only because the one who is envious thinks that someone else's good diminishes his own. Now it is impossible that God should be sad, because He is not subject to evil of any kind. Nor can His goodness be diminished by someone else's goodness, since every good flows from His goodness as from an unfailing spring. Hence Plato also said that there is no envy of any kind in God.[3] But the poets have lied not only in this matter but in many others, as is stated in the common proverb.

64. **Nor must we think** (32).

Here he proves the fourth attribute, namely, that this is the most honorable science, by the following argument. That science which is most divine is most honorable, just as God Himself is also the most honorable of all things. But this science is the most divine, and is therefore the most honorable. The minor premise is proved in this way: a science is said to be divine in two ways, and only this science is said to be divine in both ways. First, the science which God has is said to be divine; and second, the science which is about divine matters is said to be divine. But it is evident that only this science meets both of these requirements, because, since this science is about first causes and principles, it must be about God; for God is understood in this way by all inasmuch as He is one of the causes and a principle of things. Again, such a science which is about God and first causes, either God alone has or, if not He alone, at least He has it in the highest degree. Indeed, He alone has it in a perfectly comprehensive way. And He has it in the highest degree inasmuch as it is also had by men in their own way, although it is not had by them as a human possession, but as something borrowed from Him.

65. From these considerations he draws the further conclusion that all other sciences are more necessary than this science for use in practical life, for these sciences are sought least of all for themselves. But none of the other sciences can be more excellent than this one.

66. **But it is necessary** (33).

He now gives the goal toward which this science moves. He says that its progression comes to rest, or is terminated, in the contrary of what was previously found in those who first sought this science, as also happens in the case of natural generations and motions. For each motion is terminated in the contrary of that from which the motion begins. Hence, since investigation is a kind of movement towards knowledge, it must be terminated in the contrary of that from which it begins. But, as was stated above (27:C 53), the investigation of this science began with man's wonder about all things, because the first philosophers wondered about less important matters and subsequent philosophers about more hidden ones. And the object of their wonder was whether the case was like that of strange chance occurrences, i.e., things which seem to happen mysteriously by chance. For things which happen as if by themselves are called chance occurrences. For men wonder most of all when things happen by chance in this way, supposing that they were foreseen or determined by some cause. For chance occurrences are not determined by a cause, and wonder results from ignorance of a cause. Therefore when men were not yet able to recognize the causes of things, they wondered about all things as if they were chance occurrences; just as they wondered about changes in the course of the sun, which are two in number, namely, the solstices, that of winter and that of summer. For at the summer solstice the sun begins to decline toward the south, after previously declining toward the

[3] *Phaedrus,* 247A; *Timaeus,* 29E.

26

north. But at the winter solstice the opposite occurs. And they wondered also that the diagonal of a square is not commensurable with a side. For since to be immeasurable seems to belong to the indivisible alone (just as unity alone is what is not measured by number but itself measures all numbers), it seems to be a matter of wonder that something which is not indivisible is immeasurable, and consequently that what is not a smallest part is immeasurable. Now it is evident that the diagonal of a square and its side are neither indivisible nor smallest parts. Hence it seems a matter of wonder if they are not commensurable.

67. Therefore, since philosophical investigation began with wonder, it must end in or arrive at the contrary of this, and this is to advance to the worthier view, as the common proverb agrees,[4] which states that one must always advance to the better. For what that opposite and worthier view is, is evident in the case of the above wonders, because when men have already learned the causes of these things they do not wonder. Thus the geometrician does not wonder if the diagonal is incommensurable with a side. For he knows

the reason for this, namely, that the proportion of the square of the diagonal to the square of a side is not as the proportion of the square of a number to the square of a number, but as the proportion of two to one. Hence it follows that the proportion of a side to the diagonal is not as the proportion of number to number. And from this it is evident that they cannot be made commensurable. For only those lines are commensurable which are proportioned to each other as number to number. Hence the goal of this science to which we should advance will be that in knowing the causes of things we do not wonder about their effects.

68. From what has been said, then, it is evident what the nature of this science is, namely, that it is speculative and free, and that it is not a human possession but a divine one; and also what its aim is, for which the whole inquiry, method, and art must be conducted. For its goal is the first and universal causes of things, about which it also makes investigations and establishes the truth. And by reason of the knowledge of these it reaches this goal, namely, that there should be no wonder because the causes of things are known.

[4] *Paroemiographi Graeci*, I, 62.

LESSON 4

Opinions about the Material Cause

ARISTOTLE'S TEXT   Chapter 3: 983a 24-984a 16

34. It is evident, then, that one must acquire scientific knowledge of those causes which stand at the beginning, for we say that we have scientific knowledge of each thing when we think we comprehend its first cause. Now causes are spoken of in four ways. Of these we say that one is the substance or quiddity [1] of a thing, for the first "why" of a thing is reduced to its ultimate intelligible structure, and the first why of a thing is a cause or principle; another is the matter or subject; a third is the source of motion; and a fourth is the cause which is opposite to this, namely, that for the sake of which, or the good; for this is the goal of every generation and motion. There has been sufficient consideration of these in our works on nature.[2]

35. However, let us examine those who have undertaken an investigation of existing things and have philosophized about the truth before us. For evidently they too speak of certain principles and causes. Therefore, to us who come later [their views] will serve as an introduction to the study which we are now making; for we shall either discover some other class of cause, or be more convinced of those which have just been expounded.

36. Most of those who first philosophized thought that only the things which belong to the class of matter are the principles of all things. For that of which all things are composed, from which they first come to be, and into which they are finally dissolved, while their substance remains although it is changed in its attributes—this they call the element and principle of existing things.

37. And for this reason they thought that nothing is either generated or corrupted, as if such a reality always remained in existence. And just as we do not say that Socrates comes to be in an unqualified sense when he becomes good or musical, or is corrupted when he loses these states, because the subject Socrates himself remains, in the same way they say that nothing else is generated or corrupted. For there must be some matter, either one or more than one, from which other things come to be, and which itself remains in existence. However, they do not all speak in the same way about the number and nature of such a principle.

38. Thales, the originator of this kind of philosophy,[3] says that this principle is water; and this is why he also claimed that the earth rests upon water.

39. For presumably he took this position because he saw that the nutriment of all things is moist, that heat itself is generated from this, and that animal life comes from this. But that from which each thing comes to be is a principle

---

[1] The term *quiddity* is used here to translate the expression *quod quid erat esse*, which is a literal translation of Aristotle's τὸ τί ἦν εἶναι. The expression is often used interchangeably with *quod quid est* and *quod quid est esse*. See St. Thomas, *De Ente et Essentia*, 1.

[2] *Physica*, II, 3 (194b 15); 7 (198a 14).

[3] The Ionian school, whose chief representatives are Thales, Anaximander and Anaximenes.

of all things. He bases his opinion on this, then, and on the fact that the seeds of all things have a moist nature, whereas water is by nature the principle of moist things.

40. Moreover, there are some [4] who think that the ancients who lived long before the present generation and were the first to speculate about the gods also held this view about the nature of things. For they [5] made Oceanus and Tethys the parents of generation, and held the oath of the gods to be by a body of water, to which the poets gave the name Styx.[6] For what is oldest is most honorable, and what is most honorable is that by which one swears. Whether this view of nature is in fact the ancient and primary one is perhaps uncertain. Thales is said to have expressed himself in this way about the first cause, but no one could say that Hippo [7] is to be included in this group, because of the weakness of his understanding.

41. Anaximenes and Diogenes hold that air is prior to water and is the most fundamental of the simple bodies.

42. Hippasus of Metopontium and Heraclitus of Ephesus [8] hold that fire [is the primary principle].

43. Empedocles holds that there are four [simple bodies], since he adds a fourth—earth—to those already mentioned. For he says that these always remain and only become many or few in number by being combined into a unity and separated out of a unity.

44. Anaxagoras of Clazomenae, who was prior to Empedocles in years but later in his speculations, says that the principles of things are infinite in number. For he says that nearly all bodies which are made up of parts like themselves,[9] such as fire or water, are generated or corrupted in this way, merely by combining and separating; but that otherwise they are neither generated nor corrupted but always remain in existence.[10] From these views, then, one might think that the only cause is the one which is said to belong to the class of matter.

[4] See Plato, *Theaetetus* 152 E, 180 C-D; *Cratylus* 402 B.
[5] See Homer, *Iliad*, XIV, 201, 246.
[6] *Ibid.*, II, 755; XIV, 271; XV, 37.
[7] See *De Anima*, I, 2 (405b 2).
[8] Diels, *Die Fragmente der Vorsokratiker*, Frag. 17.
[9] Aristotle describes the homoeomeries of Anaxagoras in *De Gen. et Corr.*, I, 1 (314a 24) and *De Coelo*, III, 3 (302a 28).
[10] Diels, Frag. 4.

COMMENTARY

69. Having set forth a preface in which he indicates the aim of this science, its dignity and goal, Aristotle begins to deal with this science; and this is divided into two parts. In the first (34:C 70), he explains what the first philosophers had to say about the causes of things. In the second (144:C 274), he begins to pursue the truth of this science. He does this in Book II ("Theoretical, i.e., speculative, knowledge").

The first part is divided into two members. First, he gives the opinions of the philosophers about the causes of things. Second (86:C 181), he criticizes them insofar as their statements are unsatisfactory ("Therefore all those").

In regard to the first he does two things. First, he takes up again the enumeration of causes which was treated in greater detail in Book II of the *Physics*.[1] Second (35:C 72), he presents the opinions of the philosophers ("However, let us examine").

70. Accordingly, he says, first (34), that since it is evident that wisdom speculates about causes, we ought to begin by acquiring knowledge from the causes of things. This also seems to be in keeping with the intelligible structure of science, because we say that we know each thing scientifically when we think we are not ignorant of its cause. Now causes are spoken of in four ways. One of these is the formal cause, which is the very substance of a thing by which we know what each thing is. For it is well known, as is stated in Book II of the *Physics*,[2] that we do not say that anything has a nature before it has received a form. Now it is clear that a form is a cause, because the question "Why is something so?" we reduce to its formal cause as its ultimate explanation, beginning with proximate forms and proceeding to the ultimate form. But evidently the "why?" asks about a cause and principle. Hence it is evident that a form is a cause. A second cause is the material cause. A third is the efficient cause, which is the source of motion. A fourth is the final cause, which is opposite to the efficient cause as a goal is to a starting-point; for motion begins with the efficient cause and terminates with the final cause. This [latter] cause is also that for the sake of which a thing comes to be, and the good of each nature.

71. He makes the final cause known by three considerations. It is the goal of motion, and thus is opposite to the source of motion, which is the efficient cause. It is first in intention, and for this reason is said to be that for the sake of which [something is done]. It is desirable of itself, and for this reason is called a good; for the good is what all desire. Hence, in explaining how the final cause is opposite to the efficient cause, he says that it is the goal [or end] of every process of generation and motion, whose starting-point is the efficient cause. By these two types of change he seems to imply that there is a twofold goal. For the goal of a process of generation is the form itself, which is a part of a thing. But the goal of motion is something sought for outside the thing moved. He says that he has treated these causes at sufficient length in the *Physics*,[3] lest he should be asked to make a more extensive treatment of them.

72. **However, let us examine** (35).

Here he states what the philosophers had to say about the causes; and in regard to this he does two things. First, he gives the reasons why this must be done; and, second (36:C 73), he begins to carry out his plan ("Most of those").

Accordingly, he says that even though there is a treatise on the causes in the *Physics*,[4] it is still necessary to consider the opinions of the philosophers who first undertook an investigation of the natures of existing things, and have philosophized about the truth before him; because they too set down causes and principles. Therefore, for us who have come later, a consideration of their opinions will be "a first [step]," [5] or preamble, "to the investigation," i.e., to the art which we are now seeking. Hence the text

---

[1] *Physica*, II, 3 (194b 15).
[2] *Physica*, II, 1 (193b 7).
[3] *Physica*, II, 3 (194b 15).
[4] *Ibid*.
[5] The word *prius*, which St. Thomas uses here, is not found in the Latin version. Apparently St. Thomas had before him the reading *prius methodo* instead of *prae opere methodo* found in the Latin version of Cathala's edition.

of Boethius [6] also says: "Therefore as we enter upon the task of this science, their opinions will constitute a preamble to the road that is now to be travelled." Another text has: "Therefore to us who are beginning this inquiry it will be a certain vital work in the investigation that now confronts us," and it must be read in this way: "Therefore, as we enter upon our present course," i.e., upon the present study and art, it will be necessary to consider the opinion of these men "as a work of life," that is to say, as necessary, like works which are done for the preservation of life, so that this reading is interpreted as a metaphorical way of speaking, meaning by "work of life" anything necessary. Now this is useful, because from the opinions of these men we will either discover another class of causes over and above those already enumerated, or be more convinced of the things that have just been stated about the causes, namely, that there are four classes of them.

73. **Most of those** (36).

Here he begins to deal with the opinions of the ancient philosophers; and in regard to this he does two things. First (36), he states their opinions; and, second (86:C 181) he finds fault with them ("Therefore all those").

In regard to the first he does two things. First, he states the opinions which each one of the philosophers held about the causes. Second (79:C 171), he summarizes the discussion ("We have examined").

The first part is divided into two members. In the first (36:C 74), he gives the opinions of those who omitted the formal cause. In the second (69:C 151), he gives the opinion of Plato, who was the first to posit a formal cause ("After the philosophies").

In regard to the first he does two

things. First, he gives the opinion of those who claimed that certain evident things are principles. Second (55:C 112), he gives the opinions of those who devised extrinsic principles ("Leucippus").

In regard to the first he does two things. First, he touches on the opinions which the ancient philosophers held about the material cause; and, second (45:C 93), on their opinions about the efficient cause ("But as men").

In regard to the first he does two things.[7] First, he states in a general way the views of those who posited a material cause. Second (38:C 77), he examines their views in detail ("Thales, the originator").

In regard to the first he does two things. First, he states their opinions about the material cause. Second (37:C 75), he states their opinions about the generation of things, which follow from the first ("And for this reason").

74. Accordingly he says, first (36), that most of those who first philosophized about the natural world held that the principles of all things are merely those which are referred to the class of material cause. In regard to this it must be said that they took the four conditions of matter which seem to belong to the notion of a principle. For, [first], that of which a thing is composed seems to be a principle of that thing. But matter is such a thing; for we say that a thing that has matter is *of* its matter, as a knife is of iron. [Second], that from which a thing comes to be, being also a principle of the process of generation of that thing, seems to be one of its causes, because a thing comes into being by way of generation. But a thing first comes to be from matter, because the matter of things precedes their pro-

[6] I.e., the *littera Boethii* of Aristotle's *Metaphysics*.
[7] The sentence following this in the Latin version: *Primo ponit quid sensuerint de causa materiali* along with the following *Et*, appears to be an intrusion from the following paragraph. It has therefore been deleted.

duction. And a thing does not come from matter in an accidental way; for a thing is generated in an accidental way from its contrary or privation, as when we say that white comes from black. Third, that into which all things are ultimately dissolved by corruption seems to be a principle of things. For just as principles are first in the process of generation, in a similar way they are last in the process of dissolution; and obviously this too pertains to matter. Fourth, since a principle must remain in existence, then that which remains throughout the process of generation and corruption seems to be a principle. Now the matter which they said is the substance of a thing remains throughout every transmutation, although its attributes, such as its form and everything that accrues to it over and above its material substance, are changed. From all these considerations they concluded that matter is the element and principle of all beings.

75. **And for this reason** (37).

Then he gives, as a secondary point, what they held as following from the above, namely, that in the world nothing is generated or corrupted in an absolute sense. For when some change occurs with regard to a thing's attributes, and its substance remains unchanged, we do not say that it is generated or corrupted in an absolute sense, but only in a qualified one; for example, when Socrates becomes good or musical, we do not say that he simply comes to be, but comes to be this. And similarly when he loses a state of this kind, we do not say that he is corrupted in an absolute sense, but only in a qualified one. But matter, which is the substance of things according to them, always remains; and every change affects some of a thing's accidents, such as its attributes. From this they concluded that nothing is generated or corrupted in an absolute sense, but only in a qualified one.

76. Yet even though they all agreed on this point, in positing a material cause, nevertheless they differed in their position in two respects: first, with respect to the number of material causes, because some held that there is one, and others many; and second, with respect to its nature, because some held that it is fire, others water, and so on. Similarly, among those who posited many material causes, some assigned certain ones as the material principles of things, and some the others.

77. **Thales, the originator** (38).

Here he begins to give the opinions of each of the philosophers about the material cause. First (38), he gives the opinions of those who posited one material cause; and second (43:C 88), the opinions of those who posited many ("Empedocles").

In regard to the first he does three things. First, he gives the opinions of those who claimed that water is the principle of all things; second (41:C 86), he gives the opinion of those who made air the principle of things ("Anaximenes"); and third (42:C 87), the opinion of those who claimed that fire is the principle of things ("Hippasus").

In regard to the first he does two things. First, he gives the opinion of Thales, who said that water is the principle of things; and second (39:C 79), the reason for this opinion ("For presumably").

He says then (38) that Thales, the originator of this kind of philosophy, i.e., speculative philosophy, said that water is the first principle of all things. Thales is said to have been the originator of speculative philosophy because he was the only one of the seven wise men, who came after the theological poets, to make an investigation into the causes of things, the other sages being concerned with moral matters. The names of the seven wise men are as follows. The first was Thales of Miletus, who lived during the time of Romulus and when Achaz, King of Israel, was reigning over the Hebrews. The second was Pittacus of Mitylene, who lived when Sedecias was reigning over the Hebrews and when Tarquinius Priscus was reigning over the Romans. The other five sages were Solon of Athens, Chilo of Lacedaemon, Periander of Corinth, Cleobulus of Lydia, and Bias of Prienne, all of whom lived during the period of the Babylonian captivity.[8] Hence, since Thales alone among these men investigated the natures of things and distinguished himself by committing his arguments to writing, he is described here as the originator of this science.

78. Nor should it be thought unfitting if he touches here on the opinions of those who have treated only the philosophy of nature; because according to the ancients, who knew no other substance except the corporeal and mobile, it was necessary that first philosophy be the philosophy of nature, as is stated in Book IV.[9] And from this position Thales next adopted this one, that the earth rests upon water, as anything having a principle is based on its principle.

79. **For presumably he took** (39).

Here he gives the reasons by which Thales could be led to the above position. First, he shows how he was led to this position by his own reasoning; and second (40:C 82), by the authority of his predecessors ("Moreover, there are some").

Now he was led by two lines of reasoning; one is taken from the cause itself of a thing, and the other from a consideration of the generation of things ("And on the fact"). Therefore these premises are related. For the second follows from the first, because that which is a principle of being of other things is also the first principle from which things are generated. The third

follows from the second, because by corruption each thing is dissolved into that from which it was generated. The fourth follows from the second and the third; for that which precedes the generation of things and remains after they have been corrupted must always remain in being.

80. In the first line of reasoning he uses three indications to show that water is the principle of being of things. The first of these is that the nutriment of living things must be moist. But living things derive nourishment and being from the same principle; and thus moisture appears to be the principle of being of things. The second indication is that the being of any physical thing, and especially of a living one, is conserved by its proper and natural heat. But heat seems to be generated from moisture, since moisture itself is in a sense the matter of heat. Hence from this it appears that moisture is a principle of being of things. The third indication is that animal life depends on moisture. Hence an animal dies as a result of its natural moisture being dried up and is kept in existence as a result of its moisture being preserved. But in living things to live is to be. Hence it is also evident from this that moisture is a principle of being of things. These three indications also have a natural connection with one another. For an animal is nourished by moisture, because its natural heat is sustained by moisture. And from these two it follows that animal life is always due to moisture. But that from which a thing comes to be, i.e., from which a thing gets its being, is a principle of everything that derives being from it. And for this reason he adopted this opinion that moisture is the principle of all things.

81. In a similar way he also draws

[8] See St. Augustine, *De Civitate Dei*, VIII, 2 (PL 41:225-6); XVIII, 24-26 (PL 41:581-3).
[9] Aristotle makes this point in Book VI, chapter 1 (542:C 1170) as St. Thomas again notes in Book III, Lesson 6 (C 398); and in Book XI, Lesson 7, (962:C 2267).

33

an indication of this from the generation of things, because the processes of generation of living things, which are the noblest of [natural] beings, come from seed. But the seed or spermata of all living things have a moist nature. Hence from this it also appears that moisture is a principle of generation of things. Again, if we add to all of the above points the fact that water is the principle of moisture, it follows that water is the first principle of things.

82. **Moreover, there are** (40).

Here he shows how Thales was led to the above position by the authority of the ancients. He says that prior to Thales and many years before the men of Aristotle's time there were some men, the first to speculate about the gods, who seem to have held this opinion about nature, namely, that water is the principle of all things.

83. With a view to making this clear, we must bear in mind that among the Greeks the first who were famous for their learning were certain theological poets, so called because of the songs which they wrote about the gods. These poets, who were three in number, Orpheus, Museus and Linus,[10] of whom Orpheus was the more famous, lived during the time when the judges ruled over the Jewish people. Hence it is clear that they lived long before Thales and much longer before Aristotle, who lived during the time of Alexander. These poets dealt to some extent with the nature of things by means of certain figurative representations in myths. For they said that Oceanus [i.e., the ocean], where the greatest aggregation of waters is found, and Tethys, which is the name they gave to the goddess of the waters, are the parents of generation, implying by this, under the form of a myth, that water is the principle of generation.

84. They cloaked this view in another fabulous story, saying that the oath or vow of the gods was by a certain body of water, which the poets call Styx and describe as an underground swamp. And when they said that the gods swore by water, they implied that water was nobler than the gods themselves, because an oath or vow is taken on what is most honorable. Now that [11] which is prior is more honorable; for the perfect is prior absolutely to the imperfect, both in nature and in time, although in a particular being imperfection is prior temporally to perfection. Hence, from this it is evident that they thought that water is prior to the gods themselves, whom they thought to be celestial bodies. And since these earliest thinkers said that water is the principle of things, if there was any opinion about natural bodies prior to theirs, we do not know what it was. Thus what Thales is said to have thought about the first cause of things is now clear.

85. A certain philosopher named Hippo was not credited with adding anything to those mentioned because of the imperfection of his knowledge or understanding. Hence, in *The Soul*,[12] Hippo is placed among the ruder [thinkers]; for in that work it is stated that Hippo, basing his argument on the seeds of things, as was said here of Thales, held water to be the soul and principle of things. Hence it is clear that he adds nothing to Thales' view. Or the statement can mean that, since he spoke imperfectly, he did not make himself worthy to have his doctrine included here with the others.

86. **Anaximenes and Diogenes** (41).

Here he gives the opinions of those who held that air is the principle of things, namely, Diogenes and Anaxim-

---

[10] See St. Augustine, *Op. cit.,* XVIII, 14 (PL 41:572).
[11] Reading *hoc* for *hos,* as given in the original Cathala edition.
[12] *De Anima,* I, 2 (405b 1).

enes, who held that air is naturally prior to water and is the principle of all simple bodies, i.e., of the four elements, and thus of all other things. Anaximenes is the third philosopher after Thales and the disciple of Anaximander, who was the disciple of Thales; and Diogenes is said to have been the disciple of Anaximenes. Yet there is this difference between the opinion of Diogenes and that of Anaximenes: Anaximenes held that air is the principle of things in an absolute sense, whereas Diogenes said that air could be the principle of things only if it possessed a divine nature. From this comes the opinion which is touched on in *The Soul,* Book I.[13] Now the reason why he held that air is the principle of things could be taken from the process of respiration, by which the life of animals is conserved, and because the processes whereby things are generated and corrupted seem to be modified as a result of changes in the air.

87. **Hippasus of Metopontium** (42).

Here he states that the two philosophers, Hippasus and Heraclitus, held that fire is the material principle of things. And they could have been influenced by its subtileness, as is said below.

88. **Empedocles** (43).

Here he gives the opinions of those who posited many material principles. First, he gives the opinion of Empedocles, who held that there are a limited number of such principles; and second (44:C 90), that of Anaxagoras, who held that there are an infinite number ("Anaxagoras").

First (43), he gives Empedocles' opinion regarding the three elements mentioned above, water, air, and fire, which he says are the principles of things, adding to them a fourth, earth.

89. Second, he gives Empedocles'

opinion about the permanence of these elements; for, like those who hold that there is one material cause, he holds that these elements always remain and are neither generated nor corrupted. However, he said that other things are generated from and dissolved into these elements according as a greater or smaller number of them are combined or separated out, i.e., inasmuch as these four are united by the process of combination and lose their unity by the process of separation.

90. **Anaxagoras** (44).

Here he gives the opinion of Anaxagoras, who was the other disciple of Anaximenes and the classmate of Diogenes. A native of Clazomenae, he was prior to Empedocles in years but later in his activity or work, either because he began to philosophize later, or because his explanation of the number of principles is less satisfactory than that of Empedocles. For he said that there are an infinite number of material principles, whereas it is better to take a limited and smaller number, as Empedocles did, as is stated in Book I of the *Physics.*[14] For Anaxagoras not only said that fire, water, and the other elements are the principles of things, as Empedocles did, but also claimed that all things having like parts, such as flesh, bones, marrow and so forth, whose smallest parts are infinite in number, are the principles of things. For he claimed that in each being there are an infinite number of parts of each type of thing, because he found that in the case of inferior things one of these can be generated from another. He said, in fact, that things could be generated only by being separated out from a mixture, as Aristotle has explained more fully in the *Physics,* Book I.[15]

91. Second, Anaxagoras also agrees

---

[13] *Op. cit.,* I, 2 (405a 21).
[14] *Physica,* I, 4 (188a 16).
[15] *Physica,* I, 4 (187a 20).

with Empedocles on this point, namely, that things are generated and corrupted only insofar as the parts of these infinite principles are combined or separated out, and that if this were not the case nothing would be generated or corrupted. But he said that the infinite number of principles of this kind, from which the substances of things are produced, always remain in being.

92. From the opinions of these philosophers, then, Aristotle concludes that the only cause which these men recognized was the one which belongs to the class of material cause.

LESSON 5

Opinions about the Efficient Cause

ARISTOTLE'S TEXT   Chapters 3 & 4: 984a 16-984b 32

45. But as men proceeded in this way, reality itself again opened up a path and forced them to make investigations. For if every process of generation and corruption is from some one thing or more than one, why does this occur, and what is the cause? For certainly the subject itself does not cause itself to change. I mean, for example, that neither wood nor bronze is the cause of the change undergone by either one of them; for wood does not produce a bed, or bronze a statue, but something else is the cause of the change. But to seek this is to seek another principle, as if one were to say that from which the beginning of motion comes.

46. Now in general those who have taken such a course from the very beginning, and who said that the subject is one, created no difficulty for themselves when they said that everything is one. [But some [1] of those who say that it is one],[2] being baffled, so to speak, by this question, say that this [one subject] and the whole of nature is immobile not only with respect to generation and corruption (for this is an ancient opinion and one which all men confess to be true), but also with respect to every other change. This opinion is peculiar to them. Hence, of those who said that the [universe] itself is one, it occurred [3] to none of them to conceive of such a cause, except perhaps Parmenides, and to him only insofar as he claims that there is not one cause but also in a sense two causes.[4] But for those who make the elements of things many, such as the hot and cold, or fire and earth, a better explanation is possible, because they use fire as if it were a material principle which is active in nature, but water and earth and the like they use in the opposite way.[5]

47. After these men and such principles, as if they were insufficient to generate the natures of existing things, men were again compelled (as we said [45]) by the truth itself to seek for the next principle. For perhaps it is unlikely that either fire or earth or anything else of this kind should be the cause of the good dispositions of things which are or come to be; nor was it consistent that they should think this to be the case. Nor again would it be right to attribute so important a matter to chance occurrence and fortune.

48. And when someone [6] said that there is one intellect present in nature as in animals, and that this is the cause of the world and the arrangement of the whole, he seemed to atone for the untenable statements made by his predecessors.

---

[1] I.e., the Eleatics.
[2] This statement is omitted in the Latin version, but see Greek text (984a 30) and St. Thomas (C 95).
[3] Reading *contingit* for *convenit.*
[4] Diels, Frag. 8.
[5] Probably Empedocles.
[6] I.e., Anaxagoras; see Plato, *Phaedo,* 97 B-98 B.

We know that Anaxagoras expressed these views, although Hermotimus of Clazomenae was the first to speak of such a cause. Those, therefore, who held these opinions likewise posited a principle in existing things which is the cause of their goodness, and that sort of cause which is the source of motion in the world.

Chapter 4

49. Now someone might have suspected that Hesiod was the first to have investigated this sort of cause, or anyone else who held that love or desire is a principle in existing things, as Parmenides did. For in the place where he attempts to explain the generation of the universe, he says that "Love, the first of all the gods, was made." [7] And Hesiod says that "The first of all things to be made was chaos, then broad earth, and love, who is pre-eminent among the immortals" [8]—as though there must be in the world some cause which moves things and brings them together. How one must arrange these thinkers in sequence will be decided later on.

[7] Diels, Frag. 13.
[8] *Theogony,* 116-20.

COMMENTARY

93. Having given the philosophers' opinions about the material cause, Aristotle now gives their opinions about the efficient cause, which is the source of motion. This is divided into two parts. First (45:C 93), he gives the opinion of those who assigned without qualification a cause of motion and generation. Second (47:C 97), he examines the opinion of those who posited an efficient cause, which is also the principle of good and evil in the world ("After these men").

In regard to the first he does two things. First, he gives the reasoning which compelled them to posit an efficient cause. Second (46:C 94), he shows the different positions which different men have held regarding this ("Now in general").

He says (45), then, that some philosophers have proceeded in this way in positing a material cause, but that the very nature of reality clearly provided them with a course for understanding or discovering the truth, and compelled them to investigate a problem which led them to the efficient cause. This problem is as follows: no thing or subject changes itself; for example, wood does not change itself so that a bed comes from it, nor does bronze cause itself to be changed in such a way that a statue comes from it; but there must be some other principle which causes the change they undergo, and this is the artist. But those who posited a material cause, whether one or more than one, said that the generation and corruption of things come from this cause as a subject. Therefore there must be some other cause of change, and to seek this is to seek another class of principle and cause, which is called the source of motion.

94. **Now in general** (46).

He shows here that the philosophers have adopted three positions with respect to the foregoing issue. For those who adopted this course from the very beginning, and said that there is one material cause, were not greatly con-

cerned with the solution of this problem. For they were content with their
view of matter and neglected the cause
of motion altogether.

95. But others, who said that all
things are one, being defeated as it
were by this issue, as they were unable
to go so far as to assign a cause of
motion, denied motion altogether.
Hence they said that the whole universe is one immobile being. In this
respect they differed from the first
philosophers of nature, who said that
one cause is the substance of all things
although it is moved by rarefaction and
condensation, so that in this way many
things come to be in some measure
from one principle. However, they did
not say that this principle is subject
to generation and corruption in an
absolute sense. For the view that nothing was generated or corrupted without qualification is an ancient one
admitted by all of them, as is clear
from what was said above (37:C 75).
But it was peculiar to these later thinkers to say that the whole of reality is
one immobile being, devoid of every
kind of motion. These men were
Parmenides and Melissus, as will be
explained below (65:C 138). Hence it
is evident that it was impossible for
those who said that the whole is one
immobile being to conceive of "such a
cause," i.e., a cause of motion. For,
by the very fact that they did away with
motion, they sought in vain for a cause
of motion. An exception was Parmenides; for even though he held that
there is only one thing according to
reason, he held that there are many
things according to the senses, as will
be stated below (49:C 101). Hence,
inasmuch as Parmenides held that there
are many things, it was in keeping
with his position to hold that there
are many causes, one of which would
be a mover and the others something
moved. For just as he held that there
are many things according to the
senses, in a similar way it was neces-

sary for him to hold that there is motion according to the senses, because
a plurality of things can be understood
to be produced from one subject only
by some kind of motion.

96. Third, there were those who, in
making the substances of things many,
assented to the aforesaid reasoning by
positing a cause of motion. For they
maintained that the hot or the cold,
i.e., fire or earth, are causes; and of
these they used fire as having a mobile,
i.e., an active, nature, but water, earth
and air they used in the opposite way,
i.e., as having a passive nature. Thus
fire was a sort of efficient cause, but
the others a sort of material cause.

97. **After these men** (47).

Here he gives the opinion of those
who posited an efficient cause, not only
as a principle of motion, but also as
a principle of good and evil in things.
In regard to this he does two things.
First (47:C 97), he expounds their
views. Second (51:C 107), he shows
in what respect they failed in assigning the causes of things ("These
thinkers").

In regard to the first he does two
things. First, he gives the reasons for
their position by which they were induced to posit another cause besides
the foregoing one. Second (48:C 100),
he shows how they posited this kind of
cause in different ways ("And when
someone").

He says first (47), then, that after
the foregoing philosophers who held
that there is only one material cause,
or many bodies, one of which was
active and the others passive, and after
the other first principles given by them,
men were again compelled by the
truth itself, "as we have said," i.e., as
was stated above (45:C 93), to seek
the "next" principle, i.e., the one
which naturally follows the foregoing
one, namely, the cause of good, which
is really the final cause, although it
was held by them only incidentally,
as will be seen below (84:C 177). For

they held that there is a cause of goodness in things only after the manner of an efficient cause. They were compelled to do this because the foregoing principles were not sufficient to account for the generation of the natural world, in which some things are found to be well disposed. The fact that bodies are conserved in their proper places and are corrupted outside of them proves this; and so do the benefits resulting from the parts of animals, which are found to be disposed in this manner according as this is in keeping with an animal's good state of being.

98. But neither fire nor earth nor any such bodies were held to be adequate causes of this kind of good disposition or state of being which some things already have but others acquire by some kind of production. For these bodies act in one definite way according to the necessity of their proper forms, as fire heats things and tends upward, and water cools things and tends downward. But the aforesaid benefits and good states of being of things must have a cause which is not limited to one effect only, since the parts of different animals are found to be disposed in different ways, and in each one insofar as it is in keeping with its nature.

99. Hence, it is not reasonable that fire or earth or the like should be the cause of the aforesaid good state of being which things have, nor was it reasonable that these men should have thought this to be the case. Nor again would it be reasonable to say that these things are chance occurrences, i.e., that they are accidental or come about by chance, and that their causality is changed only fortuitously; although some of these thinkers had said this, as Empedocles and all those who posited a material cause, as is evident in Book II of the *Physics*.[1] However,

this is also seen to be false by reason of the fact that good dispositions of this kind are found either always or for the most part, whereas things that come about by chance or fortune do not occur always or for the most part but seldom. For this reason, then, it was necessary to discover besides the four elements some other principle which would account for the good dispositions of things. Another text has "Nor would it be right that these should be attributed to chance occurrence and fortune," but this means the same as the above.

100. **And when someone said** (48).

Here he gives in detail the opinions about the aforesaid principle. First (48), he gives the opinions of those who held that there is one [efficient] cause; and second (50:C 104), the opinions of those who held that there are two such causes ("But since there would seem").

In regard to the first he does two things. First, he gives the views of those who held that the first efficient cause is an intellect; and second (49:C 101), the opinions of those who held that it is love ("Now someone might").

He says (48), then, that after the foregoing doctrine someone appeared who said that there is an intellect present in nature at large, just as there is in animals, and that this is the cause of the world and the order of the whole, i.e., of the universe, in which order the good of the entire universe and that of every single part consists. And this man atoned for the first philosophers by reducing to pure truth those who said unreasonable things and did not mention this kind of cause. Now Anaxagoras clearly stated this doctrine, although another philosopher —Hermotimus of Clazomenae—first gave him the idea of proposing this opinion. Hence it is evident that those who held this opinion claimed at the

---

[1] *Physica*, II, 4 (196a 21).

same time that the principle by which things are well disposed and the one which is the source of motion in things, are one and the same.

101. **Now someone might** (49).

Here he gives the opinion of those who claimed that love is the first principle, although they did not hold this very explicitly or clearly. Accordingly, he says that some suspected that Hesiod had sought for such a principle to account for the good disposition of things, or anyone else who posited love or desire in nature. For when Parmenides attempted to explain the generation of the universe, he said that in the establishing of the universe "Love, the first of all the gods, was made." Nor is this opposed to his doctrine that there is one immobile being, of which Aristotle speaks here; because this man held that there are many things according to the senses, although there is only one thing according to reason, as was stated above and will be stated below. Moreover, he called the celestial bodies, or perhaps certain separate substances, gods.

102. But Hesiod said that first of all there was chaos, and then broad earth was made, to be the receptacle of everything else; for it is evident[2] that the receptacle [or void] and place are principles, as is stated in Book IV of the *Physics*.[3] And he also held that love, which instructs all the immortals, is a principle of things. He did this because the communication of goodness seems to spring from love, for a good deed is a sign and effect of love. Hence, since corruptible things derive their being and every good disposition from immortal beings of this kind, this must be attributed to the love of the immortals. Furthermore, he held that the immortals are either the celestial bodies themselves, or material principles themselves. Thus he posited chaos and love as though there had to be in existing things not only a material cause of their motions, but also an efficient cause which moves and unites them, which seems to be the office of love. For love moves us to act, because it is the source of all the emotions, since fear, sadness and hope proceed only from love. That love unites things is clear from this, that love itself is a certain union between the lover and the thing loved, seeing that the lover regards the beloved as himself. This man Hesiod is to be numbered among the poets who lived before the time of the philosophers.

103. Now, as to which one of these thinkers is prior, i.e., more competent in knowledge, whether the one who said that love is the first principle, or the one who said that intellect is, can be decided later on, that is, where God is discussed. He calls this decision an arrangement, because the degree of excellence belonging to each man is allotted to him in this way. Another translation states this more clearly: "Therefore, in what order it is fitting to go over these thinkers, and who in this order is prior, can be decided later on."

[2] The context requires *patet* rather than *posuerunt*.
[3] *Physica*, IV, 1 (208b 25).

LESSON 6

Love and Hate as Efficient Causes of Good and Evil

ARISTOTLE'S TEXT   Chapter 4: 984b 32-985b 4

50. But since there would seem to be in nature things which are contrary to those that are good, and not only order and good but also disorder and what is base, and evil things more numerous than good ones, and base things more numerous than noble ones, for this reason another thinker introduced love and strife as causes, each of its own type of effects. For if anyone grasps what Empedocles said, taking it according to its meaning rather than according to its faltering expression, he will find that love is the cause of things which come to be by aggregation,[1] and strife [2] the cause of evil things. Hence, if anyone were to say that Empedocles, in a sense, both said and was the first to say that good and evil are principles, he would perhaps speak correctly, i.e., if the cause of all good things is good and that of all evil things is evil.

51. These thinkers, then, as we have said, to this extent have touched on two of the causes which we established in the *Physics*,[3]—matter and the source of motion—though only obscurely and with no clarity, much as untrained men conduct themselves in battle. For the latter, though encircled, often deal telling blows, but without science. In the same way these thinkers do not seem to be aware of what they are saying. For it seems that they almost never make use of the causes except to a small degree.

52. Anaxagoras uses "intellect" [4] in an artificial way in generating the world. For when he is in difficulty as to what is necessarily the cause of something, he drags in this intellect; but in other cases he makes everything but intellect the cause of what comes to be.[5]

53. Empedocles, it is true, makes greater use of causes than Anaxagoras, though not sufficiently; nor does one find in his use of them what he professed. In many places he argues that love separates things, and that strife brings them together. For when being itself is separated out into its elements by strife, then fire and each of the other elements are brought together into a unity. But when they are united by love, the particles must again be separated out from each element.

54. In contrast to the first philosophers, then, Empedocles was the first to introduce this cause, dividing it in such a way as to make the source of motion not a single principle but different and contrary ones. Moreover, he was the first to claim that the elements, which are said to belong to the class of matter, are four in number, although he does not use them as four but as two, taking fire by itself alone, and its opposites—earth, air, and water—as a single nature (46).

---

[1] The Greek text reads: "love is the cause of good things."
[2] Diels, Frags. 17, 26.
[3] *Physica*, II, 3 (194b 15).
[4] *Op. cit.*, Frag. 12.
[5] See Plato, *Laws*, 967 B; *Phaedo* 98 B.

But anyone may see this by studying his basic sayings.[6] This philosopher, then, as we have said, has spoken in this way about the principles of things and their number.

[6] Diels, Frag. 62.

COMMENTARY

104. Here Aristotle gives the opinion of those who posited contrariety in beings of this kind, and the reason which moved them, which is as follows. There would seem to be in nature things which are contrary to those that are good, because in nature one finds not only things which are ordered and good, but sometimes things which are disordered and base. Now it cannot be said that evil things have no cause but happen by chance, because evil things are more numerous than good ones, and base things more numerous than those which are unqualifiedly noble. But those things which come to be by chance without a definite cause do not occur for the most part but in the smaller number of cases. Hence, since contrary effects have contrary causes, it was necessary to hold as a cause of things not only love, from which the order and good in things originate, but also hate, which is the source of disorder and baseness or evil in things, so that in this way particular instances of evil and good have their own type of causes.

105. That this was the reason which moved Empedocles is evident if anyone grasps what he says, taking his statement according to its meaning rather than according to the words which he used imperfectly and, as it were, in a faltering way. For he said that it is the office of love to bring the elements together, and of hate to separate them. But since the generation of things is a result of the coming together [of the elements], by reason of which there is being and good in things, and their corruption a result of the separation [of the elements], which is the way to non-being and evil, it is now evident that he wanted love to be the cause of things which come to be by aggregation, i.e., of good things, and hate the cause of evil things. Thus if one were to say that Empedocles was the first to maintain that good and evil are principles, he would perhaps speak correctly.

106. That is to say, this would follow if Empedocles did hold that good is the cause of all good things, and evil the cause of all evil things. For it is evident that he posited evil as the cause of some evil things, namely, of corruption, and good as the cause of some good things, namely, of generation. But because it would not follow that all good things would be caused by friendship or all evil things by hate, since the parts of the world would be differentiated by hate and fused together by friendship, therefore he did not always hold that good is the cause of good things, and evil the cause of evil things.

107. **These thinkers** (51).

Here he shows that in giving these causes the philosophers treated them inadequately. First (51:C 107), he mentions them in a general way. Second (52:C 108), he treats each one individually ("Anaxagoras").

He says first (51), then, that these philosophers—Anaxagoras and Empedocles—arrived at a doctrine of two of the causes which have been established

43

in the *Physics*,[1] namely, matter and the cause of motion, although they treated these obscurely and with no clarity, because they did not explain that those principles which they held to be the causes of things could be reduced to these classes of causes. But insofar as they posited two of these causes, they may be likened to untrained warriors who, though encircled by the enemy, sometimes strike good blows, not by art but by chance. This is evident from the fact that, even though they happen to do this sometimes, this does not occur always or for the most part. In like manner, too, these philosophers were not accustomed to express themselves accurately, nor was it their custom to speak with awareness, i.e., as men who know. Hence another translation has, "But these men neither have science, nor are they to be compared with men who realize what they are saying." This is shown by the fact that, although they had proposed these causes, they hardly ever used them, because they employed them in few instances. Hence it seems that they introduced them not as a result of art but by accident, because they were moved to do so by necessity.

108. **Anaxagoras** (52).

Here he shows in what particular respect the view of each is unsatisfactory. First, he speaks of Anaxagoras; and second (53:C 109), of Empedocles ("Empedocles").

He says first, then, that Anaxagoras uses "intellect" to generate the world, and in so doing he seems to speak of it in an artificial way. For [2] when he inquires about the causes of the world's generation, he drags it in of necessity, i.e., he invents this intelligence only because he is unable to attribute the generation of the world to any other cause which would differentiate things

except to one which is essentially distinct and unmixed, and intellect is a thing of this kind. But in all other cases he draws his causes from any other source rather than intellect, for example, in the case of the particular natures of things.

109. **Empedocles** (53).

Here he shows in what respect Empedocles' doctrine is inadequate; and in regard to this he does two things. First, he shows in what respect Empedocles' doctrine is inadequate. Second (54:C 111), he explains what Empedocles himself held in contrast to the other philosophers ("In contrast").

He says, first (53), that Empedocles, in dealing with the particular natures of things, "makes greater use of the causes" posited by him (the four elements, and love and hate) than Anaxagoras did, because he reduced the generation and corruption of particular things to these causes, and not to intelligence as Anaxagoras did. But Empedocles failed in two ways.

First, he failed because he does not treat causes of this kind adequately enough; for he uses things which are not self-evident as though they were self-evident axioms, as is stated in the *Physics*, Book I,[3] that is, insofar as he assumed that they are self-evident, because at one definite time strife has dominion over the elements and at another, love.

110. Second, he failed because in the matters which he investigates, one does not find what he has professed, i.e., what he held as a principle, namely, that love combines things and that strife separates them, because in many places love must on the contrary "separate" or divide things, and strife "bring them together," i.e., unite them. For when the universe itself "is separated out," i.e., divided into its parts,

[1] *Physica*, II, 3 (194b 15).
[2] *Non* in the Latin version should read *nam*.
[3] *Physica*, I, 5 (189a 4).

44

by hate, as occurs when the world is generated, all particles of fire are then combined into one whole, and so also are the individual particles of the other elements "brought together," i.e., joined to each other. Hence, strife not only separates the particles of fire from those of air, but also brings together the particles of fire. But, on the other hand, when the elements come together through love, which occurs when the universe is destroyed, the particles of fire must then be separated from each other, and so also must the particles of the other elements. For fire can be mixed with air only if the particles of fire are separated from each other; and the same is true of the particles of air only if these elements penetrate one another, so that love not only unites unlike things but also separates like things, according to what follows from his position.

111. **In contrast** (54).

Here he shows in what respect Empedocles' own doctrine differs from that of the other philosophers. He says that Empedocles maintained two things in contrast to the others. First, he divided the cause which is the source of motion into two contrary parts. Second, he held the material cause to be constituted of four elements—not that he uses the four elements as four, but rather as two, because he contrasts fire with the other three, saying that fire is active in nature and the others passive in nature. Anyone can gather this from the elements of things treated by him, or from his "basic sayings" in the sense of the rudiments of the doctrine which he propounded. Another version reads "from his verses," because he is said to have written his philosophy in meters. And still another version, which says "from his statements," agrees with this. As has been stated, then, this philosopher was the first to stipulate in this way that the principles of things are so many in number, namely, four, and to speak of those which have been mentioned.

LESSON 7

The Views of the Atomists and the Pythagoreans

ARISTOTLE'S TEXT   Chapters 4 & 5: 985b 4-986a 13

55. Leucippus and his colleague Democritus say that the elements of things are the full and the void, calling the one being and the other non-being. Of these they say that the full or solid is being, and the void, non-being. For this reason too they say that being no more *is* than non-being, because the void no more *is* than body; and they hold that these are the material causes of things.

56. And just as those who make the underlying substance one generate other things from this by means of its attributes, holding that rarity and density are the principles of these attributes, in the same way these men say that the differences [1] [of the atoms] are the causes of other things. These differences, they say, are three: shape, arrangement, and position. For they claim that what exists differs only by rhythm, inter-contact, and turning; and of these rhythm means shape, inter-contact arrangement, and turning position. For A differs from N in shape, AN from NA in arrangement, and Z from N in position. But with regard to motion, from whence it comes or how it is present in things, these men carelessly dismissed this question as the other thinkers did. As we have said before, then, these two types of causes seem to have been investigated to this extent by the first thinkers.

Chapter 5

57. But during the time of these and prior to them, lived the group called the Pythagoreans, who dealt with mathematics and were the first to develop it; and having been brought up in these sciences, they thought that their principles were the principles of all things. But since among these principles numbers are naturally first, they thought they saw in numbers,[2] more than in fire and earth, many resemblances to things which are and come to be, because [according to them] this particular attribute of numbers is justice, another is soul and mind, and still another is opportunity. The case is the same, so to speak, with every other thing.

58. Moreover, since they considered the attributes and ratios of harmonies in terms of numbers, and since other things in their whole nature seemed to be likened to numbers, and since numbers are the first things in the whole of nature, they thought that the elements of numbers are the elements of all things, and that the whole heaven is a harmony and number. And whatever they had revealed in the case of numbers and harmonies [which they could] show [to be in agreement] with the motions and parts of the heavens, and its whole arrangement, they collected and adapted to these. And if anything was lacking anywhere,

[1] Reading *differentias* for *differentes*.
[2] Aristotle investigates this view at greater length in *Metaphysics*, XIV, 6 (1092b 26).

they called it in in order that their undertaking might be complete. I mean that since the number ten seems to be the perfect number and to comprise the whole nature of numbers, they said that the bodies which move in the heavens are ten in number; but as only nine are observable they therefore invented a tenth, the counter-earth. These things have been dealt with more exactly in another work.[3]

[3] *De Coelo*, II, 13 (293a 24).

COMMENTARY

112. Here he begins to give the positions of those who held strange and obscure views about the principles of things. First (55:C 112), he gives the position of those who held that there are many principles of things; and second (63:C 134), the position of those who held that there is only one being ("But there are some").

In regard to the first he does two things. First, he gives the opinion of Leucippus and Democritus, who held that the principles of things are corporeal. Second (57:C 119), he gives the opinion of the Pythagoreans, who held that the principles of things are incorporeal entities ("But during the time").

In regard to the first he does two things. First, he gives the opinion of Democritus and Leucippus about the material cause of things; and second (56:C 115), their opinion about the cause of diversity, that is, how matter is differentiated into many things. In this discussion the cause of the generation and corruption of things also becomes evident; and this is a point on which these men agreed with the ancient philosophers ("And just as those who").[1]

He says (55), then, that two philosophers, Democritus and Leucippus, who are called friends because they followed each other in all things, held that the principles of things are the full and the void or empty, of which the full is being, and the void or empty, non-being.

113. Now in order to clarify this opinion we must recall what the Philosopher says in Book I of *Generation*,[2] where he treats it more fully. For certain philosophers had held that everything is one continuous immobile being, because it seems that there cannot be motion without a void, or any distinction between things, as they said. And though they could not comprehend the privation of continuity, by reason of which bodies must be understood to be differentiated, except by means of a void, they claimed that the void existed in no way. Democritus, who came after them, and who agreed with their reasoning but was unable to exclude diversity and motion from things, held that the void existed, and that all bodies are composed of certain indivisible bodies [i.e., the atoms]. He did this because it seemed to him that no reason could be given why the whole of being should be divided in one part rather than another. And lest he should hold that the whole of being is continuous, he therefore chose to maintain that this whole is divided everywhere and in its entirety; and this could not be the case if anything divisible remained undivided. And according to him indivisible bodies of this

[1] Reading *Et quemadmodum qui unum* for *Et quemadmodum in unum*.
[2] *De Generatione*, I, 8 (325a 1-326b 29).

kind can neither exist nor be joined together except by means of the void. For if the void did not come between any two of them, one continuous whole would result from the two; which he did not hold for the above reason. Hence he said that the continuous quantity of each body is constituted both of those indivisible bodies filling indivisible spaces and of certain empty spaces,[3] which he called pores, coming between these indivisible bodies.

114. And since the void is non-being and the full is being, it is evident from this that he did not hold that a thing was constituted by being rather than non-being, because the [indivisible] bodies did not constitute things more than the void, or the void more than bodies; but he said that a body is composed at once of these two things, as is clear in the text. Hence he held that these two things are the causes of beings as their matter.

115. **And just as those** (56).

Here he shows in what respect these philosophers agreed with the ancients who claimed that there is only one matter. He indicates agreement in two respects.

First, just as the ancient philosophers held that there is one matter, and from that one matter generated something else according to the different attributes of matter (i.e., the rare and dense, which they accepted as the principles of all other attributes), in a similar way these philosophers—Democritus and Leucippus—said that there were different causes of different things (namely, of the bodies composed of these indivisible bodies), i.e., that different beings were produced as a result of certain differences of these indivisible bodies and their pores.

116. Now they said that these differences are, first, differences in shape, which is noted from this that things are angular, circular or square; second,

differences in arrangement, i.e., insofar as the indivisible bodies are prior or subsequent; and, third, differences in position, i.e., insofar as these bodies are in front or behind, right or left, or above and below. Hence they said that one being differs from another "either by rhythm," which is shape, "or by inter-contact," which is arrangement, "or by turning," which is position.

117. He illustrates this by using the letters of the Greek alphabet, which differ from each other in shape just as in our alphabet one letter also differs from another; for A differs from N in shape. Again, AN differs from NA in arrangement, because one letter is placed before the other. And one letter also differs from another in position, as Z from N, just as in our language we also see that semivowels cannot stand after liquids preceded by mutes in the same syllable. Therefore, just as tragedy and comedy come from the same letters as a result of the letters being disposed in different ways because of this threefold difference, in a similar fashion different species of things are produced from the same indivisible bodies as a result of the latter being disposed in different ways.

118. The second respect in which these philosophers agreed with the ancients is this: just as the ancient philosophers neglected to posit a cause which accounts for motion in things, so also did these men, although they would say that these indivisible bodies are capable of self-motion. Thus it is evident that these philosophers mentioned only two of the causes, i.e., all of them spoke of the material cause, and some of the efficient cause.

119. **But during the time of these** (57).

Here he gives the opinions of the Pythagoreans, who held that numbers are the substances of things. In regard

---

[3] Reading *spatiis* for *spatii.*

to this he does two things. First (57:C 119), he gives their opinions about the substance of things; and second (59:C 124), their opinions about the principles of things ("But the reason").

In regard to the first he gives two reasons by which they were led to assert that numbers are the substances of things. He gives the second reason (58:C 121) where he says "Moreover, since they considered."

He says (57) that the Pythagoreans were philosophers who lived "during the time of these," i.e., they were contemporaries of some of the foregoing philosophers; "and prior to them," because they preceded some of them. Now it must be understood that there were two groups of philosophers.[4] One group was called the Ionians, who inhabited the land which is now called Greece. This group originated with Thales, as was pointed out above (38:C 77). The other group of philosophers were the Italians, who lived in that part of Italy which was once called Greater Greece and is now called Apulia and Calabria. The leader of these philosophers was Pythagoras, a native of Samos, so called from a certain city of Calabria. These two groups of philosophers lived at the same time, and this is why he says that they lived "During the time of these and prior to them."

120. These Italian philosophers, also called Pythagoreans, were the first to develop certain mathematical entities, so that they said that these are the substances and principles of sensible things. He says that they were "the first" because the Platonists were their successors. They were moved to bring in mathematics because they were brought up in the study of these sciences, and therefore they thought that the principles of mathematics are the principles of all existing things. For men are wont to judge about things

in terms of what they already know. And since among mathematical entities numbers are first, these men therefore tried to see resemblances of natural things, both as regards their being and generation, in numbers rather than in the sensible elements—earth, water and the like. For just as the foregoing philosophers adapted the attributes of sensible things to those of natural things because of a certain resemblance which they bear to the properties of fire, water, and bodies of this kind, in a similar fashion these mathematicians adapted the properties of natural things to the attributes of numbers when they said that some one attribute of number is the cause of justice, another the cause of soul and intellect, and still another the cause of opportunity, and so on for other things. And in this way the attributes of numbers are understood to be the intelligible structures and principles of all things appearing in the sensible world, both in the realm of voluntary matters, signified by justice, and in that of the substantial forms of natural things, signified by soul and intellect, and in that of accidents, signified by opportunity.

121. **Moreover, since they** (58).

Here he gives the second reason which motivated them. For they thought of the attributes of harmonies, musical consonants and their ratios, i.e., proportions, in terms of the nature of numbers. Hence, since harmonious sounds are certain sensible things, they attempted by the same reasoning to liken all other sensible things, both in their intelligible structure and in their whole nature, to numbers, so that numbers are the first things in the whole of nature.

122. For this reason too they thought that the principles of numbers are the principles of all existing things, and they said that the whole heaven is merely a kind of nature and harmony

---

[4] See St. Augustine, *De Civitate Dei*, VIII, 2 (PL 41:225).

of numbers, i.e., a kind of numerical proportion similar to the proportion found in harmonies. Hence, whatever they had "revealed," i.e., had shown, which they could adapt to numbers and harmonies, they also adapted both to the changes undergone by the heavens, as its motion, eclipses and the like; and to its parts, as the different orbs; and to the whole arrangement of the heavens, as the different stars and different figures in the constellations.

123. And if anything was lacking in the observable order of things which did not seem to be adapted to numbers, "they called it in," i.e., they invented something new "in order that their whole undertaking might be complete," i.e., in order that their whole undertaking, which was to adapt sensible things to numbers, might be made complete, until they had adapted all sensible things to numbers, as is evident in one example. For the number ten seems to be the perfect number, because it constitutes the first limit and contains within itself the nature of all numbers; for all other numbers are merely a kind of repetition of the number ten. This is why Plato counted up to ten, as Aristotle says in the *Physics,* Book IV.[5] Hence Pythagoras also said that the spheres which move in the heavens are ten in number,

although only nine of these are observable; because we observe seven in the motions of the planets, an eighth in the motion of the fixed stars, and a ninth in the daily motion, which is the first motion. But Pythagoras adds a tenth sphere, which was that of the "counter-earth," i.e., which is moved in the opposite direction to the motion in the lower spheres and therefore produces a contrary sound. For he said that a kind of harmony results from the motion of the celestial bodies, so that just as a harmony is produced from a proportion of contrary sounds, i.e., of low and high notes, in a similar way he claimed that in the heavens there was a single motion in the opposite direction to that of the other motions in order that a harmony might result. According to this position the daily motion belonged to the tenth sphere, which moves from east to west, the other spheres being revolved in the opposite direction from west to east. In fact, according to him, it could have been the ninth sphere which first revolved all the lower spheres in the opposite direction to the first motion. The things that pertain to this opinion of Pythagoras are considered more extensively and more definitely in the last books [6] of this science.

[5] *Physica,* III, 6 (206b 33).
[6] Books XIII & XIV.

LESSON 8

The Pythagorean Doctrine about Contraries

ARISTOTLE'S TEXT   Chapter 5: 986a 13-986b 10

59. But the reason we have come [to examine these philosophers] is that we may also learn from them what they hold the principles of things to be, and how these principles fall under the causes already described. Now these men also seem to think that number is the principle of existing things both as their matter and as their attributes and states. According to them the elements of number are the even and odd, and of these the latter is limited and the former, unlimited. The unit is composed of both of these, since it is both even and odd, and number is derived from the unit. And number, as has been stated (58), constitutes the whole heaven.

60. But other members of the same school say that the principles of things are ten in number, which they give as co-elements: the limited and unlimited, even and odd, one and many, right and left, masculine and feminine, rest and motion, straight and curved, light and darkness, good and evil, square and oblong.

61. Alcmaeon of Croton seems to have formed his opinion in the same way, and either he derived the theory from them or they from him; for Alcmaeon (who had reached maturity when Pythagoras was an old man) expressed views similar to those of the Pythagoreans. For he says that many things in the realm of human affairs are in twos [i.e., pairs], calling them contrarieties, not distinguished as these men had distinguished them, but such as are taken at random, for example, white and black, sweet and bitter, good and evil, small and great. It is true that this philosopher threw out vague remarks about the other contrarieties, but the Pythagoreans have declared both what the contrarieties are and how many there are.

62. From both of these,[1] then, we can gather this much, that contraries are the principles of existing things; but how many they are and that they are these [determinate ones must be learned] from other thinkers. The way in which many principles can be brought together under the causes described is not clearly expressed by them, although they seem to allot their elements to the class of matter; for they say that substance is composed and moulded out of these as something inherent. From these remarks, then, it is possible to get an adequate understanding of the meaning of the ancient philosophers who said that the elements of things are many.

[1] I.e., Alcmaeon and the Pythagoreans.

COMMENTARY

124. Here he states what the Pythagoreans had to say about the principles of things. In regard to this he
does two things. First (59:C 124), he
expounds their opinions about the
principles of things; and second (62:C
132), he indicates to what class of cause
the principles laid down by them are
reduced ("From both of these").

In regard to the first he gives three
opinions. The second (60:C 127) begins at the words "But other members"; and the third (61:C 131), where
he says "Alcmaeon of Croton."

He says first (59), then, that the
reason he came to examine the opinions of the Pythagoreans is that he
might show from their opinions what
the principles of things are and how
the principles laid down by them fall
under the causes given above. For the
Pythagoreans seem to hold that number is the principle of existing things
as matter,[1] and that the attributes of
number are the attributes and states of
existing things. By "attributes" we
mean transient accidents, and by
"states," permanent accidents. They
also held that the attribute of any number according to which any number is
said to be even is justice, because of
the equality of division, since such a
number is evenly divided into two parts
right down to the unit. For example,
the number eight is divided into two
fours, the number four into two twos,
and the number two into two units.
And in a similar way they likened the
other accidents of things to the accidents of numbers.

125. In fact, they said that the even
and odd, which are the first differences

of numbers, are the principles of numbers. And they said that even number
is the principle of unlimitedness and
odd number the principle of limitation,
as is shown in the *Physics,* Book III,[2]
because in reality the unlimited seems
to result chiefly from the division of
the continuous. But an even number is
capable of division; for an odd number
includes within itself an even number
plus a unit, and this makes it indivisible. He also proves this as follows:
when odd numbers are added to each
other successively, they always retain
the figure of a square, whereas even
numbers change their figure. For when
the number three is added to the unit,
which is the principle of numbers, the
number four results, which is the first
square [number], because $2 \times 2 = 4$.
Again, when the number five, which
is an odd number, is added to the
number four, the number nine results,
which is also a square number; and
so on with the others. But if the number two, which is the first even number, is added to the number one, a
triangular number results, i.e., the
number three. And if the number four,
which is the second even number, is
added to the number three, there results a septangular number, i.e., the
number seven. And when even numbers are added to each other successively
in this way, they do not retain the same
figure. This is why they attributed the
unlimited to the even and the limited
to the odd. And since limitedness pertains to form, to which active power
belongs, they therefore said that even
numbers are feminine, and odd numbers, masculine.

[1] Reading *sicut materiam* for *sicut numerum* on basis of discussion in text, n. 59.
[2] *Physica,* III, 4 (203a 10).

126. From these two, namely, the even and odd, the limited and unlimited, they produced not only number but also the unit itself, i.e., unity. For unity is virtually both even and odd; because all differences of number are virtually contained in the unit; for all differences of number are reduced to the unit. Hence, in the list of odd numbers the unit is found to be the first. And the same is true in the list of even numbers, square numbers, and perfect numbers. This is also the case with the other differences of number, because even though the unit is not actually a number, it is still virtually all numbers. And just as the unit is said to be composed of the even and odd, in a similar way number is composed of units. In fact, [according to them], the heavens and all sensible things are composed of numbers. This was the sequence of principles which they gave.

127. **But other members** (60).

Here he gives another opinion which the Pythagoreans held about the principles of things. He says that among these same Pythagoreans there were some who claimed that there is not just one contrariety in principles, as the foregoing did, but ten principles, which are presented as co-elements, that is, by taking each of these principles with its co-principle, or contrary. The reason for this position was that they took not only the first principles but also the proximate principles attributed to each class of things. Hence, they posited first the limited and the unlimited, as did those who have just been mentioned; and subsequently the even and the odd, to which the limited and unlimited are attributed. And because the even and odd are the first principles of things, and numbers are first produced from them, they posited, third, a difference of numbers, namely, the one and the many, both of which are produced from the even and the odd. Again, be-

cause continuous quantities are composed of numbers, inasmuch as they understood numbers to have position (for according to them the point was merely the unit having position, and the line the number two having position), they therefore claimed next that the principles of positions are the right and left; for the right is found to be perfect and the left imperfect. Therefore the right is determined from the aspect of oddness, and the left from the aspect of evenness. But because natural bodies have both active and passive powers in addition to mathematical extensions, they therefore next maintained that masculine and feminine are principles. For masculine pertains to active power, and feminine to passive power; and of these masculine pertains to odd number and feminine to even number, as has been stated (C 125).

128. Now it is from active and passive power that motion and rest originate in the world; and of these motion is placed in the class of the unlimited and even, because it partakes of irregularity and otherness, and rest in the class of the unlimited and odd. Furthermore, the first differences of motions are the circular and straight, so that as a consequence of this the straight pertains to even number. Hence they said that the straight line is the number two; but that the curved or circular line, by reason of its uniformity, pertains to odd number, which retains its undividedness because of the form of unity.

129. And they not only posited principles to account for the natural operations and motions of things, but also to account for the operations of living things. In fact, they held that light and darkness are principles of knowing, but that good and evil are principles of appetite. For light is a principle of knowing, whereas darkness is ascribed to ignorance; and good is that to which

appetite tends, whereas evil is that from which it turns away.

130. Again, [according to them] the difference of perfection and imperfection is found not only in natural things and in voluntary powers and motions, but also in continuous quantities and figures. These figures are understood to be something over and above the substances of continuous quantities, just as the powers responsible for motions and operations are something over and above the substances of natural bodies. Therefore with reference to this they held that what is quadrangular, i.e., the square and oblong, is a principle. Now a square is said to be a figure of four equal sides, whose four angles are right angles; and such a figure is produced by multiplying a line by itself. Therefore, since it is produced from the unit itself, it belongs to the class of odd number. But an oblong is defined as a figure whose angles are all right angles and whose opposite sides alone, not all sides, are equal to each other. Hence it is clear that, just as a square is produced by multiplying one line by itself, in a similar way an ob-oblong is produced by multiplying one line by another. Hence it pertains to the class of even number, of which the first is the number two.

131. **Alcmaeon of Croton** (61).

Here he gives the third opinion of the Pythagoreans, saying that Alcmaeon of Croton, so named from the city in which he was raised, seems to maintain somewhat the same view as that expressed by these Pythagoreans, namely, that many contraries are the principles of things. For either he derives the theory from the Pythagoreans, or they from him. That either of these might be true is clear from the fact that he was a contemporary of the Pythagoreans, granted that he began to philosophize when Pythagoras was an old man. But whichever happens to be true, he expressed views similar to those of the Pythagoreans. For he said that many of

the things "in the realm of human affairs," i.e., many of the attributes of sensible things are arranged in pairs, understanding by pairs opposites which are contrary. Yet in this matter he differs from the foregoing philosophers, because the Pythagoreans said that determinate contraries are the principles of things. But he throws them in, as it were, without any order, holding that any of the contraries which he happened to think of are the principles of things, such as white and black, sweet and bitter, and so on.

132. **From both of these** (62).

Here he gathers together from the above remarks what the Pythagoreans thought about the principles of things, and how the principles which they posited are reduced to some class of cause.

He says, then, that from both of those mentioned above, namely, Alcmaeon and the Pythagoreans, it is possible to draw one common opinion, namely, that the principles of existing things are contraries; which was not expressed by the other thinkers. This must be understood with reference to the material cause. For Empedocles posited contrariety in the case of the efficient cause; and the ancient philosophers of nature posited contrary principles, such as rarity and density, although they attributed contrariety to form. But even though Empedocles held that the four elements are material principles, he still did not claim that they are the first material principles by reason of contrariety but because of their natures and substance. These men, however, attributed contrariety to matter.

133. The nature of the contraries posited by these men is evident from the foregoing discussion. But how the aforesaid contrary principles posited by them can be "brought together under," i.e., reduced to, the types of causes described, is not clearly "expressed," i.e., distinctly stated, by them. Yet it seems

that such principles are allotted to the class of material cause; for they say that the substance of things is composed and moulded out of these principles as something inherent, and this is the notion of a material cause. For matter is that from which a thing comes to be as something inherent. This is added to distinguish it from privation, from which something also comes to be but which is not inherent, as the musical is said to come from the non-musical.

LESSON 9

The Opinions of the Eleatics and Pythagoreans about the Causes of Things

ARISTOTLE'S TEXT   Chapter 5: 986b 10-987a 28

63. But there are some [the Eleatics] who spoke of the whole as if it were a single nature, although the statements which they made are not all alike either with regard to their acceptableness or their conformity with nature.

64. Therefore a consideration of these men pertains in no way to the present investigation of causes. For they do not, like certain of the philosophers [the early physicists] who supposed being to be one, still generate it from the one as matter; but they speak of this in another way. For the others assume motion when they generate this whole, whereas these thinkers say it is immobile.

65. Yet their opinion is relevant to the present investigation to some extent; for Parmenides seems to touch on unity according to intelligible structure and Melissus on unity according to matter. This is why the former says that it is limited,[1] and the latter that it is unlimited.[2] Xenophanes, the first of those to speak of the one (for Parmenides is said to have been his disciple), made nothing clear, nor does he seem to have touched on either [3] of these. But with regard to the whole heaven he says that the one is God.

66. As we have stated, then, these men must be dismissed for the purposes of the present inquiry. In fact, two of them—Xenophanes and Melissus—are to be disregarded altogether as being a little too rustic. Parmenides, however, seems to speak with more insight; for he thought that besides being there is only non-being, and this is nothing. This is why he thinks that being is necessarily one and nothing else. We have discussed this point more clearly in the *Physics*.[4] But being compelled to follow the observed facts, and having assumed that what is one from the viewpoint of reason is many from the viewpoint of the senses, he postulates in turn two principles, i.e., two causes, the hot and cold, calling the one fire and the other earth; and of these he ranks the hot with being and the cold with non-being.

67. From what has been said, then, and from the wise men who have already agreed with this reasoning, we have acquired these things. From the first philosophers we have learned that the principle of things is corporeal, because water and fire and the like are bodies; and from some we have learned that there is one corporeal principle, and from others, many; although both suppose that these belong to the class of matter. And from others we have learned that in addition to this cause there is the source from which motion begins, which some claim to be one and others two. Down to the Italian philosophers, then, and independent

---

[1] Diels, Frag. 8.
[2] *Op. cit.,* Frag. 3.
[3] Reading *neutrorum* for *neuter.*
[4] *Physica,* I, 3 (186b 5).

of them, others have spoken of these things in a more trivial way, except that, as we have said, they have used two kinds of causes, and one of these—the source of motion—some thinkers consider as one and others as two.

68. Now the Pythagoreans have spoken of these two principles in the same way, but added this much, which is peculiar to them, that they did not think that the limited, unlimited and one are different natures, like fire or earth or anything else of this kind, but that the unlimited itself and the one itself are the substance of the things of which they are predicated. And this is why they considered number as the substance of all things. These thinkers, then, have expressed themselves thus with regard to these things, and they began to discuss and define the "what" itself of things, although they treated it far too simply. For they defined things superficially and thought that the substance of a thing is that to which a given definition first applies; just as if one supposed that double and two are the same because that to which the double first belongs is the number two. But perhaps "to be double" is not the same as "to be two"; and if they are not, then the one itself will be many. This, indeed, is the conclusion which they reached. From the first philosophers and others, then, this much can be learned.

COMMENTARY

134. Here he gives the opinions of those philosophers who spoke of the whole universe as one being; and in regard to this he does two things. First (63:C 134), he gives the opinion which they held in common; and second (64:C 135), he shows how a consideration of this opinion is relevant to the present treatise, and how it is not ("Therefore a consideration").

He says (63), then, that there were certain philosophers, other than those just mentioned, who spoke "of the whole," i.e., of the universe, as if it were of one nature, i.e., as if the whole universe were a single being or a single nature. However, not all maintained this position in the same way, as he will make clear below (65-68:C 138-49). Yet in the way in which they differ their statements are neither acceptable nor in conformity with nature. None of their statements are in conformity with nature, because they did away with motion in things. And none of them are acceptable, because they held an

impossible position and used sophistical arguments, as is clear in Book I of the *Physics*.[1]

135. **Therefore a consideration** (64).
Here he shows how a consideration of this position pertains to the present investigation and how it does not. He shows, first, that it has no bearing on this investigation if we consider their position itself; and, second (65:C 137), that it does have a bearing on this investigation if the reasoning or method behind their position is considered ("Yet their opinion").

He says (64), then, that since these philosophers held that there is only one being, and a single thing cannot be its own cause, it is clear that they could not discover the causes. For the position that there is a plurality of things demands a diversity of causes in the world. Hence, a consideration of their statements is of no value for the purposes of the present study, which deals with causes. But the situation is different in the case of the ancient philoso-

[1] *Physica*, I, 8 (191a 26-191b 25).

phers of nature, who held that there is
only one being, and whose statements
must be considered here. For they generated many things from that one principle as matter, and thus posited both
cause and effect. But these men with
whom we are now dealing speak of
this in a different way. For they do
not say that all things are one materially, so that all things are generated
from one matter, but that all things
are one in an absolute sense.

136. The reason for this difference is
that the ancient philosophers of nature
added motion to the view of those who
posited one being and one principle,
and said that this one being is mobile;
and therefore different things could be
generated from that one principle by a
certain kind of motion, i.e., by rarefaction and condensation. And they said
that the whole universe with respect
to the diversity found in its parts is generated in this way. Yet since they held
that the only change affecting substance
is accidental, as was stated above (37:C
75), the conclusion then followed that
the whole universe is one thing substantially but many things accidentally.
But these thinkers [i.e., the Eleatics],
said that the one being which they
posited is immobile in an absolute
sense; and therefore a diversity of
things could not be produced from that
one being. For since this being is immobile they could not posit any plurality in the world, either substantial or
accidental.

137. **Yet their opinion** (65).
Here he shows how their opinion is
relevant to the present inquiry. First
(65), he deals with all of these thinkers
in general; and second (66:C 142),
with Parmenides in particular ("As we
have stated").

He says, first (65), that although
they did away with diversity in the
world, and consequently with causality,

nevertheless their opinion is relevant
to the present study to this extent, let
us say: as regards the method by which
they establish their position and the
reason for their position.

138. Parmenides, who was a member of this group, seems to touch on
unity according to intelligible structure,
i.e., according to form; for he argued
as follows: besides being there is only
non-being, and non-being is nothing.
Therefore besides being there is nothing. But being is one. Therefore, besides the one there is nothing. In this
argument he clearly considered the intelligible structure itself of being, which
seems to be one, because nothing can
be understood to be added to the concept of being by which it might be
diversified. For whatever is added to
being must be other than being. But
anything such as this is nothing. Hence
it does not seem that this can diversify
being; just as we also see that differences added to a genus diversify it, even
though these differences are outside
the substance of that genus. For differences do not participate in a genus, as is
stated in the *Topics,* Book IV,[2] otherwise a genus would have the substance
of a difference. And definitions would
be nonsense if when a genus is given
the difference were added, granted
that the genus were the substance of
the difference, just as it would be nonsense if the species were added. Moreover a difference would not differ in
any way from a species. But those
things which are outside the substance
of being must be non-being, and thus
cannot diversify being.

139. But they were mistaken in this
matter, because they used being as if
it were one in intelligible structure and
in nature, like the nature of any genus.
But[3] this is impossible. For being is not
a genus but is predicated of different

[2] *Topica,* IV, 1 (121a 10).
[3] Reading *autem* for *enim.*

things in many ways. Therefore in Book I of the *Physics* [4] it is said that the statement "Being is one" is false. For being does not have one nature like one genus or one species.

140. But Melissus considered being in terms of matter. For he argued that being is one by reason of the fact that being is not generated from something prior, and this characteristic pertains properly to matter, which is ungenerated. For he argued in this way: whatever is generated has a starting-point. But being is not generated and therefore does not have a starting-point. But whatever lacks a starting-point lacks an end and therefore is unlimited. And if it is unlimited, it is immobile, because what is unlimited has nothing outside itself by which it is moved. That being is not generated he proves thus. If being were generated, it would be generated either from being or from non-being. But it is not generated from non-being, because non-being is nothing and from nothing nothing comes. Nor is it generated from being, because then a thing would be before it came to be. Therefore it is not generated in any way. In this argument he obviously treats being as matter, because it is of the very nature of matter not to be generated from something prior. And since limitation pertains to form, and unlimitedness to matter, Melissus, who considered being under the aspect of matter, said that there is one unlimited being. But Parmenides, who considered being under the aspect of form, said that being is limited. Hence, insofar as being is considered under the aspect of form and matter, a study of these men is relevant to the present investigation; because matter and form are included among the causes.

141. But Xenophanes, who was the first of those to say that everything is one (and therefore Parmenides was his disciple), did not explain by what reasoning he maintained that all things are one, either by arguing from the viewpoint of matter, or from that of form. Hence, with respect to neither nature, i.e., neither matter nor form, does he seem "to come up to these men," [5] that is, to reach and equal them in their irrational manner of arguing. But concerning the whole heaven he says that the one is God. For the ancients said that the world itself is God. Hence, seeing that all parts of the universe are alike insofar as they are bodies, he came to think of them as if they were all one. And just as the foregoing philosophers held that beings are one by considering those things which pertain either to matter or to form, in a similar way these philosophers maintained this position regarding the composite itself.

142. **As we have stated** (66).

His aim here is to explain in a special way how the opinion of Parmenides pertains to the present investigation. He concludes from the foregoing that, since these men did away with diversity in the world and therefore with causality, all of them must be disregarded so far as the present study is concerned. Two of them—Xenophanes and Melissus—must be disregarded altogether, because they are a little too "rustic," i.e., they proceeded with less accuracy. But Parmenides seems to have expressed his views "with more insight," i.e., with greater understanding. For he employs the following argument: besides being there is only non-being, and whatever is non-being "is thought to be nothing"; i.e., he considers it worthy to be nothing. Hence he thought that it necessarily followed that being is one, and that whatever is other than being is nothing. This argu-

[4] *Physica,* I, 2 (185a 20).
[5] St. Thomas' interpretation here does not agree with the thought of the Greek text or the Latin version. *Tangere hos* suggests that he followed a different reading.

ment has been treated more clearly in the *Physics,* Book I.[6]

143. But even though Parmenides was compelled by this argument to hold that all things are one, yet, because there appeared to the senses to be many things in reality, and because he was compelled to accept what appeared to the senses, it was his aim to make his position conform to both of these, i.e., to what is apprehended both by the senses and by reason. Hence he said that all things are one according to reason but many according to the senses. And inasmuch as he held that there is a plurality of things according to the senses, he was able to hold that there is in the world both cause and effect. Hence he posited two causes, namely, the hot and the cold, one of which he ascribed to fire, and the other to earth. And one of these—the hot or fire—seemed to pertain to the efficient cause, and the other—cold or earth—to the material cause. And lest his position should seem to contradict the conclusion of his own argument that whatever is besides being is nothing, he said that one of these causes—the hot—is being, and that the other cause—the one besides being, or the cold—is non-being, according to both reason and the truth of the thing itself, and is a being only according to sensory perception.

144. Now in this matter he comes very close to the truth; for the material principle, which he held to be earth, is not an actual being. And in a similar way, too, one of two contraries is a privation, as is said in Book I of the *Physics.*[7] But privation does not belong to the intelligible constitution of being. Hence in a sense cold is the privation of heat, and thus is non-being.

145. **From what has been said** (67). Here he summarizes the remarks which have been made about the doctrines of the ancient philosophers; and in regard to this he does two things.

[6] *Physica,* I, 3 (186b 5).

First (67), he summarizes the remarks made about the doctrines of the ancient philosophers of nature; and second (68:C 147), those made about the doctrines of the Pythagoreans, who introduced mathematics ("Now the Pythagoreans").

Therefore from the above remarks he concludes, first (67), that from the foregoing philosophers, who adopted the same opinion, namely, that the material cause is the substance of things, and who were already beginning by the use of reason to know the causes of things by investigating them, we learn the causes which have been mentioned. For from the first philosophers it was learned that the principle of all things is corporeal. This is evident from the fact that water and the like, which are given as the principles of things, are bodies. However, they differed in this respect, that some, such as Thales, Diogenes and similar thinkers, claimed that there is only one corporeal principle, whereas others, such as Anaxagoras, Democritus and Leucippus, held that there are several corporeal principles. Yet both groups, i.e., both those who posited one principle and those who posited many, placed such corporeal principles in the class of material cause. And some of them not only posited a material cause but added to this the cause from which motion begins: some holding it to be one, as Anaxagoras did in positing intellect, and Parmenides, love, and others to be two, as Empedocles did in positing love and hate.

146. Hence, it is clear that these philosophers who lived down to the time of the Italians, or Pythagoreans, "and [were] independent of them," i.e., who had their own opinions about reality and were unaware of those of the Pythagoreans, spoke obscurely about the principles of things; for they did not designate to what class of cause such principles might be reduced. Yet

[7] *Physica,* I, 9 (192a 3).

they made use of two causes, i.e., the source from which motion begins and matter: some saying that the former—the source from which motion begins—is one, and others two; as has been pointed out (67:C 145).

147. **Now the Pythagoreans** (68).

Here he summarizes the opinions expressed by the Pythagoreans, both what they held in common with the foregoing philosophers, and what was peculiar to themselves. Now the opinion common to some of the foregoing philosophers and to the Pythagoreans was this that they posited, in a sense, two principles in the same way as the foregoing philosophers did. For Empedocles held that there are two contrary principles, one being the principle of good things, and the other the principle of evil things, and the Pythagoreans did the same thing, as is clear from the co-ordination of contrary principles which they posited.

148. However, they did not do this in the same way; because Empedocles placed these contrary principles in the class of material cause, as was stated above (54:C 111), whereas the Pythagoreans added their own opinion to that of the other thinkers. The first thing that they added is this: they said that what I call the one, the limited [8] and the unlimited are not accidents of any other natures, such as fire or earth or the like, but claimed that what I call the one, the limited and the unlimited constitute the substance of the same things of which they are predicated. From this they concluded that number, which is constituted of units, is the substance of all things. But while the other philosophers of nature posited the one, the limited and the unlimited, they nevertheless attributed these to another nature, as accidents are attributed to a subject, for example, to fire or water or something of this kind.

149. The second addition which they made to the views of the other philoso-

phers is this: they began to discuss and to define "the whatness itself," i.e., the substance and quiddity of things, although they treated this far too simply by defining things superficially. For in giving definitions they paid attention only to one thing; because they said that, if any given definition were to apply primarily to some thing, this would be the substance of that thing; just as if one were to suppose that the ratio "double" is the substance of the number two, because such a ratio is found first in the number two. And since being was found first in the one rather than in the many (for the many is composed of ones), they therefore said that being is the substance itself of the one. But this conclusion of theirs is not acceptable; for although the number two is double, the essence of twoness is not the same as that of the double in such a way that they are the same conceptually, as the definition and the thing defined. But even if their statements were true, it would follow that the many would be one. For some plurality can belong primarily to something one; for example, evenness and the ratio double belong first to the number two. Hence [according to them] it would follow that the even and the double are the same. And it would likewise follow that that to which the double belongs is the same as the number two, so long as the double is the substance of the number two. This, indeed, is also the conclusion which the Pythagoreans drew; for they attributed plurality and diversity to things as if they were one, just as they said that the properties of numbers are the same as the properties of natural beings.

150. Hence, Aristotle concludes that it is possible to learn this much from the early philosophers, who posited only one material principle, and from the later philosophers, who posited many principles.

---

[8] Reading here and below *unum et finitum* for *unum finitum;* see Aristotle's text (68).

LESSON 10

The Platonic Theory of Ideas

ARISTOTLE'S TEXT   Chapter 6: 987a 29-988a 17

69. After the philosophies described came the system of Plato, which followed them in many respects, but also had other [theses] of its own in addition to the philosophy of the Italians. For Plato agreeing at the very beginning with the opinions of Cratylus (362) and Heraclitus that all sensible things are always in a state of flux,[1] and that there is no scientific knowledge of them, also accepted this doctrine in later years. However, when Socrates, concerning himself with moral matters and neglecting nature as a whole, sought for the universal in these matters and fixed his thought on definition, Plato accepted him because of this kind of investigation, and assumed that this consideration refers to other entities and not to sensible ones. For [according to him] it is impossible that there should be a common definition of any one of these sensible things which are always changing. Such entities, then, he called Ideas or Forms (*species*); and he said that all sensible things exist because of them and in conformity with them;[2] for there are many individuals of the same name because of participation in these Forms. With regard to participation, he [merely] changed the name; for while the Pythagoreans say that things exist by imitation of numbers, Plato says that they exist by participation, changing the name. Yet what this participation or imitation of Forms is they commonly neglected to investigate.

70. Further, he says that besides sensible things and Ideas there are the objects of mathematics, which constitute an intermediate class. These differ from sensible things in being eternal and immobile; and from the Ideas in that there are many alike, whereas each Idea is itself only one.

71. And since the Forms [or Ideas] are the causes of other things, he thought that the elements of these are the elements of all existing things. Hence, according to him, the great and small are principles as matter, and the one as substance [or form]; for it is from these by participation in the one that the Ideas are numbers.

72. Yet Plato said that the one is substance and that no other being is to be called one, just as the Pythagoreans did; and like them too he said that numbers are the causes of real substance.

73. But to posit a dyad in place of the indeterminate one, and to produce the unlimited out of the great and small, is peculiar to him. Moreover, he says that numbers exist apart from sensible things, whereas they say that things themselves are numbers. Further, they do not maintain that the objects of mathematics are an intermediate class.

74. Therefore, his making the one and numbers to exist apart from things and not in things, as the Pythagoreans did, and his introducing the separate

---

[1] See Plato, *Cratylus* 402 A.
[2] Reading *propter haec* and *secundum haec* for *propter hoc* and *secundum hoc*.

Forms, were due to his investigation into the intelligible structures of things; for the earlier philosophers were ignorant of dialectic.

75. But his making the dyad [or duality] to be a different nature was due to the fact that all numbers, with the exception of prime numbers, are naturally generated from the number two as a matrix.

76. Yet what happens is the contrary of this. For this view is not a reasonable one; because the Platonists produce many things from matter but their form generates only once.

77. And from one matter one measure [3] seems to be produced, whereas he who induces the form, even though he is one, produces many measures. The male is also related to the female in a similar way; for the latter is impregnated by one act, but the male impregnates many females. And such are the changes [4] in these principles. Concerning the causes under investigation, then, Plato defines them thus.

78. From the foregoing account it is evident that Plato used only two causes: one being the whatness of a thing, and the other, matter; for the Forms are the cause of the quiddity in other things, and the one is the cause of the quiddity in the Forms. What the underlying matter is of which the Forms are predicated in the case of sensible things, and the one in the case of the Forms, is also evident, namely, that it is this duality, the great and small. Moreover, he assigned the cause of good and evil to these two elements, one to each of them; which is rather a problem, as we say (48:C 100), that some of the first philosophers, such as Empedocles and Anaxagoras, [have attempted] to investigate.

[3] According to the Greek text which has "table," the Latin version, which reads *mensura* twice, should read *mensa*. St. Thomas reads *mensura*: see C 167.

[4] According to the Greek text, for *mutationes* the Latin version should read *imitationes* (imitations). St. Thomas reads *mutationes*.

COMMENTARY

151. Having given the opinion of the ancient phiolsophers about the material and efficient cause, he gives a third opinion, that of Plato, who was the first to clearly introduce the formal cause. This is divided into two parts. First (69:C 151), he gives Plato's opinion. Second (79:C 171), from all of the foregoing remarks he makes a summary of the opinions which the other philosophers expressed about the four classes of causes ("We have examined").

In regard to the first he does two things. First, he gives Plato's opinion about the substances of things; and second (71:C 159), his opinion about the principles of things ("And since the Forms").

In regard to the first he does two things. First, he gives Plato's opinion insofar as he posited Ideas; and second (70:C 157), insofar as he posited intermediate substances, namely, the separate mathematical entities ("Further, he says").

He says, first (69), that after all the foregoing philosophers came the system of Plato, who immediately preceded Aristotle; for Aristotle is considered to have been his disciple. And even if Plato followed in many respects the natural philosophers who preceded him, such as Empedocles, Anaxagoras and the like, he nevertheless had certain other doctrines of his own in addition to those of the preceding philosophers, because of the philosophy of the Italians, or Pythagoreans. For insofar as he was devoted to the study of truth he sought out the philosophers of all lands in order to learn their teachings. Hence he came to Tarentum in Italy, and was instructed in the teachings of the Pythagoreans by Archytas of Tarentum, a disciple of Pythagoras.

152. Now Plato would seem to follow the natural philosophers who lived in Greece; and of this group some of the later members held that all sensible things are always in a state of flux, and that there can be no scientific knowledge of them (which was the position of Heraclitus and Cratylus). And since Plato became accustomed to positions of this kind from the very beginning, and agreed with these men in this position, which he acknowledged to be true in later years, he therefore said that scientific knowledge of particular sensible things must be abandoned. And Socrates (who was Plato's master and the disciple of Archelaus, a pupil of Anaxagoras), because of this position, which arose in his time, that there can be no science of sensible things, was unwilling to make any investigation into the nature of physical things, but only busied himself with moral matters. And in this field he first began to investigate what the universal is, and to insist upon the need for definition.

153. Hence, Plato, being Socrates' pupil, "accepted Socrates," i.e., followed him, and adopted this method for the purpose of investigating natural beings. He did so believing that in their case the universal in them could successfully be grasped and a definition be assigned to it, with no definition being given for any sensible thing; because, since sensible things are always "changing," i.e., being changed, no common intelligible structure can be assigned to any of them. For every definition must

conform to each thing defined and must always do so, and thus requires some kind of immutability. Hence universal entities of this kind, which are separate from sensible things and that to which definitions are assigned, he called the Ideas or Forms of sensible things. He called them Ideas, or exemplars, inasmuch as sensible things are made in likeness to them; and he called them Forms inasmuch as [sensible things] have substantial being by participating in them. Or he called them Ideas inasmuch as they are principles of being, and Forms inasmuch as they are principles of knowledge. Hence all sensible things have being because of them and in conformity with them. They have being because of the Ideas insofar as the Ideas are the causes of the being of sensible things, and "in conformity with them" insofar as they are the exemplars of sensible things.

154. The truth of this is clear from the fact that "many individuals of the same name" are attributed to one Form alone, i.e., there are many individuals which have the same Form predicated of them, and predicated by participation. For the Form or Idea [of man] is the specific nature itself by which there exists *man* essentially. But an individual is man by participation inasmuch as the specific nature [man] is participated in by this designated matter. For that which is something in its entirety does not participate in it but is essentially identical with it, whereas that which is not something in its entirety but has this other thing joined to it, is said properly to participate in that thing. Thus, if heat were a self-subsistent heat, it would not be said to participate in heat, because it would contain nothing but heat. But since fire is something other than heat, it is said to participate in heat.

155. In a similar way, since the separate Idea of man contains nothing but the specific nature itself, it is man es-

sentially; and for this reason it was called by him man-in-itself. But since Socrates and Plato have in addition to their specific nature an individuating principle, which is designated matter, they are therefore said to participate in a Form, according to Plato.

156. Now Plato took this term *participation* from Pythagoras, although [in doing so] he made a change in the term. For the Pythagoreans said that numbers are the causes of things, just as the Platonists said that the Ideas are, and claimed that sensible things of this kind exist as certain imitations of numbers. For inasmuch as numbers, which have no position of themselves, received positions, they caused bodies. But because Plato held that the Ideas are unchangeable in order that there might be scientific knowledge of them, he did not agree that the term *imitation* could be used of the Ideas, but in place of it he used the term participation. However, it must be noted that, even though the Pythagoreans posited participation or imitation, they still did not investigate the way in which a common Form is participated in by individual sensible things or imitated by them. But the Platonists have treated this.

157. **Further, he says** (70).

Here he gives Plato's opinion about the mathematical substances. He says that Plato posited other substances—the objects of mathematics—in addition to the Forms and sensible things. Moreover, he said that beings of this kind were an intermediate class among the three kinds of substances; or that they were above sensible substances and below the Forms, and differed from both. The mathematical substances differed from sensible substances, because sensible substances are corruptible and changeable, whereas the mathematical substances are eternal and immobile. The Platonists got this idea from the way in which mathematical science conceives its objects; for mathematical science abstracts from motion. The mathematical substances also differed from the Forms, because the objects of mathematics are found to be numerically different and specifically the same, otherwise the demonstrations of mathematics would prove nothing. For unless two triangles belonged to the same class, geometry would attempt in vain to demonstrate that some triangles are alike; and the same thing is true of other figures. But this does not happen in the case of the Forms. For, since a Form is just the specific nature itself of a thing, each Form can only be unique. For even though the Form of man is one thing, and the Form of ass another thing, nevertheless the Form of man is unique, and so is the Form of ass; and the same thing is true of other things.

158. Now to one who carefully examines Plato's arguments it is evident that Plato's opinion was false, because he believed that the mode of being which the thing known has in reality is the same as the one which it has in the act of being known. Therefore, since he found that our intellect understands abstractions in two ways: in one way as we understand universals abstracted from singulars, and in another way as we understand the objects of mathematics abstracted from sensible things, he claimed that for each abstraction of the intellect there is a corresponding abstraction in the essences of things. Hence he held that both the objects of mathematics and the Forms are separate. But this is not necessary. For even though the intellect understands things insofar as it becomes assimilated to them through the intelligible form by which it is put into act, it still is not necessary that a form should have the same mode of being in the intellect that it has in the thing known; for everything that exists in something else exists there according to the mode of the recipient. Therefore, considering the

nature of the intellect, which is other than the nature of the thing known, the mode of understanding, by which the intellect understands, must be one kind of mode, and the mode of being, by which things exist, must be another. For although the object which the intellect understands must exist in reality, it does not exist there according to the same mode [which it has in the intellect]. Hence, even though the intellect understands mathematical entities without simultaneously understanding sensible substances, and understands universals without understanding particulars, it is not therefore necessary that the objects of mathematics should exist apart from sensible things, or that universals should exist apart from particulars. For we also see that sight perceives color apart from flavor, even though flavor and color are found together in sensible substances.

159. **And since the Forms** (71).

Here he gives Plato's opinion concerning the principles of things; and in regard to this he does two things. First (71), he states the principles which Plato assigned to things; and second (78:C 169), the class of cause to which they are reduced ("From the foregoing").

In regard to the first he does two things. First, he tells us what kind of principles Plato had assigned to things. Second (72:C 160), he shows in what respect Plato agreed with the Pythagoreans, and in what respect he differed from them ("Yet Plato").

He says, first (71), that, since the Forms are the causes of all other beings according to Plato, the Platonists therefore thought that the elements of the Forms are the elements of all beings. Hence, they assigned as the material principle of things the great and small, and said that "the substance of things," i.e., their form, is the one. They did this because they held these to be the

principles of the Forms. For they said that just as the Forms are the formal principles of sensible things, in a similar way the one is the formal principle of the Forms. Therefore, just as sensible things are constituted of universal principles by participation in the Forms, in a similar way the Forms, which he said are numbers, are constituted "of these," i.e., of the great and small. For the unit constitutes different species of numbers by addition and subtraction, in which the notion of the great and small consists. Hence, since the one was thought to be the substance of being (because he did not distinguish between the one which is the principle of number, and the one which is convertible with being), it seemed to him that a plurality of different Forms might be produced from the one, which is their common substance, in the same way that a plurality of different species of numbers is produced from the unit.

160. **Yet Plato** (72).

Here he compares the position of Plato with that of Pythagoras. First (72), he shows in what respect they agreed; and second (73:C 160), in what respect they differed ("But to posit").

Now they agreed in two positions; and the first is that the one is the substance of things. For the Platonists, like the Pythagoreans, said that what I call the one is not predicated[1] of some other being as an accident is of a subject, but signifies a thing's substance. They said this, as we have pointed out (71:C 159), because they did not distinguish between the one which is convertible with being and the one which is the principle of number.

161. The second position follows from the first; for the Platonists, like the Pythagoreans, said that numbers are the causes of the substance of all

---

[1] Reading *praedicatur* instead of *probatur*.

beings; and they held this because [in their opinion] number is just a collection of units. Hence if the one is substance, number must also be such.

162. **But to posit** (73).

Here he shows in what respect they differed; and in regard to this he does two things. First, he states how they differed. Second (74:C 164), he gives the reason for this difference ("Therefore, his making").

Now this difference involves two things. First, the Pythagoreans, as has already been stated, posited two principles of which things are constituted, namely, the limited and the unlimited, of which one, i.e., the unlimited, has the character of matter. But in place of this one principle—the unlimited—which the Pythagoreans posited, Plato created a dyad, holding that the great and small have the character of matter. Hence the unlimited, which Pythagoras claimed to be one principle, Plato claimed to consist of the great and small. This is his own opinion in contrast with that of Pythagoras.

163. The second difference is that Plato held that numbers are separate from sensible things, and this in two ways. For he said that the Forms themselves are numbers, as was pointed out above (71:C 159); and he also held, as was stated above (70:C 157), that the objects of mathematics are an intermediate class between the Forms and sensible things, and that they are numbers by their very essence. But the Pythagoreans said that sensible things themselves are numbers, and did not make the objects of mathematics an intermediate class between the Forms and sensible things; nor again did they hold that the Forms are separate from things.

164. **Therefore, his making** (74).

Here he gives the reason for the difference. First (74), he gives the reason for the second difference; and then

(75:C 165), the reason for the first difference ("But his making").

He says, then, that the Platonists adopted the position that both the one and numbers exist apart from sensible things and not in sensible things, as the Pythagoreans claimed; and they also introduced separate Forms because of the investigation "which was made into the intelligible structures of things," i.e., because of their investigation of the definitions of things, which they thought could not be attributed to sensible substances, as has been stated (69:C 151). This is the reason they were compelled to hold that there are certain things to which definitions are assigned. But the Pythagoreans, who came before Plato, were ignorant of dialectic, whose office it is to investigate definitions and universals of this kind, the study of which led to the introduction of the Ideas.

165. **But his making** (75).

Here he gives the reason for the other difference, that is, the one concerning matter. First (75), he gives the reason for such a difference. Second (76:C 166), he shows that Plato was not reasonably motivated ("Yet what happens").

He accordingly says (75) that the Platonists made the dyad [or duality] to be a number of a different nature than the Forms, because all numbers with the exception of prime numbers are produced from it. They called prime numbers those which are not measured by any other number, such as three, five, seven, eleven, and so on; for these are produced immediately from unity alone. But numbers which are measured by some other number are not called prime numbers but composite ones, for example, the number four, which is measured by the number two; and in general every even number is measured by the number two. Hence even numbers are attributed to matter, since unlimitedness, which belongs to matter, is attributed to them, as has been stated above (59:C 125). This is why he posited the dyad, from which as "a matrix," or exemplar, all other even numbers are produced.

166. **Yet what happens** (76).

Here he proves that Plato made unreasonable assumptions; and in regard to this he does two things. For, first (76), he proves this by an argument from nature. Second (77:C 167), he gives the argument based on the nature of things, which led Plato to adopt this position ("And from one matter").

He says (76) that, although Plato posited a dyad on the part of matter, still what happens is the contrary of this, as the opinions of all the other natural philosophers testify; for they claimed that contrariety pertains to form and unity to matter, as is clear in Book I of the *Physics*.[2] For they held that the material principle of things is air or water or something of this kind, from which the diversity of things is produced by rarefaction and condensation, which they regarded as formal principles; for Plato's position is not a reasonable one. Now the natural philosophers adopted this position because they saw that many things are generated from matter as a result of a succession of forms in matter. For that matter which now supports one form may afterwards support many forms as a result of one form being corrupted and another being generated. But one specifying principle or form "generates only once," i.e., constitutes the thing which is generated. For when something is generated it receives a form, and the same form numerically cannot become the form of another thing that is generated[3] but ceases to be when that which was generated undergoes corruption. In this argument it is clearly apparent that one matter is related to many forms, and not the reverse, i.e., one form to

many matters. Thus it seems more reasonable to hold that unity pertains to matter but duality or contrariety to form, as the philosophers of nature claimed. This is the opposite of what Plato held.

167. **And from one matter** (77).

Here he gives an opposite argument taken from sensible things according to the opinion of Plato. For Plato saw that each thing is received in something else according to the measure of the recipient. Hence receptions seem to differ according as the capacities of recipients differ. But one matter is one capacity for reception. And Plato also saw that the agent who induces the form, although he is one, causes many things to have this form; and this comes about because of diversity on the part of matter. An example of this is evident in the case of male and female; for a male is related to a female as an agent and one who impresses a form on matter. But a female is impregnated by one act of a male, whereas one male can impregnate many females. This is why he held that unity pertains to form and duality to matter.

168. Now we must note that this difference between Plato and the philosophers of nature is a result of the fact that they considered things from different points of view. For the philosophers of nature considered sensible things only insofar as they are subject to change, in which one subject successively acquires contrary qualities. Hence they attributed unity to matter and contrariety to form. But Plato, because of his investigation of universals, went on to give the principles of sensible things. Therefore, since the cause of the diversity of the many singular things which come under one universal is the division of matter, he held that diversity pertains to matter and unity to form. "And such are the

[2] *Physica*, I, 4 (187a 16).
[3] Reading *generato* instead of *generatio*.

changes of those principles" which Plato posited, i.e., participations, or, as I may say, influences in the things generated. For Pythagoras understands the word change in this way. Or Aristotle says "changes" inasmuch as Plato changed the opinion which the first philosophers of nature had about principles, as is evident from the foregoing. Hence it is evident from the foregoing that Plato dealt thus with the causes which we are investigating.

169. **From the foregoing** (78).

Here he shows to what class of cause the principles given by Plato are referred. He says that it is evident from the foregoing that Plato used only two kinds of causes. For he used as "one" cause of a thing the cause of its "whatness," i.e., its quiddity, or its formal cause, which determines its quiddity; and he also used matter itself. This is also evident from the fact that the Forms which he posited "are the causes of other things," i.e., the causes of the whatness of sensible things, namely, their formal causes, whereas the formal cause of the Forms themselves is what I call the one, which seems to be the substance of which the Forms are composed. And just as he holds that the one is the formal cause of the Forms, in a similar fashion he holds

that the great and small are their material cause, as was stated above (71:C 159). And these causes—the formal and the material cause—are referred not only to the Forms but also to sensible substances, because [there is some subject of which] the one is predicated in the case of the Forms. That is to say, that which is related to sensible substances in the same way as the one is to the Forms is itself a Form, because that duality which relates to sensible things as their matter is the great and small.

170. Furthermore, Plato indicated the cause of good and evil in the world, and he did this with reference to each of the elements which he posited. For he made Form the cause of good and matter the cause of evil. However, some of the first philosophers attempted to investigate the cause of good and evil, namely, Anaxagoras and Empedocles, who established certain causes in the world with this special end in view that by means of these causes they might be able to give the principles of good and evil. And in touching upon these causes of good and evil they came very close to positing the final cause, although they did not posit this cause directly but only indirectly, as is stated below (84:C 177).

LESSON 11

A Summary of the Early Opinions about the Causes

ARISTOTLE'S TEXT   Chapter 7: 988a 18-988b 21

79. We have examined, then, in a brief and summary way those philosophers who [1] have spoken about the principles of things and about the truth, and the way in which they did this. Yet we have learned from them this much: that none of those who have discussed principle and cause have said anything beyond the points established by us in the *Physics*.[2]

80. Yet all have approached these causes obscurely.

81. For some speak of the [first] principle as matter, whether they suppose it to be one or many, and whether they assume it to be a body or something incorporeal, as Plato speaks of the great and small; the Italians of the unlimited; Empedocles of fire, earth, water and air; and Anaxagoras of an infinite number of like parts. All these have touched on this kind of cause, and so also have those who make the first principle air or fire or water or something denser than fire or rarer than air. For they have said that some such body is the primary element.[3] These thinkers, then, have touched only on this cause.

82. But others [have introduced] the source of motion, for example, those who make friendship and strife, or intellect, or love, or something besides these a principle of things.

83. But the quiddity or substance no one has presented clearly. Those who express it best are those who posit the Ideas and the intelligible natures inherent in the Ideas. For they do not think of the Ideas and the things inherent in them as the matter of sensible things; nor do they think of them as the source from which motion originates, for [4] they say that these things are the causes rather of immobility and of that which is at rest. But [according to them] the Forms are responsible for the quiddity of all other things, and the one for the quiddity of the Forms.

84. That for the sake of which there are actions and changes and motions they affirm in some way to be a cause, but not in the way we are determining causes, or in the way in which it is truly a cause. For while those who speak of intellect or love posit these causes as good, they do not say that anything exists or comes to be because of them, but claim that the motion of things stems from them. In like manner those who say that the one or being is such a reality, say that it is the cause of substance, but not that things either are or come to be for the sake of this. Hence, it happens to them that in a way they both say

---

[1] Reading *qui* for *quid*.
[2] *Physica*, II, 3 (194b 15-195b 30).
[3] This statement in the Latin version is not an accurate rendering of the Greek text, but it has been retained because St. Thomas accepted it. See C 173. The text should read: "For *some* have said that such a body is the primary element."
[4] Reading *enim* for *autem*.

and do not say that the good is a cause; for they do not speak of it in its principal aspect but in a secondary one.

85. Therefore all these philosophers, being unable to touch on any other cause, seem to bear witness to the fact that we have dealt correctly with the causes, both as to their number and their kinds. Moreover, it is evident that all principles must be sought in this way or in some similar one. As to the way in which each of these philosophers has spoken, and how they have raised possible problems about the principles of things, let us discuss these points next.

COMMENTARY

171. Here he makes a summary of everything that the early philosophers have said about causes; and in regard to this he does three things. First (79:C 171), he shows that the early philosophers were unable to add another kind of cause to the four classes of causes given above (34:C 70). Second (80:C 172), he indicates the way in which they touched upon these causes ("Yet all"). Third (85:C 180) he draws the conclusion at which he chiefly aims ("Therefore, all these").

He says, first (79), that in giving this brief and summary account he has stated who the philosophers are, and how they have spoken of the principles of things and of what is true of the substance itself of things. And from their statements this much can be learned: that none of those who have spoken about causes and principles were able to mention any causes other than those distinguished in Book II of the *Physics*.[1]

172. **Yet all** (80).

Here he gives the way in which they dealt with each of the causes. He does this, first (80), in a general way: and, second (81:C 172), in a special way ("For some speak").

Accordingly he says, first, that they not only have not added anything, but in the way in which they approached these causes they proceeded obscurely

and not clearly. For they have not stated to what class of cause the principles posited by them would belong; but they gave as principles things that can be adapted to some class of cause.

173. **For some speak** (81).

Here he shows in a special way how they touched on each of these causes. He shows, first (81), how they touched on the material cause; second (82:C 174), on the efficient cause ("But others"); third (83:C 175), on the formal cause ("But the quiddity"); and fourth (84:C 177), on the final cause ("That for the sake of which").

He says, first (81), then, that those philosophers, i.e., the early ones, all agree insofar as they assign some material cause to things. Yet they differ in two respects. First, they differ in that some, such as Thales, Diogenes and the like, held that the material principle is one, whereas others, such as Empedocles, claimed that it is many; and second, they differ in that some, such as the first group above, held that the material principle of things is a body, whereas others, such as Plato, who posited a dyad, claimed that it is something incorporeal. For Plato posited the great and small, which the Platonists do not speak of as a body. The Italians, or Pythagoreans, posited the unlimited; but neither is this a body. Empedocles, on the other hand,

[1] *Physica*, II, 3 (194b 15-195b 30).

posited the four elements, which are bodies; and Anaxagoras also posited "an infinite number of like parts," i.e., [he claimed] that the principles of things are an infinite number of like parts. All of these thinkers have touched on "this kind of cause," i.e., the material cause, and so also have those who said that the principle of things is air or water or fire or something midway between these elements, i.e., what is denser than fire and rarer than air. For all philosophers such as those just mentioned have claimed that some kind of body is the first element of things. Thus Aristotle's statement is evident, namely, that in the light of the foregoing remarks these philosophers have posited only the material cause.

174. **But others** (82).

Here he gives their opinions about the efficient cause. He says that some of the foregoing philosophers have posited, in addition to the material cause, a cause from which motion begins, for example, those who made love or hate or intellect a cause of things, or those who introduced some other active principle distinct from these, as Parmenides, who made fire an efficient cause.

175. **But the quiddity** (83).

Here he gives their opinions about the formal cause. He says that the cause through which a thing's substance is known, i.e., the formal cause, no one attributed to things with any clarity. And if the ancient philosophers touched on something that might pertain to the formal cause, as Empedocles did when he claimed that bone and flesh contain some proportion [of the elements], by which they are things of this kind, nevertheless they did not treat what belongs to the formal cause after the manner of a cause.

176. But among the other philosophers, those who posited the Forms and those intelligible aspects which belong to the Forms, such as unity, number and the like, came closest to positing the formal cause. For the Forms and everything that belongs to the Forms in the aforesaid way, such as unity and number, are not acknowledged or assumed by them to be the matter of sensible things, since they place matter rather on the side of sensible things; nor do they claim that the Forms are the causes from which motion originates in the world, but rather that they are the cause of immobility in things. For they said that whatever is found to be necessary in sensible things is caused by the Forms, and that these, i.e., the Forms, are immobile. For they claimed that the Forms, because immobile, are uniform in being, as has been said (69:C 156), so that definitions can be given of them and demonstrations made about them. But according to the opinion of these men the Forms are responsible for the quiddity of particular things after the manner of a formal cause, and the one is responsible for the quiddity of the Forms.

177. **That for the sake of which** (84).

Here he gives the opinions of certain thinkers about the final cause. He says that in one sense the philosophers say that the goal for the sake of which motions, changes and activities occur is a cause, and in another sense they do not. And they neither speak of it in the same way, nor in the way in which it is a true cause. For those who affirm that intellect or love is a cause, posit these causes as good. For they said that things of this kind are the causes of things being well disposed, since the cause of good can only be good. Hence it follows that they could make intellect and love to be causes, just as the good is a cause. But good can be understood in two ways: in one way as a final cause, in the sense that something comes to be for the sake of some good; and in another way as an efficient cause, as we say that the good man does good. Now these philosophers did not say that the foregoing causes are good in the sense that they are the reason for the existence or coming to be of some beings, which pertains to the intelligibility of the final cause, but in the sense that there proceeds from these causes—intellect and will—a kind of motion toward the being and coming-to-be of things; and this pertains to the intelligibility of the efficient cause.

178. In a similar way the Pythagoreans and Platonists, who said that the substance of things is the one itself or being, also attributed goodness to the one or being. Thus they said that such a reality, i.e., the good, is the cause of the substance of sensible things, either in the manner of a formal cause, as the Platonists maintained, or in the manner of a material cause, as the Pythagoreans claimed. However, they did not say that the being and coming-to-be of things exists for the sake of this, i.e., the one or being; and this is something that pertains to the intelligibility of the final cause. Hence, just as the philosophers of nature claimed that the good is a cause in the manner of an efficient cause and not in that of a formal cause, in a similar way the Platonists claimed that the good is a cause in the manner of a formal cause, and not in that of a final cause. The Pythagoreans, on the other hand, considered it to be a cause in the manner of a material cause.

179. It is evident, then, that in one sense they happened to speak of the good as a cause and in another not. For they did not speak of it as a cause in its principal aspect but in a secondary one; because according to its proper intelligible structure the good is a cause in the manner of a final cause. This is clear from the fact that the good is what all desire. Now that to which an appetite tends is a goal. Therefore according to its proper intelligible structure the good is a cause

in the manner of a goal. Hence those who make the good a cause in its principal aspect claim that it is a final cause. But those who attribute a different mode of causality to the good claim that the good is a cause but only in a secondary way; because they do not hold that it is such by reason of being good, but by reason of that to which good happens to belong—by reason of its being active or perfective. Hence it is clear that those philosophers posited a final cause only incidentally, because they posited as a cause something that is fitting to be an end, namely, the good. However, they did not claim that it is a cause in the manner of a final cause, as has been stated.

180. **Therefore all these** (85).

Here he draws the conclusion at which he chiefly aims: that the things established about the causes, both as to their number and their kinds, are correct. For the foregoing philosophers seem to bear witness to this in being unable to add another class of cause to those discussed above. This is one of the useful pieces of information resulting from the account of the foregoing views. Another is that evidently the principles of things must be investigated in this science, either all those which the ancient philosophers posited, and which have been established above, or some of them. For this science considers chiefly the formal and final cause, and also in a sense the efficient cause. Now it is not only necessary that the above views be discussed, but after this examination it is also necessary to describe the way in which each of these men has spoken (both in what sense their statements are acceptable and in what sense not), and how the statements which have been made about the principles of things contain a problem.

LESSON 12

Criticism of the Views about the Number of Material Principles

ARISTOTLE'S TEXT   Chapter 8: 988b 22-989b 24

86. Therefore all those who hold that the whole is one and say that there is a certain single nature as matter, and that this is corporeal and has measure, are clearly at fault in many ways. For they give only the elements of bodies and not those of incorporeal things, as if incorporeal things did not exist.

87. And in attempting to state the cause of generation and corruption, and in treating all things according to the method of natural philosophy, they do away with the cause of motion.

88. Furthermore, they did not claim that the substance or whatness of a thing is a cause of anything.

89. And they were wrong in holding that any of the simple bodies except earth is a principle, without considering how they are generated from each other.

90. I mean fire, earth, water and air; for some of these are generated from each other by combination and others by separation. Now it makes the greatest difference as to which of these is prior and which subsequent.

91. For in one way it would seem that the most basic element of all is that from which a thing first comes to be by combination. But such an element will be one which has the smallest parts and is the subtlest of bodies. Hence all those who posit fire as the first principle make statements that conform most closely to this theory. But each of the other thinkers admits that the primary element of bodies is something of this kind.

92. For none of the later thinkers, and none of those who spoke about the one, wanted earth to be an element, evidently because of the size of its particles. But each of the other three elements finds some supporter, for some say that this primary element is fire, others water, and others air. But why do they not say that it is earth, as in a sense most men do? For they say that everything is earth. And Hesiod says that earth is the first of bodies to be generated; [1] for this happens to be the ancient and common view. Therefore, according to this theory, if anyone says that any of these bodies with the exception of fire is the primary element of things, or if anyone holds that it is something denser than air but rarer than water, [2] he will not speak the truth.

93. However, if that which is later in generation is prior in nature, and if that which is condensed and compounded is later in generation, then the reverse will be true—water will be prior to air, and earth to water. Let these points suffice, then, regarding those who posit one cause such as we have described.

94. The same consequence will also be true if anyone posits many elements, as Empedocles says that the four [elemental] bodies are the matter of things. For these same consequences must befall this man, as well as some which are

[1] *Theogony*, 116-120.
[2] See *Physica*, VIII, 6 (187a 14-189b 3).

peculiar to himself. For we see things being generated from each other in such a way that the same body does not always remain fire or earth. But we have spoken of these matters in our physical treatises.[3]

95. And concerning the cause of things in motion, whether one or more than one must be posited, it must not be thought that what has been said is either entirely correct or reasonable.

96. And in general those who speak thus must do away with alteration, because the cold will not come from the hot, nor the hot from the cold. For what is it that undergoes these contraries, and what is the one nature which becomes [4] fire and water? Such a thing Empedocles does not admit.

97. But if anyone were to maintain that Anaxagoras speaks of two elements, they would acknowledge something fully in accord with a theory which he himself has not stated articulately, although he would have been forced to follow those who express this view. For to say, as he did, that in the beginning all things are mixed together is absurd, both because it would be necessary to understand that things previously existed in an unmixed state, and because it is not fitting that anything should be mixed with just anything; and also because properties and accidents could be separated from substances (for there is both mixture and separation of the same things). Yet, if anyone were to follow him up and articulate what he means, his statement would perhaps appear more astonishing. For when nothing was distinct from anything else, evidently nothing would be truly predicated of that substance. I mean that it would neither be white nor black nor tawny, nor have any color, but would necessarily be colorless; for otherwise it would have one of these colors. And, similarly, it would be without humors. And for the same reason it would have no other similar attribute. For it could not have any quality or quantity or whatness, because, if it had, some of the attributes described as formal principles would inhere in it. But this is obviously impossible, since all things are mixed together; for they would already be distinct from each other. But he said that all things are mixed together except intellect, and that this alone is unmixed and pure.[5] Now from these statements it follows for him that there are two principles, one being the intellect itself (for this is unmixed in an absolute sense), and the other being the kind of thing we suppose the indeterminate to be before it is limited and participates in a form. Hence, what he says is neither correct nor clear, although he intends something similar to what later thinkers said and what is now more apparent. But these thinkers are concerned only with theories proper to generation, corruption and motion; for usually it is only of this kind of substance that these men seek the principles and causes.

[3] *De Gen. et Cor.*, II, 6 (333a 15 ff.); *De Coelo*, III, 7 (305a 34 ff.).
[4] Reading *fit* for *sit*. See Greek text 989a 30.
[5] Diels, Frag. 12.

COMMENTARY

181. Having stated the opinions which the philosophers held about the principles of things, Aristotle begins here to criticize them; and this is divided into two parts. First (86:C 181), he criticizes each opinion. Second

(143:C 272), he summarizes his discussion and links it up with what follows ("From the foregoing").

The first is divided into two parts. First, he criticizes the opinions of those who have treated things according to the method of natural philosophy. Second (98:C 201), he criticizes the opinions of those who have not treated things according to the method of natural philosophy, i.e., Pythagoras and Plato, because they posited higher principles than the natural philosophers did ("But all those").

In regard to the first part he does two things. First, he criticizes the opinions of those who posited one material cause; and second (94:C 190), the opinions of those who posited many ("The same consequence").

In regard to the first he does two things. First, he criticizes the foregoing opinions in a general way; and second (89:C 183), in a special way ("And they were wrong").

He criticizes these opinions in a general way by means of three arguments. The first (86) is this: in the world there are not only bodies but also certain incorporeal things, as is clear from *The Soul*.[1] But these men posited only corporeal principles, which is clear from the fact that they maintained that "the whole is one," i.e., that the universe is one thing substantially, and that there is a single nature as matter, and that this is corporeal and has "measure," i.e., dimension. But a body cannot be the cause of an incorporeal thing. Therefore it is evident that they were at fault in this respect that they treated the principles of things inadequately. And they were at fault not only in this respect but in many others,

as is clear from the following arguments.

182. **And in attempting** (87).

Here he gives the second argument, which runs thus: whoever feels obliged to establish the truth about motion must posit a cause of motion. But these philosophers felt obliged to treat motion, which is clear for two reasons: first, because they tried to state the causes of generation and corruption in the world, which do not occur without motion; and second, because they wanted to treat things according to the method of natural philosophy. But since a treatment of things according to this method involves motion (because nature is a principle of motion and rest, as is clear in Book II of the *Physics*[2]), they should therefore have dealt with that cause which is the source of motion. And since they did away with the cause of motion by saying nothing about it, obviously they were also at fault in this respect.

183. **Furthermore, they did not** (88).

Here he gives the third argument: every natural being has "a substance," i.e., a *form of the part,* "and whatness," i.e., quiddity, which is the *form of the whole.*[3] He says *form* inasmuch as it is a principle of subsistence, and *whatness* inasmuch as it is a principle of knowing, because *what a thing is* is known by means of this. But the foregoing philosophers did not claim that form is a cause of anything. They treated things inadequately, then, and were also at fault in neglecting the formal cause.

184. **For none of the later** (92).

Here he criticizes their opinions in a special way; and he does this with respect to two things. First (92:C 184), he criticizes them for maintaining that

---

[1] *De Anima*, I, 5 (411a 23).

[2] *Physica*, II, 1 (192b 22).

[3] The expression *form of the part* (*forma partis*) designates the formal cause or principle which, together with matter, makes up a thing's essence. The expression *form of the whole* (*forma totius*) designates the whole essence of a thing, i.e., both its form and matter. See Book VII, L.9:C 1467-69.

all the elements with the exception of fire are the principles of things. Second (93:C 187), he criticizes them for omitting earth ("However, if").

First (92), he takes up once more the position of those who claimed that each of the simple bodies except earth is the [primary] element of things. The reason which he gives for this position is that these men saw that the simple bodies are generated from each other in such a way that some come from others [4] by combination or compacting, as grosser things come from more refined ones.

185. He also explains how to proceed against their opinions from their own arguments. For they claimed that one of these elements is the principle of things by arguing that other things are generated from it either by combination or by separation. Now it makes the greatest difference as to which of these two ways is prior and which subsequent, for on this depends the priority or posteriority of that from which something is generated. For, on the one hand, that seems to be prior from which something is produced by combination; and he gives this argument first. Yet, on the other hand, that seems to be prior from which something is produced by rarefaction; and he bases his second argument on this.

186. For the fact that the primary element is that from which something is produced by combination supports the opinion which is now held that the most basic element is that from which other things are produced by combination. This in fact is evident both from reason and from the things that they held. It is evident from reason, because that from which other things are produced by combination is the most refined type of body, and the one having the smallest parts; and this seems to be the simpler body. Hence, if the simple is prior to the composite, this body seems to be first. It is also evident from the things that they held, because all those who posited fire as the principle of things asserted that it is the first principle. Similarly, others have been seen to follow this argument, for they thought that the primary element of bodies is the one having the finest parts. This is evident from the fact that none of the later philosophers followed the theological poets, who said that earth is the primary element of things. Evidently they refused to do this "because of the size of its parts," i.e., because of the coarseness of its parts. However, it is a fact that each of the other three elements finds some philosopher who judges it to be the principle of things. But their refusal to make earth a principle is not to be explained by a refusal to reject a common opinion; for many men thought that earth is the substance of things. Hesiod, who was one of the theological poets, also said that earth is the first of all bodies to come into being. Thus the opinion that earth is the principle of things is evidently an ancient one, because it was maintained by the theological poets, who preceded the philosophers of nature. It was also the common opinion, because many men accepted it. It follows, then, that the later philosophers avoided the position that earth is a principle only because of the coarseness of its parts. But it is certain that earth has coarser parts than water, and water than air, and air than fire; and if there is any intermediate element, it is evident that it is grosser than fire. Hence by following this argument it is clear that none of them spoke correctly, except him who held that fire is the first principle. For as soon as some element is held to be a principle by reason of its minuteness, the most minute element must be held to be the first principle of things.

---

[4] Reading *aliis* for *illis,* i.e., some from others.

187. **However, if that which** (93).

Here he gives another argument, and according to it the opposite seems to be true, namely, that earth is the most basic element of things. For it is evident that whatever is subsequent in generation is prior in nature, because nature tends to the goal of generation as the first thing in its intention. But the denser and more composite something is, the later it appears in the process of generation; for the process of generation proceeds from simple things to composite ones, just as mixed bodies come from the elements, and the humors and members [of a living body] from mixed bodies. Hence, whatever is more composite and condensed is prior in nature. In this way a conclusion is reached which is the opposite of that following from the first argument; i.e., water is now prior to air and earth to water as the first principle of things.

188. It should be noted, however, that it is a different thing to look for what is prior in one and the same entity and for what is prior without qualification. For if one seeks what is prior without qualification, the perfect must be prior to the imperfect, just as actuality is prior to potentiality; because a thing is brought from a state of imperfection to one of perfection, or from potentiality to actuality, only by something completely actual. Therefore, if we speak of what is first in the whole universe, it must be the most perfect thing. But in the case of one particular thing which goes from potentiality to complete actuality, potentiality is prior to actuality in time, although it is subsequent in nature. It is also clear that the first of all things must be one that is simplest; for the composite depends on the simple, and not the reverse. It was necessary, then, that the ancient philosophers should attribute both of these

properties (the greatest perfection along with the greatest simplicity) to the first principle of the whole universe. However, these two properties cannot be attributed simultaneously to any corporeal principle, for in bodies subject to generation and corruption the simplest entities are imperfect. They were compelled, then, as by contrary arguments, to posit different principles. Yet they preferred the argument of simplicity, because they considered things only insofar as something passes from potentiality to actuality, and in this order it is not necessary that anything which is a principle should be more perfect. But this kind of opposition can be resolved only by maintaining that the first principle of things is incorporeal, because this principle will be the simplest one, as Aristotle will prove below (1076:C 2548).

189. Last of all he concludes that for the purpose of the present discussion enough has been said about the positions of those who affirm one material cause.

190. **The same consequence** (94).

Here he gives the arguments against those who posited many material causes. First (94:C 190), he argues against Empedocles; and second (97:C 194), against Anaxagoras ("But if anyone").

First (94), he says that the same consequence faces Empedocles, who held that the four [elemental] bodies are the matter of things, because he experienced the same difficulty with regard to the above contrariety. For according to the argument of simplicity fire would seem to be the most basic principle of bodies; and according to the other argument earth would seem to be such, as has been stated (93:C 187). And while Empedocles faced some of the same absurd conclusions as the preceding philosophers (i.e.,[5] he did not posit either a formal cause or

---

[5] Reading *scilicet* for *sicut*.

the aforesaid contrariety of simplicity and perfection in corporeal things), there is no argument against him for doing away with the cause of motion. But he did face certain other absurd conclusions besides those that confronted the philosophers who posited one material cause.

191. This is shown by three arguments, of which the first is as follows. First principles are not generated from each other, because a principle must always remain in existence, as is pointed out in Book I of the *Physics*.[6] But we perceive that the four elements are generated from each other, and for this reason their generation is dealt with in natural philosophy. Hence his position that the four elements are the first principles of things is untenable.

192. **And concerning the cause** (95).

Here he gives the second absurdity, which has to do with the cause of motion. For to posit many and contrary causes of motion is not at all correct or reasonable; because if the causes of motion are understood to be proximate ones, they must be contraries, since their effects seem to be contraries. But if the first cause is understood, then it must be unique, as is apparent in Book XII (1056:C 2492) of this work, and in Book VIII of the *Physics*.[7] Therefore, since he intends to posit the first causes of motion, his position that they are contraries is untenable.

193. **And in general** (96).

Here he gives the third argument which leads to an absurdity: in every process of alteration it must be the same subject which undergoes contraries. This is true because one contrary does not come from another in such a way that one is converted into the other; for example, the cold does not come from the hot in such a way that heat itself becomes cold or the

reverse, although the cold does come from the hot when the underlying[8] subject is one only inasmuch as the single subject which is now the subject of heat is afterwards the subject of cold. But Empedocles did not hold that contraries have one subject. In fact he held that they are found in different subjects, as heat in fire and cold in water. Nor again did he hold that there is one nature underlying these two. Therefore he could not posit alteration in any way. Yet it is absurd that alteration should be done away with altogether.

194. **But if anyone** (97).

Here he deals with Anaxagoras' opinion; and in regard to this he does two things. First, he shows in general in what respect Anaxagoras' opinion should be accepted as true, and in what respect not. Second (97), he explains each of these in particular ("For to say").

He says, first, that if anyone wishes to maintain that Anaxagoras' opinion is true insofar as he posited two principles, i.e., matter and efficient cause, let him understand this according to the reasoning which Anaxagoras himself seems to have followed, as if compelled by some need for truth, inasmuch as he would have followed those who expressed this theory. But "he himself has not stated it articulately"; i.e., he has not expressed it distinctly. Therefore, with reference to what he has not expressly stated his opinion is true; but with reference to what he has expressly stated his opinion is false.

195. This is made clear in particular as follows. If his opinion is taken in its entirety according to a superficial understanding of his statements, a greater absurdity will appear for four reasons. First, his opinion that all things were mixed together at the

[6] *Physica*, I, 5 (188a 26).
[7] *Physica*, VIII, 6 (259a 14).
[8] Reading *supposito* for *suppositum*. See Parma ed., Vol. XX, p. 275.

beginning of the world is absurd; for in Aristotle's opinion the distinction between the parts of the world is thought to be eternal. The second reason is this: what is unmixed is related to what is mixed as the simple to the composite. But simple bodies are prior to composite ones, and not the reverse. Therefore what is unmixed must be prior to what is mixed. This is the opposite of what Anaxagoras said. The third reason is this: in the case of bodies not anything at all is naturally disposed to be mixed with anything else, but only those things are naturally disposed to be mixed which are naturally inclined to pass over into each other by some kind of alteration; for a mixture is a union of the altered things which are capable of being mixed. But Anaxagoras held that anything is mixed with just anything. The fourth reason is this: there is both mixture and separation of the same things; for only those things are said to be mixed which are naturally disposed to exist apart. But properties and accidents are mixed with substances, as Anaxagoras said. Therefore it follows that properties and accidents can exist apart from substances. This is evidently false. These absurdities appear then, if Anaxagoras' opinion is considered in a superficial way.

196. Yet if anyone were to follow him up "and articulate," i.e., investigate clearly and distinctly, the things which Anaxagoras "means," i.e., what he intended, although he did not know how to express this, his statement would appear to be more astonishing and subtler than those of the preceding philosophers. This will be so for two reasons. First, he came closer to a true understanding of matter. This is clear from the fact that in that mixture of things, when nothing was distinguished from anything else but all things were mixed together, nothing could be truly predicated of that substance which is so mixed, which

he held to be the matter of things. This is clear in the case of colors; for no special color could be predicated of it so that it might be said to be white or black or have some other color; because, according to this, that color would necessarily be unmixed with other things. Nor, similarly, could color in general be predicated of it so that it might be said to be colored; because everything of which a generic term is predicated must also have a specific term predicated of it, whether the predication be univocal or denominative. Hence, if that substance were colored, it would necessarily have some special color. But this is opposed to the foregoing statement. And the argument is similar with respect to "humors," i.e., savors, and to all other things of this kind. Hence the primary genera themselves could not be predicated of it in such a way that it would have quality or quantity or some attribute of this kind. For if these genera were predicated of it, some particular species would necessarily belong to it. But this is impossible, if all things are held to be mixed together. For this species which would be predicated of that substance would already be distinguished from the others. And this is the true nature of matter, namely, that it does not have any form actually but is in potentiality to all forms. For the mixed body itself does not have actually any of the things which combine in its mixture, but has them only potentially. And it is because of this likeness between prime matter and what is mixed that he seems to have posited the above mixture; although there is some difference between the potentiality of matter and that of a mixture. For even though the elements which constitute a mixture are present in the mixture potentially, they are still not present in a state of pure passive potency; for they remain virtually in the mixture. This can be shown from the fact that a mixture has motion and operations as a result of the bodies of which the mixture is composed. But this cannot be said of the things which are present potentially in prime matter. And there is also another difference, namely, that even though a mixture is not actually any of the mixed bodies which it contains, yet it is something actual. This cannot be said of prime matter. But Anaxagoras seems to do away with this difference, because he has not posited any particular mixture but the universal mixture of all things.

197. The second reason is this: he spoke more subtly than the others, because he came closer to a true understanding of the first active principle. For he said that all things are mixed together except intellect, and that this alone is unmixed and pure.

198. From these things it is clear that he posited two principles: one of these he claimed to be the intellect itself, insofar as it is simple and unmixed with other things; and the other is prime matter, which we claim is like the indeterminate before it is limited and participates in a form. For since [prime] matter is [the subject] of an infinite number of forms, it is limited by a form and acquires some species by means of it.

199. It is clear, then, that, in regard to the things which he stated expressly, Anaxagoras neither spoke correctly nor clearly. Yet he would seem to say something directly which comes closer to the opinions of the later philosophers, which are truer (namely, to those of Plato and Aristotle, whose judgments about prime matter were correct) and which were then more apparent.

200. In concluding Aristotle excuses himself from a more diligent investigation of these opinions, because the statements of these philosophers belong to the realm of physical discussions, which treat of generation and corruption. For these men usually posited principles and causes of this kind of substance, i.e., of material and corruptible substance. He says "usually," because, while they did not treat other substances, certain of the principles laid down by them can also be extended to other substances. This is most evident in the case of intellect. Therefore, since they have not posited principles common to all substances, which pertains to this science, but only principles of corruptible substances, which pertains to the philosophy of nature, a diligent study of the foregoing opinions belongs rather to the philosophy of nature than to this science.

LESSON 13

Criticism of the Pythagoreans' Opinions

ARISTOTLE'S TEXT   Chapters 8 & 9: 989b 24-990a 34

98. But all those who make a study of all existing things, and who claim that some are sensible and others not, evidently make a study of both classes. And for this reason one should dwell at greater length on the statements they have made, whether they be acceptable or not, for the purposes of the present study which we now propose to make.

99. Therefore, those who are called Pythagoreans used principles and elements which are foreign to the physicists; and the reason is that they did not take them from sensible things. For the objects of mathematics, with the exception of those that pertain to astronomy, are devoid of motion. Nevertheless they discuss and treat everything that has to do with the physical world; for they generate the heavens and observe what happens in regard to its parts, affections and operations. And in doing this they use up their principles and causes, as though they agreed with the others, i.e., the physicists, that whatever exists is sensible and is contained by the so-called heavens. But, as we have stated, the causes and principles [of which they speak] are sufficient to extend even to a higher class of beings, and are better suited to these than to their theories about the physical world.

100. Yet how there will be motion if only the limited and unlimited and even and odd are posited as principles, they do not say. But how can there be generation or corruption, or the activities of those bodies which traverse the heavens, if there is no motion or change?

101. And further, whether one grants them that continuous quantities come from these things, or whether this is demonstrated, how is it that some bodies are light and others heavy? For from what they suppose and state, they say nothing more about mathematical bodies than they do about sensible ones. Hence they have said nothing about fire, earth and other bodies of this kind, since they have nothing to say that is proper to sensible things.

102. Further, how are we to understand that the attributes of number and number itself are [the causes] of what exists and comes to pass in the heavens, both from the beginning and now? And how are we to understand that there is no other number except that of which the world is composed? For when they [place] opportunity and opinion in one part of the heavens, and a little above or below them injustice and separation or mixture, and when they state as proof of this that each of these is a number, and claim that there already happens to be in this place a plurality of quantities constituted [of numbers], because these attributes of number correspond to each of these places, [we may ask] whether this number which is in the heavens is the same as that which we understand each [sensible] thing to be, or whether there is another kind of number in addition to this? For Plato says there is another. In fact, he also thinks that both

82

these things and their causes are numbers, but that some are intellectual causes and others sensible ones.

Chapter 9

Regarding the Pythagoreans, then, let us dismiss them for the present; for it is enough to have touched upon them [1] to the extent that we have.

[1] Reading *ipsos* or *eos* for *ipsa* in the Latin version. See St. Thomas, C 207.

COMMENTARY

201. Here he argues dialectically against the opinions of Pythagoras and Plato, who posited different principles than those which pertain to the philosophy of nature. In regard to this he does two things. First (98:C 201), he shows that a study of these opinions rather than those mentioned above belongs to the present science. Second (99:C 202), he begins to argue dialectically against these opinions ("Therefore those who").

He says, first (98), then, that those who "make a study," i.e., an investigation, of all existing things, and hold that some are sensible and others nonsensible, make a study of both classes of beings. Hence an investigation of the opinions of those who spoke either correctly or incorrectly, belongs rather to the study which we now propose to make in this science. For this science deals with all beings and not with some particular class of being. Hence, the things which pertain to every class of being are to be considered here rather than those which pertain to some particular class of being.

202. **Therefore those who** (99).

Here he argues against the opinions of the foregoing philosophers. First (99), he argues against Pythagoras; and second (103:C 208), against Plato ("But those who posited Ideas").

[1] *Physica*, II, 2 (194a 8).

In regard to the first he does two things. First, he shows in what way Pythagoras agreed with the philosophers of nature, and in what way he differed from them. Second (100:C 204), he argues against Pythagoras' position ("Yet how").

We must understand (99), then, that in one respect the Pythagoreans agreed with the philosophers of nature, and in another respect they differed from them. They differed from them in their position regarding principles, because they employed principles of things in a way foreign to the philosophers of nature. The reason is that they did not take the principles of things from sensible beings, as the natural philosophers did, but from the objects of mathematics, which are devoid of motion, and are therefore not physical. And the statement that the objects of mathematics are devoid of motion must be referred to those sciences which are purely mathematical, such as arithmetic and geometry. Astronomy considers motion, because astronomy is a science midway between mathematics and natural philosophy. For astronomy and the other intermediate sciences apply their principles to natural things, as is clear in Book II of the *Physics*.[1]

203. Now Pythagoras agreed with the philosophers of nature concerning

the things whose principles he sought; for he discussed and treated all natural beings. He dealt with the generation of the heavens, and observed everything that happens to the parts of the heavens, by which are meant the different spheres, or also the different stars. He also considered what happens to its affections, or to the eclipses of the luminous bodies; and what happens to the operations and motions of the heavenly bodies, and their effects on lower bodies. And he used up causes on particular things of this kind by applying to each one its proper cause. He also seemed to agree with the other philosophers of nature in thinking that that alone has being which is sensible and is contained by the heavens which we see. For he did not posit an infinite sensible body as the other philosophers of nature did. Nor again did he hold that there are many worlds, as Democritus did. He therefore seemed to think that there are no beings except sensible ones, because he assigned principles and causes only for such substances. However, the causes and principles which he laid down are not proper or limited to sensible things, but are sufficient for ascending to higher beings, i.e., intellectual ones. And they were better fitted to these than the theories of the natural philosophers which could not be extended beyond sensible things, because these philosophers claimed that principles are corporeal. But since Pythagoras posited incorporeal principles, i.e., numbers, although he only posited principles of sensible bodies, he came very close to positing principles of intelligible beings, which are not bodies, as Plato did later on.

204. **Yet how** (100).

Here he gives three arguments against the opinion of Pythagoras. The first is this: Pythagoras could not explain how motion originates in the world, because he posited as principles only the limited and unlimited and the even and odd, which he held to be principles as substance, or material principles. But he had to admit that there is motion in the world. For how could there be generation and corruption in bodies, and how could there be any activities of the heavenly bodies, which occur as a result of certain kinds of motion, unless motion and change existed? Evidently they could not exist in any way. Hence, since Pythagoras considered generation and corruption and the operations of the heavenly bodies without assigning any principle of motion, his position is clearly unsatisfactory.

205. **And further** (101).

Here he gives the second argument. For Pythagoras claimed that continuous quantities are composed of numbers. But whether he proves this or takes it for granted, he could not give any reason on the part of numbers as to why some things are heavy and others light. This is clear from the fact that his theories about numbers are no more adapted to sensible bodies than they are to the objects of mathematics, which are neither heavy nor light. Hence they obviously said nothing more about sensible bodies than they did about the objects of mathematics. Therefore, since sensible bodies, such as earth and fire and the like, considered in themselves, add something over and above the objects of mathematics, it is evident that they said nothing proper in any true sense about these sensible bodies. Thus it is also evident that the principles which they laid down are not sufficient, since they neglected to give the causes of those [attributes] which are proper to sensible bodies.

206. **Further, how are we** (102).

Here he gives the third argument, which is based on the fact that Pythagoras seemed to hold two contrary [positions]. For, on the one hand, he held that number and the attributes of number are the cause both of those events which occur in the heavens and of all generable and corruptible things from the beginning of the world. Yet, on the other hand, he held that there is no other number besides that of which the substance of things is composed; for he held that number is the substance of things. But how is this to be understood, since one and the same thing is not the cause of itself? For Pythagoras says that the former position may be demonstrated from the fact that each one of these sensible things is numerical in substance; because in this part of the universe there are contingent beings, about which there is opinion, and which are subject to time inasmuch as they sometimes are and sometimes are not. But if generable and corruptible things were partly above or partly below, there would be disorder in the order of the universe: either after the manner of injustice, i.e., insofar as some being would receive a nobler or less noble place than it ought to have; or after the manner of separation, i.e., in the sense that, if a body were located outside its own place, it would be separated from bodies of a like nature; or after the manner of mixture and mingling, provided that a body located outside its proper place must be mixed with some other body, for example, if some part of water occupied a place belonging to air or to earth. In this discussion he seems to touch on two ways in which a natural body conforms to its proper place: one pertains to the order of position, according to which nobler bodies receive a higher place, in which there seems to be a kind of justice; and the other pertains to the similarity or dissimilarity between bodies in place, to which separation and mingling may be opposed. Therefore, insofar as things have a definite position, they are fittingly situated in the universe. For if [2] their position were

changed ever so little, something unfitting would result, inasmuch as it has been stated and shown that all parts of the universe are arranged in a definite proportion; for every definite proportion is numerical. And it was from this that Pythagoras showed that all things would be numbers. But, on the other hand, we see that the continuous quantities established in different places are many and different, because the particular places in the universe correspond to the proper attributes by which bodies are differentiated. For the attributes of bodies which are above differ from those which are below. Hence, since Pythagoras by means of the above argument affirms that all sensible things are numbers, and we see that the difference in sensible bodies is attributable to difference in place, the question arises whether the number which exists "in the heavens," i.e., in the whole visible body which comprises the heavens, is merely the same as that which must be understood to be the substance of each sensible thing, or whether besides this number which constitutes the substance of sensible things there is another number which is their cause. Now Plato said that there is one kind of number which is the substance of sensible things, and another which is their cause. And while both Plato himself and Pythagoras thought that numbers are both sensible bodies themselves and their causes, Plato alone considered intellectual numbers to be the causes of things that are not sensible, and sensible numbers to be the causes and forms of sensible things. And since Pythagoras did not do this, his position is unsatisfactory.

207. In concluding Aristotle says that these remarks about the Pythagoreans' opinions will suffice; for it is enough to have touched upon them to this extent.

---

[2] Reading *si* before *situs*. The argument requires a conditional statement.

LESSON 14

Arguments against the Platonic Ideas

ARISTOTLE'S TEXT   Chapter 9: 990a 34-991a 8

103. But those who posited Ideas, and were the first to seek an understanding of the causes of sensible things, introduced other principles equal in number to these—as though one who wishes to count things thinks that this cannot be done when they are few, but believes that he can count them after he has increased their number. For the separate Forms are almost equal to, or not fewer than, these sensible things in the search for whose causes these thinkers have proceeded from sensible things to the Forms. For to each thing there corresponds some homogeneous entity bearing the same name; and with regard to the substances of other things there is a *one-in-many*,[1] both in the case of these sensible things and in those which are eternal.

104. Furthermore, with regard to the ways in which we prove that there are Forms, according to none of these do they become evident. For from some no syllogism necessarily follows, whereas from others there does; and [according to these] there are Forms of things of which we do not think there are Forms.

105. For according to those arguments from [the existence of] the sciences there will be Forms of all things of which there are sciences; and according to the argument of the one-in-many there will also be Forms of negations.

106. Again, according to the argument that there is some understanding of corruption, there will be Forms of corruptible things; for of these there is some sensible image.

107. Again, according to the most certain arguments [for the Forms] some establish Forms of relations,[2] of which they deny there is any essential class; whereas others lead to "the third man."[3]

108. And in general the arguments for the Forms do away with the existence of the things which those who speak of the Forms are more anxious to retain than the Forms themselves. For [4] it happens that the dyad [or duality] is not first, but that number is; and that the relative is prior to that which exists of itself. And all the other [conclusions] which some [5] [reach] by following up the opinions about the Ideas are opposed to the principles [of the theory].[6]

109. Again, according to the opinion whereby we claim that there are Ideas [or Forms], there will be Forms not only of substances but also of many other things. For there is one concept not only in the case of substances but also in that

---

[1] For Plato's argument see *Republic* 596 A.

[2] See *Phaedo*, 74 A-77 A; *Republic* 479 A-480 A.

[3] See *Parmenides*, 132 A-133 A; see also Aristotle, *Metaphysics*, VII, 13 (656:C 1586) and *Sophistical Refutations*, 22 (178b 36-179a 10).

[4] The sense of the text requires *enim* for *autem*.

[5] Reading *aliqui* for *aliquid*.

[6] St. Thomas interprets *opposuerunt principiis* in the Latin version to mean opposed to self-evident principles. The Greek text does not justify this interpretation.

of other things; and there are sciences not only of substance itself but also of other things. And a thousand other such [difficulties] face them.

110. But according to logical necessity and the opinions about the Ideas, if the Forms are participated in, there must be Ideas only of substances. For they are not participated in according to what is accidental. But things must participate in each Form in this respect: insofar as each Form is not predicated of a subject. I mean that if anything participates in doubleness itself, it also participates in the eternal, but only accidentally; for it is an accident of doubleness to be eternal. Hence the Forms will be substances.

111. But these things signify substance both here and in the ideal world; [otherwise] why is it necessary that a one-in-many appear in addition to these sensible things? Indeed, if the form of the Ideas and that of the things which participate in them are the same, there will be something in common. For why should duality be one and the same in the case of corruptible [7] twos and in those which are many but eternal, rather than in the case of this [Idea of duality] and a particular two? But if the form is not the same, there will be pure equivocation; just as if one were to call both Callias and a piece of wood man, without observing any common attribute which they might have.[8]

[7] Reading *in corruptibilibus* for *incorruptibilibus*. See Greek text and St. Thomas, C 222.
[8] See *Metaphysics*, XIII, 4 (1078b 34-1079b 3).

COMMENTARY

208. Here he argues disputatively against Plato's opinion. This is divided into two parts. First (103:C 208), he argues against Plato's opinion with reference to his position about the substances of things; and second (133:C 259), with reference to his position about the principles of things ("And in general").

The first is divided into two parts. First, he argues against Plato's position that the Forms are substances; and second (122:C 239), against the things that he posited about the objects of mathematics ("Further, if the Forms").

In regard to the first he does two things. First, he argues against this position of Plato; and second (104:C 210), against the reasoning behind it ("Furthermore, with regard to").

He says, first (103), that the Platonists, in holding that the Ideas are certain separate substances, seemed to be at fault in that, when they sought for the causes of these sensible beings, they neglected sensible beings and invented certain other new entities equal in number to sensible beings. This seems to be absurd, because one who seeks the causes of certain things ought to make these evident and not add other things, the premising of which only adds to the number of points which have to be investigated. For it would be similar if a man who wished to count certain things which he did not think he was able to count because they are few, believed that he could count them by increasing their number through the addition of certain other things. But it is evident that such a man has a foolish motive, because the path is clearer when there are fewer things; for it is better and easier to make certain of fewer things than of many. And the smaller a number is, the more certain it is to us, inasmuch as it is nearer to the unit, which is the most accurate measure. And just as the process of counting things is the measure we use to make certain of their number, in a similar fashion an investigation of the causes of things is the accurate measure for making certain of their natures. Therefore, just as the number of fewer numerable things is made certain of more easily, in a similar way the nature of fewer things is made certain of more easily. Hence, when Plato increased the classes of beings to the extent that he did with a view to explaining sensible things, he added to the number of difficulties by taking what is more difficult in order to explain what is less difficult. This is absurd.

209. That the Ideas are equal in number to, or not fewer than, sensible things, whose causes the Platonists seek (and Aristotle includes himself among their number because he was Plato's disciple), and which they established by going from sensible things to the aforesaid Forms, becomes evident if one considers by what reasoning the Platonists introduced the Ideas. Now they reasoned thus: they saw that there is a one-in-many for all things having the same name. Hence they claimed that this one-in-many is a Form. Yet with respect to all substances of things other than the Ideas we see that there is found to be a one-in-many which is predicated of them univocally inasmuch as there are found to be many things which are specifically one. This occurs not only in the case of sensible things but also in that of the objects of mathematics, which are eternal; because among these there are also many things which are specifically one, as was stated above (70:C 157). Hence it follows that some Idea corresponds to each species of sensible things; and therefore each Idea is something having the same name as these sensible things, because the Ideas agree with them in name. For just as Socrates is called man, so also is the Idea of man. Yet they differ conceptually; for the

intelligible structure of Socrates contains matter, whereas that of the ideal man is devoid of matter. Or, according to another reading, each Form is said to be something having the same name [as these sensible things] inasmuch as it is a one-in-many and agrees with the things of which it is predicated so far as the intelligible structure of the species is concerned. Hence he says that they are equal to, or not fewer than, these things. For either there are held to be Ideas only of species, and then they would be equal in number to these sensible things (granted that things are counted here insofar as they differ specifically and not individually, for the latter difference is infinite); or there are held to be Ideas not only of species but also of genera, and then there would be more Ideas than there are species of sensible things, because all species would be Ideas and in addition to these each and every genus [would be an Idea]. This is why he says that they are either not fewer than or more. Or, in another way, they are said to be equal inasmuch as he claimed that they are the Forms of sensible things. And he says not fewer than but more inasmuch as he held that they are the Forms not only of sensible things but also of the objects of mathematics.

210. **Furthermore, with regard to** (104).

Here he argues dialectically against the reasoning behind Plato's position; and in regard to this he does two things. First (104), he gives a general account of the ways in which Plato's arguments fail. Second (105:C 211), he explains them in detail ("For according to those").

He says, first (104), that with regard to the ways in which we Platonists prove the existence of the Forms, according to none of these are the Forms seen to exist. The reason is that "no syllogism follows" necessarily from some of these ways, i.e., from certain arguments of Plato, because they cannot demonstrate with necessity the existence of the Ideas. However, from other arguments a syllogism does follow, although it does not support Plato's thesis; for by certain of his arguments there are proved to be Forms of certain things of which the Platonists did not think there are Forms, just as there are proved to be Forms of those things of which they think there are Forms.

211. **For according to** (105).

Here he examines in detail the arguments by which the Platonists establish Ideas. First, he examines the second argument; and he does this by showing that from Plato's argument it follows that there are Forms of some things for which the Platonists did not posit Forms. Second (112:C 225), he examines the first argument; and he does this by showing that Plato's arguments are not sufficient to prove that Ideas exist ("But the most").

In regard to the first member of this division he gives seven arguments. The first is this: one of the arguments that induced Plato to posit Ideas is taken from scientific knowledge; for since science is concerned with necessary things, it cannot be concerned with sensible things, which are corruptible, but must be concerned with separate entities which are incorruptible. According to the argument taken from the sciences, then, it follows that there are Forms of every sort of thing of which there are sciences. Now there are sciences not only of that which is one-in-many, which is affirmative, but also of negations; for just as there are some demonstrations which conclude with an affirmative proposition, in a similar way there are demonstrations which conclude with a negative proposition. Hence it is also necessary to posit Ideas of negations.

212. **Again, according to the argument** (106).

Here he gives the second argument. For in the sciences it is not only understood that some things always exist in the same way, but also that some things are destroyed; otherwise the philosophy of nature, which deals with motion, would be destroyed. Therefore, if there must be Ideas of all the things which are comprehended in the sciences, there must be Ideas of corruptible things as such, i.e., insofar as these are singular sensible things; for thus are things corruptible. But according to Plato's theory it cannot be said that those sciences by which we understand the processes of corruption in the world attain any understanding of the processes of corruption in sensible things; for there is no comprehension of these sensible things, but only imagination or phantasy, which is a motion produced by the senses in their act of sensing, as is pointed out in *The Soul*, Book II.[1]

213. **Again, according to the most** (107).

Here he gives the third argument, which contains two conclusions that he says are drawn from the most certain arguments of Plato. One conclusion is this: if there are Ideas of all things of which there are sciences, and there are sciences not only of absolutes but also of things predicated relatively, then in giving this argument it follows that there are also Ideas of relations. This is opposed to Plato's view. For, since the separate Ideas are things which exist of themselves, which is opposed to the intelligibility of a relation, Plato did not hold that there is a class of Ideas of relations, because the Ideas are said to exist of themselves.

214. The second conclusion is one which follows from other most certain arguments, namely, that there is "a third man." This phrase can be understood in three ways. First, it can mean that the ideal man is a third man dis-

---

[1] *De Anima*, II, 3 (428b 10).

tinct from two men perceived by the senses, who have the common name man predicated of both of them. But this does not seem to be what he has in mind, even though it is not mentioned in the *Sophistical Refutations,* Book II; [2] for this is the position against which he argues. Hence according to this it would not lead to an absurdity.

215. The second way in which this expression can be understood is this: the third man means one that is common to the ideal man and to one perceived by the senses. For since both a man perceived by the senses and the ideal man have a common intelligible structure, like two men perceived by the senses, then just as the ideal man is held to be a third man in addition to two men perceived by the senses, in a similar way there should be held to be another third man in addition to the ideal man and one perceived by the senses. But neither does this seem to be what he has in mind here, because he leads us immediately to this absurdity by means of another argument. Hence it would be pointless to lead us to the same absurdity here.

216. The third way in which this expression can be understood is this: Plato posited three kinds of entities in certain classes of things, namely, sensible substances, the objects of mathematics and the Forms. He does this, for example, in the case of numbers, lines and the like. But there is no reason why intermediate things should be held to exist in certain classes rather than in others. Hence in the class of man it was also necessary to posit an intermediate man, who will be a third man midway between the man perceived by the senses and the ideal man. Aristotle also gives this argument in the later books of this work (906:C 2160).[3]

217. **And in general** (108).

Here he gives the fourth argument, which runs as follows. Whoever by his own reasoning does away with certain [principles] which are better known to him than the ones which he posits, adopts an absurd position. But these theories about the Forms which Plato held do away with certain principles whose reality the Platonists (when they said that there are Ideas) were more convinced of than the existence of the Ideas. Therefore Plato's position is absurd. The minor premise is proved in this way. According to Plato the Ideas are prior both to sensible things and to the objects of mathematics. But according to him the Ideas themselves are numbers; and they are odd numbers rather than even ones, because he attributed odd number to form and even number to matter. Hence he also said that the dyad [or duality] is matter. Therefore it follows that other numbers are prior to the dyad, which he held to be the matter of sensible things, and identified with the great and small. Yet the Platonists asserted the very opposite of this, that is to say, that the dyad is first in the class of number.

218. Again, if, as has been proved by the above argument (107:C 213), there must be Ideas of relations, which are self-subsistent relations, and if the Idea itself is prior to whatever participates in the Idea, it follows that the relative is prior to the absolute, which is said to exist of itself. For sensible substances of this kind, which participate in Ideas, are said to be in an unqualified sense. And in like manner whatever those who follow the opinion about the Ideas say of all things is opposed to self-evident principles which even they themselves are most ready to acknowledge.

[2] *De Sophisticis Elenchis,* chap. 22. This work was formerly divided into two books, the second beginning at chap. 16 of the current single-book arrangement. The present chap. 22 fell within Book II, chap. 3. Cf. the edition of *Aristotelis Opera Omnia* with the commentary of Sylvester Maurus, vol. I (Paris: Lethielleux, 1885).

[3] See also Book XIII, 5 (1079b 13).

219. **Again, according to the opinion** (109).

Here he gives the fifth argument, which is as follows: Ideas were posited by Plato in order that the intelligible structures and definitions of things given in the sciences might correspond to them, and in order that there could be sciences of them. But there is "one concept," i.e., a simple and indivisible concept, by which the quiddity of each thing is known, i.e., not only the quiddity of substances "but also of other things," namely, of accidents. And in a similar way there are sciences not only of substance and about substance, but there are also found to be sciences "of other things," i.e., of accidents. Hence according to the opinion by which you Platonists acknowledge the existence of Ideas, it evidently follows that there will be Forms not only of substances but also of other things, i.e., of accidents. This same conclusion follows not only because of definitions and the sciences, but there also happen to be many "other such" [reasons],[4] i.e., very many reasons why it is necessary to posit Ideas of accidents according to Plato's arguments. For example, he held that the Ideas are the principles of being and of becoming in the world, and of many such aspects which apply to accidents.

220. But, on the other hand, according to Plato's opinion about the Ideas and according to logical necessity, insofar as the Ideas are indispensable to sensible things, i.e., "insofar"[5] as they are capable of being participated in by sensible things, it is necessary to posit Ideas only of substances. This is proved thus: things which are accidental are not participated in. But an Idea must be participated in by each thing insofar as it is not predicated of a subject. This

becomes clear as follows: if any sensible thing participates in "doubleness itself," i.e., in a separate doubleness (for Plato spoke of all separated things in this way, namely, as self-subsisting things), it must participate in the eternal. But it does not do this essentially (because then it would follow that any double perceived by the senses would be eternal), but accidentally, i.e., insofar as doubleness itself, which is participated in, is eternal. And from this it is evident that there is no participation in things which are accidental, but only in substances. Hence according to Plato's position a separate Form was not an accident but only a substance. Yet according to the argument taken from the sciences there must also be Forms of accidents, as was stated above (109:C 219).

221. **But these things** (111).

Then he gives the sixth argument, which runs thus: these sensible things signify substance both in the case of things perceived by the senses and in that of those in the ideal world, i.e., in the case of intelligible things, which signify substance; because they held that both intelligible things and sensible ones are substance. Therefore it is necessary to posit in addition to both of these substances—intelligible and sensible ones—some common entity which is a one-in-many. For the Platonists maintained that the Ideas exist on the grounds that they found a one-in-many which they believed to be separate from the many.

222. The need for positing a one apart from both sensible substances and the Forms he proves thus: the Ideas and the sensible things which participate in them either belong to one class or not. If they belong to one class, and

4 According to the Greek text Aristotle is talking about "other such" absurd conclusions which face those who accept the theory of Ideas. St. Thomas is either following a different reading, or has misinterpreted Aristotle's thought. As the text stands it could be interpreted in the sense in which he takes it.
5 The quotation marks suggest that St. Thomas is following a different reading. In the Latin version "inquantum" appears only in a later sentence, i.e., at "insofar as doubleness."

it is necessary to posit, according to Plato's position, one common separate Form for all things having a common nature, then it will be necessary to posit some entity common to both sensible things and the Ideas themselves, which exists apart from both. Now one cannot answer this argument by saying that the Ideas, which are incorporeal and immaterial, do not stand in need of any higher Forms; because the objects of mathematics, which Plato places midway between sensible substances and the Forms, are similarly incorporeal and immaterial. Yet since many of them are found to belong to one species, Plato held that there is a common Form for these things, in which not only the objects of mathematics participate but also sensible substances. Therefore, if the twoness [or duality] which is the Form or Idea of twoness is identical with that found in sensible twos, which are corruptible (just as a pattern is found in the things fashioned after it), and with that found in mathematical twos, which are many in one class (but are nevertheless eternal), then for the same reason in the case of the same twoness, i.e., the Idea two, and in that of the other twoness, which is either mathematical or sensible, there will be another separate twoness. For no reason can be given why the former should exist and the latter should not.

223. But if the other alternative is admitted—that sensible things, which participate in the Ideas, do not have the same form as the Ideas—it follows that the name which is predicated of both the Ideas and sensible substances is predicated in a purely equivocal way. For those things are said to be equivocal which have only a common name and differ in their intelligible structure. And it follows that they are not only equivocal in every way but equivocal in an absolute sense, like those things on which one name is imposed without regard for any common attribute, which are said to be equivocal by chance; for example, if one were to call both Callias and a piece of wood man.

224. Now Aristotle added this because someone might say that a name is not predicated of an Idea and of a sensible substance in a purely equivocal way, since a name is predicated of an Idea essentially and of a sensible substance by participation. For, according to Plato, the Idea of man is called "man in himself," whereas this man whom we apprehend by the senses is said to be a man by participation. However, such an equivocation is not pure equivocation. But a name which is predicated by participation is predicated with reference to something that is predicated essentially; and this is not pure equivocation but the multiplicity of analogy. However, if an Idea and a sensible substance were altogether equivocal by chance, it would follow that one could not be known through the other, as one equivocal thing cannot be known through another.

LESSON 15

The Destruction of the Platonists' Arguments for Ideas

ARISTOTLE'S TEXT   Chapter 9: 991a 8-991b 9

112. But the most important problem of all that one might raise is what the Forms contribute to sensible things, either to those which are eternal or to those which are generated and corrupted.

113. For they are not the cause of motion or of any change whatever in these things.

114. Nor are they of any assistance in knowing other things; for they are not the substance of other things, because if they were they would exist in them. Nor do they contribute anything to the being of other things; for they are not present in the things which participate in them. For if they were they would perhaps seem to be causes, as whiteness mixed with some white thing. But this theory, which was first stated by Anaxagoras [1] and later by Hesiod [2] and certain other thinkers, is easily disposed of. For it is easy to bring many absurd conclusions against such a view. In fact other things are not derived from the Forms in any of the customary senses.

115. Again, to say that they are exemplars, and that other things participate in them, is to speak with empty talk and to utter poetic metaphors.

116. For what is the work which looks towards the Ideas [as an examplar]? [3] For one thing may both be and become similar to another thing and not be made in likeness to it. So whether Socrates exists or not, a man such as Socrates might come to be.

117. Similarly, it is evident that this will be the case even if Socrates is eternal. And there will be many exemplars of the same thing, and for this reason many Forms, as animal and two-footed and man-in-himself will be the Form of man.

118. Further, the Forms will be the exemplars not only of sensible things but also of the Forms themselves, as the genus of the species. Hence the same thing will be both an exemplar and a copy.

119. Again, it is thought to be impossible that the substance of a thing and that of which it is the substance should exist apart. Hence, if the Forms are the substances of things, how will they exist apart from them?

120. But in the *Phaedo* [4] it is stated that the Forms are the causes both of being and of coming to be. Yet even if the Forms do exist, still the things which participate in them will not come to be unless there is something which produces motion.

121. And many other things come to be, such as a house and a ring, of which

[1] Diels, Frag. 12.
[2] Instead of *Hesiodus,* found in the Latin, the Greek text has Eudoxus.
[3] See Plato, *Timaeus* 28 C & 29 A.
[4] *Phaedo* 100 D.

we do not say that there are any Forms. It is evident, then, that other things can exist and come to be because of such causes as those [responsible for the things] just mentioned.

COMMENTARY

225. Here Aristotle attacks the opinion of Plato insofar as he did not draw the conclusion which he intended to draw. For Plato intended to conclude that there are Ideas by this argument that they are necessary in some way for sensible things. Hence, Aristotle, by showing that the Ideas cannot contribute anything to sensible things, destroys the arguments by which Plato posits Ideas. Thus he says (112) that of all the objections which may be raised against Plato the foremost is that the Forms which Plato posited do not seem to contribute anything to sensible things, either to those which are eternal, as the celestial bodies, or to those which are generated and corrupted, as the elemental bodies. He shows (113) that this criticism applies to each of the arguments by which Plato posited Ideas ("For they are not").

226. At this point in the text (113) he begins to present his five objections [against the Platonic arguments for Ideas].

He argues, first (113:C 226), that they are useless in explaining motion; second (114:C 227), that they are useless in explaining our knowledge of sensible things ("Nor are they"); third (115:C 231), that they are of no value as exemplars ("Again, to say"); fourth (119:C 236), that they are of no value as the substances of things ("Again, it is thought"); and fifth (120:C 237), that they are of no value as causes of generation ("But in the *Phaedo*").

Accordingly, he says, first (113), that the Forms cannot contribute anything to sensible things in such a way as to be the cause of motion or of any kind of change in them. He does not give the reason for this here but mentioned it above (120:C 237), because it is clear that the Ideas were not introduced to explain motion but rather to explain immutability. For since it seemed to Plato that all sensible things are always in motion, he wanted to posit something separate from sensible things that is fixed and immobile, of which there can be certain knowledge. Hence, according to him, the Forms could not be held to be sensible principles of motion, but rather to be immutable things and principles of immutability; so that, undoubtedly, whatever is found to be fixed and constant in sensible things will be due to participation in the Ideas, which are immutable in themselves.

227. **Nor are they of any assistance** (114).

Second, he shows that the Forms do not contribute anything to the knowledge of sensible things, by the following argument: knowledge of each thing is acquired by knowing its own substance, and not by knowing certain substances which are separate from it. But these separate substances, which they call Forms, are altogether other than sensible substances. Therefore a knowledge of them is of no assistance in knowing other sensible things.

228. Nor can it be said that the Forms are the substances of these sensible things; for the substance of each thing is present in the thing whose substance it is. Therefore, if these Forms were the substances of sensible things, they would be present in sensible things. This is opposed to Plato's opinion.

229. Nor again can it be said that the Forms are present in these sensible substances as in things which participate in them; for Plato thought that some Forms are the causes of sensible things in this way. For just as we might understand whiteness itself existing of itself as a certain separate whiteness to be mingled with the whiteness in a subject, and to participate in whiteness, in a similar way we might say that man [in himself], who is separate, is mingled with this man who is composed of matter and the specific nature in which he participates. But this argument is easily "disposed of," i.e., destroyed; for Anaxagoras, who also held that forms and accidents are mingled with things, was the first to state it. Hesiod [1] and certain other thinkers were the second to mention it. Therefore I say that it is easily disposed of, because it is easy to bring many absurd conclusions against such an opinion. For it would follow, as he pointed out above (97:C 194) against Anaxagoras, that accidents and forms could exist without substances. For only those things can exist separately which are naturally disposed to be mixed with other things.

230. It cannot be said, then, that the Forms contribute in any way to our knowledge of sensible things as their substances. Nor can it be said that they are the principles of being in these substances by way of participation. Nor again can it be said that from these Forms as principles other things— sensible ones—come to be in any of the ways in which we are accustomed to speak. Therefore, if principles of being and principles of knowledge are the same, the Forms cannot possibly make any contribution to scientific knowledge, since they cannot be principles of being. Hence he says "in any of the customary ways" of speaking, because Plato invented many new ways of deriving knowledge of one thing from something else.

231. **Again, to say** (115).

Here he gives the third objection against the arguments for separate Forms. He says that the Forms are of no value to sensible things as their exemplars. First (115), he states his thesis; and second (116:C 232), he proves it ("For what is the work").

Accordingly he says, first (115), that to say that the Forms are the exemplars both of sensible things and the objects of mathematics (because the latter participate in causes of this kind), is untenable for two reasons. First, because it is vain and useless to posit exemplars of this kind, as he will show; and second, because this manner of speaking is similar to the metaphors which the poets introduce, which do not pertain to the philosopher. For the philosopher ought to teach by using proper causes. Hence he says that this manner of speaking is metaphorical, because Plato likened the generation of natural substances to the making of works of art, in which the artisan, by looking at some exemplar, produces something similar to his artistic idea.

232. **For what is the work** (116).

Here he proves his thesis by three arguments. For the work, i.e., the use, of an exemplar, seems to be this, that the artisan by looking at an exemplar induces a likeness of the form in his own artifact. But in the operations of natural beings we see that like things are generated by like, as man is generated by man. Therefore this likeness arises in things which are generated, either because some agent looks toward an exemplar or not. If not, then what is "the work," or utility, of the agent's so looking toward the Ideas as exemplars?—as if to say, none. But if the likeness results from looking at a separate exemplar, then it cannot be said that the cause of this likeness in

---

[1] St. Thomas follows the Latin version in reading *Hesiodus* for *Eudoxus*.

the thing generated is the form of an inferior agent. For something similar would come into being with reference to this separate exemplar and not with reference to this sensible agent. And this is what he means when he says "and not be like it," i.e., like the sensible agent. From this the following absurdity results: someone similar to Socrates will be generated whether Socrates is held to exist or not. This we see is false; for unless Socrates plays an active part in the process of generation, no one similar to Socrates will ever be generated. Therefore, if it is false that the likeness of things which are generated does not depend on proximate agents, it is pointless and superfluous to posit separate exemplars of any kind.

233. However, it should be noted that, even though this argument does away with the separate exemplars postulated by Plato, it still does not do away with the fact that God's knowledge is the exemplar of all things. For since things in the physical world are naturally inclined to induce their likeness in things which are generated, this inclination must be traced back to some directing principle which ordains each thing to its end. This can only be the intellect of that being who knows the end and the relationship of things to the end. Therefore this likeness of effects to their natural causes is traced back to an intellect as their first principle. But it is not necessary that this likeness should be traced back to any other separate forms; because in order to have the above-mentioned likeness this direction of things to their end, according to which natural powers are directed by the first intellect, is sufficient.

234. **Similarly, it is evident** (117).

Here he gives the second argument, which runs as follows: just as Socrates because he is Socrates adds something to man, in a similar way man adds something to animal. And just as Socrates participates in man, so does man participate in animal. But if besides this Socrates whom we perceive there is held to be another Socrates who is eternal, as his exemplar, it will follow that there are several exemplars of this Socrates whom we perceive, i.e., the eternal Socrates and the Form man. And by the same reasoning the Form man will have several exemplars; for its exemplar will be both animal and two-footed and also "man-in-himself," i.e., the Idea of man. But that there should be several exemplars of a single thing made in likeness to an exemplar is untenable. Therefore it is absurd to hold that things of this kind are the exemplars of sensible things.

235. **Further** (118).

Here he gives the third argument, which runs thus: just as a Form is related to an individual, so also is a genus related to a species. Therefore, if the Forms are the exemplars of individual sensible things, as Plato held, there will be also certain exemplars of these Forms, that is to say, their genus. But this is absurd, because then it would follow that one and the same thing, i.e., Form, would be an exemplar of one thing, namely, of the individual whom we perceive by the senses, and a copy made in likeness to something else, namely, a genus. This seems to be absurd.

236. **Again, it is thought** (119).

Here he proves his fourth objection, namely, that the Forms contribute nothing to sensible things as their substances or formal causes; because "It is thought by him," that is to say, it is a matter of opinion (to put this impersonally), that it is impossible for a thing's substance to exist apart from the thing whose substance it is. But the Forms exist apart from the things of which they are the Forms, i.e., apart from sensible things. Therefore they are not the substances of sensible things.

237. **But in the "Phaedo"** (120).

Here he shows that the Forms are of no value in accounting for the coming to be of sensible things, although

Plato said "in the *Phaedo*," [2] i.e., in one of his works, that the Forms are the causes both of the being and of the coming to be of sensible things.

But Aristotle disproves this by two arguments. The first is as follows: to posit the cause is to posit the effect. However, even if the Forms exist, the particular or individual things which participate in the Forms will come into being only if there is some agent which moves them to acquire form. This is evident from Plato's opinion that the Forms are always in the same state. Therefore, assuming that these Forms exist, if individuals were to exist or come into being by participating in them, it would follow that individual substances of this kind would always be. This is clearly false. Therefore it cannot be said that the Forms are the causes of both the coming to be and the being of sensible things. The chief reason is that Plato did not hold that the Forms are efficient causes, as was

[2] *Phaedo* 100 D.

stated above (113:C 226). For Aristotle holds that the being and coming to be of lower substances proceeds from immobile separate substances, inasmuch as these substances are the movers of the celestial bodies, by means of which generation and corruption are produced in these lower substances.

238. **And many other** (121).

Here he gives the second argument, which runs thus: just as artifacts are related to artificial causes, so are natural bodies to natural causes. But we see that many other things besides natural bodies come into being in the realm of these lower bodies, as a house and a ring, for which the Platonists did not posit any Forms. Therefore "other things," namely, natural things, can both be and come to be because of such proximate causes as those just mentioned, i.e., artificial ones; so that, just as artificial things come to be as a result of proximate agents, so also do natural things.

LESSON 16

Arguments against the View that Ideas Are Numbers

ARISTOTLE'S TEXT   Chapter 9: 991b 9-992a 24

122. Further, if the Forms are numbers, in what way will they be causes? Will it be because existing things are other numbers, so that this number is man, another Socrates, and still another Callias? In what respect, then, are the former the cause of the latter? For it will make no difference if the former are eternal and the latter are not. But if it is because the things here are ratios of numbers, like a harmony, then clearly there will be one kind of thing of which they are the ratios. And if this is matter, evidently the numbers themselves will be certain ratios of one thing to something else. I mean that, if Callias is a numerical ratio of fire, water, earth and air, [his Idea will also be a ratio of certain things],[1] and man-in-himself, whether it be a number or not, will still be a numerical ratio of certain things and not just a number; nor will it be any number because of these.

123. Again, one number will come from many numbers, but how or in what way can one Form come from [many] Forms?

124. But if one number is not produced from them but from the units which they contain, as the units in the number ten thousand, how are the units related? For if they are specifically the same, many absurdities will follow; and if they are not, neither will they be the same as one another nor all the others the same as all.

125. For in what way will they differ, if they have no attributes? For these statements are neither reasonable nor in accord with our understanding.

126. Further, [if the Forms are numbers], it is necessary to set up some other class of number: that with which arithmetic deals. And all the things which are said to be intermediate, from what things or what principles in an absolute sense will they come, or why [2] will they be [an intermediate class] between [3] the things at hand and those [in the ideal world]?

127. Again, each of the units which are contained in the number two will come from a prior two. But this is impossible.

128. Further, why is a number something composed of these?

129. And, again, in addition to what has been said, if the units are different, it will be necessary to speak of them in the same way as do those who say that the elements are four or two. For none of them designate as an element what is common, namely, body, but fire and earth, whether body is something in common or not. But now we are speaking of the one as if it were one thing made up of like parts, as fire or water. But if this is the case, numbers will not be substances.

---

[1] This statement in the Greek text is not rendered in the Latin version in the Cathala edition. St. Thomas presumably follows a different reading. See C 242.

[2] Reading *quare* for *quale*.

[3] Reading *intra* for *infra*.

Yet it is evident that, if the one itself is something common and a principle, then the one is used in different senses; otherwise this will be impossible.

130. Now when we wish to reduce substances to their principles, we claim that lengths come from the long and short, i.e., from a kind of great and small; and the plane from the wide and narrow; and body from the deep and shallow.

131. Yet how will a surface contain a line, or a solid a line or surface? For the wide and narrow is a different class from the deep and shallow. Hence, just as number is not present in these, because the many and few differ from these, it is evident that no one of the other higher classes will be present in the lower. And the broad is not in the class of the deep, for then the solid would be a kind of surface.

132. Further, from what will points derive being? Plato was opposed to this class of objects as a geometrical fiction, but he called them the principle of a line. And he often holds that there are indivisible lines. Yet these must have some [limit]. Therefore any argument that proves the existence of the line also proves the existence of the point.

COMMENTARY

239. Here he destroys Plato's opinion about the Forms inasmuch as Plato claimed that they are numbers. In regard to this he does two things. First (122:C 239), he argues dialectically against Plato's opinion about numbers; and second (130:C 254), against his opinion about the other objects of mathematics ("Now when we wish").

In regard to the first part he gives six arguments. The first (122) is this: in the case of things which are substantially the same, one thing is not the cause of another. But sensible things are substantially numbers according to the Platonists and Pythagoreans. Therefore, if the Forms themselves are numbers, they cannot be the cause of sensible things.

240. But if it is said that some numbers are Forms and others are sensible things, as Plato literally held (as though we were to say that this number is man and another is Socrates and still another is Callias), even this would not seem to be sufficient; for according to this view the intelligible structure of number will be common both to sensible things and the Forms. But in the case of things which have the same intelligible structure, one does not seem to be the cause of another. Therefore the Forms will not be the causes of sensible things.

241. Nor again can it be said that they are causes for the reason that, if those numbers are Forms, they are eternal. For this difference, namely, that some things differ from others in virtue of being eternal and non-eternal in their own being considered absolutely, is not sufficient to explain why some things are held to be the causes of others. Indeed, things differ from each other as cause and effect rather because of the relationship which one has to the other. Therefore things that differ numerically do not differ from each other as cause and effect because some are eternal and some are not.

242. Again, it is said that sensible things are certain "ratios" or proportions of numbers, and that numbers are the causes of these sensible things, as we also observe to be the case "in harmonies," i.e., in the combinations

of musical notes. For numbers are said to be the causes of harmonies insofar as the numerical proportions applied to sounds yield harmonies. Now if the above is true, then just as in harmonies there are found to be sounds in addition to numerical proportions, in a similar way it was obviously necessary to posit in addition to the numbers in sensible things something generically one to which the numerical proportions are applied, so that the proportions of those things which belong to that one genus would constitute sensible things. However, if that to which the numerical proportion in sensible things is applied is matter, evidently those separate numbers, which are Forms, had to be termed proportions of some one thing to something else. For this particular man, called Callias or Socrates, must be said to be similar to the ideal man, called "man-in-himself," or humanity. Hence, if Callias is not merely a number, but is rather a kind of ratio or numerical proportion of the elements, i.e., of fire, earth, water and air, and if the ideal man-in-himself is a kind of ratio or numerical proportion of certain things, the ideal man will not be a number by reason of its own substance. From this it follows that there will be no number "apart from these," [1] i.e., apart from the things numbered. For if the number which constitutes the Forms is separate in the highest degree, and if it is not separate from things but is a kind of proportion of numbered things, no other number will now be separate. This is opposed to Plato's view.

243. It also follows that the ideal man is a proportion of certain numbered things, whether it is held to be a number or not. For according to those who held that substances are numbers, and according to the philosophers of nature, who denied that num-

bers are substances, some numerical proportions must be found in the substances of things. This is most evident in the case of the opinion of Empedocles, who held that each one of these sensible things is composed of a certain harmony or proportion [of the elements].

244. **Again, one number** (123).

Here he gives the second argument which runs thus: one number is produced from many numbers. Therefore, if the Forms are numbers, one Form is produced from many Forms. But this is impossible. For if from many things which differ specifically something specifically one is produced, this comes about by mixture, in which the natures of the things mixed are not preserved; just as a stone is produced from the four elements. Again, from things of this kind which differ specifically one thing is not produced by reason of the Forms, because the Forms themselves are combined in such a way as to constitute a single thing only in accordance with the intelligible structure of individual things, which are altered in such a way that they can be mixed together. And when the Forms themselves of the numbers two and three are combined, they give rise to the number five, so that each number remains and is retained in the number five.

245. But since someone could answer this argument, in support of Plato, by saying that one number does not come from many numbers, but each number is immediately constituted of units, Aristotle is therefore logical in rejecting this answer (124) ("But if one number").

For if it is said that some greater number, such as ten thousand, is not produced "from them," namely, from twos or many smaller numbers, but from "units," i.e., ones, this question

---

[1] The phrase *praeter ea* to which St. Thomas refers in his commentary does not agree with the Latin version or with the Greek text. He is either following a different reading or misreads *praeter ea* for *propterea*.

will follow: How are the units of which numbers are composed related to each other? For all units must either conform with each other or not.

246. But many absurd conclusions follow from the first alternative, especially for those who claim that the Forms are numbers. For it will follow that different Forms do not differ substantially but only insofar as one Form surpasses another. It also seems absurd that units should differ in no way and yet be many, since difference is a result of multiplicity.

247. But if they do not conform, this can happen in two ways. First, they can lack conformity because the units of one number differ from those of another number, as the units of the number two differ from those of the number three, although the units of one and the same number will conform with each other. Second, they can lack conformity insofar as the units of one and the same number do not conform with each other or with the units of another number. He indicates this distinction when he says, "For neither will they be the same as one another (125)," i.e., the units which comprise the same number, "nor all the others the same as all," i.e., those which belong to different numbers. Indeed, in whatever way there is held to be lack of conformity between units an absurdity is apparent. For every instance of non-conformity involves some form or attribute, just as we see that bodies which lack conformity differ insofar as they are hot and cold, white and black, or in terms of similar attributes. Now units lack qualities of this kind, because they have no qualities, according to Plato. Hence it will be impossible to hold that there is any non-conformity or difference between them of the kind caused by a quality. Thus it is evident that Plato's opinions about the Forms and numbers are neither "reasonable" (for example, those proved by an apodictic argument), nor "in accord with our understanding" (for example, those things which are self-evident and verified by [the habit of] intellect alone, as the first principles of demonstration).

248. **Further, [if the Forms]** (126).

Here he gives the third argument against Plato, which runs thus: all objects of mathematics, which Plato affirmed to be midway between the Forms and sensible substances, are derived unqualifiedly from numbers, either as proper principles, or as first principles. He says this because in one sense numbers seem to be the immediate principles of the other objects of mathematics; for the Platonists said that the number one constitutes the point, the number two the line, the number three surface, and the number four the solid. But in another sense the objects of mathematics seem to be reduced to numbers as first principles and not as proximate ones. For the Platonists said that solids are composed of surfaces, surfaces of lines, lines of points, and points of units, which constitute numbers. But in either way it followed that numbers are the principles of the other objects of mathematics.

249. Therefore, just as the other objects of mathematics constituted an intermediate class between sensible substances and the Forms, in a similar way it was necessary to devise some class of number which is other than the numbers that constitute the Forms and other than those that constitute the substance of sensible things. And arithmetic, which is one of the mathematical sciences, evidently deals with this kind of number as its proper subject, just as geometry deals with mathematical extensions. However, this position seems to be superfluous; for no reason can be given why number should be midway "between the things at hand," or sensible things, and "those in the ideal world," or the Forms, since both sensible things and the Forms are numbers.

250. **Again, each of the units** (127).

Here he gives the fourth argument, which runs thus: those things which exist in the sensible world and those which exist in the realm of mathematical entities are caused by the Forms. Therefore, if some number two is found both in the sensible world and in the realm of the objects of mathematics, each unit of this subsequent two must be caused by a prior two, which is the Form of twoness. But it is "impossible" that unity should be caused by duality. For it would be most necessary to say this if the units of one number were of a different species than those of another number, because then these units would acquire their species from a Form which is prior to the units of that number. And thus the units of a subsequent two would have to be produced from a prior two.

251. **Further, why is** (128).

Here he gives the fifth argument, which runs thus: many things combine so as to constitute one thing only by reason of some cause, which can be considered to be either extrinsic, as some agent which unites them, or intrinsic, as some unifying bond. Or if some things are united of themselves, one of them must be potential and another actual. However, in the case of units none of these reasons can be said to be the one "why a number," i.e., the cause by which a number, will be a certain "combination," [2] i.e., collection of many units; as if to say, it will be impossible to give any reason for this.

252. **And, again, in addition** (129).

Here he gives the sixth argument, which runs thus: if numbers are the Forms and substances of things, it will be necessary to say, as has been stated before (124:C 245), either that units are different, or that they conform. But if they are different, it follows that unity as unity will not be a principle.

This is clarified by a similar case drawn from the position of the natural philosophers. For some of these thinkers held that the four [elemental] bodies are principles. But even though being a body is common to these elements, these philosophers did not maintain that a common body is a principle, but rather fire, earth, water and air, which are different bodies. Therefore, if units are different, even though all have in common the intelligible constitution of unity, it will not be said that unity itself as such is a principle. This is contrary to the Platonists' position; for they now say that the unit is the principle of things, just as the natural philosophers say that fire or water or some body with like parts is the principle of things. But if our conclusion against the Platonists' theory is true—that unity as such is not the principle and substance of things—it will follow that numbers are not the substances of things. For number is held to be the substance of things only insofar as it is constituted of units, which are said to be the substances of things. This is also contrary to the Platonists' position which is now being examined, i.e., that numbers are Forms.

253. But if you say that all units are undifferentiated, it follows that "the whole," [3] i.e., the entire universe, is a single entity, since the substance of each thing is the one itself, and this is something common and undifferentiated. Further, it follows that the same entity is the principle of all things. But this is impossible by reason of the notion involved, which is inconceivable in itself, namely, that all things should be one according to the aspect of substance. For this view contains a contradiction, since it claims that the one is the substance of all things, yet maintains that the one is a principle. For one and the same thing is not its

---

[2] St. Thomas is apparently following a different reading. The Latin version has *collectus* not *comprehensum*, as given above.

[3] *Quod omne* does not appear in the Latin version of Aristotle's text.

own principle, unless, perhaps, it is said that "the one" is used in different senses, so that when the senses of the one are differentiated all things are said to be generically one and not numerically or specifically one.

254. **Now when we wish** (130).

Here he argues against Plato's position with reference to his views about mathematical extensions. First (130), he gives Plato's position; and second (131:C 255), he advances an argument against it ("Yet how will").

He says, first, that the Platonists, wishing to reduce the substances of things to their first principles, when they say that continuous quantities themselves are the substances of sensible things, thought they had discovered the principles of things when they assigned line, surface and solid as the principles of sensible things. But in giving the principles of continuous quantities they said that "lengths," i.e., lines, are composed of the long and short, because they held that contraries are the principles of all things. And since the line is the first of continuous quantities, they first attributed to it the great and small; for inasmuch as these two are the principles of the line, they are also the principles of other continuous quantities. He says "from the great and small" because the great and small are also placed among the Forms, as has been stated (108:C 217). But insofar as they are limited by position, and are thus particularized [4] in the class of continuous quantities, they constitute first the line and then other continuous quantities. And for the same reason they said that surface is composed of the wide and narrow, and body of the deep and shallow.

255. **Yet how will a surface** (131).

Here he argues against the foregoing position, by means of two arguments. The first is as follows. Things whose principles are different are them-

selves different. But the principles of continuous quantities mentioned above are different, according to the foregoing position, for the wide and narrow, which are posited as the principles of surface, belong to a different class than the deep and shallow, which are held to be the principles of body. The same thing can be said of the long and short, which differ from each of the above. Therefore, line, surface and body all differ from each other. How then will one be able to say that a surface contains a line, and a body a line and a surface? In confirmation of this argument he introduces a similar case involving number. For the many and few, which are held to be principles of things for a similar reason, belong to a different class than the long and short, the wide and narrow, and the deep and shallow. Therefore number is not contained in these continuous quantities but is essentially separate. Hence, for the same reason, the higher of the above mentioned things will not be contained in the lower; for example, a line will not be contained in a surface or a surface in a body.

256. But because it could be said that certain of the foregoing contraries are the genera of the others, for example, that the long is the genus of the broad, and the broad the genus of the deep, he destroys this [objection] by the following argument: things composed of principles are related to each other in the same way as their principles are. Therefore, if the broad is the genus of the deep, surface will also be the genus of body. Hence a solid will be a kind of plane, i.e., a species of surface. This is clearly false.

257. **Further, from what will** (132).

Here he gives the second argument, which involves points; and in regard to this Plato seems to have made two errors. First, Plato claimed that a point

---

[4] Reading *particularizatur* for *particulari*.

is the limit of a line, just as a line is the limit of a surface and a surface the limit of a body. Therefore, just as he posited certain principles of which the latter are composed, so too he should have posited some principle from which points derive their being. But he seems to have omitted this.

258. The second error is this: Plato seems to have held different opinions about points. For sometimes he maintained that the whole science of geometry treats this class of things, namely, points, inasmuch as he held that points are the principles and substance of all continuous quantities. And he not only implied this but even explicitly stated that a point is the principle of a line, defining it in this way. But many times he said that indivisible lines are the principles of lines and other continuous quantities, and that this is the class of things with which geometry deals, namely, indivisible lines. Yet by reason of the fact that he held that all continuous quantities are composed of indivisible lines, he did not avoid the consequence that continuous quantities are composed of points, and that points are the principles of continuous quantities. For indivisible lines must have some limits, and these can only be points. Hence, by whatever argument indivisible lines are held to be the principles of continuous quantities, by the same argument too the point is held to be the principle of continuous quantity.

LESSON 17

Arguments against the View that the Ideas Are Principles of Being and Knowledge

ARISTOTLE'S TEXT   Chapters 9 & 10: 992a 24-993a 27

133. And, in general, even though wisdom investigates the causes of apparent things, we have neglected this study. For we [1] say nothing about the cause from which motion originates. And while we think that we are stating the substance of these sensible things, we introduce other substances. But the way in which we explain how the latter are the substances of the former is empty talk; for to participate, as we have said before (115), signifies nothing. Moreover, that which we see to be the cause in the sciences, that by reason of which all intellect and all nature operates, on that cause which we say is one of the principles the Forms do not touch in any way. But mathematics has been turned into philosophy by present-day thinkers (566), although they say [2] that mathematics must be treated for the sake of other things.

134. Further, one might suppose that the underlying substance [which they consider] as matter is too mathematical, and that it is rather a predicate and difference of substance and matter, like the great and small; just as the philosophers of nature speak of the rare and dense (56), which they say are the primary differences of the underlying subject; for [3] these are a kind of excess and defect.

135. And with regard to motion, if these entities [the great and small] are motion, evidently the Forms are moved; but if they are not, from what does motion come? For [if it has no cause], the whole study of nature is destroyed.

136. And what seems easy to show is that all things are not one; for from their position all things do not become one. But if someone [4] should assert that all things are some one thing, not even this is true unless one grants that the universal is a class; and in certain other cases this is impossible.

137. For they do not have any theory about the lengths, widths, and solids which come after the numbers: either as to how they now exist or will exist, or what importance they have. For it is impossible that they should be Forms (since they are not numbers), or intermediate things (for those are the objects of mathematics), or corruptible things; but, on the contrary, it seems that they form a fourth class.

138. And, in general, to look for the elements of existing things without distinguishing the different senses in which things are said to be, makes it impossible to discover them. And [their view is unsatisfactory] in another way,[5] i.e.,

---

[1] Aristotle is speaking as a Platonist.
[2] See Plato, *Republic* 531 C, D; 533 B-E.
[3] Reading *enim* for *autem*.
[4] Reading *quis* for *siquis*.
[5] According to the Greek text this statement should read: "And especially if they seek in this way for the elements of which things are composed." St. Thomas follows the reading of the Latin version. See C 266.

in the way in which they seek for the elements of which things are composed. For it is impossible to understand of what things action or passion or straightness is composed. But if this is possible only in the case of substances, then to look for the elements of all existing things, or to think that we have found them, is a mistake.

139. But how will one acquire knowledge of the elements of all things? For it is clearly impossible to have prior knowledge of anything. For just as one acquiring knowledge of geometry must have a prior knowledge of other things, but not of the things which this science [investigates], and which he is to learn, so it is in the case of the other sciences. Hence, if there is a science of all things (and there must be a science of these),[6] as some say, the one learning this science does not have any prior knowledge of it. But all learning proceeds from things previously known, either all or some of them, whether the learning be by demonstration or by definitions. For [the parts] of which definitions are composed must already be known beforehand and be evident. The same thing is true in the case of things discovered by induction.

140. But if this science were connatural,[7] it is a wonder how we could be unconscious of having the most important of the sciences.

141. Again, how is anyone to know the elements of which things are composed, and how is this to be made evident? For this also presents a difficulty; because one might argue in the same way as one does about certain syllables. For some say that *sma* is made up of *s, m* and *a,* whereas others say that it is a totally different sound and not any of those which are known to us.

142. Again, how could one know the things of which a sense is cognizant without having that sense? Yet this will be necessary if they [i.e., sensible things] are the elements of which all things are composed, just as spoken words are composed of their proper elements.

Chapter 10 [8]

143. From the foregoing, then, it is evident that all [the early philosophers] seem to seek the causes mentioned in the *Physics,*[9] and that we cannot state any other in addition to these. But they understood these obscurely; and while in one sense all causes have been mentioned before, in another sense they have not been mentioned at all. Indeed, the earliest philosophy seems to speak in a faltering way about all subjects inasmuch as it was new as regards principles and the first of its kind. For even Empedocles says that ratios are present in bone, and that this is the quiddity or substance of a thing. But [if this is true], there must likewise be a ratio of flesh and of every other thing or of nothing. For it is because of this that flesh and bone and every other thing exists, and not because of their matter, which he says is fire, earth, air and water. But if someone else had said this, he would have been forced to agree to the same thing. But he has not said this. Such things as these, then, have been explained before. So let us return again to whatever problems one might raise about the same subject; for perhaps in the light of these we shall be able to make some investigation into subsequent problems.

[6] This statement—*Et de quibus oportet*—has no counterpart in the Greek text. Nor does St. Thomas mention it. It is probably an intrusion from the preceding sentence.

[7] See Plato, *Meno* 81 C; *Phaedo* 72 E.

[8] The chapter heading is missing in the Latin version.

[9] *Physica,* II, 3 (194b 16); 7 (198a 14).

COMMENTARY

259. Here Aristotle destroys Plato's opinion about the principles of things. First (133:C 259), he destroys Plato's opinion about principles of being; and second (139:C 268), his opinion about principles of knowledge ("But how will one").

In regard to the first part he gives six arguments. The first is based on the fact that Plato neglected to deal with the classes of causes. Thus he says that, "in general, wisdom," or philosophy, has as its aim to investigate the causes "of apparent things," i.e., things apparent to the senses. For men began to philosophize because they sought for the causes of things, as was stated in the prologue (27:C 53). But the Platonists, among whom he includes himself, neglected the principles of things, because they said nothing about the efficient cause, which is the source of change. And by positing the Ideas they thought they had given the formal cause of things. But while they thought that they were speaking of the substance of these things, i.e., sensible ones, they posited the existence of certain other separate substances which differ from these. However, the way in which they assigned these separate substances as the substances of sensible things "is empty talk," i.e., it proves nothing and is not true. For they said that the Forms are the substances of sensible things inasmuch as they are participated in by sensible things. But what they said about participation is meaningless, as is clear from what was said above (112:C 225). Furthermore, the Forms which they posited have no connection with the final cause, although we see that this is a cause in

certain sciences which demonstrate by means of the final cause, and that it is by reason of this cause that every intellectual agent and every natural one operates, as has been shown in the *Physics*, Book II.[1] And just as they do not touch on that cause which is called an end [or goal], when they postulate the existence of the Forms (78:C 169), neither do they treat of that cause which is called the source of motion, namely, the efficient cause, which is the opposite, so to speak, of the final cause. But the Platonists by omitting causes of this kind (since they did omit a starting-point and end of motion), have dealt with natural things as if they were objects of mathematics, which lack motion. Hence they said that the objects of mathematics should be studied not only for themselves but for the sake of other things, i.e., natural bodies; inasmuch as they attributed the properties of the objects of mathematics to sensible bodies.

260. **Further, one might** (134).

Here he gives the second argument, which runs thus: that which is posited as the matter of a thing is the substance of a thing, and is predicable of a thing to a greater degree than something which exists apart from it. But a Form exists apart from sensible things. Therefore, according to the opinion of the Platonists, one[2] might suppose that the underlying substance as matter is the substance of the objects of mathematics rather than a separate Form. Furthermore, he admits that it is predicated of a sensible thing rather than the above Form. For the Platonists held that the great and small is a difference of substance or matter;

---

[1] *Physica*, II, 8 (199a 10).
[2] Reading *aliquis* for *aliquid* in keeping with Aristotle's text.

for they referred these two principles to matter, just as the philosophers of nature (56:C 115) held that rarity and density are the primary differences of the "underlying subject," or matter, by which matter is changed, and spoke of them in a sense as the great and small. This is clear from the fact that rarity and density are a kind of excess and defect. For the dense is what contains a great deal of matter under the same dimensions, and the rare is what contains very little matter. Yet the Platonists said that the Forms are the substance of sensible things rather than the objects of mathematics, and that they are predicable of them to a greater degree.

261. **And with regard** (135).

Here he gives the third argument, which runs thus: if those attributes which exist in sensible things are caused by separate Forms, it is necessary to say either that there is an Idea of "motion" among the Forms or there is not. If there is a Form or Idea of motion among the Forms, and there cannot be motion without something that is moved, it also follows that the Forms must be moved. But this is opposed to the Platonists' opinion, for they claimed that the Forms are immobile. On the other hand, if there is no Idea of motion, and these attributes which exist in sensible things are caused by the Ideas, it will be impossible to assign a cause for the motion which occurs in sensible things; and thus the entire investigation of natural philosophy, which studies mobile things, will be destroyed.

262. **And what seems easy** (136).

Then he gives the fourth argument, which runs thus: if unity were the substance of all things, as the Platonists assumed, it would be necessary to say that all things are one, just as the philosophers of nature also did in claiming that the substance of all things is

water, and so on for the other elements. But it is easy to show that all things are not one. Hence the position that unity is the substance of all things is not held in high repute.

263. But let us assume that someone might say that it does not follow, from Plato's position, that all things are one in an unqualified sense but in a qualified sense,[3] just as we say that some things are one generically or specifically. And if someone wished to say that all things are one in this way, even this could be held only if what I call the one were a genus or universal predicate of all things. For then we could say that all things are one specifically, just as we say that both a man and an ass are animal substantially. But in certain cases it seems impossible that there should be one class of all things, because the difference dividing this class would necessarily not be one, as will be said in Book III (229:C 432). Therefore, in no way can it be held that the substance of all things is one.

264. **For they do not have** (137).

Here he gives the fifth argument, which runs thus: Plato placed lengths, widths and solids after numbers as the substances of sensible things, i.e., that of which they are composed. But according to Plato's position there seems to be no reason why they should be held to exist either now or in the future. Nor does this notion seem to have any efficacy to establish them as the causes of sensible things. For things which exist "now" must mean immobile things (because these always exist in the same way), whereas things which "will exist" must mean those which are capable of generation and corruption, which acquire being after non-being. This becomes clear thus: Plato posited three classes of things— sensible things, the Forms and the objects of mathematics, which are an intermediate class. But such lines and

---

[3] Reading *secundum aliquid* for *aliquod*.

surfaces as those of which sensible bodies are composed cannot be Forms; for the Forms are essentially numbers, whereas such things [i.e., the lines and surfaces composing bodies] come after numbers. Nor can such lines and surfaces be said to be an intermediate class between the Forms and sensible things; for the things in this intermediate class are the objects of mathematics, and exist apart from sensible things; but this cannot be said of the lines and surfaces of which sensible bodies are composed. Nor again can such lines and surfaces be sensible things; for the latter are corruptible, whereas these lines and surfaces are incorruptible, as will be proved below in Book III (250:C 466). Therefore these things are either nothing at all or they constitute a fourth class of things, which Plato omitted.

265. **And, in general** (138).

Here he gives the sixth argument, which runs thus: it is impossible to discover the principles of anything that is spoken of in many senses, unless these many senses are distinguished. Now those things which agree in name only and differ in their intelligible structure cannot have common principles; otherwise they would have the same intelligible structure, since the intelligible structure of a thing is derived from its own principles. But it is impossible to assign distinct principles for those things which have only the name in common, unless it be those whose principles must be indicated to differ from each other. Therefore, since being is predicated both of substance and the other genera in different senses and not in the same sense, Plato assigned inadequate principles for things by failing to distinguish beings from each other.

266. But since someone could assign principles to things which differ in their intelligible structure and have a common name, by adjusting proper principles to each without distinguish-

ing the many senses of the common name, and since the Platonists have not done this, then "in another way," i.e., by another argument, they assigned inadequate principles to things when they looked for the elements of which things are made, i.e., in the way in which they sought for them, inasmuch as they did not assign principles which are sufficient for all things. For from their statements it is impossible to understand the principles of which either action and passion, curvature and straightness, or other such accidents, are composed. For they only indicated the principles of substances and neglected accidents.

267. But if in defense of Plato someone wished to say that it is possible for the elements of all things to have been acquired or discovered at the moment when the principles of substances alone happen to have been acquired or discovered, this opinion would not be true. For even if the principles of substances are also in a sense the principles of accidents, nevertheless accidents have their own principles. Nor are the principles of all genera the same in all respects, as will be shown below in Book XI (912:C 2173) and Book XII (1042:C 2455) of this work.

268. **But how will one** (139).

Here he argues dialectically against Plato's position that the Ideas are the principles of our scientific knowledge.

He gives four arguments, of which the first is this: if our scientific knowledge is caused by the Ideas themselves, it is impossible for us to acquire knowledge of the principles of things. But it is evident that we do acquire knowledge. Therefore our knowledge is not caused by the Ideas themselves. That it would be impossible to acquire knowledge of anything, he proves thus: no one has any prior knowledge of that object of which he ought to acquire knowledge; for example, even though in the case of geometry one has prior knowledge of other things which are necessary for demonstration, nevertheless the objects of which he ought to acquire knowledge he must not know beforehand. The same thing is also true in the case of the other sciences. But if the Ideas are the cause of our knowledge, men must have knowledge of all things, because the Ideas are the intelligible structures of all knowable things. Therefore we cannot acquire knowledge of anything, unless one might be said to acquire knowledge of something which he already knew. If it is held, then, that someone acquires knowledge, he must not have any prior knowledge of the thing which he comes to know, but only of certain other things through which he becomes instructed; i.e., one acquires knowledge through things previously known, [either] "all," i.e., universals, "or some of them," i.e., singular things. One learns through universals in the case of those things which are discovered by demonstration and definition, for in the case of demonstrations and definitions the things of which definitions or universals are composed must be known first. And in the case of things which are discovered by induction singular things must be known first.

269. **But if this science** (140).

Here he gives the second argument, which runs thus: if the Ideas are the cause of our knowledge, it must be connatural to us; for men grasp sensible things through this proper nature, because sensible things participate in Ideas according to the Platonists. But the most important knowledge or science is one that is connatural to us and which we cannot forget, as is evident of our knowledge of the first principles of demonstration, of which no one is ignorant. Hence there is no way in which we can forget the knowledge of all things caused in us by the Ideas. But this is contrary to the Platonists' opinion, who said that the soul as a result of its union with the body forgets the knowledge which it has of all things by nature, and that by teaching a man acquires knowledge of something that he previously knew, as though the process of acquiring knowledge were merely one of remembering.

270. **Again, how is anyone** (141).

Here he gives the third argument, which runs thus: in order to know things a man must acquire knowledge not only of the forms of things but also of the material principles of which they are composed. This is evident from the fact that occasionally questions arise regarding these; for example, with regard to this syllable *sma*, some raise the question whether it is composed of the three letters *s, m* and *a*, or whether it is one letter which is distinct from these and has its own sound. But only the formal principles of things can be known through the Ideas, because the Ideas are the forms of things. Hence the Ideas are not a sufficient cause of our knowledge of things when material principles remain unknown.

271. **Again, how could** (142).

Here he gives the fourth argument, which runs thus: in order to know reality we must know sensible things, because sensible things are the apparent material element of which all things are composed, just as complex sounds (such as syllables and words) are composed of their proper elements. If, then, knowledge is caused in us by the Ideas, our knowledge of sensible things must be caused by the Ideas. But the knowledge which is caused in us by the Ideas is grasped without the senses, because we have no connection with the Ideas through the senses. Therefore in the act of perception it follows that anyone who does not have a sense can apprehend the object of that sense. This is clearly false; for a man born blind cannot have any knowledge of colors.

272. **From the foregoing** (143).

Here he summarizes the statements made by the ancient philosophers. He says that from what has been said above it is evident that the ancient philosophers attempted to investigate the cause which he [Aristotle] dealt with in the *Physics*,[4] and that in their statements we find no cause in addition to those established in that work. However, these men discussed these causes obscurely; and while in a sense they have mentioned all of these causes, in another sense they have not mentioned any of them. For just as young children at first speak imperfectly and in a stammering way, in a similar fashion this philosophy, since it was new, seems to speak imperfectly and in a stammering way about the principles of all things. This is borne out by the fact that Empedocles was the first to say that bones have a certain ratio, or proportional mixture [of the elements], and that this is a thing's quiddity or substance. But the same thing must also be true of flesh and of every other single thing or of none of them, for all of these things are mixtures of the elements. And for this reason it is evident that flesh and bone and all things of this kind are not what they are because of their matter, which he identified with the four elements, but because of this principle—their form. However, Empedocles, compelled as it were by the need for truth, would have maintained[5] this view if it had been expressed more clearly by someone else, but he did not express it clearly. And just as the ancient philosophers have not clearly expressed the nature of form, neither have they clearly expressed the nature of matter, as was said above about Anaxagoras (44:C 90). Nor have they clearly expressed the nature of any other principles. Therefore, concerning such things as have been stated imperfectly, we have spoken of this before (94:C 190). And with regard to these matters we will restate again in Book III (220:C 423) whatever difficulties can be raised on both sides of the question. For perhaps from such difficulties we will discover some useful information for dealing with the problems which must be examined and solved later on throughout this whole science.

[4] *Physica*, II, 3 (194b 16); 7 (198a 14).
[5] Reading *posuisset* for *posuit*. See Cathala-Spiazzi ed., p. 78.

BOOK II

The Search for Truth and Causes

CONTENTS

Book II

LESSON 1

The Acquisition of Truth: Its Ease and Its Difficulty

ARISTOTLE'S TEXT   Chapter 1: 993a 30-993b 19

144. Theoretical, i.e., speculative, knowledge of truth is in one sense difficult and in another, easy.

145. An indication of this is found in the fact that, while no one can attain an adequate knowledge of it, all men together do not fail, because each one is able to say something true about nature.

146. And while each one individually contributes nothing or very little to the truth, still as a result of the combined efforts of all a great amount of truth becomes known.

147. Therefore, if the situation in the case of truth seems to be like the one which we speak of in the proverb "Who will miss a door?" then in this respect it will be easy to know the truth.

148. But the fact that we cannot simultaneously grasp a whole and its parts shows the difficulty involved.[1]

149. However, since the difficulty is twofold, perhaps its cause is not in things but in us; for just as the eyes of owls are to the light of day, so is our soul's intellective power to those things which are by nature the most evident of all.

150. Now it is only right that we should be grateful not merely to those with whose views we agree but also to those who until now have spoken in a superficial way; for they too have made some contribution because they have made use of the habit which we now exercise. Thus if there had been no Timotheus, we would not have a great part of our music; and if there had been no Phrynis, there would have been no Timotheus. The same is true of those who have made statements about the truth; for we have accepted certain opinions from some of them, and others have been the cause of them attaining their knowledge as they have been the cause of us attaining ours.

[1] St. Thomas interprets this statement to mean the whole and the parts of truth in general, see C 278. Aristotle, however, seems to mean simply the whole and the parts of a thing or of a particular question.

COMMENTARY

273. Having criticized the ancient philosophers' opinions about the first principles of things, with which first philosophy is chiefly concerned, the Philosopher now begins to establish what is true.

First philosophy considers truth in a different way than the particular sciences do. Each of the particular sciences considers a particular truth about a definite class of beings; e.g., geometry deals with the continuous quantities of bodies, and arithmetic with numbers; whereas first philosophy considers what is universally true of beings. Therefore, it pertains to this science to consider in what respects man is capable of knowing the truth.

274. This part is divided into two sections. In the first (144:C 274) he deals with the things that belong to a universal consideration of truth. In the second (176:C 338) he begins to investigate what is true of first principles and of everything else with which this philosophy deals. He does this in Book III, which begins with the words "With a view to."

The first part is again divided into three parts. In the first of these he explains in what respects man is capable of knowing the truth. In the second (151:C 290) he indicates to what science the knowledge of truth principally belongs ("It is only right to call"). In the third (171:C 331) he explains the method by which truth is investigated ("The way in which people are affected").

In regard to the first he does three things. First, he shows in what respect it is easy to know the truth. Second (149:C 279), he gives the reason for the difficulty involved ("However, since the difficulty is twofold"). Third (150:C 287), he shows how men assist each other to know the truth ("Now it is only right").

In regard to the first he does two things. First, he states what he intends to prove. He says that "theoretical knowledge," i.e., the contemplative or speculative understanding of truth, is in one sense easy and in another, difficult.

275. **An indication of this** (145).

Second, he explains what he intends to prove: first, in what sense it is easy to know the truth; and second

(148:C 278), in what sense it is difficult ("But the fact").

He shows in what sense it is easy to know the truth, by giving three indications. The first is this: while no man can attain a complete knowledge of the truth, still no man is so completely devoid of truth that he knows nothing about it. This is shown by the fact that anyone can make a statement about the truth and the nature of things, which is a sign of intellectual reflection.

276. **And while each one individually** (146).

Here he gives the second indication. He says that, while the amount of truth that one man can discover or contribute to the knowledge of truth by his own study and talents is small compared with a complete knowledge of truth, nevertheless what is known as a result of "the combined efforts" of all, i.e., what is discovered and collected into one whole, becomes quite extensive. This can be seen in the case of the particular arts, which have developed in a marvelous manner as a result of the studies and talents of different men.

277. **Therefore, if the situation** (147).

Third, he shows that the same thing is true by citing a common proverb. He concludes from the foregoing that since anyone can attain some knowledge of the truth, even though it be little, the situation in the case of knowledge is like the one that we speak of in the proverb "Who will miss a door?" i.e., the outer door of a house. For it is difficult to know what the interior of a house is like, and a man is easily deceived in such matters; but just as no one is mistaken about the entrance of a house, which is evident to all and is the first thing that we perceive, so too this is the case with regard to the knowledge of truth; for those truths through which we enter into a knowledge of others are known to all, and no man is mistaken about them. Those first principles which are naturally apprehended are truths of this sort, e.g., "It is impossible both to affirm and deny something at the same time," and "Every whole is greater than each of its parts," and so on. On the other hand, there are many ways in which error may arise with respect to the conclusions into which we enter through such principles as through an outer door. Therefore, it is easy to know the truth if we consider that small amount of it which is comprised of self-evident principles, through which we enter into other truths, because this much is evident to all.

278. **But the fact that we cannot** (148).

Here he explains in what sense it is difficult to know the truth. He says that our inability to grasp the whole truth and a part of it shows the difficulty involved in the search for truth. In support of this we must consider his statement that the truth through which we gain admission to other truths is known to all. Now there are two ways in which we attain knowledge of the truth. The first is the method of analysis, by which we go from what is complex to what is simple or from a whole to a part, as it is said in Book I of the *Physics* [1] that the first objects of our knowledge are confused wholes. Now our knowledge of the truth is perfected by this method when we attain a distinct knowledge of the particular parts of a whole. The other method is that of synthesis, by which we go from what is simple to what is complex; and we attain knowledge of truth by this method when we succeed in knowing a whole. Thus the fact that man is unable to know perfectly in things a whole and a part shows the

difficulty involved in knowing the truth by both of these methods.

279. **However, since the difficulty is twofold** (149).

He gives the reason for this difficulty. Here too it must be noted that, in all cases in which there is a certain relationship between two things, an effect can fail to occur in two ways, i.e., because of either one of the things involved. For example, if wood does not burn, this may happen either because the fire is not strong enough or because the wood is not combustible enough. And in a similar way the eye may be prevented from seeing a visible object either because the eye is weak or because the visible object is in the dark. Therefore, in like manner, it may be difficult to know the truth about things either because things themselves are imperfect in some way or because of some weakness on the part of our intellect.

280. Now it is evident that we experience difficulty in knowing the truth about some things because of the things themselves; for since each thing is knowable insofar as it is an actual being, as will be stated below in Book IX (805:C 1894) of this work, then those things which are deficient and imperfect in being are less knowable by their very nature; e.g., matter, motion, and time are less knowable because of the imperfect being which they have, as Boethius says in his book *The Two Natures*. [2]

281. Now there were some philosophers who claimed that the difficulty experienced in knowing the truth is wholly attributable to things themselves, because they maintained that nothing is fixed and stable in nature but that everything is in a state of continual change, as will be stated in Book IV (362:C 683) of this work. But the Philosopher denies this, saying that even though the difficulty

---

[1] *Physica*, I, 1 (184a 21).
[2] *Liber de Persona et Duabus Naturis*, Chap. 7 (PL 64:1337).

experienced in knowing the truth can perhaps be twofold because of different things, i.e., our intellect and things themselves, still the principal source of the difficulty is not things but our intellect.

282. He proves this in the following way. If this difficulty were attributable principally to things, it would follow that we would know best those things which are most knowable by nature. But those things which are most knowable by nature are those which are most actual, i.e., immaterial and unchangeable things, yet we know these least of all. Obviously, then, the difficulty experienced in knowing the truth is due principally to some weakness on the part of our intellect. From this it follows that our soul's intellectual power is related to those immaterial beings, which are by nature the most knowable of all, as the eyes of owls are to the light of day, which they cannot see because their power of vision is weak, although they do see dimly lighted things.

283. But it is evident that this simile is not adequate; for since a sense is a power of a bodily organ, it is made inoperative as a result of its sensible object being too intense. But the intellect is not a power of a bodily organ and is not made inoperative as a result of its intelligible object being too intelligible. Therefore, after understanding objects that are highly intelligible our ability to understand less intelligible objects is not decreased but increased, as is stated in Book III of *The Soul*.[3]

284. Therefore it must be said that a sense is prevented from perceiving some sensible object for two reasons: first, because a sensory organ is rendered inoperative as a result of its sensible object being too intense (this does not occur in the case of the in-

tellect); second, because of some deficiency in the ability of a sensory power to perceive its object; for the powers of the soul in all animals do not have the same efficacy. Thus, just as it is proper to man by nature to have the weakest sense of smell, in a similar way it is proper to an owl to have the weakest power of vision, because it is incapable of perceiving the light of day.

285. Therefore, since the human soul occupies the lowest place in the order of intellective substances, it has the least intellective power. As a matter of fact, just as it is by nature the actuality of a body, although its intellective power is not the act of a bodily organ, in a similar way it has a natural capacity to know the truth about corporeal and sensible things. These are less knowable by nature because of their materiality, although they can be known by abstracting sensible forms from phantasms. And since this process of knowing truth befits the nature of the human soul insofar as it is the form of this kind of body (and whatever is natural always remains so), it is possible for the human soul, which is united to this kind of body, to know the truth about things only insofar as it can be elevated to the level of the things which it understands by abstracting from phantasms. However, by this process it cannot be elevated to the level of knowing the quiddities of immaterial substances because these are not on the same level as sensible substances. Therefore it is impossible for the human soul, which is united to this kind of body, to apprehend separate substances by knowing their quiddities.

286. For this reason the statement which Averroes makes at this point in his *Commentary*[4] is evidently false, i.e., that the Philosopher does not prove

[3] *De Anima*, III, 4 (429b 1).
[4] *In II Metaph.*, com. 1 (VIII, 14v).

here that it is just as impossible for us to understand abstract substances as it is for a bat to see the sun. The argument that he gives is wholly ridiculous; for he adds that, if this were the case, nature would have acted in vain because it would have made something that is naturally knowable in itself to be incapable of being known by anything else. It would be the same as if it had made the sun incapable of being seen.

This argument is not satisfactory for two reasons. First, the end of separate substances does not consist in being understood by our intellect, but rather the converse. Therefore, if separate substances are not known by us, it does not follow that they exist in vain; for only that exists in vain which fails to attain the end for which it exists. Second, even though the quiddities of separate substances are not understood by us, they are understood by other intellects. The same is true of the sun; for even though it is not seen by the eye of the owl, it is seen by the eye of the eagle.

287. **Now it is only right** (150).

He shows how men assist each other to know the truth; for one man assists another to consider the truth in two ways—directly and indirectly.

One is assisted directly by those who have discovered the truth; because, as has been pointed out, when each of our predecessors has discovered something about the truth, which is gathered together into one whole, he also introduces his followers to a more extensive knowledge of truth.

One is assisted indirectly insofar as those who have preceded us and who were wrong about the truth have bequeathed to their successors the occasion for exercising their mental powers, so that by diligent discussion the truth might be seen more clearly.

288. Now it is only fitting that we should be grateful to those who have helped us attain so great a good as knowledge of the truth. Therefore he says that "It is only right that we should be grateful," not merely to those whom we think have found the truth and with whose views we agree by following them, but also to those who, in the search for truth, have made only superficial statements, even though we do not follow their views; for these men too have given us something because they have shown us instances of actual attempts to discover the truth. By way of an example he mentions the founders of music; for if there "had been no Timotheus," who discovered a great part of the art of music, we would not have many of the facts that we know about melodies. But if Timotheus had not been preceded by a wise man named "Phrynis," he would not have been as well off in the subject of music. The same thing must be said of those philosophers who made statements of universal scope about the truth of things; for we accept from certain of our predecessors whatever views about the truth of things we think are true and disregard the rest. Again, those from whom we accept certain views had predecessors from whom they in turn accepted certain views and who were the source of their information.

LESSON 2

The Supreme Science of Truth, and Knowledge of Ultimate Causes

ARISTOTLE'S TEXT   Chapters 1 & 2: 993b 19-994b 11

151. It is only right to call philosophy the science of truth. For the end of theoretical knowledge is truth, whereas that of practical knowledge is action; for even when practical men investigate the way in which something exists, they do not consider it in itself but in relation to some particular thing and to the present moment. But we know a truth only by knowing its cause. Now anything which is the basis of a univocal predication about other things has that attribute in the highest degree. Thus fire is hottest and is actually the cause of heat in other things. Therefore that is also true in the highest degree which is the cause of all subsequent things being true. For this reason the principles of things that always exist must be true in the highest degree, because they are not sometimes true and sometimes not true. Nor is there any cause of their being, but they are the cause of the being of other things. Therefore insofar as each thing has being, to that extent it is true.

Chapter 2

152. Further, it is evident that there is a [first] principle, and that the causes of existing things are not infinite either in series or in species. For it is impossible that one thing should come from something else as from matter in an infinite regress, for example, flesh from earth, earth from air, air from fire, and so on to infinity. Nor can the causes from which motion originates proceed to infinity, as though man were moved by the air, the air by the sun, the sun by strife, and so on to infinity. Again, neither can there be an infinite regress in the case of the reason for which something is done, as though walking were for the sake of health, health for the sake of happiness, and happiness for the sake of something else, so that one thing is always being done for the sake of something else. The same is true in the case of the quiddity.

COMMENTARY

289. Having shown how man is disposed for the study of truth, the Philosopher now shows that the knowledge of truth belongs pre-eminently to first philosophy. Regarding this he does two things. First (151:C 290), he shows that a knowledge of truth belongs pre-eminently to first philosophy. Second (152:C 299), he rejects a false doctrine that would render his proof untenable ("Further it is evident").

In regard to the first he does two

things. First, he shows that knowledge of the truth belongs to first philosophy. Second (151:C 290), that it belongs in the highest degree to this science ("But we know a truth").

He proves these two propositions from two things established above in the prologue of this book, i.e., that wisdom is not a practical but a speculative science (27:C 53), and that it knows first causes (23:C 48).

290. He argues from the first of these to the first conclusion in this way. Theoretical, i.e., speculative, knowledge differs from practical knowledge by its end; for the end of speculative knowledge is truth, because it has knowledge of the truth as its objective. But the end of practical knowledge is action, because, even though "practical men," i.e., men of action, attempt to understand the truth as it belongs to certain things, they do not seek this as an ultimate end; for they do not consider the cause of truth in and for itself as an end but in relation to action, either by applying it to some definite individual, or to some definite time. Therefore, if we add to the above the fact that wisdom or first philosophy is not practical but speculative, it follows that first philosophy is most fittingly called the science of truth.

291. But since there are many speculative sciences, which consider the truth, such as geometry and arithmetic, therefore it was necessary to show that first philosophy considers truth in the highest degree inasmuch as it has been shown above that it considers first causes (23:C 48). Hence he argues as follows. We have knowledge of truth only when we know a cause. This is apparent from the fact that the true things about which we have some knowledge have causes which are also true, because we cannot know what is true by knowing what is false, but

only by knowing what is true. This is also the reason why demonstration, which causes science, begins with what is true, as is stated in Book I of the *Posterior Analytics*.[1]

292. Then he adds the following universal proposition. When a univocal predicate is applied to several things, in each case that which constitutes the reason for the predication about other things has that attribute in the fullest sense. Thus fire is the cause of heat in compounds. Therefore, since heat is predicated univocally both of fire and of compound bodies, it follows that fire is hottest.

293. Now he says "univocal" because sometimes it happens that an effect does not become like its cause, so as to have the same specific nature, because of the excellence of that cause; for example, the sun is the cause of heat in these lower bodies, but the form which these lower bodies receive cannot be of the same specific nature as that possessed by the sun or any of the celestial bodies, since they do not have a common matter. This is why we do not say that the sun is hottest, as we say fire is, but that it is something superior to the hottest.

294. Now the term *truth* is not proper to one class of beings only, but is applied universally to all beings. Therefore, since the cause of truth is one having the same name and intelligible structure as its effect, it follows that whatever causes subsequent things to be true is itself most true.

295. From this he again concludes that the principles of things which always exist, i.e., the celestial bodies, must be most true. He does this for two reasons. First, they are not "sometimes true and sometimes not true," and therefore surpass the truth of things subject to generation and corruption, which sometimes exist and sometimes do not. Second, these principles have

[1] *Analytica Posteriora*, I, 6 (74b 5).

no cause but are the cause of the being of other things. And for this reason they surpass the celestial bodies in truth and in being; and even though the latter are incorruptible, they have a cause not only of their motion, as some men thought, but also of their being, as the Philosopher clearly states in this place.

296. Now this is necessary, because everything that is composite in nature and participates in being must ultimately have as its causes those things which have existence by their very essence. But all corporeal things are actual beings insofar as they participate in certain forms. Therefore a separate substance which is a form by its very essence must be the principle of corporeal substance.

297. If we add to this conclusion the fact that first philosophy considers first causes, it then follows, as was said above (151:C 291), that first philosophy considers those things which are most true. Consequently this science is pre-eminently the science of truth.

298. From these conclusions he draws a corollary: since those things which cause the being of other things are true in the highest degree, it follows that each thing is true insofar as it is a being; for things which do not always have being in the same way do not always have truth in the same way, and those which have a cause of their being also have a cause of their truth. The reason for this is that a thing's being is the cause of any true judgment which the mind makes about a thing; for truth and falsity are not in things but in the mind, as will be said in Book VI (558:C 1230) of this work.

299. **Further, it is evident** (152).

He rejects a position that would render the above proof untenable; for this proof proceeded on the supposition that first philosophy considers first causes. But if there were an infinite regress in causes, this proof would be destroyed, for then there would be no first cause. So his aim here is to refute this position. Concerning this he does two things. First (152), he points out what he intends to prove. Second (153:C 301), he proceeds to do so ("For intermediate things").

He says, first, that from what has been said it can clearly be shown that there is some [first] principle of the being and truth of things. He states that the causes of existing things are not infinite in number because we cannot proceed to infinity in a series of causes belonging to one and the same class, e.g., the class of efficient causes. Nor again are causes infinite in species, as though the classes of causes were infinite in number.

300. Then he explains his statement about an infinite number of causes in a series. He does this, first, in regard to the class of material causes. For it is impossible to have an infinite series in the sense that one thing always comes from something else as its matter, e.g., that flesh comes from earth, earth from air, and air from fire, and that this does not terminate in some first entity but goes on to infinity. Second, he gives an example of this in the class of efficient cause. He says that it is impossible to have an infinite series in the class of cause which we define as the source of motion; e.g., when we say that a man is moved to put aside his clothing because the air becomes warm, the air having been heated in turn by the sun, the sun having been moved by something else, and so on to infinity. Third, he gives an example of this in the class of final causes. He says that it is also impossible to proceed to infinity in the case of "the reason for which" something is done, i.e., the final cause; for example, if we were to say that a journey or a walk is undertaken for the sake of health, health for the sake of happiness, happiness

for the sake of something else, and so on to infinity. Finally, he mentions the formal cause. He says that it is also impossible to proceed to infinity in the case of the "quiddity," i.e., the formal cause, which the definition signifies. However, he omits examples because these are evident, and because it was shown in Book I of the *Posterior Analytics* [2] that it is impossible to proceed to infinity in the matter of predication, as though animal were predicated quidditatively of man, living of animal, and so on to infinity.

[2] *Analytica Posteriora*, I, 19 (81b 10).

LESSON 3

The Existence of a First Efficient Cause and of a First Material Cause

ARISTOTLE'S TEXT   Chapter 2: 994a 11-994b 9

153. For intermediate things in a series limited by some first and last thing must have as their cause the first member of the series, which they follow; because if we had to say which one of these three is the cause of the others, we would say that it is the first. What is last is not the cause, since what is last is not a cause of anything. Neither is the intermediate the cause, because it is the cause of only one; for it makes no difference whether one or several intermediates exist, or an infinite or finite number. Indeed, in series that are infinite in this way or in the infinite in general, all parts are intermediates to the same degree right down to the present one. Therefore, if there is nothing first in the whole series, nothing in the series is a cause.

154. Neither is it possible to proceed to infinity in a downward direction, where there is a starting-point in an upward direction, so that water comes from fire, earth from water, and some other class of things always being generated in this way.

155. Now there are two ways in which one thing comes *from* (*ex*) another. I do not mean *from* in the sense of *after,* as the Olympian games are said to come *from* the Isthmian, but either in the way in which a man comes from a boy as a result of a boy changing, or in the way in which air comes from water.

156. We say, then, that a man comes from a boy in the sense that what has come into being comes from what is coming into being, or in the sense that what has been completed comes from what is being completed. For generation is always midway between being and non-being, and thus whatever is coming into being is midway between what is and what is not. Now a learner is one who is becoming learned, and this is the meaning of the statement that the man of science comes from the learner. But water comes from air in the sense that it comes into being when the latter ceases to be.

157. This is why changes of the former kind are not reversible, and thus a boy does not come from a man. The reason is that the thing which comes into being does not come *from* generation but exists *after* generation. This is the way in which the day comes *from* the dawn, i.e., in the sense that it exists *after* the dawn; and this is why the dawn cannot come from the day. On the other hand, changes of the latter sort are reversible.

158. Now in neither way is it possible to proceed to infinity; for existing intermediaries must have some end, and one thing may be changed into the other because the corruption of one is the generation of the other.

159. At the same time it is impossible that an eternal first cause should be corrupted; for since generation is not infinite in an upward direction, then a first principle by whose corruption something else is produced could not be eternal.

COMMENTARY

301. Having assumed above that the causes of beings are not infinite in number, the Philosopher now proves this. First (153:C 301), he proves that there are not an infinite number of causes in a series; and second (170:C 330), that the classes of causes are not infinite in number ("Again, if the classes of causes").

In regard to the first he does four things. First, he proves his assumption in the case of efficient or moving causes; second (154:C 305), in the case of material causes ("Neither is it possible"); third (160:C 316), in the case of final causes ("Again, that for the sake of which"); and fourth (164:C 320), in the case of formal causes ("Nor can the quiddity").

In regard to the first he proceeds as follows. First, he lays down this premise: in the case of all those things which lie between two extremes, one of which is last and the other first, the first is necessarily the cause of those which come after it, namely, what is intermediate and what is last.

302. Then he proves this premise by a process of elimination. For if we had to say which of the three, i.e., the first, the intermediate, or the last, is the cause of the others, we would have to say that the first is the cause. We could not say that what is last is the cause of all the others, because it is not a cause of anything; for in other respects what is last is not a cause, since an effect follows a cause. Nor could we say that the intermediate is the cause of all the others, because it is the cause of only one of them, namely, what is last.

303. And lest someone should think that an intermediate is followed by only one thing, i.e., what is last (for

this occurs only when there is a single thing between two extremes), in order to exclude this interpretation he adds that it makes no difference to the premise given above whether there is only one intermediate or several, because all intermediates are taken together as one insofar as they have in common the character of an intermediate. Nor again does it make any difference whether there are a finite or infinite number of intermediates, because so long as they have the nature of an intermediate they cannot be the first cause of motion. Further, since there must be a first cause of motion prior to every secondary cause of motion, then there must be a first cause prior to every intermediate cause, which is not an intermediate in any sense, as though it had a cause prior to itself. But if we were to hold that there is an infinite series of moving causes in the above way, then all causes would be intermediate ones. Thus we would have to say without qualification that all parts of any infinite thing, whether of a series of causes or of continuous quantities, are intermediate ones; for if there were a part that was not an intermediate one, it would have to be either a first or a last; and both of these are opposed to the nature of the infinite, which excludes every limit, whether it be a starting-point or a terminus.

304. Now there is another point that must be noted, i.e., that if there are several intermediate parts in any finite thing, not all parts are intermediate to the same degree; for some are closer to what is first, and some to what is last. But in the case of some infinite thing in which there is neither a first nor last part, no part can be closer

to or farther away from either what is first or what is last. Therefore all parts are intermediates to the same degree right down to the one you designate now. Consequently, if the causes of motion proceed to infinity in this way, there will be no first cause. But a first cause is the cause of all things. Therefore it will follow that all causes are eliminated; for when a cause is removed the things of which it is the cause are also removed.

305. **Neither is it possible** (154).

He shows that it is impossible to proceed to infinity in the case of material causes. First (154:C 305), he states what he intends to prove. Second (155:C 308), he proceeds with his proof ("Now there are two ways").

In regard to the first it must be noted that a patient is subjected to the action of an agent. Therefore to pass from agent to agent is to proceed in an upward direction, whereas to pass from patient to patient is to proceed in a downward direction. Now just as *action* is attributed to the cause of motion, so is *undergoing action* attributed to matter. Therefore among the causes of motion the process is in an upward direction, whereas among material causes the process is in a downward direction. Consequently, since he showed among moving causes that it is impossible to proceed to infinity, as it were, in an upward direction, he adds that it is impossible to proceed to infinity in a downward direction, i.e., in the process of material causes, granted that there is a starting-point in an upward direction among the causes of motion.

306. He illustrates this by way of the process of natural bodies, which proceeds in a downward direction, as if we were to say that water comes from fire, earth from water, and so on to infinity. He uses this example in accordance with the opinion of the ancient philosophers of nature, who held that one of these elements is the

source of the others in a certain order.

307. However, this can also be explained in another way, inasmuch as we understand that in the case of moving causes there are evident to the senses certain ultimate effects which do not move anything else. Therefore we do not ask if there is an infinite regress in the lower members of that class, but if there is an infinite regress in the higher ones. But in regard to the class of material causes, he assumes that there is one first cause which is the foundation and basis of the others; and he inquires whether there is an infinite regress in a downward direction in the process of those things which are generated from matter. The example which he gives illustrates this, because he does not say that fire comes from water and this in turn from something else, but the converse, i.e., that water comes from fire, and something else again from this. For this reason first matter is held to exist; and he asks whether the things that are generated from matter proceed to infinity.

308. **Now there are two ways in which** (155).

He proves his original thesis. Concerning this he does four things. First (155:C 308), he distinguishes between the two ways in which one thing *comes from* something else. Second (156:C 310), he shows that these two ways differ in two respects ("We say, then, that a man"). Third (158:C 312), he shows that it is impossible to proceed to infinity in either of these ways ("Now in neither way"). Fourth (159:C 314), he shows in which of these ways other things come from the first material principle ("At the same time").

He says, first, that one thing "comes from" another properly and essentially in two ways. He speaks thus in order to exclude that way in which something is said in an improper sense to *come from* something else only by reason of the fact that it *comes after* it, as when it is said that certain feasts of the Greeks called the Olympian come from those called the Isthmian, or as if we were to say that the feast of the Epiphany comes from the feast of the Nativity. But this is an improper use of the word, because the process of coming to be is a change, and in a change it is not only necessary that an order exist between the two limits of the change but also that both limits have the same subject. Now this is not the case in the above example, but we speak in this way insofar as we think of time as the subject of different feasts.

309. Now properly speaking it is necessary to say that one thing *comes from* something else when some subject is changed from *this* into *that*. This occurs in two ways: first, as when we say that a man comes from a boy in the sense that a boy is changed from boyhood to manhood; second, as when we say that air comes from water as a result of substantial change.

310. **We say, then, that a man** (156).
He explains the twofold sense in which these two ways differ. First, we say that a man comes from a boy in the sense that what has already come into being comes from what is coming into being, or in the sense that what has already been completed comes from what is being completed. For anything in a state of becoming and of being completed is midway between being and non-being, just as generation is midway between existence and non-existence. Therefore, since we reach an extreme through an intermediate, we say that what has been generated comes from what is being generated, and that what has been completed comes from what is being completed. Now this is the sense in which we say that a man comes from a boy, or a man of science from a learner, because a learner is one who is becoming a man of science. But in the other sense, i.e., the one in which we say that water comes from fire, one of the limits of

the change is not related to the other as a passage or intermediate, as generation is to being, but rather as the limit from which a thing starts in order to reach another limit. Therefore one comes from the other when the other is corrupted.

311. **This is why changes** (157).
He infers another difference from the foregoing one. For since, in the first way, one thing is related to the other as generation is to being, and as an intermediate to a limit, it is evident that one is naturally ordained to the other. Therefore they are not reversible so that one comes from the other indifferently. Consequently we do not say that a boy comes from a man, but the reverse. The reason for this is that those two things, of which one is said to come from the other in this way, are not related to each other in the same way as the two limits of a change, but as two things one of which comes after the other in sequence. And this is what he means when he says that "what has come into being" (i.e., the terminus of generation or being) does not come from generation as though generation itself were changed into being, but is that which exists after generation, because it follows generation in a natural sequence; just as one's destination comes after a journey, and as what is last comes after what is intermediate. Therefore, if we consider these two things, i.e., generation and being, the way in which they are related does not differ from the one we have excluded, in which sequence alone is considered, as when we say that the day comes from the dawn because it comes after the dawn. Moreover, this natural sequence prevents us from saying in an opposite way that the dawn comes "from the day," i.e., after the day; and for the same reason a boy cannot come from a man. But in the other sense in which one thing comes from another, the process is reversible; for just as water is generated

by reason of air being corrupted, in a similar way air is generated by reason of water being corrupted. The reason is that these two are not related to each other in a natural sequence, i.e., as an intermediate to a limit, but as two limits, either one of which can be first or last.

312. **Now in neither way** (158).

He shows that it is impossible to proceed to infinity in either of these ways. First, in the way in which we say that a man comes from a boy; for the thing from which we say something else comes as a man comes from a boy has the position of an intermediary between two limits, i.e., between being and non-being. But an infinite number of intermediates cannot exist when certain limits are held to exist, since limits are opposed to infinity. Therefore, it is impossible to have an infinite series in this way.

313. In like manner it is impossible to have an infinite series in the other way; for in that way one limit is converted into the other, because the corruption of one is the generation of the other, as has been explained. Now wherever a reversible process exists there is a return to some first thing in the sense that what was at first a starting-point is afterwards a terminus. This cannot occur in the case of things that are infinite, in which there is neither a starting-point nor a terminus. Consequently, there is no way in which one thing can come from another in an infinite regress.

314. **At the same time it is impossible** (159).

He shows in which of these ways something comes from first matter. Now it must be noted that in this place Aristotle uses two common suppositions accepted by all of the ancient philosophers: first, that there is a primary material principle, and therefore that in the process of generation there is no infinite regress on the part of the higher, i.e., of that from which a thing is generated; second, that matter is eternal. Therefore, from this second supposition he immediately concludes that nothing comes from first matter in the second way, i.e., in the way in which water comes from air as a result of the latter's corruption, because what is eternal cannot be corrupted.

315. But since someone could say that the philosophers did not hold that the first material principle is eternal because it remains numerically one eternally but because it is eternal by succession (as if the human race were held to be eternal), he therefore excludes this from the first supposition. He says that since generation is not infinite in an upward direction but stops at a first material principle, then if there is a first material principle by reason of whose corruption other things come into being, it must not be the eternal principle of which the philosophers speak. The reason is that the first material principle cannot be eternal if other things are generated by reason of its corruption, and it in turn is generated by the corruption of something else. It is evident, then, that a thing comes from this first material principle as something imperfect and potential which is midway between pure non-being and actual being, but not as water comes from air by reason of the latter's corruption.

LESSON 4

The Existence of a First in Final and Formal Causes

·

ARISTOTLE'S TEXT   Chapter 2: 994b 9-994b 31

160. Again, that for the sake of which something comes to be is an end. Now such a thing is not for the sake of something else, but other things are for its sake. Therefore, if there is such a thing as an ultimate end, there will not be an infinite regress; but if there is no ultimate end, there will be no reason for which things come to be.

161. Now those who posit infinity do away with the nature of the good without realizing it.

162. But no one will attempt to do anything unless he thinks he can carry it through to its term.

163. Nor will there be any intelligence in such matters, because one who has intelligence always acts for the sake of something since this limit is the end of a thing.

164. Nor can the quiddity be reduced to a definition which adds to the defining notes.

165. For a prior definition is always more of a definition, whereas a subsequent one is not; and where the first note does not apply, neither does a later one.

166. Again, those who speak in this way do away with science, because it is impossible to have science until we reach what is undivided.

167. Nor will knowledge itself exist; for how can one understand things which are infinite in this way?

168. This case is not like that of a line, whose divisibility has no limit, for it would be impossible to understand a line if it had no limits. This is why no one will count the sections, which proceed to infinity.

169. But it is necessary to understand that there is matter in everything that is moved, and that the infinite involves nothingness, but essence does not. But if there is no infinite, what essence [i.e., definition] does the infinite have? [1]

170. Again, if the classes of causes were infinite in number, it would also be impossible to know anything; for we think that we have scientific knowledge when we know the causes themselves of things; but what is infinite by addition cannot be traversed in a finite period of time.

---

[1] This sentence in the Greek text, which differs from that of the Latin version, expresses Aristotle's thought more clearly: "But if it does not [i.e., if the infinite does not exist], the essence of the infinite is not infinite."

COMMENTARY

316. Having shown that there is no infinite regress either among the causes of motion or among material causes, the Philosopher now shows that the same thing is true of the final cause, which is called "that for the sake of which" something comes to be (160).

He proves this by four arguments. The first is as follows. That for the sake of which something comes to be has the character of an end. But an end does not exist for the sake of other things, but others exist for its sake. Now such a thing either exists or not. If there is something of such a kind that all things exist for its sake and not it for the sake of something else, it will be the last thing in this order; and thus there will not be an infinite regress. However, if no such thing exists, no end will exist; and thus the class of cause called "that for the sake of which" will be eliminated.

317. **Now those who posit infinity** (161).

He gives the second argument, which is derived from the foregoing one; for from the first argument he concluded that those who posit an infinite regress in final causes do away with the final cause. Now when the final cause is removed, so also is the nature and notion of the good; because *good* and *end* have the same meaning, since the good is that which all desire, as is said in Book I of the *Ethics*.[1] Therefore those who hold that there is an infinite regress in final causes do away completely with the nature of the good, although they do not realize this.

318. **But no one will attempt** (162).

He gives the third argument, which is as follows. If there were an infinite number of final causes, no one could

reach a last terminus, because there is no last terminus in an infinite series. But no one will attempt to do anything unless he thinks he is able to accomplish something as a final goal. Therefore, those who hold that final causes proceed to infinity do away with every attempt to operate and even with the activities of natural bodies; for a thing's natural movement is only toward something which it is naturally disposed to attain.

319. **Nor will there be** (163).

He states the fourth argument, which is as follows. One who posits an infinite number of final causes does away with a limit, and therefore with the end for the sake of which a cause acts. But every intelligent agent acts for the sake of some end. Therefore it would follow that there is no intellect among causes which are productive; and thus the practical intellect is eliminated. But since these things are absurd, we must reject the first position, from which they follow, i.e., that there is an infinite number of final causes.

320. **Nor can the quiddity** (164).

He shows that there is not an infinite number of formal causes. In regard to this he does two things. First (164:C 320), he states what he intends to prove. Second (165:C 322), he proves it ("For a prior definition").

Regarding the first we must understand that each thing derives its particular species from its proper form, and this is why the definition of a species signifies chiefly a thing's form. Therefore we must understand that a procession of forms is consequent upon a procession of definitions; for one part of a definition is prior to another just as genus is prior to difference

---

[1] *Ethica Nicomachea*, I, 1 (1094a 2).

and one difference is prior to another. Therefore an infinite regress in forms and in the parts of a definition is one and the same thing. Now since Aristotle wishes to show that it is impossible to proceed to infinity in the case of formal causes, he holds that it is impossible to proceed to infinity in the parts of a definition. Hence he says that it is impossible for a thing's quiddity to be reduced to another definition, and so on to infinity, so that the defining notes are always increased in number. For example, one who defines man gives animal in his definition, and therefore the definition of man is reduced to that of animal, and this in turn to the definition of something else, thereby increasing the defining notes. But to proceed to infinity in this way is absurd.

321. Now we do not mean by this that there are the same number of forms in each individual as there are genera and differences, so that in man there is one form by which he is man, another by which he is animal, and so on; but we mean that there must be as many grades of forms in reality as there are orders of genera and differences [in knowledge]. For we find in reality one form which is not the form of a body, another which is the form of a body but not of an animated body, and so on.

322. **For a prior definition** (165).

He proves his premise by four arguments. The first is this. Wherever there are a number of forms or defining notes, a prior definition is always "more of a definition." This does not mean that a prior form is more complete (for specific forms are complete), but that a prior form belongs to more things than a subsequent form, which is not found wherever a prior form is found; e.g., the definition of man is not found wherever that of animal is found. From this he argues that if the

first note [of a series] does not fit the thing defined, "neither does a later one." But if there were an infinite regress in definitions and forms, there would be no first definition or definitive form. Hence all subsequent definitions and forms would be eliminated.

323. **Again, those who speak** (166).

He gives the second argument, which is as follows. It is impossible to have scientific knowledge of anything until we come to what is undivided. Now in this place "undivided" cannot mean the singular, because there is no science of the singular. However, it can be understood in two other ways. First, it can mean the definition itself of the last species, which is not further divided by essential differences. In this sense his statement can mean that we do not have complete knowledge of a thing until we reach its last species; for one who knows the genus to which a thing belongs does not yet have a complete knowledge of that thing. According to this interpretation we must say that, just as the first argument concluded that it is impossible to have an infinite regress in an upward direction among formal causes, in a similar fashion this second argument concludes that it is impossible to have an infinite regress in a downward direction, otherwise it would be impossible to reach a last species. Therefore this position destroys any complete knowledge.

324. Now a formal division exists not only when a genus is divided by differences (and when such division is no longer possible the last species can be said to be undivided), but also when the thing defined is divided into its definitive parts, as is evident in Book I of the *Physics*.[2] Therefore in this place "undivided" can also mean a thing whose definition cannot be resolved into any definitive parts. Now according to this the supreme genus is un-

2 *Physica*, I, 1 (184a 11).

divided; and from this point of view his statement can mean that we cannot have scientific knowledge of a thing by definition unless we reach its supreme genera; because when these remain unknown it is impossible to know its subsequent genera. And according to this the second argument concludes, as the former one did, that it is impossible to proceed to infinity in an upward direction among formal causes.

325. Or, in order to reach the same conclusion, "undivided" can be explained in another way, i.e., in the sense that an immediate proposition is undivided. For if it were possible to proceed to infinity in an upward direction in the case of definitions, there would be no immediate proposition, and thus science as such, which is about conclusions derived from immediate principles, would be destroyed.

326. **Nor will knowledge** (167).

He gives the third argument, which proceeds to [show that such an infinite regress would] destroy not only science but any kind of human knowing whatsoever. In regard to this argument he does two things. First (167:C 326), he gives his argument. Second (168:C 327), he refutes an objection raised against it ("This case is not like").

The argument is as follows. We know each thing by understanding its form. But if there were an infinite regress in forms, these forms could not be understood, because the intellect is incapable of understanding the infinite as infinite. Therefore this position destroys knowing in its entirety.

327. **This case is not like** (168).

He disposes of an objection; for someone could say that a thing having an infinite number of forms can be understood in the same way as a line which is divided to infinity. But he denies this. He says that this case is not the same as that of a line, whose divisions do not stop but go on to in-

finity. For it is impossible to understand anything unless some limit is set to it. Therefore a line can be understood inasmuch as some actual limit is given to it by reason of its extremes. However, it cannot be understood insofar as its division does not terminate. Hence no one can count the divisions of a line insofar as they are infinite. But as applied to forms "infinite" means actually infinite, and not potentially infinite as it does when applied to the division of a line. Therefore, if there were an infinite number of forms, there would be no way in which a thing could be known either scientifically or in any way at all.

328. **But it is necessary** (169).

He gives the fourth argument, which runs thus. Matter must be understood to exist in everything that is moved; for whatever is moved is in potentiality, and what is in potentiality is matter. But matter itself has the character of the infinite, and nothingness belongs to the infinite in the sense of matter, because matter taken in itself is understood without any of kind of form. And since nothingness belongs to the infinite, it follows contrariwise that the principle by which the infinite is a being is itself not infinite, and that it does not belong "to the infinite," i.e., to matter, to be infinite in being. But things are by virtue of their form. Hence there is no infinite regress among forms.

329. However, it must be noted that in this place Aristotle holds that the infinite involves the notion of nothingness, not because matter involves the notion of privation (as Plato claimed when he failed to distinguish between privation and matter), but because the infinite involves the notion of privation. For a potential being contains the notion of the infinite only insofar as it comes under the nature of privation, as is evident in Book III of the *Physics*.[3]

---

[3] *Physica*, III, 7 (207b 35).

330. **Again, if the classes** (170).

He shows that the classes of causes are not infinite in number, and he uses the following argument. We think that we have scientific knowledge of each thing when we know all its causes. But if there were an infinite number of causes in the sense that one class of cause may be added to another continuously, it would be impossible to traverse this infinity in such a way that all causes could be known. Hence in this way too the knowing of things would be destroyed.

LESSON 5

The Method to Be Followed in the Search for Truth

ARISTOTLE'S TEXT   Chapter 3: 994b 32-995a 20

171. The way in which people are affected by what they hear depends upon the things to which they are accustomed; for it is in terms of such things that we judge statements to be true, and anything over and above these does not seem similar but less intelligible and more remote. For it is the things to which we are accustomed that are better known.

172. The great force which custom has is shown by the laws, in which legendary and childish elements prevail over our knowledge of them, because of custom.

173. Now some men will not accept what a speaker says unless he speaks in mathematical terms; and others, unless he gives examples; while others expect him to quote a poet as an authority. Again, some want everything stated with certitude, while others find certitude annoying, either because they are incapable of comprehending anything, or because they consider exact inquiry to be quibbling; for there is some similarity. Hence it seems to some men that, just as liberality is lacking in the matter of a fee for a banquet, so also is it lacking in arguments.

174. For this reason one must be trained how to meet every kind of argument; and it is absurd to search simultaneously for knowledge and for the method of acquiring it; for neither of these is easily attained.

175. But the exactness of mathematics is not to be expected in all cases, but only in those which have no matter. This is why its method is not that of natural philosophy; for perhaps the whole of nature contains matter. Hence we must first investigate what nature is; for in this way it will become evident what the things are with which natural philosophy deals, and whether it belongs to one science or to several to consider the causes and principles of things.

COMMENTARY

331. Having shown that the study of truth is in one sense difficult and in another easy, and that it belongs preeminently to first philosophy, the Philosopher now exposes the proper method of investigating the truth. In regard to this he does two things. First (171:C 331), he gives the different methods which men follow in the study

of truth. Second (174:C 335), he shows which method is the proper one ("For this reason one must").

In regard to the first he does two things. First, he shows how powerful custom is in the study of truth. Second (173:C 334), he concludes that the different methods which men employ in the study of truth depend on the different things to which they are accustomed ("Now some men").

In regard to the first he does two things. First, he shows how powerful custom is in the study of truth. Second (172:C 333), he makes this clear by an example ("The great force").

He says, first, that the way in which people are affected by what they hear depends upon the things to which they are accustomed, because such things are more willingly heard and more easily understood. For things spoken of in a manner to which we are accustomed seem to us to be acceptable; and if any things are said to us over and above what we have been accustomed to hear, these do not seem to have the same degree of truth. As a matter of fact they seem less intelligible to us and further removed from reason just because we are not accustomed to them; for it is the things which we are accustomed to hear that we know best of all.

332. Now the reason for this is that things which are customary become natural. Hence a habit, which disposes us in a way similar to nature, is also acquired by customary activity. And from the fact that someone has some special sort of nature or special kind of habit, he has a definite relationship to one thing or another. But in every kind of cognition there must be a definite relationship between the knower and the object of cognition. Therefore, to the extent that natures and habits differ, there are diverse kinds of cognition. For we see that there are innate first principles in men because of their human nature, and that what is proper to some special virtue appears good to one who has this habit of virtue; and, again, that something appears palatable to the sense of taste because of its disposition. Therefore, since custom produces a habit which is similar to nature, it follows that what is customary is better known.

333. **The great force** (172).

Here he makes his previous statement clear by giving a concrete case. He says that the laws which men pass are positive evidence of the force of custom; for the legendary and childish elements in these laws are more effective in winning assent than is knowledge of the truth. Now the Philosopher is speaking here of the laws devised by men, which have as their ultimate end the preservation of the political community. Therefore the men who have established these laws have handed down in them, in keeping with the diversity of peoples and nations involved, certain directives by which human souls might be drawn away from evil and persuaded to do good, although many of them, which men had heard from childhood and of which they approved more readily than of what they knew to be true, were empty and foolish. But the law given by God directs men to that true happiness to which everything false is opposed. Therefore there is nothing false in the divine law.

334. **Now some men** (173).

Here he shows how men as a result of custom use different methods in the study of truth. He says that some men listen to what is said to them only if it is mathematical in character; and this is acceptable to those who have been educated in mathematics because of the habits which they have. Now since custom is like nature, the same thing can also happen to certain men because they are poorly disposed in some respect, e.g., those who have a strong imagination but little intelligence. Then there are others who do not wish to accept anything unless they are given a concrete example, either because they are accustomed to this or because their sensory powers dominate and their intellect is weak. Again, there are some who think that nothing is convincing enough unless a poet or some authority is cited. This is also a result either of custom or of poor judgment, because they cannot decide for themselves whether the conclusion of an argument is certain; and therefore, having no faith in their own judgment, as it were, they require the judgment of some recognized authority. Again there are others who want everything said to them with certitude, i.e., by way of careful rational investigation. This occurs because of the superior intelligence of the one making the judgment and the arguments of the one conducting the investigation, provided that one does not look for certitude where it cannot be had. On the other hand there are some who are annoyed if some matter is investigated in an exact way by means of a careful discussion. This can occur for two reasons. First, they lack the ability to comprehend anything; for since their reasoning power is poor they are unable to understand the order in which premises are related to conclusions. Second, it occurs because of quibbling, i.e., reasoning about the smallest matters, which bears some resemblance to the search for certitude since it leaves nothing undiscussed down to the smallest detail. Then there are some who think that, just as liberality is lacking when the smallest details are taken into account in estimating the fee for a banquet, in a similar way there is a lack of civility and liberality when a man also wishes to discuss the smallest details in the search for truth.

335. For this reason one must be trained (174).

He exposes the proper method of investigating the truth. Concerning this he does two things. First (174:C 335), he shows how a man can discover the proper method of investigating the truth. Second (175:C 336), he explains that the method which is absolutely the best should not be demanded in all matters ("But the exactness of mathematics").

He says, first, that since different men use different methods in the search for truth, one must be trained in the method which the particular sciences must use to investigate their subject. And since it is not easy for a man to undertake two things at once (indeed, so long as he tries to do both he can succeed in neither), it is absurd for a man to try to acquire a science and at the same time to acquire the method proper to that science. This is why a man should learn logic before any of the other sciences, because logic considers the general method of procedure in all the other sciences. Moreover, the method appropriate to the particular sciences should be considered at the beginning of these sciences.

336. But the exactness of mathematics (175).

He shows that the method which is absolutely the best should not be demanded in all the sciences. He says that the "exactness," i.e., the careful and certain demonstrations, found in mathematics should not be demanded in the case of all things of which we have science, but only in the case of those things which have no matter; for things that have matter are subject to motion and change, and therefore in their case complete certitude cannot be had. For in the case of these things we do not look for what exists always and of necessity, but only for what exists in the majority of cases. Now immaterial things are most certain by their very nature because they are unchangeable, although they are not certain to us because our intellectual power is weak, as was stated above (149:C 279). The separate substances are things of this kind. But while the things with which mathematics deals are abstracted from matter, they do not surpass our understanding; and therefore in their case most certain reasoning is demanded. Again, because the whole of nature involves matter, this method of most certain reasoning does not belong to natural philosophy. However, he says "perhaps" because of the celestial bodies, since they do not have matter in the same sense that lower bodies do.

337. Now since this method of most certain reasoning is not the method proper to natural science, therefore in order to know which method is proper to that science we must investigate first what nature is; for in this way we will discover the things which natural philosophy studies. Further, we must investigate "whether it belongs to one science," i.e., to natural philosophy, or to several sciences, to consider all causes and principles; for in this way we will be able to learn which method of demonstration is proper to natural philosophy. He deals with this method in Book II of the *Physics*,[1] as is obvious to anyone who examines it carefully.

[1] *Physica*, II, 1 (193b 23).

BOOK III

Metaphysical Problems

CONTENTS

Book III

LESSON 1

The Need of Questioning Everything in the Search for Universal Truth

ARISTOTLE'S TEXT   Chapter 1: 995a 24-995b 4

176. With a view to the science under investigation we must attack first those subjects which must first be investigated. These are all the subjects about which some men have entertained different opinions, and any other besides these[1] which has been omitted.

177. Now for those who wish to investigate the truth it is worth the while to ponder these difficulties well. For the subsequent study of truth is nothing else than the solution of earlier problems. For it is impossible to untie a knot without knowing it. But a perplexity on the part of the mind makes this evident in regard to the matter at hand; for insofar as the mind is perplexed, to that extent it experiences something similar to men who are bound; for in both cases it is impossible to move forward. For this reason, then, it is first necessary to consider all the difficulties and the reasons for them.[2]

178. [This is also necessary] for another reason, namely, that those who make investigations without first recognizing the problem are like those who do not know where they ought to go.

179. Again, one would not even know when he finds the thing which he is seeking [and when not];[3] for the goal is not evident to such a man, but it is evident to one who previously discussed the difficulties.

180. Furthermore, one who has heard all the arguments of the litigants, as it were, and of those who argue the question, is necessarily in a better position to pass judgment.

---

[1] Reading *haec* for *hoc*.
[2] According to the Greek text (995a 33 ff.) the last part of this sentence and the first part of the following one (#178) should read: ". . . all the difficulties, both for the reasons given, and because those who make. . . ." St. Thomas follows the version given in the text; see C 339.
[3] *An non* is missing in the Latin version.

COMMENTARY

338. Having indicated in Book II (171:C 331), the method of considering the truth, the Philosopher now proceeds with his study of the truth. First (176:C 338), he proceeds disputatively, indicating those points which are open to question so far as the truth of things is concerned. Second (294:C 529), he

141

begins to establish what is true, and he does this in Book IV, which begins: "There is a certain science."

The first part is divided into two sections. In the first, he states what he intends to do. In the second (181:C 346), he proceeds to do it ("The first problem").

In regard to the first he does two things. First, he states what he intends to do. Second (177:C 339), he gives the reasons for this ("Now for those").

He says first (176), then, that with a view to this science which we are seeking about first principles and what is universally true of things, we must attack, first of all, those subjects about which it is necessary to raise questions before the truth is established. Now there are disputed points of this kind for two reasons, either because the ancient philosophers entertained a different opinion about these things than is really true, or because they completely neglected to consider them.

339. **Now for those** (177).

Here he gives four arguments in support of this thesis. First, he says that for those who wish to investigate the truth it is "worth the while," i.e., worth the effort, "to ponder these difficulties well," i.e., to examine carefully those matters which are open to question. This is necessary because the subsequent study of truth is nothing else than the solution of earlier difficulties. Now in loosening a physical knot it is evident that one who is unacquainted with this knot cannot loosen it. But a difficulty about some subject is related to the mind as a physical knot is to the body, and manifests the same effect. For insofar as the mind is puzzled about some subject, it experiences something similar to those who are tightly bound. For just as one whose feet are tied cannot move forward on an earthly road, in a similar way one who is puzzled, and whose mind is bound, as it were, cannot move forward on the road of speculative knowledge. There-

fore, just as one who wishes to loosen a physical knot must first of all inspect the knot and the way in which it is tied, in a similar way one who wants to solve a problem must first survey all the difficulties and the reasons for them.

340. [**This is also necessary**] (178).

Here he gives the second argument. He says that those who wish to investigate the truth without first considering the problem are like those who do not know where they are going. This is true for this reason, that, just as the terminus of a journey is the goal intended by one who travels on foot, in a similar way the solution of a problem is the goal intended by one who is seeking the truth. But it is evident that one who does not know where he is going cannot go there directly, except perhaps by chance. Therefore, neither can one seek the truth directly unless he first sees the problem.

341. **Again, one would** (179).

Here he gives the third argument. He says that, just as one who is ignorant of where he is going does not know whether he should stop or go further when he reaches his appointed goal, in a similar way one who does not know beforehand the problem whose solution marks the terminus of his search cannot know when he finds the truth which he is seeking and when not. For he does not know what the goal of his investigations is, but this is evident to one who knew the problem beforehand.

342. **Furthermore** (180).

He gives the fourth argument, which is taken from the viewpoint of a judge. For a judge must pass judgment on the things which he hears. But just as one can pass judgment in a lawsuit only if he hears the arguments on both sides, in a similar way one who has to pass judgment on a philosophy is necessarily in a better position to do so if he will hear all the arguments, as it were, of the disputants.

343. Now it must be noted that it

was for these reasons that Aristotle was accustomed, in nearly all his works, to set forth the problems which emerge before investigating and establishing what is true. But while in other works Aristotle sets down the problems one at a time in order to establish the truth about each one, in this work he sets forth all the problems at once, and afterwards in the proper order establishes the things that are true. The reason for this is that other sciences consider the truth in a particular way, and therefore it belongs to them to raise problems of a particular kind about individual truths. But just as it belongs to this science to make a universal study of truth, so also does it belong to it to discuss all the problems which pertain to the truth. Therefore it does not discuss its problems one at a time but all at once.

344. There can also be another reason [why Aristotle proceeds in this way], namely, that those problems on which he touches are chiefly those about which the philosophers have held different opinions. However, he does not proceed to investigate the truth in the same order as the other philosophers did. For he begins with things which are sensible and evident and proceeds to those which are separate from matter, as is evident below in Book VII (650:C 1566), whereas the other philosophers wanted to apply intelligible and abstract principles to sensible things. Hence, because he did not intend to establish the truth in the same order as that followed by the other philosophers, and from whose views these problems arise, he therefore decided to give first all the problems in a separate section, and afterwards to solve these problems in their proper order.

345. Averroes [1] gives another reason [for Aristotle's procedure]. He says that Aristotle proceeds in this way because of the relationship of this science to logic, which will be touched on below in Book IV (319:C 588); and therefore he made dialectical discussion a principal part of this science.

[1] *In III Metaph.,* com. 1 (VIII, 18r).

LESSON 2

Questions Concerning the Method of This Science

ARISTOTLE'S TEXT   Chapter 1: 995b 4-995b 27

181. The first problem concerns the things about which we raised questions in our introductory statements, i.e., whether it belongs to one science or to many to speculate about the causes.[1]

182. And there is also the problem whether it belongs to this science to know only the principles of substance, or also the principles on which all sciences base their demonstrations, e.g., whether it is possible to affirm and deny one and the same thing at the same time or not; and other such principles.[2] And if this science deals with substance, there is the question whether one science deals with all substances, or many sciences. And if many, whether all are cognate, or whether some should be called wisdom and others something else.[3]

183. It is also necessary to inquire whether sensible substances alone must be said to exist, or whether there are other substances in addition to these; and whether they are unique, or whether there are many classes of substances, as was claimed by those who created the Forms and made the objects of mathematics an intermediate class between these Forms and sensible substances. As we have said, then, it is necessary to examine these questions.[4]

184. There is also the problem whether this speculation has to do with substances alone or also with the proper accidents of substances. And we must inquire about sameness and difference, likeness and unlikeness, contrariety, priority and posteriority, and all other such things which the dialecticians attempt to treat (basing their investigations only on probabilities); for to them too it belongs to theorize about all these things. Furthermore, we must investigate all those essential accidents of these same things; and not only what each one of them is, but also whether there is one contrary for each one.[5]

[1] This problem was first raised in I, L.2 (14-26:C 36-51). It is discussed dialectically in III, L.4 (190-197:C 369-386) and answered in IV, L.1 (294-296:C 529-533).
[2] Discussed in III, L.5 (198-201:C 387-392). Answered in IV, L.5 (319-325:C 588-595).
[3] Discussed III, L.6 (202-204:C 393-398). Answered in IV, L.2 (305:C 563).
[4] Discussed in III, L.7 (208-219:C 403-422). Answered in XII, L.6-10 (1059-1088:C 2500-2599).
[5] Discussed in III, L.6 (205-207:C 399-402). Answered in IV, L.3 & 4 (306-318:C 564-587).

COMMENTARY

346. Following out his announced plan, the Philosopher begins to set down the problems which are en- countered in establishing the truth; and he divides this into two parts. In the first (181:C 346), he gives these

problems; and in the second (190:C 369), he gives the reasons for these problems, by indicating the arguments on either side of the question ("Therefore let us discuss").

Now it was stated in Book II (174:C 335) that it is necessary to seek the method of a science before seeking the science itself. Therefore he gives, first (181:C 346), the problems which pertain to this science's method of investigation. Second (185:C 355), he gives the problems which pertain to the first principles with which this science deals, as has been stated in Book I (14:C 36) ("And we must inquire").

Now a science is concerned with two things, as was said in Book II (175:C 336), namely, a study of the causes by which it demonstrates and the things with which it deals. Hence in regard to the first point he does two things. First (181:C 346), he presents a problem concerning the investigation of causes. Second (182:C 347), he presents several problems concerning the things with which this science deals ("And there is also the problem").

He says (181), then, that the first problem is one which we proposed in the issues raised at the end of Book II (175:C 336), which is, so to speak, the prologue to the whole of science, i.e., whether a study of the four causes in their four classes belongs to one science or to many different sciences. And this is to ask whether it belongs to one science, and especially to this science, to demonstrate by means of all the causes, or rather whether some sciences demonstrate by one cause and some by another.

347. **And there is also the problem** (182).

Here he raises problems about the things which this science considers. First (182:C 347), he inquires about the things which this science considers about substances; and second (183:C 350), about substances themselves ("It is also necessary").

In regard to the first (182) he raises three questions. For if it is supposed, from what was said in Book I (13:C 35), that this science considers first principles, the first question here will be whether it belongs to this science to know only the first principles of substances, or also to consider the first principles of demonstration, by means of which all sciences demonstrate. For example, should this science consider whether it is possible to affirm and deny one and the same thing at the same time or not? And the same thing applies to the other first and self-evident principles of demonstration.

348. And if this science considers substance as the primary kind of being, the second question is whether there is one science which considers all substances, or whether there are many sciences which consider different substances. For it seems that there should be many sciences which consider many substances.

349. And if there are many sciences which consider many substances, the third question is whether all are "cognate," i.e., whether all belong to one class, as geometry and arithmetic belong to the class of mathematical science, or whether they do not, but some to the class of wisdom and some to another class, for example, to the class of natural philosophy or to that of mathematical science. For according to the first point of view it seems that they do not belong to one class, since material and immaterial substances are not known by the same method.

350. **It is also necessary** (183).

Here he adds to the number of questions about substance; and he does this by raising two questions. The first question is whether sensible substances alone must be held to exist, as the philosophers of nature claimed, or whether there are in addition to sensible substances other immaterial and intelligible substances, as Plato claimed.

351. And if there are some sub-

stances separate from sensible things, the second question is whether "they are unique," i.e., whether they belong only to one class, or whether there are many classes of such substances. For certain men, understanding that there is a twofold abstraction, namely, of the universal from the particular, and of the mathematical form from sensible matter, held that each class is self-subsistent. Thus they held that there are separate substances which are subsisting abstract universals, and between these and particular sensible substances they placed the objects of mathematics —numbers, continuous quantities, and figures—which they regarded as separate subsisting things. Concerning the questions which have now been raised, then, it is necessary to investigate them below. He does this, first, by arguing both sides of the question, and, second, by determining its truth.

352. **There is also the problem** (184). Here he asks whether this science's investigations extend to accidents; and he raises three questions. The first is whether this science, seeing that it is called the philosophy of substance, speculates about substance alone, or whether it also speculates about the proper accidents of substance; for it seems to be the office of the same science to consider a subject and the proper accidents of that subject.

353. The second question is whether this science considers certain things which seem to be proper accidents of being and which belong to all beings, namely, sameness and difference, likeness and unlikeness, contrariety, priority, and posteriority, and all others of this kind which are treated by the dialecticians, who deal with all things. However, they do not examine such things according to necessary premises but according to probable ones. For from one point of view it seems that, since these accidents are common ones, they pertain to first-philosophy; but from another point of view it seems that, since they are considered by the dialecticians, whose office it is to argue from probabilities, an examination of them does not belong to the consideration of the philosopher, whose office it is to demonstrate.

354. And since certain proper attributes naturally flow from these common accidents of being, the third question is whether it is the function of the philosopher to consider in regard to the common accidents only their quiddity or also their properties; for example, whether there is one opposite for each one.

LESSON 3

Questions Concerning the Things with Which This Science Deals

ARISTOTLE'S TEXT   Chapter 1: 995b 27-996a 17

185. And we must inquire whether it is genera that constitute the principles and elements of things, or the parts into which each existing thing is divided. And if it is genera, whether it is those that are predicated of individuals first or last. And we must also inquire whether animal or man is a principle, and exists more truly than the singular.[1]

186. But most of all it is necessary to investigate and treat the question whether besides matter there is any cause in the proper sense or not; and whether it is separable or not; and whether it is numerically one or many. And we must ask whether there is anything besides the *synolon* (and by synolon I mean matter when something is predicated of it), or nothing; or whether this is true of some things but not of others,[2] [and what these things are].[3]

187. Further, we must inquire whether the principles of things are limited in number or in kind,[4] both those in the intelligible structures of things and those in the underlying subject; and whether the principles of corruptible and of incorruptible things are the same or different; and whether they are all incorruptible, or whether those of corruptible things are corruptible.[5] And the most difficult question of all, and the most disputed one, is whether unity and being are not something different from the substances of existing things, as the Pythagoreans and Plato say, or whether this is not the case, but the underlying subject is something different,[6] as Empedocles holds of love, another thinker of fire, another of water, and another of air. And we must inquire whether the principles of things are universals or singular things.

188. Again, we must inquire whether they exist potentially or actually. And also whether they are principles of things in some other way or in reference to motion; for these questions present great difficulty.

189. And in addition to these questions we must inquire whether numbers or lengths and points are somehow substances or not. And if they are substances, whether they are separate from sensible things or are found in them.[7] Concerning

---

[1] Discussed in III, L.8 (220-234:C 423-442). Answered in VII, L.9 & 10 (622-628:C 1460-1500); 12 & 13 (640-658:C 1537-1591).
[2] Discussed in III, L.9 (235-244:C 443-455). Answered in VII, L.8 (611-614:C 1417-1453); 13 & 14 (650-668:C 1566-1605); XII, 6-12 (1055-1122:C 2488-2663).
[3] This statement is omitted from the Latin version. See Greek text 995b 36.
[4] Discussed in III, L.10 (249:C 464-465). Answered in XII, L.4 (1042-1054:C 2455-2487).
[5] Discussed in III, L.11 (250-265:C 466-487). Dealt with in VII, L.6 (598-625:C 1381-1500); XII, L.1-8 (1023-1077:C 2416-2552).
[6] Discussed in III, L.12 (266-274:C 488-501). Answered in VII, L.16 (678:C 1637-1639); X, L.3 (829-832:C 1961-1982).
[7] Discussed in III, L.13 (275-283:C 502-514). The answer to this problem, which Aristotle gives in Books XIII & XIV, was not commented on by St. Thomas. See *Metaphysics*, XIII, 1, 2, 6-9; XIV, 1-3, 5, 6.

all of these matters it is not only difficult to discover what is true, but it is not even easy to state the problems well.[8]

[8] The foregoing problems are also discussed in XII, L.1, 2 (899-923:C 2146-2193).

COMMENTARY

355. Having raised questions pertaining to the method of investigation which this science uses, the Philosopher now raises questions pertaining to the things which this science considers. And since this science considers first principles, as has been stated in Book I (13:C 35), he therefore raises here questions pertaining to the principles of things.

Now both the Forms and the objects of mathematics were held to be the first principles of things. Therefore, first (185:C 355), he raises questions concerning the Forms; and second (189:C 366), concerning the objects of mathematics ("And in addition to these").

In regard to the first he does two things. First, he asks what things are principles; and second (187:C 361), what sort of beings they are ("Further, we must inquire").

And since separate universals were held to be the principles of things, he asks, first, whether universals are the principles of things; and second (186:C 357), whether separate entities are the principles of things ("But most of all").

Concerning the first (185) he asks two questions. The first is whether genera constitute the principles and elements of things, or the ultimate parts into which each individual thing is dissolved. This question arises because an element is that of which a thing is first composed and into which it is ultimately dissolved. Now we find a twofold mode of composition and dissolution. One has to do with the in-

telligible constitution, in which species are resolved into genera, and according to this mode genera seem to be the principles and elements of things, as Plato claimed. The other mode of composition and dissolution has to do with the real order; for example, natural bodies are composed of fire, air, water and earth, and are dissolved into these. It was for this reason that the natural philosophers claimed that the elements constitute the first principles of things.

356. And assuming that genera are the principles of things, the second question is whether the principles of things are to be identified with the universals which are predicated of individual things, i.e., the lowest species, which he calls genera after the usage of the Platonists, because the lowest species contain under themselves many individuals just as genera contain many species; or whether it is rather the first and most common genera that constitute principles, for example, which of the two is more of a principle, animal or man; for man is a principle according to the Platonists, and is more real than any singular man. Now this problem arises because of two divisions which reason makes. One of these is that whereby we divide genera into species, and the other is that whereby we resolve species into genera. For it seems that whatever is the last term in a process of division is always the first principle and element in a process of composition.

357. But most of all (186).
Here he inquires whether separate

entities are the principles of things; and he raises four questions. For since the first philosophers of nature posited only a material cause, the first question is whether besides matter there is anything else that is a cause in the proper sense or not.

358. And granted that there is some other cause besides matter, the second question is whether it is separable from matter, as Plato held, or as Pythagoras held.

359. And if there is something separable from matter, the third question is whether it is a single thing, as Anaxagoras claimed, or many, as Plato and Aristotle himself claimed.

360. The fourth question is whether there is anything "besides the *synolon*," i.e., the concrete whole, or nothing; or whether there is something in certain cases and not in others; and what kind of things they are in those cases in which there is something else, and what kind of things they are in those in which there is not. And he explains what a *synolon* or concrete whole is; i.e., it is matter when something is predicated of it. Now in order to understand this we must note that Plato claimed that man and horse, and universals which are predicated in this way, are certain separate Forms; and that man is predicated of Socrates or Plato by reason of the fact that sensible matter participates in a separate Form. Hence Socrates or Plato is called a *synolon* or concrete whole, because each is constituted as a result of matter participating in a separate form. And each is, as it were, a kind of predicate of matter. Hence the Philosopher asks here whether the whatness of the individual thing is something else in addition to the individual thing itself, or not; or also whether it is something else in the case of some things and not in that of others. The Philosopher will answer this question in Book VII (588:C 1356).

361. **Further, we must inquire (187).**

Here he raises questions about the way in which principles exist. And since being is divided by the one and many, and by act and potency, he asks, first, whether these principles are one or many; and second (188:C 365), whether they are actual or potential ("Again, we must inquire").

In regard to the first he asks four questions. The first is whether the principles of things are limited in number or in kind; as we say, for example, that there are three principles of nature. Now the statement that they are limited in number can mean that the principle of nature is numerically a single form and a single matter and privation. And the statement that they are limited in kind can mean that there are many material principles which have in common the specific nature of material principle, and so on for the rest. And since some of the philosophers, such as the Platonists, attributed formal causes to things, while others, such as the ancient natural philosophers, attributed only material causes to things, he adds that this question is applicable both "in the intelligible structures," i.e., in formal causes, "and in the underlying subject," i.e., in material causes.

362. The second question is whether the principles of corruptible and of incorruptible things are the same or different. And if they are different, whether all are incorruptible, or whether the principles of corruptible things are corruptible and those of incorruptible things are incorruptible.

363. The third question is whether unity and being signify the very substance of things and not something added to the substance of things, as the Pythagoreans and Platonists claimed; or whether they do not signify the substance of things, but something else is the subject of unity and being, for example, fire or air or something else of this kind, as the ancient philosophers of nature held. Now he

says that this question is the most difficult and most puzzling one, because
on this question depends the entire
thought of Plato and Pythagoras, who
held that numbers are the substance
of things.

364. The fourth question is whether
the principles of things are "somehow
universals or are in some sense singular things," [1] i.e., whether those
things which are held to be principles
have the character of a principle in
the sense of a universal intelligible
nature, or according as each is a particular and singular thing.

365. **Again, we must inquire** (188).
Here he asks whether these principles exist potentially or actually. This
question seems to refer especially to
material principles; for it can be a
matter of dispute whether the first
material principle is some actual body,
such as fire or air, as the ancient philosophers of nature held, or something
which is only potential, as Plato held.
And since motion is the actualization
of something in potency, and is, in a
sense, midway between potentiality and
actuality, he therefore adds another
question: whether the principles of
things are causes only in reference to
motion, as the philosophers of nature
posited only principles of motion, either
material or efficient, or also whether

they are principles which act in some
other way than by motion, as Plato
claimed that sensible things are caused
by immaterial entities by a certain participation in these.[2] Futhermore, he
says that these questions have been
raised because they present the greatest
difficulty, as is clear from the manner
in which the philosophers have disa-
greed about them.

366. **And in addition to these** (189).
Here he raises questions concerning
the objects of mathematics, which are
posited as the principles of things. He
raises two questions. The first is
whether numbers, lengths, figures and
points are somehow substances, as the
Pythagoreans or Platonists held, or
whether they are not, as the philosophers of nature held.

367. And if they are substances, the
second question is whether they are
separate from sensible things, as the
Platonists held, or exist in sensible
things, as the Pythagoreans held.

368. Now these questions are raised
as problems which must be debated
and settled below, because in these
matters it is not only difficult to discover the truth, but it is not even
easy to debate the matter adequately
by finding probable arguments for
either side of the question.

[1] From the citation which St. Thomas gives it appears that he is following a different reading from that given in the Latin version.
[2] Reading *horum* for *hujus*.

LESSON 4

Are All the Classes of Causes Studied by One Science or by Many?

ARISTOTLE'S TEXT   Chapter 2: 996a 18-996b 26

190. Therefore let us discuss first the problem about which we first spoke (181): whether it is the office of one science or of many to study all the classes of causes.

191. For how will it be the office of one science to come to principles since they are not contrary?

192. Furthermore, in the case of many existing things not all the principles are present. For how can a principle of motion be present in all immobile things, or how can the nature of the good be found there? For everything which is a good in itself and by reason of its own nature is an end and thus a cause, because it is for its sake that other things come to be and exist. Further, the end and that for the sake of which something comes to be is the terminus of some action. But all actions involve motion. Therefore it would be impossible for this principle to be present in immobile things, nor could there be an *autoagathon*, i.e., a good in itself. Hence in mathematics too nothing is proved by means of this cause, nor is there any demonstration on the grounds that a thing is better or worse. Nor does anyone make any mention at all of anything of this kind. And for this reason some of the Sophists, for example, Aristippus, disregarded these. For in the other arts, even in the servile ones, such as building and cobbling, all things are to be explained on the grounds that they are better or worse; but the mathematical sciences give no account of things which are good or evil.

193. But on the other hand, if there are many sciences of the causes, and different sciences for different principles, which of these must be said to be the one that is being sought, or which one of those who have them is best informed about the subject under investigation?

194. For it is possible for the same thing to have all the classes of causes; for example, in the case of a house the source of motion is the art and the builder, the reason for which is its function, the matter is earth and stones, and the form is the plan.

195. Therefore, from the things which were established a little while ago (14-26:C 36-51) as to which of the sciences one should call wisdom, there is reason for calling every one of them such. For inasmuch as wisdom takes precedence and is a more authoritative science, and one which the others, like slaves, have no right to contradict, then the science which deals with the end and the good is such a science, because other things are for the sake of this.

196. But insofar as wisdom has been defined (24:C 49) as the science of first causes and of what is most knowable, such a science will be about substance. For while a subject may be known in many ways, we say that he who knows what a thing is in its being knows it better than he who knows it in its non-being. And in the former case one knows better than another, especially he who

knows what a thing is, and not how great it is or of what sort it is or anything that it is naturally disposed to do or to undergo. Further, in the case of other things too we think that we know every single thing, and those of which there are demonstrations, when we know what each is, for example, what squaring is, because it is finding the middle term. The same thing is true in other cases.

197. But with regard to processes of generation and actions and every change, we think that we know these perfectly when we know the principle of motion. But this differs from and is opposite to the end of motion. And for this reason it seems to be the province of a different science to speculate about each one of these causes.

COMMENTARY

369. Having raised the questions which cause difficulty in this science, Aristotle begins here to treat them dialectically. This is divided into three parts. In the first part (190:C 369), he treats the questions which pertain to the method of investigation of this science. In the second (208:C 403), he treats the questions which pertain to substances ("Furthermore, there is"). In the third (220:C 423), he treats the questions which pertain to the principles of substances ("Concerning the principles").

In regard to the first he does three things. First, he argues dialectically about this science's method of investigation, with reference to the causes by means of which it demonstrates; second (196:C 387), with reference to the first principles of demonstration ("But insofar"); and third (202:C 393), with reference to substances themselves ("And there is the problem").

In regard to the first he does two things. First (190), he takes up again the question about which he plans to argue dialectically, concluding from the order in which the questions have been listed that it is necessary first to debate those issues which were stated first in the list of questions, namely, whether it is the function of one science or of many to investigate all the classes of causes; so that in this way the order of argument corresponds to the order in which the questions have been raised.

370. **For how will it be** (191).

Second, he gives the arguments relating to this question; and in regard to this he does three things. First (191), he gives an argument for the purpose of showing that it is not the office of a single science to consider all the classes of causes. Second (193:C 376), assuming that it belongs to different sciences to consider the different classes of causes, he asks which class of cause it is that is investigated by first philosophy. He argues on both sides of this question ("But on the other hand"). Third (197:C 386), he draws from this second dispute the conclusion of the first arguments ("But with regard to").

In regard to the first (191) he gives two arguments. He says that since it belongs to one science to consider contraries, how will it belong to one science to consider principles since they are not contrary? This view, if it is considered superficially, seems to be of no importance; for it appears to follow from the destruction of the antecedent, as if one were to argue thus: if principles are contraries, they belong to one science; therefore, if they are not contraries, they do not belong to one science.

371. Therefore it can be said that in these disputes the Philosopher not only uses probable arguments but sometimes also uses sophistical ones when he gives arguments introduced by others. But it does not seem reasonable that in such an important matter so great a philosopher would have introduced an argument which is both trifling and insignificant. Hence a different explanation must be given, namely, that if one rightly considers the nature of the various things which belong to the same science, some belong to a single science insofar as they are different, but others insofar as they are reduced to some one thing. Hence many other different things are found to belong to one science insofar as they are reduced to one thing, for example, to one whole, one cause, or one subject. But contraries and all opposites belong essentially to one science by reason of the fact that one is the means of knowing the other. And from this comes this probable proposition that all different things which are contraries belong to one science. Therefore, if principles were different and were not contraries, it would follow that they would not belong to one science.

372. **Furthermore, in the case of** (192).

Here he gives the second argument, which runs thus. In the case of different things which belong to one science, whatever science considers one also considers another. This is evident in the case of contraries, which are different and belong essentially to one science without being reduced to some other unity. But not every science which considers one cause considers all causes. Therefore the study of all the causes does not belong to a single science.

373. He proves the minor premise thus: Different sciences deal with different beings, and there are many beings to which all the causes cannot be assigned. He makes this clear, first, with regard to that cause which is called the source of motion; for it does not seem that there can be a principle of motion in immobile things. Now certain immobile things are posited, especially by the Platonists, who claim that numbers and substances are separate entities. Hence, if any science considers these, it cannot consider the cause which is the source of motion.

374. Second, he shows that the same thing is true of the final cause, which has the character of good. For it does not seem that the character of goodness can be found in immobile things, if it is conceded that everything which is good in itself and by reason of its own nature is an end. And it is a cause in the sense that all things come to be and exist because of it and for its sake. However, he says "everything which is good in itself and by reason of its own nature" in order to exclude the useful good, which is not predicated of the end but of the means to the end. Hence those things which are said to be good only in the sense that they are useful for something else are not good in themselves and by reason of their own nature. For example, a bitter potion is not good in itself but only insofar as it is directed to the end, health, which is a good in itself. But an end, or that for the sake of which something comes to be, seems to be the terminus of an action. But all actions seem to involve motion. Therefore it seems to follow that this principle, i.e., the final cause, which has the character of goodness, cannot exist in immobile things. Further, since those things which exist of themselves apart from matter must be immobile, it therefore does not seem possible that "an *autoagathon*," i.e., a good-in-itself, exists, as Plato held. For he called all immaterial and unparticipated things entities which exist of themselves, just

as he called the Idea of man, man-in-himself, as though not something participated in matter. Hence he also called the good-in-itself that which is its own goodness unparticipated, namely, the first principle of all things.

375. Moreover, with a view to strengthening this argument he introduces an example. For, from the fact that there cannot be an end in the case of immobile things, it seems to follow that in the mathematical sciences, which abstract from matter and motion, nothing is proved by means of this cause, as in the science of nature, which deals with mobile things, something is proved by means of the notion of good. For example, we may give as the reason why man has hands that by them he is more capable of executing the things which reason conceives. But in the mathematical sciences no demonstration is made in this way, that something is so because it is better for it to be so, or worse if it were not so; as if one were to say, for example, that the angle in a semi-circle is a right angle because it is better that it should be so than be acute or obtuse. And because there can be, perhaps, another way of demonstrating by means of the final cause (for example, if one were to say that, if an end is to be, then what exists for the sake of an end must first be), he therefore adds that in the mathematical sciences no one makes any mention at all of any of those things which pertain to the good or to the final cause. And for this reason certain sophists, as Aristippus, who belonged to the Epicurean school, completely disregarded any demonstrations which employ final causes, considering them to be worthless in view of the fact that in the servile or mechanical arts, for example, in the "art of building," i.e., in carpentry, and in that of "cobbling," all things are explained on the grounds that something is better or worse; whereas in the mathematical sciences, which are the noblest and

most certain of the sciences, no mention is made of things good and evil.

376. **But on the other hand** (193).

Here he interjects another question. First, he states this question, which has two parts. The first part of the question is this. If different causes are considered by many sciences, so that a different science considers a different cause, then which of these sciences should be called the one "that is being sought," i.e., first philosophy? Is it the one which considers the formal cause, or the one which considers the final cause, or the one which considers one of the other causes? The second part of the question is this: If there are some things which have many causes, which one of those who consider those causes knows that subject best?

377. **For it is possible** (194).

He clarifies the second part of the question by the fact that one and the same thing is found to have every type of cause. For example, in the case of a house the source of motion is the art and the builder; the reason for which, or the final cause of the house, "is its function," i.e., its use, which is habitation; its material cause is the earth, from which the walls and floor are made; and its specifying or formal cause is the plan of the house, which the architect, after first conceiving it in his mind, gives to matter.

378. **Therefore from the things** (195).

Here he takes up again the question as to which of the aforesaid sciences we can call wisdom on the basis of the points previously established about wisdom at the beginning of this work (14:C 36), namely, whether it is the science which considers the formal cause, or the one which considers the final cause, or the one which considers one of the other causes. And he gives in order arguments relating to each of the three causes, saying that there seems to be some reason why "every one of the sciences," i.e., any one which proceeds by means of any cause at all, should be called by the name of wisdom. First, he speaks of that science which proceeds by means of the final cause. For it was stated at the beginning of this work that this science, which is called wisdom, is the most authoritative one, and the one which directs others as subordinates. Therefore, inasmuch as wisdom "takes precedence," i.e., is prior in the order of dignity and more influential in its authoritative direction of the other sciences (because it is not right that the others should contradict it but they should take their principles from it as its servants), it seems that that science "which deals with the end and the good," i.e., the one which proceeds by means of the final cause, is worthy of the name of wisdom. And this is true because everything else exists for the sake of the end, so that in a sense the end is the cause of all the other causes. Thus the science which proceeds by means of the final cause is the most important one. This is indicated by the fact that those arts which are concerned with ends are more important than and prior to the other arts; for example, the art of navigation is more important than and prior to the art of ship-building. Hence, if wisdom is pre-eminent and regulative of the other sciences, it seems that it proceeds especially by means of the final cause.

379. **But insofar as wisdom** (196). Here he introduces the arguments relating to the formal cause. For it was said in the prologue of this work (26:C 51) that wisdom is concerned with first causes and with whatever is most knowable and most certain. And according to this it seems to be concerned with "substance," i.e., it proceeds by means of the formal cause. For among the different ways of knowing things, we say that he who knows that something exists, knows more perfectly than he who knows that it does not exist. Hence in the *Posterior Analytics*[1] the Philosopher proves that an affirmative demonstration is preferable to a negative demonstration. And among those who know something affirmatively, we say that one knows more perfectly than another. But we say that he knows more perfectly than any of the others who knows what a thing is, and not he who knows how great it is, or what it is like, or what it can do or undergo. Therefore, to know a thing itself in the most perfect way absolutely is to know what it is, and this is to know its substance. But even in knowing other things, for example, a thing's properties, we say that we know best every single thing about which there are demonstrations when we also know the whatness of their accidents and properties; because whatness is found not only in substance but also in accidents.

380. He gives the example of squaring, i.e., squaring a surface of equally distant sides which is not square but which we say we square when we find a square equal to it. But since every rectangular surface of equally distant sides is contained by the two lines which contain the right angle, so that the total surface is simply the product of the multiplication of one of these lines by the other, then we find a square equal to this surface when we find a line which is the proportional mean between these two lines. For example, if line A is to line B as line B is to line C, the square of line B is equal to the surface contained by C and A, as is proved in Book VI of Euclid's *Elements*.[2]

381. This becomes quite evident in the case of numbers. For 6 is the proportional mean between 9 and 4; for 9 is related to 6 in the ratio of $1\frac{1}{2}$ to 1, and so also is 6 to 4. Now the square

[1] *Analytica Posteriora*, I, 25 (86b 35).
[2] Book VI, Proposition 17.

of 6 is 36, which is also produced by
multiplying 4 by 9; for $4 \times 9 = 36$.
And it is similar in all other cases.

382. **But with regard to processes**
(197).

Here he gives an argument pertaining to the cause of motion. For in
processes of generation and actions and
in every change we see that we may
say that we know a thing when we
know its principle of motion, and that
motion is nothing else than the actuality of something mobile produced
by a mover, as is stated in the *Physics,*
Book III.[8] He omits the material cause,
however, because that cause is a principle of knowing in the most imperfect
way; for the act of knowing is not
caused by what is potential but by what
is actual, as is stated below in Book IX
(805:C 1894).

383. Then after having given those
arguments which pertain to the second
question, he introduces an argument
which is based on the same reasons as
were given above (191:C 370 ff.) in
reference to the first question, namely,
that it is the office of a different science
to consider all these causes by reason
of the fact that in different subject-
matters different causes seem to have
the principal role, for example, the
source of motion in mobile things, the
quiddity in demonstrable things, and
the end in things which are directed
to an end.

384. However, we do not find that
Aristotle explicitly solves this question
later on, though his solution can be
ascertained from the things which he
establishes below in different places. For
in Book IV (296:C 533) he establishes
that this science considers being as
being, and therefore that it also belongs
to it, and not to the philosophy of
nature, to consider first substances; for
there are other substances besides mobile ones. But every substance is either
a being of itself, granted that it is only

a form; or it is a being by its form,
granted that it is composed of matter
and form. Hence inasmuch as this
science considers being, it considers the
formal cause before all the rest. But
the first substances are not known by
us in such a way that we know what
they are, as can be understood in some
way from the things established in
Book IX (810:C 1904); and thus in
our knowledge of them the formal
cause has no place. But even though
they are immobile in themselves, they
are nevertheless the cause of motion in
other things after the manner of an
end. Hence inasmuch as this science
considers first substances, it belongs to
it especially to consider the final cause
and also in a way the efficient cause.
But to consider the material cause in
itself does not belong to it in any way,
because matter is not properly a cause
of being but of some definite kind of
being, namely, mobile substance. However, such causes belong to the consideration of the particular sciences,
unless perhaps they are considered by
this science inasmuch as they are contained under being; for it extends its
analysis to all things in this way.

385. Now when these things are
seen it is easy to answer the arguments
which have been raised. For, first,
nothing prevents the different causes
in this science from belonging to a
single existing thing, even though they
are not contraries, because they are
reducible to one thing—being in general—as has been stated (C 384). And
in a similar way, even though not
every science considers all of the causes,
still nothing prevents one science from
being able to consider all of the causes
or several of them insofar as they are
reducible to some one thing. But to be
more specific, it must be said that in
the case of immobile things nothing
prevents the source of motion and the

8 *Physica*, III, 2 (202a 5).

end or good from being investigated. By immobile things I mean here those which are still causes of motion, as the first substances. However, in the case of those things which are neither moved nor cause motion there is no investigation of the source of motion, or of the end in the sense of the end of motion, although an end can be considered as the goal of some operation which does not involve motion. For if there are held to be intellectual substances which do not cause motion, as the Platonists claimed, still insofar as they have an intellect and will it is necessary to hold that they have an

⁴ See also Book XIII, 3 (1078a 31).

end and a good which is the object of their will. However, the objects of mathematics neither are moved nor cause motion nor have a will. Hence in their case the good is not considered under the name of good and end, although in them we do consider what is good, namely, their being and what they are. Hence the statement that the good is not found in the objects of mathematics is false, as he proves below in Book IX (805:C 1888).⁴

386. The reply to the second question is already clear; for a study of the three causes, about which he argued dialectically, belongs to this science.

LESSON 5

Are the Principles of Demonstration and Substance Considered by One Science or by Many?

ARISTOTLE'S TEXT   Chapter 2: 996b 26-997a 15

198. But with respect to the principles of demonstration there is also the problem whether they are studied by one science or by many. By principles of demonstration I mean the common axioms from which [all] demonstrations proceed, e.g., "everything must either be affirmed or denied," and "it is impossible both to be and not to be at the same time," and all other such propositions. Is there one science which deals with these principles and with substance or are there different sciences? And, if not one, which of the two must be called the one that is now being sought?

199. Now it would be unreasonable that these things should be studied by one science; for why should the study of these be proper to geometry rather than to any other science? In a similar way, then, if this study pertains to any science but cannot pertain to all, an understanding of these principles is no more proper to the science which studies substance than it is to any other science.

200. But at the same time how will there be a science of these principles? For we already know what each one of them is; and therefore the other arts use them as something known. However, if there is demonstration of them, there will have to be some subject-genus, and some of the principles will have to be properties and others axioms. For there cannot be demonstration of all things, since demonstration must proceed from something, and be about something, and [be demonstration] of certain things. It follows, then, that there is a single genus of demonstrable things; for all demonstrative sciences use axioms.

201. But on the other hand, if the science which considers substance differs from the one which considers axioms, which of these sciences is the more important and prior one? For axioms are most universal and are the principles of all things. And if it does not belong to the philosopher to establish the truth and falsity [of these principles], to what other person will it belong? [1]

---

[1] For the answer to this question see IV, L.5 (319-325:C 588-595).

COMMENTARY

387. Having debated the first question, which had to do with the study of causes, Aristotle's intention here is to argue dialectically about the science

which is concerned with the study of the first principles of demonstration; and in regard to this he does three things. First (198:C 387), he raises the question. Second (199:C 388), he argues one side of the question ("Now it would be"). Third (201:C 391), he argues on the other side of the question ("But on the other hand").

Accordingly, he states, first (198), the problem relating to the first principles of demonstration, namely, whether the study of these principles belongs to one science or to many. Further, he explains what the principles of demonstration are, saying that they are the common conceptions of all men on which all demonstrations are based, i.e., inasmuch as the particular principles of the proper demonstrated conclusions derive their stability from these common principles. And he gives an example of first principles, especially this one, that everything must either be affirmed or denied [of some subject]. Another principle which he mentions is that it is impossible for the same thing both to be and not to be at the same time. Hence the question arises whether these principles and similar ones pertain to one science or to many. And if they pertain to one science, whether they pertain to the science which investigates substance or to another science. And if to another science, then which of these must be called wisdom, or first philosophy, which we now seek.

388. **Now it would be** (199).

Here he argues one side of the question with a view to showing that it is not the office of one science to consider all first principles, i.e., the first principles of demonstration and substance. He gives two arguments, of which the first runs thus: since all sciences employ these principles of demonstration, there seems to be no reason why the study of them should pertain to one science rather than to another; nor again does it seem reasonable that they should be studied by all sciences, because then it would follow that the same thing would be treated in different sciences; but that

would be superfluous. Hence it seems to follow that no science considers these principles. Therefore, for the very same reason that it does not belong to any of the other sciences to give us a knowledge of such principles, for this reason too it follows that it does not belong to the science whose function it is to consider substance.

389. **But at the same time** (200).

Here he gives the second argument, which runs thus. In the sciences there are two methods by which knowledge is acquired. One is that by which the whatness of each thing is known, and the other is that by which knowledge is acquired through demonstration. But it does not belong to any science to give us a knowledge of the principles of demonstration by means of the first method, because such knowledge of principles is assumed to be prior to all the sciences. For "we already know" what each one of them is, i.e., we know from the very beginning what these principles signify, and by knowing this the principles themselves are immediately known. And since such knowledge of principles belongs to us immediately, he concludes that all the arts and sciences which are concerned with other kinds of cognitions make use of these pinciples as things naturally known by us.

390. But it is proved in the same way that a knowledge of these principles is not presented to us in any science by means of demonstration, because if there were demonstration of them, then three principles would have to be considered, namely, some subject-genus, its properties and the axioms. In order to clarify this he adds that there cannot be demonstration of all things; for subjects are not demonstrated but properties are demonstrated of subjects. Concerning subjects, however, it is necessary to know beforehand whether they exist and what they are, as is stated in Book I of the *Pos-*

terior Analytics.[1] The reason is that demonstration must proceed from certain things as principles, which are the axioms, and be about something, which is the subject, and [be demonstration] of certain things, which are properties. Now according to this it is immediately evident of one of these three, i.e., the axioms, that they are not demonstrated, otherwise there would have to be certain axioms prior to the axioms; but this is impossible. Therefore, having dismissed this method of procedure as obvious, he proceeds to consider the subject-genus. For since one science has one subject-genus, then that science which would demonstrate axioms would have one subject-genus. Thus there would have to be one subject-genus for all demonstrative sciences, because all demonstrative sciences use axioms of this kind.

391. **But on the other hand** (201). Here he argues the other side of the question. For if it is said that there is one science which deals with such principles, and another which deals with substance, the problem will remain as to which of these sciences is the more important and prior one. For, on the one hand, since the axioms are most universal and are the principles of everything that is treated in any of the sciences, it seems that the science which deals with such principles is the most important one. Yet, on the other hand, since substance is the first and

[1] *Analytica Posteriora*, I, 1 (71a 10).

principal kind of being, it is evident that first-philosophy is the science of substance. And if it is not the same science which deals with substance and with the axioms, it will not be easy to state to which of the other sciences it belongs to consider the truth and falsity of these axioms, i.e., if it does not belong to first philosophy, which considers substance.

392. The Philosopher answers this question in Book IV (321:C 590) of this work. He says that the study of the axioms belongs chiefly to the [first] philosopher inasmuch as it pertains to him to consider being in general, to which first principles of this kind essentially belong, as is most evident in the case of the very first principle: it is impossible for the same thing both to be and not to be [at the same time]. Hence all the particular sciences use principles of this kind just as they use being itself, although it is the first philosopher who is chiefly concerned with this. And the first argument is solved in this way. But the second argument is solved thus: the [first] philosopher does not consider principles of this kind in such a way as to make them known by defining them or by demonstrating them in an absolute sense, but by refutation, i.e., by arguing disputatively against those who deny them, as is stated in Book IV (331:C 608).

LESSON 6

Are All Substances Considered by One Science or by Many? Does the Science of Substance Consider the Essential Accidents of Substance?

ARISTOTLE'S TEXT   Chapter 2: 997a 15-997a 34

202. And there is the problem whether there is one science which deals with all substances, or many sciences.

203. If there is not one science, then with what substances must this science deal?

204. But it is unreasonable that there should be one science of all substances; for then one science would demonstrate all essential accidents, i.e., if it is true that every demonstrative science speculates about the essential accidents of some subject by proceeding from common opinions. Hence it is the office of the same science to study the essential accidents of the same subject-genus by proceeding from the same opinions. For it belongs to one science to consider that something is so, and it belongs to one science to consider the principles from which demonstrations proceed, whether to the same science or to a different one. Hence it belongs to one science to consider accidents, whether they are studied by these sciences or by one derived from them.[1]

205. Further, there is the problem whether this science is concerned only with substances or also with accidents. I mean, for example, that if a solid is a kind of substance, and also lines and surfaces, the question arises whether it is the function of the same science to know these and also the accidents of each class of things about which the mathematical sciences make demonstrations, or whether it is the concern of a different science.

206. For if it is the concern of the same science, a particular one will undertake these demonstrations and this will be the one which deals with substance. However, there does not seem to be any demonstration of the quiddity.

207. But if it is the concern of a different science, which science will it be that studies the accidents of substances? For to solve this is very difficult.[2]

[1] For the answer to this question see IV, L.2 (304-305:C 561-563); VI, L.1 (532-542: C 1144-1170).
[2] For the answer to this question see IV, L.3 & 4 (306-318:C 564-587).

COMMENTARY

393. Having debated the questions which pertain to the scope of investigation of this science, he now treats the third question, which pertains to the study of substances and accidents. This is divided into two parts inasmuch

as he discusses two questions on this point. The second (208:C 403) begins where he says, "Furthermore, there is."

In regard to the first he does three things. First (202:C 393), he raises the question whether there is one science that considers all substances, or whether there are many sciences that consider different substances.

394. If there is not (203).

Second, he argues the first side of the question with a view to showing that there is one science of all substances. For if there were not one science of all substances, then apparently it would be impossible to designate the substance which this science considers, because substance as substance is the primary kind of being. Hence it does not seem that one substance rather than another belongs to the consideration of the basic science.

395. But it is unreasonable (204).

Third, he argues the other side of the question, saying that it is unreasonable to hold that there is one science of all substances. For it would follow that there would be one demonstrative science of all essential accidents. And this is true because every science which demonstrates certain accidents speculates about the essential accidents of some particular subject, and it does this from certain common conceptions. Therefore, since a demonstrative science considers the accidents only of some particular subject, it follows that the study of some subject-genus belongs to the same science that is concerned with the study of the essential accidents of that genus and vice versa, so long as demonstrations proceed from the same principles.

396. But sometimes it happens to be the function of some science to demonstrate from certain principles that a thing is so, and sometimes it happens

to be the function of some science to demonstrate the principles from which it was demonstrated that a thing is so, sometimes to the same science and sometimes to a different one. An example of its being the function of the same science is seen in the case of geometry, which demonstrates that a triangle has three angles equal to two right angles in virtue of the principle that the exterior angle of a triangle is equal to the two interior angles opposite to it; for to demonstrate this belongs to geometry alone. And an example of its being the function of a different science is seen in the case of music, which proves that a tone is not divided into two equal semitones by reason of the fact that a ratio of 9 to 8, which is superparticular,[1] cannot be divided into two equal parts. But to prove this does not pertain to the musician but to the arithmetician. It is evident, then, that sometimes sciences differ because their principles differ, so long as one science demonstrates the principles of another science by means of certain higher principles.

397. But if it is assumed that the principles are identical, sciences could not differ so long as the accidents are the same and the subject-genus is the same, as if one science considered the subject and another its accidents.[2] Hence it follows that that science which considers a substance will also consider its accidents, so that if there are many sciences which consider substances, there will be many sciences which consider accidents. But if there is only one science which considers substances, there will be only one science which considers accidents. But this is impossible, because it would then follow that there would be only one science, since there is no science which does not demonstrate the accidents of some subject. Therefore it is the function of one

---

[1] I.e., containing a number and some aliquot part of it.
[2] The sense of the argument demands *et alia ejus accidentia* or *ejusdem accidentia* rather than *et eadem accidentia*.

science to consider all substances.

398. This is treated in Book IV (299a:C 546) of this work, where it is shown that the examination of substance as substance belongs to the first science, whose province it is to consider being as being; and thus it considers all substances according to the common aspect of substance. Therefore it belongs to this science to consider the common accidents of substance. But it belongs to the particular sciences, which deal with particular substances, to consider the particular accidents of substances, just as it belongs to the science of nature to consider the accidents of mobile substance. However, among substances there is also a hierarchy, for the first substances are immaterial ones. Hence the study of them belongs properly to first-philosophy, just as the philosophy of nature would be first philosophy if there were no other substances prior to mobile corporeal substances, as is stated below in Book VI (542:C 1170).

399. **Further, there is the problem** (205).

Here he raises another question regarding the study of substance and accidents. Concerning this he does three things. First, he raises the question whether the investigation of this science is concerned with substance alone or also with the attributes that are accidents of substances. For example, if we say that lines, surfaces and solids are substances of some sort, as some held, the question arises whether it belongs to the same science to consider such things and also their proper accidents, which are demonstrated in the mathematical sciences, or whether it belongs to another science.

400. **For if it is the concern** (206).

Second, he argues one side of the question. For if it belongs to the same science to consider accidents and substances, then, since a science which considers accidents demonstrates accidents, it follows that a science which considers substance demonstrates substances. But this is impossible; for the definition of a substance, which expresses the quiddity, is indemonstrable. Hence it will belong to the same science to consider substances and accidents.

401. **But if it is the concern** (207).

Third, he argues the other side of the question: if different sciences consider substance and accident, it will not be possible to state which science it is that speculates about the accidents of substance; because the science which would do this would consider both, although this would seem to pertain to all sciences; for every science considers the essential accidents of its subject, as has been explained.

402. The Philosopher answers this question in Book IV (310:C 570) of this work, saying that it is also the office of that science which is concerned with the study of substance and being to consider the proper accidents of substance and being. Yet it does not follow that it would consider each in the same way, i.e., by demonstrating substance as it demonstrates accidents, but by defining substance and by demonstrating that accidents either belong to or do not belong to it, as is explained more fully at the end of Book IX (806:C 1895) of this work.

LESSON 7

Are There Certain Other Substances Separate from Sensible Things? Criticism of the Different Opinions Regarding the Objects of Mathematics

ARISTOTLE'S TEXT   Chapters 2 & 3: 997a 34-998a 21

208. Furthermore, there is the problem whether sensible substances alone must be said to exist,[1] or others besides these. And whether there is one genus or many genera of substances, as is held by those who speak of the Forms and the intermediate entities with which they say the mathematical sciences deal.

209. Now the way in which we say that the Forms are both causes and substances in themselves has been treated in our first discussions concerning all of these things (69).

210. But while they involve difficulty in many respects, it is no less absurd to say that there are certain other natures besides those which exist in the heavens, and that these are the same as sensible things, except that the former are eternal whereas the latter are corruptible. For they [i.e., the Platonists] say nothing more or less than that there is a man-in-himself and horse-in-itself and health-in-itself, which differ in no respect [from their sensible counterparts]; in which they act like those who say that there are gods and that they are of human form. For just as the latter made nothing else than eternal men, in a similar way the former make the Forms nothing else than eternal sensible things.

211. Furthermore, if anyone holds that there are intermediate entities in addition to the Forms and sensible substances, he will face many problems. For evidently there will be, in like manner, lines in addition to ordinary sensible lines,[2] and the same will be true of other classes of things. Therefore, since astronomy is one of these [mathematical sciences], there will be a heaven in addition to the one we perceive, and a sun and moon, and the same will be true of the other celestial bodies. And how are we to accept these things? For it is unreasonable that a heaven should be immobile, but that it should be mobile is altogether impossible. The same thing is true of the things with which the science of perspective is concerned, and of harmonics in mathematics, because for the same reasons it is also impossible that these should exist apart from sensible things. For if there are intermediate sensible objects and senses, evidently there will be intermediate animals between animals-in-themselves and those which are corruptible.

212. Again, one might also raise the question as to what things these sciences must investigate. For if geometry, which is the art of measuring the earth, differs from geodesy, which is the art of dividing the earth, only in this respect that

---

[1] Deleting *causae* from the Latin version. The term does not occur in the Greek text or in Aquinas' reading.

[2] The Latin version here differs from the Greek text which appears to say "in addition to lines-in-themselves and to sensible lines."

the latter deals with things which are perceptible by the senses, whereas the former deals with those which are imperceptible, evidently there will be, in addition to the science of medicine, another science midway between the science of medicine itself and this particular science of medicine; and this will be true of the other sciences. But how is this possible? For then there will be certain healthy things besides those which are sensible and besides health-in-itself.

213. Similarly, neither does it seem that geodesy is concerned with continuous quantities which are sensible and corruptible. For in this case it would be destroyed when they are destroyed.

214. Nor again will astronomy deal with sensible continuous quantities, or with this heaven. For the lines we perceive by the senses are not such as those of which geometry speaks, since none of the things perceived by the senses are straight or round in this way. For the circle does not touch the rule at a point, but in the way in which Protagoras spoke in arguing against the geometricians. Neither are the motions or revolutions of the heavens similar to the things of which geometry speaks, nor do points have the same nature as the stars.

215. However, there are also some who say that these intermediate entities, which are below the Forms and above sensible things, do not exist outside of sensible things but in them. But to enumerate all the impossible consequences which follow from this theory would require too long a discussion. It will be sufficient to propose the following consideration.

216. It is unreasonable that this should be so only in the case of such things, but evidently it is also possible for the Forms to exist in sensible things, because both of these views depend on the same argument.

217. Furthermore, it would be necessary for two solids to occupy the same place.

218. And [the objects of mathematics] would not be immobile since they exist in sensible things, which are moved.

219. Moreover, on the whole, to what end would anyone hold that they exist but exist in sensible things? For the same absurdities as those described will apply to these suppositions. For there will be a heaven in addition to the one which we perceive, although it will not be separate but in the same place; but this is quite impossible.

Chapter 3

In these matters, then, it is difficult to see how it is possible to have any positive truth.

COMMENTARY

403. Having debated the questions which pertain to the scope of this science, the Philosopher now treats dialectically the questions which pertain to the substances themselves with which this science is chiefly concerned. In regard to this he does three things. First (208:C 403), he raises the ques-

tions. Second (209:C 406), he indicates the source from which arguments can be drawn in support of one side of the question ("Now the way"). Third (210:C 407), he argues on the other side of the question ("But while they involve").

In regard to the first part of this

division he raises two questions. The first question is whether sensible substances alone are found in the universe, as certain of the ancient philosophers of nature claimed, or whether besides sensible substances there are certain others, as the Platonists claimed.

404. And assuming that besides sensible substances there are certain others, the second question is whether these substances belong to one genus, or whether there are many genera of substances. For he considers both opinions. For some thinkers held that in addition to sensible substances there are only separate Forms, i.e., an immaterial man-in-himself and horse-in-itself and so on for the other classes of things, whereas others held that there are certain other substances midway between the Forms and sensible things, namely, the objects of mathematics, with which they said the mathematical sciences deal.

405. The reason for this view is that they posited on the part of the intellect a twofold process of abstracting things: one whereby the intellect is said to abstract the universal from the particular, and according to this mode of abstraction they posited separate Forms, which subsist of themselves; and another [whereby the intellect is said to abstract] from sensible matter certain forms in whose definition sensible matter is not given, for example, the abstraction of circle from brass. And according to this mode of abstraction they posited separate objects of mathematics, which they said are midway between the Forms and sensible substances, because they have something in common with both: with the Forms inasmuch as they are separate from sensible matter, and with sensible substances inasmuch as many of them are found in one class, as many circles and many lines.

406. **Now the way in which** (209).

Then he shows how it is possible to argue one side of the question, saying that it has been stated "in our first discussions," i.e., in Book I (69:C 151), how the Forms are held to be both the causes of sensible things and substances which subsist of themselves. Hence, from the things which have been said there in presenting the views of Plato, arguments can be drawn in support of the affirmative side of the question.

407. **But while they involve** (210).

Here he advances reasons for the negative side. He does this, first (210), for the purpose of showing that the Forms are not separate from sensible things; and, second (211:C 410), for the purpose of showing that the objects of mathematics are not separate ("Furthermore, if anyone").

Now above in Book I (103:C 208) he gave many arguments against those who posited separate Forms; and, therefore, passing over those arguments, he gives the line of reasoning which seems most effective. He says (210) that while the position of those who posit separate Forms contains many difficulties, the position of those which is now given is no less absurd than any of the others, i.e., that someone should say that there are certain natures in addition to the sensible ones which are contained beneath the heavens. For the heavens constitute the limit of sensible bodies, as is proved in Book I of *The Heavens and the World*.[1] But those who posited the Forms did not place them below the heavens or outside of it, as is stated in Book III of the *Physics*.[2] Hence, in accordance with this he says that they posited certain other natures in addition to those which exist in the heavens. And they said that these opposite natures are the same as these sensible things both in kind and in their intelligible constitution, and that they exist in these sensible things; or rather they said that

---

[1] *De Coelo et Mundo*, I, 9 (278b 23).
[2] *Physica*, III, 4 (203a 5).

those natures are the Forms of these sensible things. For example, they said that a separate man constitutes the humanity of this particular man who is perceived by the senses, and that a man who is perceived by the senses is a man by participating in that separate man. Yet they held that these differ in this respect, that those immaterial natures are eternal, whereas these sensible natures are corruptible.

408. That they hold those natures to be the same as these sensible things is clear from the fact that, just as man, horse, and health are found among sensible things, in a similar way they posited among these natures "a man-in-himself," i.e., one lacking sensible matter; and they did the same with regard to horse and health. Moreover, they claimed that nothing else existed in the class of separate substances except [the counterpart of] what existed materially in the sensible world. This position seems to be similar to that of those who held that the gods are of human form, which was the position of the Epicureans, as Tully states in *The Nature of the Gods*.[3] For just as those who held that the gods are of human form did nothing else than make men eternal in nature, in a similar way those who claimed that there are Forms do nothing else than hold that there are eternal sensible things, such as horse, ox, and the like.

409. But it is altogether absurd that what is naturally corruptible should be specifically the same as what is naturally incorruptible; for it is rather the opposite that is true, namely, that corruptible and incorruptible things differ in kind to the greatest degree, as is said below in Book X (895:C 2137) of this work. Yet it can happen that what is naturally corruptible is kept in being perpetually by Divine power.

410. **Furthermore, if anyone** (211). Then he argues against those who

claimed that the objects of mathematics are midway between the Forms and sensible things. First (211:C 410), he argues against those who held that the objects of mathematics are intermediate entities and are separate from sensible things; and, second (215:C 417), against those who held that the objects of mathematics exist but exist in sensible things ("However, there are").

In regard to the first he does two things. First, he introduces arguments against the first position. Second (214:C 416), he argues in support of this position ("Nor again").

He brings up three arguments against the first position. The first argument is this: just as there is a mathematical science about the line, in a similar way there are certain mathematical sciences about other subjects. If, then, there are certain lines in addition to the sensible ones with which geometry deals, by the same token there will be, in all other classes of things with which the other mathematical sciences deal, certain things in addition to those perceived by the senses. But he shows that it is impossible to hold this with regard to two of the mathematical sciences.

411. He does this, first, in the case of astronomy, which is one of the mathematical sciences and which has as its subject the heavens and the celestial bodies. Hence, according to what has been said, it follows that there is another heaven besides the one perceived by the senses, and similarly another sun and another moon, and so on for the other celestial bodies. But this is incredible, because that other heaven would be either mobile or immobile. If it were immobile, this would seem to be unreasonable, since we see that it is natural for the heavens to be always in motion. Hence the astronomer also makes some study of the motions of the heavens. But to say that a

---

[3] Cicero, *De Natura Deorum*, I, 18.

heaven should be both separate and mobile is impossible, because nothing separate from matter can be mobile.

412. Then he shows that the same view is unacceptable in the case of other mathematical sciences, for example, in that of perspective, which considers visible lines, and "in the case of harmonics," i.e., in that of music, which studies the ratios of audible sounds. Now it is impossible that there should be intermediate entities between the Forms and sensible things; because, if these sensible things—sounds and visible lines—were intermediate entities, it would also follow that there are intermediate senses. And since senses exist only in an animal, it would follow that there are also intermediate animals between the Form animal, and corruptible animals; but this is altogether absurd.

413. **Again, one might** (212).

The second argument [which he uses against the possibility of the objects of mathematics being an intermediate class of entities separate from sensible things] is as follows. If in those classes of things with which the mathematical sciences deal there are three classes of things—sensible substances, Forms and intermediate entities, then since the intelligible structure of all sensible things and of all Forms seems to be the same, it appears to follow that there are intermediate entities between any sensible things at all and their Forms. Hence there remains the problem as to what classes of things are included in the scope of the mathematical sciences. For if a mathematical science such as geometry differs from geodesy, which is the science of sensible measurements, only in this respect that geodesy deals with sensible measurements, whereas geometry deals with intermediate things which are not sensible, there will be in addition to all the sciences which consider sensible things certain [other] mathematical sciences which

deal with these intermediate entities. For example, if the science of medicine deals with certain sensible bodies, there will be in addition to the science of medicine, and any like science, some other science which will be intermediate between the science of medicine which deals with sensible bodies and the science of medicine which deals with the Forms. But this is impossible; for since medicine is about "healthy things," i.e., things which are conducive to health, then it will also follow, if there is an intermediate science of medicine, that there will be intermediate health-giving things in addition to the health-giving things perceived by the senses and absolute health, i.e., health-in-itself, which is the Form of health separate from matter. But this is clearly false. Hence it follows that these mathematical sciences do not deal with certain things which are intermediate between sensible things and the separate Forms.

414. **Similarly, neither** (213).

Then he gives the third argument [against the possibility of the objects of mathematics being an intermediate class]; and in this argument one of the points in the foregoing position is destroyed, namely, that there would be a science of continuous quantities which are perceptible; and thus, if there were another science of continuous quantities, it would follow from this that there would be intermediate continuous quantities. Hence he says that it is not true that geodesy is a science of perceptible continuous quantities, because such continuous quantities are corruptible. It would follow, then, that geodesy is concerned with corruptible continuous quantities. But it seems that a science is destroyed when the things with which it deals are destroyed; for when Socrates is not sitting, our present knowledge that he is sitting will not be true. Therefore it would follow that geodesy, or geosophics as other readings say, is destroyed when sensible continuous quantities are destroyed; but this is contrary to the character of science, which is necessary and incorruptible.

415. Yet this argument can be brought in on the opposite side of the question inasmuch as one may say that he intends to prove by this argument that there are no sciences of sensible things, so that all sciences must be concerned with either the intermediate entities or the Forms.

416. **Nor again will** (214).

Here he argues in support of this position, as follows: it belongs to the very notion of science that it should be concerned with what is true. But this would not be the case unless it were about things as they are. Therefore the things about which there are sciences must be the same in themselves as they are shown to be in the sciences. But perceptible lines are not such as geometry says they are. He proves this on the grounds that geometry demonstrates that a circle touches "the rule," i.e., a straight line, only at a point, as is shown in Book III of Euclid's *Elements*.[4] But this is found to be true of a circle and a line in the case of sensible things. Protagoras used this argument when he destroyed the certainties of the sciences against the geometricians. Similarly, the movements and revolutions of the heavens are not such as the astronomers describe them; for it seems to be contrary to nature to explain the movements of the celestial bodies by means of eccentrics and epicycles and other different movements which the astronomers describe in the heavens. Similarly, neither are the quantities of the celestial bodies such as the astronomers describe them to be, for they use stars as points even though they are still bodies having extension. It seems, then, that geometry does not deal with perceptible continuous quantities, and that astronomy does not deal

with the heaven which we perceive. Hence it remains that these sciences are concerned with certain other things, which are intermediate.

417. **However, there are** (215).

Here he argues against another position. First, he states the point at issue. Second (216:C 418), he brings in arguments germane to his purpose ("It is unreasonable").

Accordingly, he says, first (215), that some thinkers posit natures midway between the Forms and sensible things, yet they do not say that these natures are separate from sensible things but exist in sensible things themselves. This is clear regarding the opinion of those who held that there are certain self-subsistent dimensions which penetrate all sensible bodies, which some thinkers identify with the place of sensible bodies, as is stated in Book IV of the *Physics*[5] and is disproved there. Hence he says here that to pursue all the absurd consequences of this position is a major undertaking, but that it is now sufficient to touch on some points briefly.

418. **It is unreasonable** (216).

Then he brings four arguments against this position. The first runs as follows. It seems to be for the same reason that in addition to sensible things the Forms and objects of mathematics are posited, because both are held by reason of abstraction on the part of the intellect. If, then, the objects of mathematics are held to exist in sensible things, it is fitting that not only they but also the Forms themselves should exist there. But this is contrary to the opinion of those who posit [the existence of] the Forms. For they hold that these are separate, and not that they exist anywhere in particular.

419. **Furthermore, it would be** (217).

Here he gives the second argument, which runs thus: if the objects of

4 *Elements*, III, prop. 16.
5 *Physica*, IV, 2 (209b 32).

mathematics differ from sensible things yet exist in them, since a body is an object of mathematics, it follows that a mathematical body exists simultaneously with a sensible body in the same subject. Therefore "two solids," i.e., two bodies, will exist in the same place. This is impossible not only for two sensible bodies but also for a sensible body and a mathematical one, because each has dimensions, by reason of which two bodies are prevented from being in the same place.

420. **And [the objects of mathematics]** (218).

Here he gives the third argument. For when something is moved, anything that exists within it is moved. But sensible things are moved. Therefore, if the objects of mathematics exist in sensible things, it follows that the objects of mathematics are moved. But this is contrary to the intelligible constitution of mathematical objects, which abstract not only from matter but also from motion.

421. **Moreover, on the whole** (219).

Then he gives the fourth argument, which runs thus: no position is thought to be reasonable unless it is based on one of the causes, and especially if a more untenable conclusion follows from such a position. But this position is held without a cause. For the same absurdities face those who hold the objects of mathematics to be intermediate entities and to exist in sensible things, as face those who hold that they do not exist in sensible things,

as well as certain other peculiar and greater difficulties, as is clear from what has been said above. Hence, this position is an unreasonable one. In concluding he states that the questions mentioned above involve much difficulty as to what is true in these matters.

422. Now the Philosopher treats these questions below in Books XII, XIII and XIV of this work,[6] where he shows that there are neither separate mathematical substances nor Forms. The reasoning which moved those who posited the objects of mathematics and the Forms, which are derived from an abstraction of the intellect, is given at the beginning of Book XIII.[7] For nothing prevents a thing which has some particular attribute from being considered by the intellect without its being viewed under this aspect and yet be considered truly, just as a white man can be considered without white being considered. Thus the intellect can consider sensible things not inasmuch as they are mobile and material but inasmuch as they are substances or continuous quantities; and this is to abstract the thing known from matter and motion. However, so far as the thing known is concerned, the intellect does not abstract in such a way that it understands continuous quantities and forms to exist without matter and motion. For then it would follow either that the intellect of the one abstracting is false, or that the things which the intellect abstracts are separate in reality.

[6] See XII, L.5 (1056:C 2492); L.9 (1078:C 2492); XIII, chaps. 1-5; and XIV, chaps. 2, 3, 5 & 6.
[7] See XIII, 2 (1077b 1 ff.); 3 (1078a 20 ff.); 4 (1078b 30 ff.).

LESSON 8

Are Genera Principles of Things? And If So, Does This Apply to The Most Universal Genera or to Those Nearest to Individuals?

ARISTOTLE'S TEXT   Chapter 3: 998a 20-999a 23

220. Concerning the principles of things there is the problem whether genera must be regarded as the elements and principles of things, or rather the first things of which each thing is composed inasmuch as they are intrinsic.

221. Just as the elements and principles of a word seem to be those things of which all words are first composed, but not word in common. And just as we say that the elements of diagrams are those things whose demonstrations are found in the demonstrations of others, either of all or of most of them.

222. Furthermore, those who say that the elements of bodies are many, and those who say that they are one, call the things of which bodies are composed and constituted their principles, as Empedocles says that fire and water and those things which are included with these are the elements from which existing things derive their being; but he does not speak of them as the genera of existing things.

223. And again if anyone wished to speculate about the nature of other things, in finding out in regard to each (a bed, for example) of what parts it is made and how it is put together, he will come to know its nature. And according to these arguments genera are not the principles of existing things.

224. But if we know each thing through definitions, and genera are the principles of definitions,[1] genera must be the principles of the things defined.

225. And if in order to acquire scientific knowledge of existing things it is necessary to acquire scientific knowledge of their species, according to which they are said to be beings, then genera are the principles of species.

226. Moreover, some of those who say that the elements of existing things are the one or being or the great and small, seem to use these as genera.

227. But it is not possible to speak of principles in both ways; for the meaning of substance is one. Therefore a definition by means of genera will differ from one which gives the intrinsic constituents.

228. Again, if genera are the principles of things in the fullest sense, there is the question whether the first genera must be thought to be principles, or those which are lowest and are predicated of individual things. For this also raises a problem.

229. For if universals are the principles of things to a greater degree, evidently these must be the highest genera, because it is most properly these which are predicated of all existing things. Therefore there will be as many principles of existing things as there are first genera. Hence being and unity will be principles and substances, for it is these especially which are predicated of all existing things.

---

[1] Reading *definitionum* in place of *definitorum*.

It is impossible, however, that unity or being should be a single genus of existing things; for it is necessary both that the differences of each genus exist and that each be one. But it is impossible either that species be predicated of the differences of their own genera, or that a genus be so predicated independently of its species. If, then, unity or being is a genus, no difference will be one and a being. But if unity and being are not genera, neither will they be principles, supposing that genera are principles.

230. Further, those things which are intermediate and are taken along with differences will be genera down to individuals. But some seem to be such, whereas others do not. Again, differences are principles to a greater degree than genera; and if they are principles, principles will be infinite in number, so to speak. And [this will appear] in another way also if one holds that the first genus is a principle.

231. But, on the other hand, if unity is a specific principle to a greater degree, and unity is indivisible, and everything indivisible is such either in quantity or in species, and what is indivisible in species is prior, and genera are divisible into species, then it will be rather the lowest predicate which is one. For man is not the genus of particular men.

232. Further, in the case of those things to which prior and subsequent apply, it is not possible in their case that there should be something which exists apart from them. For example, if the number two is the first of numbers, there will not be any number apart from the species of numbers; nor, likewise, any figure apart from the species of figures. But if the genera of these things do not [exist apart from the species], then in the case of other things the teaching [2] will be that there are genera apart from the species; for of these things there seem especially to be genera. But among individual things one is not prior and another subsequent.

233. Further, where one thing is better and another worse, that which is better is always prior; so that there will be no genus of these things. From these considerations, then, it seems that it is the terms predicated of individuals, rather than genera, which are principles.

234. But again it is not easy to state how one must conceive these to be the principles of things. For a principle or cause must be distinct from the things of which it is the principle or cause, and must be able to exist apart from them. But why should one think that anything such as this exists apart from singular things, except that it is predicated universally and of all things? But if this is the reason, then the more universal things are, the more they must be held to be principles. Hence the first genera will be principles of things.

[2] The term σχολῇ, in the Greek text, which is rendered in the Latin version as *schola*, does not mean *school* or *teaching* (which is the meaning that St. Thomas accepts in his commentary), but means *scarcely* or *hardly*. Hence the statement should rather read: "But if [the genera] of these things do not exist [apart from the species], the genera of other things will scarcely exist apart from the species."

COMMENTARY

423. Having debated the questions which were raised about substances, the Philosopher now treats dialectically the questions which were raised about principles. This is divided into two parts. In the first (220:C 423) he discusses the questions which asked what the principles of things are; and in the second (245:C 456), the questions which asked what kind of things the principles are ("Again, there is the problem").

In the first part of this division he discusses two questions: first, whether universals are the principles of things; and second (235:C 443), whether any principles are separate from matter ("But there is a problem").

In regard to the first he discusses two questions, of which the first is whether genera are the principles of things. The second (228:C 431) asks which genera these are, whether the first genera or the others ("Again, if genera").

In regard to the first he does two things: first, he raises the question; and second (221:C 424), he treats it dialectically ("Just as the elements").

The first question (220) has to do with the principles of things: whether it is necessary to accept or believe that those genera which are predicated of many things are the elements and principles of things, or rather that those parts of which every single thing is composed must be called the elements and principles of things. But he adds two conditions, one of which is "inasmuch as they are intrinsic," which is given in order to distinguish these parts from a contrary and a privation. For white is said to come from black, or the non-white, although these are not intrinsic to white. Hence they are not its elements. The other condition is what he calls "the first things," which is given in order to distinguish them from secondary components. For the bodies of animals are composed of flesh and nerves, which exist within the animal; yet these are not called the elements of animals, because they are not the first things of which an animal is composed, but rather fire, air, water and earth, from which flesh and nerves derive their being.

424. **Just as the elements** (221).

Here he treats this question dialectically; and in regard to this he does three things. First, he shows that the first things of which anything is composed are its principles and elements. Second (224:C 427), he argues the opposite side of the question ("But if we know"). Third (227:C 430), he rejects one answer by which it could be said that both of these [i.e., genera and constituent parts] are the principles and elements of things ("But it is not").

In regard to the first he gives three arguments. The first of these proceeds from natural phenomena, in which he makes his thesis evident by two examples. The first example which he gives if that of a word, whose principle and element is not said to be the common term word but rather the first constituents of which all words are composed, which are called letters. He gives as a second example, diagrams, i.e., the demonstrative descriptions of geometrical figures. For the elements of these diagrams are not said to be the common term diagram but rather those theorems whose demonstrations are found in the demonstrations of other geometrical theorems, either of all or of most of them, because the other demonstrations proceed from the supposition of the first demonstrations. Hence the book of Euclid is called *The Book of Elements,* because the first theorems of geometry, from which the other demonstrations proceed, are demonstrated therein.

425. **Furthermore, those who** (222).

Here he gives the second argument, which also employs certain examples drawn from nature. He says that those who hold that the elements of bodies are either one or many, say that the principles and elements of bodies are those things of which bodies are composed and made up as intrinsic constituents. Thus Empedocles says that the elements of natural bodies are fire and water and other things of this kind, which along with these he calls the elements of things; and natural bodies are constituted of these first things inasmuch as they are intrinsic. Moreover, they [i.e., the philosophers of nature] held that in addition to these two principles there are four others—air, earth, strife and friendship—as was stated in Book I (50:C 104). But neither Empedocles nor the other philosophers of nature said that the genera of things are the principles and elements of these natural bodies.

426. **And again if anyone** (223).

Here he gives the third argument, which involves things made by art. He says that if someone wished to "speculate about their nature," i.e., about the definition which indicates the essence of other bodies than natural ones, namely, of bodies made by human art, for example, if one wished to know a bed, it would be necessary to consider of what parts it is made and how they are put together; and in this way he would know the nature of a bed. And after this he concludes that genera are not the principles of existing things.

427. **But if we know** (224).

Here he argues the other side of the question. He gives three arguments, the first of which is as follows. Each thing is known through its definition.

Therefore, if a principle of being is the same as a principle of knowing, it seems that anything which is a principle of definition is also a principle of the thing defined. But genera are principles of definitions, because definitions are first composed of them. Hence genera are the principles of the things defined.

428. **And if in order to** (225).

Here he gives the second argument, which runs thus. Scientific knowledge of each thing is acquired by knowing the species from which it gets its being, for Socrates can be known only by understanding that he is man. But genera are principles of species, because the species of things are composed of genera and differences. Therefore genera are the principles of existing things.

429. **Moreover, some of those** (226).

Here he gives a third argument, which is based on the authority of the Platonists, who held that the one and being are the principles of things, and also the great and small, which are used as genera. Therefore genera are the principles of things.

430. **But it is not possible** (227).

Here he excludes one answer which would say that both of these are principles. He says that it is impossible to say that both of these are "principles," i.e., both the elements, or the parts of which something is composed, and genera. He proves this by the following argument. Of each thing there is one definite concept which exposes its substance, just as there is also one substance of each thing. But the definitive concept which involves genera is not the same as the one which involves the parts of which a thing is composed. Hence it cannot be true that each definition indicates a thing's substance. But the definitive concept which indicates a thing's substance cannot be taken from its principles. Therefore it is impossible that both genera and the parts of which things are composed should be simultaneously the principles of things.

431. **Again, if genera** (228).

Then he treats the second question dialectically. First, he raises the question; and second (229:C 432), he brings up arguments relative to this question ("For if universals").

Accordingly, he says that if we hold that genera are the principles of things in the fullest sense, which of these genera should be considered to be the principles of things to a greater degree? Must we consider those "genera" which are first in number, namely, the most common, or also the lowest genera, which are proximately predicated of the individual, i.e., the lowest species. For this is open to question, as is clear from what follows.

432. **For if universals** (229).

Here he argues about the question which was proposed; and in regard to this he does three things. First, he introduces arguments to show that the first genera cannot be principles. Second (231:C 436), he introduces arguments to show that the last species should rather be called the principles of things ("But, on the other hand"). Third (234:C 441), he debates the proposed question ("But again it is").

In regard to the first (229) he gives three arguments, of which the first runs thus: if genera are principles to the extent that they are more universal, then those which are most universal, i.e., those which are predicated of all things, must be the first genera and the principles of things in the highest degree. Hence there will be as many principles of things as there are most common genera of this kind. But the most common of all genera are unity and being, which are predicated of all things. Therefore unity and being will be the principles and substances of all things. But this is impossible, because unity and being cannot be genera of all things. For, since unity and being are most universal, if they were principles of genera, it would follow that genera would not be the principles of things. Hence the position which maintains that the most common genera are principles is an impossible one, because from it there follows the opposite of what was held, namely, that genera are not principles.

433. That being and unity cannot be genera he proves by this argument: since a difference added to a genus constitutes a species, a species cannot be predicated of a difference without a genus, or a genus without a species. That it is impossible to predicate a species of a difference is clear for two reasons. First, because a difference applies to more things than a species, as Porphyry says;[1] and second, because, since a difference is given in the definition of a species, a species can be predicated essentially of a difference only if a difference is understood to be the subject of a species, as number is the subject of evenness in whose definition it is given. This, however, is not the case; but a difference is rather a formal principle of a species. Therefore a species cannot be predicated of a difference except, perhaps, in an incidental way. Similarly too neither can a genus, taken in itself, be predicated of a difference by essential predication. For a genus is not given in the definition of a difference, because a difference does not share in a genus, as is stated in Book IV of *The Topics;*[2] nor again is a difference given in the definition of a genus. Therefore a genus is not predicated essentially of a difference in any way. Yet it is predicated of that which "has a difference," i.e., of a species, which actually contains a difference. Hence he says that a species is not predicated of the proper differences

---

[1] *Isagoge* (translation of Boethius), c. "De differentia" (CG, IV, i, 37. 6-7).
[2] *Topica*, IV, 2 (122b 20).

of a genus, nor is a genus independently of its species, because a genus is predicated of its differences inasmuch as they inhere in a species. But no difference can be conceived of which unity and being are not predicated, because any difference of any genus is a one and a being, otherwise it could not constitute any one species of being. It is impossible, then, that unity and being should be genera.

434. **Further, those things** (230).

Then he gives the second argument, which runs thus: if genera are called principles because they are common and predicated of many things, then for a like reason all those things which are principles because they are common and predicated of many will have to be genera. But all things which are intermediate between the first genera and individuals, namely, those which are considered together with some differences, are common predicates of many things. Hence they are both principles and genera. But this is evidently false. For some of them are genera, as subaltern species, whereas others are not, as the lowest species. It is not true, then, that the first or common genera are the principles of things.

435. Further, if the first genera are principles, because they are the principles by which we know species, then differences will be principles to a greater degree, because differences are the formal principles of species; and form or actuality is chiefly the principle of knowing. But it is unfitting that differences should be the principles of things, because in that case there would be an infinite number of principles, so to speak; for the differences of things are infinite, so to speak; not infinite in reality but to us. That they are infinite in number is revealed in two ways: in one way if we consider the multitude of differences in themselves; in another

way if we consider the first genus as a first principle, for evidently innumerable differences are contained under it. The first genera, then, are not the principles of things.

436. **But on the other hand** (231).

Then he shows that the lowest species are principles to a greater degree than genera. He gives three arguments, of which the first runs thus: according to the Platonists it is the one which seems to have "the nature," [3] or character, of a principle to the greatest degree. Indeed, unity has the character of indivisibility, because a one is merely an undivided being. But a thing is indivisible in two ways, namely, in quantity and in species: in quantity, as the point and unit, and this is a sort of indivisibility opposed to the division of quantity; and in species, as what is not divided into many species. But of these two types of indivisibility the first and more important one is indivisibility in species, just as the species of a thing is prior to its quantity. Therefore that which is indivisible in species is more of a principle because it is indivisible in quantity. And in the division of quantity the genus seems to be more indivisible, because there is one genus of many species; but in the division of species one species is more indivisible. Hence the last term which is predicated of many, which is not a genus of many species, namely, the lowest species, is one to a greater degree in species than a genus; for example, man or any other lowest species is not the genus of particular men. Therefore a species is a principle to a greater degree than a genus.

437. **Further, in the case of** (232).

Then he gives the second argument, which is based on a certain position of Plato; for at one time Plato held that there is some one thing which is predicated of many things without priority

[3] The term "speciem" which St. Thomas cites here in place of the "principium speciale" of the Latin version suggests that he is following a different reading.

and posteriority, and that this is a separate unity, as man is separate from all men; and at another time he held that there is some one thing which is predicated of many things according to priority and posteriority, and that this is not a separate unity. This is what Aristotle means when he says "in the case of those things to which prior and subsequent apply," i.e., that when one of the things of which a common term is predicated is prior to another, it is impossible in such cases that there should be anything separate from the many things of which this common term is predicated. For example, if numbers stand in such a sequence that two is the first species of number, no separate Idea of number will be found to exist apart from all species of numbers. And on the same grounds no separate figure will be found to exist apart from all species of figures.

438. The reason for this can be that a common attribute is held to be separate so as to be some first entity in which all other things participate. If, then, this first entity is a one applicable to many in which all other things participate, it is not necessary to hold that there is some separate entity in which all things participate. But all genera seem to be things of this kind, because all types of genera are found to differ insofar as they are more or less perfect, and thus insofar as they are prior and subsequent in nature. Hence, if in those cases in which one thing is prior to another it is impossible to regard anything common as a separate entity, on the supposition that there is a genus apart from species, then "in the case of other things the teaching" will [differ], i.e., there will be another doctrine and rule concerning them, and the foregoing rule will not apply to them. But considering the individuals of one species, it is evident that one of these is not prior and another subsequent in nature but only in time. And

thus according to Plato's teaching a species is separate. Since, then, these common things are principles inasmuch as they are separate, it follows that a species is a principle to a greater degree than a genus.

439. **Further, where one thing** (233).

Here he gives the third argument, which makes use of the notions "better or worse." For in all those cases where one thing is better than another, that which is better is always prior in nature. But there cannot be held to be one common genus of those things which exist in this way. Hence there cannot be held to be one separate genus in the case of those things in which one is better and another worse; and thus the conclusion is the same as the above. For this argument is introduced to strengthen the preceding one, so to speak, i.e., with a view to showing that there is priority and posteriority among the species of any genus.

440. And from these three arguments he draws the conclusion in which he is chiefly interested, namely, that the lowest species, which are predicated immediately of individuals, seem to be the principles of things to a greater degree than genera.

441. **But again it is not** (234).

Here he argues the opposite side of the question, as follows: a principle and a cause are distinct from the things of which they are the principle and cause, and are capable of existing apart from them. And this is true, because nothing is its own cause. He is speaking here of extrinsic principles and causes, which are causes of a thing in its entirety. But the only thing that is held to exist apart from singular things is what is commonly and universally predicated of all things. Therefore the more universal a thing is, the more separate it is, and the more it should be held to be a principle. But the first genera are most universal.

Therefore the first genera are the principles of things in the highest degree.

442. Now the solution to these questions is implied in this last argument. For according to this argument genera or species are held to be universal principles inasmuch as they are held to be separate. But the fact that they are not separate and self-subsistent is shown in Book VII (659:C 1592) of this work. Hence the Commentator also shows, in Book VIII,[4] that the principles of things are matter and form, to which genus and species bear some likeness. For a genus is derived from matter and difference from form, as will be shown in the same book (716:C 1721). Hence, since form is more of a principle than matter, species will consequently be principles more than genera. But the objection which is raised against this, on the grounds that genera are the principles of knowing a species and its definitions, is answered in the same way as the objection raised about their separateness. For, since a genus is understood separately by the mind without understanding its species, it is a principle of knowing. And in the same way it would be a principle of being, supposing that it had a separate being.

---

[4] *In VIII Metaph.*, com. 6 (VIII, 101r).

LESSON 9

Do Any Universals Exist Apart from the Singular Things Perceived by the Senses and from Those Which Are Composed of Matter and Form?

ARISTOTLE'S TEXT   Chapter 4: 999a 24-999b 20

235. But there is a problem connected with these things, which is the most difficult of all and the most necessary to consider, with which our analysis is now concerned.

236. For if there is nothing apart from singular things, and singular things are infinite in number, how is it possible to acquire scientific knowledge of them? For insofar as there is something that is one and the same, and insofar as there is something universal [which relates to singular things], to that extent we acquire knowledge of them.

237. But if this is necessary, and there must be something apart from singular things, it will be necessary that genera exist apart from singular things, and they will be either the last or the first. But the impossibility of this has already appeared from our discussion.

238. Further, if there is something apart from the concrete whole (which is most disputable), as when something is predicated of matter, if there is such a thing, the problem arises whether it must exist apart from all concrete wholes, or apart from some and not from others, or apart from none.

239. If, then, there is nothing apart from singular things, nothing will be intelligible, but all things will be sensible, and there will be no science of anything, unless one might say that sensory perception is science.

240. Further, neither will anything be eternal or immobile; for all sensible things perish and are subject to motion.

241. But if there is nothing eternal, neither can there be generation; for there must be something which has come to be and something from which it comes to be; and the last of these must be ungenerated, since [1] the process of generation must have a limit, and since it is impossible for anything to come to be from non-being.

242. Further, since generation and motion exist, there must be a terminus; for no motion is infinite but every motion has a terminus. And that which is incapable of coming to be cannot be generated. But that which has come to be must exist as soon as it has come to be.

243. Further, if matter exists because it is ungenerated, it is much more reasonable that substance should exist, since that is what it (matter) eventually comes to be. For if neither the one nor the other exists, nothing at all will exist. But if this is impossible, there must be something besides the *synolon,* and this is the form or specifying principle.

---

[1] Reading *siquidem* for *si.*

244. But again if anyone holds this to be true, the problem arises in what cases one may hold this and in what not. For evidently this is not thought to be so in all cases. For we do not hold that there is a house apart from particular houses.

COMMENTARY

443. Having debated the question whether universals are the principles of things, the Philosopher now raises a question about their separability, namely, whether there is anything separate from sensible things as their principle. In regard to this he considers two questions. The first (235:C 443) of these is whether universals are separate from singular things. The second (238:C 447) is whether there is any formal [principle] separate from things which are composed of matter and form ("Further, if there is something").

In regard to the first he does three things. First, he describes the problem. Second (236:C 444), he argues one side of the question ("For if there is nothing"). Third (237:C 445), he argues the other side of the question ("But if this is").

Accordingly, this problem arises with regard to a point mentioned in the last argument of the preceding question, namely, whether a universal is separate from singular things, as the aforesaid argument supposed. He describes this problem as "the one with which our analysis is now concerned (235)," i.e., the one which immediately preceded the foregoing argument. And he speaks of it in this way: first, that "it is connected with," i.e., is a consequence of, the foregoing one, because, as has already been stated, the consideration of the preceding question depends on this. For if universals are not separate, they are not principles; but if they are separate, they are principles. Second, he speaks of this problem as the most difficult of all the problems in this sci-

ence. This is shown by the fact that the most eminent philosophers have held different opinions about it. For the Platonists held that universals are separate, whereas the other philosophers held the contrary. Third, he says that this problem is one which it is most necessary to consider, because the entire knowledge of substances, both sensible and immaterial, depends on it.

444. **For if there is nothing** (236).

Here he advances an argument to show that universals are separate from singular things. For singular things are infinite in number, and what is infinite cannot be known. Hence all singular things can be known only insofar as they are reduced to some kind of unity which is universal. Therefore there is science of singular things only inasmuch as universals are known. But science is only about things which are true and which exist. Therefore universals are things which exist of themselves apart from singular things.

445. **But if this is** (237).

Then he argues the other side of the question in this way: if it is necessary that universals be something apart from singular things, it is necessary that genera exist apart from singular things, either the first genera or also the last, which are immediately prior to singular things. But this is impossible, as is clear from the preceding discussion. Therefore universals are not separate from singular things.

446. The Philosopher solves this problem in Book VII (659:C 1592) of this work, where he shows in many ways that universals are not substances

which subsist of themselves. Nor is it necessary, as has often been said, that a thing should have the same mode of being in reality that it has when understood by the intellect of a knower. For the intellect knows material things immaterially, and in a similar way it knows universally the natures of things which exist as singulars in reality, i.e., without considering the principles and accidents of individuals.

447. **Further, if there is something** (238).

Here he raises another question, namely, whether anything is separate from things composed of matter and form; and in regard to this he does two things. First, he raises the question. Second (239:C 448), he proceeds to deal with it ("If, then, there is").

In regard to the first it should be observed that he first raises the question whether a universal is separate from singular things. Now it happens to be the case that some singular things are composed of matter and form. But not all singular things are so composed, either according to the real state of affairs, since separate substances are particular because existing and operating of themselves, or even according to the opinion of the Platonists, who held that even among separate mathematical entities there are particulars inasmuch as they held that there are many of them in a single species. And while it is open to dispute whether there is anything separate in the case of those things which are not composed of matter and form, as the universal is separate from the particular, the problem is chiefly whether there is anything separate in the case of things which are composed of matter and form. Hence he says that the point which causes most difficulty is whether there is something "apart from the concrete whole," i.e., apart from the thing composed of matter and form.

The reason why a composite thing is called a concrete whole he explains by adding "when something is predicated of matter." For Plato held that sensible matter participates in separate universals, and that for this reason universals are predicated of singular things. These participations in universal forms by material sensible things constitute a concrete whole inasmuch as a universal form is predicated of matter through some kind of participation. Now in regard to these things he raises a question which has three parts, namely, whether there is anything that exists apart from all things of this kind, or apart from some and not from others, or apart from none.

448. **If, then, there is** (239).

Here he proceeds to deal with this problem; and concerning it he does two things. First, he argues against the position that nothing can be held to be separate from things composed of matter and form. Second (244:C 454), he argues the other side of the question ("But again if anyone holds this").

In regard to the first (239) he advances two arguments. First, he argues from the principle that those things which are composed of matter and form are sensible things; and therefore he proposes that those things which are composed of matter and form are singulars. However, singular things are not intelligible but sensible. Therefore, if there is nothing apart from singular things which are composed of matter and form, nothing will be intelligible but all beings will be sensible. But there is science only of things which are intelligible. Therefore it follows that there will be no science of anything, unless one were to say that sensory perception and science are the same, as the ancient philosophers of nature held, as is stated in Book I of *The Soul*.[1] But both of these conclusions are untenable, namely, that there

---

[1] *De Anima*, I, 2 (404b 8).

is no science and that science is sensory perception. Therefore the first position is also untenable, namely, that nothing exists except singular things which are composed of matter and form.

449. **Further, neither will anything** (240).

Second, he argues on the grounds that things composed of matter and form are mobile. He gives the following argument. All sensible things composed of matter and form perish and are subject to motion. Therefore, if there is nothing apart from beings of this kind, it will follow that nothing is eternal or immobile.

450. **But if there is** (241).

Here he shows that this conclusion is untenable, namely, that nothing is eternal and immobile. He does this, first, with respect to matter; and second (242:C 451), with respect to form ("Further, since generation").

Accordingly, he says first (241) that if nothing is eternal, it is impossible for anything to be generated. He proves this as follows. In every process of generation there must be something which comes to be and something from which it comes to be. Therefore, if that from which a thing comes to be is itself generated, it must be generated from something. Hence there must either be an infinite regress in material principles, or the process must stop with some first thing which is a first material principle that is ungenerated, unless it might be said, perhaps, that it is generated from non-being; but this is impossible. Now if the process were to go on to infinity, generation could never be completed, because what is infinite cannot be traversed. Therefore it is necessary to hold either that there is some material principle which is ungenerated, or that it is impossible for any generation to take place.

451. **Further, since generation** (242).

Here he proves the same thing with respect to the formal cause; and he gives two arguments, the first of which is as follows. Every process of generation and motion must have some terminus. He proves this on the grounds that no motion is infinite, but that each motion has some terminus. This is clear in the case of other motions which are completed in their termini. But it seems that a contrary instance is had [2] in the case of circular motion, which can be perpetual and infinite, as is proved in Book VIII of the *Physics*.[3] And even though motion is assumed to be eternal, so that the entire continuity of circular motion is infinite insofar as one circular motion follows another, still each circular motion is both complete in its species and finite. That one circular motion should follow another is accidental so far as the specific nature of circular motion is concerned.

452. The things which he said about motion in general he proves specially in regard to generation; for no process of generation can be infinite, because that thing cannot be generated whose process of generation cannot come to an end, since the end of generation is to have been made. That its being made is the terminus of generation is clear from the fact that what has been generated must exist "as soon as it has come to be," i.e., as soon as its generation is first terminated. Therefore, since the form whereby something is, is the terminus of generation, it must be impossible to have an infinite regress in the case of forms, and there must be some last form of which there is no generation. For the end of every generation is a form, as we have said. Thus it seems that just as the matter from which a thing is generated must itself be ungenerated because it is impossible to have an infinite regress, in a similar

[2] Reading *haberi instantia* for *habere instantiam*.
[3] *Physica*, VIII, 1 (251b 20).

way there must be some form which is ungenerated because it is impossible to have an infinite regress in the case of forms.

453. **Further, if matter exists** (243).

He gives the second argument, which runs thus. If there is some first matter which is ungenerated, it is much more reasonable that there should be some substance, i.e., some form, which is ungenerated, since a thing has being through its form, whereas matter is rather the subject of generation and transmutation. But if neither of these is ungenerated, then absolutely nothing will be ungenerated, since everything which exists has the character of matter or form or is composed of both. But it is impossible that nothing should be ungenerated, as has been proved (242:C 452). Therefore it follows that there must be something else "besides the *synolon*," or concrete whole, i.e., besides the singular thing which is composed of matter and form. And by something else I mean the form or specifying principle. For matter in itself cannot be separated from singular things, because it has being only by reason of something else. But this seems to be true rather of form, by which things have being.

454. **But again if anyone** (244).

Here he argues the other side of the question. For if one holds that there is some form separate from singular things which are composed of matter and form, the problem arises in which cases this must be admitted and in which not. For obviously this must not be held to be true in the case of

all things, especially in that of those made by art. For it is impossible that there should be a house apart from this sensible house, which is composed of matter and form.

455. Now Aristotle solves this problem partly in Book XII (1055:C 2488) of this work, where he shows that there are certain substances separate from sensible things and intelligible in themselves; and partly in Book VII (630:C 1503), where he shows that the forms or specifying principles of sensible things are not separate from matter. However, it does not follow that no science of sensible things can be had or that science is sensory perception. For it is not necessary that things have in themselves the same mode of being which they have in the intellect of one who knows them. For those things which are material in themselves are known in an immaterial way by the intellect, as has also been stated above (C 446). And even though a form is not separate from matter, it is not therefore necessary that it should be generated; for it is not forms that are generated but composites, as will be shown in Book VII (611:C 1417) of this work. It is clear, then, in what cases it is necessary to posit separate forms and in what not. For the forms of all things which are sensible by nature are not separate from matter, whereas the forms of things which are intelligible by nature are separate from matter. For the separate substances do not have the nature of sensible things, but are of a higher nature and belong to another order of existing things.

LESSON 10

Do All Things Have a Single Substance? Do All Things Have the Same or Different Principles?

ARISTOTLE'S TEXT   Chapter 4: 999b 20-1000a 4

245. Again, there is the problem whether all things, for example, all men, have a single substance.

246. But this is absurd; for not all things whose substance is one are themselves one, but are many and different. But this too is untenable.

247. And at the same time there is the problem how matter becomes each of the many things and a concrete whole.[1]

248. And again one might also raise this problem about principles. For if they are specifically one, there will be nothing that is numerically one. Nor again will unity itself and being be one. And how will there be science unless there is some unity in all things?

249. But, on the other hand, if they are numerically one, each of the principles will also be one, and not as in the case of sensible things, different for different things; for example, if the syllable *ba* is taken as a species, its principles in every case are specifically the same, for they are numerically different. However, if this is not so, but the things which are the principles of beings are numerically one, there will be nothing else besides the elements. For it makes no difference whether we say "numerically one" or "singular," because it is in this way that we say each thing is numerically one. But the universal is what exists in these. For example, if the elements of a word were limited in number, there would have to be as many letters as there are elements. Indeed, no two of them would be the same, nor would more than two.[2]

[1] These questions are answered in VII, L.7 (611-614:C 1417-1435); L.12-14 (640-668:C 1537-1605); XII, L.5-12 (1055-1122:C 2488-2663); see Bk. XIII, 10 (1086b 13 ff.).

[2] This problem is answered in XII, L.4 (1042-1054:C 2455-2487). See also Book XIII, 10 (1086b 13 ff.).

COMMENTARY

456. Having asked what the principles are, and whether some are separate from matter, the Philosopher now asks what the principles are like. First (245:C 456), he asks whether the principles are one or many; second (287:C 519), whether they exist potentially or actually ("And connected with these problems"); and third (290:C 523), whether they are universals or singular things ("And there is also the problem").

In regard to the first he does two things. First (245:C 456), he inquires how the principles stand with respect to unity; and second (266:C 488), what relationship unity has to the notion of principle ("But the most difficult").

In regard to the first he does three things. First, he inquires specially about the formal principle: whether all things that are specifically the same have a single form. Second (248:C 460), he asks the same question of all principles in general ("And again one might"). Third (250:C 466), he asks whether corruptible and incorruptible things have the same principles or different ones ("Again there is the problem").

In regard to the first he does two things. First, he introduces the problem. Second (246:C 457), he debates it ("But this is absurd").

The problem (245), then, is whether all things that belong to the same species, for example, all men, have a single substance or form.

457. But this is absurd (246).

Then he advances arguments on one side of the question, to show that all things belonging to one species do not have a single form. He does this by means of two arguments, the first of which runs thus. Things that belong to one species are many and different. Therefore, if all things that belong to one species have a single substance, it follows that those which have a single substance are many and different. But this is unreasonable.

458. And at the same time (247).

Then he gives the second argument, which runs thus. That which is one and undivided in itself is not combined with something divided in order to constitute many things. But it is evident that matter is divided into different singular things. Hence, if substance in the sense of form is one and the same for all things, it will be impossible to explain how each of these singular things is a matter having a

substance of the kind that is one and undivided, so that as a singular thing it is a concrete whole having two parts: a matter and a substantial form which is one and undivided.

459. Now he does not argue the other side of the question, because the very same arguments which were advanced above regarding the separateness of universals are applicable in the inquiry which follows it against the arguments just given. For if a separate universal exists, it must be held that things having the same species have a single substance numerically, because a universal is the substance of singular things. Now the truth of this question will be established in Book VII (588:C 1356) of this work, where it is shown that the whatness or essence of a thing is not other than the thing itself, except in an accidental way, as will be explained in that place.

460. And again one might (248).

Here he raises a difficulty concerning the unity of principles in general: whether the principles of things are numerically the same, or only specifically the same and numerically distinct. And in regard to this he does two things. First, he advances arguments to show that they are numerically the same. Second (249:C 464), he argues on the other side of the question ("But, on the other hand").

In regard to the first (248) he gives three arguments; and he introduces the problem, saying that the same question which was raised about substance can be raised about principles in general, i.e., whether the principles of things are numerically the same.

461. He introduces the first argument to show that they are numerically the same. For things composed of principles merely contain what they receive from these principles. Therefore, if principles are not found to be one numerically but only specifically, the things composed of these principles

will not be one numerically but only specifically.

462. The second argument runs thus: unity itself or being itself must be numerically one. And by unity itself or being itself he means unity or being in the abstract. Hence, if the principles of things are not one numerically but only specifically, it will follow that neither unity itself or being itself will subsist of themselves.

463. The third argument is this: science is had of things because there is found to be a one-in-many, as man in common is found in all men; for there is no science of singular things but of the unity [i.e., common attribute] found in them. Moreover, all science or cognition of things which are composed of principles depends on a knowledge of these principles. If, then, principles are not one numerically but only specifically, it will follow that there is no science of beings.

464. **But, on the other hand** (249). Here he argues the opposite side of the question in the following fashion. If principles are numerically one so that each of the principles considered in itself is one, it will be impossible to say that the principles of beings exist in the same way as the principles of sensible things. For we see that the principles of different sensible things are numerically different but specifically the same, just as the things of which they are the principles are numerically different but specifically the same. We see, for example, that syllables which are numerically distinct but agree in species have as their principles letters which are the same specifically though not numerically. And if anyone were to say that this is not true of the principles of beings, but that the principles of all beings are the same numerically, it would follow that nothing exists in the world except the elements, because what is numerically one is a singular

thing. For what is numerically one we call singular, just as we call universal what is in many. But what is singular is incapable of being multiplied, and is encountered only as a singular. Therefore, if it is held that numerically the same letters are the principles of all syllables, it will follow that those letters could never be multiplied so that there could be two of them or more than two. Thus a could not be found in these two different syllables ba or da. And the argument is the same in the case of other letters. Therefore, by the same reasoning, if the principles of all beings are numerically the same, it will follow that there is nothing besides these principles. But this seems to be untenable; because when a principle of anything exists it will not be a principle unless there is something else besides itself.

465. Now this question will be solved in Book XII (1046:C 2464); for it will be shown there that the principles which things have, namely, matter and form or privation, are not numerically the same for all things but analogically or proportionally the same. But those principles which are separate, i.e., the intellectual substances, of which the highest is God, are each numerically one in themselves. Now that which is one in itself and being is God; and from Him is derived the numerical unity found in all things. And there is science of these, not because they are numerically one in all, but because in our conception there is a one in many. Moreover, the argument which is proposed in support of the opposite side of the question is true in the case of essential principles but not in that of separate ones, which is the class to which the agent and final cause belong. For many things can be produced by one agent or efficient cause, and can be directed to one end.

LESSON 11

Do Corruptible and Incorruptible Things Have the Same or Different Principles?

ARISTOTLE'S TEXT   Chapter 4: 1000a 5-1001a 3

250. Again, there is a problem which has been neglected no less by the moderns than by their predecessors: whether the principles of corruptible and incorruptible things are the same or different.

251. For if they are the same, how is it that some things are incorruptible and others corruptible? And what is the cause?

252. The followers of Hesiod and all those who were called theologians paid attention only to what was plausible to themselves and have neglected us. For,[1] making the principles of things to be gods or generated from the gods, they say that whatever has not tasted nectar and ambrosia became mortal.

253. And it is clear that they are using these terms in a way known to themselves, but what they have said about the application of these causes is beyond our understanding. For if it is for the sake of pleasure that the gods partake of these things, nectar and ambrosia are not the cause of their being. But if they partake of them to preserve their being, how will the gods be eternal in requiring food?

254. But with regard to those who have philosophized by using fables, it is not worth our while to pay any serious attention to them.

255. However, from those who make assertions by means of demonstration it is necessary to find out, by questioning them, why some of the things which are derived from the same principles are eternal in nature and others are corrupted. But since these philosophers mention no cause, and it is unreasonable that things should be as they say, it is clear that the principles and causes of these things will not be the same.

256. For the explanation which one will consider to say something most to the point is that of Empedocles, who has been subject to the same error. For he posits a certain principle, hate, which is the cause of corruption.

257. Yet even hate would seem to generate everything except the one. For all things except God are derived from this. Hence he says: "From which have blossomed forth all that was and is [and will be]:[2] trees, and men and women, and beasts and flying things, and water-nourished fish, and the long-lived gods."[3] And apart from these things it is evident that, if hate did not exist in the world, all things would be one, as he says: "For when they have come together, then hate will stand last of all."[4]

258. For this reason too it turns out that God, who is most happy, is less wise

---

[1] Reading *enim* for *autem*.
[2] Omitted in the Latin version. See Greek text 1000a 30.
[3] Diels, Frag. 21, 9-12.
[4] Diels, Frag. 36, 7.

than other beings. For he does not know all the elements, because hate he does not have, and knowledge is of like by like. "For one knows earth by earth, water by water, affection by affection, and hate by mournful hate." [5]

259. But it is also clear (and this is where our discussion began) that hate no more turns out to be the cause of corruption than of being.

260. Nor, similarly, is love the cause of existence; for in blending things together into a unity it corrupts other things.

261. Moreover, he does not speak of the cause of change itself, except to say that it was naturally disposed to be so.

262. [He says]: "But thus mighty hate was nourished among the members and rose to a position of honor when the time was fulfilled, which being changeable dissolved the bond." [6] Hence change is a necessity, but he gives no reason for its necessity.

263. Yet he alone speaks expressly to this extent. For he does not make some beings corruptible and others incorruptible, but makes all things corruptible except the elements. But the problem that has been stated is why some things are corruptible and others are not, supposing that they come from the same principles. To this extent, then, it has been said that the principles of things will not be the same.

264. But if the principles are different, one problem is whether they will be incorruptible or corruptible. For supposing that they are corruptible, it is evident that they must also come from certain things, because all things that are corrupted are dissolved into those elements from which they come. Hence it follows that there are other principles prior to these principles. But this is also unreasonable, whether the process stops or goes on to infinity. Further, how will corruptible things exist if their principles are destroyed? But if they are incorruptible, why will corruptible things come from incorruptible principles, and incorruptible things from others? For this is unreasonable, and is either impossible or requires a great deal of reasoning.

265. Further, no one has attempted to say that these things have different principles, but [all thinkers] say that all things have the same principles. But they admit the first problem, considering it a trifling matter.

[5] Diels, Frag. 109.
[6] Diels, Frag. 30. The Latin version differs from the original text, which reads: "But when hate waxed strong among the members, it rose to a position of honor as the time was fulfilled which is appointed for them in turn by a mighty oath."

COMMENTARY

466. Having investigated in a general way whether all principles belonging to one species are numerically the same, the Philosopher inquires here whether the principles of corruptible and incorruptible things are numerically the same. In regard to this he does three things. First (250:C 466), he raises the question. Second (251:C 467), he introduces an argument to show that the principles of corruptible and those of incorruptible things are not the same ("For if they are the same"). Third (264:C 483), he introduces arguments to show that they are not different ("But if the principles").

He says first (250), then, that there is a problem which has been neglected no less by the modern philosophers, who followed Plato, than by the ancient philosophers of nature, who also were puzzled whether the principles of corruptible and incorruptible things are the same or different.

467. **For, if they are the same** (251).

Here he advances an argument to show that the principles of corruptible and of incorruptible things are not the same. In regard to this he does three things. First (251:C 467), he gives the argument. Second (252:C 468), he criticizes the solution of the proposed argument which the theological poets gave ("The followers of Hesiod"). Third (255:C 472), he criticizes the solution which some philosophers of nature gave ("However, from those who").

He says first (251), then, that if the principles of corruptible and of incorruptible things are held to be the same, since from the same principles there follow the same effects, it seems that either all things are corruptible or all are incorruptible. Therefore the question arises how some things are corruptible and others incorruptible, and what the reason is.

468. **The followers of Hesiod** (252).

He criticizes the solution given by the theological poets. First (252:C 468), he gives their solution. Second (253:C 470), he argues against it ("And it is clear that"). Third (254:C 471), he gives the reason why he does not criticize this position with more care ("But with regard to those").

Concerning the first (252) it must be noted that there were among the Greeks, or philosophers of nature, certain students of wisdom, such as Orpheus, Hesiod and certain others, who were concerned with the gods and hid the truth about the gods under a cloak of fables, just as Plato hid philosophical truth under mathematics, as Simplicius says in his *Commentary on the Categories*.[1] Therefore he says that the followers of Hesiod, and all those who were called theologians, paid attention to what was convincing to themselves and have neglected us, because the truth which they understood was treated by them in such a way that it could be known only to themselves. For if the truth is obscured by fables, then the truth which underlies these fables can be known only to the one who devised them. Therefore the followers of Hesiod called the first principles of things gods, and said that those among the gods who have not tasted a certain delectable food called nectar or manna became mortal, whereas those who had tasted it became immortal.

469. But some part of the truth could lie hidden under this fable, provided that by nectar or manna is understood the supreme goodness itself of the first principle. For all the sweetness of love and affection is referred to goodness. But every good is derived from a first good. Therefore the meaning of these words could be that some things are incorruptible by reason of an intimate participation in the highest good, as those which participate perfectly in the divine being. But certain things because of their remoteness from the first principle, which is the meaning of not to taste manna and nectar, cannot remain perpetually the same in number but only in species, as the Philosopher says in Book II of *Generation*.[2] But whether they intended to treat this obscurely or something else, cannot be

[1] Perhaps *In Categorias*, Prooem. (CG, VIII, 6.28-7.6); but cf. *In I De Coelo*, c. 10 (CG, VII, 293.11-14; 294.7-10; 296.3-30, esp. 5-6, 26-29). See Th. Deman, O.P., "Remarques critiques de s. Thomas sur Aristote interprète de Platon," *Les Sciences Philosophiques et Théologiques*, 1941-42, 134-48.
[2] *De Generatione*, II, 11 (338b 12).

perceived any more fully from this statement.

470. **And it is clear** (253).

He argues against the aforesaid position. He says that the meaning which these followers of Hesiod wished to convey by the terms nectar or manna was known to them but not to us. Therefore their explanation of the way in which these causes are meant to solve this question and preserve things from corruption is beyond our understanding. For if these terms are understood in their literal sense, they appear to be inadequate, because the gods who tasted nectar or manna did so either for the sake of pleasure or because these things were necessary for their existence, since these are the reasons why men partake of food. Now if they partook of them for the sake of pleasure, nectar and manna could not be the cause of their existence so as to make them incorruptible, because pleasure is something that follows on being. But if they partook of the aforesaid nourishment because they needed it to exist, they would not be eternal, having repeated need of food. Therefore it seems that gods who are first corruptible, as it were, standing as they do in need of food, are made incorruptible by means of food. This also seems to be unreasonable, because food does not nourish a thing according to its species unless it is corrupted and passes over into the species of the one nourished. But nothing that is corruptible can be responsible for the incorruptibility of something else.

471. **But with regard to those** (254).

Here he gives his reason for not investigating this opinion with more care. He says that it is not worth our while to pay any attention to those who have philosophized "by using fables," i.e., by hiding philosophical truth under fables. For if anyone argues against their statements insofar as they are taken in a literal sense, these statements are ridiculous. But if one wishes to inquire into the truth hidden by these fables, it is not evident. Hence it is understood that Aristotle, in arguing against Plato and other thinkers of this kind who have treated their own doctrines by hiding them under something else, does not argue about the truth which is hidden but about those things which are outwardly expressed.

472. **However, from those who make assertions** (255).

Then he argues against the answer given by some of the philosophers of nature; and in regard to this he does three things. First (255:C 472), he gives the argument. Second (256:C 473), he gives the answer ("For the explanation"). Third (257:C 474), he criticizes it ("Yet even hate").

Accordingly, he says, first (255), that, having dismissed those who treated the truth by using fables, it is necessary to seek information about the aforesaid question from those who have treated the truth in a demonstrative way, by asking them why it is that, if all beings are derived from the same principles, some beings are eternal by nature and others are corrupted. And since these men give no reason why this is so, and since it is unreasonable that things should be as they say (that in the case of beings having the same principles some should be corruptible and others eternal), it seems clearly to follow that corruptible and eternal things do not have the same principles or the same causes.

473. **For the explanation** (256).

Then he gives one solution. He says that the explanation given to the aforesaid question which seems to fit it best is the one which Empedocles gave, although he was subject to the same error as the others, because the explanation which he gave is no more adequate than theirs, as is about to be shown. For he maintained that corruptible and incorruptible things have certain common principles, but that a special principle, hate, causes the corruption of the elements in such a way that the coming together of this cause and another principle produces corruption in the world.

474. **Yet even hate** (257).

Here he criticizes Empedocles' argument, and he does this in three ways. First (257:C 474), he does this by showing that the argument which Empedocles gave is not in keeping with his position; second (261:C 478), by showing that it is not adequate ("Moreover, he does not"); third (263:C 481), by showing that it is not to the point ("Yet he alone speaks").

In regard to the first he does three things. First, he shows that Empedocles' argument does not agree with his other views about hate; second (258:C 476), that it does not agree with his view about God himself ("For this reason"); and third (260:C 477), that it does not agree with his view about love ("Nor, similarly").

Accordingly, he says, first (257), that Empedocles' position that hate is the cause of corruption is untenable, because according to his position hate also seems to be the cause of the generation of all things except one. For he held that everything else is composed essentially of hate along with the other principles, with the exception of God alone, whom he claimed to be composed of the other principles without hate. Moreover, he called the heavens God, as was stated above in Book I (49:C 101), because Xenophanes, after reflecting upon the whole heaven, said that the one itself is God. And Empedocles, considering the indestructibleness of the heavens, held that the heavens are composed of the four elements and love, but not of strife or hatred. But in the case of other things he said that all those

which are or were or will be, come from hate, such as sprouting trees, and men and women, and beasts (which are terrestial animals), and vultures (which are flying and long-lived animals), and fish (which are nourished in the water), and the long-lived gods. And by the gods he seems to mean either the stars, which he held are sometimes corrupted, although after a long period of time, or the demons, which the Platonists held to be ethereal animals. Or by the gods he also means those beings whom the Epicureans held to be of human form, as was stated above (210:C 408). Therefore, from the fact that all living things except one are generated from hate, it can be said that hate is the cause of generation.

475. And in addition to this there is another reason [why hate can be said to be the cause of generation]; for according to Empedocles' position it is evident that, if hate did not exist in the world, all things would be one, since hate is the reason why things are distinct, according to Empedocles. Hence he quotes Empedocles' words to the effect that, when all things come together into a unity, for example, when chaos comes into being, hate will stand last of all, separating and dissolving things. Hence the text of Boethius says: "When [3] it comes together, then chaos knows the ultimate discord." Thus it is clear that, since the being of the world consists in the distinction of things, hate is the cause of the world's generation.

476. **For this reason** (258).

Here he gives a second argument, which pertains to the deity. He says that, since Empedocles would hold that hate is not a constituent of the divine composition, it follows, according to his arguments, that God, who is said by all men to be most happy, and consequently most knowing, is less prudent than all other beings who have

[3] *Ea enim* in the Latin version appears to be a misreading for *quando* or *cum*.

knowledge. For according to Empedocles' position it follows that God does
not know the elements because He
does not contain hate. Hence He does
not know himself. And like knows like
according to the opinion of Empedocles, who said that by earth we know
earth, by water water, "and by affection," i.e., love or concord, we know
affection, or love or concord. And in
a similar way we know "hate by hate,"
which is sadness, whether unpleasant
or evil, according to the text of
Boethius, who says that "by evil discord
we know discord." It is evident, then,
that Aristotle thought this untenable
and contrary to the position that God
is most happy because He himself
would not know some of the things
that we know. And since this argument seemed to be beside the point,
therefore, returning to his principal
theme, he says (259) that, in returning
to the point from which the first argument began, it is evident, so far as
Empedocles is concerned, that hate is
no more a cause of corruption than of
being.

477. **Nor, similarly, is love** (260).

Here he gives the third argument,
which pertains to love. He says that
in like manner love is not the cause
of generation or being, as Empedocles
claimed, if another position of his is
considered. For he said that, when all
the elements are combined into a unity,
the corruption of the world will then
take place; and thus love corrupts all
things. Therefore, with respect to the
world in general, love is the cause of
corruption, whereas hate is the cause
of generation. But with respect to singular things, hate is the cause of corruption and love of generation.

478. **Moreover, he does** (261).

Here he shows that Empedocles' argument is not adequate. For Empedocles said that there exists in the world
a certain alternation of hate and friendship, in such a way that at one time
love unites all things and afterwards

hate separates them. But as to the
reason why this alternation takes place,
so that at one time hate predominates
and at another time love, he said nothing more than that it was naturally
disposed to be so.

479. And next he gives Empedocles'
words, which, because they are written
in Greek verse, are difficult and differ
from the common way of speaking.
These words are (262): "But thus
mighty hate was nourished among the
members and rose to a position of
honor when the time was fulfilled,
which being changeable dissolved the
bond." But the text of Boethius runs
thus: "But when mighty discord in
the members was promoted to a place
of honor, because it marched forward
in a completed year, which, when these
things have been changed, returns to
a full bond." Now in order to understand this it must be noted that he
speaks poetically of the whole world
as though it were a single living thing
in whose members and parts there is
found at first the greatest harmony,
which he calls love or concord, and
afterwards there begins to exist little
by little a certain dissonance, which he
calls discord. And, similarly, in the
parts of the universe at first there was
maximum concord, and afterwards hate
was nourished little by little until it
acquired "the place of honor," i.e., it
acquired dominion over the elements.
This comes about when a completed
time is reached or a year is completed,
as Empedocles held, "which" (hate or
discord, or the year), being changeable,
dissolves "the bond," i.e., the former
union of the elements; or the year or
hate returns to a full bond, because by
a certain ability and hidden power it
returns to predominate over things.

480. After these words of Empedocles, Aristotle, in giving the meaning
of the word "changeable" which he
used, adds the explanation as though
change were necessary; for he says
that Empedocles made the foregoing

statements as though it were necessary that there should be an alternation of hate and love, but he gives no reason for this necessity. For in the case of this one living thing it is evident that what causes the alternation of hate and love is the motion of the heavens which causes generation and corruption in the world. But no such cause can be assigned why the whole should be changed in this way by love and hate. Hence it is clear that his argument was inadequate.

481. **Yet he alone** (263).

Here he shows that this argument of Empedocles is not to the point. He says that Empedocles seems to say "expressly," i.e., clearly, only that he does not hold that some of the things derived from these principles are corruptible and others incorruptible, but he holds that all things are corruptible with the exception of the elements alone. Thus he seems to avoid the foregoing problem inasmuch as the question remains why some things are corruptible and some not, if they come from the same principles. Hence it is also clear that his argument is not to the point, because he neglects the very point that requires explanation.

482. But it can be asked how he can say here that Empedocles held all things to be corruptible except the elements, since Empedocles has said above that the one is God, i.e., what is composed of the other principles except hate. It must be noted, however, that Empedocles posited two processes of corruption in the world, as is clear from what was said above. He posited one with respect to the blending of the whole universe, which was brought about by love; and from this process he did not make even God immune, because in God he placed love, which caused other things to be mixed with God. And he posited another process of corruption for singular things, and the principle of this process is hate. But he excluded this kind of corruption

from God, seeing that he did not posit hate in God. In summing up, then, Aristotle concludes that this much has been said for the purpose of showing that corruptible and incorruptible things do not have the same principles.

483. **But if the principles** (264).

Here he argues the other side of the question, with two arguments. The first is this: if the principles of corruptible and incorruptible things are not the same, the question arises whether the principles of corruptible things are corruptible or incorruptible. If one says that they are corruptible, he proves that this is false by two arguments. The first runs thus: every corruptible thing is dissolved into the principles of which it is composed. If, then, the principles of corruptible things are corruptible, it will be necessary to hold also that there are other principles from which they are derived. But this is untenable, unless an infinite regress is posited. Now it was shown in Book II (152:C 299) that it is impossible to have an infinite regress in principles in any class of cause. And it would be just as untenable for someone to say that this condition applies in the case of corruptible principles, since corruption seems to come about as a result of something being dissolved into prior principles.

484. The second argument runs thus. If the principles of corruptible things are corruptible, they must be corrupted, because every corruptible thing will be corrupted. But after they have been corrupted they cannot be principles, for what is corrupted or has been corrupted cannot cause anything. Therefore, since corruptible things are always caused in succession, the principles of corruptible things cannot be said to be corruptible.

485. Again, if it is said that the principles of corruptible things are incorruptible, evidently the principles of incorruptible things are incorruptible. Therefore the question remains why

it is that from certain incorruptible principles corruptible effects are produced, and from certain others incorruptible effects are produced; for this seems to be unreasonable and is either impossible or requires considerable explanation.

486. **Further, no one** (265).

Then relative to his main thesis he gives his second argument, which is drawn from the common opinions of all men. For no one has attempted to say that corruptible and incorruptible things have different principles, but all say that all things have the same principles. Yet the first argument, given in favor of the first part of the question, all pass over lightly, as though it were of little importance; but this is to acknowledge its truth. Hence the text of Boethius says: "But they swallow the first argument as though they considered it a minor matter."

---

[4] *Physica*, I, 7 (190a 33).

487. Now the solution to this problem is given in Book XII (1078:C 2553), where the Philosopher shows that the first active or motive principles of all things are the same but in a certain sequence. For the first principles of things are unqualifiedly incorruptible and immobile, whereas the second are incorruptible and mobile, i.e., the celestial bodies, which cause generation and corruption in the world as a result of their motion. Now the intrinsic principles of corruptible and of incorruptible things are the same, not numerically but analogically. Still the intrinsic principles of corruptible things, which are matter and form, are not corruptible in themselves but only in reference to something else. For it is in this way that the matter and form of corruptible things are corrupted, as is stated in Book I of the *Physics*.[4]

LESSON 12

Are Unity and Being the Substance and Principle of All Things?

ARISTOTLE'S TEXT   Chapter 4: 1001a 4-1001b 25

266. But the most difficult problem which has to be considered, and the one which is most necessary for a knowledge of the truth, is whether unity and being are the substance of existing things, and whether each of them is nothing else than unity and being. Or whether it is necessary to investigate what being and unity themselves are, as though there were some other nature which underlies them.

267. For some think that reality is of the former sort, and some of the latter. For Plato and the Pythagoreans thought that being and unity were nothing else [than themselves], and that this is their nature, their substance being simply unity and being. But among the other philosophers [there are different opinions] about the nature of unity. Empedocles, for example, as though reducing it to something better known, says that unity is being; for he would seem to say that this is love, since this is the cause why unity belongs to all things. Others say that this unity and being of which existing things consist and have been made is fire, and others say it is air. And those who hold that there are many elements say the same thing; for they must also speak of unity and being in as many ways as they say there are principles.

268. But if anyone holds that unity and being are not substances, it will follow that no other universals are such; for these are the most universal of all. But if there is no one-in-itself or being-in-itself, there will hardly be any other things that exist apart from what are called singular things. Further, if unity is not a substance, evidently number will not exist as another reality separate from existing things; for number is units, and a unit is truly something one. But if there is a one-in-itself and being-in-itself, the substance of these must be unity itself and being itself. For nothing else is predicated universally of all things but these two.

269. But, on the other hand, if there is to be a one-in-itself and being-in-itself, there is great difficulty in seeing how there will be anything else besides these. I mean, how will there be more beings than one? For that which differs from being does not exist. Hence according to Parmenides' argument it must follow that all beings are one, and that this is being.

270. But there is a difficulty in either case; for whether unity itself is not a substance, or whether there is a unity itself, it is impossible for number to be a substance. Now it has already been stated why this follows if unity is not a substance; but if it is, the same difficulty will arise with regard to being. For from something outside of being something else will be one; for it must be not one. But all beings are either one or many, each of which is a one.

271. Further, if unity itself is indivisible, according to Zeno's axiom it will be nothing. For that which when added does not make a thing greater or when

subtracted does not make it smaller, this, he says, does not belong to the realm of existing things, as though it were evident that whatever has being is a continuous quantity.[1] And if it is a continuous quantity, it is corporeal; for this in every respect is a being. But other quantities, for example, a surface and a line, when added in one way will make a thing greater, but in another way they will not; and a point and a unit will do so in no way.

272. But this philosopher speculates clumsily, and it is possible for a thing to be indivisible in such a way that some answer may be made against him; for when something of this kind is added it will not make a thing greater but more.

273. Yet how will continuous quantity come from such a unity or from many of them? For this would be like saying that a line is made up of points.

274. But even if someone were to think that the situation is such that number has come, as some say, from unity itself and from something else that is not one, none the less it would be necessary to inquire why and how the thing which has come to be would sometimes be a number and sometimes a continuous quantity, if that not-one were inequality and the same nature in either case. For it is not clear how continuous quantities would be produced from unity and this principle, or from some number and this principle.[2]

[1] Diels, Frag. 2.
[2] This problem is answered in VII, L.16 (678-679:C 1637-1640); X, L.3 (829-832:C 1961-1982); see also Book XIII, chap. 8.

COMMENTARY

488. Having asked whether the principles of things are the same or different, the Philosopher now asks how unity itself could have the nature of a principle; and in regard to this he does three things. First (266:C 488), he asks whether unity itself is a principle; second (275:C 502), he asks whether numbers, which arise or follow from unity, are the principles of things ("And connected with"); and third (284:C 515), whether the Forms, which are certain separate unities, are the principles of things ("But in general").

In regard to the first he does three things. First, he raises the question. Second (267:C 489), he gives the opinions on both sides ("For some think"). Third (268:C 490), he advances arguments on both sides ("But if anyone").

He says, first (266), that of all the

different questions which have been raised, one is more difficult to consider because of the weight of the arguments on both sides, and that this question is also one about which it is necessary to know the truth, because our decision about the substances of things depends on it. Now this question is whether unity and being are the substances of things, not so that either of them must be attributed to some other nature which would be informed, as it were, by unity and being, but rather so that the unity and being of a thing are its substance; or, in an opposite way, whether it is necessary to ask what that thing is to which unity and being properly belong, as though there were some other nature which is their subject.

489. **For some think** (267).

Here he gives the opinions on each side of the question. He says that some philosophers thought that reality was of one kind, and some of another. For Plato and the Pythagoreans did not hold that unity and being are the attributes of some nature, but that they constitute the nature of things, as though being itself and unity itself were the substance of things. But some philosophers, in speaking about the natural world, attributed unity and being to certain other natures, as Empedocles reduced the one to something better known, which he[1] said is unity and being; and this seems to be love, which is the cause of unity in the world. But other philosophers of nature attributed these to certain elementary causes, whether they posited one first principle, as fire or air, or more than one. For since they would hold that the material principles of things are the substances of things, it was necessary that each of these should constitute the unity and being of things; so that whichever one of these anyone might hold to be a principle, he would logically think that through it being and unity would be attributed to all things, whether he posited one principle or more than one.

490. **But if anyone** (268).

Here he gives arguments on both sides of the question. First, he gives arguments in support of the view of Plato and Pythagoras. Second (269:C 493), he gives arguments on the other side of the question, in support of the view of the philosophers of nature ("But, on the other hand").

In regard to the first (268), he makes use of elimination as follows. It is necessary to hold either that unity and being, separate and existing apart, are a substance, or not. Now if it is said that unity and being are not a substance, two untenable consequences will follow. The first of these is this: unity and being are said to be the most universal of all, and therefore, if unity and

being are not separate in such a way that unity itself or being itself is a certain substance, it will then follow that no universal is separate. Thus it will follow that there is nothing in the world except singular things, which seems to be inappropriate, as has been stated in earlier questions (C 443).

491. The other untenable consequence is this. Number is nothing else than units, because number is composed of units; for a unit is nothing else than unity itself. Therefore, if unity itself is not separate as a substance existing of itself, it will follow that number will not be a reality separate from those things which are found in matter. This can be shown to be inappropriate in view of what has already been stated above. Hence it cannot be said that unity and being are not a substance which exists by itself.

492. Therefore, if the other part of the division is conceded, that there is something which is unity itself and being itself, and that this exists separately, it must be the substance of all those things of which unity and being are predicated. For everything that is separate and is predicated of many things is the substance of those things of which it is predicated. But nothing else is predicated of all things in as universal a way as unity and being. Therefore unity and being will be the substance of all things.

493. **But, on the other hand** (269).

Then he argues the other side of the question; and he gives two arguments. The second (271:C 496) of these begins where he says, "Further, if unity itself."

In regard to the first he does two things. First, he gives the argument. Second (270:C 494), he shows how the question is made difficult as a result of the argument given ("But there is a difficulty in either case").

The first (269) argument, then, is

[1] Reading *dicebat* for *dicebant*.

as follows: if there is something which is itself being and unity as something existing separately, it will be necessary to say that unity is the very same thing as being. But that which differs from being is non-being. Therefore it follows, according to the argument of Parmenides, that besides the one there is only non-being. Thus all things will have to be one, because it could not be held that that which differs from the one, which is essentially separate, is a being.

494. **But there is a difficulty** (270).

Here he shows how this argument creates a difficulty in the case of the position of Plato, who held that number is the substance of things. He says that Plato faces a difficulty in either case, whether it is said that this separate one is a substance or not. For whichever view is held, it seems impossible that number should be the substance of things. For if it is held that unity is not a substance, it has already been stated (269:C 493) why number cannot be held to be a substance.

495. But if unity itself is a substance, the same problem will arise with respect to both unity and being. For either there is some other unity besides this unity which exists separately of itself, or there is not. And if there is no other, a multitude of things will not exist now, as Parmenides said. But if there is another unity, then that other unity, since it is not unity itself, must have as a material element something that is other than unity itself, and, consequently, other than being. And that material element from which this second unity comes to be, will have not to be a being. Thus a multitude of beings cannot be constituted from this unity which exists apart from unity itself, because all beings are either one or many, each of which is a one. But this one has as its material element something that is neither unity nor being.

496. **Further, if unity** (271).

Here he gives the second argument; and in regard to this he does three things. First (271:C 496), he gives the argument. Second (272:C 498), he criticizes it ("But this"). Third (273:C 499), he shows that the difficulty remains ("Yet how will continuous quantity").

He says first (271), then, that if this separate unity is indivisible, there follows from this the other position, which Zeno assumed, that nothing exists. For Zeno supposed that that which when added does not make a thing greater and when taken away does not make it smaller, is nothing in the real order. But he makes this assumption on the grounds that continuous quantity is the same as being. For it is evident that this is not a continuous quantity—I mean that which when added does not make a thing greater and when subtracted does not make it smaller. Therefore, if every being were a continuous quantity, it would follow that that which when added does not make a thing greater and when subtracted does not make it smaller, is non-being.

497. And better still, if any particular thing were to bear this out, every being would have to be a corporeal continuous quantity. For anything added to or subtracted from a body in any one of its dimensions, makes the body greater or less. But other continuous quantities, such as lines and surfaces, become greater insofar as one dimension is added, whereas others do not. For line added to line in length causes increase in length but not in width; and surface added to surface causes increase in width and in length but not in depth. But a point and a unit do not become greater or less in any way. Hence according to Zeno's axiom it would follow that a point and a unit are non-beings in an absolute sense, whereas a body is a being in every respect, and surfaces and lines are

beings in one respect and non-beings in another respect.

498. But this (272).

Here he criticizes the argument which has been given. He says that Zeno, by proposing such an axiom, speculated "clumsily," i.e., in an unskilled and rude manner, so that according to him there cannot by anything indivisible. And for this reason some answer must be given to the foregoing argument; and if not to the point at issue, at least to the man. Now we say that even though a unity when added to something else does not make it larger, it does cause it to be more. And it is sufficient for the notion of being that in the case of what is continuous it should make a thing larger, and that in the case of what is discrete it should make it more.

499. Yet how will (273).

Then he states the difficulty which still faces the Platonists after the above solution. And he advances two difficulties. The first of these is that the Platonists held that the one which is indivisible is the cause not only of number, which is a plurality, but also of continuous quantity. Therefore, if it is granted that when a one is added it makes a thing more, as would seem to suffice for the one which is the cause of number, how will it be possible for continuous quantity to come from an indivisible one of this kind, or from many such ones, as the Platonists held? For this would seem to be the same thing as to hold that a line is composed of points. For unity is indivisible just as a point is.

500. But even if someone (274).

Here he gives the second difficulty. He says that if anyone were to think that the situation is such that number is the result of the indivisible one and of something else which is not one, but participates in the one as a kind of material nature, as some say, the question would still remain why and how that which comes from the one as form

and from another material nature, which is called the not-one, is sometimes a number and sometimes a continuous quantity. The difficulty would be most acute if that material not-one were inequality, as is implied in the continuously extended, and were to be the same reality. For it is not clear how numbers come from this inequality as matter and from the one as form; nor again is it clear how continuous quantities come from some number as form and from this inequality as matter. For the Platonists held that number comes from a primary one and a primary two, and that from this number and material inequality continuous quantity is produced.

501. The solution of this problem is treated by Aristotle in the following books. For the fact that there is something separate, which is itself one and being, he will prove below in Book XII (1078:C 2553), when he establishes the oneness of the first principle which is separate in an absolute sense, although it is not the substance of all things which are one, as the Platonists thought, but is the cause and principle of the unity of all things. And insofar as unity is predicated of other things it is used in two ways. In one way it is interchangeable with being, and in this way each thing is one by its very essence, as is proved below in Book IV (301:C 548); and unity in this sense adds nothing to being except merely the notion of undividedness. Unity is used in another way insofar as it has the character of a first measure, either in an absolute sense or with respect to some genus. And this unity if it is both a minimum in the absolute sense and indivisible, is the one which is the principle and measure of number. But if it is not both a minimum in an absolute sense and indivisible, it will not be a unit and measure in an absolute sense, as a pound in the case of weights and a half-tone in the case of

melodies, and a foot in the case of lengths. And nothing prevents continuous quantities from being composed of this kind of unity. He will establish this in Book X (822:C 1940) of this work. But because the Platonists thought that the one which is the principle of number and the one which is interchangeable with being are the same, they therefore held that the one which is the principle of number is the substance of each thing, and consequently that number, inasmuch as it is composed of many substantial principles, makes up or comprises the substance of composite things. But he will treat this question at greater length in Books XIII and XIV of this work.

LESSON 13

Are Numbers and Continuous Quantities the Substances and Principles of Sensible Things?

ARISTOTLE'S TEXT   Chapter 5: 1001b 26-1002b 11

275. And connected with these is the question whether numbers and bodies and surfaces and points are substances, or not.

276. For if they are not, we are in a quandary as to what being is, and what the substances of things are. For affections and motions and relations and dispositions and their complex conceptions do not seem to signify substance; because all are predicated of some subject, and no one of them is a particular thing. And those things which seem to signify substance most of all, as fire, water, earth [and air],[1] of which composite bodies are constituted, their heat and cold and similar affections, are not substances. And it is only the body which undergoes these that remains as a being and is a substance.

277. Yet a body is a substance to a lesser degree than a surface, and this than a line, and this in turn than a unit and a point; for a body is defined by means of these, and these seem to be capable of existing without a body, but that a body should exist without these is impossible.

278. For this reason many of the natural philosophers, including the first, thought that substance and being are bodies, and that other things are attributes of this kind of thing; and hence too that the principles of bodies are the principles of beings. But the later philosophers, who were wiser than these, thought that the principles of things are numbers. Therefore, as we have said, if these are not substance, there is no substance or being at all; for the accidents of these things are not worthy to be called beings.

279. But if it is admitted that lengths and points are substances to a greater degree than bodies, and we do not see to what sort of bodies these belong (because it is impossible for them to exist in sensible bodies), there will then be no substance at all.

280. Further, all of these seem to be dimensions of bodies, one according to width, another according to depth, and another according to length.

281. And, similarly, any figure whatever already exists in a solid. Hence if neither Mercury is in the stone, nor one half of a cube in a cube as something segregated, neither will surface exist in a solid; for if this were true of anything whatever, it would also be true of that which divides a thing in half. And the same argument would apply in the case of a line, a point and a unit. If, then, a body is substance in the highest degree, and these things are such to a greater degree than it is, and these do not exist and are not substances, it escapes our understanding as to what being itself is and what the substance of beings is.

[1] This phrase is found in the Greek text but not in the Latin version. See St. Thomas' Commentary: C 503.

201

282. For along with what has been said there happen to be certain unreasonable views about generation and corruption. For if substance, not existing before, exists now, or existing before, does not exist afterwards, it seems to suffer these changes through generation and corruption. But it is impossible for points and lines and surfaces either to come to be or to be destroyed, even though they sometimes exist and sometimes do not. For when bodies are joined or divided, at one time, when they are joined, they [i.e., the two surfaces] simultaneously become one, and at another time, when they are divided, two surfaces are produced; because it [i.e., one of the two surfaces in question] is not in the bodies which have been joined but has perished.[2] And when bodies are divided surfaces exist which did not exist before. For the indivisible point is not divided into two, and if things are generated and corrupted, they are generated from something.

283. And it is similar with regard to the now in time, for this cannot be generated and corrupted. Yet it seems always to exist, although it is not a substance. It is also clear that this is true of points, lines and surfaces, because the argument is the same; for they are all similarly either limits or divisions.[3]

[2] Inverting the Latin text and changing its punctuation to read: *quia compositorum non est sed corruptum est, divisorumque sunt prius non existentes.*

[3] Aristotle shows that the objects of mathematics are not substances in XIII, 1-3, 6-9; XIV, 1-3, 5, 6.

COMMENTARY

502. Having inquired whether unity and being are the substances of sensible things, the Philosopher now asks whether numbers and continuous quantities are the substances of sensible things; and in regard to this he does three things. First (275:C 502), he presents the question. Second (276:C 503), he argues in support of one side of the question ("For if they are not"). Third (279:C 507), he argues on the other side ("But if it is admitted").

Accordingly he says, first (275), that "connected with these," i.e., following from the foregoing problem, there is the question whether numbers and continuous quantities, i.e., bodies, surfaces, and their extremities, such as points, are either substances that are separate from sensible things, or are the substances of sensible things themselves, or not. He says that this problem is a result of the foregoing one, because in the foregoing problem it was asked whether unity is the substance of things. Now unity is the principle of number. But number seems to be the substance of continuous quantity inasmuch as a point, which is a principle of continuous quantity, seems to be merely the number one having position, and a line to be the number two having position, and the primary kind of surface to be the number three having position, and a body the number four having position.

503. **For if they are not** (276).

Then he advances an argument to show that these are the substances of sensible things; and in regard to this he does two things. First (276:C 503), he introduces an argument to show that these are the substances of sensible things. Second (278:C 506), he shows how the early philosophers followed out the first arguments ("For this reason").

In regard to the first he does two things. For, first, he advances an argument to show that body is the substance of things; and second (277:C 504), to show that many other things are substances to an even greater degree ("Yet a body").

He says, first (276), that if these things are not substances, we are in a quandary as to what being is essentially, and what the substances of beings are. For it is evident that affections and motions and relations and dispositions or arrangements, and their complex conceptions [1] according as they are put into words, do not seem to signify the substance of anything; because all things of this kind seem to be predicated of a subject as something belonging to the genus of quantity, and no one of them seems to signify "this particular thing," i.e., something that is complete and subsists of itself. This is especially evident in regard to the foregoing things, which are not said to be complete things but things whose nature consists in a kind of relation. But of all things those which especially seem to signify substance are fire, earth, and water, of which many bodies are composed. But he omits air,[2] because it is less perceptible; and this is the reason why some thought air to be nothing. But in these bodies there are found certain dispositions, namely, hot and cold and other affections and passible qualities of this kind, which are not substances according to what has been said. It follows, then, that body alone is substance.

504. **Yet a body** (277).

Here he proceeds to examine those things which appear to be substance to an even greater degree than a body. He says that a body seems to be a substance to a lesser degree than a surface, and a surface than a line, and a line than a point or a unit. He proves this in two ways, of which the first is as follows. That by which a thing is defined seems to be its substance, for a definition signifies substance. But a body is defined by a surface, a surface by a line, a line by a point, and a point by a unit, because they say that a point is a unit having position. Therefore surface is the substance of body, and so on for the others.

505. The second argument runs as follows. Since substance is the primary kind of being, whatever is prior seems to be substance to a greater degree. But a surface is naturally prior to a body, because a surface can exist without a body but not a body without a surface. Therefore a surface is substance to a greater degree than a body. The same reasoning can be applied to all the others in turn.

506. **For this reason** (278).

Then he shows how the earlier philosophers followed out the foregoing arguments. He says that it was because of the foregoing arguments that many of the ancient philosophers, especially the first, thought that body alone was being and substance, and that all other things were accidents of bodies. Hence when they wanted to study the principles of beings, they studied the principles of bodies, as was stated above in Book I (36:C 74) with regard to the positions of the ancient natural philosophers. But the other philosophers who came later, and were reputed to be wiser than the aforesaid philosophers inasmuch as they dealt more profoundly with the principles of things, i.e., the Pythagoreans and Platonists, were of the opinion that numbers are the substances of sensible things inasmuch as numbers are composed of units. And the unit seems to be one substance of things. Hence, according to the foregoing arguments and opinions of the philosophers, it seems that if these things—numbers, lines, surfaces, and bodies—are not the substances of things, there will be no being

---

[1] See *In I Perih.*, Lesson 2, for the meaning of *orationes* in this context.
[2] Aristotle mentions air, but the Latin version which St. Thomas reads omits it.

at all. For if these are not beings, it is unfitting that their accidents should be called beings.

507. **But if it is** (279).

Then he argues in support of the other side of the question; and he gives four arguments, the first of which is as follows. If anyone were to admit that lengths and points are substances to a greater degree than bodies, then supposing that things of this sort are not substances, it also follows that bodies are not substances. Consequently, no substance will exist, because the accidents of bodies are not substances, as has been stated above (C 503). But points, lines and surfaces are not substances. For these must be the limits of some bodies, because a point is the limit of a line, a line the limit of a surface, and a surface the limit of a body. But it is not evident to what sort of bodies these surfaces, lines and points, which are substances, belong. For it is evident that the lines and surfaces of sensible bodies are not substances, because they are altered in the same way as the other accidents in reference to the same subject. Therefore it follows that there will be no substance whatever.

508. **Further, all of these** (280).

Here he gives the second argument, which is as follows. All of the above-mentioned things seem to be certain dimensions of bodies, either according to width, as a surface, or according to depth, as a solid, or according to length, as a line. But the dimensions of a body are not substances. Therefore things of this kind are not substances.

509. **And, similarly** (281).

Here he gives a third argument, which is as follows. Any figure which can be educed from a solid body according to some dimension is present in that body in the same way, i.e., potentially. But in the case of a large piece of stone which has not yet been cut, it is evident that "Mercury," i.e.,

the figure of Mercury, is not present in it actually but only potentially. Therefore, in like manner, "in a cube," i.e., in a body having six square surfaces, one half of the cube, which is another figure, is not present actually; but it becomes actual in this way when a cube has already been divided into two halves. And since every eduction of a new figure in a solid which has been cut is made according to some surface which limits a figure, it is also evident that such a surface will not be present in a body actually but only potentially. For if each surface besides the external one were actually present in a solid body, then for the same reason the surface which limits one half of the figure would also be actually present in it. But what has been said of a surface must also be understood of a line, a point, and a unit; for these are actually present in the continuum only insofar as they limit the continuum, and it is evident that these are not the substance of a body. But the other surfaces and lines cannot be the substance of a body, because they are not actually present in it; for [3] substance is actually present in the thing whose substance it is. Hence he concludes that of all of these body especially seems to be substance, and that surfaces and lines seem to be substance to a great degree than bodies. Now if these are not actual beings or substances, it seems to escape our comprehension as to what being is and what the substances of things are.

510. **For along with** (282).

Here he gives the fourth argument. First, he states it, and second (283:C 513), he clarifies it by using a similar case ("And it is similar").

Accordingly, he says, first (282), that along with the other untenable consequences mentioned there also happen to be certain unreasonable views about generation and corruption on the part

[3] Reading *enim* for *autem*.

of those who hold that lines and surfaces are the substances of sensible things. For every substance which at first did not exist and later does exist, or which first was and afterwards is not, seems to suffer this change by way of generation and corruption. This is most evident in the case of all those things which are caused by way of motion. But points and lines and surfaces sometimes are and sometimes are not. Yet they are not generated or corrupted. Neither, then, are they substances.

511. He then proves each assumption. The first of these, is that they sometimes are and sometimes are not. For it happens that bodies which were at first distinct are afterwards united, and that those which were at first united are afterwards divided. For when bodies which were initially separated are united, one surface is produced for the two of them, because the parts of a continuous body are united in having one common boundary, which is one surface. But when one body is divided into two, two surfaces are produced, because it cannot be said that when two bodies are brought together their surfaces remain intact, but that both "perish," i.e., cease to be. In like manner, when bodies are divided there begin to exist for the first time two surfaces which previously did not exist. For it cannot be said that a surface, which is indivisible according to depth, is divided into two surfaces according to depth; or that a line, which is indivisible according to width, is divided according to width; or that a point, which is indivisible in every respect, is divided in any respect whatsoever. Thus it is clear that two things cannot be produced from one thing by way of division, and that one thing cannot be produced from two of these things by way of combination. Hence it follows that points, lines and surfaces some-

times begin to be and sometimes cease to be.

512. After having proved this, he proves the second assumption, namely, that these things are neither generated nor corrupted. For everything that is generated is generated from something, and everything that is corrupted is dissolved into something as its matter. But it is impossible to assign any matter whatever from which these things are generated and into which they are dissolved, because they are simple. Therefore they are neither generated nor corrupted.

513. **And it is similar** (283).

Then he makes the foregoing argument clear by using a similar case. For the now in time stands to time as a point to a line. But the now in time does not seem to be generated and corrupted, because if it were its generation and corruption would have to be measured by some particular time or instant. Thus the measure of this now either would be another now and so on to infinity, or would be time itself. But this is impossible. And even though the now is not generated or corrupted, still each now always seems to differ, not substantially but existentially, because the substance of the now corresponds to the mobile subject. But the difference of the now in terms of existence corresponds to the variation in motion, as is shown in Book IV of the *Physics*.[4] Therefore the same thing seems to be true of a point in relation to a line, and of a line in relation to a surface, and of a surface in relation to a body, namely, that they are neither corrupted nor generated, although some variation is observable in things of this kind. For the same holds true of all of these, because all things of this kind are, in like manner, limits if regarded as at the extremities, or divisions if they are found in between. Hence, just as the now varies existen-

---

[4] *Physica*, IV, 11 (219b 12).

tially as motion flows by, although it remains substantially the same because the mobile subject remains the same, so also does the point vary. And it does not become different because of the division of a line, even though it is not corrupted or generated in an absolute sense. The same holds true of the others.

514. But the Philosopher will treat this question in Books XIII and XIV.[5] And the truth of the matter is that mathematical entities of this kind are not the substances of things, but are accidents which accrue to substances. But this mistake about continuous quantities is due to the fact that no distinction is made between the sort of body which belongs to the genus of substance and the sort which belongs to the genus of quantity. For body belongs to the genus of substance according as it is composed of matter and form; and dimensions are a natural consequence of these in corporeal matter. But dimensions themselves belong to the genus of quantity, and are not substances but accidents whose subject is a body composed of matter and form. The same thing too was said above (C 501) about those who held that numbers are the substances of things; for their mistake came from not distinguishing between the one which is the principle of number and that which is interchangeable with being.

5 See XIII, 1-3; XIV, 1-3, 5, 6.

LESSON 14

Are There Separate Forms in Addition to the Objects of Mathematics and Sensible Things?

ARISTOTLE'S TEXT   Chapter 6: 1002b 12-1002b 32

284. But in general one will wonder why, in addition to sensible things and those which are intermediate, it is necessary to look for certain other things which we posit as the specific essences (or Forms) of sensible things.

285. For if it is because the objects of mathematics differ in one respect from the things which are at hand, they do not differ in being many things that are specifically the same. Hence the principles of sensible things will not be limited in number but only in species; unless one were to consider the principles of this particular syllable or word, for these are limited in number. And this is likewise true of the intermediate entities; for in their case too there are an infinite number of things that are specifically the same. Hence, if in addition to sensible substances and the objects of mathematics there are not certain other things, such as some call the Forms, there will be no substance which is one both numerically and specifically. Nor will the principles of beings be limited in number, but only in species. Therefore, if this is necessary, it will also be necessary on this account that there should be Forms. And even if those who speak of the Forms do not express themselves clearly, although this is what they wanted to say, they must affirm that each of the Forms is a substance, and that nothing accidental pertains to them.

286. But if we hold that the Forms exist, and that principles are one numerically but not specifically, we have stated the untenable conclusions that follow from this view.

COMMENTARY

515. Having inquired whether the objects of mathematics are the principles of sensible substances, the Philosopher now inquires whether in addition to the objects of mathematics there are certain other principles, such as those which we call Forms, which are the substances and principles of sensible things. In regard to this he does three things. First (284:C 515), he presents the question. Second (285:C 516),

he argues one side of the question ("For if it is because"). Third (286:C 518), he argues the other side ("But if we hold").

Accordingly, he says, first (284), that if one assumes that the objects of mathematics are not the principles of sensible things and their substances, one will next have the problem why, in addition to both sensible things and the objects of mathematics (which are an in-

207

termediate class between sensible things and the Forms), it is necessary to posit a third class of entities, namely, the specific essences, i.e., the Ideas or separate Forms.

516. **For if it is because** (285).

Here he argues one side of the question. The reason why it is necessary to posit separate Forms over and above sensible substances and the objects of mathematics seems to be that the objects of mathematics differ in one respect "from the things at hand," i.e., from sensible things, which exist in the universe; for the objects of mathematics abstract from sensible matter. Yet they do not differ but rather agree in another respect. For just as we find many sensible things which are specifically the same but numerically different, as many men or many horses, in a similar way we find many objects of mathematics which are specifically the same but numerically different, such as many equilateral triangles and many equal lines. And if this is true, it follows that, just as the principles of sensible things are not limited in number but in species, the same thing is true "of the intermediate entities"—the objects of mathematics. For since in the case of sensible things there are many individuals of one sensible species, it is evident that the principles of sensible things are not limited in number but in species, unless of course we can consider the proper principles of a particular individual thing, which are also limited in number and are individual. He gives as an example words; for in the case of a word expressed in letters it is clear that the letters are its principles, yet there are not a limited number of individual letters taken numerically, but only a limited number taken specifically, some of which are vowels and some consonants. But this limitation is according to species and not according to number. For *a* is not only one but many, and the same applies to

other letters. But if we take those letters which are the principles of a particular syllable, whether written or spoken, then they are limited in number. And for the same reason, since there are many objects of mathematics which are numerically different in one species, the mathematical principles of mathematical science could not be limited in number but only in species. We might say, for example, that the principles of triangles are three sides and three angles; but this limitation is according to species, for any of them can be multiplied to infinity. Therefore, if there were nothing besides sensible things and the objects of mathematics, it would follow that the substance of a Form would be numerically one, and that the principles of beings would not be limited in number but only in species. Therefore, if it is necessary that they be limited in number (otherwise it would happen that the principles of things are infinite in number), it follows that there must be Forms in addition to the objects of mathematics and sensible things.

517. This is what the Platonists wanted to say, because it necessarily follows from the things which they held that in the case of the substance of sensible things there is a single Form to which nothing accidental belongs. For something accidental, such as whiteness or blackness, pertains to an individual man, but to this separate man, who is a Form, according to the Platonists, there pertains nothing accidental but only what belongs to the definition of the species. And although they wanted to say this, they did not "express themselves" clearly; i.e., they did not clearly distinguish things.

518. **But if we hold that** (286).

Then he counters with an argument for the other side of the question. He says that, if we hold that there are separate Forms and that the principles of things are limited not only in species but also in number, certain impossible consequences will follow, which are touched on above in one of the questions (249:C 464). But the Philosopher will deal with this problem in Book XII (1040:C 2450) and Book XIV [1] of this work. And the truth of the matter is that, just as the objects of mathematics do not exist apart from sensible things,

neither do Forms exist apart from the objects of mathematics and from sensible substances. And while the efficient and moving principles of things are limited in number, the formal principles of things, of which there are many individuals in one species, are not limited in number but only in species.

[1] See XIV, 6 (1093a 1 ff.).

LESSON 15

Do First Principles Exist Actually or Potentially, and Are They Universal or Singular?

ARISTOTLE'S TEXT   Chapter 6: 1002b 32-1003b 17

287. And connected with these problems there is the question whether the elements of things exist potentially or in some other way.

288. If they exist in some other way, then there will be something else prior to [first] principles. For potentiality is prior to that cause, but the potential need not exist in that way.

289. But if the elements exist potentially, it is possible for nothing to exist; for even that which does not yet exist is capable of existing, because that which does not exist may come to be. But nothing that is incapable of existing may come to be. It is necessary, then, to investigate these problems.

290. And there is also the problem whether [first] principles are universals or singular things, as we maintain.

291. For if they are universals, they will not be substances, because a common term signifies not a particular thing but what sort of thing; and a substance is a particular thing.

292. But if it is a particular thing, and is held to be the common whatness which is predicated of things, Socrates himself will be many animals: [himself] and man and animal; i.e., if each of these signifies a particular thing and a one. If, then, the first principles of things are universals, these consequences will follow.

293. However, if they are not universals but have the nature of singular things, they will not be knowable; for all scientific knowledge is universal. Hence, if there is to be any scientific knowledge of [first] principles, there will have to be different principles which are predicated universally and are prior to [first] principles.[1]

---

[1] This problem is answered in VII, L.13-15 (650-676:C 1566-1630); see also Aristotle XIII, 10.

COMMENTARY

519. Having inquired what the principles are, the Philosopher now asks how they exist. First (287:C 519), he asks whether they exist potentially or actually; and second (290:C 523), whether they are universals or singulars ("And there is also the problem").

In regard to the first he does three things. First, he raises the question. Second (288:C 520), he argues one side

("If they exist"). Third (289:C 501), he argues the opposite side ("But if the elements").

His first question (287), then, is whether first principles exist potentially or "in some other way," i.e., actually. This problem is introduced because of the ancient philosophers of nature, who held that there are only material principles, which are in potency. But the Platonists, who posited separate Forms as formal principles, claimed that they exist actually.

520. **If they exist** (288).

He proves that principles exist potentially. For if they were to exist "in some other way," i.e., actually, it would follow that there would be something prior to principles; for potentiality is prior to actuality. This is clear from the fact that one thing is prior to another when the sequence of their being cannot be reversed; for if a thing exists, it follows that it can be, but it does not necessarily follow that, if a thing is possible, it will exist actually. But it is impossible for anything to be prior to a first principle. Therefore it is impossible for a first principle to exist in any other way than potentially.

521. **But if the elements** (289).

Here he argues the other side of the question. If the principles of things exist potentially, it follows that no beings exist actually; for that which exists potentially does not yet exist actually. He proves this on the grounds that that which is coming to be is not a being. For that which exists is not coming to be; but only that comes to be which exists potentially. Therefore everything that exists potentially is nonbeing. Hence if principles exist only potentially, beings will not exist. But if principles do not exist, neither will their effects. It follows, then, that it is possible for nothing to exist in the order of being. And in summing this up he concludes that according to what has been said it is necessary to inquire

about the principles of things for the reasons given.

522. This question will be answered in Book IX (778:C 1844) of this work, where it is shown that actuality is prior to potentiality in an unqualified sense, but that in anything moved from potentiality to actuality, potentiality is prior to actuality in time. Hence it is necessary that the first principle exist actually and not potentially, as is shown in Book XII (1059:C 2500) of this work.

523. **And there is also the problem** (290).

Here he asks whether the principles of things exist as universals or as singular things; and in regard to this he does three things. First (290:C 253), he presents the question. Second (291:C 254), he argues one side ("For if they are universals"). Third (293:C 527), he argues the other side ("However, if they are not universals").

The problem (290), then, is whether principles are universals or exist in the manner of singular things.

524. **For if they are** (291).

Then he proves that principles are not universals, by the following argument. No predicate common to many things signifies a particular thing, but signifies such and such a thing or of what sort a thing is; and it does this not according to accidental quality but according to substantial quality, as is stated below in Book V (487:C 987) of this work. The reason for this is that a particular thing is said to be such insofar as it subsists of itself. But that which subsists of itself cannot be something that exists in many, as belongs to the notion of common. For that which exists in many will not subsist of itself unless it is itself many. But this is contrary to the notion of common, because what is common is what is one-in-many. Hence it is clear that a particular thing does not signify anything common, but signifies a form existing in many things.

525. Further, he adds the minor premise, namely, that substance signifies a particular thing. And this is true of first substances, which are said to be substances in the full and proper sense, as is stated in the *Categories;* [1] for substances of this kind are things which subsist of themselves. Thus it follows that, if principles are universals, they are not substances. Hence either there will be no principles of substances, or it will be necessary to say that the principles of substances are not substances.

526. But since it is possible for someone to affirm that some common predicate might signify this particular thing, he therefore criticizes this when he says "But if it is (292)."

He explains the untenable consequence resulting from this. For if a common predicate were a particular thing, it would follow that everything to which that common predicate is applied would be this particular thing which is common. But it is clear that both animal and man are predicated of Socrates, and that each of these— animal and man—is a common predicate. Hence, if every common predicate were a particular thing, it would follow that Socrates would be three particular things; for Socrates is Socrates, which is a particular thing; and he is also a man, which is a particular thing according to the above; and he is also an animal, which is similarly a particular thing. Hence he would be

three particular things. Further, it would follow that there would be three animals; for animal is predicated of itself, of man, and of Socrates. Therefore, since this is impossible, it is also impossible for a common predicate to be a particular thing. These, then, will be the impossible consequences which follow if principles are universals.

527. **However, if they are not (293).**
He argues the other side of the question. Since all sciences are universal, they are not concerned with singulars but with universals. Therefore, if some principles were not universals but were singular things, they would not be knowable in themselves. Hence, if any science were to be had of them, there would have to be certain prior principles, which would be universals. It is necessary, then, that first principles be universals in order that science may be had of things; because if principles remain unknown, other things must remain unknown.

528. This question will be answered in Book VII (655:C 1584) of this work, where it is shown that universals are neither substances nor the principles of things. However, it does not follow for this reason that, if the principles and substances of things were singulars, there could be no science of them, both because immaterial things, even though they subsist as singulars, are nevertheless also intelligible, and also because there is science of singulars according to their universal concepts which are apprehended by the intellect.

---

[1] *Categoriae,* 5 (2b 15).

BOOK IV

Being and First Principles

CONTENTS

LESSON 1

The Proper Subject Matter of This Science:
Being as Being, and Substance and Accidents

ARISTOTLE'S TEXT   Chapters 1 & 2: 1003a-1003b 22

294. There is a certain science which studies being as being and the attributes which necessarily belong to being.

295. This science is not the same as any of the so-called particular sciences; for none of the other sciences attempt to study being as being in general, but cutting off some part of it they study the accidents of this part. This, for example, is what the mathematical sciences do.

296. Now since we are seeking the principles and ultimate causes of things, it is evident that these must be of themselves the causes of some nature. Hence, if those who sought the elements of beings sought these principles, they must be the elements of beings not in any accidental way but inasmuch as they are beings. Therefore the first causes of being as being must also be understood by us.

Chapter 2

297. The term *being* is used in many senses, but with reference to one thing and to some one nature and not equivocally. Thus everything healthy is related to health, one thing because it preserves health, another because it causes it, another because it is a sign of it (as urine) and still another because it is receptive of it. The term *medical* is related in a similar way to the art of medicine; for one thing is called medical because it possesses the art of medicine,[1] another because it is receptive of it, and still another because it is the act of those who have the art of medicine. We can take other words which are used in a way similar to these. And similarly there are many senses in which the term being is used, but each is referred to a first principle. For some things are called beings because they are substances; others because they are affections of substances; others because they are a process toward substance, or corruptions or privations or qualities of substance, or because they are productive or generative principles of substance, or of things which are related to substance, or the negation of some of these or of substance. For this reason too we say that non-being *is* non-being.

298. Therefore, just as there is one science of all healthy things, so too the same thing is true in other cases. For it is the office of one and the same science to study not only those things which are referred to one thing but also those which are referred to one nature. For those too in a sense are referred to one thing.

299. It is evident, then, that it is the function of one science to study beings as beings.

---

[1] Reading *medicinam* for *medicinas*.

299a. But in every respect a science is concerned with what is primary, and that on which other things depend, and from which they derive their name. Hence, if this is substance, it must be of substances that the philosopher possesses the principles and causes.

300. Now of every single class of things there is one sense and one science; for example, grammar, which is one science, studies all words. And for this reason too it belongs to a general science to study all species of being as being and the species of these species.

COMMENTARY

529. In the preceding book the Philosopher proceeded to treat dialectically the things which ought to be considered in this science. Here he begins to proceed demonstratively by establishing the true answer to those questions which have been raised and argued dialectically.

In the preceding book he treated dialectically both the things which pertain to the method of this science, namely, those to which the consideration of this science extends, as well as those which fall under the consideration of this science. And because it is first necessary to know the method of a science before proceeding to consider the things with which it deals, as was explained in Book II (174:C 335), this part is therefore divided into two members. First (294:C 529), he speaks of the things which this science considers; and second (403:C 749), of those which fall under its consideration. He does this in Book V ("In one sense the term *principle*").

The first part is divided into two members. First, he establishes what the subject matter of this science is. Second (297:C 534), he proceeds to answer the questions raised in the preceding book about the things which this science considers ("The term *being*").

In regard to the first he does three things. First, he submits that there is a science whose subject is being. Second

(295:C 532), he shows that it is not one of the particular sciences ("But this science"); and third (296:C 533), he shows that it is the science with which we are now dealing ("Now since").

Now because a science should investigate not only its subject but also the proper accidents of its subject, he therefore says, first (294), that there is a science which studies being as being, as its subject, and studies also "the attributes which necessarily belong to being," i.e., its proper accidents.

530. He says "as being" because the other sciences, which deal with particular beings, do indeed consider being (for all the subjects of the sciences are beings), yet they do not consider being as being, but as some particular kind of being, for example, number or line or fire or the like.

531. He also says "and the attributes which necessarily belong to being," and not just those which belong to being, in order to show that it is not the business of this science to consider those attributes which belong accidentally to its subject, but only those which belong necessarily to it. For geometry does not consider whether a triangle is of bronze or of wood, but only considers it in an absolute sense according as it has three angles equal to two right angles. Hence a science of this kind, whose subject is being, must not consider all the attributes which belong accidentally to

being, because then it would consider the accidents investigated by all sciences; for all accidents belong to some being, but not inasmuch as it is being. For those accidents which are the proper accidents of an inferior thing are related in an accidental way to a superior thing; for example, the proper accidents of man are not the proper accidents of animal. Now the necessity of this science, which considers being and its proper accidents, is evident from this, that such things should not remain unknown since the knowledge of other things depends on them, just as the knowledge of proper objects depends on that of common objects.

532. **This science** (295).

Then he shows that this science is not one of the particular sciences, and he uses the following argument. No particular science considers universal being as such, but only some part of it separated from the others; and about this part it studies the proper accidents. For example, the mathematical sciences study one kind of being, quantitative being. But the common science considers universal being as being, and therefore it is not the same as any of the particular sciences.

533. **Now since** (296).

Here he shows that the science with which we are dealing has being as its subject, and he uses the following argument. Every principle is of itself the principle and cause of some nature. But we are seeking the first principles and ultimate causes of things, as was explained in Book I (26:C 57), and therefore these are of themselves the causes of some nature. But this nature can only be the nature of being. This is clear from the fact that all philosophers, in seeking the elements of things inasmuch as they are beings, sought principles of this kind, namely, the first and ultimate ones. Therefore in this science we are seeking the principles of being as being. Hence being is the sub-

ject of this science, for any science seeks the proper causes of its subject.

534. **The term "being"** (297).

Then he proceeds to answer the questions raised in the preceding book about the things which this science considers, and this is divided into three parts. First (297:C 534), he answers the question whether this science considers substances and accidents together, and whether it considers all substances. Second (301:C 548), he answers the question whether it belongs to this science to consider all of the following: one and many, same and different, opposites, contraries, and so forth ("Now although"). Third (319:C 588), he answers the question whether it belongs to this science to consider the principles of demonstration ("Moreover, it is necessary").

In regard to the first he does three things. First, he shows that it is the office of this science to consider both substances and accidents. Second (299a: C 546), he shows that this science is chiefly concerned with substances ("But in every respect"). Third (300:C 547), he shows that it pertains to this science to consider all substances ("Now of every").

In regard to the first part he uses this kind of argument: those things which have one term predicated of them in common, not univocally but analogously, belong to the consideration of one science. But the term being is thus predicated of all beings. Therefore all beings, i.e., both substances and accidents, belong to the consideration of one science which considers being as being.

535. Now in this argument he gives, first (297:C 535), the minor premise; second (298:C 544), the major premise ("Therefore, just as"); and third (299:C 545), the conclusion ("It is evident, then").

He accordingly says, first (297), that the term being, or what is, has several meanings. But it must be noted that a term is predicated of different things in various senses. Sometimes it is predicated of them according to a meaning which is entirely the same, and then it is said to be predicated of them univocally, as animal is predicated of a horse and of an ox. Sometimes it is predicated of them according to meanings which are entirely different, and then it is said to be predicated of them equivocally, as *dog* is predicated of a star and of an animal. And sometimes it is predicated of them according to meanings which are partly different and partly not (different inasmuch as they imply different relationships, and the same inasmuch as these different relationships are referred to one and the same thing), and then it is said "to be predicated analogously," i.e., proportionally, according as each one by its own relationship is referred to that one same thing.

536. It must also be noted that the one thing to which the different relationships are referred in the case of analogical things is numerically one and not just one in meaning, which is the kind of oneness designated by a univocal term. Hence he says that, although the term being has several senses, still it is not predicated equivocally but in reference to one thing; not to one thing which is one merely in meaning, but to one which is one as a single definite nature. This is evident in the examples given in the text.

537. First, he gives the example of many things being related to one thing as an end. This is clear in the case of the term *healthy* or *healthful*. For the term healthy is not predicated univocally of food, medicine, urine and an animal; because the concept healthy as applied to food means something that preserves health; and as applied to medicine it means something that causes health; and as applied to urine

it means something that is a sign of health; and as applied to an animal it means something that is the recipient or subject of health. Hence every use of the term healthy refers to one and the same health; for it is the same health which the animal receives, which urine is a sign of, which medicine causes, and which food preserves.

538. Second, he gives the example of many things being related to one thing as an efficient principle. For one thing is called medical because it possesses the art of medicine, as the skilled physician. Another is called medical because it is naturally disposed to have the art of medicine, as men who are so disposed that they may acquire the art of medicine easily (and according to this some men [1] can engage in medical activities as a result of a peculiar natural constitution). And another is called medical or medicinal because it is necessary for healing, as the instruments which physicians use can be called medical. The same thing is also true of the things called medicines, which physicians use in restoring health. Other terms which resemble these in having many senses can be taken in a similar way.

539. And just as the above-mentioned terms have many senses, so also does the term being. Yet every being is called such in relation to one first thing, and this first thing is not an end or an efficient cause, as is the case in the foregoing examples, but a subject. For some things are called beings, or are said to be, because they have being of themselves, as substances, which are called beings in the primary and proper sense. Others are called beings because they are affections or properties of substances, as the proper accidents of any substance. Others are called beings because they are processes toward substance, as generation and motion. And others are called beings

[1] Reading *quidam* for *quaedam*.

218

because they are corruptions of sub-stances; for corruption is the process toward non-being just as generation is the process toward substance. And since corruption terminates in privation just as generation terminates in form, the very privations of substantial forms are fittingly called beings. Again, certain qualities or certain accidents are called beings because they are productive or generative principles of substances or of those things which are related to substance according to one of the fore-going relationships or any other rela-tionship. And similarly the negations of those things which are related to substances, or even substance itself, are also called beings. Hence we say that non-being *is* non-being. But this would not be possible unless a negation pos-sessed being in some way.

540. But it must be noted that the above-mentioned modes of being can be reduced to four. For one of them, which is the most imperfect, i.e., nega-tion and privation, exists only in the mind. We say that these exist in the mind because the mind busies itself with them as kinds of being while it affirms or denies something about them. In what respect negation and privation differ will be treated below (306:C 564).

541. There is another mode of being inasmuch as generation and corruption are called beings, and this mode by reason of its imperfection comes close to the one given above. For generation and corruption have some admixture of privation and negation, because motion is an imperfect kind of actuality, as is stated in the *Physics*, Book III.[2]

542. The third mode of being admits of no admixture of non-being, yet it is still an imperfect kind of being, because it does not exist of itself but in some-thing else, for example, qualities and quantities and the properties of sub-stances.

543. The fourth mode of being is the one which is most perfect, namely, what has being in reality without any admixture of privation, and has firm and solid being inasmuch as it exists of itself. This is the mode of being which substances have. Now all the others are reduced to this as the pri-mary and principal mode of being; for qualities and quantities are said to be inasmuch as they exist in substances; and motions and generations are said to be inasmuch as they are processes tending toward substance or toward some of the foregoing; and negations and privations are said to be inasmuch as they remove some part of the preced-ing three.

544. **Therefore, just as** (298).

Here he gives the major premise of the first argument. He says that it is the office of one science to study not only those things which are referred "to one thing," i.e., to one common notion, but also those which are re-ferred to one nature according to differ-ent relationships. And the reason for this is that the thing to which they are referred is one; just as it is clear that one science, medicine, considers all health-giving things. The same thing holds true of other things which are spoken of in the same way.

545. **It is evident** (299).

Then he draws his intended con-clusion. This is evident of itself.

546. **But in every** (299a).

Then he shows that this science, even though it considers all beings, is chiefly concerned with substances. He uses the following argument. Every science which deals with many things that are referred to one primary thing is properly and principally concerned with that primary thing on which other things depend for their being and from which they derive their name; and this is true in every case. But substance is the primary kind of being. Hence the

---

[2] *Physica*, III, 2 (201b 31).

philosopher who considers all beings ought to consider primarily and chiefly the principles and causes of substances. Therefore his consideration extends primarily and chiefly to substances.

547. **Now of every** (300).

Then he shows by the following argument that it is the business of the first philosopher to consider all substances. There is one sense and one science of all things belonging to one class; for example, sight is concerned with all colors, and grammar with all words. Therefore, if all beings somehow belong to one class, all species of being must belong to the consideration of one science which is a general science, and different species of being must belong to the different species of that science. He says this because it is not necessary for one science to consider all the species of one genus according to the special notes of every single species, but only inasmuch as they agree generically. But according to their specific notes the different species of one genus belong to the special sciences, as happens in the present case. For inasmuch as all substances are beings or substances, they belong to the consideration of this science; but inasmuch as they are a particular kind of substance, as a lion or an ox, they belong to the special sciences.

LESSON 2

This Science Considers Being and Unity. The Parts of Philosophy Based on the Divisions of Being and Unity

ARISTOTLE'S TEXT   Chapter 2: 1003b 22-1004a 9

301. Now although being and unity are the same and are a single nature in the sense that they are associated like principle and cause, they are not the same in the sense that they are expressed by a single concept. Yet it makes no difference even if we consider them to be the same; in fact this will rather support our undertaking.

302. For *one man* and *human being* and *man* are the same thing; and nothing different is expressed by repeating the terms when we say, "This is a human being, a man, and one man." And it is evident that they are not separated either in generation or in corruption. The same holds true of what is one. Hence it is evident that any addition to these expresses the same thing, and that unity is nothing else than being.

303. Further, the substance of each thing is one in no accidental way; and similarly it is something that is.

304. Hence there are as many species of being as there are of unity, of which it is the office of the same general science to treat. I mean, for example, sameness and likeness and other such attributes. And almost all contraries may be referred to this starting point. But these have been studied by us in our selection, i.e., in our explanation or treatment, of contraries.

305. And there are just as many parts of philosophy as there are substances, so that there must be a first philosophy and one which is next in order to it. For being and unity are things which straightway have genera; and for this reason the sciences will correspond to these. For the term *philosopher* is used like the term *mathematician;* for mathematics too has parts, and there is a first and a second science and then others [1] following these among the mathematical sciences.

[1] Reading *aliae* for *alia.*

COMMENTARY

548. Here he proceeds to show that the study of common attributes such as one and many and same and different belongs to the consideration of one and the same science; and in regard to this he does two things. First (301:C 548), he shows that this is true of each attribute taken separately by arguing from proper or specific principles. Second (310:C 570), he shows that this

is true of all attributes taken together by arguing from common principles ("And it is also evident").

In regard to the first he does two things. First, he shows that the philosopher ought to investigate all these attributes.[1] Second (308:C 568), he tells us how to investigate them ("Hence, since the term").

In regard to the first he does two things. First, he shows that it is the office of this science to consider unity and its species. Second (306:C 564), he shows that it is the office of one and the same science to consider all opposites ("Now since").

In regard to the first he does two things. First, he shows that it is the office of this science to consider unity. Second (304:C 561), he shows that it also belongs to it to examine the species of unity ("Hence there are").

He therefore says, first (301), that being and unity are the same and are a single nature. He says this because some things are numerically the same which are not a single nature but different natures, for example, Socrates, this white thing, and this musician. Now the terms *one* and *being* do not signify different natures but a single nature. But things can be one in two ways; for some things are one which are associated as interchangeable things, like principle and cause; and some are interchangeable not only in the sense that they are one and the same numerically [or in subject] but also in the sense that they are one and the same conceptually, like garment and clothing.

549. Now the terms one and being signify one nature according to different concepts, and therefore they are like the terms principle and cause, and not like the terms tunic and garment, which are wholly synonymous.—Yet it makes no difference to his thesis if we consider them to be used in the same sense, as those things which are one both numerically and conceptually. In fact this will "rather support our undertaking," i.e., it will serve his purpose better; for he intends to prove that unity and being belong to the same study, and that the species of the one correspond to those of the other. The proof of this would be clearer if unity and being were the same both numerically and conceptually rather than just numerically and not conceptually.

550. He proves that they are the same numerically by using two arguments. He gives the first where he says, "For one man," and it runs as follows. Any two things which when added to some third thing cause no difference are wholly the same. But when one and being are added to man or to anything at all, they cause no difference. Therefore they are wholly the same. The truth of the minor premise is evident; for it is the same thing to say "man" and "one man." And similarly it is the same thing to say "human being" and "the thing that is man;" and nothing different is expressed when in speaking we repeat the terms, saying, "This is a human being, a man, and one man." He proves this as follows.

551. It is the same thing for man and the thing that is man to be generated and corrupted. This is evident from the fact that generation is a process toward being, and corruption a change from being to non-being. Hence a man is never generated without a human being being generated, nor is a man ever corrupted without a human being being corrupted; and those things which are generated and corrupted together are themselves one and the same.

552. And just as it has been said that being and man are not separated either in generation or in corruption,

---

[1] For *hic* reading *his,* with former Cathala edition.

so too this is evident of what is one; for when a man is generated, one man is generated, and when a man is corrupted, one man is also corrupted. It is clear, then, that the apposition of these [i.e., of one or being to man] expresses the same thing, and that just because the term one or being is added to man it is not to be understood that some nature is added to man. And from this it is clearly apparent that unity does not differ from being, because any two things which are identical with some third thing are identical with each other.

553. It is also evident from the foregoing argument that unity and being are the same numerically but differ conceptually; for if this were not the case they would be wholly synonymous, and then it would be nonsense to say, "a human being," and "one man." For it must be borne in mind that the term *man* is derived from the quiddity or the nature of man, and the term *thing* from the quiddity only; but the term *being* is derived from the act of being, and the term *one* from order or lack of division; for what is one is an undivided being. Now what has an essence, and a quiddity by reason of that essence, and what is undivided in itself, are the same. Hence these three—thing, being, and one—signify absolutely the same thing but according to different concepts.

554. **Further, the substance** (303).

Then he gives the second argument, which has to do with sameness or identity of subject. This argument is as follows. Any two attributes which are predicated essentially and not accidentally of the substance of each thing are the same in subject, or numerically. But unity and being are such that they are predicated essentially and not accidentally of the substance of each thing; for the substance of a thing is one in itself and not accidentally. Therefore

the terms being and one signify the same thing in subject.

555. That the terms being and one are predicated essentially and not accidentally of the substance of each thing can be proved as follows. If being and one were predicated of the substance of each thing by reason of something added to it [i.e., accidentally], being would have to be predicated also of the thing added, because anything at all is one and a being. But then there would be the question whether being is predicated of this thing (the one added) either essentially or by reason of some other thing that is added to it in turn. And if the latter were the case, then the same question would arise once again regarding the last thing added, and so on to infinity. But this is impossible. Hence the first position must be held, namely, that a thing's substance is one and a being of itself and not by reason of something added to it.

556. But it must be noted that Avicenna felt differently about this; for he said [2] that the terms being and one do not signify a thing's substance but something added to it. He said this of being because, in the case of anything that derives its existence from something else, the existence of such a thing must differ from its substance or essence. But the term being signifies existence itself. Hence it seems that being, or existence, is something added to a thing's essence.

557. He spoke in the same way of one, because he thought that the one which is interchangeable with being and the one which is the principle of number are the same. And the one which is the principle of number must signify a reality added to the substance, otherwise number, since it is composed of ones, would not be a species of quantity, which is an accident added to substance. He said that this kind of one

[2] *Metaphysica*, III, 3 (79rab); I, 2 (70vb).

is interchangeable with being, not in the sense that it signifies the very substance of a thing or being, but in the sense that it signifies an accident belonging to every being, just as the ability to laugh belongs to every man.

558. But in regard to the first point he does not seem to be right; for even though a thing's existence is other than its essence, it should not be understood to be something added to its essence after the manner of an accident, but something established, as it were, by the principles of the essence. Hence the term being, which is applied to a thing by reason of its very existence, designates the same thing as the term which is applied to it by reason of its essence.

559. Nor does it seem to be true that the one or unity which is interchangeable with being and that which is the principle of number are the same; for nothing that pertains to some special class of being seems to be characteristic of all beings. Hence the unity which is limited to a special class of being—discrete quantity—does not seem to be interchangeable with universal being. For, if unity is a proper and essential accident of being, it must be caused by the principles of being as being, just as any proper accident is caused by the principles of its subject. But it is not reasonable that something having a particular mode of being should be adequately accounted for by the common principles of being as being. It cannot be true, then, that something which belongs to a definite genus and species is an accident of every being.

560. Therefore the kind of unity which is the principle of number differs from that which is interchangeable with being; for the unity which is interchangeable with being signifies being itself, adding to it the notion of undividedness, which, since it is a negation or a privation, does not posit any reality added to being. Thus unity differs from being in no way numeri-cally but only conceptually; for a negation or a privation is not a real being but a being of reason, as has been stated (297:C 540). However, the kind of unity which is the principle of number adds to substance the note of a measure, which is a special property of quantity and is found first in the unit. And it is described as the privation or negation of division which pertains to continuous quantity; for number is produced by dividing the continuous. Hence number belongs to mathematical science, whose subject cannot exist apart from sensible matter but can be considered apart from sensible matter. But this would not be so if the kind of unity which is the principle of number were separate from matter in being and existed among the immaterial substances, as is true of the kind of unity which is interchangeable with being.

561. **Hence there are** (304).

Then he concludes that it is the business of the philosopher to consider the parts of unity, just as it is to consider the parts of being. First, he proves this; and second (305:C 563), he shows that there are different parts of philosophy corresponding to the different parts of being and unity ("And there are").

He says, first (304), that since being and unity signify the same thing, and the species of things that are the same are themselves the same, there must be as many species of being as there are of unity, and they must correspond to each other. For just as the parts of being are substance, quantity, quality, and so on, in a similar way the parts of unity are sameness, equality and likeness. For things are the same when they are one in substance, equal when they are one in quantity, and like when they are one in quality. And the other parts of unity could be taken from the other parts of being, if they were given names. And just as it is the office of one science, philosophy, to consider all parts of being, in a similar way it is the office of this same science to consider all parts of unity, i.e., sameness, likeness and so forth. And to this "starting point," i.e., unity, "almost" all contraries may be referred.

562. He adds this qualification because in some cases this point is not so evident. Yet it must be true; for since one member of every pair of contraries involves privation, they must be referred back to certain primary privatives, among which unity is the most basic. And plurality, which stems from unity, is the cause of otherness, difference and contrariety, as will be stated below. He says that this has been treated "in our selection," or extract, "of contraries," i.e., a treatise which is the part selected to deal with contraries, namely, Book X (836-40:C 2000-21) of this work.

563. **And there are** (305).

Here he shows that the parts of philosophy are distinguished in reference to the parts of being and unity. He says that there are as many parts of philosophy as there are parts of substance, of which being and unity chiefly are predicated, and of which it is the principal intention or aim of this science to treat. And because the parts of substance are related to each other in a

certain order, for immaterial substance is naturally prior to sensible substance, then among the parts of philosophy there must be a first part. Now that part which is concerned with sensible substance is first in the order of instruction, because any branch of learning must start with things which are better known to us. He treats of this part in Books VII (577:C 1300) and VIII [3] of this work. But that part which has to do with immaterial substance is prior both in dignity and in the aim of this science. This part is treated in Book XII (1055:C 2488) of this work. Yet whatever parts are first must be continuous with the others, because all parts have unity and being as their genus. Hence all parts of this science are united in the study of being and unity, although they are about different parts of substance. Thus it is one science inasmuch as the foregoing parts are things which correspond to "these," [4] i.e., to unity and being, as common attributes of substance. In this respect the philosopher resembles the mathematician; for mathematical science has different parts, one of which is primary, as arithmetic, another secondary, as geometry, and others [5] following these in order, as optics, astronomy and music.

---

[3] I.e., the general development in Book VIII.
[4] Reading *haec* for *hoc*.
[5] Reading *aliae* for *alia*.

LESSON 3

The Same Science Considers Unity and Plurality and All Opposites. The Method of Treating These

ARISTOTLE'S TEXT   Chapter 2: 1004a 9-1004a 34

306. Now since it is the office of a single science to study opposites, and plurality is the opposite of unity, it is also the office of a single science to study negation and privation, because in both cases we are studying the unity of which there is negation or privation. And this (negation or privation) is what is stated either absolutely because an attribute is not present in a thing or (not absolutely) because it is not present in some determinate class. Therefore this difference is present in unity over and above what is implied in negation; for negation is the absence of the thing in question. But in the case of privation there is an underlying subject of which the privation is predicated.

307. But plurality is the opposite of unity.[1] Hence the opposites of the above-mentioned concepts, otherness, unlikeness, and inequality, and any others which are referred to plurality or unity, must come within the scope of the science mentioned above. And contrariety is one of these; for contrariety is a kind of difference, and difference is a kind of otherness.

308. Hence, since the term *one* is used in many senses,[2] the terms designating the foregoing opposites will also be used in many senses. Yet it is the business of one science to know them all. For even if some term is used in many senses, it does not therefore follow that it belongs to another science. Hence if terms are not used with one meaning, and their concepts are not referred to one thing, then it is the office of a different science to study them. But since all things are referred to some primary thing, as all things which are one are referred to a primary one, the same thing must hold true of sameness, otherness, and the contraries. It is necessary, then to distinguish all the senses in which each term is used and then refer them back to the primary thing signified in each of the predicates in question to see how each is related to it. For one thing is given a particular predicate because it possesses it, another because it produces it, and others in other ways.

309. Hence it is evident, as has been stated in our problems, that it is the office of a single science to give an account of these predicates as well as of substance; and this was one of the problems (181:C 346; 202:C 393).

[1] See Book X (868:C 2075).
[2] See Book V (423:C 842).

COMMENTARY

564. Here he shows that it is the office of this science to consider opposites; and in regard to this he does two things. First (306:C 564), he shows that it is the office of this science to consider privation and negation; and second (307:C 567), to consider contraries ("But plurality").

He accordingly says (306) that, since it pertains to one science to consider opposites (for example, it belongs to medicine to consider health and sickness, and to grammar to consider agreement and disagreement), and since plurality is the opposite of unity, the study of privation and negation must belong to that science which deals with unity and plurality. For the consideration "of both" involves unity; that is, the study of unity, whose concept entails negation and privation, depends on both of these. For, as has been said above (302:C 553), what is one is an undivided being, and division relates to plurality, which is the opposite of unity. Hence the study of negation and privation belongs to that science whose business it is to consider unity.

565. Now there are two kinds of negation: simple negation, by which one thing is said absolutely not to be present in something else, and negation in a genus, by which something is denied of something else, not absolutely, but within the limits of some determinate genus. For example, not everything that does not have sight is said absolutely to be blind, but something within the genus of an animal which is naturally fitted to have sight. And this difference is present in unity over and above "what is implied in negation"; i.e., it is something by which it differs

from negation, because negation expresses only the absence of something, namely, what it removes, without stating a determinate subject. Hence simple negation can be verified both of a non-being, which is not[1] naturally fitted to have something affirmed of it, and of a being which is naturally fitted to have something affirmed of it and does not. For *unseeing* can be predicated both of a chimera and of a stone and of a man. But in the case of privation there is a determinate nature or substance of which the privation is predicated; for not everything that does not have sight can be said to be blind, but only that which is naturally fitted to have sight. Thus since the negation which is included in the concept of unity is a negation in a subject (otherwise a non-being could be called one), it is evident that unity differs from simple negation and rather resembles the nature of privation, as is stated below in Book X (865:C 2069) of this work.

566. But it must be noted that, although unity includes an implied privation, it must not be said to include the privation of plurality; for, since a privation is subsequent in nature to the thing of which it is the privation, it would follow that unity would be subsequent in nature to plurality. And it would also follow that plurality would be given in the definition of unity; for a privation can be defined only by its opposite. For example, if someone were to ask what blindness is, we would answer that it is the privation of sight. Hence, since unity is given in the definition of plurality (for plurality is an aggregate of units), it would follow that there would be circularity

---

[1] Reading *quod non est natum habere* (with the sense of the text) for *quod est natum habere*.

in definitions. Hence it must be said that unity includes the privation of division, although not the kind of division that belongs to quantity; for this kind of division is limited to one particular class of being and cannot be included in the definition of unity. But the unity which is interchangeable with being implies the privation of formal division, which comes about through opposites, and whose primary root is the opposition between affirmation and negation. For those things are divided from each other which are of such a kind that one is not the other. Therefore being itself is understood first, and then non-being, and then division, and then the kind of unity which is the privation of division, and then plurality, whose concept includes the notion of division just as the concept of unity includes the notion of undividedness. However, some of the things that have been distinguished in the foregoing way can be said to include the notion of plurality only if the notion of unity is first attributed to each of the things distinguished.

567. **But plurality** (307).

Here he shows that it is the business of the philosopher to consider contraries, or opposites; for plurality is the opposite of unity, as has been said (306:C 564), and it is the office of one science to consider opposites. Hence, since this science considers unity, sameness, likeness and equality, it must also consider their opposites, plurality, otherness or diversity, unlikeness and inequality, and all other attributes which are reduced to these or even to unity and plurality. And contrariety is one of these; for contrariety is a kind of difference, namely, of things differing in the same genus. But difference is a kind of otherness or diversity, as is said in Book X (840:C 2017). Therefore contrariety belongs to the consideration of this science.

568. **Hence, since** (308).

Then he deals with the method by which the philosopher ought to establish these things. He says that, since all of the above-mentioned opposites are derived from unity, and the term one is used in many senses, all of the terms designating these must also be used in many senses, i.e., *same, other,* and so on. Yet even though all of these are used in many senses, it is still the work of one science, philosophy, to know the things signified by each of these terms. For if some term is used in many senses, it does not therefore follow that it belongs to another or different science. For if the different things signified are not referred to "with one meaning," or according to one concept, i.e., univocally, or are not referred to one thing in different ways, as in the case of analogous things, then it follows that it is the office of another, i.e., of a different, science, to consider them; or at least it is the office of one science accidentally, just as astronomy considers a star in the heavens, i.e., the dog star, and natural science considers a dog-fish and a dog.—But all of these are referred to one starting point. For things signified by the term one, even though diverse, are referred back to a primary thing signified as one; and we must also speak in the same way of the terms same, other, contrary, and others of this kind. Regarding each of these terms, then, the philosopher should do two things. First, he should distinguish the many senses in which each may be used; and second, he should determine regarding "each of the predicates," i.e., each of the names predicated of many things, to what primary thing it is referred. For example, he should state what the first thing signified by the term same or other is, and how all the rest are referred to it; one inasmuch as it possesses it, another inasmuch as it produces it, or in other ways of this kind.

569. **Hence it is evident** (309).

He draws his conclusion from what has been said, namely, that it belongs to this science to reason about these common predicates and about substance; and this was one of the problems investigated in the questions treated dialectically in Book III (181:C 346; 202:C 393).

LESSON 4

First Philosophy Considers All Contraries. Its Distinction from Logic

ARISTOTLE'S TEXT   Chapter 2: 1004a 34-1005a 18

310. And it is also evident that it is the function of the philosopher to be able to study all things. For if it is not the function of the philosopher, who is it that will investigate whether Socrates and Socrates sitting are the same person, or whether one thing has one contrary, or what a contrary is, or how many meanings it has? And the same applies to other questions of this kind. Therefore, since these same things are the essential properties of unity as unity and of being as being, but not as numbers or lines or fire, evidently it is the office of this science to know both the quiddities of these and their accidents. Therefore those who have been studying these things do not err by being unphilosophical, but because substance, to which they pay no attention, is first. Now there are properties of number as number, for example, oddness and evenness, commensurability and equality, excess and defect, and these belong to numbers either in themselves or in relation to one another. And similarly there are properties of the solid, and of what is changeable and what is unchangeable, and of what is heavy and what is light. And in a similar fashion there are properties of being as being; and these are the ones about which the philosopher has to investigate the truth.

311. An indication of this is the following. Dialecticians and sophists assume the same guise as the philosopher, for sophistry [1] is apparent wisdom, and dialecticians dispute about all things, and being is common to all things. But evidently they dispute about these matters because they are common to philosophy.[2] For sophistry and dialectics are concerned with the same class of things as philosophy.

312. But philosophy differs from the latter in the manner of its power, and from the former in the choice, i.e., selection, of a way of life. For [3] dialectics is in search of knowledge of what the philosopher actually knows, and sophistry has the semblance of wisdom but is not really such.

313. Further, one corresponding member of each pair of contraries is privative, and all contraries are referred to being and to non-being and to unity and to plurality; for example, rest pertains to unity and motion to plurality.

314. And almost all men admit that substance and beings are composed of contraries; for all say that principles are contraries. For some speak of the odd and even, others of the hot and cold, others of the limited and unlimited, and others of love and hate.

315. And all the other contraries seem to be reducible to unity and plurality. Therefore let us take that reduction for granted. And all the principles which have to do with other things [4] fall under unity and being as their genera.

---

[1] Reading *sophistica* (with Greek) for *sophistae*.
[2] Reading *philosophiae* for *sophistae.*   [3] Reading *enim* for *autem*.
[4] To conform with the Greek text the Latin version should read: *Principia vero et omnia quae ab aliis* (i.e., "And all principles which are given by other thinkers . . .") in place of *Principia*

316. It is clear from these discussions, then, that it is the office of one science to study being as being. For all beings are either contraries or composed of contraries, and the principles of contraries are unity and plurality. And these belong to one science, whether they are used in one sense or not. And perhaps the truth is that they are not. Yet even if the term one is used in many senses, all will be referred to one primary sense; and the same is true of contraries. Hence, even if unity or being is not a universal and the same in all things or is something separate (as presumably it is not), still in some cases the thing will be referred to unity and in others it will be referred to what follows on unity.

317. And for this reason it is not the province of geometry to examine what a contrary is, or what the perfect is, or what unity is, or what sameness or otherness is, but to assume them.

318. It is evident, then, that it is the office of one science to study both being as being and the attributes which belong to being as being. And it is evident too that the same science studies not only substances but also their accidents, both those mentioned above, and *prior* and *subsequent, genus* and *species, whole* and *part,* and others such as these.

vero et omnia quae de aliis. St. Thomas follows the Latin text as given in the Cathala-Spiazzi edition; see C 583.

COMMENTARY

570. Here he uses arguments based on common principles to prove what the philosopher ought to consider regarding all of the foregoing attributes. First (310:C 570), he proves his thesis; and second (318:C 587), he introduces his intended conclusion ("It is evident").

In regard to the first part he does two things. First, he proves his thesis; and second (317:C 586), he draws a corollary from what has been said ("And for this reason").

He gives three arguments to prove his thesis. The second (311:C 572) begins where he says, "An indication of this"; and the third (313:C 578), at "Further, one corresponding."

The first argument (310) is as follows. All questions that can be raised must be answered by some science. But questions are raised about the common attributes mentioned above, for example, that raised about sameness and otherness: whether Socrates and Socrates sitting are the same; and that

raised about contraries: whether one thing has one contrary, and how many meanings the term contrary has. Hence these questions must be answered by some science which considers sameness and contrariety and the other attributes mentioned above.

571. That this is the job of the philosopher and of no one else he proves thus: that science whose office is to consider being as being is the one which must consider the first properties of being. But all of the above-mentioned attributes are proper accidents of unity and being as such. For number as number has properties, such as excess, equality, commensurability, and so on, some of which belong to a number taken absolutely, as even and odd, and some to one number in relation to another, as equality. And even substance has proper attributes, "as the resistant," or body, and others of this kind. And in a similar way being as being has certain properties, which are the com-

mon attributes mentioned above; and therefore the study of them belongs to the philosopher. Hence those dealing with philosophy have not erred in their treatment of these things "by being unphilosophical," i.e., by considering them in a way that does not pertain to the investigations of philosophy, but because in treating them they pay no attention to substance, as though they were completely unmindful of it despite the fact that it is the first thing which the philosopher ought to consider.

572. **An indication** (311).

Then he gives a second argument to prove the same point. This argument employs an example and runs thus: dialecticians and sophists assume the same guise as the philosopher inasmuch as they resemble him in some respect. But the dialectician and sophist dispute about the above-mentioned attributes. Therefore the philosopher should also consider them. In support of his first premise he shows how dialectics and sophistry resemble philosophy and how they differ from it.

573. Dialectics resembles philosophy in that it is also the office of the dialectician to consider all things. But this could not be the case unless he considered all things insofar as they agree in some one respect; because each science has one subject, and each art has one matter on which it operates. Therefore, since all things agree only in being, evidently the subject matter of dialectics is being and those attributes which belong to being; and this is what the philosopher also investigates. And sophistry likewise resembles philosophy; for sophistry has "the semblance of wisdom," or is apparent wisdom, without being wisdom. Now anything that takes on the appearance of something else must resemble it in some way. Therefore the philosopher, the dialectician and the sophist must consider the same thing.

574. Yet they differ from each other. The philosopher differs from the dialectician in power, because the consideration of the philosopher is more efficacious than that of the dialectician. For the philosopher proceeds demonstratively in dealing with the common attributes mentioned above, and thus it is proper to him to have scientific knowledge of these attributes. And he actually knows them with certitude, for certain or scientific knowledge is the effect of demonstration. The dialectician, however, proceeds to treat all of the above-mentioned common attributes from probable premises, and thus he does not acquire scientific knowledge of them but a kind of opinion. The reason for this difference is that there are two kinds of beings: beings of reason and real beings. The expression *being of reason* is applied properly to those notions which reason derives from the objects it considers, for example, the notions of genus, species and the like, which are not found in reality but are a natural result of the consideration of reason. And this kind of being, i.e., being of reason, constitutes the proper subject of logic. But intellectual conceptions of this kind are equal in extension to real beings, because all real beings fall under the consideration of reason. Hence the subject of logic extends to all things to which the expression *real being* is applied. His conclusion is, then, that the subject of logic is equal in extension to the subject of philosophy, which is real being. Now the philosopher proceeds from the principles of this kind of being to prove the things that have to be considered about the common accidents of this kind of being. But the dialectician proceeds to consider them from the conceptions of reason, which are extrinsic to reality. Hence it is said that dialectics is in search of knowledge, because in searching it is proper to proceed from extrinsic principles.

575. But the philosopher differs from the sophist "in the choice," i.e., in the selection or willing,[1] or in the desire, of a way of life. For the philosopher and sophist direct their life and actions to different things. The philosopher directs his to knowing the truth, whereas the sophist directs his so as to appear to know what he does not.

576. Now although it is said that philosophy is scientific knowledge, and that dialectics and sophistry are not, this still does not do away with the possibility of dialectics and sophistry being sciences. For dialectics can be considered both from the viewpoint of theory and from that of practice. From the viewpoint of theory it studies these conceptions and establishes the method by which one proceeds from them to demonstrate with probability the conclusions of the particular sciences; and it does this demonstratively, and to this extent it is a science. But from the viewpoint of practice it makes use of the above method so as to reach certain probable conclusions in the particular sciences; and in this respect it falls short of the scientific method. The same must be said of sophistry, because from the viewpoint of theory it treats by means of necessary and demonstrative arguments the method of arguing to apparent truth. From the viewpoint of practice, however, it falls short of the process of true argumentation.

577. But that part of logic which is said to be demonstrative is concerned only with theory, and the practical application of it belongs to philosophy and to the other particular sciences, which are concerned with real beings. This is because the practical aspect of the demonstrative part of logic consists in using the principles of things, from which proceeds demonstration (which properly belongs to the sciences that deal with real beings), and not in using the conceptions of logic. Thus it appears that some parts of logic are at the same time scientific, theoretical, and practical, as exploratory dialectics and sophistry; and one is concerned with theory and not practice, namely, demonstrative logic.

578. **Further, one corresponding** (313).
Then he gives the third argument in support of his thesis. It runs as follows: everything that is reducible to unity and being should be considered by the philosopher, whose function is to study unity and being. But all contraries are reducible to unity and being. Therefore all contraries belong to the consideration of the philosopher, whose function is to study unity and being.

579. Then he proves that all contraries are reducible to unity and being. He does this, first, with regard to being; and he proceeds thus: of any two contraries which the philosophers posited as the principles of things, as is said in Book I (62:C 132), one contrary is always the correlative of the other and is related to it as its privation. This is clear from the fact that one of two contraries is always something imperfect when compared with the other, and thus implies some privation of the perfection of the other. But a privation is a kind of negation, as was stated above (306:C 564), and thus is a non-being. Hence it is clear that all contraries are reducible to being and non-being.

580. He also shows by an example that all contraries are reducible to unity and plurality. For rest or repose is reducible to unity, since that is said to be at rest which is in the same condition now as it was before, as is stated in Book VI of the *Physics*.[2] And motion is reducible to plurality, because

[1] Reading *voluntate* for *voluptate*.
[2] *Physica*, VI, 3 (234b 5).

whatever is in motion is in a different condition now than it was before, and this implies plurality.

581. **And almost all** (314).

Then he uses another argument to show that contraries are reducible to being. Both the principles of things and the things composed of them belong to the same study. But the philosophers admit that contraries are the principles of being as being; for all say that beings and the substances of beings are composed of contraries, as was stated in Book I of the *Physics*[3] and in the first book of this work (62:C 132). Yet while they agree on this point, that the principles of beings are contraries, still they differ as to the contraries which they give. For some give the even and odd, as the Pythagoreans; others the hot and cold, as Parmenides; others "the end" or terminus "and the unlimited," i.e., the finite and infinite, as did the same Pythagoreans (for they attributed limitedness and unlimitedness to the even and the odd, as is stated in Book I (59:C 124); and still others gave friendship and strife, as Empedocles. Hence it is clear that contraries are reducible to the study of being.

582. **And all the other** (315).

He says that the above-mentioned contraries are reducible not only to being but also to unity and plurality. This is evident. For oddness by reason of its indivisibility is affiliated with unity, and evenness by reason of its divisibility has a natural connection with plurality. Thus end or limit pertains to unity, which is the terminus of every process of resolution, and lack of limit pertains to plurality, which may be increased to infinity. Again, friendship also clearly pertains to unity, and strife to plurality. And heat pertains to unity inasmuch as it can unite homogeneous things, whereas cold pertains to plurality inasmuch as it can

separate them. Further, not only these contraries are reducible in this way to unity and plurality, but so also are the others. Yet this "reduction," or introduction, to unity and plurality let us now accept or "take for granted," i.e., let us now assume it, because to examine each set of contraries would be a lengthy undertaking.

583. Next he shows that all contraries are reducible to unity and being. For it is certain that all principles, inasmuch as they have to do "with other things," i.e., the things composed of them, fall under unity and being as their genera, not in the sense that they truly are genera, but in the sense that they bear some likeness to genera by reason of what they have in common. Hence, if all contraries are principles or things composed of principles, they must be reducible to unity and being.— Thus it is clear that he shows that contraries are reducible to being for two reasons: first, because of the nature of privation, and second, by reason of the fact that contraries are principles. He shows that they are reducible to unity by giving an example and by using a process of reduction. Last, he shows that they are reducible to unity and being inasmuch as they have the character of genera.

584. **It is clear** (316).

Here he proves in a converse way that this science considers being because it considers the things mentioned above. His argument is this: all beings are reducible to contraries because they are either contraries or composed of contraries. And contraries are reducible to unity and plurality because unity and plurality are the principles of contraries. But unity and plurality belong to one science, philosophy. Therefore it is the office of this science to consider being as being. Yet it must be noted that all the contraries mentioned above fall under the consideration of

---

[3] *Physica*, I, 5 (188a 19).

one science whether they are used "in one sense," i.e., univocally, or not, as perhaps is the case. However, even if the term one is used in many senses, all the others, i.e., all the other senses, are reducible to one primary sense. Hence, even if unity or being is not one universal, like a genus, as was stated above (whether a universal is said to be a one-in-all, as we maintain, or something separate from things, as Plato thought, and as is presumably not the case), still each is used in a primary and a secondary sense. And the same holds true in the case of other terms, for some senses are referred to one primary sense, and others are secondary with respect to that primary sense. An adverb designating uncertainty is used inasmuch as we are now assuming things that will be proved below.

585. But nevertheless it must be borne in mind that the statement which he made, that all beings are either contraries or composed of contraries, he did not give as his own opinion but as one which he took from the ancient philosophers; for unchangeable beings are not contraries or composed of contraries. And this is why Plato did not posit any contrariety in the unchangeable sensible substances; for he attributed unity to form and contrariety to matter. But the ancient philosophers claimed that only sensible substances exist and that these must contain contrariety inasmuch as they are changeable.

586. **And for this reason** (317).

Then he draws a corollary from what

has been said. He says that it is not the province of geometry to investigate the foregoing things, which are accidents of being as being, i.e., to investigate what a contrary is, or what the perfect is, and so on. But if a geometer were to consider them, he would "assume them," i.e., presuppose their truth, inasmuch as he would take them over from some prior philosopher from whom he accepts them insofar as they are necessary for his own subject matter. What is said about geometry must be understood to apply also in the case of any other particular science.

587. **It is evident** (318).

He now summarizes the points established above. He says that obviously the consideration of being as being and the attributes which belong to it of itself pertain to one science. Thus it is clear that that science considers not only substances but also accidents since being is predicated of both. And it considers the things which have been discussed, namely, sameness and otherness, likeness and unlikeness, equality and inequality, privation and negation, and contraries—which we said above are the proper accidents of being. And it considers not only those things which fall under the consideration of this science, about which demonstration was made individually by means of arguments based on proper principles, but it in like manner also considers prior and subsequent, genus and species, whole and part, and other things of this kind, because these too are accidents of being as being.

LESSON 5

Answers to Questions Raised in Book III about Principles of Demonstration

ARISTOTLE'S TEXT   Chapter 3: 1005a 19-1005b 8

319. Moreover, it is necessary to state whether it is the office of one science or of different sciences to inquire about those principles which are called axioms in mathematics, and about substance.

320. Now it is evident that it is the office of one science—that of the philosopher—to investigate these.

321. For these principles apply to all beings and not to some class distinct from the others. And all men employ them, because they pertain to being as being; for each class is being. But they employ them just so far as to satisfy their needs, i.e., so far as the class contains the things about which they form demonstrations. Hence, since it is evident that these principles pertain to all things inasmuch as they are beings (for this is what they have in common), the investigation of them belongs to him who considers being as being.

322. Hence no one who is making a special inquiry attempts to say anything about their truth or falsity, neither the geometer nor the arithmetician.

323. However, some of the philosophers of nature have done this, and with reason; for they thought that they alone were inquiring about the whole of nature and about being. But since there is one kind of thinker who is superior to the philosopher of nature (for nature is only one class of being), the investigation of these principles will belong to him who studies the universal and deals with first substance. The philosophy of nature is a kind of wisdom, but it is not the first.

324. And whatever certain ones of [1] those who speak about the truth attempt to say concerning the way in which it must be accepted, they do this through ignorance of analytics. For they must know these principles in order to attain scientific knowledge and not be seeking them when they are learning a science.

325. It is evident, then, that it is also the business of the philosopher, i.e., of him who investigates all substance insofar as its nature permits, to investigate all syllogistic principles.

[1] Reading *quaecumque . . . quidam* (with the Greek and St. Thomas) for *quicumque*.

COMMENTARY

588. Here he answers another question raised in Book III (198:C 387): whether it belongs to this science to consider the first principles of demonstration. This is divided into two parts. In the first (319:C 588) he shows that

it belongs to this science to make a general study of all these principles; and in the second (326:C 596) he shows that it also belongs to it to make a special study of the first of these principles ("And it is fitting").

In regard to the first he does three things. First, he raises the question whether it belongs to one or to different sciences to consider substance and the principles which are called axioms in the mathematical sciences. He assigns these principles more to the mathematical sciences because such sciences have more certain demonstrations and use these self-evident principles in a more manifest way inasmuch as they refer all of their demonstrations to them.

589. **Now it is evident** (320).

Second, he answers this question by saying that a single science investigates both of the foregoing things, and that this is the philosophy with which we are now concerned.

590. **For these principles** (321).

Third, he proves his proposed answer, and in regard to this he does two things. First (321:C 590), he proves it. Second (325:C 595), he introduces his main conclusion ("It is evident").

Now he proves his proposed answer in two ways. He does this, first, by an argument; and second (322:C 592), by an example ("Hence no one").

The argument is as follows: whatever principles pertain to all beings, and not just to one class of beings distinct from the others, belong to the consideration of the philosopher. But the above-mentioned principles are of this kind. Therefore they belong to the consideration of the philosopher. He proves the minor premise as follows. Those principles which all sciences use pertain to being as being. But first principles are principles of this kind. Therefore they pertain to being as being.

591. The reason which he gives for saying that all sciences use these principles is that the subject genus of each science has being predicated of it. Now the particular sciences do not use the foregoing principles insofar as they are common principles, i.e., as extending to all beings, but insofar as they have need of them; that is, insofar as they extend to the things contained in the class of beings which constitutes the subject of a particular science, about which it makes demonstrations. For example, the philosophy of nature uses them insofar as they extend to changeable beings and no further.

592. **Hence no one** (322).

Then he proves what he had said by using an example. First, he introduces the proof; and second (323:C 593), he rejects a false notion held by some men ("However, some").

He accordingly says, first (322), that no one whose chief intention is to hand down scientific knowledge of some particular being has attempted to say anything about the truth or falsity of first principles. Neither the geometer nor the arithmetician does this even though they make the greatest use of these principles, as was said above (319:C 588). Hence it is evident that the investigation of these principles belongs to this science.

593. **However, some** (323).

Here he rejects the false notion held by some men, and in regard to this he does two things. First, he rejects the false notion of those who occupied themselves with these principles even though they did not concern them. Second, (324:C 594), he rejects the false notion of those who wanted to deal with these principles in a different way than they should be dealt with ("And whatever").

He accordingly says, first (323), that even though none of the particular sciences ought to deal with the above-mentioned principles, nevertheless some of the natural philosophers have dealt with them; and they did so not without reason. For the ancients did not think that there was any substance besides the changeable corporeal substance with which the philosophy of nature is concerned. Hence they believed that they alone established the truth about the whole of nature and therefore about being, and thus about first principles, which must be considered along with being. But this is false, because there is still a science which is superior to the science of nature. For nature itself, i.e., natural being, which has its own principle of motion, constitutes in itself one class of universal being. But not every being is of this kind, because it has been proved in the *Physics,* Book VIII,[1] that an unchangeable being exists. Now this unchangeable being is superior to and nobler than changeable being, with which the philosophy of nature is concerned. And since the consideration of common being belongs to that science which studies the primary kind of being, then the consideration of common being belongs to a different science than the philosophy of nature. And the consideration of common principles of this kind will also belong to this science. For the philosophy of nature is a part of philosophy but not the first part, which considers common being and those attributes which belong to being as being.

594 **And whatever** (324).

Then he rejects the other false notion, which concerns the way in which such principles should be treated. For some men investigated these principles with the aim of demonstrating them. And whatever they said about the truth of these principles, i.e., how they must be accepted as true by force of demonstration, or how the truth found

in all these principles must be reached, they did through ignorance of, or lack of skill in, "analytics," which is that part of logic in which the art of demonstration is treated.[2] For "they must know these principles in order to attain scientific knowledge"; i.e., every science acquired by demonstration depends on these principles. But "those who are learning," i.e., the pupils who are being instructed in some science, must not seek these principles as something to be demonstrated. Or, according to another text, "those who have scientific knowledge must attain science from these principles"; i.e., those who attain knowledge by demonstration must come to know common principles of this kind and not ask that they be demonstrated to them.

595. **It is evident** (325).

He draws the conclusion primarily intended, namely, that it will be the function of the philosopher to consider every substance as such and also the first syllogistic principles. In order to make this clear it must be noted that self-evident propositions are those which are known as soon as their terms are known, as is stated in Book I of the *Posterior Analytics*.[3] This occurs in the case of those propositions in which the predicate is given in the definition of the subject, or is the same as the subject. But it happens that one kind of proposition, even though it is self-evident in itself, is still not self-evident to all, i.e., to those who are ignorant of the definition of both the subject and the predicate. Hence Boethius says in the *Hebdomads*[4] that there are some propositions which are self-evident to the learned but not to all. Now those are self-evident to all whose terms are comprehended by all. And common

[1] *Physica,* VIII, 5 (256a 3 ff.).
[2] I.e., the *Prior Analytics* and *Posterior Analytics,* in which Aristotle treats the form and matter of demonstration.
[3] *Analytica Posteriora,* I, 3 (72b 18).
[4] *De Hebdomadibus* (i.e., *Quomodo Substantiae*) (PL 64, 1311).

238

principles are of this kind, because our knowledge proceeds from common principles to proper ones, as is said in Book I of the *Physics*.[5] Hence those propositions which are composed of such common terms as whole and part (for example, every whole is greater than one of its parts) and of such terms as equal and unequal (for example, things equal to one and the same thing are equal to each other), constitute the first principles of demonstration. And the same is true of similar terms. Now since common terms of this kind belong to the consideration of the philosopher, then it follows that these principles also fall within his scope. But the philosopher does not establish the truth of these principles by way of demonstration, but by considering the meaning of their terms. For example, he considers what a whole is and what a part is; and the same applies to the rest. And when the meaning of these terms becomes known, it follows that the truth of the above-mentioned principles becomes evident.

[5] *Physica*, I, 1 (184a 21).

LESSON 6

First Philosophy Must Examine the First Principle of Demonstration. The Nature of This Principle. The Errors about It

ARISTOTLE'S TEXT   Chapters 3 & 4: 1005b 8-1006a 18

326. And it is fitting that the person who is best informed about each class of things should be able to state the firmest principles of his subject. Hence he who understands beings as beings should be able to state the firmest principles of all things. This person is the philosopher.

327. And the firmest of all principles is that about which it is impossible to make a mistake; for such a principle must be both the best known (for all men make mistakes about things which they do not know) and not hypothetical. For the principle which everyone must have who understands anything about beings is not hypothetical; and that which everyone must know who knows anything must be had by him when he comes to his subject. It is evident, then, that such a principle is the firmest of all.

328. And let us next state what this principle is. It is that the same attribute cannot both belong and not belong to the same subject at the same time and in the same respect; and let us stipulate any other qualifications that have to be laid down to meet dialectical difficulties. Now this is the firmest of all principles, since it answers to the definition given; for it is impossible for anyone to think that the same thing both is and is not, although some are of the opinion that Heraclitus speaks in this way; for what a man says he does not necessarily accept. But if it is impossible for contraries to belong simultaneously to the same subject (and let us then suppose that the same things are established here as in the usual proposition [1]), and if one opinion which expresses the contradictory of another is contrary to it, evidently the same man at the same time cannot think that the same thing can both be and not be; for one who is mistaken on this point will have contrary opinions at the same time. And it is for this reason that all who make demonstrations reduce their argument to this ultimate position. For this is by nature the starting point of all the other axioms.

Chapter 4

329. Now as we have said (328), there are some who claimed that the same thing can both be and not be, and that this can be believed. And many of those who treat of nature adopt this theory. But now we take it to be impossible for a thing both to be and not be at the same time, and by means of this we shall show [2] that this is the firmest of all principles.

330. But some deem it fitting that even this principle should be demonstrated, and they do this through want of education. For not to know of what things one

---

[1] Reading *propositione* for *positione*.
[2] The Greek has the past tense: we showed.

should seek demonstration and of what things one should not shows want of education. For it is altogether impossible that there should be demonstration of all things, because there would then be an infinite regress so that there would still be no demonstration. But if there are some things of which it is not necessary to seek demonstration, these people cannot say what principle they think to be more indemonstrable.

331. But even in this case it is possible to show by refutation that this view is impossible, if only our opponent will say something. But if he says nothing, it is ridiculous to look for a reason against one who has no reason, on the very point on which he is without reason; for such a man is really like a plant. Now I say that demonstration by refutation is different from demonstration [in the strict sense], because he who would demonstrate this principle in the strict sense would seem to beg the question.[3] But when someone argues for the sake of convincing another there will be refutation, not demonstration.

[3] Reading . . . *demonstraret, videretur quaerere quod a principio erat* (with the *versio recens* of Parma) for . . . *demonstrat quidem in principio.*

COMMENTARY

596. He shows here that it is the first philosopher who is chiefly concerned with the first principle of demonstration; and in regard to this he does two things. First (326:C 596), he shows that it is the business of the first philosopher to consider this principle; and second (332:C 611), he begins to examine this principle ("The starting point").

In regard to the first he does three things. First, he shows that it is the office of this science to consider the first principle of demonstration. Second (327:C 597), he indicates what this principle is ("And the firmest"). Third (329:C 606), he rejects certain errors regarding this same principle ("Now as we have said").

In regard to the first point he uses the following argument. In every class of things that man is best informed who knows the most certain principles, because the certitude of knowing depends on the certitude of principles. But the first philosopher is best informed and most certain in his knowledge; for this was one of the conditions

of wisdom, as was made clear in the prologue of this work (13:C 35), namely, that he who knows the causes of things has the most certain knowledge. Hence the philosopher ought to consider the most certain and firmest principles of beings, which he considers as the subject-genus proper to himself.

597. **And the firmest** (327).

Then he shows what the firmest or most certain principle is; and in regard to this he does two things. First (327:C 597), he states the conditions for the most certain principle; and then (328:C 600) he shows how they fit a single principle ("And let us").

He accordingly gives, first (327), the three conditions for the firmest principle. The first is that no one can make a mistake or be in error regarding it. And this is evident because, since men make mistakes only about those things which they do not know, then that principle about which no one can be mistaken must be the one which is best known.

598. The second condition is that

241

it must "not be hypothetical," i.e., it must not be held as a supposition, as those things which are maintained through some kind of common agreement. Hence another translation reads "And they should not hold a subordinate place," i.e., those principles which are most certain should not be made dependent on anything else. And this is true, because whatever is necessary for understanding anything at all about being "is not hypothetical," i.e., it is not a supposition but must be self-evident. And this is true because whatever is necessary for understanding anything at all must be known by anyone who knows other things.

599. The third condition is that it is not acquired by demonstration or by any similar method, but it comes in a sense by nature to the one having it inasmuch as it is naturally known and not acquired. For first principles become known through the natural light of the agent intellect, and they are not acquired by any process of reasoning but by having their terms become known. This comes about by reason of the fact that memory is derived from sensible things, experience from memory, and knowledge of those terms from experience. And when they are known, common propositions of this kind, which are the principles of the arts and sciences, become known. Hence it is evident that the most certain or firmest principle should be such that there can be no error regarding it; that it is not hypothetical; and that it comes naturally to the one having it.

600. **And let us next** (328).

Then he indicates the principle to which the above definition applies. He says that it applies to this principle, as the one which is firmest: it is impossible for the same attribute both to belong and not belong to the same subject at the same time. And it is necessary to add "in the same respect";

and any other qualifications that have to be given regarding this principle "to meet dialectical difficulties" must be laid down, since without these qualifications there would seem to be a contradiction when there is none.

601. That this principle must meet the conditions given above he shows as follows: it is impossible for anyone to think, or hold as an opinion, that the same thing both is and is not at the same time, although some believe that Heraclitus was of this opinion. But while it is true that Heraclitus spoke in this way, he could not think that this is true; for it is not necessary that everything that a person says he should mentally accept or hold as an opinion.

602. But if one were to say that it is possible for someone to think that the same thing both is and is not at the same time, this absurd consequence follows: contraries could belong to the same subject at the same time. And "let us suppose that the same things are established," or shown, here as in the usual proposition established in our logical treatises. For it was shown at the end of the *Perihermineas* [1] that contrary opinions are not those which have to do with contraries but those which have to do with contradictories, properly speaking. For when one person thinks that Socrates is white and another thinks that he is black, these are not contrary opinions in the primary and proper sense; but contrary opinions are had when one person thinks that Socrates is white and another thinks that he is not white.

603. Therefore, if someone were to think that two contradictories are true at the same time by thinking that the same thing both is and is not at the same time, he will have contrary opinions at the same time; and thus contraries will belong to the same thing at the same time. But this is impossible.

[1] *De Interpretatione*, 14 (23b 23).

It is impossible, then, for anyone to be mistaken in his own mind about these things and to think that the same thing both is and is not at the same time. And it is for this reason that all demonstrations reduce their propositions to this proposition as the ultimate opinion common to all; for this proposition is by nature the starting point and axiom of all axioms.

604. The other two conditions are therefore evident, because, insofar as those making demonstrations reduce all their arguments to this principle as the ultimate one by referring them to it, evidently this principle is not based on an assumption. Indeed, insofar as it is by nature a starting point, it clearly comes unsought to the one having it and is not acquired by his own efforts.

605. Now for the purpose of making this evident it must be noted that, since the intellect has two operations, one by which it knows quiddities, which is called the understanding of indivisibles, and another by which it combines and separates, there is something first in both operations. In the first operation the first thing that the intellect conceives is *being,* and in this operation nothing else can be conceived unless being is understood. And because this principle—it is impossible for a thing both to be and not be at the same time—depends on the understanding of being (just as the principle, every whole is greater than one of its parts, depends on the understanding of whole and part), then this principle is by nature also the first in the second operation of the intellect, i.e., in the act of combining and separating. And no one can understand anything by this intellectual operation unless this principle is understood. For just as a whole and its parts are understood only by understanding being, in a similar way the principle that every whole is greater than one of its parts is understood only if the firmest principle is understood.

606. **Now as we have said** (329).

Then he shows how some men erred regarding this principle; and in regard to this he does two things. First, he touches on the error of those who rejected the foregoing principle; and second (330:C 607) he deals with those who wished to demonstrate it ("But some").

He accordingly says that some men, as was stated above about Heraclitus (328:C 601), said that the same thing can both be and not be at the same time, and that it is possible to hold this opinion; and many of the philosophers of nature adopt this position, as will be made clear below (354:C 665). For our part, however, we now take as evident that the principle in question is true, i.e., the principle that the same thing cannot both be and not be; but from its truth we show that it is most certain. For from the fact that a thing cannot both be and not be it follows that contraries cannot belong to the same subject, as will be said below (353:C 663). And from the fact that contraries cannot belong to a subject at the same time it follows that a man cannot have contrary opinions and, consequently, that he cannot think that contradictories are true, as has been shown (328:C 603).

607. **But some** (330).

Then he mentions the error of certain men who wished to demonstrate the above-mentioned principle; and in regard to this he does two things. First, he shows that it cannot be demonstrated in the strict sense; and second (331:C 608), that it can be demonstrated in a way ("But even").

Thus he says, first (330), that certain men deem it fitting, i.e., they wish, to demonstrate this principle; and they do this "through want of education," i.e., through lack of learning or instruction. For there is want of education when a man does not know what to seek demonstration for and what not to; for not all things can be demonstrated. For if all things were demonstrable, then, since a thing is not demonstrated through itself but through something else, demonstrations would either be circular (although this cannot be true, because then the same thing would be both better known and less well known, as is clear in Book I of the *Posterior Analytics* [2]), or they would have to proceed to infinity. But if there were an infinite regress in demonstrations, demonstration would be impossible, because the conclusion of any demonstration is made certain by reducing it to the first principle of demonstration. But this would not be the case if demonstration proceeded to infinity in an upward direction. It is clear, then, that not all things are demonstrable. And if some things are not demonstrable, these men cannot say that any principle is more indemonstrable than the above-mentioned one.

608. **But even in this case** (331).

Here he shows that the above-mentioned principle can be demonstrated in a certain respect. He says that it may be demonstrated by disproof. In Greek the word is ἐλεγκτικῶς, which is better translated as *by refutation,* for an ἔλεγχος is a syllogism that establishes the contradictory of a proposition, and so is introduced to refute some false position. And on these grounds it can be shown that it is impossible for the same thing both to be and not be. But this kind of argument can be employed only if the one who denies that principle because of difficulties "says something," i.e., if he signifies some-

thing by a word. But if he says nothing, it is ridiculous to look for a reason against one who does not make use of reason in speaking; for in this dispute anyone who signifies nothing will be like a plant, for even brute animals signify something by such signs.

609. For it is one thing to give a strict demonstration of this principle, and another to demonstrate it argumentatively or by refutation. For if anyone wished to give a strict demonstration of this principle, he would seem to be begging the question, because any principle that he could take for the purpose of demonstrating this one would be one of those that depend on the truth of this principle, as is clear from what has been said above (330:C 607). But when the demonstration is not of this kind, i.e., demonstration in the strict sense, there will then be disproof or refutation at most.

610. Another text states this better by saying, "But when one argues for the sake of convincing another, there will then be refutation but not demonstration"; i.e., when a process of this kind from a less well known to a better known principle is employed for the sake of convincing another man who denies this, there will then be disproof or refutation but not demonstration; i.e., it will be possible to have a syllogism which contradicts his view, since what is less known absolutely is admitted by the opponent, and thus it will be possible to proceed to demonstrate the above-mentioned principle so far as the man is concerned but not in the strict sense.

---

[2] *Analytica Posteriora,* I, 2 (72a 30); 3 (72b 5 ff.).

LESSON 7

Contradictories Cannot Be True at the Same Time

ARISTOTLE'S TEXT   Chapter 4: 1006a 18-1007b 18

332. The starting point of all such discussions is not the desire that someone shall state that something either is or is not, for this might perhaps be thought to be begging the question, but that he shall state something significant both for himself and for someone else; for this he must do if he is to say anything. For if he does not, no discussion will be possible for such a person either with himself or with another. But if anyone will grant this, demonstration will be possible; for there will already be something definite. But this will not have the effect of demonstrating but of upholding, for he who destroys reason upholds reason.

333. First of all, then, it is evident that this at least is true, that the term *to be* or *not to be* signifies something, so that not everything will be so and not so.

334. Again, if the term *man* signifies one thing, let this be a two-footed animal.

335. Now by signifying one thing I mean this: granted that man is a two-footed animal, then if something is a man, this will be what *being a man* is. And it makes no difference even if someone were to say that this term signifies many things, provided that there are a definite number; for a different term might be assigned to each concept. I mean, for example, that if one were to say that the term man signifies not one thing but many, one of which would have a single concept, namely, two-footed animal, there might still be many others, if only there are a limited number; for a particular term might be assigned to each concept. However, if this were not the case, but one were to say that a term signifies an infinite number of things, evidently reasoning would be impossible; for not to signify one thing is to signify nothing. And if words signify nothing, there will be no discourse with another or even with ourselves. For it is impossible to understand anything unless one understands one thing; but if this does happen, a term may be assigned to this thing. Let it be assumed, then, as we said at the beginning (332), that a term signifies something, and that it signifies one thing.

336. It is impossible, then, that *being a man* should mean *not being a man,* if the term man not only signifies something about one subject but also signifies one thing. For we do not think it fitting to identify *signifying one thing* with *signifying something about one subject,* since the terms *musical, white* and *man* would then signify one thing. And therefore all things would be one, because all would be synonymous. And it will be impossible to be and not to be the same thing, except in an equivocal sense, as occurs if one whom we call *man* others call *not-man.* But the problem is not whether the same thing can at the same time be and not be a man in name, but whether it can in fact.

337. Now if man and not-man do not signify something different, it is evident that *not being a man* will not differ from *being a man.* Thus *being a man* will be identical with *not being a man,* for they will be one thing. For being one

means this: being related as clothing and garment are, if they are taken in the same sense. And if *being a man* and *not being a man* are to be one, they must signify one thing. But it has been shown that they signify different things.

338. Therefore, if it is true to say that something is a man, it must be a two-footed animal, for this is what the term man signifies. But if this is necessary, it is impossible for this very thing not to be a two-footed animal; for this is what to-be-necessary means, namely, unable not to be. Hence it cannot be true to say that the same thing is and is not a man at the same time. The same argument also applies to *not being a man*.

339. For *being a man* and *not being a man* signify different things, since *being white* and *being a man* are different; for there is much greater opposition in the former case, so that they signify different things. And if one were to say also that *white* signifies the same thing as man and is one in concept, we shall say the same thing as was said before (335), namely, that all things are one, and not merely opposites. But if this is impossible, then what has been said will follow.

340. That is to say, it will follow if our opponent answers the question. And if in giving a simple answer to the question he also adds the negations, he is not answering the question. For there is nothing to prevent the same thing from being man and white and a thousand other things numerically. Still if one asks whether it is or is not true to say that this is a man, his opponent should reply by stating something that means one thing and not add that it is also white or black or large. Indeed, it is impossible to enumerate the accidents of being, which are infinite in number; so therefore let him enumerate either all or none. Similarly, even if the same thing is a thousand times a man and a not-man, he must not, in answering the question whether this is a man, add that it is also at the same time a not-man, unless he also gives all the other corresponding accidents, whatever are so or are not so. And if he does not do this, there will be no debate with him.

341. And those who say this do away completely with substance or essence, for they must say that all attributes are accidents, and that there is no such thing as *being a man* or *being an animal*. For if there is to be such a thing as *being a man*, this will not be *being a not-man* or *not being a man;* in fact these are the negations of it. For there was one thing which the term signified, and this was the substance of something. And to signify the substance of a thing is to signify that its being is not something else. And if being essentially a man is being essentially a not-man, then the being of man will be something else. Hence they are compelled to say that nothing will have such a concept as this, but that all attributes are accidental. For this distinguishes substance from accident; for white is an accident of man, because while some man is white he is not the essence of whiteness.

342. Moreover, if all attributes are accidental predicates, there will be no first universal. And if the accidental always implies a predication about some subject, the process must go on to infinity. But this is impossible; for not more than two terms are combined in accidental predication. For an accident is an accident of an accident only because both are accidents of the same subject. I mean, for example, that white is an accident of musical and musical of white [1] only because both are accidental to man; but Socrates is not musical in the sense that both are accidental to something else. Therefore, since some accidents are predicated in the latter and some in the former sense, all those that are predicated as white

---

[1] Reading *album musico et hoc albo* for *album musico et homo albo*.

is predicated of Socrates cannot form an infinite series in an upward direction so that there should be another accident of white Socrates; for no one thing results from all of these. Nor again will white have another accident, such as musical; for this is no more an accident of that than that of this. And at the same time it has been established that some things are accidents in this sense and some in the sense that musical is an accident of Socrates. And whatever attributes are predicated accidentally in the latter sense are not accidents of accidents but only those predicated in the former sense. Not all attributes, then, are said to be accidents; and thus there must be some term which also signifies substance. And if this is so, then we have proved that contradictories cannot be predicated at the same time of the same subject.

COMMENTARY

611. Here he begins to argue dialectically against those who deny the foregoing principle, and this is divided into two parts. In the first (332:C 611) he argues against those who say that contradictories are true at the same time; and in the second (383:C 720), against those who say that they are false at the same time ("Neither can there be").

In regard to the first he does two things. First, he argues in a general way against those who make the aforesaid errors. Second (353:C 663), he shows how we must argue specifically against different positions ("But the same method").

In regard to the first he does two things. First, he argues dialectically against the reasoning of those who deny the foregoing principle. Second (352:C 661), he shows that Protagoras' opinion is fundamentally the same as the one just mentioned ("The doctrine of Protagoras").

In regard to the first point he gives seven arguments. He gives the second (341:C 624) at the words "And those who"; the third (343:C 636) at "Furthermore, if all"; the fourth (347:C 642) at "Again, either this"; the fifth (348:C 652) at "Again, how"; the sixth

(349:C 654) at "It is most evident"; and the seventh (351:C 659) at "Further, even if all."

In regard to the first he does two things. First, he indicates the starting point from which one must proceed to argue against those who deny the first principle. Second (333:C 612), he proceeds to argue from that starting point ("First of all, then").

He therefore says, first (332), that with respect to all such unreasonable positions there is no need for us to take as a starting point that someone [1] wishes to suppose that this thing definitely is "or is not"; i.e., it is not necessary to take as a starting point some proposition in which some attribute is either affirmed or denied of a subject (for this would be a begging of the question, as was said above [331:C 609]), but it is necessary to take as a starting point that a term signifies something both to the one who utters it, inasmuch as he himself understands what he is saying, and to someone else who hears him. But if such a person does not admit this, he will not say anything meaningful either for himself or for someone else, and it will then be idle to dispute with him. But when he has admitted this, a demonstration

---

[1] Reading *aliquis* for *aliquid*.

will at once be possible against him; for there is straightway found to be something definite and determinate which is signified by the term distinct from its contradictory, as will become clear below. Yet this will not strictly be a demonstration of the foregoing principle but only an argument upholding this principle against those who deny it. For he who "destroys reason," i.e., his own intelligible expression, by saying that a term signifies nothing, must uphold its significance, because he can only express what he denies by speaking and by signifying something.

612. **First of all, then** (333).

He proceeds from the assumption he had made to prove what he intends. First, he deals with one particular case; and second (334:C 612), he treats all cases in a general way ("Again, if the term").

He accordingly says, first (333), that if a term signifies something, it will be evident first of all that this proposition will be true, and that its contradictory, which he denies, will be false; and thus this at least will be true, that not every affirmation is true together with its negation.

613. **Now by signifying** (335).

Then he shows that this applies universally to all cases, namely, that contradictories are not true at the same time. In regard to this he does four things. First, he makes certain assumptions which are necessary for drawing his intended conclusion. Second (338:C 620), he draws his conclusion ("Therefore, if it is true"). Third (339:C 622), he proves one assumption which he had made ("For *being a man*"). Fourth (340:C 623), he rejects a quibble ("That is to say").

In regard to the first he does three things. First, he shows that a term signifies one thing; and second (336:C 616), he shows from this that the term man signifies what being a man is, but not what it is not ("It is impossible,

then"). Third (337:C 619), he shows that the term *man* signifies one thing ("Now if man").

He accordingly says, first (335), that if the term man signifies one thing, let this be two-footed animal. For a term is said to signify this one thing which is the definition of the thing signified by the term, so that if "two-footed animal" is the being of man, i.e., if this is what the essence of man is, this will be what is signified by the term man.

614. But if one were to say that a term signifies many things, it will signify either a finite or an infinite number of them. But if it signifies a finite number, it will differ in no way, according to another translation, from the term which is assumed to signify one thing; for it signifies many finite concepts of different things, and different terms can be fitted to each single concept. For example, if the term man were to signify many concepts, and the concept two-footed animal is one of them, one term is assigned to the concept man. And if there are many other concepts, many other terms may be assigned so long as those concepts are finite in number. Thus he will be forced back to the first position, that a term signifies one thing.

615. But if a term does not signify a finite but an infinite number of concepts, evidently neither reasoning nor debate will be possible. This becomes clear as follows: any term that does not signify one thing signifies nothing. This is proved thus: terms signify something understood, and therefore if nothing is understood, nothing is signified. But if one thing is not understood, nothing is understood, because anyone who understands anything must distinguish it from other things. If a term does not signify one thing, then, it signifies nothing at all; and if terms signify nothing, discourse will be impossible, both the kind which establishes truth and the kind which re-

futes an assertion. Hence it is clear that, if terms signify an infinite number of things, neither reasoning nor dispute will be possible. But if it is possible to understand one thing, a term may be given to it. So let it be held then that a term signifies something.

616. **It is impossible** (336).

He proves the second point, namely, that the term *man* does not signify *not being a man;* for a term that signifies one thing signifies not only what is one in subject (and is therefore said to be one because it is predicated of one subject) but what is one absolutely, i.e., in concept. For if we wanted to say that a term signifies one thing because it signifies the attributes which are verified of one thing, it would then follow that the terms musical, white and man all signify one thing, since all are verified of one thing. And from this it would follow that all things are one; for if white is predicated of man and is therefore identical with him, then when it is also predicated of a stone it will be identical with a stone; and since those things which are identical with one and the same thing are identical with each other, it would follow that a man and a stone are one thing and have one concept. Thus the result would be that all terms are univocal, i.e., one in concept, or synonymous, as another text says, i.e., meaning absolutely the same thing in subject and in concept.

617. Now although being and nonbeing are verified of the same subject according to those who deny the first principle, still being a man and not being a man must differ in concept, just as white and musical differ in concept even though they are verified of the same subject. Hence it is evident that being and non-being cannot be the same in concept and in subject in the sense that they are signified by one univocal term.

618. Now it must be noted that the

expression *being a man* or *to be a man* or *having the being of a man* is taken here for the quiddity of man, and therefore it is concluded from this that the term man does not signify not being a man as its proper concept. But because he had said above (335:C 614) that the same term can signify many things according to different concepts, he therefore adds "except in an equivocal sense" in order to make clear that the term man does not signify in a univocal sense both being a man and not being a man, but it can signify both in an equivocal sense; i.e., in the sense that what we call man in one language others might call not-man in another language. For we are not debating whether the same thing can both be and not be man in name, but whether it can in fact.

619. **Now if man** (337).

Then he proves the third point: that the terms *man* and *not-man* do not signify the same thing, and he uses the following argument. The term man signifies being a man or what man is, and the term not-man signifies not being a man or what man is not. If, then, man and not man do not signify something different, being a man will not differ from not being a man, or being a not-man, and therefore one of these will be predicated of the other. And they will also have one concept; for when we say that some terms signify one thing, we mean that they signify one concept, as the terms clothing and garment do. Hence, if being a man and not being a man are one in this way, i.e., in concept, there will then be one concept which will signify both being a man and not being a man. But it has been granted or demonstrated that the term which signifies each is different; for it has been shown that the term man signifies man and does not signify not-man. Thus it is clear that being a man and not being a man do not have a single concept, and therefore the thesis that man and not-man signify different things becomes evident.

620. **Therefore, if it is true** (338).

Here he proves his main thesis from the assumptions made earlier, and he uses the following argument. A man must be a two-footed animal, as is true from the foregoing, for this is the concept which the term man signifies. But what is necessary cannot not be; for this is what the term necessary means, namely, unable not to be, or incapable of not being, or impossible not to be. Hence it is not possible, or incapable, or impossible for man not to be a two-footed animal, and therefore it is evident that the affirmation and the negation cannot both be true; i.e., it cannot be true that man is both a two-footed animal and not a two-footed animal. The same reasoning based on the meanings of terms can be understood to apply to what is not-man, because what is not-man must be not a two-footed animal, since this is what the term signifies. Therefore it is impossible that a not-man should be a two-footed animal.

621. Now the things demonstrated above are useful to his thesis, because if someone were to think that the terms man and not-man might signify the same thing, or that the term man might signify both being a man and not being a man, his opponent could deny the proposition that man must be a two-footed animal. For he could say that it is no more necessary to say that man must be a two-footed animal than to say that he is not a two-footed animal, granted that the terms man and not-man signify the same thing, or granted that the term man signifies both of these—being a man and not being a man.

622. **For being a man** (339).

Then he proves one of the assumptions which he had made; for in order to prove that the term man does not signify not being a man, he assumed that being a man and not being a man

are different, even though they might be verified of the same subject. His aim here is to prove this by the following argument. There is greater opposition between being a man and not being a man than between man and white; but man and white have different concepts, although they may be the same in subject. Therefore being a man and not being a man also have different concepts. He proves the minor thus: if all attributes which are predicated of the same subject have the same concept and are signified by one term, it follows that all are one, as has been stated and explained (336:C 616). Now if this is impossible, the position we have maintained follows, namely, that being a man and not being a man are different. And for this reason the final conclusion given above will follow, namely, that man is a two-footed animal, and that it is impossible for him to be what is not a two-footed animal.

623. **That is to say** (340).

He rejects one quibble by which the foregoing process of reasoning could be obstructed. For when an opponent has been asked whether man must be a two-footed animal, he need not reply either affirmatively or negatively but could say that man must be both a two-footed animal and not a two-footed animal. But the philosopher rejects this here, saying that the foregoing conclusion follows so long as an opponent wishes to give a simple answer to the question. But if in giving a simple answer to the question on the side of the affirmative he also wishes to include in his answer the negative aspect, he will not be answering the question. He proves this as follows. One and the same thing can be both a man and white and a thousand other things of this kind. Yet if it is asked here whether a man is white, we must give in our answer only what is signified by one word, and not add all the other attributes. For example, if one asks whether this is a man, we must answer that it is a man, and not add that it is both a man and white and large and the like; for we must give either all of the accidents of a thing at once or not. But not all accidents can be given at once since they are infinite in number; for there are an infinite number of accidents belonging to one and the same thing by reason of its relationship to an infinite number of antecedents and consequents, and what is infinite in number cannot be traversed. In answering the question, then, we must not give any of the attributes which are accidental to the thing about which the question is raised but only the attribute which is asked for. Hence, even if it is supposed a thousand times that man and not-man are the same, still, when the question is asked about man, the answer must not include anything about not-man, unless all those things which are accidental to man are given. And if this were done, no dispute would be possible, because it would never reach completion, since an infinite number of things cannot be traversed.

624. **And those who** (341).

Then he gives the second argument, and it is based on the notion of substantial and accidental predicates. This is his argument: if an affirmation and a negation are verified of the same subject, it follows that no term will be predicated quidditatively, or substantially, but only accidentally; and therefore there will have to be an infinite regress in accidental predicates. But the consequent is impossible, and thus the antecedent must be impossible.

625. In this argument he does two things. First, he gives a conditional proposition. Second (342:C 629), he gives a proof that destroys the consequent ("Moreover, if all").

Regarding the first part he proceeds as follows. He says that those who state that an affirmation and a negation may be true at the same time completely do away with "substance," i.e., with a

substantial predicate, "or essence," i.e., with an essential predicate; for they must say "that all attributes are accidents," or accidental predicates, and that there is no such thing as being a man or being an animal, and that what the quiddity of man or the quiddity of animal signifies does not exist.

626. He proves this as follows: if there is something which is being a man, i.e., which is the substantial essence of man, which is predicated of man, it will not be not being a man or being a not-man; for these two, i.e., not being a man and being a not-man, are the negations of being a man. It is clear, then, that an affirmation and a negation are not verified of the same subject, for not being a man or being a not-man is not verified of being a man.

627. And the assumption made, namely, that if there is such a thing as being a man, this will not be not being a man or being a not-man, he proves in the following way. It was posited and proved above that the thing which a term signifies is one. And it was also posited that the thing which a term signifies is the substance of something, namely, a thing's quiddity. Hence it is clear that some term signifies a thing's substance, and that the thing which was signified is not something else. Therefore, if the essence or quiddity of man should be either not being a man or being a not-man, it is quite clear that it would differ from itself. It would be necessary to say, then, that there is no definition signifying a thing's essence. But from this it would follow that all predicates are accidental ones.

628. For substance is distinguished from accident, i.e., a substantial predicate is distinguished from an accidental one, in that each thing is truly what is predicated substantially of it. Thus it cannot be said that a substantial predicate is not one thing, for each thing exists only if it is one. But man is said

251

to be white because whiteness or white is one of his accidents, although not in such a way that he is the very essence of white or whiteness. It is not necessary, then, that an accidental predicate should be one only, but there can be many accidental predicates. A substantial predicate, however, is one only; and thus it is clear that what being a man is is not what not being a man is. But if a substantial predicate is both, it will no longer be one only, and thus will not be substantial but accidental.

629. **Moreover, if all** (342).

He destroys the consequent. He shows that it is impossible that all predicates should be accidental and none substantial because, if all were accidental, there would be no universal predicate. (And universal predicate here means the same thing as it does in the *Posterior Analytics*,[2] i.e., an attribute which is predicated of something in virtue of itself and in reference to what it itself is). But this is impossible; for if one attribute is always predicated of another accidentally, there will be an infinite regress in accidental predication; but this is impossible for this reason.

630. For there are only two ways in which accidental predication occurs. One way is had when one accident is predicated accidentally of another; and this happens because both are accidents of the same subject, for example, when white is predicated of musical because both are accidents of man. The other way is had when an accident is predicated of a subject (as when Socrates is said to be musical), not because both are accidents of some other subject, but because one of them is an accident of the other. Hence, even though there are two ways in which accidents may be predicated, in neither way can there be an infinite regress in predication.

631. For it is clear that there cannot

be an infinite regress in that way in which one accident is predicated of another, because one must reach some subject. For it has been stated already that the essential note of this kind of predication is that both accidents are predicated of one subject. And thus by descending from a predicate to a subject, the subject itself can be found to be the terminus.

632. And there cannot be an infinite regress in an upward direction in the way of predicating in which an accident is predicated of a subject, as when Socrates is said to be white, by ascending from a subject to a predicate so as to say that white is an accident of Socrates and that some other attribute is an accident of white Socrates. For this could occur only in two ways. One way would be that one thing would come from white and Socrates; and thus just as Socrates is one subject of whiteness, in a similar way white Socrates would be one subject of another accident. But this cannot be so, because one thing does not come from all of these predicates. For what is one in an absolute sense does not come from a substance and an accident in the way that one thing comes from a genus and a difference. Hence it cannot be said that white Socrates is one subject.

633. The other way would be that, just as Socrates is the subject of whiteness, in a similar way some other accident, such as musical, would have whiteness as its subject. But neither can this be so, and for two reasons. First, there can be no special reason why musical should be said to be an accident of white rather than the reverse; neither white nor musical will be prior to the other, but they will rather be of equal rank. Second, in conjunction with this it has been established or determined at the same time that this way of predicating in which an accident is

2 *Analytica Posteriora*, I, 4 (73b 27).

predicated of an accident differs from that in which an accident is predicated of a subject, as when musical is predicated of Socrates. But in the way of which he is now speaking accidental predication does not mean that an accident is predicated of an accident; but it is to be so taken in the way we first described.

634. It is evident, then, that an infinite regress in accidental predication is impossible, and therefore that not all predications are accidental. And it is also evident that there will be some term which signifies substance; and again, that contradictories are not true of the same subject.

635. Now with regard to the argument given it must be noted that, even though one accident is not the subject of another, and thus one accident is not related to the other as its subject, still one is related to the other as cause and thing caused. For one accident is the cause of another. Heat and moistness, for example, are the cause of sweetness, and surface is the cause of color. For by reason of the fact that a subject is receptive of one accident it is receptive of another.

LESSON 8

Other Arguments Against the Foregoing Position

ARISTOTLE'S TEXT   Chapter 4: 1007b 18-1008b 2

343. Furthermore, if all contradictories are true of the same subject at the same time, it is evident that all things will be one. For the same thing will be a trireme, a wall and a man, if it is possible either to affirm or to deny anything of everything.

344. And this is what must follow for those who agree with Protagoras' view. For if it appears to anyone that a man is not a trireme, it is evident that he is not a trireme; so that he also is a trireme if contradictories are true. And thus there arises the view of Anaxagoras [1] that all things exist together at the same time, so that nothing is truly one. Hence they seem to be speaking about the indeterminate; and while they think they are speaking about being, they are speaking about non-being; for the indeterminate is what exists potentially and is not complete.

345. But the affirmation and the negation of every predicate of every subject must be admitted by them; for it would be absurd if each subject should have its own negation predicated of it while the negation of something else which cannot be predicated of it should not be predicated of it. I mean that, if it is true to say that a man is not a man, evidently it is also true to say that he is not a trireme. Therefore, if the affirmation is predicable of him, so also must the negation be. But if the affirmation is not [2] predicable of him, the negation of the other term will be predicable of him to a greater degree than his own negation. If, then, the latter negation is predicable of him, the negation of trireme will also be predicable of him; and if this is predicable of him, the affirmation will be too. This is what follows, then, for those who hold this view.

346. And it also follows for them that it is not necessary either to affirm or to deny. For if it is true that the same thing is both a man and a not-man, evidently it will be neither a man nor a not-man; for of the two affirmations there are two negations. And if the former is taken as a single proposition composed of the two, the latter also will be a single proposition opposed to the former.

347. Again, either this is true of all things, and a thing is both white and not-white, and both being and not-being, and the same applies to other affirmations and negations; or it is not true of all but is true of some and not of others. And if not of all, the exceptions will be admitted. But if it is true of all, then either the negation will be true of everything of which the affirmation is, and the affirmation will be true of everything of which the negation is, or the negation will be true of everything of which the affirmation is, but the affirmation will not always be true of everything of which the negation is. And if the latter is true, there will be something that certainly is not, and this will be an unshakeable opinion.

[1] Frag. 1.
[2] *Non* is omitted in the Cathala-Spiazzi edition.

And if that it is not is something certain and knowable, more known indeed will be the opposite affirmation than the negation. But if in denying something it is equally possible to affirm what is denied, it is necessary to state what is true about these things, either separately (for example, to say that a thing is white and that it is not-white), or not. And if it is not true to affirm them separately, then an opponent will not be saying what he professes to say, and nothing will exist. But how could non-existent things speak or walk, as he does? Again, [according to this view] all things will be one, as has been said before (336:C 616), and man and God and a trireme and their contradictories will be the same. Similarly, if this is true of each thing, one thing will differ in no respect from another; for if it differs, this difference will be something true and proper to it. And similarly if it is possible for each to be true separately, the results described will follow. And to this we may add that all will speak the truth and all speak falsely; and that each man will admit of himself that he is in error. And at the same time it is evident that up to this point the discussion is about nothing at all, because our opponent says nothing. For he does not say that a thing is so or is not so, but that it is both so and not so; and again he denies both of these and says that it is neither so nor not so. For if this were not the case there would already be some definite statement. Further, if when the affirmation is true the negation is false, and if when the negation is true the affirmation is false, it will be impossible both to affirm and to deny the same thing truly at the same time. But perhaps someone will say that this was the contention from the very beginning.

COMMENTARY

636. Then he gives a third argument, which involves oneness and difference. The argument runs thus: if an affirmation and a negation are true of the same subject at the same time, all things will be one. But the consequent is false. Hence the antecedent must be false. In regard to this argument he does three things.

First (343:C 636), he lays down a conditional proposition and gives an example, namely, that if contradictories are true of the same subject at the same time, it will follow that the same thing will be a trireme (i.e., a ship with three banks of oars), a wall and a man.

637. **And this is what** (344).

Then he shows that the same impossible conclusion follows with regard to two other positions. He does this, first, with regard to the opinion of Protagoras, who said that whatever seems so to anyone is wholly true for him; for if it seems to someone that a man is not a trireme, then he will not be a trireme; and if it seems to someone else that a man is a trireme, he will be a trireme; and thus contradictories will be true.

638. Second, he does this with regard to the opinion of Anaxagoras, who said that all things exist together, so that nothing which is truly one is distinguished from other things, but all are one in a kind of mixture. For he said that everything is found in everything else, as has been shown in Book I of the *Physics*.[1] This is the position which Anaxagoras adopted because he seems to be speaking about indeterminate be-

[1] *Physica*, I, 4 (187a 30).

ing, i.e., what has not been made actually determinate. And while he thought
he was speaking about complete being,
he was speaking about potential being,
as will become clear below (355:C
667). But the indeterminate is what exists potentially and is not "complete,"
i.e., actual; for potency is made determinate only by actuality.

639. **But the affirmation** (345).

Third, he proves that the first conditional proposition is true. He does
this, first, on the grounds that all things
would have to be affirmed to be one;
and second (346:C 640), on the
grounds that affirmations would not be
distinguished from their negations
from the viewpoint of truth and falsity
("And it also follows").

He accordingly says, first (345), that
the first conditional proposition must
be admitted by them inasmuch as they
hold than an affirmation and a negation
are true of the same subject at the same
time because an affirmation and a negation are true of anything at all. For it
is clear that the negation of some other
thing seems to be predicable of each
thing to a greater degree than its own
negation. For it would be absurd if
some subject should have its own negation predicated of it and not the negation of something else by which it is
signified that this other thing is not
predicable of it. For example, if it is
true to say that a man is not a man, it
is much truer to say that a man is not
a trireme. Hence it is clear that anything of which a negation must be
predicated must also have an affirmation predicated of it. Therefore a negation will be predicated of it since an
affirmation and a negation are true at
the same time; or if an affirmation is
not predicated of it, the negation of the
other term will be predicated of it to a
greater degree than its own negation.
For example, if the term trireme is not
predicable of man, non-trireme will be
predicated of him inasmuch as it may
be said that a man is not a trireme. But

if the affirmation is predicable, so also
must the negation be, since they are
verified of the same thing. A man, then,
must be a trireme, and he must also be
anything else on the same grounds.
Hence all things must be one. Therefore this is what follows for those who
maintain the position that contradictories are true of the same subject.

640. **And it also follows** (346).

He now draws the other impossible
conclusion which follows from this
view, namely, that a negation will not
be distinguished from an affirmation as
regards falsity, but each will be false.
Thus he says that not only the foregoing impossible conclusions follow
from the above-mentioned position,
but also the conclusion that it is not
necessary "either to affirm or to deny,"
i.e., it is not necessary that either the
affirmation or the negation of a thing
should be true, but each may be false;
and so there will be no difference between being true and being false. He
proves this as follows.

641. If it is true that something is
both a man and a not-man, it is also
true that it is neither a man nor a not-
man. This is evident. For of these two
terms, *man* and *not-man,* there are two
negations, *not man* and *not not-man.*
And if one proposition were formed
from the first two, for example, if one
were to say that Socrates is neither a
man nor a not-man, it would follow
that neither the affirmation nor the negation is true but that both are false.

642. **Again, either this** (347).

Then he gives a fourth argument,
and this is based on certitude in knowing. It runs thus. If an affirmation and
a negation are true at the same time,
either this is true of all things, or it is
true of some and not of others. But if it
is not true of all, then those of which
it is true will be "admitted"; i.e., they
will be conceded simply and absolutely,
or according to another translation
"they will be certain," i.e., true with
certainty; that is, in their case the nega-

tion will be true because the affirmation is false, or the reverse.

643. But if it is true in all cases that contradictories are verified of the same subject, this might happen in two ways. In one way anything of which affirmations are true, negations are true, and the reverse. In another way anything of which affirmations are true, negations are true, but not the reverse.

644. And if the second is true, this impossible conclusion will follow: there will be something that firmly or certainly is not; and so there will be an unshakeable opinion regarding a negative proposition. And this will be the case because a negation is always true since whenever an affirmation is true its negation is also true. But an affirmation will not always be true, because it was posited that an affirmation is not true of anything at all of which a negation is true; and thus a negation will be more certain and knowable than an affirmation. But this seems to be false because, even though non-being is certain and knowable, an affirmation will always be more certain than its opposite negation; for the truth of a negation always depends on that of some affirmation. Hence a negative conclusion can be drawn only if there is some kind of affirmation in the premises. But an affirmative conclusion can never be drawn from negative premises.

645. Now if one were to speak in the first way and say that of anything of which an affirmation is true the negation is also true, and similarly that of anything of which the negation is true the affirmation is also true, inasmuch as affirmation and negation are interchangeable, this might happen in two ways. For if an affirmation and a negation are both true at the same time, either it will be possible to state what is true of each separately, for example, to say that each of these propositions is true separately—"Man is white" and "Man is not white"; or it will not be possible to state that each

is true separately but only both together. For example, if we were to say that this copulative proposition is true —"Man is white and man is not white."

646. And if we were to speak in the second way and say that neither one is true separately but only both together, two impossible conclusions would then follow. The first is that "an opponent will not be saying what he professes to say," i.e., he will assert neither the affirmation nor the negation of something, and "neither will exist," i.e., both will be false; or according to another text, "nothing will exist," i.e., it will follow that nothing is true, neither the affirmation nor the negation. And if nothing is true it will be impossible to understand or to express anything. For how can anyone understand or express non-being? Implied is the reply: in no way.

647. The second impossible conclusion would be that all things are one, as has been stated in a previous argument (345:C 639). For it would follow that a man and God and a trireme, and also their contradictories, a not-man, not-God and not-trireme, are the same. Thus it is clear that, if an affirmation and a negation are true of any subject at the same time, one thing will not differ from another. For if one were to differ from another, something would have to be predicated of the one which is not predicated of the other; and so it would follow that something is definitely and properly true of this thing which does not fit the other. Therefore an affirmation and a negation will not be true of anything whatever. But it is clear that things which differ in no way are one. Thus it would follow that all things are one.

648. But if one were to speak in the first way and say that it is possible for an affirmation and a negation to be true, not only together but also separately, four impossible conclusions will follow. The first is that this position "indicates that this statement is true";

i.e., it proves that the statement just made is true. Hence another text reads, "the results described will follow," i.e., all things will be one, because it will then be possible both to affirm and to deny each thing, and one will not differ from the other.

649. A second impossible conclusion is that all will speak the truth, because anyone at all must make either an affirmation or a negation, and each will be true. And each man will also admit of himself that he is wrong when he says that the affirmation is true; for, since he says that the negation is true, he admits that he was in error when he made the affirmation.

650. A third impossible conclusion is that up to this point there obviously could not be any investigation or dispute. For it is impossible to carry on a dispute with someone who admits nothing, because such a person really says nothing since he does not say absolutely that something is so or is not so; but he says that it is both so and not so. And again he denies both of these, for he says that it is neither so nor not so, as is evident from the preceding argument. For if he does not deny all of these he will know that something is definitely true, and this is contrary to his original position. Or according to another translation which expresses this more clearly, "there would already be some definite statement."

651. A fourth impossible conclusion will follow because of the definition of the true and the false. For truth exists when one says that what is, is, or that what is not, is not. But falsity exists when one says that what is, is not, or that what is not, is. Hence from the definition of the true and the false it is clear that, when an affirmation is true, its negation is false; for one then says that what is, is not. And when a negation is true, its affirmation is false; for what is not is then said to be. Therefore it is impossible both to affirm and to deny the same thing truly. But perhaps an opponent could say that this last argument is begging the question; for he who claims that contradictories are true at the same time does not accept this definition of the false: the false is to say that what is not, is, or that what is, is not.

LESSON 9

Three Further Arguments Against Those Who Deny the First Principle

ARISTOTLE'S TEXT   Chapters 4 & 5: 1008b 2-1009a 16

348. Again, how is that man wrong who judges that a thing is so or is not so, and is he right who judges both? For if the second is right, what will his statement mean except that such is the nature of beings? And if he is not right, he is more right than the one who holds the first view, and beings will already be of a certain nature, and this will be true and not at the same time not true. But if all men are equally right and wrong, anyone who holds this view can neither mean nor state anything; for he will both affirm and not affirm these things at the same time. And if he makes no judgment but equally thinks and does not think, in what respect will he differ from plants?

349. It is most evident, then, that no one, either among those who profess this theory or any others, is really of this mind. For why does a man walk home [1] and not remain where he is when he thinks he is going there? He does not at dawn walk directly into a well or into a brook if he happens on such; but he seems to be afraid of doing so because he does not think that to fall in is equally good and not good. Therefore he judges that the one is better and the other not. And if this is so in the case of what is good and what is not good, it must also be so in the case of other things. Thus he must judge that one thing is a man and another not a man, and that one thing is sweet and another not sweet. For when he thinks that it is better to drink water and to see a man and then seeks these things, he does not make the same judgment about all of them, though this would be necessary if the same thing were equally a man and not a man. But according to what has been said there is no one who does not seem to fear some things and not others. Hence, as it appears, all men make an unqualified judgment, and if not about all things, still about what is better or worse.

350. And if they do not have science but opinion, they ought to care all the more about the truth, just as one who is ill ought to care more about health than one who is well. For one who has opinion in contrast to one who has science is not healthily disposed towards the truth.

351. Further, even if all things are so and not so as much as you like, still difference of degree belongs to the nature of beings. For we should not say that two and three are equally even; and he who thinks that four is five is not equally as wrong as he who thinks that it is a thousand. Therefore, if they are not equally wrong, obviously one is less wrong and so more right. Hence, if what is truer is nearer to what is true, there must be some truth to which the truer is nearer. And even if there is not, still there is already something truer and more certain,

---

[1] The Greek text reads: "to Megara." St. Thomas follows the reading of the Latin version.

and we shall be freed from that intemperate theory which prevents us from determining anything in our mind.

Chapter 5

352. The doctrine of Protagoras proceeds from the same opinion, and both of these views must be alike either true or not true. For if all things which seem or appear are true, everything must be at once true and false. For many men have opinions which are contrary to one another, and they think that those who do not have the same opinions as themselves are wrong. Consequently the same thing must both be and not be. And if this is so, it is necessary to think that all opinions are true; for those who are wrong and those who are right entertain opposite opinions. If, then beings are such, all men will speak the truth. Hence it is evident that both contraries proceed from the same way of thinking.

COMMENTARY

652. Here he gives a fifth argument, which is based on the notion of truth, and it runs as follows. It has been stated that both the affirmation and the negation of something are held to be true at the same time. Therefore he who judges or thinks that "a thing is so," i.e., that the affirmation alone is true, "or is not so," i.e., that the negation alone is true, is wrong; and he who judges that both are true at the same time is right. Hence, since truth exists when something is such in reality as it is in thought, or as it is expressed in words, it follows that what a man expresses will be something definite in reality; i.e., the nature of beings will be such as it is described to be; so that it will not be at once the subject both of an affirmation and of a negation. Or according to another text, "beings will already be of a certain nature," as if to say that since the statement is definitely true, it follows that a thing has such a nature. However, if one were to say that it is not he who judges that an affirmation and a negation are true at the same time that has a true opinion, but rather he who thinks that either the affirmation alone is true or the negation

alone is true, it is evident that beings will already exist in some determinate way. Hence another translation says more clearly, "and in a sense this will be definitely true and not at the same time not true," because either the affirmation alone is true or the negation alone is true.

653. But if all of those just mentioned, i.e., both those who affirm both parts of a contradiction and those who affirm one of the two, "are wrong," and all are also right, it will be impossible to carry on a dispute with anyone who maintains this, or even to say anything that might provoke a dispute with him. Or according to another text, "such a man will not affirm or assert anything." For, as another translation says, "he cannot assert or affirm anything of this kind," because he equally affirms and denies anything at all. And if this man takes nothing to be definitely true, and similarly thinks and does not think, just as he similarly affirms and denies something in speech, he seems to differ in no way from plants; because even brute animals have certain definite conceptions. Another text reads, "from those disposed by nature," and this

means that such a one who admits nothing does not differ in what he is actually thinking from those who are naturally disposed to think but are not yet actually thinking. For those who are naturally disposed to think about any question do not affirm either part of it, and similarly neither do the others.

654. **It is most evident** (349).

Then he gives a sixth argument, which is based on desire and aversion. In regard to this he does two things. First, he gives the argument. Second (350:C 658), he rejects an answer which is a quibble ("And if they").

He accordingly says, first (349), that it is evident that no man is of such a mind as to think that both an affirmation and a negation can be verified of the same subject at the same time. Neither those who maintain this position nor any of the others can think in this way. For if to go home were the same as not to go home, why would someone go home rather than remain where he is, if he were of the opinion that to remain where he is is the same as to go home? Therefore, from the fact that someone goes home and does not remain where he is it is clear that he thinks that to go and not to go are different.

655. Similarly, if someone walks along a path which happens to lead directly to a well or a brook, he does not proceed straight along that path but seems to fear that he will fall into the well or brook. This happens because he judges that to fall into a well or a brook is not equally good and not good, but he judges absolutely that it is not good. However, if he were to judge that it is both good and not good, he would not avoid the above act any more than he would desire it. Therefore, since he avoids doing this and does not desire it, obviously he judges or thinks that the one course is better, namely, not to fall into the well, because he knows that it is better.

656. And if this is true of what is good and what is not good, the same thing must apply in other cases, so that clearly one judges that one thing is a man and another not a man, and that one thing is sweet and another not sweet. This is evident from the fact that he does not seek all things to the same degree or make the same judgment about them, since he judges that it is better to drink water which is sweet than to drink that which is not sweet; and that it is better to see a man than to see something which is not a man. And from this difference in opinion it follows that he definitely desires the one and not the other; for he would have to desire both equally, i.e., both the sweet and the not-sweet, and both man and not-man, if he thought that contradictories were the same. But, as has been said before (349:C 655), there is no one who does not seem to avoid the one and not the other. So by the very fact that a man is differently disposed to various things inasmuch as he avoids some and desires others, he must not think that the same thing both is and is not.

657. It is evident, then, that all men think that truth consists in affirmation alone or in negation alone and not in both at the same time. And if they do not think that this applies in all cases, they at least are of the opinion that it applies in the case of things which are good or evil or of those which are better or worse; for this difference accounts for the fact that some things are desired and others are avoided.

658. **And if they** (350).

Then he rejects a quibble. For someone could say that men desire some things inasmuch as they are good and avoid others inasmuch as they are not good, not because they know the truth but because they are of the opinion that the same thing is not both good and not good, although this amounts to the same thing in reality. But if it is true

that men do not have science but opinion, they ought to care all the more
about learning the truth. This is made
clear as follows: one who is ill cares
more about health than one who is
well. But one who has an untrue opinion, in comparison with one who has
scientific knowledge, is not healthily
disposed towards the truth, because he
is in the same state with regard to
scientific knowledge as a sick man is
with regard to health; for a false opinion is a lack of scientific knowledge
just as illness is a lack of health. Thus
it is evident that men ought to care
about discovering the truth. However,
this would not be the case if nothing
were definitely true, but only if something were both true and not true at
the same time.

659. **Further, even if all** (351).

Then he gives a seventh argument,
which is based on the different degrees
of falsity. He says that even if it should
be most true that everything is so and
not so, i.e., that an affirmation and its
negation are true at the same time,
still it is necessary that different degrees
of truth should exist in reality. For obviously it is not equally true to say
that two is even and that three is even;
nor is it equally false to say that four
is five, and that it is a thousand. For
if both are equally false, it is evident
that one is less false, i.e., it is less false
to say that four is five than to say that
it is a thousand. But what is less
false is truer, or nearer to the truth,
just as that is also less black which is
nearer to white. Therefore it is clear
that one of them speaks more truly,
i.e., he comes nearer to the truth; and
this is the one who says that four is
five. But nothing would be closer or
nearer to the truth unless there were
something which is absolutely true in
relation to which the nearer or closer
would be truer and less false. It follows,
then, that it is necessary to posit something which is unqualifiedly true, and
that not all things are both true and

false, because otherwise it would follow from this that contradictories are
true at the same time. And even if it
does not follow from the foregoing
argument that there is something which
is unqualifiedly true, still it has been
stated already that one thing is truer
and firmer or more certain than another (351:C 659); and thus affirmation and negation are not related in the
same way to truth and certitude. Hence
as a result of this argument and the
others given above we shall be freed
or liberated from this theory, i.e., from
this non-mixed opinion, or one that is
not tempered (and for this reason another text has "intemperate"); for an
opinion is well tempered when the
predicate is not repugnant to the subject. But when an opinion involves opposite notions, it is not well tempered;
and the position mentioned above,
which says that contradictories can be
true, is an opinion of this kind.

660. Further, this position prevents
us from being able to define or settle
anything in our mind. For the first notion of difference is considered in affirmation and negation. Hence he who
says that an affirmation and a negation
are one does away with all definiteness
or difference.

661. **The doctrine of Protagoras**
(352).

Here he shows that the opinion of
Protagoras is reduced to the same position as the one mentioned above. For
Protagoras said that everything which
seems to be true to anyone is true. And
if this position is true, the first one
must also be true, namely, that an affirmation and its negation are true at
the same time. Hence all things must
be true and false at the same time inasmuch as this follows from this position, as has been shown above (351:C
659). He proves this as follows. Many
men have opinions which are contrary
to one another, and they think that
those who do not have the same opin-

ions as themselves are wrong, and vice versa. If, then, whatever seems so to anyone is true, it follows that both are wrong and both are right, because the same thing is and is not. Hence according to the opinion of Protagoras it follows that both parts of a contradiction are true at the same time.

662. Similarly, if it is true that both parts of a contradiction are true at the same time, the opinion of Protagoras must be true, namely, that all things which seem true to anybody are true.

For it is clear that people have different opinions, and some of these are false and others are true because they have opinions which are opposed to each other. If, then, all opposites are true at the same time (and this follows if contradictories are true at the same time), the result must be that all are right, and that what seems so to anyone is true. Thus it is clear that each position contains the same opinion, theory, or way of thinking, because one necessarily follows from the other.

LESSON 10

The Procedure Against Those Who Say that Contradictories Are True at the Same Time

ARISTOTLE'S TEXT   Chapter 5: 1009a 16-1009a 38

353. But the same method of discussion is not applicable in all of these cases, because some men need persuasion and others force. For the ignorance of those who have formed their opinions as a result of difficulties is easily cured, because refutation is directed not against their words but against their thought. But the cure for all of those who argue for the sake of argument consists in refuting what they express in speech and in words.

354. Those who have experienced difficulties have formed this opinion because of things observed in the sensible world, i.e., the opinion that contradictories and contraries can both be true at the same time, inasmuch as they see that contraries are generated from the same thing. Therefore, if it is impossible for non-being to come into being, the thing must have existed before as both contraries equally. This is Anaxagoras' view, for he says [1] that everything is mixed in everything else. And Democritus is of the same opinion, for he holds [2] that the void and the full are equally present in any part, and yet one of these is non-being and the other being.

355. Concerning those who base their opinions on these grounds, then, we say that in one sense they speak the truth, and that in another they do not know what they are saying. For *being* has two meanings, so that in one sense a thing can come to be from non-being and in another sense it cannot. Hence the same thing can both be and not be at the same time, but not in the same respect; for while the same thing can be potentially two contraries at the same time, it cannot in complete actuality.

356. Further, we shall expect them to believe that among beings there is also another kind of substance to which neither motion nor generation nor corruption belongs in any way.

[1] Diels, Frag. 1; see also *Physica*, I, 4 (187a 30).
[2] Burnet, *E.G.P.*, 171 ff.; and see 55:C 112.

COMMENTARY

663. Having raised arguments against those who deny the first principle, and having settled the issue, here the Philosopher indicates how one must proceed differently against various men who adopted different versions of the above-mentioned error. This is divided into two parts.

In the first (353:C 663) he shows that one must proceed differently against different men. In the second (354:C 665) he begins to proceed in a different way than he did above ("Those who").

He accordingly says, first (353), that the same method "of discussion," i.e., of popular address (or "of good grammatical construction," according to another translation, or of well ordered argument "or intercession," as is said in the Greek, i.e., of persuasion) is not applicable to all of the foregoing positions; that is, to the position that contradictories can be true, and to the position that truth consists in appearances. For some thinkers adopt the foregoing positions for two reasons. Some do so because of some difficulty; for since certain sophistical arguments occur to them, from which the foregoing positions seem to follow, and they do not know how to solve them, they accept the conclusion. Hence their ignorance is easily cured. For one must not oppose them or attack the arguments which they give, but must appeal to their thought, clearing up the mental difficulties which have led them to form such opinions; and then they will give up these positions.

664. Others adopt the foregoing positions, not because of any difficulty which leads them to such positions, but only because they want to argue "for the sake of argument," i.e., because of a certain insolence, inasmuch as they want to maintain impossible theories of this kind for their own sake since the contrary of these cannot be demonstrated. The cure for these men is the refutation or rejection "of what they express in speech and in words," i.e., on the grounds that the word in a statement has some meaning. Now the meaning of a statement depends on the meaning of the words, so that it is necessary to return to the princi-

[1] Diels, Frag. 1.

ple that words signify something. This is the principle which the Philosopher used above (332:C 611).

665. **Those who** (354).

Since the Philosopher met the difficulties above on this point by considering the meaning of words, he begins here to meet those who are in difficulties by solving their problems.

First (354), he deals with those who held that contradictories are true at the same time; and second (357:C 669), he deals with those who held that everything which appears so is true ("And similarly").

In regard to the first he does two things. First, he sets forth the difficulty which led some men to admit that contradictories are true at the same time. Second (355:C 667), he clears up this difficulty ("Concerning those").

He says, then, that the opinion on this point, that the parts of a contradiction may be true at the same time, was formed by some men as a result of a difficulty which arose with regard to sensible things, in which generation and corruption and motion are apparent. For it seemed that contraries were generated from the same thing; for example, air, which is warm, and earth, which is cold, both come from water. But everything which is generated comes from something that existed before; for non-being cannot come into being, since nothing comes from nothing. A thing therefore had to have in itself contradictories simultaneously, because if both the hot and the cold are generated from one and the same thing, then it turns out to be hot and not-hot itself.

666. It was because of such reasoning that Anaxagoras claimed [1] that everything is mixed in everything else. For from the fact that anything at all seemed to come from anything else he thought that one thing could come from another only if it already existed

in it. Democritus also seems to have agreed with this theory, for he claimed [2] that the void and the full are combined in any part of a body. And these are like being and non-being, because the full has the character of being and the void the character of non-being.

667. Concerning those (355).

Here he solves the foregoing difficulty in two ways. First, he says that the opinion of those who have adopted the foregoing absurd views because of some difficulty must be met by appealing to their thought, as has been stated (353:C 663). Therefore "concerning those who base their opinions," i.e., those who think that contradictories are true at the same time, "on these grounds," i.e., on the reasoning mentioned above, we say that in one sense they speak the truth and in another they do not know what they are saying since their statements are absurd. For being has two meanings: actual being and potential being; and therefore when they say that being does not come from non-being, in one sense they are right and in another they are not. For being does not come from actual being but from potential being. Hence in one sense the same thing can be at the same time both being and non-being,

and in another sense it cannot; for the same thing can be contraries potentially, but it cannot be both "in complete actuality," i.e., actually. For if something warm is potentially both hot and cold, it still cannot be actually both.

668. Further, we shall (356).

Then he gives the second solution. He says that we deem it fitting that they should accept or think that there is some kind of substance to which neither motion nor generation nor corruption belongs, as is proved in Book VIII of the *Physics*.[3] Now one could not conclude to the existence of this kind of substance by reason of what has been said above, namely, that contraries belong to it, because nothing is generated from them. This solution seems to be like the one reached by the Platonists, who, because of the changeable character of sensible things, were compelled to posit unchangeable separate Forms (i.e., those of which definitions are given, and demonstrations made, and certain knowledge is had) on the grounds that there could be no certain knowledge of sensible things because of their changeableness and the mixture of contrariety which they contain. But the first solution is a better one.

[2] Burnet, *E.G.P.*, 171 ff.
[3] *Physica*, VIII, 5 (258b 5).

LESSON 11

The Reason Why Some Considered Appearances to Be True

ARISTOTLE'S TEXT   Chapter 5: 1009a 38-1009b 12

357. And similarly the theory that truth consists in appearances comes to some thinkers from sensible things. For they think that the truth should not be judged by the large or small number who uphold some view; and they point out that the same thing appears to be sweet to some when they taste it and bitter to others. Hence, if all men were ill or all were mad, and only two or three were healthy or in possession of their wits, the latter would appear ill or mad and not the former. Further, they say that the impressions made upon many of the other animals are contrary to those made upon us, and that to the senses of each person things do not always appear to be the same. Therefore it is not always evident which of these views is true or which is false, but both appear equally so. And it is for this reason that Democritus says [1] that either nothing is true or it is not evident to us.

[1] Ritter and Preller, 204.

COMMENTARY

669. Having solved the difficulty which led the ancient philosophers to maintain that contradictories are true at the same time, the Philosopher now dispels the difficulty which led some thinkers to maintain that every appearance is true.

This part is divided into two. First (351:C 669), he gives the difficulties which led some thinkers to hold the position mentioned above. Second (363:C 685), he dispels these difficulties ("But in reply").

In regard to the first he does two things. First, he gives the reason which led these men to maintain that every appearance is true. Second (358:C 672), he explains why they reasoned in this way ("In general").

He therefore says, first (357), that, just as the opinion which maintained that contradictories are true at the same time came from certain sensible things in which it happens that contradictories come from the same thing, so too "the theory that truth consists in appearances," or the opinion about the truth of appearances, is derived from certain sensible things; that is, by those who are not perverse but are drawn into this position because of difficulties. This occurs because they find that different men hold contrary opinions about the same sensible things; and they give three reasons in support of their position. First, they point out that the same thing appears to taste sweet to some and bitter to others, so that men

267

have contrary opinions about all sensible things. Second, they note that many animals make judgments about sensible things which are contrary to ours; for what seems tasty to the ox or to the ass is judged by man to be unpalatable. Third, they say that the same man at different times makes different judgments about sensible things; for what now appears to be sweet and palatable to him at another time seems bitter or tasteless.

670. And no certain reason can be given that clearly indicates which of these opinions is true or which is false, because one of these seems no truer to one person than the other does to another person. Therefore they must be equally true or equally false. Hence Democritus said[1] that either nothing is definitely true or, if anything is true, it is not evident to us; for even though we acquire our knowledge of things through the senses, their judgment is not certain since they do not always judge in the same way. Hence we do not seem to have any certainty regarding the truth so that we can say that this opinion is definitely true and its contrary definitely false.

671. But someone could say, in opposing this position, that some rule can be adopted whereby a person can discern among contrary opinions the one that is true. That is, we might say that the judgment which healthy people make about sensible things is right, and the one which sick people make is not; and that the judgment which wise and intelligent people make in matters of truth is right, and the one which foolish or ignorant people make is not. He rejects this reply at the very start on the grounds that no certain judgment about the truth of any theory can be fittingly based on the number, large or small, of persons who hold it, according to which that would be said to be true which seems so to many, and that to be false which seems so to a few; for sometimes what many believe is not simply true. Now health and sickness or wisdom and foolishness do not seem to differ only by reason of the greater or smaller number of people involved. For if all or most persons were like those who are now thought to be ignorant or foolish, they would be considered wise, and those who are now thought to be wise would be considered foolish. The same applies in the case of health and sickness. Hence the judgment regarding truth and falsity of one who is healthy and wise is no more credible than the judgment of one who is ill and foolish.

[1] Ritter and Preller, 204.

LESSON 12

Two Reasons Why Some Identify Truth with Appearances

ARISTOTLE'S TEXT   Chapter 5: 1009b 12-1010a 15

358. And in general it is because these philosophers think that discretion is sensory perception, and that this in turn is alteration, that they say that what appears to the senses is necessarily true.

359. For it is for these reasons that both Empedocles and Democritus and, we may probably say, every one of the other philosophers became involved in such opinions. For Empedocles also says that when men change their condition they change their knowledge, "for understanding varies in men in relation to what is seen," according to him.[1] And elsewhere he says, "Insofar as they are changed into a different nature, to that extent it is proper for them always to think other thoughts." [2] And Parmenides also speaks in the same way: "For just as each has his mixture of many-jointed limbs, so intellect is present in men; for it is the same thing, the nature of the limbs, which exercises discretion in men—in all and in each; for that which is more is intellect." [3] Anaxagoras is also recorded as saying to some of his companions that things were such to them as they thought them to be. And men also say that Homer maintained this view,[4] because he made Hector,[5] after he was stunned by the blow, think other thoughts; implying that people of sound and unsound mind both think but not the same thoughts. It is evident, then, that if both of these states of mind are forms of knowledge, beings must also be so and not so at the same time.

360. Hence their conclusion happens to be the most serious one. For if those who have seen most clearly the truth which it is possible for us to have (and these are those who seek and love it most), maintain such opinions and express such views about the truth, how is it unfitting that those who are trying to philosophize should abandon the attempt? For to seek the truth will be like chasing birds.[6]

361. Now the reason these men held this opinion is that, while they investigated the truth about beings, they thought that sensible things alone exist; and in these much of the nature of the indeterminate, i.e., the kind of being which we have described (355), is present. Hence, while they speak in a plausible way, they do not say what is true; for it is more plausible to speak as they do than as Epicharmus did to Xenophanes.[7]

362. Again, since they saw that the whole of the natural world is in motion, and that we can say nothing true about what is undergoing change, they came to

[1] Diels, Frag. 106.
[2] Diels, Frag. 108.
[3] Diels, Frag. 16.
[4] *Iliad,* xxiii, 698.
[5] The passage refers to Euryalus, not Hector.
[6] *Paroemiographi Graeci,* ii, 677.
[7] Kaibel, Frag. 252.

the conclusion that it is impossible to say anything true about what is always changing altogether. For it was from this view that the most extreme of the opinions mentioned above blossomed forth; that is, the opinion held by those who are said to Heraclitize, and such as Cratylus expressed, who finally thought that he should say nothing but only moved his finger, and criticized Heraclitus for saying that it is impossible to step into the same river twice; for he himself thought that this could not be done even once.

COMMENTARY

672. He gives the reason why these philosophers adopted the foregoing position. First (358:C 672), he shows how sensory perception provided one reason for adopting this position; and second (361:C 681), how sensible objects provided another ("Now the reason").

In regard to the first part he does three things. First, he explains how sensory perception provided one reason for adopting this position. Second (359:C 674), he recounts the opinions of different men which have this reason as their common basis ("For it is"). Third (360:C 680), he attacks these opinions ("Hence their conclusion").

He accordingly says, first (358), that the ancients were of the opinion that discretion, i.e., wisdom or science, is merely sensory perception; for they did not make any distinction between sense and intellect. Now sensory perception comes about through a certain alteration of a sense with reference to sensible objects. And so the fact that a sense perceives something results from the impression which a sensible thing makes on the sense. Thus a sensory perception always corresponds to the nature of the sensible object as it appears. Hence, according to these thinkers, whatever appears to the senses is necessarily true; and since we must add that all knowing is sensory, it follows that whatever appears in any way at all to anyone is true.

673. But this argument fails, not only because it holds that sense and intellect are the same, but also because it maintains that the judgment which a sense makes about sensible objects is never false. For while a sense may make a mistake about common and accidental sensible objects, it does not do this with regard to its proper sensible object, except perhaps when the sensory organ is indisposed. And even though a sense is altered by its sensible object, the judgment of a sense does not have to conform to the conditions of the sensible object; for it is not necessary that the action of an agent be received in the patient according to the mode of being of the agent but only according to that of the patient or subject. This is why a sense sometimes is not disposed to receive the form of a sensible object according to the mode of being which the form has in the sensible object, and it therefore sometimes judges a thing to be otherwise than it really is.

674. **For it is** (359).
He presents the opinions which different men held for the reasons stated above. Now all of the statements of these men which he adduces imply two things: first, that intellect is the same as sense, and, second, that every appearance is true. Thus he says that it is for the reasons mentioned above that Empedocles and Democritus and each of the other philosophers became in-

volved in such opinions about reality "we may probably say," i.e., we can conjecture on the basis of their statements.

675. For Empedocles said [1] that those who change "their condition," i.e., some bodily disposition, also change their understanding; implying that the intellect, to which knowledge belongs, depends on a condition of the body, just as a sense does. For understanding increases in men "in relation to what is seen"; that is, an increase in knowledge takes place in a man by reason of the fact that something new begins to appear to him, and this comes about as a result of some change in a bodily disposition. Another translation states this more clearly, saying, "For purpose or decision develops in man in relation to what is at hand"; as if to say, according to the different dispositions which are actually present in men, new decisions or new purposes or new judgments develop in them. And the implication is that decision or purpose does not depend on any intellective power in man over and above the senses but only on a disposition of the body, which is changed with the presence of different things. But in other works [2] of his Empedocles says that, to the extent that alteration occurs, that is, to the extent that men are changed to another bodily disposition, to that extent, he says, there is always thoughtfulness in them; that is, thought, concern, or planning arises in them proportionately. This translation is a difficult one to understand, but another states this notion more clearly, saying, "to the extent that men have been changed, to that extent they are always determined to think other thoughts or even foolish ones." Or according to another text, "It is proper for them [always to think other thoughts]," as if to say

that, insofar as a man is changed in some bodily disposition, to that extent his basic outlook is different—implying that he has a different understanding and a different outlook.

676. Then he gives Parmenides' opinion in this matter. He says that Parmenides speaks about the truth of things in the same way that Empedocles does, for Parmenides says [3] that, just as each man has an arrangement of jointed members, or "of many-jointed limbs," according to another text, so intellect is present in men; implying that there is a great deal of variety and circumvolution in the members of man in order that such an arrangement of members may be adjusted for the operation of the intellect, which depends on the way in which the members are combined, according to him. For he says that it is the same thing "which cares for," i.e., which has the care or supervision of the members because of the nature of the members, and which is "in each," i.e., in the individual parts of the universe, and "in all," i.e., in the whole universe. Yet insofar as it is present in the whole universe and in its individual parts and in men, it is designated by different names. In the whole universe it is called God, in the individual parts it is called nature, and in men it is called thought. Thus it is present to a greater degree in man than it is in the other parts of the universe; for in man this power thinks as a result of the determinate way in which his members are combined, but this does not apply in the case of other things. In this statement he also wants it understood that thought is a result of the way in which the body is composed, and thus does not differ from sensory perception. Another translation states this more clearly, saying, "For

[1] Diels, Frag. 106.
[2] Diels, Frag. 108.
[3] Diels, Frag. 16.

it is the same thing, the nature of the limbs, which exercises discretion in men—in all and in each; for that which is more is intellect."

677. Then he gives the opinion of Anaxagoras, who expressed it to some of his companions and friends and had them commit it to memory, namely, that things are such to them as they take or believe them to be. This is the second point which is touched on in these statements of the philosophers, namely, that truth depends on opinion.

678. Then he gives the view of Homer, who seemed to be of the same opinion according to what people said of him. For in his story [4] he made Hector [5] lie, as it were, in a trance from the blow which he had been dealt, "lingering in another place," i.e., to think other thoughts than he had thought before, or, according to another text, to be of a different opinion from the one which he had before; as if in lingering and not lingering, i.e., in the state in which he lay after being struck down, he would both think and not think, although not about the same thing. For he knew those things which then appeared to him, but not those which he had known before and had then ceased to know. Another translation expresses the idea thus: "Implying that people of sound and unsound mind both think but not the same thoughts"; as if to say that, just as this is true of Hector, who had strange opinions after the blow, so too it is possible for others to have sound and foolish opinions at the same, although not about the same things but about different ones.

679. Now from all of the foregoing views of the philosophers he draws his intended conclusion that, if both of these states of mind constitute knowledge, i.e., those states in which a man thinks contrary things when he is changed from one state to another, it follows that whatever anyone thinks is true; for knowing would not consist in thinking what is false. Hence it follows that beings are equally so and not so.

680. **Hence, their conclusion** (360).

Here he attacks the above-mentioned philosophers. He says that the conclusion which they drew is the most serious one. For if those who have seen the truth most clearly, insofar as it is possible for man to see it (namely, the foregoing philosophers, who are also the ones that love and seek it most of all) offer such opinions and views about the truth, how is it unfitting that these philosophers should grieve about the ineffectualness of their study if truth cannot be found? Another text reads, "How is it unfitting that those who are trying to philosophize should give up or abandon the attempt?" i.e., that a man should not cling to those who want to philosophize but despise them. For, if a man can know nothing about the truth, to seek the truth is to seek something which he cannot attain. In fact he resembles someone who chases or hunts birds; for the more he pursues them the farther they get away from him.

681. **Now the reason** (361).

He indicates how sensible things influenced this opinion, i.e., how they provided a basis for the above-mentioned position. For, since sensible things are naturally prior to the senses, the dispositions of the senses must depend on those of sensible things. He gives two ways in which sensible things provided a basis for this position. The second (362) is treated at the words, "Again, since they."

He accordingly says, first, that the reason why the foregoing philosophers adopted this position is this: since they aimed to know the truth about beings, and it seemed to them that sensible things alone exist, they therefore based

---

[4] *Iliad,* xxiii, 698.

[5] The reference is to Euryalus, not Hector.

their doctrine about truth in general on the nature of sensible things. Now in sensible things much of the nature of the infinite or indeterminate is present, because they contain matter, which is not in itself limited to one form but is in potency to many; and in these the nature of being is also found just as we have pointed out: the being of sensible things is not determinate but is open to various determinations. It is not to be wondered at, then, if he does not assign a definite knowledge to the senses, but one kind of knowledge to one sense, and another kind to another sense.

682. And for this reason the above-mentioned philosophers use the foregoing argument plausibly or fittingly, though they are not right in claiming that there is nothing definite in sensible things; for even though matter in itself is indeterminately disposed for many forms, nevertheless by a form it is determined to one mode of being. Hence, since things are known by their form rather than by their matter, it is wrong to say that we can have no definite knowledge of them. Yet, since the opinion of these philosophers has some plausibility, it is more fitting to speak as they do than as Epicharmus did to Xenophanes, who seems to have said that all things are immovable, necessary and known with certainty.

683. **Again, since they** (362).

He gives the second way in which sensible things provided a basis for this opinion. He says that the philosophers saw that the whole of the natural world, i.e., the sensible world, is in motion, and they also saw that no attribute can be predicated of anything that is being changed insofar as it is being changed; for whatever is being changed insofar as it is being changed is neither white nor black. Hence, if the nature of sensible things is being changed always and "altogether," i.e., in all respects, so that there is nothing fixed in reality, it is impossible to make

any statement about them that is definitely true. Thus it follows that the truth of an opinion or proposition does not depend on some determinate mode of being in reality but rather on what appears to the knower; so that it is what appears to each individual that is true for him.

684. That such was their argument becomes clear as follows. For from this assumption or opinion there sprouted "the most serious or extreme" opinion of the philosophers of whom we have spoken, i.e., the opinion which is found to be the most serious or extreme in this class. And this is the one which he called "Heraclitizing," i.e., following the opinion of Heraclitus, or the opinion of those who were disciples of Heraclitus, according to another text, or of those who professed to follow the opinion of Heraclitus, who claimed that all things are in motion and consequently that nothing is definitely true. This opinion also was maintained by Cratylus, who finally arrived at such a pitch of madness that he thought that he should not express anything in words, but in order to express what he wanted he would only move his finger. He did this because he believed that the truth of the thing which he wanted to express would pass away before he had finished speaking. But he could move his finger in a shorter space of time. This same Cratylus also reprimanded or rebuked Heraclitus. For Heraclitus said that a man cannot step into the same river twice, because before he steps in a second time the water of the river already has flowed by. But Cratylus thought that a man cannot step into the same river even once, because even before he steps in once the water then in the river flows by and other water replaces it. Thus a man is incapable not only of speaking twice about anything before his disposition is changed but even of speaking once.

LESSON 13

Change in Sensible Things Not Opposed to Their Truth

ARISTOTLE'S TEXT   Chapter 5: 1010a 15-1010b 1

363. But in reply to this theory we shall also say that there is some reason why these men should think that what is changing, when it is changing, does not exist.

364. Yet there is a problem here; for what is casting off some quality retains something of what is being cast off, and something of what is coming to be must already exist. And in general if a thing is ceasing to be, there must be something which is; and if a thing is coming to be, there must be something from which it comes to be and something by which it comes to be; and this process cannot proceed to infinity.

365. But setting aside these considerations, let us say that change in quantity and change in quality are not the same. Let it be granted, then, that a thing does not remain the same in quantity; but it is by reason of its form that we know each thing.

366. Again, those who hold this view deserve to be criticized, because what they saw in the case of a very small number of sensible things they asserted to be true also of the whole universe. For it is only that region of the sensible world about us which is always in process of generation and corruption. But this is, so to speak, not even a part of the whole, so that it would have been juster for them to have esteemed the changing because of the whole than to misjudge as they did the whole because of its changing part.

367. Further, it is evident that in answering these men we shall say the same things as we said before (356); for we must show them and make them understand that there is a kind of nature which is immobile.

368. And those who say that the same thing both is and is not at the same time can also say that all things are at rest rather than in motion. For according to this view there is nothing into which anything may be changed, since everything is already present in everything.

COMMENTARY

685. He argues against the foregoing opinions. First (363:C 685), he argues against the views that were held about the changeable character of sensible things; and second (369:C 692), against the statements that were made regarding sensory appearances ("Now concerning the truth").

In regard to the first part (363) he gives six arguments. The first of these is as follows: he who thinks that what is not does not exist, has a true opinion and makes a true statement if he expresses this. But what is being changed, while it is being changed, is neither that to which it is being changed nor that from which it is being changed; and thus some true statement can be made about a thing that is undergoing change. Hence, in opposing the foregoing theory or "account" (i.e., the opinion that no true statement can be made about anything which is changing), we can say that there is some ground or valid reason "in their case," i.e., according to the opinion of the foregoing philosophers, for thinking "that what is changing," or what is being changed, "when it is changing," i.e., while it is undergoing change, does not exist; that is, there is some reason for thinking that it has no being.

686. **Yet there is** (364).

Then he gives the second argument, and it runs thus: everything which is being changed already has some part of the terminus to which it is being changed, because what is being changed, while it is being changed, is partly in the terminus to which it is being changed, and partly in the terminus from which it is being changed, as is proved in Book VI of the *Physics* [1] (or, according to another text, "that which is casting off some quality retains something of what is being cast off"). And by this statement we are given to understand that anything which is being moved retains some part of the terminus from which it is being moved, because so long as a thing is being moved it is casting off the terminus from which it is being moved; and it is possible only to cast off some quality which belongs to a mobile subject. And something of what is coming to be must already exist, because everything

which is coming to be was coming to be, as is proved in Book VI of the *Physics*.[2] And it is also evident that, if something is ceasing to be, there must be something which is; for if it did not exist in any way at all, it already would have ceased to be and would not be ceasing to be. Similarly, if something is coming to be, there must be a matter from which it is coming to be and an agent by which it is coming to be. But this cannot go on to infinity, because, as is proved in Book II (153:C 301), there cannot be an infinite regress either in the case of material causes or in that of efficient causes. Hence a major problem faces those who say that no true statement can be made about anything which is being moved or generated, both because each thing which is being moved or generated has some part of the terminus to which it is being moved, and because in every process of generation or motion there must be held to be something unproduced and unchangeable both on the part of the matter and on that of the agent.

687. **But setting aside** (365).

Then he gives the third argument, and this rejects the very ground on which these thinkers base their opinion that all sensible things are always in motion. For they were led to make this statement because of things which increase as a result of growth. For they saw that a thing increases in quantity to a very small degree during one year, and they thought that the motion of growth was continuous, so that quantity, in which increase is observed, might be divided in proportion to the parts of time. Thus an increase in some part of quantity would take place in some part of time, and this part of quantity would be related to a whole quantity as some part of a period of time to the whole of that period. And

[1] *Physica*, VI, 5 (235b 6).
[2] *Physica*, VI, 6 (237b 10).

since this kind of motion is imperceptible, they also thought that things which appear to be at rest are being moved, although by an imperceptible motion.

688. In opposing these thinkers, then, he says that, even apart from the considerations which have been made, it is clear that change in quantity and in quality or form are not the same. And although they admit that change in quantity is continuous in reality, and that all things are always being moved imperceptibly by this motion, it is not therefore necessary for this reason that all things should be being moved in quality or form. Hence it will be possible to have a definite knowledge of things, because things are known by their form rather than by their quantity.

689. **Again, those who** (366).

Then he gives the fourth argument. He says that "those who think in this way," i.e., those who entertain the opinion that all sensible things are always being moved because they find a small number of sensible things of which this is true, deserve to be criticized; for there are many sensible things which are capable of being moved only from the viewpoint of local motion. For it is obvious that it is only the sensible things around us here in the sphere of active and passive things which are in process of generation and corruption. But this sphere or place amounts to nothing, so to speak, in comparison with the whole universe; for the entire earth has no sensible quantity in comparison with the outermost sphere. Hence this place is related to the universe as its central point, as the astronomers prove on the grounds that the six signs of the zodiac always appear above the earth. But this would not be the case if the

earth were to hide from us some part of the heavens which are perceived by the senses. For it would be foolish to make a judgment about the whole sensible world in the light of these few things. Indeed, it would have been more acceptable if the whole sensible world had been judged according to the motion of the celestial bodies, which far surpass the others in quantity.

690. **Further, it is evident** (367).

He gives the fifth argument. He says that we must also use the same arguments against these men as were used above in this same book; that is, we must show them that there is a kind of nature which is immobile, namely, that of the primary mover, as is proved in Book VIII of the *Physics*.[3] And this argument must be used against them, and they ought to accept it, as has been proved elsewhere (356:C 668). It is not true, then, that all things are always in motion, and that it is impossible to make any true statement about anything.

691. **And those who say** (368).

He gives the sixth argument. He says that their position that all things are being moved is opposed to their first position, that contradictories are true of the same subject at the same time, because if something is and is not at the same time, it follows that all things are at rest rather than in motion. For nothing is being changed in terms of any attribute which already belongs to it; for example, what is already white is not being changed as regards whiteness. But if it is possible for the same thing both to be and not be at the same time, all attributes will be present in all things, as has been proved above (345:C 639), because all will be one. Hence there will not be anything to which a thing can be changed.

---

[3] *Physica*, VIII, 5 (258b 5).

LESSON 14

Seven Arguments against the View that Truth Consists in Appearances

ARISTOTLE'S TEXT   Chapter 5: 1010b 1-1011a 2

369. Now concerning the truth that not everything which appears is true, the following points must be taken into consideration: first, that a sense is not false with regard to its proper object, but imagination is not the same as a sense.

370. Second, that it is surprising if some should raise the question whether continuous quantities are as great and colors really such as they appear to those who are at a distance or as they appear to those who are close at hand, and whether things are such as they appear to those who are healthy or to those who are ailing, and whether heavy things are such as they appear to those who are weak or to those who are strong, and whether those things are true which appear to those who are asleep or to those who are awake. For it is clear that they do not think so. Therefore no one who is in Lybia, having dreamed that he was in Athens, would go to the Odeon.

371. Again, concerning future things, as Plato says,[1] the opinion of a physician and that of a person who is ignorant of the art of medicine are not of equal value as to whether someone will get well or not.

372. Again, in the case of the senses the perception of a foreign object and that of a proper object, or that of a kindred object and that of the object of the sense concerned, are not of equal value. In the case of colors it is sight and not taste which passes judgment; and in the case of flavors it is taste and not sight which does this.

373. And no one of these senses ever affirms at the same time about the same subject that it is simultaneously both so and not so. Nor at another time does it experience any difficulty about a modification, but only about the object of which the modification is an accident. I mean, for example, that the same wine, either as a result of a change in itself or in the body, might seem at one time sweet and at another not. But sweetness, such as it is when it exists, has never changed; but one is always right about it, and sweetness itself is necessarily such as it is.

374. Yet all these theories destroy this, for just as things will have no substance, neither will they have any necessity; for that is necessary which cannot be in one way and in another. Hence, if anything is necessary, it will not be both so and not so.

375. And in general if only the sensible actually exists, there would be nothing if living things did not exist; for there would be no senses. Therefore the position that neither sensible objects nor sensory perceptions would exist is perhaps true, for these are modifications of the one sensing. But that the underlying subjects which cause perception should not exist apart from perception is impossible; for a perception is not the perception of itself, but there is some other

[1] *Theaetetus*, 171e, 178c.

thing besides the perception which must be prior to the perception. For that which causes motion is naturally prior to that which is moved, and this is no less true if they are correlative terms.

COMMENTARY

692. Here he begins to argue dialectically against the opinion that truth if equivalent to appearances; and in regard to this he does two things. First (369:C 718), he rejects this opinion. Second (381:C 718), he draws his intended conclusion ("Let this suffice").

In regard to the first he does two things. First, he argues dialectically against those who held this opinion because of some theory or difficulty. Second (376:C 708), he argues against those who held this opinion because of insolence ("Now there are some").

In regard to the first part (369) he gives seven arguments. The first of these is as follows: it has been shown (367:C 690) that not all things are changeable, and "concerning the truth that not everything which appears is true," these points must be considered. First, the proper cause of falsity is not the senses but the imagination, which is not the same as the senses. That is to say, the diversity of judgments made about sensible objects is not attributable to the senses but to the imagination, in which errors are made about sensory perceptions because of some natural obstacle. Now imagination is not the same as perception, as is proved in Book III of *The Soul*,[1] but is a motion produced as a result of actual sensing. Therefore in attributing to the senses this diversity of judgments by which one person is considered to have a false perception of a particular object about which another has a true perception, they do not proceed as they should.

Another translation states this better, saying, "And, first, it must be understood that a sense is not false with regard to its proper object," implying that no sense makes a mistake about its own proper object; for example, sight is not mistaken about colors. From this it is evident that the judgment which a sense makes about its proper sensible object is a definite one, so that there must be some definite truth in the world.

693. And if someone raises the objection that error sometimes arises even with regard to proper sensibles, his answer is that this is attributable not to the senses but to the imagination; for when the imagination is subject to some sort of abnormality, it sometimes happens that the object apprehended by a sense enters the imagination in a different way than it was apprehended by the sense. This is evident, for example, in the case of madmen, in whom the organ of imagination has been injured.

694. **Second, that it is** (370).

Then he gives his second argument, and it runs thus: it is surprising if some "should raise the question," or "be puzzled," as another text says, whether continuous quantities are such as they appear to those who are at a distance or to those who are close at hand. For it is just about self-evidently true that a sense judges quantities which are close at hand to be such as they are, and those which are far away to be smaller than they are, be-

[1] *De Anima*, III, 3 (428b 10).

cause what seems farther away appears small, as is proved in the science of optics.

695. The same thing applies if someone raises the question whether colors are such as they appear to those who are close at hand; for it is evident that the farther an agent's power is extended when it acts, the more imperfect is its effect; for fire heats those things which are far away to a lesser degree than those which are close at hand. And for the same reason the color of a perfect sensible body does not change that part of the transparent medium which is far away from it as completely as it changes that part which is close to it. Hence the judgment of a sense is truer about sensible colors in things close at hand than it is about those in things far away.

696. The same thing is also true if someone asks whether things are such as they appear to those who are healthy or "to those who are ailing," i.e., those who are ill. For healthy people have sensory organs which are well disposed, and therefore the forms of sensible things are received in them just as they are; and for this reason the judgment which healthy people make about sensible objects is a true one. But the organs of sick people are not properly disposed, and therefore they are not changed as they should be by sensible objects. Hence their judgment about such objects is not a true one. This is clear with regard to the sense of taste; for when the organ of taste in sick people has been rendered inoperative as a result of the humors being destroyed, things which have a good taste seem tasteless to them.

697. The same thing also applies regarding the question whether things having weight are as heavy as they seem to those who are weak or to those who are strong; for it is clear that the strong judge about heavy things as they really are. But this is

not the case with the weak, who find it difficult to lift a weight not only because of the heaviness of it (and this sometimes happens even with the strong) but also because of the weakness of their power, so that even less heavy things appear heavy to them.

698. The same thing again applies if the question is raised whether the truth is such as it appears to those who are asleep or to those who are awake. For the senses of those who are asleep are fettered, and thus their judgment about sensible things cannot be free like the judgment of those who are awake and whose senses are unfettered. For it has been pointed out above that it would be surprising if they should be perplexed, because it appears from their actions that they are not perplexed, and that they do not think that all of the above-mentioned judgments are equally true. For if someone in Lybia seems in his dreams to be in Athens, or if someone in Paris seems in his dreams to be in Hungary, he does not when he awakens act in the same way that he would if he were to perceive this when he is awake. For, if he were awake in Athens, he would go to the Odeon, i.e., a building in Athens; but he would not do this if he had merely dreamed it. It is clear, then, that he does not think that what appears to him when he is asleep and what appears when he is awake are equally true.

699. We can argue in the same way with regard to the other issues mentioned above; for even though men often raise questions about these issues, they are not in their own mind perplexed about them. Hence it is clear that their reason for holding to be true everything which appears, is invalid; for they held this position because of the impossibility of deciding which of several opinions is the truer, as has been stated above (353:C 663).

700. **Again, concerning future** (371).

Here he gives his third argument. He says that in the case of future events, as Plato points out,[2] the opinion of a physician and that of a person who is ignorant of the art of medicine are not "of equal value," i.e., equally important, certain, true or acceptable, as to the future possibility of some sick person being cured or not. For, while a physician knows the cause of health, this is unknown to someone who is ignorant of the art of medicine. It is clear, then, that the opinion which some held that all opinions are equally true is a foolish one.

701. **Again, in the case** (372).

He gives his fourth argument, which runs thus: in the case of sensible objects the judgment which a sense makes about some sensible object foreign to it and that which it makes about its proper sensible object are not of equal "value," i.e., equally true and acceptable; for example, sight and taste do not make the same sort of judgment about colors and flavors, but in the case of colors the judgment of sight must be accepted, "and in the case of flavors," or savors, the judgment of taste must be accepted. Hence, if sight judges a thing to be sweet and taste judges it to be bitter, taste must be accepted rather than sight.

702. And in the same way too the judgment which a sense makes about its proper sensible object and the one which it makes about something akin to its proper object are not of equal value. Now those things which are said here to be akin to proper sensible objects are called common sensibles, for example, size, number and the like, about which a sense is deceived to a greater degree than it is about its proper sensible object, although it is deceived about them to a lesser degree than it is about the sensible objects of another sense or about things which are called accidental sensible objects.

Hence it is clearly foolish to say that all judgments are equally true.

703. **And no one** (373).

He now gives his fifth argument. He says that no sense affirms at one instant of time that a thing is simultaneously both so and not so. For sight does not at the same moment affirm that something is white and not white or that it is two cubits and not two cubits or that it is sweet and not sweet. But while a sense's power of judging may seem at different times to form opposite judgments about the same thing, still from this judgment no difficulty ever arises about the sensible modification itself, but only about the subject of this modification. For example, if we take the same subject, wine, sometimes it appears to the sense to taste sweet and sometimes not. This happens either because of some change in the sentient body, i.e., in the organ, which is infected by bitter humors, so that whatever it tastes does not seem sweet to it, or else because of some change in the wine itself. But the sense of taste never changes its judgment without judging sweetness itself to be such as it considered it to be in the sweet thing when it judged it to be sweet; but about sweetness itself it always makes a true affirmation, and always does this in the same way. Hence, if the judgment of a sense is true, as these men claimed, it also follows that the nature of sweetness is necessarily such as it is; and thus something will be definitely true in reality. And it also follows that both an affirmation and a negation can never be true at the same time, because a sense never affirms that something is both sweet and not sweet at the same time, as has been stated.

704. **Yet all these** (374).

He gives the sixth argument. He says that, just as all of the above-mentioned theories or opinions destroy substantial

---

[2] *Theaetetus,* 171e, 178c.

predicates, as has been shown above (341:C 625), in a similar way they destroy all necessary predicates. For it follows that nothing could ever be predicated of anything else either substantially or necessarily. That nothing could be predicated of anything else substantially is clear from what has been stated above. That nothing could be predicated of anything else necessarily is proved as follows. That is necessary which cannot be otherwise than it is; therefore, if everything which is can exist in one way or in another way, as is held by those who say that contradictories and opposite opinions are true at the same time, it follows that nothing is necessary in the world.

705. **And in general** (375).

Then he gives the seventh argument. He says that, if everything which appears is true, and a thing is true only insofar as it appears to the senses, it follows that a thing exists only insofar as it is actually being sensed. But if something exists only in this way, i.e., insofar as it is being sensed, then it follows that nothing would exist if the senses did not exist; and this would follow if there were no animals or living things. But this is impossible.

706. For this can be true, that sensibles under the aspect of their sensibility do not exist; i.e., if they are considered under the aspect of sensibles actualized, they do not exist apart from the senses, for they are sensibles actualized insofar as they are present in a sense. And according to this every actualized sensible is a certain modification of the subject sensing, although this would be impossible if there were no sensory beings. But that the sensible objects which cause this modification in a sense should not exist is impossible. This becomes clear as follows: when some subsequent thing is removed it does not follow that a prior thing is removed. But the thing producing the modification in a sense is not the perception itself, because a perception is not the perception of itself but of something else, and this must be naturally prior to the perception just as a mover is prior to the thing which is moved. For sight does not see itself but sees color.

707. And even if someone were to raise the objection that a sensible object and a sense are correlative and thus naturally simultaneous, so that when one is destroyed the other is destroyed, Aristotle's thesis is still true; for what is potentially sensible is not said to be relative to a sense because it is referred to a sense, but because the sense is referred to it, as is stated in Book V of this work (496:C 1027). It is clearly impossible, then, to say that some things are true because they appear to the senses; yet this is what those men maintain who claim that all appearances are true, as is evident from the foregoing statements.

LESSON 15

Refutation of the View that Contradictories Can Be Shown to Be True at the Same Time. Contraries Cannot Belong to the Same Subject at the Same Time

ARISTOTLE'S TEXT   Chapter 6: 1011a 3-1011b 22

376. Now there are some, both of those who have been convinced by theories of this kind and of those who merely state them, who raise a difficulty; for they ask who it is that judges a man to be healthy, and in general who it is that judges rightly in each particular case. But such difficulties are like wondering whether we are now asleep or awake; and all such difficulties amount to the same thing. For these people think it fitting that there should be a reason for everything; for they are seeking a starting point, and they think they can get this by demonstration. Yet that sometimes they are not convinced they make evident in their actions. But according to what we have said this is characteristic of them; for they are seeking a reason for things for which no reason can be given, because the starting point of demonstration is not demonstration. These men, then, might easily believe this truth, for it is not difficult to grasp.

377. But those who seek compulsion only in words are seeking the impossible. For they deem it right to speak as they do, and immediately say contrary things.

378. Yet if not all things are relative but some things are absolute, not everything which appears will be true; for that which appears appears to someone. Thus he who says that all things which appear are true, makes all things which are, relative. Hence, those who look for compulsion in words, and think it fitting to maintain this view at the same time, must be careful to add that it is not what appears that is true, but what appears for him to whom it appears, and at the time when it appears, and in the manner in which it appears, and so on. And if they maintain their view but not in this way, it will soon happen that they are saying contrary things. For it is possible that the same thing may appear to be honey to the sense of sight but not to the sense of taste, and that, since we have two eyes, things will not appear the same to each if their sight is unequal. Now, as we have stated, there are some who say, for the reasons already given (357), that what appears is true, and that all things are therefore equally true and false, because they do not always appear the same to all men or to the same man (for they do not always happen to be the same) but often have contrary appearances at the same time. For touch says there are two objects when the fingers are crossed, but sight says there is one. And in answering these men we must say that what appears is true, but not for the same man and in the same way and at the same time, so that when these qualifications are added what appears will be true. But perhaps it is for this reason that those who argue thus, not because of some difficulty but for the sake of argument, must say that this is not true but true for this person.

379. And, as has been said before (378), they must make everything relative both to opinion and to perception, so that nothing has come to be or will come to be unless someone has first formed an opinion about it. But if something has come to be or will come to be, it is evident that not all things depend on opinion.

380. Further, if a thing is one, it is relative to one thing or to a determinate number; and if the same thing is both half and equal, still the equal is not relative to the double or the half to the equal. If, then, in relation to the thinking subject, *man* and the object of thought are the same, *man* will not be the thinking subject but the object of thought. And if each thing is relative to the thinking subject, the thinking subject will be relative to things infinite in species.

381. Let this suffice, then, regarding the points under discussion: that the firmest opinion of all is the one which asserts that opposite statements are not true at the same time; the conclusions that follow for those who say that they are true; and why they speak as they do.

382. But since it is impossible for contradictories to be true of the same subject at the same time, it is evident that contraries cannot belong to the same subject at the same time; for one of two contraries is a privation. But a privation is nothing less than the negation of substance from some determinate genus. Therefore, if it is impossible to affirm and deny something truly at the same time, it is also impossible for contraries to belong to the same subject at the same time; but either both belong in a certain respect, or the one in a certain respect and the other absolutely.

COMMENTARY

708. He argues against those who adopted the above-mentioned theory not because of any reason but merely because they are obstinate; and in regard to this he does two things. First (376:C 708), he shows how these men were moved to adopt this opinion; and second (377:C 711), how this opinion must be dealt with ("But those who").

He accordingly says, first (376), that, besides the foregoing thinkers who adopted the above-mentioned opinion because of certain difficulties, there are some "among those who have been persuaded to accept these views," or opinions (i.e., those who continue to deceive themselves and have only these arguments to support their view), who raise a question. Another translation reads: "Now there are some, both of those who have been convinced by theories of this kind and of those who merely state them, who are puzzled or raise a question." And this statement means that some of those who are puzzled, i.e., some of those who hold the above-mentioned opinion, consider only these difficulties and use the arguments which are given below. For if someone says to them that in the case of contrary opinions we should believe those persons who are healthy rather than those who are ill, and those who are wise rather than those who are ignorant, and those who are awake rather than those who are asleep, they will immediately ask how it is possible to distinguish with certainty between a healthy person and a sick one, and one who is awake and one who is asleep, and one who is wise and one who is foolish. In short, regarding all differences of opinion they will ask how it is possible to decide which one of these judges rightly in each particular case; for a man may seem to be wise to some and foolish to others, and the same applies in other cases.

709. But these questions are foolish, for they are similar to the question whether we are now asleep or awake; for the distinction between all of these is not essential. Yet all of the foregoing difficulties amount to the same thing since they have a common root. For these sophists desire that demonstrative arguments should be given for all things; for it is obvious that they wanted to take some starting point which would be for them a kind of rule whereby they could distinguish between those who are healthy and those who are ill, and between those who are awake and those who are asleep. And they were not content to know this rule in just any way at all but wanted to acquire it by demonstration. That these men were in error, then, becomes evident from their actions, according to what has been said. And from these considerations it appears that their position is false; for if the judgments of one who is asleep and of one who is awake were equally good, then the same thing would result from each judgment when men act. But this is clearly false. Another text says, "But that sometimes they are not convinced they make evident in their actions"; and this statement is the clearer one in the light of the things laid down above. For although these men maintain this view and raise such questions, still they are not deceived in their own mind so that they believe the judgment of one who is asleep and the judgment of one who is awake to be equally true. And this is clear from their actions, as has been pointed out.

710. But even though they are not deceived so as to be perplexed in this matter, this "nevertheless is characteristic of them," i.e., this weakness of mind that they should seek a demonstrative argument for things for which no demonstration can be given. For "the starting point of demonstration is not demonstration"; i.e., there can be no demonstration of it. And this is easy for them to believe, because this too is not difficult to grasp by demonstration; for a demonstrative argument proves that not all things can be demonstrated, otherwise there would be an infinite regress.

711. **But those who** (377).

He now argues against the other philosophers, i.e., against those who were not moved to maintain that all appearances are true on the grounds that no rule can be established demonstratively whereby it is possible to distinguish with certainty between those who judge rightly and those who do not, but who hold the above-mentioned theory or view only because they are insolent.

In regard to this he does three things. First (377:C 711), he shows that such insolence tends to lead to an impossible conclusion. Second (378:C 712), he indicates the way in which it seems necessary to oppose them ("Yet if not all things"). Third (379:C 716), he explains how we must meet their argument from the viewpoint of truth ("And, as has been").

He accordingly says, first (377), that those who seek "compulsion merely in words," i.e., those who are not moved by any reason or because of the difficulty involved in some problem or because of some failure in demonstration but depend solely on words and believe that they can say anything which cannot be disproved—such people as these want to argue to an impossible conclusion. For they want to adopt the principle that contraries are true at the same time on the grounds that all appearances are true.

712. **Yet if not all** (378).

Then he shows how we may oppose these men by using their own position and avoid the foregoing impossible conclusion. He says that, unless everything which is, is claimed to be relative, it cannot be said that every appearance is true. For if there are some things in the world which have absolute being and are not relative to perception or to opinion, being and appearing will not be the same; for appearing implies a relation to perception or to opinion, because that which appears appears to someone; and thus whatever is not an appearance must be true. It is clear, then, that whoever says that all appearances are true, makes all beings relative, i.e., to perception or to opinion. Hence, in opposing the foregoing sophists who seek compulsion in words, we may say that, if anyone thinks it fitting "to grant this view," i.e., to concede this opinion which they maintain, he must be careful, or observant, lest he be led to admit that contradictories are true at the same time; for it should not be said unqualifiedly that everything which appears is true, but that what appears is true for the one to whom it appears, and inasmuch as it appears, and when it appears, and in the manner in which it appears. We would be allowed to add these qualifications on the grounds that a thing does not have being in an absolute sense but only relatively.

713. Now this should be noted by those who want to adopt this position, because if someone were to grant them that every appearance is true, and thus not admit the above-mentioned qualifications, as has been stated, it would follow immediately that he is saying that contraries are true at the same time. For it is possible that the same thing may appear to be honey to the sense of sight because its color resembles that of honey, and not appear to be honey to the sense of taste because it does not taste like honey. And similarly when two eyes are unlike, the vision which is had through each is not the same, or the visual impressions which we get through each eye do not seem the same. For example, if the pupil of one eye were infected by some gross or dark vapor, and the other were free of this, all things would seem dark or obscure through the infected eye but not through the good one. I say, then, that one must be careful, or observant, because this is necessary in confronting the foregoing sophists, who say, for the reasons given above (376:C 708), that every appearance is true.

714. And from this position it would also follow that all things are equally true and false, because they do not appear the same to all men or even the same to one man, since the same man very often makes contrary judgments about the same thing at the same time on the basis of different senses; for example, sight judges that thing to be one which touch judges to be two, because when the fingers are crossed it happens that the same tangible object is sensed by different organs of touch; that is, the contact through different fingers affects the tactual power as though there were two tangible objects. But it does not seem to the same man through the same sense and in the same way and at the same time that this is true, namely, that contraries are true at the same time.

715. Therefore, it is perhaps necessary to use this answer against the above-mentioned sophists who argue thus not because of some difficulty but for the sake of argument (as though upholding this statement for its own sake because they are perverse), namely, that this is not true absolutely but true for this person. For it does not follow from this that contradictories are true at the same time, because it is not contradictory that something should be true for one person and not true for another.

716. **And, as has been said** (379).
He tells us that we should oppose the foregoing sophists from the standpoint of the truth and not just offer an

argument *ad hominem,* namely, not by granting the false opinion which they maintain. And he does this by means of two arguments. The first is this: as has been stated before, if everything which appears is true, they must "make all things relative," i.e., to perception or to opinion. Now from this the untenable position follows that nothing may exist or come to be if it is not thought of in some way. But if this is false (because [1] many things are and come to be of which there is neither opinion nor knowledge, for example, things which exist in the depths of the sea or in the bowels of the earth), it is evident that not all things are relative, i.e., to perception or to opinion. Hence not every appearance is true.

717. **Further, if a thing** (380).

He gives the second argument. He says that what is one is relative only to one thing, and not to any one thing at all but to a determinate one. For example, it is clear that the half and the equal may be the same in their subject, yet the double is not said to be relative to the equal but rather to the half; but equal is said to be relative to equal. Similarly, if man himself as a thinking subject is also the object of thought, man is not relative to the thinking subject as a thinking subject, but as the object of thought. If, then, all beings are relative to a thinking subject as such, it follows that what I call the thinking subject is not one, since one is relative only to one, but it is an infinite number of things in species, since an infinite number of things are related to it. But this is impossible. Hence it cannot be said that all things are said to be relative to a thinking subject, or that everything which appears so, or is thought to be so, is therefore true.

718. **Let this suffice** (381).

He now draws his intended conclu-sion, and in regard to this he does two things. First, he draws his main con-clusion; and second (382:C 719), he derives a corollary from it ("But since it is impossible").

He accordingly says, first (381), that it is clear from the above statement that the most certain of all opinions or views is the one which states that opposite statements or propositions, i.e., contradictory ones, are not true at the same time. And the impossible con-clusions which face those who say that they are true at the same time, and the reason which moved them to say this, have also been explained.

719. **But since it is impossible** (382).

He draws the corollary. He says that, since it is impossible, from what has been said, for two contradictories to be true of the same subject at the same time, it is also evident that contraries cannot belong to the same subject; for the privative character of one of two contraries is no less evident in the case of contraries than it is in the case of other opposites, although each of two contraries is a positive reality; for it does not consist in affirmation and negation or in privation and possession. For one of them is imperfect when compared with the other, as black when compared with white, and bitter with sweet; and thus it has a kind of privation added to it. But privation is negation of substance, i.e., in some determinate subject. And it is also the deprivation of some determinate genus; for it is a negation within a genus. For not everything which does not see is said to be blind, but only that which is found in the genus of seeing things. It is clear, then, that a contrary includes privation, and that privation is a kind of negation. Hence, if it is impossible both to affirm and to deny something at the same time, it is also impossible for contraries to be-long absolutely to the same subject at

---

[1] Reading *quia* (with the former Cathala edition) for *qui.*

the same time; but either "both belong to it," i.e., relatively, as when
both are present potentially or par-
tially, or one is present in a certain
respect and the other absolutely; or
one is present in many and the more
important parts, and the other only
in some part; for example, an Ethiopian
is black absolutely and white as regards his teeth.

LESSON 16

No Intermediate between Contradictories. How Heraclitus and Anaxagoras Influenced This Position

ARISTOTLE'S TEXT   Chapter 7: 1011b 23-1012a 28

383. Neither can there be an intermediate between contradictories, but of each subject it is necessary either to affirm or to deny one thing. This first becomes evident when people define what truth and falsity are; for to say that what is, is not, or that what is not, is, is false; and to say that what is, is, or that what is not, is not, is true. Hence he who affirms that something is or is not will say either what is true or what is false. But neither what is nor what is not is said to be or not to be.

384. Further, an intermediate between contradictories will be such either in the way that green is an intermediate between white and black, or as what is neither a man nor a horse is an intermediate between a man and a horse. If it is of the latter sort, there will then be no change; for change is from what is good to what is not-good, or from the latter to the former. But that this now occurs is always apparent; for change takes place only between opposites and intermediates. But if it is a true intermediate, then in this case there will be a kind of change to something white, but not from what is not-white. However, this is not now apparent.

385. Further, the mind either affirms or denies every sensible and intelligible object. This is clear from the definition, because it expresses what is true or what is false. Indeed, when the mind composes in this way by affirming or denying, it says what is true; and when it does it otherwise, it says what is false.

386. Again, there must be an intermediate in addition to all contradictories, unless one is arguing for the sake of argument. In that case one will say what is neither true nor false. And then there will be something else besides being and non-being; and therefore there will also be some kind of change besides generation and corruption.

387. Again, there will also be an intermediate in all those classes of things in which the negation of a term implies its contrary; for example, in the class of numbers there will be a number which is neither even nor odd. But this is impossible, as is evident from the definition.

388. Further, there will be an infinite regress, and there will be things which are related not only as half again as much but even more. For it will also be possible to deny the intermediate both with reference to its affirmation and to its negation; and this again will be something, for its substance is something different.

389. Again, when one answers "no" to the question whether a thing is white, he has denied nothing except that it is; and its not-being is a negation.

390. Now some men have formed this opinion in the same way that other

unreasonable opinions have been formed; for when they cannot refute eristic arguments, they assent to the argument and claim that the conclusion is true. Some men hold this view, then, for this reason, and others because they seek an explanation for everything.

391. The starting point to be used against all of these people is the definition, and the definition results from the necessity of their meaning something; for the concept, of which the word is a sign, is a definition.

392. Now the statement of Heraclitus, which says that all things are and are not, seems to make all things true; and the statement of Anaxagoras that there is an intermediate between contradictories seems to make everything false; for when all things are mixed together, the mixture is neither good nor not good, so that it is impossible to say anything true.

COMMENTARY

720. Having argued dialectically against those who maintain that contradictories are true at the same time, Aristotle now argues against those who maintain that there is an intermediate between contradictories; for these thinkers do not always say that the one or the other part of a contradiction is true. In regard to this he does two things. First (383:C 720), he argues against this position. Second (393:C 736), he argues against certain other unreasonable questions which follow from this position and from the one above ("With these points").

In regard to the first he does two things. First, he raises arguments against the position mentioned. Second (390:C 731), he gives the reason why some thinkers have been moved to hold this position ("Now some men").

In regard to the first part he gives seven arguments. He says, first (383), that, just as contradictories cannot be true at the same time, neither can there be an intermediate between contradictories, but it is necessary either to affirm or deny one or the other.

721. This first becomes evident from the definition of truth and falsity; for to say what is false is simply to say that what is, is not, or that what is

not, is. And to say what is true is simply to say that what is, is, or that what is not, is not. It is clear, then, that whoever says that something is, says either what is true or what is false; and if he says what is true, it must be so, because to say what is true is to say that what is, is. And if he says what is false, it must not be so, because to say what is false is simply to say that what is, is not. The same thing applies if he says that something is not; for if he says what is false, it must be; and if he says what is true, it must not be. Therefore, either the affirmation or the negation is necessarily true. But he who holds that there is an intermediate between contradictories does not claim that it is necessary to say that what is either is or is not; nor does he claim that it is necessary to speak in this way about what is not. Thus neither he who affirms nor he who denies need say what is true or what is false.

722. **Further, an intermediate** (384). He gives the second argument, which runs thus: an intermediate between any two contradictories can be understood in one way as something that participates in each of the extremes, and this is an intermediate in the same

genus, as green or yellow is an intermediate between white and black; or in another way as something that is the negation of each extreme, and such an intermediate is different in genus; for example, a stone, which is neither a man nor a horse, is an intermediate between a man and a horse. Therefore, if there is an intermediate between contradictories, it will be such either in the first way or in the second.

723. If it is an intermediate in the second way, there will be no change. This becomes clear as follows: every change is from what is not-good to what is good, or from what is good to what is not-good. Hence, since change is between contraries, for example, white and black, change must take place between things which are opposed as contradictories; for black is not white, as is clear from the above statements. But according to the foregoing position there cannot be change from what is not-good to what is good, or the reverse. Hence there will be no change. Yet it always appears or seems that change proceeds from what is not-good to what is good, or the reverse. That every change of this sort would be destroyed if the foregoing position is true becomes clear as follows. Change can take place only between contraries and intermediates which belong to the same genus. But there can be a change from one extreme to another only through an intermediate. Therefore, if there is an intermediate between contradictories as the negation of both, i.e., as something belonging to a different genus, it will be impossible for change to take place between an extreme and an intermediate, and therefore between one extreme and another.

724. And if it is an intermediate in the first way, so that the intermediate between contradictories belongs to the same genus by participating in both, as yellow is an intermediate between white and black, this impossible conclusion follows: there will be some process of generation which terminates in white and does not come from the not-white, because change proceeds not only from one extreme to another but also from an intermediate. But it does not seem to be true that there is any process of change terminating in the white which does not proceed from the not-white. Thus it is clear that there is no way at all in which there can be an intermediate between contradictories.

725. **Further, the mind** (385).

He gives the third argument, which runs thus: in every one of the conceptions by which the intellect knows or understands, it either affirms or denies something. Now from the definition of truth and falsity it seems that whether one affirms or denies he must say what is true or what is false; because when the intellect composes in this way, either by affirming or denying as the matter stands in reality, it expresses what is true; but when it does otherwise, it expresses what is false. Thus it is clear that a true statement must always be either an affirmation or a negation, because some opinion must be true, and every opinion is either an affirmation or a negation. Hence it must always be either an affirmation or a negation that is true; and thus there is no intermediate between contradictories.

726. **Again, there must** (386).

Then he gives the fourth argument, which runs thus: if one maintains that there must be an intermediate between contradictories, then it is necessary to say that in the case of all contradictories there must be besides the contradictories themselves something true which is an intermediate between them, unless this person is arguing "for the sake of argument," i.e., without any real reason but only because it pleases him to speak in this way. But this cannot be true in all cases, because the true and the not-true are contradictories. Thus it would follow that there is someone who says what is neither true nor false. But the opposite of this was made clear from the definition of truth and falsity.

727. Similarly, since being and non-being are contradictories, it will follow that there is something besides being and non-being, and thus there will be some kind of change besides generation and corruption; for generation is a change to being, and corruption a change to non-being. Therefore there can be no intermediate between contradictories.

728. **Again, there will** (387).

He gives the fifth argument. He says that in some genera a negation takes the place of a contrary difference; or, according to another text, "negation supplies the contrary," because one of two contraries, which must be in the same genus, derives its definition from negation, as is clear in the case of the even and the odd, and the just and unjust. Therefore, if there is an intermediate between affirmation and negation, there will be some intermediate between all these contraries, since they obviously depend on affirmation and negation; for example, in the case of number, there will be some number which is neither even nor odd. But this is clearly impossible in the light of the definition of the even and the odd; for the even is what can be divided into equal numbers, and the odd is what cannot. Therefore it follows that there cannot be an intermediate between affirmation and negation.

729. **Further, there will** (388).

He now gives the sixth argument: those who claim that there is an intermediate between an affirmation and a negation hold some third thing besides these two, which all posit in common, saying that there is nothing intermediate between them. But three is related to two "as half again as much," i.e., in a proportion of one and a half to one. Therefore, according to the opinion of those who hold an intermediate between an affirmation and a negation it appears at first sight that all things "will be related as half again as much," i.e., in a proportion of one and a half to one to the things which are given, because there will be not only affirmations and negations but also intermediates. And this is not the only conclusion that follows, but it also follows that there will be many more things in infinite regression. For it is evident that everything which can be affirmed can also be denied. But if it is possible to affirm that the following three things exist: an affirmation, a negation and an intermediate, it is then also possible to deny these three. And just as a negation differs from an affirmation, in a similar way there will also be some fourth thing which differs from the three mentioned; for it will have a different substance and intelligible structure than those just mentioned, in the same way that a negation has a different substance and intelligible structure from an affirmation. And it is possible to deny these four, and the negations of these will be true; and so on to infinity. Hence there will be infinitely more things than have just been posited. This seems absurd.

730. **Again, when one** (389).

He gives the seventh argument, and it runs as follows: if someone were to ask whether a man or some other thing is white, the one answering him must say either "yes" or "no." If he says "yes," it is plain that he says that the affirmation is true; but if he does not affirm this but says "no," it is clear that he denies this. Now the only thing which he denies is what he was asked, and the negation of this is non-being because it is negative. Therefore it follows that, when he answers this question, he must of necessity either admit the affirmative or assert the negative. Hence there is no intermediate between these two.

731. **Now some men** (390).

He gives the reason why some men adopt this opinion, and in regard to this he does three things. First, he shows why some men have held this opinion. Second (391:C 733), he explains how one can argue dialectically against them ("The starting point"). Third (392:C 734), he notes the philosophical views on which the foregoing opinions depend ("Now the statement").

He accordingly says, first (390), that the foregoing opinion, like other unreasonable opinions, is adopted by certain thinkers for one of two reasons. The first is this: when some men cannot refute "eristic arguments," i.e., disputatious or sophistical arguments, which are presented to them either by others or by themselves, they agree with the one giving the argument and assent to the conclusion, saying that what has been shown is true. And then they try to confirm this by devising other arguments.

732. The second reason why men adopt this position is that some men want to discover an argument to prove everything, and therefore whatever cannot be proved they do not want to affirm but deny. But first principles, which are the common conceptions of all men, cannot be proved. Hence these men deny them and thereby adopt unreasonable views.

733. **The starting point** (391).

He indicates the starting point from which one must proceed to argue against such opinions. He says that the starting point is derived from the definitions of truth and falsity, or from the definitions of other terms, as is clear from the arguments given above. For men must admit the definitions of things if they hold that words signify something; for the intelligible expression of a thing which a word signifies is a thing's definition. But if they do not admit that all words signify something, they do not differ from plants, as has been said above (348:C 652).

734. **Now the statement** (392).

Here he gives the opinion on which the foregoing opinions depend. He says that these opinions stem from the position of Heraclitus, who said that all things are in motion, and therefore that they both are and are not at the same time. And since what is being moved has non-being mixed with being, it follows that everything is true.

735. And from the position of Anaxagoras it follows that there is an intermediate between contradictories; for he held that everything is mixed with everything, because everything comes from everything. But neither of the extremes can be predicated of the mixture; for example, intermediate colors are neither whiteness or blackness. Hence the mixture is neither good nor not-good, neither white nor not-white; and thus there is an intermediate between contradictories. It follows, then, that everything is false; for according to the common opinion we posit nothing but affirmation and negation. Hence, if both an affirmation and its negation are false, it follows that everything is false.

LESSON 17

Rejection of the Opinions that Everything Is True and False, and that Everything Is at Rest and in Motion

ARISTOTLE'S TEXT   Chapter 8: 1012a 29-1012b 31

393. With these points settled it is evident that the theories which have been expressed univocally and about all things cannot be true as some affirm them to be. Now some say that nothing is true (for they say that there is nothing to prevent all statements from being like the statement that the diagonal of a square is commensurable with one of its sides), and others say that everything is true. These views are almost the same as that of Heraclitus; for he who says that all things are true and all false admits both views apart from his own words. Hence, if those are impossible, these also must be impossible.

394. Further, it is evident that there are contradictories which cannot be true at the same time. Nor can they all be false, though this would seem more possible from what has been said.

395. But in opposing all such views it is necessary to postulate, as has been stated in the above discussion (332), not[1] that something is or is not, but that a word signifies something. Hence it is necessary to argue from a definition, once we have accepted what truth and falsity mean. But if to say what is true is merely to deny what is false, not everything can be false. For one part of a contradiction must be true.

396. Again, if everything must be either affirmed or denied, both cannot be false; for one part of a contradiction is false.

397. And the view commonly expressed applies to all such theories—they destroy themselves; for he who says that everything is true makes the contrary of his own statement true, and thus makes his own not true; for the contrary denies that it is true. And he who says that everything is false makes his own statement false. But if the former makes an exception of the contrary statement, saying that it alone is not true, and the latter makes an exception of his own statement, saying that it is not false, still they will have to consider the truth and falsity of an infinite number of statements. For he who says that a true statement is true is right; and this process will go on to infinity.

398. Now it is evident that those who say that all things are at rest do not speak the truth, and neither do those who say that all things are in motion.

399. For if all things are at rest, the same thing will always be true and false; but this seems to be something that changes, for he who makes a statement at one time was not and again will not be.

400. And if all things are in motion, nothing will be true, and so everything will be false. But it has been shown that this is impossible.

401. Further, it must be some being which is changed; for change is from something to something.

[1] Reading *non* for *an*.

402. But it is not true that all things are at rest or in motion sometimes, and nothing always; for there is something which always moves the things that are being moved, and the first mover is itself immovable.

COMMENTARY

736. He argues dialectically against certain positions which stem from those mentioned above. First (393:C 736), he argues against certain men who destroy the principles of logic; and second (398:C 744), against certain men who destroy the principles of natural philosophy ("Now it is evident").

For first philosophy should argue dialectically against those who deny the principles of the particular sciences, because all principles are based on the principle that an affirmation and a negation are not true at the same time, and that there is no intermediate between them. Now these principles are the most specific principles of this science, since they depend on the concept of being, which is the primary subject of this branch of philosophy. But the true and the false belong specifically to the study of logic; for they depend on the kind of being which is found in the mind, with which logic deals; for truth and falsity exist in the mind, as is stated in Book VI of this work (558:C 1231). Motion and rest, on the other hand, belong properly to the study of natural philosophy, because nature is defined as a principle of motion and of rest. Now the error made about truth and falsity is a result of the error made about being and non-being, for truth and falsity are defined by means of being and non-being, as has been said above. For there is truth when one says that what is, is, or that what is not, is not; and falsity is defined in the opposite way. And similarly the error made about rest and

motion is a result of the error made about being and non-being; for what is in motion as such does not yet exist, whereas what is at rest already is. Hence, when the errors made about being and non-being have been removed, the errors made about truth and falsity and rest and motion will then also be removed.

737. Regarding the first part of this division he does two things. First (393:C 737), he gives the erroneous opinions about truth and falsity. Second (394:C 739), he criticizes these opinions ("Further, it is evident").

Thus he says (393) that, "with these points settled," i.e., with the foregoing points established which have to be used against the paradoxical positions mentioned above, it is obviously impossible that the views of some men should be true, namely, that we must form an opinion "univocally," i.e., think in the same way, about all things, so that we should say that all things are equally true or equally false. For some thinkers said that nothing is true but everything false, and that there is nothing to prevent us from saying that all statements are just as false as the statement (which is false) that the diameter of a square is commensurate with one of its sides. But others have said that all things are true. Statements of the latter kind are a result of the opinion of Heraclitus, as has been pointed out (362:C 684); for he said that a thing is and is not at the same time, and from this it follows that everything is true.

738. And lest perhaps someone might

say that besides these opinions there is also a third one, which states that everything is both true and false at the same time, he replies, as though meeting a tacit objection, that anyone who maintains this opinion also maintains both of the foregoing ones. Hence, if the first two opinions are impossible, the third must also be impossible.

739. **Further, it is evident** (394).

Then he presents arguments against the foregoing opinions, and the first of these is as follows: it is evident that there are certain contradictories which cannot be true at the same time or false at the same time, for example, the true and not-true, being and non-being. This can be better understood from what has been said. Therefore, if one of these two contradictories must be false and the other true, not all things can be true or all false.

740. **But in opposing** (395).

He gives the second argument. He says that in opposing "these views," or positions, "it is necessary to postulate," or request, not that someone should admit that something either is or is not in reality, as has been stated above (332:C 611), because this seems to be begging the question, but that he should admit that a word signifies something. Now if this is not granted, the dispute comes to an end; but if it is granted, it is then necessary to give definitions, as has already been stated above (332:C 611). Hence we must argue against these thinkers by proceeding from definitions, and in the case of the present thesis we must do this especially by considering the definition of falsity. Now if truth consists merely in affirming what it is false to deny, and vice versa, it follows that not all statements can be false, because either the affirmation or the negation of something must be true. For obviously truth consists simply in saying that what is, is, or in saying that what is not, is not; and falsity consists in saying that what is, is not, or in saying that

what is not, is. Hence it is clear that it is true to say that that is of which it is false that it is not, or to say that that is not of which it is false that it is; and it is false to say that that is of which it is true that it is not, or to say that that is not of which it is true that it is. Thus from the definition of truth and falsity it is clear that not all things are false. And for the same reason it is clear that not all things are true.

741. **Again, if everything** (396).

Here he gives the third argument, which runs thus: it is clear from what has been said above that we must either affirm or deny something of each thing since there is no intermediate between contradictories. It is impossible, then, for everything to be false. And by the same reasoning it is proved that it is impossible for everything to be true, i.e., by reason of the fact that it is impossible both to affirm and to deny something at the same time.

742. **And the view** (397).

He gives the fourth argument: all of the foregoing statements, or opinions, face this unreasonable result—they destroy themselves. This is "the view commonly expressed," i.e., a frequently heard statement made by all; and thus another text says, "It happens that it is commonly held." He proves this view as follows: anyone who says that everything is true makes the contrary of his own opinion true. But the contrary of his own opinion is that his own opinion is not true. Therefore he who says that everything is true says that his own opinion is not true; and thus he destroys his own opinion. Similarly it is evident that he who says that everything is false also says that his own opinion is false.

743. And because someone could say that he who claims that everything is true makes an exception of the one contrary to his own statement, or bars it from what holds universally (and the same thing applies to one who says that everything is false), he therefore

rejects this answer. He says that, if the one who says that everything is true makes his own contrary opinion an exception, saying that it alone is not true, and if the one who says that everything is false makes his own opinion an exception, saying that it alone is not false, none the less it follows that they will be able "to consider," or bring forward, an infinite number of true statements against those who hold that all are false, and an infinite number of false statements against those who hold that all are true. For granted that one opinion is true, it follows that an infinite number are true. And granted that one opinion is false, it follows that an infinite number are false. For if the position, or opinion, that Socrates is sitting is true, then the opinion that it is true that Socrates is sitting will also be true, and so on to infinity. For he who says that a true statement is true is always right; and he who says that a false statement is true is always wrong; and this can proceed to infinity.

744. **Now it is** (398).

He argues against those who destroy the principles of nature, i.e., motion and rest, and in regard to this he does three things.

First, he mentions the falsity of these opinions, saying that it is evident, from what has been said above, that neither the opinion which states that everything is in motion, nor the one which states that everything is at rest, is true.

745. **For if all things** (399).

Second, he shows that these opinions are false. First of all he shows that the opinion which holds that everything is at rest is false; for if everything were at rest, nothing would then be changed from the state in which it sometimes is. Hence, whatever is true would always be true, and whatever is false would always be false. But this seems to be absurd; for the truth and falsity of a proposition is changeable.

Nor is this to be wondered at, because the man who has an opinion or makes a statement at one time was not and now is and again will not be.

746. Second, he uses two arguments to show that the opinion which holds that all things are in motion is false. He gives the first (400) where he says, "And if all things." It is as follows. If all things are in motion and nothing is at rest, nothing will be true in the world; for what is true already exists, but what is in motion does not yet exist. Hence everything must be false. But this is impossible, as has been shown (395:C 740).

747. **Further, it must be** (401).

He gives the second argument, and it runs thus: everything that is undergoing change is necessarily a being, because everything that is being changed is being changed from something to something else, and everything that is being changed in something else belongs to the subject that is undergoing change. Hence it is not necessary to say that everything in the subject undergoing change is being changed, but that there is something which remains. Hence not everything is in motion.

748. **But it is not** (402).

He gives the third argument, and it disposes of a false opinion which could arise from what has been said above. For, since not all things are in motion nor all at rest, someone could therefore think that all things are sometimes in motion and sometimes at rest. In disposing of this opinion he says that, it is not true that all things are sometimes in motion and sometimes at rest, for there are certain movable things which are always being moved, namely, the celestial bodies above us, and there is a mover, namely, the first, which is always immovable and ever in the same state, as has been proved in Book VIII of the *Physics*.[1]

---

[1] *Physica*, VIII, 5 (258b 5).

BOOK V

Lexicon of Philosophical Terms

CONTENTS

Book V

LESSON 1

Five Senses of the Term "Principle." The Common Definition of Principle

ARISTOTLE'S TEXT   Chapter 1: 1012b 34-1013a 23

403. In one sense the term *principle* [beginning or starting point] means that from which someone first moves something; for example, in the case of a line or a journey, if the motion is from here, this is the principle, but if the motion is in the opposite direction, this is something different. In another sense principle means that from which a thing best comes into being, as the starting point of instruction; for sometimes it is not from what is first or from the starting point of the thing that one must begin, but from that from which one learns most readily. Again, principle means that first inherent thing from which something is brought into being, as the keel of a ship and the foundation of a house, and as some suppose the heart to be the principle in animals, and others the brain, and others anything else of the sort. In another sense it means that non-inherent first thing from which something comes into being; and that from which motion and change naturally first begins, as a child comes from its father and mother, and a fight from abusive language. In another sense principle means that according to whose will movable things are moved and changeable things are changed; in states, for example, princely, magistral, imperial, or tyrannical power are all principles. And so also are the arts, especially the architectonic arts, called principles. And that from which a thing can first be known is also called a principle of that thing, as the postulates of demonstrations. And causes are also spoken of in the same number of senses, for all causes are principles.

404. Therefore, it is common to all principles to be the first thing from which a thing either is, comes to be, or is known. And of these some are intrinsic and others extrinsic. And for this reason nature is a principle, and so also is an element, and mind, purpose, substance, and the final cause; for good and evil [1] are the principles both of the knowledge and motion of many things.

[1] The Greek text reads: "the beautiful."

COMMENTARY

749. Having established in the preceding book the things which pertain to the consideration of this science, here the Philosopher begins to deal with the things which this science considers.

And since the attributes considered in this science are common to all things, they are not predicated of various things univocally but in a prior and subsequent way, as has been stated in Book IV (297:C 535). Therefore, first (403:C 751), he distinguishes the meanings of the terms which come under the consideration of this science. Second (404:C 751), he begins to deal with the things which come under the consideration of this science. He does this in the sixth book, which begins with the words, "The principles."

Now since it is the office of each science to consider both its subject and the properties and causes of its subject, this fifth book is accordingly divided into three parts. First, he establishes the various senses of the terms which signify causes; second (423:C 843), the various senses of the terms which signify the subject or parts of the subject of this science ("The term one"); and third (499:C 1034), the various senses of the terms which signify the properties of being as being ("That thing").

The first part is divided into two members. First, he distinguishes the various senses in which the term *cause* is used. Second (416:C 827), he explains the meaning of a term which signifies something associated with a cause—the term *necessary;* for a cause is that on which something else follows of necessity (*"Necessary* means").

The first part is divided into two members. First, he distinguishes the various senses of the terms which signify cause in a general way. Second (413:C 808), he gives the meaning of a term which signifies a special kind of cause, i.e., the term *nature* ("*Nature* means").

750. The first part is divided into three members. First, he gives the various meanings of the term *principle;* second (405:C 763), of the term *cause* ("In one sense the term *cause*"); and

third (411:C 795), of the term *element* ("The inherent principle").

He follows this order because the term principle is more common than the term cause, for something may be a principle and not be a cause; for example, the principle of motion is said to be the point from which motion begins. Again, a cause is found in more things than an element is, for only an intrinsic cause can be called an element.

In regard to the first he does two things. First, he gives the meanings of the term principle. Second (404:C 761), he reduces all of these to one common notion ("Therefore, it is common").

751. Now it should be noted that, although a principle and a cause are the same in subject, they nevertheless differ in meaning; for the term principle implies an order or sequence, whereas the term cause implies some influence on the being of the thing caused. Now an order of priority and posteriority is found in different things; but according to what is first known by us order is found in local motion, because that kind of motion is more evident to the senses. Further, order is found in three classes of things, one of which is naturally associated with the other, i.e., continuous quantity, motion and time. For insofar as there is priority and posteriority in continuous quantity, there is priority and posteriority in motion; and insofar as there is priority and posteriority in motion, there is priority and posteriority in time, as is stated in Book IV of the *Physics*.[1] Therefore, because a principle is said to be what is first [2] in any order, and the order which is considered according to priority and posteriority in continuous quantity is first known by us (and things are named by us insofar as they are known to us), for this reason the term principle, properly considered, designates what is first in a

---

[1] *Physica,* IV, 11 (219a 14).
[2] Reading *Quia igitur principium dicitur quod est primum in aliquo.* . . .

continuous quantity over which motion passes. Hence he says that a principle is said to be "that from which someone first moves something," i.e., any part of a continuous quantity from which local motion begins. Or, according to another reading, "Some part of a thing from which motion will first begin"; i.e., some part of a thing from which it first begins to be moved; for example in the case of a line and in that of any kind of journey the principle is the point from which motion begins. But the opposite or contrary point is "something different or other," i.e., the end or terminus. It should also be noted that a principle of motion and a principle of time belong to this class for the reason just given.

752. But because motion does not always begin from the starting point of a continuous quantity but from that part from which the motion of each thing begins most readily, he therefore gives a second meaning of principle, saying that we speak of a principle of motion in another way "as that from which a thing best comes into being," i.e., the point from which each thing begins to be moved most easily. He makes this clear by an example; for in the disciplines one does not always begin to learn from something that is a beginning in an absolute sense and by nature, but from that from which one "is able to learn" most readily, i.e., from those things which are better known to us, even though they are sometimes more remote by their nature.

753. Now this sense of principle differs from the first. For in the first sense a principle of motion gets its name from the starting point of a continuous quantity, whereas here the principle of continuous quantity gets its name from the starting point of motion. Hence in the case of those motions which are over circular continuous quantities and have no starting point, the principle is also considered to be the point from which the movable body is best or most fittingly moved according to its nature. For example, in the case of the first thing moved [the first sphere] the starting point is in the east. The same thing is true in the case of our own movements; for a man does not always start to move from the beginning of a road but sometimes from the middle or from any terminus at all from which it is convenient for him to start moving.

754. Now from the order considered in local motion we come to know the order in other motions. And for this reason we have the senses of principle based upon the principle of generation or coming to be of things. But this is taken in two ways; for it is either "inherent," i.e., intrinsic, or "non-inherent," i.e., extrinsic.

755. In the first way, then, a principle means that part of a thing which is first generated and from which the generation of the thing begins; for example, in the case of a ship the first thing to come into being is the base or keel, which is in a certain sense the foundation on which the whole superstructure of the ship is raised. And, similarly, in the case of a house the first thing that comes into being is the foundation. And in the case of an animal the first thing that comes into being, according to some, is the heart, and according to others, the brain or some such member of the body. For an animal is distinguished from a non-animal by reason of sensation and motion. Now the principle of motion appears to be in the heart, and sensory operations are most evident in the brain. Hence those who considered an animal from the viewpoint of motion held that the heart is the principle in the generation of an animal. But those who considered an animal only from the viewpoint of the senses held that the brain is this principle; yet the first principle of sensation is also in the

heart even though the operations of the senses are completed in the brain. And those who considered an animal from the viewpoint of operation, or according to some of its activities, held that the organ which is naturally disposed for that operation, as the liver or some other such part is the first part which is generated in an animal. But according to the view of the Philosopher the first part is the heart because all of the soul's powers are diffused throughout the body by means of the heart.

756. In the second way, a principle means that from which a thing's process of generation begins but which is outside the thing. This is made clear in the case of three classes of things. The first is that of natural beings, in which the principle of generation is said to be the first thing from which motion naturally begins in those things which come about through motion (as those which come about through alteration or through some similar kind of motion; for example, a man is said to become large or white); or that from which a complete change begins (as in the case of those things which are not a result of motion but come into being through mutation alone). This is evident in the case of substantial generation; for example, a child comes from its father and mother, who are its principles, and a fight from abusive language, which stirs the souls of men to quarrel.

757. The second class in which this is made clear is that of human acts, whether ethical or political, in which that by whose will or intention others are moved or changed is called a principle. Thus those who hold civil, imperial, or even tyrannical power in states are said to have the principal places; for it is by their will that all things come to pass or are put into motion in states. Those men are said to have civil power who are put in command of particular offices in states, as judges and persons of this kind. Those are said to have imperial power who govern everyone without exception, as kings. And those hold tyrannical power who through violence and disregard for law keep royal power within their grip for their own benefit.

758. He gives as the third class things made by art; for the arts too in a similar way are called principles of artificial things, because the motion necessary for producing an artifact begins from an art. And of these arts the architectonic, which "derive their name" from the word principle, i.e., those called principal arts, are said to be principles in the highest degree. For by architectonic arts we mean those which govern subordinate arts, as the art of the navigator governs the art of ship-building, and the military art governs the art of horsemanship.

759. Again, in likeness to the order considered in external motions a certain order may also be observed in our apprehensions of things, and especially insofar as our act of understanding, by proceeding from principles to conclusions, bears a certain resemblance to motion. Therefore in another way that is said to be a principle from which a thing first becomes known; for example, we say that "postulates," i.e., axioms and assumptions, are principles of demonstrations.

760. Causes are also said to be principles in these ways, "for all causes are principles." For the motion that terminates in a thing's being begins from some cause, although it is not designated a cause and a principle from the same point of view, as was pointed out above (403:C 751).

761. **Therefore, it is** (404).

Then he reduces all of the above-mentioned senses of principle to one that is common. He says that all of the foregoing senses have something in common inasmuch as that is said to be a principle which comes first either with reference to a thing's being (as the first part of a thing is said to be a principle) or with reference to its coming to be (as the first mover is said to be a principle) or with reference to the knowing of it.

762. But while all principles agree in the respect just mentioned, they nevertheless differ, because some are intrinsic and others extrinsic, as is clear from the above. Hence nature and element, which are intrinsic, can be principles—nature as that from which motion begins, and element as the first part in a thing's generation. "And mind," i.e., intellect, and "purpose," i.e., a man's intention, are said to be principles as extrinsic ones. Again, "a thing's substance," i.e., its form, which is its principle of being, is called an intrinsic principle, since a thing has being by its form. Again, according to what has been said, that for the sake of which something comes to be is said to be one of its principles. For the good, which has the character of an end in the case of pursuing, and evil in that of shunning, are principles of the knowledge and motion of many things; that is, all those which are done for the sake of some end. For in the realm of nature, in that of moral acts, and in that of artifacts, demonstrations make special use of the final cause.

LESSON 2

The Four Classes of Causes. Several Causes of the Same Effect. Causes May Be Causes of Each Other. Contraries Have the Same Cause

ARISTOTLE'S TEXT   Chapter 2: 1013a 24-1013b 16

405. In one sense the term *cause* means that from which, as something intrinsic, a thing comes to be, as the bronze of a statue and the silver of a goblet, and the genera of these. In another sense it means the form and pattern of a thing, i.e., the intelligible expression of the quiddity and its genera (for example, the ratio of 2:1 and number in general are the cause of an octave chord) and the parts which are included in the intelligible expression. Again, that from which the first beginning of change or of rest comes is a cause; for example, an adviser is a cause, and a father is the cause of a child, and in general a maker is a cause of the thing made, and a changer a cause of the thing changed. Further, a thing is a cause inasmuch as it is an end, i.e., that for the sake of which something is done; for example, health is the cause of walking. For if we are asked why someone took a walk, we answer, "in order to be healthy"; and in saying this we think we have given the cause. And whatever occurs on the way to the end under the motion of something else is also a cause. For example, reducing, purging, drugs and instruments are causes of health; for all of these exist for the sake of the end, although they differ from each other inasmuch as some are instruments and others are processes. These, then, are nearly all the ways in which causes are spoken of.

406. And since there are several senses in which causes are spoken of, it turns out that there are many causes of the same thing, and not in an accidental way. For example, both the maker of a statue and the bronze are causes of a statue not in any other respect but insofar as it is a statue. However, they are not causes in the same way, but the one as matter and the other as the source of motion.

407. And there are things which are causes of each other. Pain, for example, is a cause of health, and health is a cause of pain, although not in the same way, but one as an end and the other as a source of motion.

408. Further, the same thing is sometimes the cause of contraries; for that which when present is the cause of some particular thing, this when absent we sometimes blame for the contrary. Thus the cause of the loss of a ship is the absence of the pilot whose presence is the cause of the ship's safety. And both of these—the absence and the presence—are moving causes.

COMMENTARY

763. Here the Philosopher distinguishes the various senses in which the term *cause* is used; and in regard to this he does two things. First (405:C 763), he enumerates the classes of causes. Second (410:C 783), he gives the modes of causes ("Now the modes").

In regard to the first part he does two things. First, he enumerates the various classes of causes. Second (409:C 777), he reduces them to four ("All the causes").

In regard to the first part he does two things. First, he enumerates the different classes of causes. Second (406:C 773), he clarifies certain things about the classes of causes ("And since").

He accordingly says, first (405), that in one sense the term cause means that from which a thing comes to be and is "something intrinsic," i.e., something which exists within the thing. This is said to distinguish it from a privation and also from a contrary; for a thing is said to come from a privation or from a contrary as from something which is not intrinsic; for example, white is said to come from black or from not-white. But a statue comes from bronze and a goblet from silver as from something which is intrinsic; for the nature bronze is not destroyed when a statue comes into being, nor is the nature silver destroyed when a goblet comes into being. Therefore the bronze of a statue and the silver of a goblet are causes in the sense of matter. He adds "and the genera of these," because if matter is the species of anything it is also its genus. For example, if the matter of a statue is bronze, its matter will also be metal, compound and body. The same holds true of other things.

764. In another sense cause means the form and pattern of a thing, i.e., its exemplar. This is the formal cause, which is related to a thing in two ways. In one way it stands as the intrinsic form of a thing, and in this respect it is called the formal principle of a thing. In another way it stands as something which is extrinsic to a thing but is that in likeness to which it is made, and in this respect an exemplar is also called a thing's form. It is in this sense that Plato held the Ideas to be forms. Moreover, because it is from its form that each thing derives its nature, whether of its genus or of its species, and the nature of its genus or of its species is what is signified by the definition, which expresses its quiddity, the form of a thing is therefore the intelligible expression of its quiddity, i.e., the formula by which its quiddity is known. For even though certain material parts are given in the definition, still it is from a thing's form that the principal part of the definition comes. The reason why the form is a cause, then, is that it completes the intelligible expression of a thing's quiddity. And just as the genus of a particular matter is also matter, in a similar way the genera of forms are the forms of things; for example, the form of the octave chord is the ratio of 2:1. For when two notes stand to each other in the ratio of 2:1, the interval between them is one octave. Hence twoness is its form; for the ratio of 2:1 derives its meaning from twoness. And because number is the genus of twoness, we may therefore say in a general way that number is also the form of the octave, inasmuch as we may say that the octave chord involves the ratio of one number to another. And not only is the

whole definition related to the thing defined as its form, but so also are the parts of the definition, i.e., those which are given directly in the definition. For just as two-footed animal capable of walking is the form of man, so also are animal, capable of walking and two-footed. But sometimes matter is given indirectly in the definition, as when the soul is said to be the actuality of a physical organic body having life potentially.

765. In a third sense cause means that from which the first beginning of change or of rest comes, i.e., a moving or efficient cause. He says "of change or of rest," because motion and rest which are natural are traced back to the same cause, and the same is true of motion and of rest which are a result of force. For that cause by which something is moved to a place is the same as that by which it is made to rest there. "An adviser" is an example of this kind of cause, for it is as a result of an adviser that motion begins in the one who acts upon his advice for the sake of safeguarding something. And in a similar way "a father is the cause of a child." In these two examples Aristotle touches upon the two principles of motion from which all things come to be, namely, purpose in the case of an adviser, and nature in the case of a father. And in general every maker is a cause of the thing made and every changer a cause of the thing changed.

766. Moreover, it should be noted that according to Avicenna [1] there are four modes of efficient cause, namely, perfective, dispositive, auxiliary and advisory.

An efficient cause is said to be perfective inasmuch as it causes the final perfection of a thing, as the one who induces a substantial form in natural things or artificial forms in things made by art, as a builder induces the form of a house.

[1] *Sufficientia,* I, 10 (19ra).

767. An efficient cause is said to be dispositive if it does not induce the final form that perfects a thing but only prepares the matter for that form, as one who hews timbers and stones is said to build a house. This cause is not properly said to be the efficient cause of a house, because what he produces is only potentially a house. But he will be more properly an efficient cause if he induces the ultimate disposition on which the form necessarily follows; for example, man generates man without causing his intellect, which comes from an extrinsic cause.

768. And an efficient cause is said to be auxiliary insofar as it contributes to the principal effect. Yet it differs from the principal efficient cause in that the principal efficient cause acts for its own end, whereas an auxiliary cause acts for an end which is not its own. For example, one who assists a king in war acts for the king's end. And this is the way in which a secondary cause is disposed for a primary cause. For in the case of all efficient causes which are directly subordinated to each other, a secondary cause acts because of the end of a primary cause; for example, the military art acts because of the end of the political art.

769. And an advisory cause differs from a principal efficient cause inasmuch as it specifies the end and form of the activity. This is the way in which the first agent acting by intellect is related to every secondary agent, whether it be natural or intellectual. For in every case a first intellectual agent gives to a secondary agent its end and its form of activity; for example, the naval architect gives these to the shipwright, and the first intelligence does the same thing for everything in the natural world.

770. Further, to this genus of cause is reduced everything that makes anything to be in any manner whatsoever, not only as regards substantial being,

but also as regards accidental being, which occurs in every kind of motion. Hence he says not only that the maker is the cause of the thing made, but also that the changer is the cause of the thing changed.

771. In a fourth sense cause means a thing's end, i.e., that for the sake of which something is done, as health is the cause of walking. And since it is less evident that the end is a cause in view of the fact that it comes into being last of all (which is also the reason why this cause was overlooked by the earlier philosophers, as was pointed out in Book I [84:C 177]), he therefore gives a special proof that an end is a cause. For to ask why or for what reason is to ask about a cause, because when we are asked why or for what reason someone walks, we reply properly by answering that he does so in order to be healthy. And when we answer in this way we think that we are stating the cause. Hence it is evident that the end is a cause. Moreover, not only the ultimate reason for which an agent acts is said to be an end with respect to those things which precede it, but everything that is intermediate between the first agent and the ultimate end is also said to be an end with respect to the preceding agents. And similarly those things are said to be causes from which motion arises in subsequent things. For example, between the art of medicine, which is the first efficient cause in this order, and health, which is the ultimate end, there are these intermediates: reducing, which is the most proximate cause of health in those who have a superfluity of humors; purging, by means of which reducing is brought about; "drugs," i.e., laxative medicine, by means of which purging is accomplished; and "instruments," i.e., the instruments by which medicine or drugs are prepared and administered. And all such things exist for the sake of the end, although one of them is the end of another. For

reducing is the end of purging, and purging is the end of purgatives. However, these intermediates differ from each other in that some are instruments, i.e., the instruments by means of which medicine is prepared and administered (and the administered medicine itself is something which nature employs as an instrument); and some—purging and reducing—are processes, i.e., operations or activities.

772. He concludes, then, that "these are the ways in which causes are spoken of (405)," i.e., the four ways; and he adds "nearly all" because of the modes of causes which he gives below. Or he also adds this because the same classes of causes are not found for the same reason in all things.

773. **And since (406).**

Then he indicates certain points which follow from the things said above about the causes, and there are four of these. The first is that, since the term cause is used in many senses, there may be several causes of one thing not accidentally but properly. For the fact that there are many causes of one thing accidentally presents no difficulty, because many things may be accidents of something that is the proper cause of some effect, and all of these can be said to be accidental causes of that effect. But that there are several proper causes of one thing becomes evident from the fact that causes are spoken of in various ways. For the maker of a statue is a proper cause and not an accidental cause of a statue, and so also is the bronze, but not in the same way. For it is impossible that there should be many proper causes of the same thing within the same genus and in the same order, although there can be many causes providing that one is proximate and another remote; or that neither of them is of itself a sufficient cause, but both together. An example would be many men rowing a boat. Now in the case in point these two things are causes of a statue in different ways: the bronze as matter, and the artist as efficient cause.

774. **And there are** (407).

Then he sets down the second fact that may be drawn from the foregoing discussion. He says that it may also happen that any two things may be the cause of each other, although this is impossible in the same class of cause. But it is evident that this may happen when causes are spoken of in different senses. For example, the pain resulting from a wound is a cause of health as an efficient cause or source of motion, whereas health is the cause of pain as an end. For it is impossible that a thing should be both a cause and something caused. Another text states this better, saying that "exercise is the cause of physical fitness," i.e., of the good disposition caused by moderate exercise, which promotes digestion and uses up superfluous humors.

775. Now it must be borne in mind that, although four causes are given above, two of these are related to one another, and so also are the other two. The efficient cause is related to the final cause, and the material cause is related to the formal cause. The efficient cause is related to the final cause because the efficient cause is the starting point of motion and the final cause is its terminus. There is a similar relationship between matter and form. For form gives being, and matter receives it. Hence the efficient cause is the cause of the final cause, and the final cause is the cause of the efficient cause. The efficient cause is the cause of the final cause inasmuch as it makes the final cause be, because by causing motion the efficient cause brings about the final cause. But the final cause is the cause of the efficient cause, not in the sense that it makes it be, but inasmuch as it is the reason for the causality of the efficient cause. For an efficient cause is a cause inasmuch as it acts, and it acts only because of the final cause. Hence the efficient cause derives its causality from the final cause. And form and matter are mutual causes of being: form is a cause of matter inasmuch as it gives actual being to matter, and matter is a cause of form inasmuch as it supports form in being. And I say that both of these together are causes of being either in an unqualified sense or with some qualification. For substantial form gives being absolutely to matter, whereas accidental form, inasmuch as it is a form, gives being in a qualified sense. And matter sometimes does not support a form in being in an unqualified sense but according as it is the form of this particular thing and has being in this particular thing. This is what happens in the case of the human body in relation to the rational soul.

776. **Further, the same thing** (408).

Then he gives the third conclusion that may be drawn from the foregoing discussion. He says that the same thing can be the cause of contraries. This would also seem to be difficult or impossible if it were related to both in the same way. But it is the cause of each in a different way. For that which when present is the cause of some particular thing, this when absent "we blame," i.e., we hold it responsible, "for the contrary." For example, it is evident that by his presence the pilot is the cause of a ship's safety, and we say that his absence is the cause of the ship's loss. And lest someone might think that this is to be attributed to different classes of causes, just as the preceding two were, he therefore adds that both of these may be reduced to the same class of cause—the moving cause. For the opposite of a cause is the cause of an opposite effect in the same line of causality as that in which the original cause was the cause of its effect.

LESSON 3

All Causes Reduced to Four Classes

ARISTOTLE'S TEXT   Chapter 2: 1013b 16-1014a 25

409. All the causes mentioned fall under one of the four classes which are most evident. For the elements of syllables, the matter of things made by art, fire and earth and all such elements of bodies, the parts of a whole, and the premises of a conclusion, are all causes in the sense of that from which things are made. But of these some are causes as a subject, for example, parts, and others as the essence, for example, the whole, the composition and the species, whereas the seed, the physician, the adviser, and in general every agent, are all sources of change or of rest. But the others are causes as the end and the good of other things. For that for the sake of which other things come to be is the greatest good and the end of other things. And it makes no difference whether we say that it is a good or an apparent good. These, then, are the causes, and this the number of their classes.

410. Now the modes of causes are many in number, but these become fewer when summarized. For causes are spoken of in many senses; and of those which belong to the same class, some are prior and some subsequent. For example, both the physician and one possessing an art are causes of health, and both the ratio of 2:1 and number are causes of the octave chord; and always those classes which contain singulars. Further, a thing may be a cause in the sense of an accident, and the classes which contain these; for example, in one sense the cause of a statue is Polyclitus and in another a sculptor, because it is accidental that a sculptor should be Polyclitus. And the universals which contain accidents are causes; for example, man is the cause of a statue, and even generally animal, because Polyclitus is a man and an animal. And of accidental causes some are more remote and some more proximate than others. Thus what is white and what is musical might be said to be the causes of a statue, and not just Polyclitus or man. Again, in addition to all of these, i.e., both proper causes and accidental causes, some are said to be causes potentially and some actually, as a builder and one who is building. And the distinctions which have been made will apply in like manner to the effects of these causes, for example, to this statue, or to a statue, or to an image generally, or to this bronze, or to bronze, or to matter in general. And the same applies to accidental effects. Again, both proper and accidental causes may be spoken of together, so that the cause of a statue may be referred to as neither Polyclitus nor a sculptor but the sculptor Polyclitus. But while all these varieties of causes are six in number, each is spoken of in two ways; for causes are either singular or generic; either proper or accidental, or generically accidental; or they are spoken of in combination or singly; and again they are either active or potential causes. But they differ in this respect, that active causes, i.e., singular causes, exist or cease to exist simultaneously with their effects, as this particular one who is healing with this particular person who is being healed,

309

and as this particular builder with this particular thing which is being built. But this is not always true of potential causes; for the builder and the thing built do not cease to exist at the same time.

COMMENTARY

777. Here the philosopher reduces all causes to the classes of causes mentioned above (409), saying that all those things which are called causes fall into one of the four classes mentioned above. For "elements," i.e., letters, are said to be the causes of syllables; and the matter of artificial things is said to be their cause; and fire and earth and all simple bodies of this kind are said to be the causes of compounds. And parts are said to be the causes of a whole, and "premises," i.e., propositions previously set down from which conclusions are drawn, are said to be the causes of the conclusion. And in all of these cases cause has a single formal aspect according as cause means that from which a thing is produced, and this is the formal aspect of material cause.

778. Now it must be noted that propositions are said to constitute the matter of a conclusion, not inasmuch as they exist under such a form, or according to their force (for in this way they would rather have the formal aspect of an efficient cause), but with reference to the terms of which they are composed. For a conclusion is constituted of the terms contained in the premises, i.e., of the major and minor terms.

779. And of those things of which something is composed, some are like a subject, for example, parts and the other things mentioned above, whereas some are like the essence, for example, the whole, the composition and the species, which have the character of a form whereby a thing's essence is made complete. For it must be borne in mind that sometimes one thing is the matter of something else in an unqualified sense (for example, silver of a goblet), and then the form corresponding to such a matter can be called the species. But sometimes many things taken together constitute the matter of a thing; and this may occur in three ways. For sometimes things are united merely by their arrangement, as the men in an army or the houses in a city; and then the whole has the role of a form which is designated by the term army or city. And sometimes things are united not just by arrangement alone but by contact and a bond, as is evident in the parts of a house; and then their composition has the role of a form. And sometimes the alteration of the component parts is added to the above, as occurs in the case of a compound; and then the compound state itself is the form, and this is still a kind of composition. And a thing's essence is derived from any one of these three—the composition, species, or whole—as becomes clear when an army, a house, or a goblet is defined. Thus we have two classes of cause.

780. But the seed, the physician and the adviser, and in general every agent, are called causes for a different reason, namely, because they are the sources of motion and rest. Hence this is now a different class of cause because of a different formal aspect of causality. He puts seed in this class of cause because he is of the opinion that the seed has active power, whereas a woman's men-

strual fluid has the role of the matter of the offspring.

781. There is a fourth formal aspect of causality inasmuch as some things are said to be causes in the sense of the end and good of other things. For that for the sake of which something else comes to be is the greatest good "and the end" of other things, i.e., it is naturally disposed to be their end. But because someone could raise the objection that an end is not always a good since certain agents sometimes inordinately set up an evil as their end, he therefore replies that it makes no difference to his thesis whether we speak of what is good without qualification or of an apparent good. For one who acts does so, properly speaking, because of a good, for this is what he has in mind. And one acts for the sake of an evil accidentally inasmuch as he happens to think that it is good. For no one acts for the sake of something with evil in view.

782. Moreover, it must be noted that, even though the end is the last thing to come into being in some cases, it is always prior in causality. Hence it is called the cause of causes, because it is the cause of the causality of all causes. For it is the cause of efficient causality, as has already been pointed out (407:C 775); and the efficient cause is the cause of the causality of both the matter and the form, because by its motion it causes matter to be receptive of form and makes form exist in matter. Therefore the final cause is also the cause of the causality of both the matter and the form. Hence in those cases in which something is done for an end (as occurs in the realm of natural things, in that of moral matters, and in that of art), the most forceful demonstrations are derived from the final cause. Therefore he concludes that the foregoing are causes, and that causes are distinguished into this number of classes.

783. **Now the modes (410).**

Then he distinguishes between the modes of causes. And causes are distinguished into classes and into modes. For the division of causes into classes is based on different formal aspects of causality, and is therefore equivalently a division based on essential differences, which constitute species. But the division of causes into modes is based on the different relationships between causes and things caused, and therefore pertains to those causes which have the same formal aspect of causality. An example of this is the division of causes into proper and accidental causes, and into remote and proximate causes. Therefore this division is equivalently a division based on accidental differences, which do not constitute different species.

784. He accordingly says that there are many modes of causes, but that these are found to be fewer in number when "summarized," i.e., when brought together under one head. For even though proper causes and accidental causes are two modes, they are still reduced to one head insofar as both may be considered from the same point of view. The same thing is true of the other different modes. For many different modes of causes are spoken of, not only with reference to the different species of causes, but also with reference to causes of the same species, namely, those which are reduced to one class of cause.

785. For one cause is said to be prior and another subsequent; and causes are prior or subsequent in two ways: In one way, when there are many distinct causes which are related to each other, one of which is primary and remote, and another secondary and proximate (as in the case of efficient causes man generates man as a proximate and subsequent cause, but the sun as a prior and remote cause); and the same thing can be considered in the case of the other classes of causes. In another way, when the cause is numerically one

and the same, but is considered according to the sequence which reason sets up between the universal and the particular; for the universal is naturally prior and the particular subsequent.

786. But he omits the first way and considers the second. For in the second way the effect is the immediate result of both causes, i.e., of both the prior and subsequent cause; but this cannot happen in the first way. Hence he says that the cause of health is both the physician and one possessing an art, who belong to the class of efficient cause: one possessing an art as a universal and prior cause, and the physician as a particular, or special, and subsequent cause. The same thing is true of the formal cause, since this cause may also be considered in two ways; for example, for an octave chord "double," or the ratio of 2:1, or the number two, is a formal cause as one that is special and subsequent, whereas number, or the ratio of one number to another or to the unit, is like a universal and prior cause. And in this way too "always those classes which contain singulars," i.e., universals, are said to be prior causes.

787. Causes are distinguished in another way inasmuch as one thing is said to be a proper cause and another an accidental cause. For just as proper causes are divided into universal and particular, or into prior and subsequent, so also are accidental causes. Therefore, not only accidental causes themselves are called such, but so also are the classes which contain these. For example, a sculptor is the proper cause of a statue, and Polyclitus is an accidental cause inasmuch as he happens to be a sculptor. And just as Polyclitus is an accidental cause of a statue, in a similar way all universals "which contain accidents," i.e., accidental causes, are said to be accidental causes, for example, man and animal, which contain under themselves Polyclitus, who is a man and an animal.

788. And just as some proper causes are proximate and some remote, as was pointed out above, so also is this the case with accidental causes. For Polyclitus is a more proximate cause of a statue than what is white or what is musical. For an accidental mode of predication is more remote when an accident is predicated of an accident than when an accident is predicated of a subject. For one accident is predicated of another only because both are predicated of a subject. Hence when something pertaining to one accident is predicated of another, as when something pertaining to a builder is predicated of a musician, this mode of predication is more remote than one in which something is predicated of the subject of an accident, as when something pertaining to a builder is predicated of Polyclitus.

789. Now it must be borne in mind that one thing can be said to be the accidental cause of something else in two ways: in one way, from the viewpoint of the cause; because whatever is accidental to a cause is itself called an accidental cause, for example, when we say that something white is the cause of a house. In another way, from the viewpoint of the effect, i.e., inasmuch as one thing is said to be an accidental cause of something else because it is accidental to the proper effect. This can happen in three ways. The first is that the thing has a necessary connection with the effect. Thus that which removes an obstacle is said to be a mover accidentally. This is the case whether that accident is a contrary, as when bile prevents coolness (and thus scammony is said to produce coolness accidentally, not because it causes coolness, but because it removes the obstacle preventing coolness, i.e., bile, which is its contrary); or even if it is not a contrary, as when a pillar hinders the movement of a stone which rests upon it, so that one who removes the pillar is said to move the stone accidentally. In a second way, some-

thing is accidental to the proper effect when the accident is connected with the effect neither necessarily nor in the majority of cases but seldom, as the discovery of a treasure is connected with digging in the soil. It is in this way that fortune and chance are said to be accidental causes. In a third way things are accidental to the effect when they have no connection except perhaps in the mind, as when someone says that he is the cause of an earthquake because an earthquake took place when he entered the house.

790. And besides the distinction of all things into causes in themselves or proper causes and accidental causes, there is a third division of causes inasmuch as some things are causes potentially and some actually, i.e., actively. For example, the cause of building is a builder in a state of potency (for this designates his habit or office), or one who is actually building.

791. And the same distinctions which apply to causes can apply to the effects of which these causes are the causes. For effects, whether particular or universal, can be divided into prior and subsequent, as a sculptor may be called the cause of this statue, which is subsequent; or of a statue, which is more universal and prior; or of an image, which is still more universal. And similarly something is the formal cause of this particular bronze; or of bronze, which is more universal; or of matter, which is still more universal. The same things can be said of accidental effects, i.e., of things produced by accident. For a sculptor who is the cause of a statue is also the cause of the heaviness, whiteness or redness which are in it as accidents from the matter and are not caused by this agent.

792. Again, he gives a fourth division of causes, namely, the division into simple causes and composite causes. A cause is said to be simple when, for example, in the case of a statue, the proper cause alone is considered, as a

sculptor, or when an accidental cause alone is considered, as Polyclitus. But a cause is said to be composite when both are taken together, for example, when we say that the cause of a statue is the sculptor Polyclitus.

793. There is moreover another way in which causes are said to be composite, i.e., when several causes act together to produce one effect, for example, when many men act together in order to row a boat, or when many stones combine in order to constitute the matter of a house. But he omits the latter way because no one of these things taken in itself is the cause, but a part of the cause.

794. And having given these different modes of causes, he brings out their number, saying that these modes of causes are six in number, and that each of these have two alternatives so that twelve result. For these six modes are either singular or generic (or, as he called them above, prior and subsequent); either proper or accidental (to which the genus of the accident is also reduced, for the genus to which an accident belongs is an accidental cause); and again, either composite or simple. Now these six modes are further divided by potency and actuality and thus are twelve in number. Now the reason why all these modes must be divided by potency and actuality is that potency and actuality distinguish the connection between cause and effect. For active causes are at one and the same time particulars and cease to exist along with their effects; for example, this act of healing ceases with this act of recovering health, and this act of building with this thing being built; for a thing cannot be actually being built unless something is actually building. But potential causes do not always cease to exist when their effects cease; for example, a house and a builder do not cease to exist at one and the same time. In some cases, however, it does happen that when the

activity of the efficient cause ceases the substance of the effect ceases. This occurs in the case of those things whose being consists in coming to be, or whose cause is not only the cause of their coming to be but also of their being. For example, when the sun's illumination is removed from the atmosphere, light ceases to be. He says "singular causes" because acts belong to singular things, as was stated in Book I of this work (7:C 21).

LESSON 4

The Proper Meaning of Element; Elements in Words, Natural Bodies, and Demonstrations. Transferred Usages of "Element" and Their Common Basis

ARISTOTLE'S TEXT   Chapter 3: 1014a 25-1014b 15

411. The inherent principle of which a thing is first composed and which is not divisible into another species is called an *element*. For example, the elements of a word are the parts of which a word is composed and into which it is ultimately divided and which are not further divided into other words specifically different from them. But if they are divided, their parts are alike, as the parts of water are water; but this is not true of the syllable. Similarly, people who speak of the elements of bodies mean the component parts into which bodies are ultimately divided and which are not divided into other bodies specifically different. And whether such parts are one or many, they call them elements. And similarly the parts of diagrams are called elements, and in general the parts of demonstrations; for the primary demonstrations which are contained in many other demonstrations are called the elements of demonstrations; and such are the primary syllogisms which are composed of three terms and proceed through one middle term.

412. People also use the term element in a transferred sense of anything which is one and small and useful for many purposes; and for this reason anything which is small and simple and indivisible is called an element. Hence it follows that the most universal things are elements, because each of them, being one and simple, is found in many things, either in all or in most of them. And to some the unit and the point seem to be principles. Therefore, since what are called genera are universal and indivisible (for their formal character is one), some men call the genera elements, and these more than a difference, since a genus is more universal. For where the difference is present the genus also follows, but the difference is not always present where the genus is. And in all these cases it is common for the element of each thing to be the primary component of each thing.

COMMENTARY

795. Here he distinguishes the different senses of the term *element*, and in regard to this he does two things. First (411:C 795), he gives the different senses in which the term element is used. Second (412:C 807), he indicates what all of them have in common ("And in all these").

In regard to the first he does two things. First, he explains how the term element is used in its proper sense; and second (412:C 802), how it is used in transferred senses ("People also use").

First (411), he gives a sort of description of an element, and from this one can gather the four notes contained in its definition. The first is that an element is a cause in the sense of that from which a thing comes to be; and from this it is clear that an element is placed in the class of material cause.

796. The second is that an element is the principle from which something first comes to be. For copper is that from which a statue comes to be, but it is still not an element because it has some matter from which it comes to be.

797. The third is that an element is inherent or intrinsic; and for this reason it differs from everything of a transitory nature from which a thing comes to be, whether it be a privation or a contrary or the matter subject to contrariety and privation, which is transitory; for example, when we say that a musical man comes from a non-musical man, or that the musical comes from the non-musical. For elements must remain in the things of which they are the elements.

798. The fourth is that an element has a species which is not divisible into different species; and thus an element differs from first matter, which has no species, and also from every sort of matter which is capable of being divided into different species, as blood and things of this kind.

Hence he says, as the first note, that an element is that of which a thing is composed; as the second, that it is that of which a thing is "first" composed; as the third, that it is "an inherent principle"; and as the fourth, that it is "not divisible into another species."

799. He illustrates this definition of element in four cases in which we use the term element. For we say that letters are the elements of a word because

every word is composed of them, and of them primarily. This is evident from the fact that all words are divided into letters as ultimate things; for what is last in the process of dissolution must be first in the process of composition. But letters are not further divided into other words which are specifically different. Yet if they should be divided in any way, the parts in which the division results would be "alike," i.e., specifically the same, just as all parts of water are water. Now letters are divided according to the amount of time required to pronounce them, inasmuch as a long letter is said to require two periods of time, and a short letter one. But while the parts into which letters are so divided do not differ as the species of words do, this is not the case with a syllable; for its parts are specifically different, since the sounds which a vowel and a consonant make, of which a syllable is composed, are specifically different.

800. He gives as a second example natural bodies, certain of which we also call the elements of certain others. For those things into which all compounds are ultimately dissolved are called their elements; and therefore they are the things of which bodies of this kind are composed. But those bodies which are called elements are not divisible into other bodies which are specifically different, but into like parts, as any part of water is water. And all those who held for one such body into which every body is dissolved and which is itself incapable of being further divided, said that there is one element. Some said that it is water, some air, and some fire. But those who posited many such bodies also said there are many elements. Now it should be borne in mind that when it is set down in the definition of an element that an element is not divisible into different species, this should not be understood of the parts into which

a thing is divided in a quantitative division (for wood would then be an element, since any part of wood is wood), but in a division made by alteration, as compounds are dissolved into simple bodies.

801. As a third example he gives the order of demonstrations, in which we also employ the word element; for example, we speak of Euclid's *Book of Elements*. And he says that, in a way similar and close to those mentioned, those things which "are parts of diagrams," i.e., the constituents of geometrical figures, are called elements. This can be said not only of the demonstrations in geometry but universally of all demonstrations. For those demonstrations which have only three terms are called the elements of other demonstrations, because the others are composed of them and resolved into them. This is shown as follows: a second demonstration takes as its starting point the conclusion of a first demonstration, whose terms are understood to contain the middle term which was the starting point of the first demonstration. Thus the second demonstration will proceed from four terms, the first from three only, the third from five, and the fourth from six; so that each demonstration adds one term. Thus it is clear that first demonstrations are included in subsequent ones, as when this first demonstration—every B is A, every C is B, therefore every C is A—is included in this demonstration—every C is A, every D is C, therefore every D is A; and this again is included in the demonstration whose conclusion is that every E is A, so that for this final conclusion there seems to be one syllogism composed of several syllogisms having several middle terms. This may be expressed thus: every B is A, every C is B, every D is C, every E is D, therefore every E is A. Hence a first demonstration, which has one middle term and only three terms, is simple and not reducible to another demonstra-

tion, whereas all other demonstrations are reducible to it. Hence first syllogisms, which come from three terms by way of one middle term, are called elements.

802. **People also use** (412).

Here he shows how the term element is used in a transferred sense. He says that some men, on the basis of the foregoing notion or meaning of element, have used the term in a transferred sense to signify anything that is one and small and useful for many purposes. For from the fact that an element is indivisible they understood that it is one; and from the fact that it is first they understood that it is simple; and from the fact that other things are composed of elements they understood that an element is useful for many purposes. Hence they set up this definition of an element in order that they might say that everything which is smallest in quantity and simple (inasmuch as it is not composed of other things) and incapable of division into different species, is an element.

803. But when they had set up this definition of element, it turned out that by using it in a transferred sense they had invented two senses of element. First, they called the most universal things elements; for a universal is one in definition and is simple (because its definition is not composed of different parts) and is found in many things, and thus is useful for many purposes, whether it be found in all things, as unity and being are, or in most things, as the other genera. And by the same reasoning it came about, second, that they called points and units principles or elements because each of them is one simple thing and useful for many purposes.

804. But in this respect they fell short of the true notion of a principle, because universals are not the matter of which particular things are composed but predicate their very substance.

317

And similarly points are not the matter of a line, for a line is not composed of points.

805. Now with this transferred notion of element established, the solution to a question disputed in Book III (228-31:C 431-36) becomes clear, i.e., whether a genus or a species is more an element, and whether a genus or a difference is more an element; for it clearly follows that genera are elements to a greater degree because genera are more universal and indivisible. For there is no concept or definition of them which must be composed of genera and differences, but it is species which are properly defined. And if a genus is defined, it is not defined insofar as it is a genus but insofar as it is a species. Hence a species is divided into different parts and thus does not have the character of an element. But a genus is not divisible into different parts, and therefore they said that genera are elements more than species. Another translation reads, "For their formal character is one," that is, indivisible, because even though genera do not have a definition, still what is signified by the term genus is a simple conception of the intellect which can be called a definition.

806. And just as a genus is more an element than a species is because it is simpler, in a similar way it is more an element than a difference is, even though a difference is simple, because a genus is more universal. This is clear from the fact that anything which has a difference has a genus, since essential differences do not transcend a genus; but not everything which has a genus necessarily has a difference.

807. Last of all he says that all of the foregoing senses of element have this note in common, that an element is the primary component of each being, as has been stated.

LESSON 5

Five Senses of the Term Nature

ARISTOTLE'S TEXT   Chapter 4: 1014b 15-1015a 20

413. *Nature* means, in one sense, the generation of things that are born, as if one were to pronounce the letter υ [in φύσις] long. And in another sense it means the immanent principle from which anything generated is first produced. Again, it means the source of the primary motion in any beings which are by nature, and it is in each inasmuch as it is such. Now all those things are said to be born which increase through something else by touching and by existing together, or by being naturally joined, as in the case of embryos. But being born together differs from touching, for in the latter case there need be nothing but contact. But in things which are naturally joined together there is some one same thing in both, instead of contact, which causes them to be one, and which makes them to be one in quantity and continuity but not in quality. Again, nature means the primary thing of which a natural being is composed or from which it comes to be, when it is unformed and immutable by its own power; for example, the bronze of a statue or of bronze articles is said to be their nature, and the wood of wooden things, and the same applies in the case of other things. For each thing comes from these though its primary matter is preserved. For it is also in this sense that men speak of the elements of natural beings as their nature; some calling it fire, others earth, others water, others air, and others something similar to these, whereas others call all of them nature. In still another sense nature means the substance of things which are by nature, as those who say that nature is the primary composition of a thing, as Empedocles says, "Of nothing that exists is there nature, but only the mixing and separating-out of what has been mixed. Nature is but the name men give to these." [1] For this reason we do not say that things which are or come to be by nature have a nature, even when that from which they can be or come to be is already present, so long as they do not have their form or species. Hence that which is composed of both of these exists by nature, as animals and their parts.

414. Again, nature is the primary matter of a thing, and this in two senses: either what is primary with respect to this particular thing, or primary in general; for example, the primary matter of bronze articles is bronze, but in general it is perhaps water, if everything capable of being liquefied is water. And nature is also a thing's form or substance, i.e., the terminus of the process of generation. But metaphorically speaking every substance in general is called nature because of form or species, for the nature of a thing is also a kind of substance.

415. Hence, from what has been said, in its primary and proper sense nature is the substance of those things which have within themselves as such the source of their motion. For matter is called nature because it is receptive of this. And

---

[1] Diels, Frag. 8.

processes of generation and growth are called nature because they are motions proceeding from it. And nature is the source of motion in those things which are by nature, and it is something present in them either potentially or in complete actuality.

COMMENTARY

808. Here he gives the different meanings of the term *nature*. And even though an investigation of the term nature appears not to belong to first philosophy but rather to the philosophy of nature, he nevertheless gives the different meanings of this term here, because according to one of its common meanings nature is predicated of every substance, as he will make clear. Hence it falls under the consideration of first philosophy just as universal substance does.

In regard to the first he does two things. First (413:C 808), he distinguishes the different senses in which the term nature is used. Second (415:C 824), he reduces all of these to one primary notion ("Hence, from what").

In regard to the first he does two things. First, he gives five principal senses in which the term nature is used. Second (414:C 821), he gives two additional senses connected with the last two of these ("Again, nature").

He accordingly says, first (413), that in one sense nature means the process of generation of things that are generated, or, according to another text which states this in a better way, "of things that are born." For not everything that is generated can be said to be born but only living things, for example, plants and animals and their parts. The generation of non-living things cannot be called nature, properly speaking, according to the common use of the term, but only the generation of living things inasmuch as nature may mean the nativity or birth of a thing—as the word seems to mean,

"as if one were to pronounce nature long." This text has been corrupted, as is evident from another translation which says, "as if one were to pronounce the υ [in φύσις] long." For, if φύσις, which means nature in the Greek, is taken to mean the generation of living things, the first υ is pronounced long; but if it is taken to mean a principle, and this is the way in which it is commonly used, the first υ is pronounced short. Yet even from this text it can be understood that the term nature means the generation of living things by a certain lengthening or extension of usage.

809. Again, from the fact that nature was first used to designate the birth of a thing there followed a second use of the term, so that nature came to mean the principle of generation from which a thing comes to be, or that from which as from an intrinsic principle something born is first generated.

810. And as a result of the likeness between birth and other kinds of motion the meaning of the term nature has been extended farther, so that in a third sense it means the source from which motion begins in any being according to its nature, provided that it is present in it insofar as it is such a being and not accidentally. For example, the principle of health, which is the medical art, is not present in a physician who is ill insofar as he is ill but insofar as he is a physician. And he is not healed insofar as he is a physician but insofar as he is ill; and thus the source of motion is not in him

insofar as he is moved. This is the definition of nature given in Book II of the *Physics*.[1]

811. And because he mentioned things that are born, he also shows what it means in the proper sense "to be born," as another text says, and in place of which this text incorrectly says "to be generated." For the generation of living things differs from that of non-living things, because a non-living thing is not generated by being joined or united to its generator, as fire is generated by fire and water by water. But the generation of a living thing comes about through some kind of union with the principle of generation. And because the addition of quantity to quantity causes increase, therefore in the generation of living things there seems to be a certain increase, as when a tree puts forth foliage and fruit. Hence he says that those things are said to be born which "increase," i.e., have some increase together with the principle of generation.

812. But this kind of increase differs from that class of motion which is called increase [or augmentation], by which things that are already born are moved or changed. For a thing that increases within itself does so because the part added passes over into the substance of that thing, as food passes over into the substance of the one nourished. But anything that is born is added to the thing from which it is born as something other and different, and not as something that passes over into its substance. Hence he says that it increases "through something distinct" or something else, as if to say that this increase comes about through the addition of something that is other or different.

813. But addition that brings about increase can be understood to take place in two ways: in one way, "by

touching," i.e., by contact alone; in another way, "by existing together," i.e., by the fact that two things are produced together and naturally connected with each other, as the arms and sinews; "and by being joined," i.e., by the fact that something is naturally adapted to something else already existing, as hair to the head and teeth to the gums. In place of this another text reads, more appropriately, "by being born together with," and "by being connected with at birth." Now in the generation of living things addition comes about not only by contact but also by a kind of joining together or natural connection, as is evident in the case of embryos, which are not only in contact in the womb, but are also bound to it at the beginning of their generation.

814. Further, he indicates the difference between these two, saying that "being fused," i.e., being bound together, or "being connected at birth," as another text says, differs from contact, because in the case of contact there need be nothing besides the things in contact which makes them one. But in the case of things which are bound together, whether naturally connected or born together and joined at birth, there must be some one thing "instead of contact," i.e., in the place of contact, which causes them "to be naturally joined," i.e., joined or bound together or born together. Moreover, it must be understood that the thing which causes them to be one makes them one in quantity and continuity but not in quality; because a bond does not alter the things bound from their own dispositions.

815. And from this it is evident that anything that is born is always connected with the thing from which it is born. Hence nature never means an extrinsic principle, but in every sense

[1] *Physica*, II, 1 (192b 22).

in which it is used it is taken to mean an intrinsic principle.

816. And from this third meaning of nature there follows a fourth. For if the source of motion in natural bodies is called their nature, and it seemed to some that the principle of motion in natural bodies is matter, it was for this reason that matter came to be called nature, which is taken as a principle of a thing both as to its being and as to its becoming. And it is also considered to be without any form, and is not moved by itself but by something else. He accordingly says that nature is spoken of as that primary thing of which any being is composed or from which it comes to be.

817. He says this because matter is a principle both of being and of becoming. Hence he says that "it is without order," i.e., form; and for this reason another text says "when it is unformed"; for in the case of some things their order (or arrangement) is regarded as their form, as in the case of an army or of a city. And for this reason he says that it is "immutable by its own power," i.e., it cannot be moved by its own power but by that of a higher agent. For matter does not move itself to acquire a form but is moved by a higher and extrinsic agent. For instance, we might say that "bronze is the nature of a statue or of bronze vessels" or "wood of wooden," as if such vessels were natural bodies.[2] The same is true of everything else that is composed of or comes to be from matter; for each comes to be from its matter though this is preserved. But in the process of generation the dispositions of a form are not preserved; for when one form is introduced another is cast out. And for this reason it seemed to some thinkers that forms are accidents and that matter alone is

substance and nature, as he points out in the *Physics*, Book II.[3]

818. They held this view because they considered the matter and form of natural bodies in the same way as they did the matter and form of things made by art, in which forms are merely accidents and matter alone is substance. It was in this sense that the philosophers of nature said that the elements are the matter of things which come to be by nature, i.e., water, air, or fire—or earth, which no philosopher has held to be the element of natural beings all by itself, although some of those who were not philosophers of nature did hold this, as was stated in Book I (63:C 134). And some philosophers, such as Parmenides, held that some of these are the elements and natures of things; others, such as Empedocles, held that all four are the elements of things; and still others, such as Heraclitus, held that something different is the element of things, for he claimed that vapor plays this role.

819. Now because motion is caused in natural bodies by the form rather than by the matter, he therefore adds a fifth sense in which the term nature is used: that in which nature means the form of a thing. Hence in another sense nature means "the substance of things," i.e., the form of things, which are by nature. It was in this sense that some said that the nature of things is the composition of mixed bodies, as Empedocles said that there is nothing absolute in the world, but that only the alteration or loosening (or mixing, according to another text) of what has been mixed is called nature by men. For they said that things composed of different mixtures have different natures.

820. Now they were led to hold that form is nature by this process of reasoning: whatever things exist or come

2 Reading *naturam* for *materiam*, and *ac si* for *si*, and dropping comma after *vasa*.
3 *Physica*, II, 1 (193a 9).

to be by nature are not said to have a nature, even though the matter from which they are naturally disposed to be or to come to be is already present, unless they have a proper species and a form through which they acquire their species. Now the term species seems to be given in place of substantial form and the term form in place of figure, which is a natural result of the species and a sign of it. Hence, if form is nature, a thing cannot be said to have a nature unless it has a form. Therefore, that which is composed of matter and form "is said to be by nature," i.e., according to nature, as animals and the parts of animals, such as flesh and bones and the like.

821. Again, nature (414).

Then he gives two meanings of nature which are connected with the last two preceding ones, and the first of these is added to the fourth sense of nature, in which it means the matter of a thing. And he says that not every kind of matter is said to be the nature of a thing but only first matter. This can be understood in two senses: either with reference to something generic, or with reference to something that is first absolutely or without qualification. For example, the first matter generically of artificial things produced from bronze is bronze; but their first matter without qualification is water; for all things which are liquefied by heat and solidified by cold have the character of water, as he says in Book IV of the *Meteors*.[4]

822. He links up the second of these additional meanings with the fifth sense of nature mentioned above, according to which nature means form. And in this sense not only the form of a part (*forma partis*) is called nature but the species is the form of the

whole (*forma totius*). For example, we might say that the nature of man is not only a soul but humanity and the substance signified by the definition. For it is from this point of view that Boethius says [5] that the nature of a thing is the specific difference which informs each thing, because the specific difference is the principle that completes a thing's substance and gives it its species. And just as form or matter is called nature because it is a principle of generation, which is the meaning of nature according to the original use of the term, in a similar way the species or substance of a thing is called its nature because it is the end of the process of generation. For the process of generation terminates in the species of the thing generated, which is a result of the union of matter and form.

823. And because of this every substance is called nature according to a kind of metaphorical and extended use of the term; for the nature which we spoke of as the terminus of generation is a substance. Thus every substance is similar to what we call nature. Boethius also gives this meaning of the term.[6] Moreover, it is because of this meaning that the term nature is distinguished from other common terms. For it is common in this way just as substance also is.

824. Hence, from what (415).

Then he reduces all of the foregoing senses of the term nature to one common notion. But it must be noted that the reduction of the other senses to one primary sense can happen in two ways: in one way, with reference to the order which things have; and in another way, with reference to the order which is observed in giving names to things. For names are given to

---

[4] *Meteor.*, IV, 11 (389a 24-389b 22).
[5] *De Duabus Naturis*, 1 (PL 64, 1342).
[6] *Ibid.*

things according as we understand them, because names are signs of what we understand; and sometimes we understand prior things from subsequent ones. Hence something that is prior for us receives a name which subsequently fits the object of that name. And this is what happens in the present case; for since the forms and powers of things are known from their activities, the process of generation or birth of a thing is the first to receive the name of nature and the last is the form.

825. But with reference to the order which things have in reality the concept of nature primarily fits the form, because, as has been said (413:C 808), nothing is said to have a nature unless it has a form.

826. Hence from what has been said it is evident that "in its primary and proper sense nature is the substance," i.e., the form, of those things which have within themselves as such the source of their motion. For matter is called nature because it is receptive of form; and processes of generation get the name of nature because they are motions proceeding from a form and terminating in further forms. And this, namely, the form, is the principle of motion in those things which are by nature, either potentially or actually. For a form is not always the cause of actual motion but sometimes only of potential motion, as when a natural motion is prevented by an external obstacle, or even when a natural action is prevented by a defect in the matter.

LESSON 6

Four Senses of the Term Necessary. Its First and Proper Sense Immobile Things, though Necessary, Are Exempted from Force

ARISTOTLE'S TEXT   Chapter 5: 1015a 20-1015b 15

416. *Necessary* means that without which, as a contributing cause, a thing cannot be or live; for example, breathing and food are necessary to an animal because it cannot exist without them.

417. And it also means that without which the good for man cannot be or come to be, and that without which one cannot get rid of or remain free of some evil; for example, the drinking of some drug is necessary in order that one may not be in distress, and sailing to Aegina is necessary in order that one may collect money.

418. Again, it means what applies force and force itself, and this is something which hinders and prevents, in opposition to desire and choice. For that which applies force is said to be necessary, and for this reason anything necessary is also said to be lamentable, as Evenus[1] says, "For every necessary thing is mournful." And force is a kind of necessity, as Sophocles[2] says, "But force compels me to do this." And necessity seems to be something blameless, and rightly so, for it is contrary to motion which stems from choice and from knowledge.

419. Again, we say that anything which cannot be otherwise is necessarily so.

420. And from this sense of the term necessary all the other senses are derived. For whatever is forced is said either to do or to undergo something necessary when it cannot do something according to its inclination as a result of force, as if there were some necessity by reason of which the thing could not be otherwise. The same thing applies to the contributing causes of life and of good. For when in the one case good, and in the other life or being, is impossible without certain contributing causes, these are necessary; and this cause is a kind of necessity.

421. Further, demonstration belongs to the class of necessary things, because whatever has been demonstrated in the strict sense cannot be otherwise. The reason for this is the principles, for the principles from which a syllogism proceeds cannot be otherwise.

422. Now of necessary things some have something else as the cause of their necessity and others do not, but it is because of them that other things are necessary. Hence what is necessary in the primary and proper sense is what is simple, for this cannot be in more ways than one. Therefore it cannot be in one state and in another; otherwise there would be more ways than one. If, then, there are any beings which are eternal and immobile, in them nothing forced or contrary to nature is found.

[1] Presumably a Sophist. See Hiller, Frag. 8.
[2] *Electra*, 256.

COMMENTARY

827. Having distinguished the different senses of the terms which signify causes, the Philosopher now gives the different senses of a term which designates something pertaining to the notion of cause, i.e., the term *necessary;* for a cause is that from which something else follows of necessity. In regard to this he does two things. First (416:C 827), he distinguishes the different senses of the term necessary. Second (420:C 836), he reduces all of these to one primary sense ("And from this sense").

In the first part (416) he gives four senses in which the term *necessary* is used. First, it means that without which a thing cannot be or live; and even when this is not the principal cause of a thing, it is still a contributing cause. Breathing, for example, is necessary to an animal which breathes, because it cannot live without this. And while breathing is not the [principal] cause of life, none the less it is still a contributing cause inasmuch as it helps to restore what is lost and prevents the total consumption of moisture, which is a cause of life. Hence things of this kind are said to be necessary because it is impossible for things to exist without them.

828. **And it also means** (417).

Then he gives a second sense in which things are said to be necessary. He says that in a second way those things are said to be necessary without which some good cannot be or come about, or some evil be avoided or expelled. For example, we say that "the drinking of some drug," i.e., a laxative medicine, is necessary, not because an animal cannot live without it, but because it is required to expel something, namely, an evil, illness, or even to avoid it. For this is necessary "in order that one may not be in distress," i.e., to avoid being ill. And similarly "sailing to Aegina," i.e., to a definite place, is necessary, not because a man cannot exist without this, but because he cannot acquire some good, i.e., money, without doing this. Hence, such a voyage is said to be necessary in order to collect a sum of money.

829. **Again, it means** (418).

Here he gives a third sense in which things are said to be necessary. He says that anything which exerts force, and even force itself, is termed necessary. For force is said to be necessary, and one who is forced is said to do of necessity whatever he is compelled to do. He shows what is meant by something that exerts force both in the case of natural beings and in that of beings endowed with will. In natural beings there is a desire for or an inclination toward some end or goal, to which the will of a rational nature corresponds; and for this reason a natural inclination is itself called an appetite. For both of these, i.e., both the desire of a natural inclination and the intention of the will, can be hindered and prevented—hindered in carrying out a motion already begun, and prevented from initiating motion. Therefore, that is said to be forced "which is done in opposition to desire," i.e., against the inclination of a natural being; and it is "something that hinders choice," i.e., the end intended in executing a voluntary motion already begun, and also something that prevents it from beginning. Another text says, "and this is according to impetuousness," i.e., according to impulse. For force is found when something is done through the impulse of an external agent and is opposed to the will and power of the subject. And that is forced which is done as a result of an impulse applying force.

830. Now from this definition of the forced he draws two conclusions. The first is that everything forced is sad or mournful. He proves this by using the statement of a certain poet or teacher, saying that everything which is necessary or forced is sad or lamentable; for force is a kind of necessity, as the poet Sophocles says: "Force," i.e., necessity, "compelled me to do this."[1] For it has been said (418:C 829) that force is something which hinders the will; and things which are opposed to the will cause sorrow, because sorrow has to do with things which happen to us against our will.

831. The second conclusion is that anything which is necessary is rightly said to be without blame or reproach. For it is said that necessity deserves forgiveness rather than blame; and this is true because we deserve to be blamed only for the things which we do voluntarily and for which we may also be reasonably rebuked. But the kind of necessity which pertains to force is opposed to the will and to reason, as has been stated (418:C 829); and thus it is more reasonable to say that things done by force are not subject to blame.

832. **Again, we say** (419).

He gives a fourth sense in which things are said to be necessary. He says that being in such a state that it cannot be otherwise we also call necessary, and this is what is necessary in an absolute sense. Things necessary in the first senses, however, are necessary in a relative sense.

833. Now whatever is absolutely necessary differs from the other types of necessity, because absolute necessity belongs to a thing by reason of something that is intimately and closely

[1] *Electra*, 256.

connected with it, whether it be the form or the matter or the very essence of a thing. For example, we say that an animal is necessarily corruptible because this is a natural result of its matter inasmuch as it is composed of contraries; and we say that an animal is necessarily capable of sensing because this is a result of its form; and we also say that an animal is necessarily a living sensible substance because this is its essence.

834. However, the necessity of something which is necessary in a relative sense and not absolutely depends on an extrinsic cause. And there are two kinds of extrinsic causes—the end and the agent. The end is either existence taken absolutely, and the necessity taken from this end pertains to the first kind; or it is well disposed existence or the possession of some good, and necessity of the second kind is taken from this end.

835. Again, the necessity which comes from an external agent pertains to the third kind of necessity. For force exists when a thing is moved by an external agent to something which it has no aptitude for by its own nature. For if something is disposed by its own nature to receive motion from an external agent, such motion will not be forced but natural. This is evident in the motion of the celestial bodies by separate substances, and in that of lower bodies by higher ones.

836. **And from this** (420).

Here he reduces all of the senses in which things are necessary to one; and in regard to this he does three things. First (420:C 836), he shows that all the types of necessity found in reality pertain to this last type. Second (421:C 838), he shows that necessity in matters of demonstration is taken in this last sense ("Further, demonstration"). Third (422:C 839), he draws a corollary from what has been set down above ("Now of necessary things").

He accordingly says, first (420), that all the other senses of the term necessary are somehow referred to this last sense. He makes this clear, first, with reference to the third way in which things are said to be necessary. For whatever is forced is said to do or to undergo something of necessity on the grounds that it cannot act through its own power because of the force exerted on it by an agent; and this is a kind of necessity by which it cannot be otherwise than it is.

837. Then he shows that the same thing is true of the first and second ways in which things are said to be necessary: in the first way with reference to the causes of living and being absolutely, and in the second with reference to the causes of good. For the term necessary was so used in these other ways: in one way to designate that without which a thing cannot be well off, and in the other to designate that without which a thing cannot live or exist. Hence that cause without which a thing cannot live or exist or possess a good or avoid an evil is said to be necessary; the supposition being that the primary notion of the necessary derives from the fact that something cannot be otherwise.

838. **Further, demonstration** (421).

Then he shows that the necessary in matters of demonstration is taken from this last sense, and this applied both to principles and to conclusions. For demonstration is said to be about necessary things, and to proceed from necessary things. It is said to be about necessary things because what is demonstrated in the strict sense cannot be otherwise. He says "demonstrated in the strict sense" in order to distinguish this from what is demonstrated by the kind of demonstration which refutes

an opponent, and does not strictly demonstrate. In the fourth book (331:C 609) he called this an *ad hominem* argument. In demonstrations of this kind which refute an opponent we conclude to the impossible from certain impossible premises. But since in demonstrations the premises are the causes of the conclusion, for demonstrations in the strict sense are productive of science and this is had only by way of a cause, the principles from which a syllogism proceeds must also be necessary and thus cannot be otherwise than they are. For a necessary effect cannot come from a non-necessary cause.

839. **Now of necessary things** (422).

Here he draws three conclusions from the points set down above, one of which follows from the other. The first is that, since in demonstrations the premises are the causes of the conclusion and both of these are necessary, it follows that some things are necessary in one of two ways. For there are some things whose necessity is caused by something else, and there are others whose necessity has no cause; and such things are necessary of themselves. This is said against Democritus, who claimed that we must not look for the causes of necessary things, as is stated in Book VIII of the *Physics*.[2]

840. The second conclusion is that, since there must be one first necessary being from which other beings derive their necessity (for there cannot be an infinite regress in causes, as was shown in the second book [152:C 301]), this first necessary being, which is also necessary in the most proper sense because it is necessary in all ways, must be simple. For composite things are changeable and thus can be in more ways than one. But things which can be in more ways than one can be now in one way and now in another, and this is opposed to the notion of

[2] *Physica*, VIII, 9 (265b 23).

necessity; for that is necessary which cannot be otherwise. Hence the first necessary being must not be now in one way and now in another, and consequently cannot be in more ways than one. Thus he must be simple.

841. The third conclusion is that, since the forced is something which is moved by an external agent in opposition to its own nature, and necessary principles are simple and unchangeable, as has been shown (422:C 840), therefore if there are certain eternal and unchangeable beings, as the separate substances are, in them there must be nothing forced or contrary to their nature. He says this lest a mistake should be made in the case of the term necessity, since it is predicated of immaterial substances without implying on this account that anything forced is found in them.

LESSON 7

The Kinds of Accidental Unity and of Essential Unity

ARISTOTLE'S TEXT   Chapter 6: 1015b 16-1016b 3

423. The term *one* is used both of what is accidentally one and of what is essentially one. A thing is said to be accidentally one, for example, when we say "Coriscus" and "musical" and "musical Coriscus." For to say "Coriscus" and "musical" and "musical Coriscus" amounts to the same thing; and this is also true when we say "just" and "musical" and "just musical Coriscus." For all of these are said to be accidentally one; just and musical because they are accidents of one substance, and musical and Coriscus because the one is an accident of the other. And similarly in a sense musical Coriscus is one with Coriscus, because one of the parts of this expression is an accident of the other. Thus musical is an accident of Coriscus and musical Coriscus is an accident of just Coriscus, because one part of each expression is an accident of one and the same subject. For it makes no difference whether musical is an accident of Coriscus [or whether just Coriscus is an accident of musical Coriscus].[1] The same thing also holds true if an accident is predicated of a genus or of any universal term, for example, when one says that man and musical man are the same; for this occurs either because musical is an accident of man, which is one substance, or because both are accidents of some singular thing, for example, Coriscus. Yet both do not belong to it in the same way, but one perhaps as the genus and substance, and the other as a habit or modification of the substance. Therefore whatever things are said to be accidentally one are said to be such in this way.

424. But in the case of things which are said to be essentially one, some are said to be such by nature of their continuity; for example, a bundle becomes one by means of a binding, and pieces of wood become one by means of glue. And a continuous line, even if it is bent, is said to be one, just as each part [of the human body] is, for example, a leg or an arm. And of these things themselves those which are continuous by nature are one to a greater degree than those which are continuous by art. And that is said to be continuous whose motion is essentially one and cannot be otherwise. And motion is one when it is indivisible, i.e., indivisible in time.

425. Again, all those things are essentially continuous which are one not merely by contact; for if you place pieces of wood so that they touch each other, you will not say that they are one, either one board or one body or any other continuous thing. Hence those things which are continuous throughout are said to be one even though they are bent. And those which are not bent are one to an even greater degree; for example, the lower leg or the thigh is one to a greater degree than the leg, because the motion of the leg may not be one. And a straight line is one to a greater degree than a bent line. But what is bent and angular

---

[1] This statement, found in the Greek, is omitted from the Latin version.

we refer to as either one or not one, because its motion may be either simultaneous or not. But the motion of a straight line is always simultaneous, and no part of it which has extension is at rest when another moves, as in a bent line.

426. Again, a thing is said to be one in another sense because its underlying subject is uniform in species; and it is uniform in species as those things whose form is indivisible from the viewpoint of sensory perception. And the underlying subject is either one that is primary or one that is last in relation to the end. For wine is said to be one and water is said to be one inasmuch as they are indivisible in species. And all liquids are said to be one, as oil, wine and fluids, because the ultimate subject of all is the same; for all of these are made up of water or of air.

427. And those things are said to be one whose genus is one and differs by opposite differences. And all these things are said to be one because the genus, which is the subject of the differences, is one; for example, man, dog and horse are one because all are animals; and it is such in a way closest to that in which matter is one. And sometimes these things are said to be one in this way, and sometimes in their higher genus, which is said to be the same if those which are higher than these are the last species of the genus; for example, the isosceles and the equilateral triangle are one and the same figure because both are triangles; but they are not the same triangles.

428. Further, any two things are said to be one when the definition expressing the essence of one is indistinguishable from that signifying the essence of the other. For in itself every definition is divisible. And what has increased and what has decreased are one in this way, because their definition is one. An example of this is found in plane figures, which are one in species.

429. And those things are altogether one and in the highest degree whose concept, which grasps their essence, is indivisible and cannot be separated either in time or in place or in its intelligible structure; and of these, all those which are substances are especially such.

COMMENTARY

842. Having given the various senses of the terms which signify causes, the Philosopher now proceeds to do the same thing with those terms which signify in some way the subject of this science. This is divided into two parts. In the first (423:C 843) he gives or distinguishes the different senses of the terms which signify the subject of this science; and in the second (445:C 908) he distinguishes the different senses of the terms which signify the parts of this subject ("Things are said to be the *same*").

Now the subject of this science can be taken either as that which has to be considered generally in the whole science, and as such it is unity and being, or as that with which this science is chiefly concerned, and this is substance. Therefore, first (423), he gives the different senses of the term *one;* second (435:C 885) of the term *being* ("The term *being*"); and third (440:C 898), of the term *substance* ("The term *substance*").

In regard to the first part of this division he does two things. First, he makes a distinction between what is essentially one and what is accidentally one, and he also indicates the various senses in which things are said to be accidentally one. Second (424:C 848), he notes the various senses in which things are said to be essentially one ("But in the case").

843. He says (423), then, that the term *one* signifies both what is essentially one and what is accidentally one. And he tells us that what is accidentally one we should consider first in the case of singular terms. Now singular terms can be accidentally one in two ways: in one way according as an accident is related to a subject; and in another way according as one accident is related to another. And in both cases three things have to be considered—one composite thing and two simple ones. For if what is accidentally one is considered to be such according as an accident is related to a subject, then there are, for example, these three things: first, Coriscus; second, musical; and third, musical Coriscus. And these three are accidentally one; for Coriscus and what is musical are the same in subject. Similarly when an accident is related to an accident, three terms must be considered: first, musical; second, just; and third, just musical Coriscus. And all these are said to be accidentally one, but for different reasons.

844. For just and musical, which are two simple terms in the second way, are said to be accidentally one because both are accidents of one and the same subject. But musical and Coriscus, which are two simple terms in the first way, are said to be accidentally one because "the one," namely, musical, "is an accident of the other," namely, of Coriscus. And similarly in regard to the relationship of musical Coriscus to Coriscus (which is the relationship of a composite term to one of two simple terms), these are said to be accidentally one in the first way, because in this expression, i.e., in the complex term, musical Coriscus, one

of the parts, namely, musical, is an accident of the other, which is designated as a substance, namely, Coriscus. And for the same reason it can be said that musical Coriscus is one with just Coriscus, which are two composites in the second way, because two of the parts of each composite are accidents of one subject, Coriscus. For if musical and musical Coriscus, and just and just Coriscus, are the same, then whatever is an accident of musical is also an accident of musical Coriscus; and whatever is an accident of Coriscus is also an accident of just Coriscus. Hence, if musical is an accident of Coriscus, it follows that musical Coriscus is an accident of just Coriscus. Therefore it makes no difference whether we say that musical Coriscus is an accident of just Coriscus, or that musical is an accident of Coriscus.

845. But because accidental predicates of this kind are first applied to singular things and then to universals (although the reverse is true of essential predicates), he therefore makes clear that what he showed in the case of singular terms also applies in that of universal terms. He says that, if an accident is used along with the name of a genus or of any universal term, accidental unity is taken in the same way as it is in the above cases when an accident is joined to a singular term; for example, when it is said that man and musical man are accidentally one, although they differ in some respect.

846. For singular substances are neither present in a subject nor predicated of a subject, so that while they are the subject of other things, they themselves do not have a subject. Now universal substances are predicated of a subject but are not present in a subject, so that while they are not the subjects of accidents, they have something as their subject. Hence, when an accident is joined to a singular substance, the expression stating this can only mean that an accident belongs to

a singular substance, as musical belongs to Coriscus when Coriscus is said to be musical.

847. But when we say musical man, the expression can mean one of two things: either that musical is an accident of man, by which substance is designated, and from this it derives its ability to be the subject of an accident; or it means that both of these, man and musical, belong to some singular thing, for example, Coriscus, in the way that musical was predicated of just, because these two belong to the same singular thing and in the same way, i.e., accidentally. But perhaps the one term does not belong to the other in the same way, but in the way that universal substance belongs to the singular as a genus, as the term *animal;* or if it is not a genus, it at least belongs to the substance of the subject, i.e., as an essential predicate, as the term *man.* But the other term, namely, musical, does not have the character of a genus or essential predicate, but that of a habit or modification of the subject, or whatever sort of accident it may be. He gives these two, habit and modification, because there are some accidents which remain in their subject, such as habits, which are moved with difficulty, and others which are not permanent but transient, such as modifications. It is clear, then, that these are the ways in which things are said to be accidentally one.

848. **But in the case** (424).

Then he gives the ways in which things are essentially one, and in regard to this he does two things. First (424), he indicates the different senses in which the term *one* is used; and second (434:C 880), the different senses in which the term *many* is used ("Moreover, it is evident").

In regard to the first he does two things. First, he gives the different senses in which things are one from the viewpoint of nature, i.e., according to the conditions found in reality; and

second (433:C 876), from the viewpoint of logic, i.e., according to the considerations of logic ("Further, some things").

In regard to the first he does two things. First, he distinguishes the different senses in which things are said to be one. Second (432:C 872), he indicates a property which accompanies unity ("But the essence of oneness").

In regard to the first he does two things. First, he sets down the different senses in which things are said to be one. Second (430:C 866), he reduces all of them to a single sense ("For in general").

In the first part (424) he gives five senses in which the term one is used.

849. The first is this: some of the things which are said to be essentially one are such "by nature of their continuity," i.e., by being continuous, or "because they are continuous," as another translation says. But things are said to be continuous in two ways; for, as another text says, some things are continuous by reason of something other than themselves, and some in themselves.

850. First, he proceeds to deal with those things which are continuous by reason of something other than themselves. He says that there are things which are continuous as a result of something else; for example, a bundle of sticks is continuous by means of a cord or binding; and in this way too pieces of wood which have been glued together are said to be one by means of the glue. Now there are also two ways in which this occurs, because the continuity of things which are fastened together sometimes takes the form of a straight line, and sometimes that of a line which is not straight. This is the case, for example, with a bent line having an angle, which results from the contact of two lines in one surface in such a way that they are not joined in a straight line. And it is in this way that the parts of an animal are said

333

to be one and continuous; for example, the leg, which is bent, and contains an angle at the knee, is said to be one and continuous; and it is the same with the arm.

851. But since this kind of continuity which comes about by reason of something else can exist or come to be both by nature and by art, those things which are continuous by nature are one to a greater degree than those which are continuous by art; for the unity that accounts for the continuity of things which are continuous by nature is not extrinsic to the nature of the thing which is made continuous by it, as happens in the case of things which are one by art, in which the binding or glue or something of the sort is entirely extrinsic to the nature of the things which are joined together. Hence those things which are joined by nature hold the first place among those which are essentially continuous, which are one in the highest degree.

852. In order to make this clear he defines the continuous. He says that that is said to be continuous which has only one motion essentially and cannot be otherwise. For the different parts of any continuous thing cannot be moved by different motions, but the whole continuous thing is moved by one motion. He says "essentially" because a continuous thing can be moved in one way essentially and in another or others accidentally. For example, if a man in a ship moves against the motion of the ship essentially, he is still moved accidentally by the motion of the ship.

853. Now in order for motion to be one it must be indivisible; and by this I mean from the viewpoint of time, in the sense that at the same time that one part of a continuous

thing is moved another is also moved. For it is impossible that one part of a continuous thing should be in motion and another at rest, or that one part should be at rest and another in motion, so that the motion of the different parts should take place in different parts of time.

854. Therefore the Philosopher defines the continuous here by means of motion, and not by means of the oneness of the boundary at which the parts of the continuous things are joined, as is stated in the *Categories,*[1] and in the *Physics;*[2] because from this definition he can consider different grades of unity in different continuous things (as will be made clear later on [425:C 856]), but he cannot do this from the definition given there.

855. Moreover, it should be noted that what is said here about the motion of a continuous thing being indivisible from the viewpoint of time is not opposed to the point proved in Book VI of the *Physics,*[3] that the time of a motion is divided according to the parts of the thing moved. For here the Philosopher is speaking of motion in an unqualified sense, because one part of a continuous thing does not begin to be moved before another part does; but there he is speaking of some designation which is made in the continuous quantity over which motion passes. For that designation, which is the first part of a continuous quantity, is traversed in a prior time, although in that prior time other parts of the continuous thing that is in motion are also moved.

856. **Again, all those** (425).

Then he proceeds to deal with things which are essentially continuous. He says that those things are essentially continuous which are said to be one not by contact. He proves this as follows: things which touch each other,

[1] *Categoriae,* 6 (5a 1).
[2] *Physica,* V, 3 (227a 10).
[3] *Physica,* VI, 4 (235a 10-24).

as two pieces of wood, are not said to be one piece of wood or one body or any other kind of one which belongs to the class of the continuous. Hence it is evident that the oneness of things which are continuous differs from that of things which touch each other. For those things which touch each other do not have any unity of continuity of themselves but by reason of some bond which unites them; but those things which are continuous are said to be essentially one even though they are bent. For two bent lines are continuous in relation to one common boundary, which is the point at which the angle is formed.

857. Yet those things are one to a greater degree which are essentially continuous and without a bend. The reason is that a straight line can have only one motion in all of its parts, whereas a bent line can have one or two motions. For the whole of a bent line can be understood to be moved in one part; and it can also be understood that when one part is at rest, the other part, which makes an angle with the part at rest, can come closer by its motion to the unmoved part; for example, when the lower leg or shin is bent in the direction of the upper leg, which here is called the thigh. Hence each of these—the shin and thigh—is one to a greater degree "than the scelos," as the Greek text says, i.e., the whole composed of the shin and thigh.

858. Further, it must be noted that the text which reads "curved" instead of "bent" is false. For, since the parts of a curved line do not contain an angle, it is evident that they must be in motion together or at rest together, just as the parts of a straight line are; but this does not happen in the case of a bent line, as has been stated (425:C 857).

859. **Again, a thing** (426).

Here he gives the second way in which things are one. He says that a thing is said to be one in a second way not merely by reason of continuous quantity but because of the fact that the whole subject is uniform in species. For some things can be continuous even though they differ in species; for example, when gold is continuous with silver or something of this kind. And then two such things will be one if quantity alone is considered but not if the nature of the subject is considered. But if the whole continuous subject is uniform in species, it will be one both from the viewpoint of quantity and from that of nature.

860. Now a subject is said to be uniform in species when the same sensible form is not divided in such a way that there are different sensible forms in different parts of the subject, as it sometimes happens, for example, that one part of a sensible body is white and another black. And this subject, which does not differ in species, can be taken in two ways: in one way as the first subject, and in another as the last or ultimate subject which is reached at the end of a division. It is evident, for example, that a whole amount of wine is said to be one because its parts are parts of one common subject which is undifferentiated specifically. The same is true of water. For all liquids or moist things are said to be one insofar as they have a single ultimate subject. For oil and wine and the like are ultimately dissolved into water or air, which is the root of moistness in all things.

861. **And those things** (427).

Then he indicates the third way in which things are said to be one. He says that those things are said to be one whose genus is one, even though it is divided by opposite differences. And this way resembles the preceding one; for some things were said to be one in the preceding way because their subject-genus is one, and now some things are said to be one because their genus, which is the subject of differences, is one; for example, a man and a horse and a dog are said to be one because they have animality in common as one genus, which is the subject of differences. Yet this way differs from the preceding, because in the preceding way the subject was one thing which was not differentiated by forms; but here the subject-genus is one thing which is differentiated by various differences, as though by various forms.

862. Thus it is evident that some things are said to be one in genus in a most proximate sense, and in a way similar to that in which some things are said to be one in matter. For those things which are said to be one in matter are also differentiated by forms. For even though a genus is not matter, because it would then not be predicated of a species since matter is part of a thing, still the notion of a genus is taken from what is material in a thing, just as the notion of a difference is taken from what is formal. For the rational soul is not the difference of man (since it is not predicated of man), but something having a rational soul (for this is what the term rational signifies). Similarly, sensory nature is not the genus of man but a part. But something having a sensory nature, which the term animal signifies, is the genus of man. In a similar fashion, then, the way in which things are one in matter is closely related to that in which they are one in genus.

863. But it must be borne in mind that to be one in generic character has two meanings. For sometimes some things are said to be one in genus, as has been stated, because they belong to one genus, whatever it may be. But sometimes some things are said

to be one in genus only in reference to a higher genus, which, along with the designation "one" or "the same," is predicated of the last species of a lower genus when there are other higher species in one of which the lower [4] species agree. For example, figure is one supreme genus which has many species under it, namely, circle, triangle, square, and the like. And triangle also has different species, namely, the equilateral, which is called isopleural, and the triangle with two equal sides, which is called equi-legged or isosceles. Hence these two triangles are said to be one figure, which is their remote genus, but not one triangle, which is their proximate genus. The reason for this is that these two triangles do not differ by any differences which divide figure, but by differences which divide triangle. And the term *same* means that from which something does not differ by a difference.

864. **Further, any two** (428).

He now describes the fourth way in which things are said to be one. He says that things such that the definition of one (which is the concept signifying its quiddity) is not distinguished from the definition of the other (which also signifies its quiddity) are also said to be one. For while every definition must be divisible or distinguishable in itself, or essentially, since it is composed of genus and difference, it is possible for the definition of one thing to be indistinguishable from that of another when the two have one definition. And this applies whether those definitions signify the total [intelligible structure] of the thing defined, as tunic and clothing (and then things whose definition is one are one in an absolute sense), or whether that common definition does not totally comprehend the intelligible structure of the two things which have it in common, as an ox and a horse have in

---

[4] Reading *inferiores* for *infinitae* in keeping with the sense of the text.

common the one definition of animal. Hence they are never one in an absolute sense, but only in a relative sense inasmuch as each is an animal. The same applies in the case of increase and decrease; for there is one common definition of the genus, because each is a motion relating to quantity. And the same thing is true of plane figures, for there is one definition of the species, plane figure.

865. **And those things** (429).

He gives the fifth way in which things are one. He says that those things are "altogether" one, i.e., perfectly, and in the highest degree, whose concept, which grasps their quiddity, is altogether indivisible, like simple things, which are not composed of material and formal principles. Hence the concept which embraces their quiddity does not comprehend them in such a way as to form a definition of them from different principles, but rather grasps them negatively, as happens in the case of a point, which has no parts; or it even comprehends them by relating them to composite things, as happens, for example, when someone defines the unit as the principle of number. And because such things have in themselves an indivisible concept, and things which are divided in any way at all can be understood separately, it therefore follows that such things are indivisible both in time and in place and in their intelligible structure. Hence these things are one in the highest degree, and especially those which are indivisible in the genus of substance. For even though what is indivisible in the genus of accident is not composite in itself, none the less it does form a composite with something else, namely, the subject in which it inheres. But an indivisible substance is neither composite in itself nor does it form a composite with something else. Or the term substance can be taken in the ablative case, and then the sense is that, even though some things are said to be one because they are indivisible in time and in place and in definition, still those things in this class which are indivisible in substance are said to be one in the highest degree. This sense is reduced to the preceding one.

LESSON 8

The Primary Sense of One. One in the Sense of Complete. One as the Principle of Number. The Ways in Which Things Are One. The Ways in Which Things Are Many

ARISTOTLE'S TEXT   Chapter 6: 1016b 3-1017a 6

430. For in general those things which do not admit of division are said to be one insofar as they do not admit of division. Thus, if two things do not admit of division insofar as they are man, they are one man; and if they do not admit of division insofar as they are animal, they are one animal; and if they do not admit of division insofar as they have continuous quantity, they are one continuous quantity. Hence many things are said to be one because they do or undergo or have or are related to [1] some other thing which is one. But those things are said to be one in a primary sense whose substance is one; and they are one either by continuity or in species or in intelligible structure. For we count as many those things which are not continuous, or those whose form is not one, or those whose intelligible structure is not one.

431. Again, in one sense we say that anything at all is one by continuity if it is quantitative and continuous; and in another sense we say that a thing is not one unless it is a whole, i.e., unless it has one form. Thus in looking at the parts of a shoe which are put together in any way at all, we would not say that they are one, except by reason of their continuity; but if they are put together in such a way as to be a shoe and to have a certain form, there would then be one thing. And for this reason among lines the circular line is one in the highest degree because it is whole and complete.

432. But the essence of oneness is to be a principle of some number; for the first measure is a principle, because that by which we first come to know each class of things is its first measure. Unity, then, is the first principle of what is knowable about each class. But this unity or unit is not the same in all classes; for in one it is the lesser half tone, and in another it is the vowel or consonant; and in the case of weight the unit is different; and in that of motion different still. But in all cases what is one is indivisible either in quantity or in species. Thus a unit is indivisible in quantity as quantity in every way and has no position; and a point is indivisible in every way and has position. A line is divisible in one dimension; a surface, in two; and a body, in three. And conversely, that which is divisible in two dimensions is a surface; in one, a line; and quantitatively indivisible in every way, a point and a unit. If it has no position, it is a unit; and if it has position, it is a point.

433. Further, some things are one in number, some in species, some in genus, and some analogically or proportionally. Those things are one in number which have one matter; in species, which have one intelligible structure; in genus,

[1] Reading *ad aliquid esse unum* for *aliquid esse unum*.

which have the same figure of predication; and proportionally, which are related to each other as some third thing is to a fourth. And the latter types of unity always follow the former. Thus things which are one in number are one in species, but not all which are one in species are one in number; and all which are one in species are one in genus, but not all which are one in genus are one in species, although they are all one proportionally. And not all which are one proportionally are one in genus.

434. Moreover, it is evident that things are said to be many in a way opposite to that in which they are one. For some things are many because they are not continuous; others, because their matter, either the first or ultimate, is divisible in species; and others because they have many conceptions expressing their essence.

COMMENTARY

866. Here the Philosopher reduces all senses in which things are said to be one to one primary sense, and in regard to this he does two things. First (430:C 866), he makes this reduction; and second (431:C 870), to those senses in which things are said to be one, which have already been given, he adds another ("Again, in one sense").

He accordingly says, first (430), that it is evident from what precedes that things which are indivisible in every way are said to be one in the highest degree. For all the other senses in which things are said to be one are reducible to this sense, because it is universally true that those things which do not admit of division are said to be one insofar as they do not admit of division. For example, those things which are undivided insofar as they are man are said to be one in humanity, as Socrates and Plato; those which are undivided in the notion of animality are said to be one in animality; and those which are undivided from the viewpoint of extension or measure are said to be one in quantity, as continuous things.

867. And from this we can also derive number and the types of unity given above, because what is one is indivisible either in an absolute sense or in a qualified one. If it is indivisible in an absolute sense, it is the last type of unity, which is a principle; but if it is indivisible in a qualified sense, it is so either in quantity alone or in nature. If it is indivisible in quantity, then it is the first type. If it is indivisible in nature, it is so either in reference to its subject or to the division which depends upon the form. If it is divisible in reference to its subject, it is so either in reference to a real subject, and then it is the second type, or to a logical subject, and then it is the third type. And indivisibility of form, which is indivisibility of intelligible structure, or definition, constitutes the fourth type.

868. Now from these senses of the term one certain others are again derived. Thus there are many things which are said to be one because they are doing one thing. For example, many men are said to be one insofar as they are rowing a boat. And some things are said to be one because they are subject to one thing; for example, many men constitute one people because they are ruled by one king. And some are said to be one because they possess one thing; for example, many owners of a field are said to be one in their ownership of it. And some things are also said to be one because they are some-

thing which is one; for example, many men are said to be one because each of them is white.

869. But considering all of these secondary senses in which things are said to be one, which have already been stated in the five ways given above, we can say that those things are one in the primary sense which are one in their substance. For a thing is one in substance either by reason of its continuity, as in the first way; or because of the species of the subject, as in the second way; and again in the third way because the unity of the genus is somewhat similar to the unity of the species; or also because of the intelligible structure, as in the fourth and fifth ways. That some things are said to be one in these ways is clear from the opposite of one. For things are many in number, i.e., they are counted as many, either because they are continuous, or because they do not have one species, or because they do not have one common intelligible structure.

870. **Again, in one sense** (431).

Then he gives an additional sense in which the term one is used, which differs from the preceding ones. This sense is not derived from the notion of indivision, as the foregoing are, but rather from the notion of division. He says that sometimes some things are said to be one because of continuity alone, and sometimes they are said to be one only if they constitute a whole and something complete. Now this happens when the thing has one form, not in the sense that a homogeneous subject is said to have one form, which pertains to the second type given above, but in the sense that the form consists in a kind of totality requiring a definite order of parts. Thus it is clear that we do not say that a thing is one, for example, some artifact such as a shoe, when we see the parts put together in any way at all (unless perhaps it is taken to be one insofar as it is continuous); but we say that all parts of a

shoe are one when they are united in such a way that the thing is a shoe and has one form—that of a shoe.

871. And from this it is clear that a circular line is one in the highest degree. For a circular line is not only continuous like a straight line, but also has a totality and completeness which a straight line does not have; for that is complete and whole which lacks nothing. Now this characteristic belongs to a circular line; for nothing can be added to a circular line, but something can be added to a straight one.

872. **But the essence** (432).

Then he indicates a property which flows from oneness or unity. He says that the essence of one consists in being the principle of some number. This is clear from the fact that the unit is the primary numerical measure by which every number is measured. Now a measure has the character of a principle, because measured things are known by their measure, and things are known by their proper principles. And it is clear from this that unity is the first principle of what is known or knowable about each thing, and that it is the principle of knowing in all classes.

873. But this unity which is the principle of knowing is not the same in all classes of things. For in the class of musical sounds it is the lesser half tone, which is the smallest thing in this class; for a lesser half tone is less than a half tone since a tone is divided into two unequal half tones one of which is called a lesser half tone. And in the class of words the first and smallest unity is the vowel or consonant; and the vowel to a greater degree than the consonant, as will be stated in Book X (831:C 1971). And in the class of heavy things or weights there is some smallest thing which is their measure, i.e., the ounce or something of this kind. And in the class of motions there is one first measure which measures the other motions, namely, the simplest and swiftest motion, which is the diurnal motion.

874. Yet all of these have this feature in common that the first measure is indivisible in quantity or in species. Hence, in order that something be one and first in the genus of quantity it must be indivisible, and indivisible in quantity. It is called a unit if it is indivisible in every way and has no position, and a point if it is altogether indivisible in quantity but has position. A line is something divisible in one dimension only; a surface, in two; and a body, in all, i.e., in three dimensions. And these descriptions are reversible; for everything that is divisible in two dimensions is a surface, and so on with the others.

875. Again, it must be noted that being a measure is the distinctive characteristic of unity insofar as it is the principle of number. But this unity or one is not the same as that which is interchangeable with being, as has been stated in Book IV (303:C 557). For the concept of the latter kind of unity involves only being undivided, but that of the former kind involves being a measure. But even though this character of a measure belongs to the unity which is the principle of number, still by a kind of likeness it is transferred to the unity found in other classes of things, as the Philosopher will show in Book X of this work (814:C 1921). And according to this the character of a measure is found in any class of things. But this character of a measure is a natural consequence of the note of undividedness, as has been explained (432:C 872). Hence the term one is not predicated in a totally equivocal sense of the unity which is interchangeable with being and of that which is the principle of number, but it is predicated of one primarily and of the other secondarily.

876. **Further, some things** (433).

Then he gives another way of dividing unity, and this division is rather from the viewpoint of logic. He says that some things are one in number, some in species, some in genus, and some analogically. Those things are one in number whose matter is one; for insofar as matter has certain designated dimensions it is the principle by which a form is individuated. And for this reason a singular thing is numerically one and divided from other things as a result of matter.

877. Those things are said to be one in species which have one "intelligible structure," or definition; for the only thing that is defined in a proper sense is the species, since every definition is composed of a genus and a difference. And if any genus is defined, this happens insofar as it is a species.

878. Those things are one in genus which have in common one of the "figures of predication," i.e., which have one way of being predicated. For the way in which substance is predicated and that in which quality or action is predicated are different; but all substances have one way of being predicated inasmuch as they are not predicated as something which is present in a subject.

879. And those things are proportionally or analogically one which agree in this respect that one is related to another as some third thing is to a fourth. Now this can be taken in two ways: either in the sense that any two things are related in different ways to one third thing (for example, the term healthy is predicated of urine because it signifies the relationship of a sign of health [to health itself]; and of medicine because it signifies the relationship of a cause to the same health); or it may be taken in the sense that the proportion of two things to two other things is the same (for example, tranquillity to the sea and serenity to the air; for tranquillity is a state of rest in the sea, and serenity is a state of rest in the air).

880. Now with regard to the ways in which things are one, the latter types

of unity always follow the former, and not the reverse; for those things which are one in number are one in species, but not the other way about. The same thing is clear in the other cases.

881. **Moreover, it is evident** (434).

From the ways in which things are said to be one he now derives the ways in which things are said to be many. He says that things are said to be many in just as many ways as they are said to be one, because in the case of opposite terms one is used in as many ways as the other. Hence some things are said to be many because they are not continuous, which is the opposite of the first way in which things are one.

882. Other things are said to be many because their matter is divisible in species, whether we understand by matter "the first," i.e., their proximate matter, or the final or ultimate matter into which they are ultimately dissolved.

Indeed, it is by the division of their proximate matter that wine and oil are said to be many, and by the division of their remote matter that wine and a stone are said to be many. And if matter be taken both for real matter and for conceptual matter, i.e., for a genus, which resembles matter, many in this sense is taken as the opposite of the second and third ways in which things are said to be one.

883. And still other things are said to be many when the conceptions which express their essence are many. And many in this sense is taken as the opposite of the fourth way in which things are said to be one.

884. But the opposite of the fifth way in which things are one does not have the notion of many except in a qualified sense and potentially; for the fact that a thing is divisible does not make it many except potentially.

LESSON 9

Division of Being into Accidental and Essential. The Types of Accidental and of Essential Being

ARISTOTLE'S TEXT   Chapter 7: 1017a 7-1017b 9

435. The term *being* (*ens*) signifies both accidental being (*ens per accidens*) and essential being (*ens per se*).

436. Accidental being is designated when we say, for example, that the just person *is* musical, and that the man *is* musical, and that the musician *is* a man. And the same thing applies when we say that the musician builds, because it is accidental to a builder to be a musician, or to a musician to be a builder. For to say that "this *is* that" means that this is an accident of that. And so it is in the cases given; for when we say that the man is musical, and that the musician is a man, or that what is musical is white, in the latter case we mean that both are accidents of the same thing, and in the former that the attribute is accidental to the being. But when we say that what is musical is a man, we mean that musical is an accident of this person. And in this sense too white is said to be, because the thing of which it is an accident is. Therefore those things which are said to be in an accidental sense are said to be such either because both belong to the same being, or because the attribute belongs to the being, or because the thing to which it belongs and of which it is predicated is.

437. On the other hand those things are said to be essentially which signify the figures of predication;[1] for being is signified in just as many ways as predications are made. Therefore, since some of these predications signify what a thing is, others what it is like, others how much, others how related, others what it does, others what it undergoes, others where, and others when, to each of these there corresponds a mode of being which signifies the same thing. For there is no difference between "the man is recovering" and "the man recovers," or between "the man is walking" or "cutting" and "the man walks" or "cuts." And the same is true in other cases.

438. Again, being signifies that something is true, and non-being signifies that something is not true but false. This also holds true of affirmation and negation. For example, to say that Socrates is musical means that this is true. Or to say that Socrates is not white means that this is true. But to say that the diagonal of a square is not incommensurable with a side means that this is false.

439. Again, to be, or being, signifies that some of the things mentioned are potentially and others actually. For in the case of the terms mentioned we predicate being both of what is said to be potentially and of what is said to be actually. And similarly we say both of one who is capable of using scientific knowledge and of one who is actually using it, that he knows. And we say that that is at rest which is already so or capable of being so. And this also applies in the case of substances;

[1] See *Categoriae*, 4 (1b 25-27).

for we say that Mercury is in the stone, and half of the line in the line, and we call that grain which is not yet ripe. But when a thing is potential and when not must be settled elsewhere (773:C 1832).

COMMENTARY

885. Here the Philosopher gives the various senses in which the term *being* is used, and in regard to this he does three things. First (435:C 885), he divides being into essential being and accidental being. Second (436:C 886), he distinguishes between the types of accidental being ("Accidental being"). Third (437:C 889), he distinguishes between the types of essential being ("On the other hand").

He says (435), then, that while things are said to be both essentially and accidentally, it should be noted that this division of being is not the same as that whereby being is divided into substance and accident. This is clear from the fact that he later divides essential being into the ten predicaments, nine of which belong to the class of accident (437:C 889). Hence being is divided into substance and accident insofar as it is considered in an absolute sense; for example, whiteness considered in itself is called an accident, and man a substance. But accidental being, in the sense in which it is taken here, must be understood by comparing an accident with a substance; and this comparison is signified by the term *is* when, for example, it is said that the man is white. Hence this whole "the man is white" is an accidental being. It is clear, then, that the division of being into essential being and accidental being is based on the fact that one thing is predicated of another either essentially or accidentally. But the division of being into substance and accident is based on the fact that a thing is

in its own nature either a substance or an accident.

886. **Accidental being** (436).

Then he indicates the various senses in which a thing is said to be accidentally. He says that this occurs in three ways: first, when an accident is predicated of an accident, as when it is said that someone just is musical: second, when an accident is predicated of a subject, as when it is said that the man is musical; and third, when a subject is predicated of an accident, as when it is said that the musician is a man. And since he has shown above (410:C 787) how an accidental cause differs from an essential cause, he therefore now shows that an accidental being is a result of an accidental cause.

887. He says that in giving an accidental cause we say that the musician builds, because it is accidental to a builder to be a musician, or vice versa; for it is evident that the statement "this is that," i.e., the musician is a builder, simply means that "this is an accident of that." The same is true of the foregoing senses of accidental being when we say that the man is musical by predicating an accident of a subject, or when we say that what is white is musical, or conversely that what is musical is white by predicating an accident of an accident. For in all of these cases *is* signifies merely accidental being: "in the latter case," i.e., when an accident is predicated of an accident, *is* signifies that both accidents are accidental to the same subject; "and in the former," i.e., when an accident is predicated of a subject, *is* signifies "that the attribute

is accidental to the being," i.e., to the subject. But when we say that what is musical is a man, we mean "that musical is an accident of this person," i.e., that musical, which holds the position of a subject, is an accident of the predicate. And the reason for making the predication is similar in a sense when a subject is predicated of an accident and when an accident is predicated of an accident. For a subject is predicated of an accident by reason of the fact that the subject is predicated of that to which the accident, which is expressed in the subject, is accidental; and in a similar fashion an accident is predicated of an accident because it is predicated of the subject of an accident. And for this reason the attribute musical is predicated not only of man but also of white, because that of which the attribute musical is an accident, i.e., the subject, is white.

888. It is evident, then, that those things which are said to be in an accidental sense are said to be such for three reasons: either "because both," namely, the subject and predicate, belong to the same thing (as when an accident is predicated of an accident); or "because the attribute," namely, the predicate, such as musical, "belongs to the being," i.e., to the subject which is said to be musical (and this occurs when an accident is predicated of a subject); or "because the thing," i.e., the subject which is expressed in the predicate, to which belongs the accident of which it (the subject) is itself predicated, itself is (and this occurs when a subject is predicated of an accident, as when we say that what is musical is a man).

889. **On the other hand** (437).

Here he distinguishes between the types of essential being; and in regard to this he does three things. First (437), he divides the kind of being which lies outside the mind, which is complete being, by the ten predicaments. Second

(438:C 895), he gives another type of being, inasmuch as being exists only in the mind ("Again, being signifies"). Third (439:C 897), he divides being by potentiality and actuality—and being divided in this way is more common than complete being, for potential being is being only imperfectly and in a qualified sense ("Again, to be").

He says, first (437), that all those things which signify the figures of predication are said to be essentially. For it must be noted that being cannot be narrowed down to some definite thing in the way in which a genus is narrowed down to a species by means of differences. For since a difference does not participate in a genus, it lies outside the essence of a genus. But there could be nothing outside the essence of being which could constitute a particular species of being by adding to being; for what is outside of being is nothing, and this cannot be a difference. Hence in Book III of this work (229:C 433) the Philosopher proved that being cannot be a genus.

890. Being must then be narrowed down to diverse genera on the basis of a different mode of predication, which flows from a different mode of being; for "being is signified," i.e., something is signified to be, "in just as many ways" (or in as many senses) as we can make predications. And for this reason the classes into which being is first divided are called predicaments, because they are distinguished on the basis of different ways of predicating. Therefore, since some predicates signify what (i.e., substance); some, of what kind; some, how much; and so on; there must be a mode of being corresponding to each type of predication. For example, when it is said that a man is an animal, *is* signifies substance; and when it is said that a man is white, *is* signifies quality; and so on.

891. For it should be noted that a predicate can be referred to a subject

in three ways. This occurs in one way when the predicate states what the subject is, as when I say that Socrates is an animal; for Socrates is the thing which is an animal. And this predicate is said to signify first substance, i.e., a particular substance, of which all attributes are predicated.

892. A predicate is referred to a subject in a second way when the predicate is taken as being in the subject, and this predicate is in the subject either essentially and absolutely and as something flowing from its matter, and then it is quantity; or as something flowing from its form, and then it is quality; or it is not present in the subject absolutely but with reference to something else, and then it is relation. A predicate is referred to a subject in a third way when the predicate is taken from something extrinsic to the subject, and this occurs in two ways. In one way, that from which the predicate is taken is totally extrinsic to the subject; and if this is not a measure of the subject, it is predicated after the manner of attire, as when it is said that Socrates is shod or clothed. But if it is a measure of the subject, then, since an extrinsic measure is either time or place, the predicament is taken either in reference to time, and so it will be *when;* or if it is taken in reference to place and the order of parts in place is not considered, it will be *where;* but if this order is considered, it will be position. In another way, that from which the predicate is taken, though outside the subject, is nevertheless from a certain point of view in the subject of which it is predicated. And if it is from the viewpoint of the principle, then it is predicated as an action; for the principle of action is in the subject. But if it is from the viewpoint of its terminus, then it will be predicated as a passion; for a passion is terminated in the subject which is being acted upon.

893. But since there are some predications in which the verb *is* is clearly not used (for example, when it is said that a man walks), lest someone think that these predications do not involve the predication of being, for this reason Aristotle subsequently rejects this, saying that in all predications of this kind something is signified to be. For every verb is reduced to the verb *is* plus a participle. For there is no difference between the statements "the man is recovering" and "the man recovers"; and it is the same in other cases. It is clear, then, that "being" is used in as many ways as we make predications.

894. And there is no truth in Avicenna's statement [1] that predicates which belong to the class of accidents primarily signify substance and secondarily accidents, as the terms *white* and *musical*. For the term white, as it is used in the categories, signifies quality alone. Now the term white implies a subject inasmuch as it signifies whiteness after the manner of an accident, so that it must by implication include the subject in its notion, because the being of an accident consists in being in something. For even though whiteness signifies an accident, it still does not signify this after the manner of an accident but after that of a substance. Hence it implies a subject in no way. For if it were to signify a subject primarily, then the Philosopher would not put accidental predicates under essential being but under accidental being. For the whole statement "the man is white" is a being in an accidental sense, as has been stated (436:C 886).

895. **Again, being signifies** (438). Then he gives another sense in which the term being is used, inasmuch as the terms being and is signify the composition of a proposition, which the intellect makes when it combines and separates. He says that being signifies the truth of a thing, or as another trans-

[1] *Metaphysica,* III, 7 (82ra).

lation better expresses it, being signifies that some statement is true. Thus the truth of a thing can be said to determine the truth of a proposition after the manner of a cause; for by reason of the fact that a thing is or is not, a discourse is true or false. For when we say that something is, we signify that a proposition is true; and when we say that something is not, we signify that it is not true. And this applies both to affirmation and to negation. It applies to affirmation, as when we say that Socrates is white because this is true; and to negation, as when we say that Socrates is not white, because this is true, namely, that he is not white. And in a similar way we say that the diagonal of a square is not incommensurable with a side, because this is false, i.e., its not being incommensurable.

896. Now it must be noted that this second way in which being is used is related to the first as an effect is to a cause. For from the fact that something is in reality it follows that there is truth and falsity in a proposition, and the intellect signifies this by the term *is* taken as a verb copula. But since the intellect considers as a kind of being something which is in itself a non-being, such as a negation and the like, therefore sometimes being is predicated of something in this second way and not in the first. For blindness is said to be in the second way on the grounds that the proposition in which something is said to be blind is true. However, it is not said to be true in the first way; for blindness does not have any being in reality but is rather a privation of some being. Now it is accidental to a thing that an attribute should be affirmed of it truly in thought or in word, for reality is not referred to knowledge but the reverse. But the act of being which each thing has in its own nature is substantial; and therefore when it is said that Socrates is, if the *is*

is taken in the first way, it belongs to the class of substantial predicates; for being is a higher predicate with reference to any particular being, as animal with reference to man. But if it is taken in the second way, it belongs to the class of accidental predicates.

897. **Again, to be, or being** (439).

Here he gives the division of being into the actual and the potential. He says that to be and being signify something which is expressible or utterable potentially or actually. For in the case of all of the foregoing terms which signify the ten predicaments, something is said to be so actually and something else potentially; and from this it follows that each predicament is divided by actuality and potentiality. And just as in the case of things which are outside the mind some are said to be actually and some potentially, so also is this true in the case of the mind's activities, and in that of privations, which are only conceptual beings. For one is said to know both because he is capable of using scientific knowledge and because he is using it; and similarly a thing is said to be at rest both because rest belongs to it already and because it is capable of being at rest. And this is true not only of accidents but also of substances. For "Mercury," we say, i.e., the image of Mercury, is present potentially in the stone; and half of a line is present potentially in a line, for every part of a continuum is potentially in the whole. And the line is included in the class of substances according to the opinion of those who hold that the objects of mathematics are substances— an opinion which he has not yet disproved. And when grain is not yet ripe, for example, when it is still in blade, it is said to be potentially. Just when, however, something is potential and when it is no longer such must be established elsewhere, namely, in Book IX of this work (773:C 1832).

LESSON 10

Meanings of Substance

ARISTOTLE'S TEXT   Chapter 8: 1017b 10-1017b 26

440. The term *substance* (*substantia*) means the simple bodies, such as earth, fire, water and the like; and in general bodies and the things composed of them, both animals and demons and their parts. All of these are called substances because they are not predicated of a subject, but other things are predicated of them.

441. In another sense substance means that which, being present in such things as are not predicated of a subject, is the cause of their being, as the soul in an animal.

442. Again, substance means those parts which, being present in such things, limit them and designate them as individuals and as a result of whose destruction the whole is destroyed; for example, body is destroyed when surface is, as some say,[1] and surface when line is. And in general it seems to some that number is of this nature; for [according to them] if it is destroyed, nothing will exist, and it limits all things.

443. Again, the quiddity of a thing, whose intelligible expression is the definition, also seems to be the substance of each thing.

444. It follows, then, that the term substance is used in two senses. It means the ultimate subject, which is not further predicated of something else; and it means anything which is a particular being and capable of existing apart. The form and species of each thing is said to be of this nature.

[1] The Pythagoreans and Platonists.

COMMENTARY

898. Aristotle now explains the various senses in which the term *substance* is used; and in regard to this he does two things. First (440:C 898), he gives the various senses in which the term substance is used. Second (444:C 903), he reduces all of these to two ("It follows").

In treating the first part he gives four senses of the term substance. First, it means particular substances, such as the simple bodies: earth, fire, water and the like. And in general it means all bodies, even though they are not simple, i.e., compound bodies of like parts, such as stones, blood, flesh and the like. Again, it means animals, which are composed of such sensible bodies, and also their parts, such as hands and feet and so on; "and demons," i.e., the idols set up in temples and worshipped as gods. Or by demons he means certain animals which the Platonists claimed are capable of reasoning, and which

348

Apuleius defines thus: demons are animals composed of an ethereal body, rational in mind, passive in soul, and eternal in time.[1] Now all of the foregoing things are called substances because they are not predicated of another subject but other things are predicated of them. This is the description of first substance given in the *Categories*.[2]

899. **In another sense** (441).

He says that in another sense substance means the cause of the being of the foregoing substances which are not predicated of a subject; and it is not extrinsic to them like an efficient cause but is intrinsic like a form. It is in this sense that the soul is called the substance of an animal.

900. **Again, substance** (442).

He gives a third meaning of substance, which is the one used by the Platonists and Pythagoreans. He says that all those parts of the foregoing substances which constitute their limits and designate them as individuals, according to the opinion of these thinkers, and by whose destruction the whole is destroyed, are also termed substances. For example, body is destroyed when surface is, as some say, and surface when line is. It is also clear that surface is the limit of body and line the limit of surface. And according to the opinion of the philosophers just mentioned the line is a part of surface and surface a part of body. For they held that bodies are composed of surfaces, surfaces of lines, and lines of points; and thus it would follow that the point is the substance of the line, the line the substance of surface, and so on for the rest. And according to this position number seems to constitute the entire substance of all things, because when number is destroyed nothing remains in the world; for what is not one is nothing. And similarly things which are not many are non-existent. And

number is also found to limit all things, because all things are measured by number.

901. But this sense of substance is not a true one. For that which is found to be common to all things and is something without which they cannot exist does not necessarily constitute their substance, but it can be some property flowing from the substance or from a principle of the substance. These philosophers also fell into error especially regarding unity and number because they failed to distinguish between the unity which is interchangeable with being and that which is the principle of number.

902. **Again, the quiddity** (443).

He says that the quiddity of each thing, which the definition signifies, is also called its substance. Now the quiddity or essence of a thing, whose intelligible expression is the definition, differs from a form, which he identified with the second meaning of substance, just as humanity differs from a soul, for a form is part of a thing's essence or quiddity, but the essence or quiddity itself of a thing includes all its essential principles. It is in this last sense, then, that genus and species are said to be the substance of the things of which they are predicated; for genus and species do not signify the form alone but the whole essence of a thing.

903. **It follows** (444).

Then he reduces the foregoing senses of substance to two. He says that from the above-mentioned ways in which the term substance is used we can understand that it has two meanings. It means the ultimate subject in propositions, and thus is not predicated of something else. This is first substance, which means a particular thing which exists of itself and is capable of existing apart because it is distinct from

[1] See St. Augustine, *De Civ. Dei*, VIII, 16 (PL 41:241).
[2] *Categoriae*, 5 (2a 10).

everything else and cannot be common to many. And a particular substance differs from universal substance in these three respects: first, a particular substance is not predicated of inferiors, whereas a universal substance is; second, universal substance subsists only by reason of a particular substance, which subsists of itself; and third, universal substance is present in many things, whereas a particular substance is not but is distinct from everything else and capable of existing apart.

904. And the form and species of a thing also "is said to be of this nature," i.e., substance. In this he includes the second and fourth senses of substance; for essence and form have this note in common that both are said to be that by which something is. However, form, which causes a thing to be actual, is related to matter, whereas quiddity or essence is related to the supposit, which is signified as having such and such an essence. Hence "the form and species" are comprehended under one thing—a being's essence.

905. He omits the third sense of substance because it is a false one, or because it is reducible to form, which has the character of a limit. And he omits matter, which is called substance, because it is not substance actually. However, it is included in the first sense of substance, because a particular substance is a substance and is individuated in the world of material things only by means of matter.

LESSON 11

The Ways in Which Things Are the Same Essentially and Accidentally

ARISTOTLE'S TEXT   Chapter 9: 1017b 27-1018a 9

445. Things are said to be the *same* accidentally; for example, "white" and "musical" are the same because they are accidents of the same subject. And "man" and "musical" are the same because the one is an accident of the other. And "musical" is the same as "man" because it is an accident of a man. And the composite is the same as each of these simple terms, and each the same as it. For both "man" and "musical" are said to be the same as "musical man," and this the same as they. And for this reason none of these predications are universal. For it is not true to say that every man is the same as the musical; for universal predicates are essential, whereas accidental predicates are not, but are said of singulars in an unqualified sense. For "Socrates" and "musical Socrates" seem to be the same because Socrates is not found in many. And for this reason we do not say "every Socrates" as we say "every man." Some things, then, are said to be the same in this way.

446. And others are said to be the same essentially, and in the same number of ways in which they are said to be one. For those things whose matter is one in species or in number, and those whose substance is one, are said to be the same. Hence it is evident that sameness (*identitas*) is a kind of unity of the being of many things or of one thing taken as many; for example, when a person says that something is the same as itself, he uses the same thing as though it were two.

COMMENTARY

906. Having given the various senses of the terms which signify the subject of this science, here the Philosopher gives those which signify the parts of such things as constitute the subject of this science. This is divided into two parts. In the first (445:C 906) he gives the various senses of the terms which signify the parts of unity; and in the second (467:C 954), those which signify the parts of being ("In one sense"). For substance, which is also posited as the subject of this science, is a single category which is not divided into many categories.

The first part is divided into two sections. In the first he gives the various senses of the terms which signify the parts of unity; and in the second (457:C 936), those which signify something that flows from the notion of unity, namely, *prior* and *subsequent* ("Things are said to be"). For to be one is to be a principle or starting point, as has been explained above (432:C 872).

351

907. The first part is divided into two sections. In the first he gives the various senses of the terms which signify the primary parts of unity and of its opposite, plurality; and in the second (451:C 922), he gives those which signify certain secondary parts of unity ("By opposites").

Now the parts of unity are *sameness,* which is oneness in substance; *likeness,* which is oneness in quality; and *equality,* which is oneness in quantity. And, opposed to these, the parts of plurality are *otherness, unlikeness* and *inequality.*

In regard to the first he does two things. First, he gives the various senses in which the term *same* is used, and the senses of its opposite. Second (449:C 918), he gives the various senses of the term *like,* and of its opposite, *unlike* ("Things are said to be *like*"). He makes no mention here, however, of the term *equal* and its opposite, because in the case of these terms plurality is not so evident.

In regard to the first part he does three things. First, he gives the various senses of the term *same;* second (447:C 913), of the term *other,* or *diverse* ("Those things are said to be *other*"); and third (448:C 916), of the term *different* ("Things are said to be *different*").

In regard to the first he does two things. First, he gives the ways in which things are said to be accidentally the same; and second (446:C 911), he gives those in which things are said to be essentially the same ("And others").

908. He says (445) that things are said to be accidentally the same (*idem per accidens*) in three ways. In one way they are the same in the sense that two accidents are; thus "white" and "musical" are said to be the same because they are accidents of the same subject. Things are accidentally the same in a second way when a predicate is said to be the same as a subject inasmuch as it is predicated of it; thus when it is

said that the man is musical, these (man and musical) are said to be the same because musical is an accident of a man, i.e., the predicate is an accident of the subject. And things are accidentally the same in a third way when the subject is said to be the same as an accident inasmuch as it is predicated of it. For example, when it is said that the musical thing is a man, it is understood that the man is the same as the musical thing; for what is predicated of some subject is identified with that subject. And sameness in this sense means that the subject is an accident of the predicate.

909. Now besides these ways in which things are accidentally the same, in which an accident and a subject are taken in themselves, there are also others, i.e., those in which an accident is taken in conjunction with a subject. And when this occurs two senses of the term same have to be distinguished. One of these is signified when an accident taken singly is predicated of the composite of subject and accident; and then the meaning is that the accident is the same as both of the simple terms taken together; for example, "musical" is the same as "musical man." The other is signified when the composite of accident and subject is predicated of the subject taken singly, as when we say that the man is a musical man; and then both of these (the composite "musical man") are signified as being the same as this, i.e., as the subject taken singly. The same notion applies if an accident is taken singly and a subject is taken in combination with the accident. This would be the case, for example, if we were to say that what is musical is a musical man, or the reverse; for both "man" and "musical" are said to be accidentally the same as "musical man," which is the composite, when these two are predicated of that one thing, and vice versa.

910. From this he draws the further conclusion that, in all of the foregoing

modes of predication in which things are said to be accidentally the same, no term is predicated universally. For it is not true to say that every man is the same as what is musical. This becomes clear as follows: Only those attributes which belong essentially to the same subject are predicated universally of universals; for a predicate is predicated essentially of a subject because the mode of predication, which is a universal one, agrees with the condition of the subject, which is universal. However, accidents are not predicated essentially of universals, but only by reason of singular things; and thus they are not predicated universally of universals. But while accidents are predicated in an unqualified sense of singular things (for Socrates and musical Socrates seem to be the same in subject), they are not predicated universally of singular things; for nothing can be predicated universally of something that is not universal. But Socrates is not universal, because he is not present in many. Hence nothing can be predicated of Socrates so that we should say "every Socrates" as we say "every man." The things of which we have spoken, then, are said to be one in this way, i.e., accidentally, as has been stated.

911. **And others** (446).

Then he gives the ways in which things are said to be essentially the same (*idem per se*). He says that things are said to be essentially the same in the same number of ways in which they are said to be essentially one. Now all of the ways in which things are said to be essentially one are reduced to two. Thus, in one sense, things are said to be essentially one because their matter is one, whether we take the matter to be the same in species or in number. The second and third ways in which things are one are reduced to this. And, in another sense, things are said to be one because their substance is one, whether by reason of continu-

ity, which pertains to the first way in which things are one, or by reason of the unity and indivisibility of their intelligible structure, which pertains to the fourth and fifth ways. Therefore some things are said to be the same in these ways too.

912. From this he further concludes that sameness (*identitas*) is a unity or union. For things which are said to be the same are either many in being, but are said to be the same inasmuch as they agree in some respect, or they are one in being, but the intellect uses this as many in order to understand a relationship; for a relationship can be understood only between two extremes. This is what happens, for example, when we say that something is the same as itself; for the intellect then uses something which is one in reality as though it were two, otherwise it could not designate the relationship of a thing to itself. Hence it is clear that, if a relationship always requires two extremes, and in relations of this kind there are not two extremes in reality but only in the mind, then the relationship of sameness according to which something is said to be absolutely the same, will not be a real relation but only a conceptual relation. This is not the case, however, when any two things are said to be the same either in genus or in species. For if the relationship of sameness were something in addition to what we designate by the term *same,* then since this reality, which is a relation, is the same as itself, it would have to have for a like reason something that is also the same as itself; and so on to infinity. Now while it is impossible to proceed to infinity in the case of real beings, nothing prevents this from taking place in the case of things which have being in the mind. For since the mind may reflect on its own act it can understand that it understands; and it can also understand this act in turn, and so on to infinity.

353

LESSON 12

Various Senses of Diverse, Different, Like, Contrary, and Diverse in Species

ARISTOTLE'S TEXT   Chapters 9 & 10: 1018a 9-1018b 8

447. Things are said to be *other* or *diverse* (*diversa*) of which either the forms or the matter or the intelligible structure of the essence is many; and in general the term *other* has senses opposite to those of *the same*.

448. Things are said to be *different* (*differentia*) which, while being diverse, are the same in some respect, and not merely in number, but in species or in genus or proportionally. And so also are those things whose genus is not the same, and contraries, and all those things which have diversity or otherness in their essence.

449. Things are said to be *like* (*similia*) which undergo the same modifications; or undergo more of the same than of different modifications; or whose quality is one.

450. And whatever has a greater number or the more important of those contraries in reference to which alteration is possible is said to be like something else. And things are said to be *unlike* (*dissimilia*) in ways opposite to those in which they are *like*.

Chapter 10

451. By *opposites* (*opposita*) we mean contraries, contradictories, relatives, and privation and possession.

452. And opposites also mean the ultimate parts of which things are composed and into which they are dissolved, as in processes of generation and corruption. And those things which cannot be present at the same time in a subject which is receptive of them are called opposites: either they themselves or the things of which they are composed. Gray and white, for example, are not present at the same time in the same subject, and therefore the things of which they are composed are opposites.

453. By *contraries* (*contraria*) we mean those attributes which, differing in genus, cannot be present at the same time in the same subject; and also those which differ most in the same genus; and those which differ most in the same subject; and those which differ most among those which come under the same power; and things which differ most either absolutely or in genus or in species.

454. Other things are called contraries either because they have contrary attributes or because they are receptive of them; and others because they are capable of causing them or undergoing them, or because they are actually causing them or undergoing them, or because they are rejections or acquisitions or possessions or privations of such attributes.

455. But since the term *being* and the term *one* are used in many ways, all other terms which are used in relation to them must follow upon them; so that the terms *same, diverse* and *contrary* vary according to each category.

354

456. Those things are said to be *diverse* (or *other*) *in species* which belong to the same genus but are not subalternate. And so are those which belong to the same genus and have a difference; and also those which have contrariety in their substance. For contraries differ from each other in species, either all of them, or those which are called such in a primary sense; and so are those things whose intelligible structures differ in the lowest species of the genus (for example, man and horse do not differ in genus but their intelligible structures are different); and those attributes which belong to the same substance and have a difference. Things which are *the same in species* are said to be such in ways opposite to to those just given.

COMMENTARY

913. Here he explains the various ways in which the term *diverse* (or *other*) is used, and he gives three senses. Thus some things are said to be diverse in species because their species are many, as an ass and an ox; others are said to be diverse in number because their matters differ, as two individuals of one species; and others are said to be diverse because "the intelligible structure of the essence," i.e., the definition designating their substance, is different. For some things may be the same in number, i.e., from the viewpoint of matter, but diverse in their intelligible structure, as Socrates and this white man.

914. And since many modes of diversity can be considered (for example, diversity in genus, and the diversity resulting from the division of the continuous), he therefore adds that the term *diverse* means the very opposite of *the same;* for to every way in which things are the same there corresponds an opposite way in which they are diverse. Hence things are said to be diverse in the same number of senses in which they are said to be the same.

915. Yet the other ways in which things are said to be one, i.e., the same, can be reduced to those stated here. For diversity of genus is included in diversity of species, and diversity of quantity is included in diversity of mat-

ter, because the parts of a quantity have the character of matter in relation to the whole.

916. **Things are said to be "different"** (448).

Then he gives the various senses in which the term *different* is used, and there are two of them. First, any two things are said properly to be different which, while being diverse, are "the same in some respect," i.e., they have some one thing in common. And this is so whether they have some one thing in common numerically, as Socrates sitting and Socrates not sitting; or whether they have some one thing in common specifically, as Socrates and Plato have man in common; or whether they have a common genus, as man and ass share in the genus animal; or whether they share in some one thing proportionally, as quantity and quality both share in being. And from this it is evident that everything different is diverse, but not the reverse. For diverse things which agree in no respect cannot properly be called different, because they do not differ in some other respect but only in themselves; but that is said to be different which differs in some particular respect. The term different is used in a second way when it is taken commonly in place of the term diverse; and then those things are also said to be different which belong to diverse genera and have nothing in common.

917. Next he indicates the kind of things which admit of difference in the first way, which is the proper one. Now those things which are said properly to differ must agree in some respect. Those which agree in species differ only by accidental differences; for example, Socrates insofar as he is white or just differs from Plato insofar as he is black or musical. And those things which agree in genus and are diverse in species differ by substantial differences. And since this is so, then those things are said to differ most properly which are the same in genus and diverse in species. For every genus is divided into contrary differences, but not every genus is divided into contrary species. Thus the species of color, white and black, are contraries, and so are their differences, expanding and contracting.[1] And the differences of animal, rational and irrational, are contraries; but the species of animal, such as man, horse, and the like, are not. Therefore things which are said to differ most properly are either those which are contrary species, as white and black, or those species of one genus which are not contrary but have contrariety in their essence because of the contrariety of differences which belong to the essence of the species.

918. **Things are said to be "like"** (449).

Here he points out the various ways in which the term *like* is used, and in regard to this he does two things. First (449:C 918), he indicates the various ways in which this term is used; and second (451:C 922), he gives those senses in which the term *unlike* is used ("By opposites").

In regard to the first he does two things. First, he gives the ways in which the term like is used; and second (450:C 920), he explains how one

thing is said to be most like another ("And whatever").

He gives three ways in which things are like. Now it is evident that oneness in quality causes likeness. Further, undergoing or affection (*passio*) is associated with quality, because undergoing is most noticeable in the case of qualitative change or alteration; and thus one species of quality is called affection or possible quality. Hence things are observed to be like not only insofar as they have a common quality but also insofar as they undergo or suffer something in common. And this can be taken from two points of view: either from that of the affection or undergoing, or from that of the subject in which the affection is terminated.

919. Some things are like, then, for three reasons. First, they undergo or suffer the same thing; for example, two pieces of wood which are consumed by fire can be said to be like. Second, several things are like merely because they are affected or undergo something, whether this be the same or different; for example, two men, one of whom is beaten and the other imprisoned, are said to be like in that they both undergo something or suffer. Third, those things are said to be like which have one quality; for example, two white things are alike in whiteness, and two stars in the heaven are alike in brightness or in power.

920. **And whatever** (450).

Then he shows how one thing is said to be most like some other thing. For when there are several contraries of the sort which are observed to be alterable, whatever resembles some other thing in having the more important of these contraries is said to be more properly like that thing. For example, garlic, which is hot and dry, is said to be more properly like fire than sugar, which is hot and moist. The same holds

[1] See Book X, L.9:T 883, n. 1.

true of any two things which are like some third thing in terms of only one quality; for whatever resembles some other thing in terms of some quality which is more proper to itself, is said to be more properly like that thing. For example, air is more properly like fire than earth; for air is like fire in reference to warmth, which is a quality proper to fire itself to a greater degree than dryness, in reference to which earth is like air.

921. Then he states that things are said to be *unlike* in ways opposite to those in which they are *like*.

922. **By "opposites"** (451).

Here he distinguishes between the secondary parts of plurality, i.e., those contained under difference and diversity, which are its primary parts; and in regard to this he does three things. First, he gives the various ways in which the term *opposite* is used; second (453:C 925), those in which the term *contrary* is used ("By contraries"); and third (456:C 931), those in which things are said to be *diverse or other in species* ("Those things are said to be").

In regard to the first he does two things. First (451), he gives the various ways in which we speak of *opposites;* and there are four of these: contradictories, contraries, privation and possession, and relatives. For one thing is contraposed or opposed to another either by reason of dependence, i.e., insofar as one depends on another, and then they are opposed as relatives, or by reason of removal, i.e., because one removes another. This occurs in three ways: either one thing removes another entirely and leaves nothing, and then there is negation; or the subject alone remains, and then there is privation; or the subject and genus remain, and then there is contrariety. For there are contraries not only in the same subject but also in the same genus.

923. **And opposites** (452).

Second, he gives two ways in which things can be recognized as opposites. The first of these pertains to motion, for in any motion or change the *terminus from which* is the opposite of the *terminus to which*. Hence those things from which motion begins and those in which it ends are opposites. This is evident in processes of generation; for the white is generated from the not-white, and fire is generated from what is not-fire.

924. The second pertains to the subject. For those attributes which cannot belong at the same time to the same subject must be the opposite of each other, either they themselves or the things in which they are present. For the same body cannot be at the same time both white and black, which are contraries; nor can the terms *man* and *ass* be predicated of the same thing, because their intelligible structures contain opposite differences, i.e., rational and irrational. The same holds true of gray and white, because gray is composed of black, which is the opposite of white. And we should note that he expressly says, "in the same subject"; for certain things cannot exist at the the same time in the same subject, not because they are opposed to each other, but because the subject is not receptive of the one or the other; for example, whiteness and music cannot exist at the same time in an ass, but they can exist at the same time in a man.

925. **By "contraries"** (453).

Then he states the various ways in which the term *contrary* is used, and in regard to this he does three things. First, he gives the principal ways in which things are said to be contrary. Among these he includes, first, one improper usage of the term, i.e., that whereby some attributes are called contraries which, while differing in genus, cannot belong at the same time to the same subject; for properly speaking contraries are attributes which belong to one genus. An example of this would be found if we were to say that heaviness and circular motion cannot belong to the same subject.

926. Then he gives a second usage of the term, which is a proper one, according to which contraries are said to be things that agree in some respect; for contraries agree in three respects, namely, in reference to the same genus, or to the same subject, or to the same power. Then he uses these three to expose the things which are real contraries. He says that those attributes which differ most in the same genus are called contraries, as white and black in the genus of color; and those which differ most in the same subject, as health and disease in an animal; and those which differ most in reference to the same power, as what is correct and what is incorrect in reference to grammar; for rational powers extend to opposites. He says "most" in order to differentiate contraries from the intermediate attributes which lie between them, which also agree in the same genus, subject and power, yet do not differ to the greatest degree.

927. Hence he adds the universal notion involved in things which are designated as contraries, namely, that contraries are things which differ most either absolutely or in the same genus or in the same species. They differ "absolutely," for example, in the case of local motion, where the extremes are separated most widely, as the most easterly and westerly points of the whole universe, which are the limits of its diameter. And they differ "in the same genus," as the specific differences which divide a genus; and "in the same species," as contrary differences of an accidental kind by which individuals of the same species differ from each other.

928. **Other things** (454).

Here he shows in what respect some things are said to be contraries in a secondary way because they are related to those things which are contraries in the primary way. For some things are

contraries either because they actually possess contraries, as fire and water are called contraries because one is hot and the other cold; or because they are the potential recipients of contraries, as what is receptive of health and of disease; or because they are potentially causing contraries or undergoing them, as what is capable of heating and of cooling, and what is able to be heated and to be cooled; or because they are actually causing contraries or undergoing them, as what is heating and cooling or being heated and being cooled; or because they are expulsions or rejections or acquisitions of contraries, or even possessions or privations of them. For the privation of white is the opposite of the privation of black, just as the possession of the former is the opposite of that of the latter.

929. It is evident, then, that he touches on a threefold relationship of contraries to things: one is to a subject which is either in act or in potency; another is to something that is active or passive in act or in potency; and a third is to processes of generation and corruption, either to the processes themselves or to their termini, which are possession and privation.

930. **But since the term** (455).

He gives a third way in which the term contrary is used, and he also shows why the foregoing terms are used in many ways. For since the terms *one* and *being* have several meanings, the terms which are based upon them must also have several meanings; for example, *same* and *diverse,* which flow from *one* and *many;* and *contrary,* which is contained under *diverse.* Hence diverse must be divided according to the ten categories just as being and one are.

931. **Those things** (456).

He now explains the various ways in which things are said to be *diverse* (or *other*) *in species,* and he gives five of these. First, they belong to the same genus and are not subalternate; for example, science and whiteness both come under quality, yet they are not distinguished from each other by opposite differences.

932. Second, they belong to the same genus and are distinguished from each other by some difference, whether such differences are contrary or not, as two-footed and four-footed.

933. Third, their subjects contain contrariety; i.e., those things which are distinguished by contrary differences, whether the subjects are contrary themselves (as white and black, which are distinguished by the differences "expanding" and "contracting") or not (as man and ass, which are distinguished by the differences "rational"

and "irrational"). For contraries must differ in species, either all of them, or those which are called contraries in the primary sense.

934. Fourth, the lowest species are diverse and are the last in some genus, as man and horse. For those things which differ only in species are said more properly to differ in species than those which differ both in species and in genus.

935. Fifth, they are accidents in the same subject, yet differ from each other; for many accidents of one and the same kind cannot exist in the same subject. And things are said to be *the same in species* in ways opposite to those given above.

LESSON 13

The Ways in Which Things Are Prior and Subsequent

ARISTOTLE'S TEXT   Chapter 11: 1018b 9-1019a 14

457. Things are said to be *prior* and *subsequent* insofar as there is some primary thing or principle in each class; for prior means what is nearer to some principle determined either in an absolute sense and by nature, or relatively, or in reference to place, or in certain other ways.

458. For example, a thing is prior in place because it is nearer either to some naturally determined place, as the middle or last, or to one that depends on chance. And what is farther away is subsequent.

459. Other things are prior in time. For some are prior because they are farther away from the present, as in the case of things which have taken place. Thus the Trojan war is prior to that of the Medes because it is farther away from the present. And others are prior in time because they are nearer to the present, as in the case of future events; for the Nemean [games] are prior to the Pythian because they are nearer to the present, provided that the present is taken as the principle or primary point.

460. Other things are prior in motion; for what is nearer to a first mover is prior; for example, the boy is prior to the man. And this too is a kind of principle in an absolute sense. Other things are prior in power; for whatever surpasses another in power, or is more powerful, is prior. And such is that according to whose will another, i.e., a subsequent, thing necessarily follows, because if the one does not move, the other is not moved, and if it does move, the other is moved; and will is a principle.

461. Other things are prior in arrangement, and these are the things which have a different place in relation to some one determinate thing according to some plan; for example, one who stands second is prior to one who stands third; and among the strings of the lyre the paranete is prior to the nete. For in the one case it is [the leader] who is taken as the principle or starting point; and in the other it is the middle string. These things, then, are said to be prior in this way.

462. In another way, whatever is prior in knowledge is considered to be prior in an absolute sense. And of such things some are prior in a different way, for some are prior in reference to reason, and others in reference to the senses. For universals are prior in reference to reason, but singulars in reference to the senses.

463. And in the intelligible structure the attribute is prior to the whole, as "musical" is prior to "musical man." For the intelligible structure is not complete without one of its parts, and "musical man" cannot exist unless there is someone who is musical.

464. Again, the attributes of prior things are said to be prior, as straightness is prior to smoothness; for the former is a property of a line considered in itself,

and the latter a property of surface. Some things, then, are said to be prior and subsequent in this way.

465. But others are said to be prior in nature and in substance, namely, all those things which can exist without others, although others cannot exist without them; and this is the division which Plato used. And since the term *being* is used in many ways, the first subject is prior, and therefore substance is prior. And things which exist potentially and those which exist actually are prior in various ways. For some things are prior in being potential, and others in being actual; for example, potentially half a line is prior to the entire line, and a part is prior to the whole, and matter is prior to substance. But in reference to actuality they are subsequent; for when the whole has been dissolved into such parts they will exist actually.

466. In a sense, then, all things which are prior and subsequent are said to be such in this [last] way. For some things can exist without others so far as the process of generation is concerned (as the whole without the parts), and some again without others so far as the process of corruption is concerned (as the parts without the whole). The same thing applies in other cases.

COMMENTARY

936. Having given the various senses of the terms which signify the parts of unity, here Aristotle gives those which signify order, namely, *prior* and *subsequent*. For unity implies a certain order, because the essence of unity consists in being a principle, as was stated above (432:C 872). In regard to the first he does two things. First (457:C 936), he indicates the common meaning of the terms prior and subsequent; and second (458:C 936), he gives the various senses in which these terms are commonly taken ("For example, a thing").

He accordingly says, first (457), that the meaning of the term *prior* depends on that of the term *principle* (or starting point); for the principle in each class of things is what is first in that class, and the term prior means what is nearest to some determinate principle. Now the relationship between a principle of this kind and something which is near it can be considered from several points of view. For something is a principle or primary thing either in

an absolute sense and by nature (as a father is a principle of a child), or "relatively," i.e., in relation to some extrinsic thing (for example, something that is subsequent by nature is said to be prior in relation to something else). Things which are prior in this last sense are such either in reference to knowledge or to perfection or to dignity, or in some such way. Or a thing is also said to be a principle and to be prior in reference to place; or even in certain other ways.

937. **For example, a thing** (458).

Then he gives the various ways in which things are said to be prior and subsequent. And since the terms prior and subsequent are used in reference to some principle, and a principle is what is first either in being or in becoming or in knowledge (as has been stated above [404:C 761]), this part is therefore divided into three sections.

In the first he explains how a thing is said to be prior in motion and in quantity, because the order found in motion flows from that found in quantity. For the prior and subsequent in motion depends on the prior and subsequent in continuous quantity, as is stated in Book IV of the *Physics*.[1] Second (462:C 946), he shows how one thing is said to be prior to another in knowledge ("In another way"). Third (465:C 950), he explains how one thing is said to be prior to another in being, i.e., in nature ("But others").

In regard to the first he does two things. First, he shows how one thing is said to be prior and another subsequent in quantity in the case of continuous things; and second (461:C 944), how one thing is prior and another subsequent in the case of discrete things ("Other things are prior in arrangement").

938. In treating the first member of this division (458) he gives three ways in which things are prior. The first has to do with place; for example, a thing is said to be prior in place inasmuch as it is nearer to some determinate place, whether that place be the middle point in some continuous quantity or an extreme. For the center of the world, to which heavy bodies gravitate, can be taken as the principle (or starting point) of the order involving place, and then we put the elements in the following order, saying that earth is first, water second, and so on. Or the outermost sphere can be taken as the principle, and then we say that fire is first, air second, and so on.

939. Now nearness to a principle of place, whatever it may be, can be taken in two ways: in one way with reference to an order naturally determined, as water is naturally nearer to the middle of the universe than air, and air nearer to the extreme, i.e., the outermost sphere; and in another way with reference to an order that depends "on chance," i.e., insofar as some things have a certain order purely as a result of chance, or on some other cause than nature. For example, in the

case of stones which lie on top of one another in a heap, the highest is prior according to one order, and the lowest according to another. And just as what is nearest to a principle is prior, in a similar way what is farther away from a principle is subsequent.

940. **Other things are prior in time** (459).

Things are understood to be prior and subsequent in a second way with reference to the order in time. And he now describes this order, saying that other things are said to be prior in time, and this in various ways. For some things are prior because they are farther away from the present, as occurs "in the case of things which have taken place," i.e., past events. For the Trojan wars are said to be prior to those of the Medes and the Persians (in which Xerxes, the king of the Persians and Medes, fought against the Greeks), because they are farther away from the present. And some things are said to be prior because they are closer or nearer to the present; for example, Meneleus is said to be prior to Pyrrho because he is nearer to some present moment in reference to which each was future. But this text seems to be false, because both of them lived before the time of Aristotle, when these words were written. And it is said in the Greek that the Nemean are prior to the Pythian, these being two holidays or feasts one of which was nearer to the moment at which these words were written although both were future.

941. Now it is clear that in this case we are using the present as a principle or starting point in time, because we say that something is prior or subsequent on the grounds that it is nearer to or farther away from the present. And those who hold that time is eternal must say this; for, when this is supposed, the only principle or starting point of time which can be taken is one that relates to some present mo-

[1] *Physica*, IV, 11 (219a 15).

ment, which is the middle point between the past and the future, inasmuch as time might proceed to infinity in both directions.

942. **Other things are prior in motion** (460).

The term prior is used in a third way with reference to the order in motion; and he first shows how this applies to natural things. He says that some things are said to be prior in the order found in motion; for what is nearer to a first cause of motion is prior. A boy, for example, is prior to a man because he is nearer to his primary mover, i.e., the one begetting him. And the latter is also said to be prior because of his nearness to some principle. For that—the one moving and begetting—is in a sense a principle, though not in just any way at all (as happened in the case of place), but in an absolute sense and by nature. Second, he also mentions this order of motion in the realm of the voluntary, saying that some things are said to be prior in power, as men who are placed in positions of authority. For one who surpasses another in power, or is more powerful, is said to be prior. This is the order of dignity.

943. Now it is evident that this order also involves motion; for one who is more powerful, or surpasses another in power, is one "according to whose will," i.e., intention, something necessarily follows, because it is through him that some subsequent thing is put in motion. Hence, when the more powerful or prior does not move, no subsequent thing moves; but when the former moves, the latter is also moved. This is the position of a prince in a state; for it is by his authority that others are moved to carry out the things which he commands, and if he does not command them they do not move. And it is clear that the term prior is used here too because of the nearness of a thing to some principle. For "the will," i.e., the intention, of the ruler is taken here as a principle, and those who are nearer to the ruler, and therefore prior, are the ones through whom his commands are made known to his subjects.

944. **Other things are prior in arrangement** (461).

He now explains how a thing is prior in the order found among discrete things. He says that some things are said to be prior in order only because they (the associated things) have some kind of arrangement, and not because of continuity, as happened in the previous cases. And things of this kind have a different place in relation to some one determinate thing from a given point of view, as one who stands second and one who stands third —the one who stands second being prior to the one who stands third. By one who stands second is meant one who stands next to someone, such as a king; and by one who stands third is meant one who stands third from the king. Hence another text reads, "The leader is prior to the one who stands third." It is evident, then, that things are understood to have different places inasmuch as one is second and another third. And in a similar way the *paranete* is prior to the *nete;* for among the strings of the lyre the low-pitched string is called the *hypate;* the high-pitched, the *nete;* and the middle, the *mese.* And the *paranete* refers to that which is next to the *nete* and nearer to the *mese.*

945. It is also evident that something is said to be prior here because of its nearness to some principle, although this happens differently in both of the examples given above. For in the former case—that of one who stands second and one who stands third—the thing which is taken as a principle is a real starting point and extreme, namely, the one who is highest among them, or the chief of the others, as a king or some other person of this kind. But in the case of the strings of the lyre it is the middle

363

one, i.e., the middle string, termed the *mese,* that is taken as the principle; and since those which are nearer to this are called the paranete, the paranete are therefore said to be prior to the nete. These things are said to be prior in this way, then, i.e., by the order in quantity, whether continuous or discrete.

946. **In another way** (462).

Here he shows how one thing is said to be prior to another in knowledge. Now what is prior in knowledge is also prior in an absolute sense and not in a qualified one, as was the case with place; for a thing is known through its principles. But since knowledge is twofold: intellectual or rational, and sensory, we say that things are prior in one way in reference to reason, and in another in reference to the senses.

947. He gives three ways in which something is prior in reference to reason or intellectual knowledge. First, there is the way in which universals are prior to singulars, although the opposite occurs in the case of sensory knowledge because there singulars are prior. For reason has to do with universals and the senses with singulars; and thus the senses know universals only accidentally inasmuch as they know the singular of which the universals are predicated. For a sense knows man inasmuch as it knows Socrates, who is a man; and in the opposite way the intellect knows Socrates inasmuch as it knows man. But what is essential is always prior to what is accidental.

948. **And in the intelligible structure** (463).

Here he gives the second way in which a thing is prior in reference to reason. He says that in the intelligible structure "the attribute is prior to the whole," i.e., to the composite of subject and attribute; thus "musical man"

cannot be known without grasping the meaning of the part "musical." And in the same way all other simple things are prior in intelligibility to the composite, although the opposite is true from the viewpoint of the senses; for it is composite things which are first offered to the senses.

949. **Again, the attributes** (464).

Then he gives the third way. He says that the attributes of prior things [2] are also said to be prior from the viewpoint of reason, as straightness is said to be prior to smoothness. For straightness is an essential property of a line, and smoothness a property of surface, and a line is naturally prior to surface. But from the viewpoint of the senses surface is prior to a line, and the attributes of composite things are prior to those of simple ones. These things, then, are said to be prior in this way, namely, according to the order in knowing.

950. **But others** (465).

He then gives the ways in which a thing is said to be prior according to the order in being, and in regard to this he does two things. First, he gives three ways in which a thing is said to be prior in being; and second (466:C 953), he reduces them to one ("In a sense, then").

He says, first (465), that some things are said to be prior in being, i.e., "in nature and substance," or according to the natural order in being. And this is so for three reasons. First, priority is attributed because of community or dependence; and according to this those things are said to be prior which can exist without others, although others cannot exist without them. And one thing is prior to another when the sequence of their being cannot be reversed, as is stated in the *Categories.*[3] "This is the division," i.e., the mode of division of prior and subsequent,

[2] Reading *priorum* with the note in the Cathala-Spiazzi edition.
[3] *Categoriae,* 12 (14a 30).

which Plato used against others; for it was because of community or dependence that he wanted universals to be prior in being to singular things, surfaces prior to bodies, lines to surfaces, and numbers to all other things.

951. Second, things are said to be prior in being because of the relationship of substance to accident. For since the term being is used in many senses and not univocally, all senses of being must be reduced to one primary sense, according to which being is said to be the subject of other things and to subsist of itself. Hence the first subject is said to be prior; and thus substance is prior to accident.

952. Third, things are said to be prior in being inasmuch as being is divided into the actual and the potential. For a thing is said to be prior in one way potentially and in another actually. A thing is said to be prior potentially in the sense that half a line is prior to an entire line, and any part to its whole, and matter "to substance," i.e., to form. For all of the first things mentioned in these instances are related to the others, to which they are said to be prior, as something potential to something actual. However, from the viewpoint of actuality the first things mentioned are said to be subsequent, since they become actual only by the dissolution of some whole. For when a whole is dissolved into its parts, the parts then begin to exist actually.

953. In a sense, then (466).

Here he concludes that all of the ways in which the terms prior and subsequent are used can be reduced to the last one given; and especially to the first of these inasmuch as the term prior means something which can exist without other things, but not the reverse. For from the viewpoint of generation some things can exist without others, and it is in this way that a whole is prior to its parts; for when a whole has been generated its parts do not exist actually but only potentially. And from the viewpoint of corruption some things can exist without others; for example, the parts can exist without the whole after the whole has been corrupted and dissolved into its parts. And in the same way too the other senses of prior and subsequent can be reduced to this sense. For it is certain that prior things do not depend upon subsequent ones, but the reverse. Hence all prior things can exist without subsequent ones, but not the reverse.

LESSON 14

Various Senses of the Terms Potency, Capable, Incapable, Possible and Impossible

ARISTOTLE'S TEXT   Chapter 12: 1019a 15-1020a 6

467. In one sense the term *potency* or *power* (*potestas*) means the principle of motion or change in some other thing as other; for example, the art of building is a potency which is not present in the thing built; but the art of medicine is a potency and is present in the one healed, but not inasmuch as he is healed. In general, then, potency means the principle of change or motion in some other thing as other.

468. Or it means the principle of a thing's being moved or changed by some other thing as other. For by reason of that principle by which a patient undergoes some change we sometimes say that it has the potency of undergoing if it is possible for it to undergo any change at all. But sometimes we do not say this by reason of every change which a thing can undergo but only if the change is for the better.

469. And in another sense potency means the ability or power to do this particular thing well or according to intention. For sometimes we say of those who can merely walk or talk but not well or as they planned, that they cannot walk or talk. And the same applies to things which are undergoing change.

470. Further, all states in virtue of which things are altogether unsusceptible to change or immutable, or are not easily changed for the worse, are called potencies or powers. For things are broken and crushed and bent and in general destroyed, not because they have a potency, but because they do not have one and are deficient in some way. And things are not susceptible to such processes when they are hardly or slightly affected by them because they have the potency and the ability to be in some definite state.

471. And since the term potency is used in these senses, the term *capable* or *potent* (*possibilis*) will be used in the same number of senses. Thus in one sense whatever has [within itself] the source of the motion or change which takes place in some other thing as other (for even something that brings another to rest is potent in a sense) is said to be capable. And in another sense that which receives such a potency or power from it is said to be capable.

472. And in still another sense a thing is said to be capable if it has the potency of being changed in some way, whether for the worse or for the better. For anything which is corrupted seems to be capable of being corrupted, since it would not have been corrupted if it had been incapable of it. But as matters stand it already has a certain disposition and cause and principle to undergo such change. Hence sometimes a thing seems to be such (i.e., capable) because it has something, and sometimes because it is deprived of something.

473. But if privation is in a sense a having, all things will be capable or potent by having something. But *being* is used in two different senses. Hence

a thing is capable both by having some privation and principle, and by having the privation of this, if it can have a privation.

474. And in another sense a thing is capable because there is no potency or power in some other thing as other which can corrupt it.

475. Again, all these things are capable either because they merely might happen to come into being or not, or because they might do so well. For this sort of potency or power is found in inanimate things such as instruments. For men say that one lyre can produce a sound, and that another [1] cannot, if it does not have a good tone.

476. *Incapacity* (*impotentia*), on the other hand, is a privation of capacity, i.e., a kind of removal of such a principle as has been described, either altogether, or in the case of something which is naturally disposed to have it, or when it is already naturally disposed to have it and does not. For it is not in the same way that a boy, a man and an eunuch are said to be incapable of begetting.

477. Again, there is an incapacity corresponding to each kind of capacity, both to that which can merely produce motion, and to that which can produce it well.

478. And some things are said to be incapable according to this sense of incapacity, but others in a different sense, namely, as *possible* and *impossible*. *Impossible* means that of which the contrary is necessarily true; thus it is impossible that the diagonal of a square should be commensurable with a side, because such a statement is false of which the contrary is not only true but also necessarily so, i.e., that the diagonal is not commensurable. Therefore, that the diagonal is commensurable is not only false but necessarily false.

479. And the contrary of this, i.e., the *possible,* is when the contrary is not necessarily false. For example, it is possible that a man should be seated, because it is not necessarily false that he should not be seated. Hence the term possible means in one sense (as has been stated), whatever is not necessarily false; and in another sense, whatever is true; and in still another, whatever may be true.

480. And what is called "a power" in geometry is called such metaphorically. These senses of capable, then, do not refer to potency.

481. But those senses which do refer to potency are all used in reference to the one primary sense of potency, namely, a principle of change in some other thing inasmuch as it is other. And other things are said to be capable [in a passive sense], some because some other thing has such power over them, some because it does not, and some because it has it in a special way. The same applies to the term *incapable*. Hence the proper definition of the primary kind of potency will be: a principle of change in some other thing as other.

[1] Reading *Aliam . . . lyram, aliam . . .* for *Alia . . . lyram, alia. . . .*

COMMENTARY

954. Having treated the various senses of the terms which signify the parts of unity, here Aristotle begins to treat those which signify the parts of being. He does this, first (467:C 954), according as being is divided by act and potency; and second (482:C 977), according as it is divided by the ten categories ("*Quantity* means").

In regard to the first, he gives the

various senses in which the term *po-tency* or *power* (*potestas*) is used. But he omits the term *act,* because he could explain its meaning adequately only if the nature of forms had been made clear first, and he will do this in Books VIII (708:C 1703) and IX (768:C 1823). Hence in Book IX he immediately settles the question about potency and act together.

This part, then, is divided into two members. In the first he explains the various senses in which the term potency is used; and in the second (481:C 975), he reduces all of them to one primary sense ("But those senses").

In regard to the first he does two things. First, he gives the various senses in which the term potency is used; and second (476:C 967), the various senses in which the term *incapacity* is used (*"Incapacity"*).

In treating the first he does two things. First, he gives the senses in which the term potency is used; and second (471:C 961), those in which the term *capable* or *potent* is used ("And since the term").

955. In dealing with the first part, then, he gives four senses in which the term *potency* or *power* is used. First, potency means a principle of motion or change in some other thing as other. For there is some principle of motion or change in the thing changed, namely, the matter, or some formal principle on which the motion depends, as upward or downward motion is a result of the forms of lightness or heaviness. But a principle of this kind cannot be designated as the active power on which this motion depends. For everything which is moved is moved by another; and a thing moves itself only by means of its parts inasmuch as one part moves another, as is proved in Book VIII of the *Physics*.[1] Hence insofar as a potency is a principle of motion in that in which motion is found,

[1] *Physica,* VIII, 5 (257b 29).

it is not included under active power but under passive potency. For heaviness in earth is not a principle causing motion but rather one which causes it to be moved. Hence active power must be present in some other thing than the one moved; for example, the power of building is not in the thing being built but rather in the builder. And while the art of medicine is an active power, because the physician heals by means of it, it may also be found in the one who is healed, not inasmuch as he is healed, but accidentally, i.e., inasmuch as the physician and the one who is healed happen to be the same. So therefore generally speaking potency or power means in one sense a principle of motion or change in some other thing as other.

956. **Or it means** (468).

Here he gives a second sense in which the term potency is used. He says that in another sense the term potency means the principle whereby something is moved or changed by another thing as other. Now this is passive potency, and it is by reason of it that a patient undergoes some change. For just as every agent or mover moves something other than itself and acts in something other than itself, so too every patient is acted upon by something other than itself, i.e., everything moved is moved by another. For that principle whereby one thing is properly moved or acted upon by another is called passive potency.

957. Now there are two ways in which we can say that a thing has the potency to be acted upon by another. Sometimes we attribute such a potency to something, whatever it may be, because it is able to undergo some change, whether it be good or bad. And sometimes we say that a thing has such a potency, not because it can undergo something evil, but because it can be changed for the better. For example,

we do not say that one who can be overpowered has a potency [in this last sense], but we do attribute such a potency to one who can be taught or helped. And we speak thus because sometimes an ability to be changed for the worse is attributed to incapacity, and the ability not to be changed in the same way is attributed to potency, as will be said below (474:C 965).

958. Another text reads, "And sometimes this is not said of every change which a thing undergoes but of change to a contrary"; and this should be understood thus: whatever receives a perfection from something else is said in an improper sense to undergo a change; and it is in this sense that to understand is said to be a kind of undergoing. But that which receives along with a change in itself something other than what is natural to it is said in a proper sense to undergo a change. Hence such undergoing is also said to be a removing of something from a substance. But this can come about only by way of some contrary. Therefore, when a thing is acted upon in a way contrary to its own nature or condition, it is said in a proper sense to undergo a change or to be passive. And in this sense even illnesses are called undergoings. But when a thing receives something which is fitting to it by reason of its nature, it is said to be perfected rather than passive.

959. **And in another sense** (469).

He now gives a third sense in which the term potency is used. He says that in another sense potency means the principle of performing some act, not in any way at all, but well or according to "intention," i.e., according to what a man plans. For when men walk or talk but not well or as they planned to do, we say that they do not have the ability to walk or to talk. And "the same thing applies when things are being acted upon," for a thing is said

to be able to undergo something if it can undergo it well; for example, some pieces of wood are said to be combustible because they can be burned easily, and others are said to be incombustible because they cannot be burned easily.

960. **Further, all states** (470).

He gives a fourth sense in which the term potency is used. He says that we designate as potencies all habits or forms or dispositions by which some things are said or made to be altogether incapable of being acted upon or changed, or to be not easily changed for the worse. For when bodies are changed for the worse, as those which are broken or bent or crushed or destroyed in any way at all, this does not happen to them because of some ability or potency but rather because of some inability and the weakness of some principle which does not have the power of resisting the thing which destroys them. For a thing is destroyed only because of the victory which the destroyer wins over it, and this is a result of the weakness of its proper active power. For those things which cannot be affected by defects of this kind, or can "hardly or only gradually" be affected by them (i.e., they are affected slowly or to a small degree) are such "because they have the potency and the ability to be in some definite state"; i.e., they have a certain perfection which prevents them from being overcome by contraries. And, as is said in the *Categories*,[2] it is in this way that *hard* or *healthy* signifies a natural power which a thing has of resisting change by destructive agents. But *soft* and *sickly* signify incapacity or lack of power.

961. **And since the term** (471).

Here he gives the senses of the term *capable* or *potent,* which correspond to the above senses of potency. And there are two senses of capable which

[2] *Categoriae,* 8 (9a 22).

correspond to the first sense of potency. For according to its active power a thing is said to be capable of acting in two ways: in one way, because it acts immediately of itself; and in another way, because it acts through something else to which it communicates its power, as a king acts through a bailiff.

Hence he says that, since the term potency is used in this number of senses, the term capable or potent must also be used in the same number of senses. Thus in one sense it means something which has an active principle of change within itself, "as what brings another to rest or to a stop"; i.e., what causes some other thing to stand still is said to be capable of bringing something different from itself to a state of rest. And it is used in another sense when a thing does not act directly but another thing receives such power from it that it can act directly.

962. **And in still another** (472).

Next, he gives a second sense in which the term capable is used, and this corresponds to the second sense of the term potency, i.e., passive potency. He says that, in a different way from the foregoing, a thing is said to be capable or potent when it can be changed in some respect, whatever it may be, i.e., whether it can be changed for the better or for the worse. And in this sense a thing is said to be corruptible because "it is capable of being corrupted," which is to undergo change for the worse, or it is not corruptible because it is capable of not being corrupted, assuming that it is impossible for it to be corrupted.

963. And what is capable of being acted upon in some way must have within itself a certain disposition which is the cause and principle of its passivity, and this principle is called passive potency. But such a principle can be present in the thing acted upon for two reasons. First, this is because it possesses something; for example, a

man is capable of suffering from some disease because he has an excessive amount of some inordinate humor. Second, a thing is capable of being acted upon because it lacks something which could resist the change. This is the case, for example, when a man is said to be capable of suffering from some disease because his strength and natural power have been weakened. Now both of these must be present in anything which is capable of being acted upon; for a thing would never be acted upon unless it both contained a subject which could receive the disposition or form induced in it as a result of the change and also lacked the power of resisting the action of an agent.

964. Now these two ways in which the principle of passivity is spoken of can be reduced to one, because privation can be designated as "a having." Thus it follows that to lack something is to have a privation, and so each way will involve the having of something. Now the designation of privation as a having and as something had follows from the fact that being is used in two different ways; and both privation and negation are called being in one of these ways, as has been pointed out at the beginning of Book IV (306:C 564). Hence it follows that negation and privation can also be designated as "havings." We can say, then, that in general something is capable of undergoing because it contains a kind of "having" and a certain principle that enables it to be acted upon; for even to lack something is to have something, if a thing can *have* a privation.

965. **And in another sense** (474).

Here he gives a third sense in which the term capable is used; and this sense corresponds to the fourth sense of potency inasmuch as a potency was said to be present in something which cannot be corrupted or changed for the worse. Thus he says that in another sense a thing is said to be capable because it does not have some potency or principle which enables it to be corrupted. And I mean by some other thing as other. For a thing is said to be potent or powerful in the sense that it cannot be overcome by something external so as to be corrupted.

966. **Again, all these** (475).

He gives a fourth sense in which the term capable is used, and this corresponds to the third sense of potency inasmuch as potency designated the ability to act or be acted upon well. He says that according to the foregoing senses of potency which pertain both to acting and to being acted upon, a thing can be said to be capable either because it merely happens to come into being or not or because it happens to come into being well. For a thing is said to be capable of acting either because it can simply act or because it can act well and easily. And in a similar way a thing is said to be capable of being acted upon and corrupted because it can be acted upon easily. And this sense of potency is also found in inanimate things "such as instruments," i.e., in the case of the lyre and other musical instruments. For one lyre is said to be able to produce a tone because it has a good tone, and another is said not to because its tone is not good.

967. **Incapacity** (476).

Then he gives the different senses of the term *incapacity,* and in regard to this he does two things. First (476:C 967), he gives the various senses in which we speak of incapacity; and second (478:C 970), he treats the different senses in which the term *impossible* is used ("And some things").

In treating the first part he does two things. First, he gives the common meaning of the term incapacity. Second (477:C 969), he notes the various ways in which it is used ("Again, there is").

He accordingly says, first (476), that incapacity is the privation of potency.

Now two things are required in the notion of privation, and the first of these is the removal of an opposite state. But the opposite of incapacity is potency. Therefore, since potency is a kind of principle, incapacity will be the removal of that kind of principle which potency has been described to be. The second thing required is that privation properly speaking must belong to a definite subject and at a definite time; and it is taken in an improper sense when taken without a definite subject and without a definite time. For properly speaking only that is said to be blind which is naturally fitted to have sight and at the time when it is naturally fitted to have it.

968. And he says that incapacity, such as it has been described, is the removal of a potency, "either altogether," i.e., universally, in the sense that every removal of a potency is called incapacity, whether the thing is naturally disposed to have the potency or not; or it is the removal of a potency from something which is naturally fitted to have it at some time or other or only at the time when it is naturally fitted to have it. For incapacity is not taken in the same way when we say that a boy is incapable of begetting, and when we say this of a man and of an eunuch. For to say that a boy is incapable of begetting means that, while the subject is naturally fitted to beget, it cannot beget before the proper time. But to say that an eunuch is incapable of begetting means that, while he was naturally fitted to beget at the proper time, he cannot beget now; for he lacks the active principles of begetting. Hence incapacity here retains rather the notion of privation. But a mule or a stone is said to be incapable of begetting because neither can do so, and also because neither has any real aptitude for doing so.

969. **Again, there is** (477).

Then he explains the various senses of *incapacity* by contrasting them with the senses of potency. For just as potency is twofold, namely, active and passive, and both refer either to acting and being acted upon simply, or to acting and being acted upon well, in a similar fashion there is an opposite sense of incapacity corresponding to each type of potency. That is to say, there is a sense of incapacity corresponding "both to that which can merely produce motion and to that which can produce it well," namely, to active potency, which is the potency to simply move a thing or to move it well, and to passive potency, which is the potency to simply be moved or to be moved well.

970. And some things (478).

Then he explains the various senses in which the term *impossible* is used; and in regard to this he does two things. First, he gives the various senses in which the term impossible is used; and then (481:C 975) he reduces them to one ("But those senses").

In regard to the first he does three things. First (478), he says that in one sense some things are said to be impossible because they have the foregoing incapacity which is opposed to potency. And impossible in this sense is used in four ways corresponding to those of incapacity.

971. Accordingly, when he says "in a different sense (478)," he gives another way in which some things are said to be impossible. And they are said to be such not because of the privation of some potency but because of the opposition existing between the terms in propositions. For since potency is referred to being, then just as being is predicated not only of things that exist in reality but also of the composition of a proposition inasmuch as it contains truth and falsity, in a similar fashion the terms possible and impossible are predicated not only of real potency and incapacity but also of

the truth and falsity found in the combining or separating of terms in propositions. Hence the term impossible means that of which the contrary is necessarily true. For example, it is impossible that the diagonal of a square should be commensurable with a side, because such a statement is false whose contrary is not only true but necessarily so, namely, that it is not commensurable. Hence the statement that it is commensurable is necessarily false, and this is impossible.

972. And the contrary (479).

Here he shows that the possible is the opposite of the impossible in the second way mentioned; for the impossible is opposed to the possible in the second way mentioned. He says, then, that the possible, as the contrary of this second sense of the impossible, means that whose contrary is not necessarily false; for example, it is possible that a man should be seated, because the opposite of this—that he should not be seated—is not necessarily false.

973. From this it is clear that this sense of possible has three usages. For in one way it designates what is false but is not necessarily so; for example, it is possible that a man should be seated while he is not seated, because the opposite of this is not necessarily true. In another way possible [3] designates what is true but is not necessarily so because its opposite is not necessarily false, for example, that Socrates should be seated while he is seated. And in a third way it means that, although a thing is not true now, it may be true later on.

974. And what is called "a power" (480).

He shows how the term *power* is used metaphorically. He says that in geometry the term power is used metaphorically. For in geometry the square of a line is called its power by

---

[3] Reading *possibilis* for *impossibilis*.

reason of the following likeness, namely, that just as from something in potency something actual comes to be, in a similar way from multiplying a line by itself its square results. It would be the same if we were to say that the number three is capable of becoming the number nine, because from multiplying the number three by itself the number nine results; for three times three makes nine. And just as the term impossible taken in the second sense does not correspond to any incapacity, in a similar way the senses of the term possible which were given last do not correspond to any potency, but they are used figuratively or in the sense of the true and the false.

975. But those senses (481).

He now reduces all senses of capable and incapable to one primary sense. He says that those senses of the term capable or potent which correspond to potency all refer to one primary kind of potency—the first active potency—which was described above (467:C 955) as the principle of change in some other thing as other; because all the other senses of capable or potent are referred to this kind of potency. For a thing is said to be capable by reason of the fact that some other thing has active power over it, and in this sense it is said to be capable according to passive potency. And some things are said to be capable because some other thing does not have power over them, as those which said to be capable because they cannot be corrupted by external agents. And others are said to be capable because they have it "in some special way," i.e., because they have the power or potency to act or be acted upon well or easily.

976. And just as all things which are said to be capable because of some potency are reduced to one primary potency, in a similar way all things which are said to be incapable because of some impotency are reduced to one primary incapacity, which is the opposite of the primary potency. It is clear, then, that the proper notion of potency in the primary sense is this: a principle of change in some other thing as other; and this is the notion of active potency or power.

LESSON 15

The Meaning of Quantity. Its Kinds. The Essentially and Accidentally Quantitative

ARISTOTLE'S TEXT   Chapter 13: 1020a 7-1020a 32

482. *Quantity* [or the *quantitative*] means what is divisible into constituent parts, both or one of which is by nature a one and a particular thing.

483. Therefore plurality [or multitude] is a kind of quantity if it is numerable; and so also is magnitude [or continuous quantity] if it is measurable. Plurality means what is potentially divisible into non-continuous parts; and magnitude means what is divisible into continuous parts. Again, of the kinds of magnitude, what is continuous in one dimension is length; in two, breadth; and in three, depth. And of these, limited plurality is number; limited length, a line; limited breadth, a surface; and limited depth, a body [or solid].

484. Again, some things are said to be quantitative essentially and others accidentally; for example, a line is quantitative essentially, but the musical accidentally.

485. And of those things which are quantitative essentially, some are such by reason of their substance, as a line is quantitative quidditatively. For in the definition expressing its quiddity some kind of quantity is found. Others are properties and states of this kind of substance, as much and little, long and short, broad and narrow, deep and shallow, heavy and light, and the like. And large and small, and larger and smaller, whether they are spoken of essentially or in relation to each other, are properties of quantity. And these terms are also transferred to other things.

486. But of things which are quantitative accidentally, some are said to be such in the sense in which the musical and the white are quantitative, i.e., because the subject to which they belong is quantitative. Others are said to be quantitative in the sense in which motion and time are, for these too are said to be in a sense quantitative and continuous because the things of which they are the properties are divisible. And I mean not the thing which is moved, but the space through which it is moved. For since space is quantitative, motion is also quantitative; and through it, i.e., motion, time is also quantitative.

COMMENTARY

977. Since being is divided not only into potency and actuality but also into the ten categories, having given the different senses of the term potency (467-70:C 954-60), the Philosopher begins here to give the different senses of the terms which designate the categories. First (482:C 977), he considers

the term *quantity;* and second (487:C 987), the term *quality* ("Quality means"). Third (492:C 1001), he gives the different meanings of the term *relative* ("Some things"). He omits the other categories because they are limited to one class of natural beings, as is especially evident of action and passion, and of place and time.

In regard to the first he does three things. First, he gives the meaning of quantity. He says that quantity means what is divisible into constituent parts. Now this is said to distinguish this kind of division from that of compounds. For a compound is dissolved into the elements, and these are not present in it actually but only virtually. Hence, in the latter case there is not just division of quantity, but there must also be some alteration by means of which a compound is dissolved into its elements. He adds that both or one of these constituents is by nature "a one," that is, something which is pointed out. He says this in order to exclude the division of a thing into its essential parts, which are matter and form; for neither one of these is fitted by nature to be a particular thing of itself.

978. **Therefore plurality** (483).

Second, he gives the kinds of quantity; and of these there are two primary kinds: plurality or multitude, and magnitude or measure. And each of these has the character of something quantitative inasmuch as plurality is numerable and magnitude is measurable. For mensuration pertains properly to quantity. However, plurality is defined as what is divisible potentially into parts which are not continuous; and magnitude as what is divisible into parts which are continuous. Now this occurs in three ways, and therefore there are three kinds of magnitude. For if magnitude is divisible into continuous

parts in one dimension only, it will be length; if into two, width; and if into three, depth. Again, when plurality or multitude is limited, it is called number. And a limited length is called a line; a limited width, surface; and a limited depth, body.[1] For if multitude were unlimited, number would not exist, because what is unlimited cannot be numbered. Similarly, if length were unlimited, a line would not exist, because a line is a measurable length (and this is why it is stated in the definition of a line that its extremities are two points). The same things holds true of surface and of body.

979. **Again, some things** (484).

Third, he gives the different ways in which things are quantitative; and in regard to this he does three things. First, he draws a distinction between what is essentially quantitative, as a line, and what is accidentally quantitative, as the musical.

980. **And of those** (485).

Second, he gives the different senses in which things are essentially quantitative, and there are two of these. For some things are said to be such after the manner of a substance or subject, as line, surface or number; for each of these is essentially quantitative because quantity is given in the definition of each. For a line is a limited quantity divisible in length. The same is true of the other dimensions.

981. And other things belong essentially to the genus of quantity and are signified after the manner of a state or property of such substance, i.e., of a line, which is essentially quantitative, or of other similar kinds of quantity. For example, much and little are signified as properties of number; long and short, as properties of a line; broad and narrow, as properties of surface; and high and low or deep, as properties of body. And the same is true of

[1] Reading *latitudo finita, dicitur superficies, profunditas finita corpus* (with the Latin version of Aristotle's text) for *latitudo finita, corpus.*

heavy and light according to the opinion of those who said that having many surfaces, or atoms, causes bodies to be heavy, and having few causes them to be light. But the truth of the matter is that heavy and light do not pertain to quantity but to quality, as he states below (489:C 993). The same thing is true of other such attributes as these.

982. There are also certain attributes which are common properties of any continuous quantity, as large and small, and larger and smaller, whether these are taken "essentially," i.e., absolutely, or "in relation to each other," as something is said to be large and small relatively, as is stated in the *Categories*.[2] But these terms which signify the properties of quantity pure and simple are also transferred to other things besides quantities. For whiteness is said to be large and small, and so also are other accidents of this kind.

983. But it must be borne in mind that of all the accidents quantity is closest to substance. Hence some men think that quantities, such as line, number, surface and body are substances. For next to substance only quantity can be divided into distinctive parts. For whiteness cannot be divided, and therefore it cannot be understood to be individuated except by its subject. And it is for this reason that only in the genus of quantity are some things designated as subjects and others as properties.

984. **But of things** (486).

Then he gives the different senses in which things are said to be accidentally quantitative. These senses are two. In one sense, things are said to be accidentally quantitative only because they are accidents of some quantity; for example, white and musical are said to be quantitative because they

are accidents of a subject which is quantitative.

985. In another sense, some things are said to be accidentally quantitative, not because of the subject in which they exist, but because they are divided quantitatively as a result of the division of some quantity; for example, motion and time (which are said to be quantitative and continuous because of the subjects to which they belong) are divisible and are themselves divided as a result of the division of the subjects to which they belong. For time is divisible and continuous because of motion, and motion is divisible because of magnitude—not because of the magnitude of the thing which is moved, but because of the magnitude of the space through which it is moved. For since that magnitude is quantitative, motion is also quantitative; and since motion is quantitative, it follows that time is quantitative. Hence these can be said to be quantitative not merely accidentally but rather subsequently, inasmuch as they receive quantitative division from something prior.

986. However, it must be noted that in the *Categories*[3] the Philosopher held that time is essentially quantitative, while here he holds that it is accidentally quantitative. There he distinguished between the species of quantity from the viewpoint of the different kinds of measure. For time, which is an external measure, has the character of one kind of measure, and continuous quantity, which is an internal measure, has a different one. Hence in the *Categories* time is given as another species of quantity, whereas here he considers the species of quantity from the viewpoint of the being of quantity. Therefore those things which only receive their quantitative being from something else he does not give

[2] *Categoriae*, 6 (5b 20).
[3] *Categoriae*, 6 (5a 5).

here as species of quantity, but as things which are accidentally quantitative, as motion and time. But motion has no other manner of measure than time and magnitude. Hence neither in this work nor in the *Categories* does he give it as a species of quantity. Place, however, is given there as a species of quantity. But it is not given as such here because it has a different manner of measure, although not a different quantitative being.

LESSON 16

The Senses of Quality

ARISTOTLE'S TEXT   Chapter 14: 1020a 33-1020b 25

487. *Quality* (the *qualified* or *of what sort* [*quale*]) means in one sense substantial difference; for example, How is man's quiddity qualified? as a two-footed animal. How is a horse's? as a four-footed animal. A circle's? as a figure which is non-angular; as if substantial difference were quality. In this one sense, then, quality (*qualitas*) means substantial difference.

488. In another sense the term applies to immobile things and to the objects of mathematics, as numbers are of a certain type (*quales*), for example, those which are compound, and not only those of one dimension but also those of which surface and solid are the counterpart (for there are numbers which are so many times so much and so many times so many times so much). And in general it means what is present in substance besides quantity. For the substance of each number is what it is once; for example, the substance of six is not two times three but six taken once, for six times one is six.

489. Again, all the modifications of substances which are moved, such as heat and cold, whiteness and blackness, heaviness and lightness, and any other attributes of this sort according to which the bodies of changing things are said to be altered, are called qualities.

490. Further, the term quality is used of virtue and vice, and in general of good and evil.

491. The senses of quality, then, come down to two; and one of these is more basic than the other. For the primary kind of quality is substantial difference. And the quality found in number is a part of this, for this is a substantial difference, but either of things which are not moved, or not of them insofar as they are moved. The others, however, are the modifications of things which are moved inasmuch as they are moved, and are the differences of motions. And virtue and vice are parts of these modifications, for they indicate clearly the differences of the motion or activity according to which things in motion act or are acted upon well or badly. For what is capable of being moved or of acting in this way is good, and what cannot do so but acts in a contrary way is bad. And good and bad signify quality especially in the case of living things, and especially in those which have the power of choice.

COMMENTARY

987. Here he gives the various senses in which the term *quality* is used, and in regard to this he does two things. First (487:C 987), he gives four senses of the term quality; and second (491:C 966), he reduces them to two ("The senses of quality").

He accordingly says, first (487), that the term quality is used in one sense as "substantial difference," i.e., the difference by which one thing is distinguished substantially from another and which is included in the definition of the substance. And for this reason it is said that a difference is predicated as a substantial qualification. For example, if one were to ask what sort of (*quale*) animal man is, we would answer that he is two-footed; and if one were to ask what sort of animal a horse is, we would answer that it is four-footed; and if one were to ask what sort of figure a circle is, we would answer that it is "non-angular," i.e., without angles; as if a substantial difference were quality. In one sense, then, quality means substantial difference.

988. Now Aristotle omits this sense of quality in the *Categories*[1] because it is not contained under the category of quality, which he deals with there. But here he is dealing with the meaning of the term quality.

989. **In another sense** (488).

Here he gives a second sense in which the term quality is used. He says that the term quality or "qualified" is used in another sense insofar as immobile things and the objects of mathematics are said to be qualified in a certain way. For the objects of mathematics are abstracted from motion, as is stated in Book VI of this

[1] *Categoriae*, 8 (8b 25).

work (536:C 1161). Such objects are numbers and continuous quantities, and of both we use the term quality. Thus we say that surfaces are qualified as being square or triangular. And similarly numbers are said to be qualified as being compound. Those numbers are said to be compound which have some common number that measures them; for example, the number six and the number nine are measured by the number three, and are not merely referred to one as a common measure. But those which are measured by no common number other than one are called uncompounded or first in their proportion.

990. Numbers are also spoken of as having quality in a metaphor taken from surface and from "solid," i.e., body. They are considered like a surface inasmuch as one number is multiplied by another, either by the same number or by a different one, as in the phrase "twice three" or "three times three." And this is what he means by "so many times so much"; for something like one dimension is designated by saying "three," and a sort of second dimension by saying "twice three" or "three times three."

991. Numbers are considered like a solid when there is a twofold multiplication, either of the same number by itself, or of different numbers by one; as in the expression "three times three times three" or "two times three times two" or "two times three times four." And this is what he means by "so many times so many times so much." For we treat of three dimensions in a number in somewhat the same way as in a solid; and in this arrangement of numbers there is something which is

379

treated as a substance, as three, or any other number that is multiplied by another. And there is something else which is treated as quantity, as the multiplication of one number by another or by itself. Thus when I say "twice three," the number two is signified after the manner of a measuring quantity, and the number three after the manner of a substance. Therefore what belongs to the substance of number besides quantity itself, which is the substance of number, is called a quality of it, as what is meant in saying twice or three times.

992. Another text reads "according to quantity," and then the substance of number is said to be the number itself expressed in an unqualified sense, as "three." And insofar as we consider the quality of a quantity, this is designated by multiplying one number by another. The rest of the text agrees with this, saying that the substance of any number is what it is said to be once; for example, the substance of six is six taken once, and not three taken twice or two taken three times; and this pertains to its quality. For to speak of a number in terms of surface or solid, whether square or cube, is to speak of its quality. And this type of quality is the fourth kind given in the *Categories*.[2]

993. **Again, all the modifications** (489).

Then he gives the third sense in which quality is used. He says that qualities also mean the modifications of mobile substances according to which bodies are changed through alteration, as heat and cold and accidents of this kind. And this sense of quality belongs to the third kind of quality given in the *Categories*.[3]

994. **Further, the term quality** (490).

Next he gives the fourth sense in which quality is used. He says that quality or "qualified" is used in a fourth sense insofar as something is disposed by virtue or vice, or in whatever way it is well or badly disposed, as by knowledge or ignorance, health or sickness, and the like. This is the first kind of quality given in the *Categories*.[4]

995. Now he omits the second of these senses of quality because it is contained rather under power, since it is signified only as a principle which resists modification. But it is given in the *Categories*[5] among the kinds of quality because of the way in which it is named. However, according to its mode of being it is contained rather under power, as he also held above (470:C 960).

996. **The senses of quality** (491).

Then he reduces to two the four senses of quality so far given, saying that a thing is said to be qualified in a certain way in two senses, inasmuch as two of these four senses are reduced to the other two. The most basic of these senses is the first one, according to which quality means substantial difference, because by means of it a thing is designated as being informed and qualified.

997. The quality found in numbers and in other objects of mathematics is reduced to this as a part. For qualities of this kind are in a sense the substantial differences of mathematical objects, because they are signified after the manner of substance to a greater degree than the other accidents, as was stated in the chapter on quantity (485:C 980). Further, qualities of this kind constitute substantial differences, "either of things which are not moved, or not of them insofar as they are moved"; and he says this in order to show that it makes no difference to

[2] *Categoriae*, 8 (10a 10).
[3] *Ibid.* (9a 28).
[4] *Ibid.* (8b 26).
[5] *Ibid.* (9a 13).

his thesis whether the objects of mathematics are self-subsistent substances, as Plato claimed, and are separate from motion; or whether they exist in substances which are mobile in reality but separate in thought. For in the first sense they would not be qualities of things which are moved; but in the second sense they would be, but not inasmuch as they are moved.

998. The second basic sense in which quality is used is that in which the modifications of things which are moved as such, and also the differences of things which are moved, are called qualities. They are called the differences of motions because alterations differ in terms of such qualities, as becoming hot and becoming cold differ in terms of heat and cold.

999. The sense in which virtue and vice are called qualities is reduced to this last sense, for it is in a way a part of this sense. For virtue and vice indicate certain differences of motion and activity based on good or bad performance. For virtue is that by which a thing is well disposed to act or be acted upon, and vice is that by which a thing is badly disposed. The same is true of other habits, whether they are intellectual, as science, or corporal, as health.

1000. But the terms *well* and *badly* relate chiefly to quality in living things, and especially in those having "election," i.e., choice. And this is true because good has the role of an end or goal. So those things which act by choice act for an end. Now to act for an end belongs particularly to living things. For non-living things act or are moved for an end, not inasmuch as they know the end, or inasmuch as they themselves act for an end, but rather inasmuch as they are directed by something else which gives them their natural inclination, just as an arrow, for example, is directed toward its goal by an archer. And non-rational living things apprehend an end or goal and desire it by an appetite of the soul, and they move locally toward some end or goal inasmuch as they have discernment of it; but their appetite for an end, and for those things which exist for the sake of the end, is determined for them by a natural inclination. Hence they are acted upon rather than act; and thus their judgment is not free. But rational beings, in whom alone choice exists, know both the end and the proportion of the means to the end. Therefore, just as they move themselves toward the end, so also do they move themselves to desire the end and the means; and for this reason they have free choice.

LESSON 17

The Senses of Relative

492. Some things are said to be *relative* (*ad aliquid*) directly, as double to half and triple to a third part; and in general what is multiplied to a part of what is multiplied, and what includes to what is included in it. And in another sense as what heats to what can be heated, and what cuts to what can be cut; and in general everything active to everything passive. And in another sense as what is measurable to a measure, and what is knowable to knowledge, and what is sensible to sense.

493. The first things which are said to be relative numerically are such, either without qualification, or in some definite relation to them, or to unity; as double is related to half as a definite number. And the multiple is related numerically to the unit, but not in a definite numerical relation such as this or that. But what is one and a half times as great as something else is related to it in a definite numerical relation to a number. And the superparticular is related to the subparticular in an indefinite relation, as what is multiple is related to a number. And what includes is related to what is included in it as something altogether indefinite in number, for number is commensurable. For what includes is related to what is included in it according to so much and something more; but this something more is indefinite. For whatever the case may be, it is either equal or not equal to it. Therefore all these relations are said to be numerical and are properties of number.

494. Further, equal, like and same are said to be relative, but in a different way, because all these terms are referred to unity. For those things are the same whose substance is one; and those are alike whose quality is one; and those are equal whose quantity is one. And unity is the principle and measure of number. Hence all these are said to be relative numerically, yet not in the same way.

495. Active and passive things are relative in virtue of active and passive potencies and the operations of potencies; for example, what can heat is relative to what can be heated, because it can heat it; and what is heating is relative to what is being heated; and what is cutting to what is being cut, inasmuch as they are doing these things. But of those things which are relative numerically there are no operations, except in the sense stated elsewhere;[1] and operations which imply motion are not found in them. Moreover, of things which are relative potentially, some are said to be relative temporally also, as what makes to what is made, and what will make to what will be made. For in this way a father is said to be the father of his son, because the former has acted, whereas the latter has been acted upon. Again, some things are said to be relative according

---

[1] *Physica*, II, 2 (193b 30); 9 (200a 23).

to the privation of potency; for example, the incapable and other terms used in this way, as the invisible.

496. Therefore things which are said to be relative numerically and potentially are all relative because the subject of the reference is itself referred to something else, not because something else is referred to it. But what is measurable and knowable and thinkable are said to be relative because in each case something else is referred to them, not because they are referred to something else. For by what is thinkable is meant that of which there may be a thought. However, a thought is not relative to the one whose thought it is, for then the same thing would be expressed twice. And similarly sight is relative to that of which it is the sight and not to the one whose sight it is (although it is true to say this); but it is relative to color or to something of this sort. But then the same thing would be said twice, that sight is of the one whose sight it is. Things which are said to be relative directly, then, are spoken of in this way.

497. And other things are said to be relative because their genera are such; for example, medicine is relative because its genus, science, seems to be relative. Furthermore, of this type are all things which are said to be relative by reason of their subject; for example, equality is said to be relative because equal is relative; and likeness, because like is relative.

498. But other things are said to be relative indirectly, as man is relative because he happens to be double, and this is relative; or [2] the white is said to be relative because the same thing [3] happens to be white and double.

[2] Reading *aut* for *ut*.
[3] Reading *eidem* for *ei*.

COMMENTARY

1001. Here the Philosopher establishes the meaning of the *relative* or *relation;* and in regard to this he does two things. First (492:C 1001), he gives the senses in which things are said to be relative directly; and second (497:C 1030), those in which things are said to be relative indirectly ("And other things").

In regard to the first he does two things. First, he enumerates the senses in which things are said to be relative directly. Second (493:C 1006), he proceeds to deal with these ("The first things").

He accordingly gives, first (492), three senses in which things are said to be relative directly. The first of these has to do with number and quantity,

as double to half and triple to a third, and "what is multiplied," i.e., the multiple, to a part "of what is multiplied," i.e., the submultiple, "and what includes to what is included in it." But what includes is here taken for what is greater in quantity. For everything which is greater in quantity includes within itself that which it exceeds. For it is this and something more; for example, five includes within itself four, and three cubits include two.

1002. The second sense is that in which some things are said to be relative according to acting and undergoing, or to active and passive potency; for example, in the realm of natural actions, as what can heat to what can be heated; and in the realm of artificial actions, as what can cut to what can be cut; and in general as everything active to everything passive.

1003. The third sense of relation is that in which something measurable is said to be relative to a measure. Here measure and measurable are not taken quantitatively (for this pertains to the first sense, in which either one is said to be relative to the other, since double is said to be relative to half and half to double), but according to the measurement of being and truth. For the truth of knowledge is measured by the knowable object. For it is because a thing is so or is not so that a statement is known to be true or false, and not the reverse. The same thing applies in the case of a sensible object and sensation. And for this reason a measure and what is measurable are not said to be related to each other reciprocally, as in the other senses, but only what is measurable is related to its measure. And in a similar fashion too an image is related to that of which it is the image as what is measurable is related to its measure. For the truth of an image is measured by the thing whose image it is.

1004. These senses are explained as follows: since a real relation consists in the bearing of one thing upon another, there must be as many relations of this kind as there are ways in which one thing can bear upon another. Now one thing bears upon another either in being, inasmuch as the being of one thing depends on another, and then we have the third sense; or according to active or passive power, inasmuch as one thing receives something from another or confers it upon the other, and then we have the second sense; or according as the quantity of one thing can be measured by another, and then we have the first sense.

1005. But the quality as such of a

thing pertains only to the subject in which it exists, and therefore from the viewpoint of quality one thing bears upon another only inasmuch as quality has the character of an active or passive power, which is a principle of action or of being acted upon. Or it is related by reason of quantity or of something pertaining to quantity; as one thing is said to be whiter than another, or as that which has the same quality as another is said to be like it. But the other classes of things are a result of relation rather than a cause of it. For the category *when* consists in a relation to time; and the category *where* in a relation to place. And *posture* implies an arrangement of parts; and *having* (attire), the relation of the thing having to the things had.

1006. **The first things** (493).

Then he proceeds to deal with the three senses of relation which have been enumerated. First (494:C 1022), he considers the first sense. Second (495:C 1023), he treats the second sense ("Active and passive"). Third (496:C 1026), he attends to the third sense ("Therefore, things").

In regard to the first he does two things. First (493), he describes the relations which are based simply on number; and second (494:C 1022), he treats those which are based simply on unity ("Further, *equal*").

He says, first (493), that the first way in which things are relative, which is numerical, is divided inasmuch as the relation is based on the ratio of one number to another or on that of a number to unity. And in either case it may be taken in two ways, for the number which is referred to another number or to unity in the ratio on which the relation is based is either definite or indefinite.[1] This is his meaning in saying that the first things which are said to be relative numerically are

[1] Reading "vel . . . indeterminate ad numerum aut ad unum, vel determinate" for "vel . . . indeterminate ad numerum, aut ad unum determinate."

said to be such "without qualification," i.e., in general or indefinitely, "or else definitely." And in both ways "to them," namely, to numbers, "or to unity," i.e., to the unit.

1007. Now it should be borne in mind that every measure which is found in continuous quantities is derived in some way from number. Hence relations which are based on continuous quantity are also attributed to number.

1008. It should also be borne in mind that numerical ratios are divided first into two classes, that of equality and that of inequality. And there are two kinds of inequality: the larger and smaller, and more and less. And the larger is divided into five kinds.

1009. For a number is larger whenever it is multiple with respect to a smaller number, i.e., when it includes it many times, as six includes two three times. And if it includes it twice, it is called double; as two in relation to one, or four to two. And if it includes it three times, it is called triple; and if four times, quadruple; and so on.

1010. But sometimes a larger number includes a whole smaller number once and some part of it besides; and then it is said to be superparticular. If it includes a whole smaller number and a half of it besides, it is called sesquialteral, as three to two; and if a third part besides, it is called sesquitertian, as four to three; and if a fourth part besides, it is called sesquiquartan, as five to four; and so on.

1011. Sometimes a larger number includes a whole smaller number once and not merely one part but many parts besides, and then it is called superpartient. And if it includes two parts, it is called superbipartient, as five to three. Again, if it includes three parts, then it is called supertripartient, as seven to four; and if it includes four parts, it is superquadripartient, and then it is related as nine to five; and so on.

1012. Sometimes a larger number includes a whole smaller number many times and some part of it besides, and then it is called multiple superparticular. If it includes it two and a half times, it is called double sesquialteral, as five to two. If it includes it three and a half times, it is called triple sesquialteral, as seven to two. And if it includes it four and a half times, it is called quadruple sesquialteral, as nine to two. And the species of this kind of ratio can also be considered in the case of the superparticular, inasmuch as we speak of the double sesquitertian ratio when a greater number includes a smaller number two and a third times, as seven to three; or of the double sesquiquartan, as nine to four; and so on.

1013. Sometimes too a larger number includes a whole smaller number many times and many parts of it besides, and then it is called multiple superpartient. And similarly a ratio can be divided from the viewpoint of the species of multiplicity, and from that of the species of the superpartient, provided that we may speak of a double superbipartient, when a greater number includes a whole smaller number twice and two parts of it, as eight to three; or even of triple superbipartient, as eleven to three; or even of double supertripartient, as eleven to four. For it includes a whole number twice and three parts of it besides.

1014. And there are just as many species of inequality in the case of a smaller number. For a smaller number is called submultiple, subpartient, submultiple superparticular, submultiple superpartient, and so on.

1015. But it must be noted that the first species of ratio, namely, multiplicity, consists in the relation of one number to the unit. For any species of it is found first in the relation of some number to the unit. Double, for example, is found first in the relation of two to the unit. And similarly a triple ratio is found in the relation of three to the unit; and so on in other cases. But the first terms in which any ratio is found give species to the ratio itself. Hence in whatever other terms it is subsequently found, it is found in them according to the ratio of the first terms. For example, the double ratio is found first between two and the unit. It is from this, then, that the ratio receives its meaning and name; for a double ratio means the ratio of two to the unit. And it is for this reason [too that we use the term in other cases; for] even though one number is said to be double another, this happens only inasmuch as a smaller number takes on the role of the unit and a larger number the role of two; for six is related to three in a double ratio, inasmuch as six is to three as two is to one. And it is similar in the case of a triple ratio, and in all other species of multiplicity. Hence he says that the relation of double is a result of the fact that a definite number, i.e., two, "is referred to unity," i.e., to the unit.

1016. But the term *multiple* implies the relation of a number to the unit, not of any definite number but of number in general. For if a definite number were taken, as two or three, there would be one species of multiplicity, as double or triple. And just as the double is related to two and the triple to three, which are definite numbers, so too the multiple is related to multiplicity, because it signifies an indefinite number.

1017. Other ratios, however, cannot be reduced to the relation of a number to the unit: either a superparticular ratio, or a superpartient, or a multiple superparticular, or a multiple superpartient. For all of these species of ratios are based on the fact that a larger number includes a smaller number once, or some part of it, and one or several parts of it besides. But the unit cannot have a part, and therefore none of these ratios can be based on the relation of a number to the unit but on the

relation of one number to another. Thus the double ratio is either that of a definite number, or that of an indefinite number.

1018. And if it is that of a definite number, then "it is what is one and a half times as great," i.e., sesquialteral, or "that which it exceeds," i.e., supersesquialteral. For a sesquialteral ratio consists first in these terms: three and two; and in the ratio of these it is found in all other cases. Hence what is called one and a half times as great, or sesquialteral, implies the relation of one definite number to another, namely, of three to two.

1019. But the relation which is called superparticular is relative to the subparticular, not according to any definite number, as the multiple is relative also to the unit, but according to an indefinite number. For the first species of inequality given above (493:C 1008) are taken according to indefinite numbers, for example, the multiple, superparticular, superpartient, and so on. But the species of these are taken according to definite numbers, as double, triple, sesquialteral, sesquiquartan, and so on.

1020. Now it happens that some continuous quantities have a ratio to each other which does not involve any number, either definite or indefinite. For there is some ratio between all continuous quantities, although it is not a numerical ratio. For there is one common measure of any two numbers, namely, the unit, which, when taken many times, yields a number. But no common measure of all continuous quantities can be found, since there are certain incommensurable continuous quantities, as the diameter of a square is incommensurable with one of its sides. The reason is that there is no ratio between it and one of its sides like the ratio of one number to another or of a number to the unit.

1021. Therefore, when it is said in the case of quantities that this quantity is greater than that one, or is related to that one as what includes is related to what is included in it, not only is this ratio not considered according to any definite species of number, but it is not even considered according to number at all, because every number is commensurable with another. For all numbers have one common measure, which is the unit. But what includes and what is included in it are not spoken of according to any numerical measure; for it is what is so much and something more that is said to have the relation of what includes to what is included in it. And this is indefinite, whether it be commensurable or incommensurable; for whatever quantity may be taken, it is either equal or unequal. If it is not equal, then it follows that it is unequal and includes something else, even though it is not commensurable. Hence it is clear that all of the above-mentioned things are said to be relative according to number and to the properties of numbers, which are commensuration, ratio, and the like.

1022. **Further, equal** (494).

He now treats those relative terms which have a reference to unity or oneness and are not based on the relation of one number to another or to the unit. He says that *equal, like* and *same* are said to be relative in a different way than the foregoing. For these are called such in reference to unity. For those things are the same whose substance is one; and those are alike whose quality is one; and those are equal whose quantity is one. Now since unity is the principle and measure of number, it is also clear that the former terms are said to be relative "numerically," i.e., in reference to something belonging to the class of number. But these last terms are not said to be relative in the same way as the first. For

the first relations seen are those of number to number, or of a number to the unit; but this relation has to do with unity in an absolute sense.

1023. **Active and passive** (495).

Here he proceeds to treat the second type of relations, which pertains to active and passive things. He says that relative beings of this kind are relative in two ways: in one way according to active and passive potency; and in a second way according to the actualizations of these potencies, which are action and passivity; for example, what can heat is said to be relative to what can be heated in virtue of active and passive potency. For it is what is capable of heating [2] that can heat, and it is what is capable of being heated that can become hot. Again, what is heating in relation to what is heated, and what is cutting in relation to what is being cut, are said to be relative according to the operations of the aforesaid potencies.

1024. Now this type of relation differs from those previously given; for those which are numerical are operations only figuratively, for example, to multiply, to divide, and so forth, as has also been stated elsewhere, namely, in Book II of the *Physics*,[3] where he shows that the objects of mathematics abstract from motion, and therefore they cannot have operations of the kind that have to do with motion.

1025. It should also be noted that among relative terms based on active and passive potency we find diversity from the viewpoint of time; for some of these terms are predicated relatively with regard to past time, as what has made something to what has been made; for instance, a father in relation to his son, because the former has begot and the latter has been begotten; and these differ as what has acted and what has been acted upon. And some

[2] Reading *calefactivum* for *calefactum*.
[3] *Physica*, II, 2 (193b 30); 9 (200a 23).

are used with respect to future time, as when what will make is related to what will be made. And those relations which are based on privation of potency, as the impossible and the invisible, are reduced to this class of relations. For something is said to be impossible for this person or for that one; and the invisible is spoken of in the same way.

1026. **Therefore, things** (496).

Next he proceeds to deal with the third type of relations. He says that this third type differs from the foregoing in this way, that each of the foregoing things is said to be relative because each is referred to something else, not because something else is referred to it. For double is related to half, and vice versa; and in a similar way a father is related to his son, and vice versa. But something is said to be relative in this third way because something is referred to it. It is clear, for example, that the sensible and the knowable or intelligible are said to be relative because other things are related to them; for a thing is said to be knowable because knowledge is had of it. And similarly something is said to be sensible because it can be sensed.

1027. Hence they are not said to be relative because of something which pertains to them, such as quality, quantity, action, or undergoing, as was the case in the foregoing relations, but only because of the action of other things, although these are not terminated in them. For if seeing were the action of the one seeing as extending to the thing seen, as heating extends to the thing which can be heated, then just as what can be heated is related to the one heating, so would what is visible be related to the one seeing. But to see and to understand and actions of this kind, as is stated in Book IX (746:C 1788) of this work, remain in the things acting and do not pass over into those which are acted upon. Hence what is visible or what is knowable is not acted

upon by being known or seen. And on this account these are not referred to other things but others to them. The same is true in all other cases in which something is said to be relative because something else is related to it, as right and left in the case of a pillar. For since right and left designate starting points of motion in living things, they cannot be attributed to a pillar or to any non-living thing except insofar as living things are related to a pillar in some way. It is in this sense that one speaks of a right-hand pillar because a man stands to the left of it. The same holds true of an image in relation to the original; and of a denarius, by means of which one fixes the price of a sale. And in all these cases the whole basis of relation between two extremes depends on something else. Hence all things of this kind are related in somewhat the same way as what is measurable and its measure. For everything is measured by the thing on which it depends.

1028. Now it must be borne in mind that, even though verbally knowledge would seem to be relative to the knower and to the object of knowledge (for we speak both of the knowledge of the knower and of the knowledge of the thing known), and thought to the thinker and to what is thought, nevertheless a thought as predicated relatively is not relative to the one whose thought it is as its subject, for it would follow that the same relative term would then be expressed twice. For it is evident that a thought is relative to what is thought about as to its object. Again, if it were relative to the thinker, it would then be called relative twice; and since the very existence of what is relative is to be relative in some way to something else, it would follow that the same thing would have two acts of existence. Similarly in the case of sight it is clear that sight is not relative to the seer but to its object, which is color, "or something of this sort." He says this because of the things which are seen at night but not by means of their proper color, as is stated in *The Soul*, Book II.[4]

1029. And although it is correct to say that sight is of him who sees, sight is not related to the seer formally as sight but as an accident or power of the seer. For a relation has to do with something external, but a subject does not, except insofar as it is an accident. It is clear, then, that these are the ways in which some things are said to be relative directly.

1030. **And other things** (497).

He now gives three ways in which some things are said to be relative not directly but indirectly. The first of these is that in which things are said to be relative because their genera are relative, as medicine is said to be rela-

tive because science is relative. For medicine is called the science of health and sickness. And science is relative in this way because it is an accident.

1031. The second way is that in which certain abstract terms are said to be relative because the concrete things to which these abstract terms apply are relative to something else. For example, equality and likeness are said to be relative because the like and the equal are relative. But equality and likeness are not considered relative as words.

1032. The third way is that in which a subject is said to be relative because of an accident. For example, a man or some white thing is said to be relative because each happens to be double; and in this way a head is said to be relative because it is a part.

---

[4] *De Anima*, II, 7 (419a 1).

LESSON 18

The Senses of Perfect

ARISTOTLE'S TEXT   Chapter 16: 1021b 12-1022a 3

499. That thing is said to be *perfect* (or *complete*) outside of which it is impossible to find even a single part; for example, the perfect time of each thing is that outside of which it is impossible to find any time which is a part of it. And those things are perfect whose ability (*virtus*) and goodness admit of no further degree in their class; for example, we speak of a perfect physician and a perfect flute player when they lack nothing pertaining to the form of their particular ability. And thus in transferring this term to bad things, we speak of a perfect slanderer and a perfect thief, since we also call them good, as a good slanderer and a good thief. For any ability is a perfection, since each thing is perfect and every substance is perfect when, in the line of its particular ability, it lacks no part of its natural measure.

500. Further, those things are said to be perfect which have a goal or end worth seeking. For things are perfect which have attained their goal. Hence, since a goal is something final, we also say, in transferring the term perfect to bad things, that a thing has been perfectly spoiled and perfectly corrupted when nothing pertaining to its corruption and evil is missing but it is at its last point. And for this reason death is described metaphorically as an end; for both of these are final things. But an end is a final purpose.

501. Things which are said to be perfect in themselves, then, are said to be such in all of these senses: some because they lack no part of their goodness and admit of no further degree and have no part outside; others in general inasmuch as they admit of no further degree in any class and have no part outside.

502. And other things are now termed perfect in reference to these, either because they make something such, or have something such, or know something such, or because they are somehow referred to things which are said to be perfect in the primary senses.

COMMENTARY

1033. Having treated the various senses of the terms which signify the causes, the subject and the parts of the subject of this science, here the Philosopher begins to treat the various senses of the terms which designate attributes having the character of properties. This is divided into two parts. In the first (499:C 1034) he gives the various senses of the terms which refer to the perfection or completeness of being. In the second (526:C 1128) he treats those which refer to a lack of being (*"False* means").

In regard to the first he does two things. First, he gives the different senses of the terms which designate attributes pertaining to the perfection of being; and second (514:C 1085), he treats those which designate the wholeness of being. For the terms *perfect* and *whole* have the same or nearly the same meaning, as is said in the *Physics,* Book III.[1] He considers the second part of this division where he says, *"To come from something."*

In regard to the first part he does two things. First, he treats the various senses of the term *perfect.* Second (503:C 1044), he treats the various senses of the terms which signify certain conditions[2] of that which is perfect ("The term *limit"*).

In regard to the first he does two things. First, he considers the senses in which things are said to be *perfect in themselves;* and second (502:C 1043), he treats those in which things are said to be *perfect by reason of something else* ("And other things").

In regard to the first he does two things. First, he gives three senses in which a thing is said to be perfect in itself. Second (501:C 1040), he shows how, according to these senses, a thing is said to be perfect in different ways ("Things which are said").

1034. He accordingly says, first (499), that in one sense that thing is said to be perfect outside of which it is impossible to find any of its parts. For example, a man is said to be perfect when no part of him is missing; and a period of time is said to be perfect when none of its parts can be found outside of it. For example, a day is said to be perfect or complete when no part of it is missing.

1035. A thing is said to be perfect in another sense with reference to some ability. Thus a thing is said to be per-

fect which admits of "no further degree," i.e., excess or superabundance, from the viewpoint of good performance in some particular line, and is not deficient in any respect. For we say that that thing is in a good state which has neither more nor less than it ought to have, as is said in Book II of the *Ethics.*[3] Thus a man is said to be a perfect physician or a perfect flute player when he lacks nothing pertaining to the particular ability by reason of which he is said to be a good physician or a good flute player. For the ability which each thing has is what makes its possessor good and renders his work good.

1036. And it is in this sense that we also transfer the term perfect to bad things. For we speak of a perfect "slanderer," or scandal monger, and a perfect thief, when they lack none of the qualities proper to them as such. Nor is it surprising if we use the term perfect of those things which rather designate a defect, because even when things are bad we predicate the term good of them in an analogous sense. For we speak of a good thief and a good scandal monger because in their operations, even though they are evil, they are disposed as good men are with regard to good operations.

1037. The reason why a thing is said to be perfect in the line of its particular ability is that an ability is a perfection of a thing. For each thing is perfect when no part of the natural magnitude which belongs to it according to the form of its proper ability is missing. Moreover, just as each natural being has a definite measure of natural magnitude in continuous quantity, as is stated in Book II of *The Soul,*[4] so too each thing has a definite amount of its own natural ability. For example, a horse has by nature a definite dimensive quantity, within certain limits; for

[1] *Physica,* III, 6 (207a 12).
[2] Reading *conditiones* instead of *perfectiones.* Cf. C 1044.
[3] *Eth. Nic.,* II, 6 (1106b 10).
[4] *De Anima,* II, 4 (416a 15).

there is both a maximum quantity and minimum quantity beyond which no horse can go in size. And in a similar way the quantity of active power in a horse has certain limits in both directions. For there is some maximum power of a horse which is not in fact surpassed in any horse; and similarly there is some minimum which never fails to be attained.

1038. Therefore, just as the first sense of the term perfect was based on the fact that a thing lacks no part of the dimensive quantity which it is naturally determined to have, in a similar way this second sense of the term is based on the fact that a thing lacks no part of the quantity of power which it is naturally determined to have. And each of these senses of the term has to do with internal perfection.

1039. **Further, those things** (500).

Here he gives the third sense in which the term perfect is used, and it pertains to external perfection. He says that in a third way those things are said to be perfect "which have a goal," i.e., which have already attained their end, but only if that end is "worth seeking," or good. A man, for instance, is called perfect when he has already attained happiness. But one who has attained some goal that is evil is said to be deficient rather than perfect, because evil is a privation of the perfection which a thing ought to have. Thus it is evident that, when evil men accomplish their will, they are not happier but sadder. And since every goal or end is something final, for this reason we transfer the term perfect somewhat figuratively to those things which have reached some final state, even though it be evil. For example, a thing is said to be perfectly spoiled or corrupted when nothing pertaining to its ruin or corruption is missing. And by this metaphor death is called an end, because it is something final.

[5] *De Coelo*, I, 1 (268a 20).

However, an end is not only something final but is also that for the sake of which a thing comes to be. This does not apply to death or corruption.

1040. **Things which are said** (501).

Here he shows how things are perfect in different ways according to the foregoing senses of perfection. He says that some things are said to be perfect in themselves; and this occurs in two ways. For some things are altogether perfect because they lack absolutely nothing at all; they neither have any "further degree," i.e., excess, because there is nothing which surpasses them in goodness; nor do they receive any good from outside, because they have no need of any external goodness. This is the condition of the first principle, God, in whom the most perfect goodness is found, and to whom none of all the perfections found in each class of things are lacking.

1041. Some things are said to be perfect in some particular line because "they do not admit of any further degree," or excess, "in their class," as though they lacked anything proper to that class. Nor is anything that belongs to the perfection of that class external to them, as though they lacked it; just as a man is said to be perfect when he has already attained happiness.

1042. And not only is this distinction made with reference to the second sense of perfection given above, but it can also be made with reference to the first sense of the term, as is mentioned at the beginning of *The Heavens.*[5] For any individual body is a perfect quantity in its class, because it has three dimensions, which are all there are. But the world is said to be universally perfect because there is absolutely nothing outside of it.

1043. **And other things** (502).

He now gives the sense in which some things are said to be perfect by reason of their relation to something else. He says that other things are said to be perfect "in reference to these," i.e., in reference to things which are perfect in themselves, either because they make something perfect in one of the preceding ways, as medicine is perfect because it causes perfect health; or because they have some perfection, as a man is said to be perfect who has perfect knowledge; or because they represent such a perfect thing, as things which bear a likeness to those that are perfect (as, for example, an image which represents a man perfectly is said to be perfect); or in any other way in which they are referred to things that are said to be perfect in themselves in the primary senses.

LESSON 19

The Senses of Limit, of "According to Which," of "In Itself," and of Disposition

ARISTOTLE'S TEXT   Chapters 17 & 18: 1022a 4-1022a 36

503. The term *limit* (*boundary* or *terminus*) means the extremity of anything, i.e., that beyond which nothing of that being can be found, and that within which everything belonging to it is contained.

504. And limit means the form, whatever it may be, of a continuous quantity or of something having continuous quantity; and it also means the goal or end of each thing. And such too is that toward which motion and action proceed, and not that from which they proceed. And sometimes it is both, not only that from which, but also that to which. And it means the reason for which something is done; and also the substance or essence of each. For this is the limit or terminus of knowledge; and if of knowledge, also of the thing.

505. Hence it is clear that the term limit has as many meanings as the term principle has, and even more. For a principle is a limit, but not every limit is a principle.

Chapter 18

506. The phrase *according to which* (*secundum quod*) has several meanings. In one sense it means the species or substance of each thing; for example, that according to which a thing is good is goodness itself. And in another sense it means the first subject in which an attribute is naturally disposed to come into being, as color in surface. Therefore, in its primary sense, "that according to which" is the form; and in its secondary sense it is the matter of each thing and the first subject of each. And in general *that according to which* is used in the same way as a reason. For we speak of that according to which he comes, or the reason of his coming; and that according to which he has reasoned incorrectly or simply reasoned, or the reason why he has reasoned or reasoned incorrectly. Further, *that according to which* [1] is used in reference to place, as according [i.e., next] to which he stands, or according to [i.e., along] which he walks; for in general these signify position and place.

507. Hence the phrase *in itself* (*secundum se*) must be used in many senses. For in one sense it means the quiddity of each thing, as Callias and the quiddity of Callias. And in another sense it means everything that is found in the quiddity of a thing. For example, Callias is an animal in himself, because animal belongs to his definition; for Callias is an animal. Again, it is used of a thing when something has been manifested in it as its first subject or in some part of it; for example, a surface is white in itself, and a man is alive in himself. For the soul is a part of man in which life is first present. Again, it means a thing which

---

[1] Here Aristotle is using the basic sense of καθ' ὅ, which has to do with place or position.

has no other cause. For there are many causes of man, namely, animal and two-footed, yet man is man in himself. Further, it means any attributes that belong to a thing alone and inasmuch as they belong to it alone, because whatever is separate is in itself.

COMMENTARY

1044. Here Aristotle proceeds to examine the terms which signify the conditions necessary for perfection. Now what is perfect or complete, as is clear from the above, is what is determinate and absolute, independent of anything else, and not deprived of anything but having whatever befits it in its own line. Therefore, first (503:C 1044), he deals with the term *limit* (*boundary* or *terminus*); second (506:C 1050), with the phrase *in itself* ("The phrase *according to which*"); and third (509:C 1062), with the term *having* ("*Having* means").

In regard to the first he does three things. First (503), he gives the meaning of *limit*. He says that limit means the last part of anything, such that no part of what is first limited lies outside this limit; and all things which belong to it are contained within it. He says "first" because the last part of a first thing may be the starting point of a second thing; for example, the now of time, which is the last point of the past, is the beginning of the future.

1045. **And limit means the form** (504).

Second, he gives four senses in which the term limit is used. The first of these applies to any kind of continuous quantity insofar as the terminus of a continuous quantity, or of a thing having continuous quantity, is called a limit; for example, a point is called the limit of a line, and a surface the limit of a body, or also of a stone, which has quantity.

1046. The second sense of limit is similar to the first inasmuch as one ex-

treme of a motion or activity is called a limit, i.e., that toward which there is motion, and not that from which there is motion, as the limit of generation is being and not non-being. Sometimes, however, both extremes of motion are called limits in a broad sense, i.e., both that from which as well as that to which, inasmuch as we say that every motion is between two limits or extremes.

1047. In a third sense limit means that for the sake of which something comes to be, for this is the terminus of an intention, just as limit in the second sense meant the terminus of a motion or an operation.

1048. In a fourth sense limit means the substance of a thing, i.e., the essence of a thing or the definition signifying what a thing is. For this is the limit or terminus of knowledge, because knowledge of a thing begins with certain external signs from which we come to know a thing's definition, and when we have arrived at it we have complete knowledge of the thing. Or the definition is called the limit or terminus of knowledge because under it are contained the notes by which the thing is known. And if one difference is changed, added, or subtracted, the definition will not remain the same. Now if it [i.e., the definition] is the limit of knowledge, it must also be the limit of the thing, because knowledge is had through the assimilation of the knower to the thing known.

1049. **Hence it is clear** (505).

Here he concludes by comparing a limit with a principle, saying that limit has as many meanings as principle has, and even more, because every principle is a limit but not every limit is a principle. For that toward which there is motion is a limit, but it is not in any way a principle, whereas that from which there is motion is both a principle and a limit, as is clear from what was said above (504:C 1046).

1050. The phrase "according to which" (506).

Here he deals with the phrase *in itself;* and in regard to this he does three things. First (506), he lays down the meaning of the phrase *according to which,* which is more common than the phrase *in itself.* Second (507:C 1054), he draws his conclusion as to the ways in which the phrase *in itself* is used ("Hence the phrase"). Third (508:C 1058), he establishes the meaning of the term *disposition* ("*Disposition* means"), because each of the senses in which we use the phrases mentioned above somehow signifies disposition.

In regard to the first (506), he gives four senses in which the phrase *according to which* is used. The first has to do with the "species," i.e., the form, or "the substance of each thing," or its essence, inasmuch as this is that according to which something is said to be; for example, according to the Platonists "the good itself," i.e., the Idea of the Good, is that according to which something is said to be good.

1051. This phrase has a second meaning insofar as the subject in which some attribute is naturally disposed to first come into being is termed "that according to which," as color first comes into being in surface; and therefore it is said that a body is colored according to its surface. Now this sense differs from the preceding one, because the preceding sense pertains to form, but this last sense pertains to matter.

1052. There is a third sense in which this phrase is used, inasmuch as any

cause or reason in general is said to be "that according to which." Hence the phrase "according to which" is used in the same number of senses as the term reason. For it is the same thing to ask, "According to what does he come?" and "For what reason does he come?" And in like manner it is the same to ask, "According to what has he reasoned incorrectly or simply reasoned, and, for what reason has he reasoned?"

1053. This phrase *according to which* [1] is used in a fourth sense inasmuch as it signifies position and place; as in the statement, "according to which he stands," i.e., next to which, and, "according to which he walks," i.e., along which he walks; and both of these signify place and position. This appears more clearly in the Greek idiom.

1054. Hence the phrase (507).

From what has been said above he draws four senses in which the phrase *in itself* or *of itself* is used. The first of these is found when the definition, which signifies the quiddity of each thing, is said to belong to each in itself, as Callias "and the quiddity of Callias," i.e., the essence of the thing, are such that one belongs to the other "in itself." And not only the whole definition is predicated of the thing defined in itself, but so too in a way everything which belongs to the definition, which expresses the quiddity, is predicated of the thing defined in itself. For example, Callias is an animal in himself. For animal belongs in the definition of Callias, because Callias is an individual animal, and this would be given in his definition if individual things could have a definition. And these two senses are included under one, because both the definition and a part of the definition are predicated of each thing in itself for the same reason. For this is the first type of es-

[1] See text 506, n. 1.

sential predication given in the *Posterior Analytics;*[2] and it corresponds to the first sense given above (506:C 1050) in which we use the phrase *according to which.*

1055. This phrase is used in a second sense when something is shown to be in something else as in a first subject, when it belongs to it of itself. This can happen in two ways: for either the first subject of an accident is the whole subject itself of which the accident is predicated (as a surface is said to be colored or white in itself; for the first subject of color is surface, and therefore a body is said to be colored by reason of its surface); or also the subject of the accident is some part of the subject, just as a man is said to be alive in himself, because part of him, namely, the soul, is the first subject of life. This is the second type of essential predication given in the *Posterior Analytics,*[3] namely, that in which the subject is given in the definition of the predicate. For the first and proper subject is given in the definition of a proper accident.

1056. This phrase is used in a third sense when something having no cause is spoken of as *in itself;* as all immediate propositions, i.e., those which are not proved by a middle term. For in *a priori* demonstrations the middle term is the cause of the predicate's belonging to the subject. Hence, although

man has many causes, for example, animal and two-footed, which are his formal cause, still nothing is the cause of the proposition "Man is man," since it is an immediate one; and for this reason man is man in himself. And to this sense is reduced the fourth type of essential predication given in the *Posterior Analytics,*[4] the case in which an effect is predicated of a cause; as when it is said that the slain man perished by slaying, or that the thing cooled was made cold or chilled by cooling.

1057. This phrase is used in a fourth sense inasmuch as those things are said to belong to something in themselves which belong to it alone and precisely as belonging to it alone. He says this in order to differentiate this sense of *in itself* from the preceding senses, in which it was not said that a thing belongs to something in itself because it belongs to it alone; although in that sense too something would belong to it alone, as the definition to the thing defined. But here something is said to be in itself by reason of its exclusiveness. For *in itself* signifies something separate, as a man is said to be by himself when he is alone. And to this sense is reduced the third sense given in the *Posterior Analytics,*[5] and the fourth sense of the phrase *according to which,* which implies position.

[2] *Analytica Posteriora,* I, 4 (73a 34).
[3] *Ibid.* (73a 38).
[4] *Ibid.* (73b 10).
[5] *Ibid.* (73b 5).

LESSON 20

The Meanings of Disposition, of Having, of Affection, of Privation, and of "To Have"

ARISTOTLE'S TEXT   Chapters 19-23: 1022b 1-1023a 25

508. Disposition means the order of what has parts, either as to place or as to potentiality or as to species. For there must be a certain position, as the term disposition itself makes clear.

Chapter 20

509. *Having* (*possession* or *habit*) means in one sense a certain activity of the haver and of the thing had, as a sort of action or motion. For when one thing makes and another is made, the making is intermediate. And likewise between one having clothing and the clothing had, the having is intermediate. It is accordingly clear that it is not reasonable to have a having; for if it were possible to have the having of what is had, this would go on to infinity. In another sense having means a certain disposition whereby the thing disposed is well or badly disposed, either in relation to itself or to something else; for example, health is a sort of having and is such a disposition. Again, the term having is used if there is a part of such a disposition. And for this reason any virtue pertaining to the powers of the soul is a sort of having.

Chapter 21

510. *Affection* (*passio*) means in one sense (*modification*), the quality according to which alteration occurs, as white and black, sweet and bitter, heavy and light, and all other such attributes. And in another sense (*undergoing*), it means the actualizations and alterations of these; and of these, particularly harmful operations and motions; and most especially those which are painful and injurious (*suffering*). Again, great rejoicing and grieving are called affections (*passions*).

Chapter 22

511. The term *privation* is used in one sense when a thing does not have one of those attributes which it is suitable for some things to have, even though that particular thing would not naturally have it. In this sense a plant is said to be deprived of eyes. And it is used in another sense when a thing is naturally disposed to have something, either in itself or according to its class, and does not have it. A man and a mole, for example, are deprived of sight but in different ways: the latter according to its class and the former in itself. Again, we speak of privation when a thing is by nature such as to have a certain perfection and

398

does not have it even when it is naturally disposed to have it. For blindness is a privation, although a man is not blind at every age but only if he does not have sight at the age when he is naturally disposed to have it. And similarly we use the term privation when a thing does not have some attribute which it is naturally disposed to have, in reference to where, and to what, and to the object in relation to which, and in the manner in which it may have it by nature if it does not have it. Again, the removal of anything by force is called a privation.

512. And in all instances in which negations are expressed by the privative particle ἀ- [i.e., un- or in-], privations are expressed. For a thing is said to be unequal because it does not have the equality which it is naturally fitted to have. And a thing is said to be invisible either because it has no color at all or because its color is deficient; and a thing is said to be footless either because it lacks feet altogether or because its feet are imperfect. Again, we use the term privation of a thing when it has something to a very small degree, for example, "unignited," [1] and this means to have it in a deficient way. And privation also designates what is not had easily or well; for example, a thing is uncuttable not only because it cannot be cut but because it cannot be cut easily or well. And we use the term privation of what is not had in any way. For it is not only a one-eyed man that is said to be blind, but one who lacks sight in both eyes. And for this reason not every man is good or bad, just or unjust, but there is an intermediate state.

Chapter 23

513. *To have* (*to possess* or *to hold*) has many meanings. In one sense it means to treat something according to one's own nature or to one's own impulse; and for this reason a fever is said to possess a man, and tyrants are said to possess cities, and people who are clothed are said to possess clothing. And in another sense a thing is said to have something when this is present in the subject which receives it; thus bronze has the form of a statue, and a body, disease. And whatever contains something else is said to have or to hold it; for that which is contained is said to be held by the container; for example, we say that a bottle holds a liquid and a city men and a ship sailors. It is in this way too that a whole has parts. Again, whatever prevents a thing from moving or from acting according to its own impulse is said to hold it, as pillars hold the weight imposed on them. It is in this sense that the poets make Atlas hold the heavens, as if otherwise it would fall on the earth, as certain of the physicists also say.[2] And it is in this sense that that which holds something together is said to hold what it holds together, because otherwise it would be separated, each according to its own impulse. And *to be in something* is expressed in a similar way and corresponds to the meanings of *to have*.

[1] For *non ignitum* (unignited) the Greek text reads ἀπύρηνον, i.e., "kernelless" or "stoneless." Possibly the translator of the text or texts which St. Thomas used mistook the term for ἀπύρωτον, i.e., "without fire."

[2] The reference is to Empedocles; see *De Coelo*, II, 1 (284a 24); 13 (295a 16).

COMMENTARY

1058. Because the phrase *according to which* signifies in one sense position, the Philosopher therefore proceeds to examine next (508:C 1058) the term *disposition*. He gives the common meaning of this term, saying that a disposition is nothing else than the order of parts in a thing which has parts. He also gives the senses in which the term disposition is used; and there are three of these. The first designates the order of parts in place, and in this sense disposition or posture is a special category.

1059. Disposition is used in a second sense inasmuch as the order of parts is considered in reference to potency or active power, and then disposition is placed in the first species of quality. For a thing is said to be disposed in this sense, for example, according to health or sickness, by reason of the fact that its parts have an order in its active or passive power.

1060. Disposition is used in a third sense according as the order of parts is considered in reference to the form and figure of the whole; and then disposition or position is held to be a difference in the genus of quantity. For it is said that one kind of quantity has position, as line, surface, body and place, but that another has not, as number and time.

1061. He also points out that the term disposition signifies order; for it signifies position, as the derivation itself of the term makes clear, and order is involved in the notion of position.

1062. **"Having" means** (509).

He now proceeds to examine the term *having*. First (509:C 1062), he gives the different senses of the term having. Second (510:C 1065), he gives the different senses of certain other terms which are closely connected with this one (*"Affection* means").

He accordingly gives, first (509), the two senses in which the term having is used. First, it designates something intermediate between the haver and the thing had. Now even though having is not an action, none the less it signifies something after the manner of an action. Therefore having is understood to be something intermediate between the haver and the thing had and to be a sort of action; just as heating is understood to be something intermediate between the thing being heated and the heater, whether what is intermediate be taken as an action, as when heating is taken in an active sense, or as a motion, as when heating is taken in a passive sense. For when one thing makes and another is made, the making stands between them. In Greek the term ποίησις is used, and this signifies making. Moreover, if one goes from the agent to the patient, the intermediate is making in an active sense, and this is the action of the maker. But if one goes from the thing made to the maker, then the intermediate is making in a passive sense, and this is the motion of the thing being made. And between a man having clothing and the clothing had, the having is also an intermediate; because, if we consider it by going from the man to his clothing, it will be like an action, as is expressed under the form "to have." But if we consider it in the opposite way, it will be like the undergoing of a motion, as is expressed under the form "to be had."

1063. Now although having is understood to be intermediate between a man and his clothing inasmuch as he has it, none the less it is evident that there cannot be another intermediate between the having and the thing had, as though there were another having midway between the haver and the intermediate having. For if one were to say that it is possible to have the having "of what is had," i.e., of the thing had, an infinite regress would then result. For the man has "the thing had," i.e., his clothing, but he does not have the having of the thing had by way of another intermediate having. It is like the case of a maker, who makes the thing made by an intermediate making, but does not make the intermediate making itself by way of some other intermediate making. It is for this reason too that the relations by which a subject is related to something else are not related to the subject by some other intermediate relation and also not to the opposite term; paternity, for example, is not related to a father or to a son by some other intermediate relation. And if some relations are said to be intermediate, they are merely conceptual relations and not real ones. Having in this sense is taken as one of the categories.

1064. In a second sense the term having means the disposition whereby something is well or badly disposed; for example, a thing is well disposed by health and badly disposed by sickness. Now by each of these, health and sickness, a thing is well or badly disposed in two ways: in itself or in relation to something else. Thus a healthy thing is one that is well disposed in itself, and a robust thing is one that is well disposed for doing something. Health is a kind of having, then, because it is a disposition such as has been described. And having (habit) designates not only the disposition of a whole but also that of a part, which is a part of the disposition of the whole. For example, the good dispositions of

an animal's parts are themselves parts of the good disposition of the whole animal. The virtues pertaining to the parts of the soul are also habits; for example, temperance is a habit of the concupiscible part, fortitude a habit of the irascible part, and prudence a habit of the rational part.

1065. "Affection" (510).

Here he proceeds to treat the terms which are associated with having. First (510), he deals with those which are associated as an opposite; and second (513:C 1080), he considers something which is related to it as an effect, namely, to have, which derives its name from having ("To have").

Now there is something which is opposed to having as the imperfect is opposed to the perfect, and this is affection (being affected). And privation is opposed by direct opposition. Hence, first (510:C 1065), he deals with affection; and second (511:C 1070), with privation ("The term privation").

He accordingly gives, first (510), four senses of the term affection. In one sense (modification) it means the quality according to which alteration takes place, such as white and black and the like. And this is the third species of quality; for it has been proved in Book VII of the *Physics* [1] that there can be alteration only in the third species of quality.

1066. Affection is used in another sense (undergoing) according as the actualizations of this kind of quality and alteration, which comes about through them, are called affections. And in this sense affection is one of the categories, for example, being heated and cooled and other motions of this kind.

1067. In a third sense (suffering) affection means, not any kind of alteration at all, but those which are harmful and terminate in some evil, and

[1] *Physica*, VII, 3 (245b 1).

which are lamentable or sorrowful; for a thing is not said to suffer insofar as it is healed but insofar as it is made ill. Or it also designates anything harmful that befalls anything at all—and with good reason. For a patient by the action of some agent which is contrary to it is drawn from its own natural disposition to one similar to that of the agent. Hence, a patient is said more properly to suffer when some part of something fitting to it is being removed and so long as its disposition is being changed into a contrary one, than when the reverse occurs. For then it is said rather to be perfected.

1068. And because things which are not very great are considered as nothing, therefore in a fourth sense (passion) affection means not any kind of harmful alteration whatsoever, but those which are extremely injurious, as great calamities and great sorrows. And because excessive pleasure becomes harmful (for sometimes people have died or become ill as a result of it), and because too great prosperity is turned into something harmful to those who do not know how to make good use of it, therefore another text reads "great rejoicing and grieving are called affections." And still another text agrees with this, saying, "very great sorrows and prosperities."

1069. Now it should be noted that because these three—disposition, habit or having, and affection—signify one of the categories only in one of the senses in which they are used, as is evident from what was said above, he therefore did not place them with the other parts of being, i.e., with quantity, quality and relation. For either all or most of the senses in which they were used pertained to the category signified by these terms.

1070. **The term "privation"** (511).

Here he gives the different senses in which the term *privation* is used.

And since privation includes in its intelligible structure both negation and the fitness of some subject to possess some attribute, he therefore gives, first (511:C 1070), the different senses of privation which refer to this fitness or aptitude for some attribute. Second (512:C 1074), he treats the various senses of negation ("And in all instances").

In regard to the first (511) he gives four senses of privation. The first has to do with this natural fitness taken in reference to the attribute of which the subject is deprived and not in reference to the subject itself. For we speak of a privation in this sense when some attribute which is naturally fitted to be had is not had, even though the subject which lacks it is not designed by nature to have it. For example, a plant is said to be deprived of eyes because eyes are naturally designed to be had by something, although not by a plant. But in the case of those attributes which a subject is not naturally fitted to have, the subject cannot be said to be deprived of them, for example, that the eye by its power of vision should penetrate an opaque body.

1071. A second sense of the term privation is noted in reference to a subject's fitness to have some attribute. For in this sense privation refers only to some attribute which a thing is naturally fitted to have either in itself or according to its class; in itself, for example, as when a blind person is said to be deprived of sight, which he is naturally fitted to have in himself. And a mole is said to be deprived of sight, not because it is naturally fitted to have it, but because the class, animal, to which the mole belongs, is so fitted. For there are many attributes which a thing is not prevented from having by reason of its genus but by reason of its differences; for example, a man is not prevented from having wings by reason of his genus but by reason of his difference.

1072. A third sense of the term privation is noted in reference to circumstances. And in this sense a thing is said to be deprived of something if it does not have it when it is naturally fitted to have it. This is the case, for example, with the privation *blindness;* for an animal is not said to be blind at every age but only if it does not have sight at an age when it is naturally fitted to have it. Hence a dog is not said to be blind before the ninth day. And what is true of the circumstance *when* also applies to other circumstances, as "to *where,*" or place. Thus *night* means the privation of light in a place where light may naturally exist, but not in caverns, which the sun's rays cannot penetrate. And it applies "to what part," as a man is not said to be toothless if he does not have teeth in his hand but only if he does not have them in that part in which they are naturally disposed to exist; and "to the object in relation to which," as a man is not said to be small or imperfect in stature if he is not large in comparison with a mountain or with any other thing with which he is not naturally comparable in size. Hence a man is not said to be slow in moving if he does not run as fast as a hare or move as fast as the wind; nor is he said to be ignorant if he does not understand as God does.

1073. Privation is used in a fourth sense inasmuch as the removal of anything by violence or force is called a privation. For what is forced is contrary to natural impulse, as has been said above (418:C 829); and thus the removal of anything by force has reference to something that a person is naturally fitted to have.

1074. **And in all** (512).

Then he gives the different senses of privation which involve negation.

For the Greeks use the prefix ἀ-, when compounding words, to designate negations and privations, just as we use the prefix *in-* or *un-;* and therefore he says that in every case in which one expresses negations designated by the prefix ἀ, used in composition at the beginning of a word, privations are designated. For *unequal* means in one sense what lacks equality, provided that it is naturally such as to have it; and *invisible* means what lacks color; and footless, what lacks feet.

1075. Negations of this kind are used in a second sense to indicate not what is not had at all but what is had badly or in an ugly way; for example, a thing is said to be colorless because it has a bad or unfitting color; and a thing is said to be footless because it has defective or deformed feet.

1076. In a third sense an attribute is signified privatively or negatively because it is had to a small degree; for example, the term ἀπύρηνον,[2] i.e., unignited, is used in the Greek text, and it signifies a situation where the smallest amount of fire exists. And in a way this sense is contained under the second, because to have something to a small degree is in a way to have it defectively or unfittingly.

1077. Something is designated as a privation or negation in a fourth sense because it is not done easily or well; for example, something is said to be uncuttable not only because it is not cut but because it is not cut easily or well.

1078. And something is designated as a privation or negation in a fifth sense because it is not had in any way at all. Hence it is not a one-eyed person who is said to be blind but one who lacks sight in both eyes.

1079. From this he draws a corollary, namely, that there is some intermediate between good and evil, just and unjust. For a person does not become evil

[2] See T 512, n. 1.

when he lacks goodness to any degree at all, as the Stoics said[3] (for they held all sins to be equal), but when he deviates widely from virtue and is brought to a contrary habit. Hence it is said in Book II of the *Ethics*,[4] that a man is not to be blamed for deviating a little from virtue.

1080. **"To have"** (513).

Then he gives four ways in which the term *to have* (to possess or hold) is used. First, to have a thing is to treat it according to one's own nature in the case of natural things, or according to one's own impulse in the case of voluntary matters. Thus a fever is said to possess a man because he is brought from a normal state to one of fever. And in the same sense tyrants are said to possess cities, because civic business is carried out according to the will and impulse of tyrants. And in this sense too those who are clothed are said to possess or have clothing, because clothing is fitted to the one who wears it so that it takes on his figure. And to have possession of a thing is also reduced to this sense of to have, because anything that a man possesses he uses as he wills.

1081. To have is used in a second way inasmuch as that in which some attribute exists as its proper subject is said to have it. It is in this sense that bronze has the form of a statue, and a body has disease. And to have a science or quantity or any accident or form is included under this sense.

1082. To have is used in a third way (to hold) when a container is said to have or to hold the thing contained, and the thing contained is said to be held by the container. For example, we say that a bottle has or "holds a liquid," i.e., some fluid, such as water or wine; and a city, men; and a ship, sailors. It is in this sense too that a

whole is said to have parts; for a whole contains a part just as a place contains the thing in place. But a place differs from a whole in this respect that a place may be separated from the thing which occupies it, whereas a whole may not be separated from its parts. Hence, anything that occupies a place is like a separate part, as is said in Book IV of the *Physics*.[5]

1083. To have is used in a fourth way (to hold up) inasmuch as one thing is said to hold another because it prevents it from operating or being moved according to its own impulse. It is in this sense that pillars are said to hold up the heavy bodies placed upon them, because they prevent these bodies from falling down in accordance with their own inclination. And in this sense too the poets said that Atlas holds up the heavens; for the poets supposed Atlas to be a giant who prevents the heavens from falling on the earth. And certain natural philosophers also say this, holding that the heavens will at some time be corrupted and fall in dissolution upon the earth. This is most evident in the opinions expressed by Empedocles,[6] for he held that the world is destroyed an infinite number of times and comes into being an infinite number of times. And the fables of the poets have some basis in reality; for Atlas, who was a great astronomer, made an accurate study of the motion of the celestial bodies, and from this arose the story that he holds up the heavens. But this sense of the term to have differs from the first. For according to the first, as was seen, the thing having compels the thing had to follow by reason of its own impulse, and thus is the cause of forced motion. But here the thing having prevents the thing had from being moved by its

[3] See Cicero, *Paradoxa Stoicorum*, III, 1.
[4] *Eth. Nic.*, II, 8 (1109b 18).
[5] *Physica*, IV, 2 (209b 22-32).
[6] See *De Coelo*, II, 1 (284a 24); 13 (295a 16).

own natural motion, and thus is the cause of forced rest. The third sense of having, according to which a container is said to have or hold the thing contained, is reduced to this sense, because the individual parts of the thing contained would be separated from each other by their own peculiar impulse if the container did not prevent this. This is clear, for example, in the case of a bottle containing water, inasmuch as the bottle prevents the parts of the water from being separated.

1084. In closing he says that the phrase *to be in a thing* is used in the same way as *to have,* and the ways of *being in a thing* correspond to those of *having a thing.* Now the eight ways of being in a thing have been treated in Book IV of the *Physics.*[7] Two of these are as follows: that in which an integral whole is in its parts, and the reverse of this. Two others are: the way in which a universal whole is in its parts, and vice versa. And another is that in which a thing in place is in a place, and this corresponds to the third sense of having, according to which a whole has parts, and a place has the thing which occupies it. But the way in which a thing is said to be in something as in an efficient cause or mover (as the things belonging to a kingdom are in the king) corresponds to the first sense of having given here (513:C 1080). And the way in which a thing is in an end or goal is reduced to the fourth sense of having given here (513:C 1083), or also to the first, because those things which are related to an end are moved or at rest because of it.

[7] *Physica,* IV, 3 (210a 14).

LESSON 21

The Meanings of "To Come from Something," Part, Whole, and Mutilated

ARISTOTLE'S TEXT   Chapters 24-27: 1023a 26-1024a 28

514. *To come from something* (*esse* or *fieri ex aliquo*) means in one sense to come from something as matter, and this in two ways: either in reference to the first genus or to the ultimate species; for example, all liquefiable things come from water, and a statue comes from bronze. And in another sense it means to come from a thing as a first moving principle; for example, From what did the fight come? From a taunt; because this was the cause of the fight. In another sense it means to come from the composite of matter and form, as parts come from a whole, and a verse from the *Iliad,* and stones from a house. For the form is an end or goal, and what is in possession of its end is complete. And one thing comes from another in the sense that a species comes from a part of a species, and man from two-footed, and a syllable from an element. For this is different from the way in which a statue comes from bronze, because a composite substance comes from sensible matter, but a species also comes from the matter of a species. These are the senses, then, in which some things are said to come from something. But other things are said to come from something if they come from a part of that thing in any of the aforesaid senses. For example, a child comes from its father and mother, and plants come from the earth, because they come from some part of them. And some things come from others only because they come one after the other in time, as night comes from day, and a storm from a calm. And some of these are so described only because they admit of change into each other, as in the cases just mentioned. And some only because they follow one another in time, as a voyage is made from the equinox because it takes place after the equinox. And feasts come one from another in this way, as the Thargelian from the Dionysian, because it comes after the Dionysian.

Chapter 25

515. *Part* means in one sense that into which a quantity is divided in any way; for what is subtracted from a quantity is always called a part of it. For example, the number two is said in a sense to be a part of the number three. And in another sense part means only such things as measure a whole. And for this reason the number two is said in a sense to be a part of the number three, and in another, not. Again, those things into which a species is divided irrespective of quantity are also called parts of this species; and it is for this reason that species are said to be parts of a genus. Again, parts mean those things into which a whole is divided or of which a whole is composed, whether the whole is a species or the thing having the species, as bronze is a part of a bronze sphere or of a bronze cube (for this is the matter in which the form inheres). An angle

also is a part. And those elements contained in the intelligible expression, which manifests what each thing is, are also parts of a whole. And for this reason the genus is also called a part of the species, although in another respect the species is called a part of the genus.

Chapter 26

516. *Whole* means that from which none of the things of which it is said to consist by nature are missing; and that which contains the things contained in such a way that they form one thing.

517. But this occurs in two ways: either inasmuch as each is the one in question, or inasmuch as one thing is constituted of them.

518. For a whole is a universal or what is predicated in general as being some one thing as a universal is one, in the sense that it contains many things, because it is predicated of each, and all of them taken singly are that one thing, as man, horse and god, because all are living things.

519. A whole is something continuous and limited when one thing is constituted of many parts which are present in it, particularly when they are present potentially; but if not, even when they are present in activity.

520. And of these same things, those which are wholes by nature are such to a greater degree than those which are wholes by art, as we also say of a thing that is one (424:C 848), inasmuch as wholeness is a kind of unity.

521. Again, since a quantity has a beginning, a middle point and an end, those quantities to which position makes no difference we designate by the term *all;* but those to which position makes a difference we designate by the term *whole;* and those to which both descriptions apply we designate by both terms— all and whole. Now these are the things whose nature remains the same in being rearranged but whose shape does not, as wax and a garment; for both all and whole are predicated of them since they verify both. But water and all moist things and number have *all* applied to them, although water and number are called wholes only in a metaphorical sense. But those things of which the term *every* is predicated with reference to one, have the term all predicated of them with reference to several, for example, all this number, all these units.

Chapter 27

522. It is not any quantity at all that is said to be *mutilated,* but it must be a whole and also divisible. For two things are not mutilated when one is taken away from the other, because the mutilated part is never equal to the remainder. And in general no number is mutilated, for its substance must remain. If a goblet is mutilated it must still be a goblet; but a number is not the same when a part is taken away. Again, all things composed of unlike parts are not said to be mutilated. For a number is like something having unlike parts, as two and three. And in general those things to which position makes no difference, such as water and fire, are not mutilated; but they must have position in their substance. And they must be continuous; for a harmony is made up of unlike parts and has position but is not mutilated.

523. Further, neither is every whole mutilated by the privation of every part. For the parts which are removed must not be things which are proper to the substance or things which exist anywhere at all; for example, a goblet is not

mutilated if a hole is made in it, but only if an ear or some extremity is removed; and a man is not mutilated if his flesh or spleen is removed, but only if an extremity is removed. And this means not any extremity whatever, but those which, when removed from the whole, cannot regenerate. Hence to have one's head shaven is not a mutilation.

COMMENTARY

1085. Here he begins to treat the things which pertain to the notion of whole and part. First (514:C 1085), he deals with those which pertain to the notion of *part;* and second (516:C 1098), with those which pertain to the notion of *whole* ("*Whole* means").

And because a whole is constituted of parts, he therefore does two things in dealing with the first member of this division. First, he explains the various ways in which a thing is said *to come from something;* and second (515:C 1093), he considers the different senses in which the term *part* is used ("*Part* means").

In regard to the first he does three things. First, he considers the ways in which a thing is said *to come from something* in the primary and proper sense. Second (514:C 1090), he indicates the ways in which one thing comes from another but not in the primary sense ("But other things"). Third (514:C 1091), he considers the ways in which one thing comes from another but not in the proper sense ("And some things").

In dealing with the first part (514) he gives four ways in which a thing is said to come from something. First, a thing is said to come from something as from matter, and this can happen in two ways: In one way, inasmuch as matter is taken to be "the matter of the first genus," i.e., common matter; as water is the matter of all liquids and liquables, all of which are said to come from water. In another way, "in reference to the ultimate species," i.e., the lowest species; as the species statue is said to come from bronze.

1086. In a second way a thing is said to come from something as "from a first moving principle," as a fight comes from a taunt, which is the principle moving the soul of the taunted person to fight. And it is in this way too that a house is said to come from a builder, and health from the medical art.

1087. In a third way one thing is said to come from another as something simple "comes from the composite of matter and form." This pertains to the process of dissolution; and it is in this way that we say parts come from a whole, "and a verse from the *Iliad*" (i.e., from the whole treatise of Homer about Troy); for the *Iliad* is divided into verses as a whole is divided into parts. And it is in the same way that stones are said to come from a house. The reason for this is that the form is the goal or end in the process of generation; for it is what has attained its end that is said to be perfect or complete, as was explained above (500:C 1039). Hence it is evident that that is perfect which has a form. Therefore, when a perfect whole is broken down into its parts, there is motion in a sense from form to matter; and in a similar way when parts are combined, there is an opposite motion from matter to form. Hence the preposition *from,* which designates a beginning, applies to both processes: both to the process of composition, because it signifies a material principle, and to that of dissolution, because it signifies a formal principle.

1088. In a fourth way a thing is said to come from something as "a species comes from a part of a species." And part of a species can be taken in two ways: either in reference to the conceptual order or to the real order. It is taken in reference to the conceptual order when we say, for example, that *two-footed* is a part of *man;* because while it is part of his definition, it is not a real part, otherwise it would not be predicated of the whole. For it is proper to the whole man to have two feet. And it is taken in reference to the real order when we say, for example, that "a syllable comes from an element," or letter, as from a part of the species. But here the fourth way in which the term is used differs from the first; for in the first way a thing was said to come from a part of matter, as a statue comes from bronze. For this substance, a statue, is composed of sensible matter as a part of its substance. But this species is composed of part of the species.

1089. For some parts are parts of a species and some are parts of matter. Those which are called parts of a species are those on which the perfection of the species depends and without which it cannot be a species. And it is for this reason that such parts are placed in the definition of the whole, as body and soul are placed in the definition of an animal, and an angle in the definition of a triangle, and a letter in the definition of a syllable. And those parts which are called parts of matter are those on which the species does not depend but are in a sense accidental to the species; for example, it is accidental to a statue that it should come from bronze or from any particular matter at all. And it is also accidental that a circle should be divided

into two semi-circles; and that a right angle should have an acute angle as part of it. Parts of this sort, then, are not placed in the definition of the whole species but rather the other way around, as will be shown in Book VII of this work (644:C 1542). Hence it is clear that in this way some things are said to come from others in the primary and proper sense.

1090. But some things are said to come from something not in the primary sense but according to a part of that thing in "any of the aforesaid senses." For example, a child is said to come from its father as an efficient principle, and from its mother as matter; because a certain part of the father causes motion, i.e., the sperm, and a certain part of the mother has the character of matter, i.e., the menstrual fluid. And plants come from the earth, although not from the whole of it but from some part.

1091. And in another way a thing is said to come from something in an improper sense, namely, from the fact that this implies order or succession alone; and in this way one thing is said to come from another in the sense that it comes after it, as "night comes from day," i.e., after the day, "and a storm from a calm," i.e., after a calm. And this is said in reference to two things. For in those cases in which one thing is said to come from another, order is sometimes noted in reference to motion and not merely to time; because either they are the two extremes of the same motion, as when it is said that white comes from black, or they are a result of different[1] extremes of the motion, as night and day are a result of different locations of the sun. And the same thing applies to winter and summer. Hence in some cases one thing is said to come from another because one is changed into

---

[1] Reading *alia* for *aliqua* (*extrema*).

the other, as is clear in the above examples.

1092. But sometimes order or succession is considered in reference to time alone; for example, it is said that "a voyage is made from the equinox," i.e., after the equinox. For these two extremes are not extremes of a single motion but pertain to different motions. And similarly it is said that the Thargelian festival [of Apollo and Artemis] comes from the Dionysian because it comes after the Dionysian, these being two feasts which were celebrated among the gentiles, one of which preceded the other in time.

1093. **"Part" means** (515).

He now gives four senses in which something is said to be a *part*. In one sense part means that into which a thing is divided from the viewpoint of quantity; and this can be taken in two ways. For, in one way, no matter how much smaller that quantity may be into which a larger quantity is divided, it is called a part of this quantity. For anything that is taken away from a quantity is always called a part of it; for example, the number two is in a sense a part of the number three. And, in another way, only a smaller quantity which measures a larger one is called a part. In this sense the number two is not a part of the number three but a part of the number four, because two times two equals four.

1094. In a second sense parts mean those things into which something is divided irrespective of quantity; and it is in this sense that species are said to be parts of a genus. For a genus is divided into species, but not as a quantity is divided into quantitative parts. For a whole quantity is not in each one of its parts, but a genus is in each one of its species.

1095. In a third sense parts mean those things into which some whole is divided or of which it is composed, whether the whole is a species or the

thing having a species, i.e., the individual. For, as has been pointed out already (514:C 1089), there are parts of the species and parts of matter, and these (species and matter) are parts of the individual. Hence bronze is a part of a bronze sphere or of a bronze cube as the matter in which the form is received, and thus bronze is not a part of the form but of the thing having the form. And a cube is a body composed of square surfaces. And an angle is part of a triangle as part of its form, as has been stated above (514:C 1089).

1096. In a fourth sense parts mean those things which are placed in the definition of anything, and these are parts of its intelligible structure; for example, animal and two-footed are parts of man.

1097. From this it is clear that a genus is part of a species in this fourth sense, but that a species is part of a genus in a different sense, i.e., in the second sense. For in the second sense a part was taken as a subjective part of a universal whole, whereas in the other three senses it was taken as an integral part. And in the first sense it was taken as a part of quantity; and in the other two senses as a part of substance; yet in such a way that a part in the third sense means a part of a thing, whether it be a part of the species or of the individual. But in the fourth sense it is a part of the intelligible structure.

1098. **"Whole" means** (516).

He proceeds to treat the things which pertain to a *whole*. First (516:C 1098), he considers a whole in a general way; and second (524:C 1119), he deals with a particular kind of whole, namely a genus ("The term *genus*").

In regard to the first part he does two things. First, he proceeds to deal with the term whole; and second (522:C 1109), with its opposite, *mutilated* ("It is not any quantity").

In regard to the first he does three things. First (516), he states the common meaning of whole, which involves two things. The first is that the perfection of a whole is derived from its parts. He indicates this when he says "a whole means that from which none of the things," i.e., the parts, "of which it is said to consist by nature," i.e., of which the whole is composed according to its own nature, "are missing." The second is that the parts become one in the whole. Thus he says that a whole is "that which contains the things contained," namely, the parts, in such a way that the things contained in the whole are some one thing.

1099. **But this occurs.** (517).

Second, he notes two ways in which a thing is a whole. He says that a thing is said to be a whole in two ways: either in the sense that each of the things contained by the containing whole is "the one in question," i.e., the containing whole, which is in the universal whole that is predicated of any one of its own parts; or in the sense that it is one thing composed of parts in such a way that none of the parts are that one thing. This is the notion of an integral whole, which is not predicated of any of its own integral parts.

1100. **For a whole** (518).

Third, he explains the foregoing senses of whole. First, he explains the first sense. He says that a whole is a universal "or what is predicated in general," i.e., a common predicate, as being some one thing as a universal is one, in the sense that it is predicated of each individual just as the universal, which contains many parts, is predicated of each of its parts. And all of these are one in a universal whole in such a way that each of them is that one whole; for example, *living thing* contains man and horse and god, because "all are living things," i.e., be-

cause living thing is predicated of each. By a god he means here a celestial body, such as the sun or the moon, which the ancients said were living bodies and considered to be gods; or he means certain ethereal living beings, which the Platonists called demons, and which were worshipped by the pagans as gods.

1101. **A whole is something** (519).

Second, he explains the meaning of whole in the sense of an integral whole; and in regard to this he does two things. First, he gives the common meaning of this kind of whole, and particularly of that which is divided into quantitative parts, which is more evident to us. He says that a whole is something "continuous and limited," i.e., perfect or complete (for what is unlimited does not have the character of a whole but of a part, as is said in Book III of the *Physics* [2]) when one thing is composed of many parts which are present in it. He says this in order to exclude the sense in which one thing comes from another as from a contrary.

1102. Now the parts of which a whole is composed can be present in it in two ways: in one way potentially, and in another actually. Parts are potentially present in a whole which is continuous, and actually present in a whole which is not continuous, as stones are actually present in a heap. But that which is continuous is one to a greater degree, and therefore is a whole to a greater degree, than that which is not continuous. Hence he says that parts must be present in a whole, especially potential parts, as they are in a continuous whole; and if not potentially, then at least "in activity," or actually. For "activity" means interior action.

1103. Now although a thing is a whole to a greater degree when its parts are present potentially than when they

[2] *Physica*, III, 6 (207a 26).

are present actually, none the less if we look to the parts, they are parts to a greater degree when they exist actually than when they exist potentially. Hence another text reads, "especially when they are present perfectly and actually; but otherwise, even when they are present potentially." And it also adds the words given above: "particularly when they are present potentially; but if not, even when they are present in activity." Hence it seems that the translator found two texts, which he translated, and then made the mistake of combining both so as to make one text. This is clear from another translation, which contains only one of these statements; for it reads as follows: "And a whole is continuous and limited when some one thing is composed of many intrinsic parts, especially when they are present potentially; but if not, when they are present actually."

1104. **And of these same things** (520).

Second, he indicates two differences within this second sense of whole. The first is that some continuous things are such by art and some by nature. Those which are continuous by nature are "such," i.e., wholes, to a greater degree than those which are such by art. And since we spoke in the same way above (424:C 848) about things which are one, saying that things which are continuous by nature are one to a greater degree, as though wholeness were oneness, it is clear from this that anything which is one to a greater degree is a whole to a greater degree.

1105. **Again, since a quantity** (521).

He gives the second difference. For since it is true that there is an order of parts in quantity, because a quantity has a beginning, a middle point and an end, and the notion of position involves these, the positions of the parts in all these quantities must be continuous. But if we consider the position of the parts, a whole is found to be continuous in three ways. For there are some wholes which are unaffected by a difference of position in their parts. This is evident in the case of water, for it makes no difference how the parts of water are interchanged. The same thing is true of other liquids, as oil and wine and the like. And in these things a whole is signified by the term *all* and not by the term *whole*. For we say all the water or all the wine or all the numbers, but not the whole, except metaphorically. This perhaps applies to the Greek idiom, but for us it is a proper way of speaking.

1106. And there are some things to which the position of the parts does make a difference, for example, a man and any animal and a house and the like. For a thing is not a house if its parts are arranged in just any way at all, but only if they have a definite arrangement; and of these we use the term whole and not the term all. And similarly a thing is not a man or an animal if its parts are arranged in just any way at all. For when we speak of only one animal, we say the whole animal and not all the animal.

1107. And there are some things to which both of these apply, because in a sense the position of their parts accounts for their differences; and of these we use both terms—all and whole. And these are the things in which, when the parts are interchanged, the matter remains the same but not the form or shape. This is clear, for example, in the case of wax; for no matter how its parts are interchanged the wax still remains, but it does not have the same shape. The same is true of a garment and of all things which have like parts and take on a different shape. For even though liquids have like parts, they cannot have a shape of their own, because they are not limited by their own boundaries but by those of other things. Hence when their parts are interchanged no change occurs in anything that is proper to them.

1108. The reason for this difference is that the term all is distributive and therefore requires an actual multitude or one in proximate potency to act; and because those things have like parts, they are divided into parts entirely similar to the whole, and in that manner multiplication of the whole takes place. For if every part of water is water, then in each part of water there are many waters, although they are present potentially, just as in one number there are many units actually. But a whole signifies a collection of parts into some one thing; and therefore in those cases in which the term whole is properly used, one complete thing is made from all the parts taken together, and the perfection of the whole belongs to none of the parts. A house and an animal are examples of this. Hence, "every animal" is not said of one animal but of many. Therefore at the end of this part of his discussion he says that those wholes of which the term every is used, as is done of one thing when reference is made to a whole, can have the term all (in the plural) used of them, as is done of several things when reference is made to them as parts. For example, one says "all this number," and "all these units," and "all this water," when the whole has been indicated, and "all these waters" when the parts have been indicated.

1109. **It is not any quantity** (522).

Here he clarifies the issue about the opposite of "whole," which is *mutilated,* in place of which another translation reads "diminished (or reduced) by a member"; but this does not always fit. For the term mutilated is used only of animals, which alone have members. Now mutilated seems to mean "cut off," and thus Boethius translated it "maimed," i.e., "defective." Hence

the Philosopher's aim here is to show what is required in order that a thing may be said to be mutilated: and first, what is required on the side of the whole; and second (523:C 1117), what is required on the side of the part which is missing ("Further, neither").

1110. Now in order that a whole can be said to be mutilated, seven things are required. First, the whole must be a quantified being having parts into which it may be divided quantitatively. For a universal whole cannot be said to be mutilated if one of its species is removed.

1111. Second, not every kind of quantified being can be said to be mutilated, but it must be one that is "divisible into parts," i.e., capable of being separated, and be "a whole," i.e., something composed of different parts. Hence the ultimate parts into which any whole is divided, such as flesh and sinew, even though they have quantity, cannot be said to be mutilated.

1112. Third, two things are not mutilated, i.e., anything having two parts, if one of them is taken away from the other. And this is true because a "mutilated part," i.e., whatever is taken away from the mutilated thing, is never equal to the remainder, but the remainder must always be larger.

1113. Fourth, no number can be mutilated no matter how many parts it may have, because the substance of the mutilated thing remains after the part is taken away. For example, when a goblet is mutilated it still remains a goblet; but a number does not remain the same no matter what part of it is taken away. For when a unit is added to or subtracted from a number, it changes the species of the number.

1114. Fifth, the thing mutilated must have unlike parts. For those things which have like parts cannot be said to be mutilated, because the nature of the whole remains verified in each

413

part. Hence, if any of the parts are taken away, the others are not said to be mutilated. Not all things having unlike parts, however, can be said to be mutilated; for a number cannot, as has been stated, even though in a sense it has unlike parts; for example, the number twelve has the number two and the number three as parts of it. Yet in a sense every number has like parts because every number is constituted of units.

1115. Sixth, none of those things in which the position of the parts makes no difference can be said to be mutilated, for example, water or fire. For mutilated things must be such that the intelligible structure of their substance contains the notion of a determinate arrangement of parts, as in the case of a man[3] or of a house.

1116. Seventh, mutilated things must be continuous. For a musical harmony cannot be said to be mutilated when a note or a chord is taken away, even though it is made up of low and high pitched sounds, and even though its parts have a determinate position; for it is not any low and high pitched sounds arranged in any way at all that constitute such a harmony.

1117. **Further, neither is** (523).

Then he indicates the conditions which must prevail with regard to the part cut off in order that a thing may be mutilated; and there are three of these. He says that, just as not every kind of whole can be said to be mutilated, so neither can there be mutilation

by the removal of every part. For, first, the part which is removed must not be a principal part of the substance, that is, one which constitutes the substance of the thing and without which the substance cannot be, because the thing that is mutilated must remain when a part is removed, as has been stated above (522:C 1113). Hence a man cannot be said to be mutilated when his head has been cut off.

1118. Second, the part removed should not be everywhere, but in some extremity. Thus, if a goblet is perforated about the middle by removing some part of it, it cannot be said to be mutilated; but this is said if someone removes "the ear of a goblet," i.e., a part which is similar to an ear, or any other extremity. Similarly a man is not said to be mutilated if he loses some of his flesh from his leg or from his arm or from his waist, or if he loses his spleen or some part of it, but if he loses one of his extremities, such as a hand or a foot.

1118a. Third, a thing is not said to be mutilated if just any part that is an extremity is removed, but if it is such a part which does not regenerate if the whole of it is removed, as a hand or a foot. But if a whole head of hair is cut off, it grows again. So if such parts are removed, the man is not said to be mutilated, even though they are extremities. And for this reason people with shaven heads are not said to be mutilated.

---

[3] Reading *homo* with the original Cathala edition.

LESSON 22

The Meanings of Genus, of Falsity, and of Accident

ARISTOTLE'S TEXT   Chapters 28-30: 1024a 29-1025a 34

524. The term *genus* (or *race*) is used if there is a continuous generation of things having the same species; for example, "as long as the genus of man lasts" means "while there is continuous generation of men." And the term also designates that from which things are first brought into being. For it is in this way that some men are called Hellenes by race and others Ionians, because the former come from Hellen and the latter from Ion as the ones who begot them. Again the term is applied to the members of the genus more from the begetter than from the material principle. For some people are also said to derive their race from the female, as those who come from Pleia. Further, the term is used in the sense that the plane is called the genus of plane figures, and the solid the genus of solid figures. For each of the figures is either a plane of such and such a kind or a solid of such and such a kind; and this is the subject underlying the differences. Again, genus means the primary element present in definitions, which is predicated quidditatively of the thing whose differences are called qualities. The term genus, then, is used in all these senses: in one as the continuous generation of a species; in another as the primary mover of the same species; and in another as matter. For that to which the difference or quality belongs is the subject which we call matter.

525. Things are said to be *diverse* (or *other*) *in species* whose first subject is diverse and cannot be resolved one into the other or both into the same thing. For example, form and matter are diverse in genus. And all things which are predicated according to a different categorical figure of being are diverse in genus. For some signify the quiddity of beings, others quality, and others something else, in the sense of our previous distinctions. For they are not analyzed into each other or into some one thing.

Chapter 29

526. *False* means in one sense what is false as a thing, and that either because it is not combined or is incapable of being combined. For example, the statement that the diagonal is commensurable or that you are sitting belong to this class; for the former is always false and the latter is sometimes so; for it is in these senses that these things are non-beings. But there are things which exist and are fitted by nature to appear either other than they are or as things that do not exist, as a shadowgraph and dreams. For these in fact are something, but not that of which they cause an image in us. Therefore things are said to be false either because they do not exist or because the image derived from them is not of something real.

527. A *false notion* inasmuch as it is false is the notion of something non-

415

existent. Hence every notion is false when applied to something other than that of which it is true; for example, the notion of a circle is false when applied to a triangle. Now of each thing there is in a sense one notion, which is its essence; but there are also in a sense many, since the thing itself and the thing with a modification are in a sense the same, as Socrates and musical Socrates. But a false notion is absolutely speaking not the notion of anything. And it is for this reason that Antisthenes entertained a silly opinion when he thought that nothing could be expressed except by its proper notion—one term always for one thing. From this it would follow that there can be no contradiction and almost no error. It is possible, however, to express each thing not only by its own notion but also by that which belongs to something else not only falsely but also truly, as eight may be said to be double through the notion of two. These are the ways, then, in which things are said to be false.

528. A *false man* is one who chooses such thoughts not for any other reason but for themselves; and one who is the cause of such thoughts in others; just as we say that those things are false which produce a false image or impression.

529. Hence, the speech in the *Hippias*,[1] which says that the same man is true and false, is refuted; for it assumes that that man is false who is able to deceive, even though he is knowing and prudent.

530. And further it assumes that one who is capable of willing evil things is better. And this false opinion is arrived at by way of induction. For one who limps voluntarily is better than one who does so involuntarily; and by limping we mean imitating a limp. For if a man were to limp voluntarily, he would be worse in this way, just as he would be in the case of moral character.

Chapter 30

531. An *accident* is what attaches to anything and which it is true to affirm is so, although not necessarily or for the most part; for example, if someone discovers a treasure while digging a hole for a plant, the discovery of the treasure is an accident to the digger. For the one does not necessarily come from the other or come after it, nor does it happen for the most part that someone will find a treasure when he digs a hole to set out a plant. And a musician may be white; but since this does not happen necessarily or for the most part, we say that it is accidental. But since something belongs to something, and some belong somewhere and at some time, then whatever attaches to a subject, but not because it is now or here,[2] will be an accident. Nor does an accident have any determinate cause, but only a contingent or chance cause, i.e., an indeterminate one. For it was by accident that someone came to Aegina; and if he did not come there in order to get there, but because he was driven there by a storm or was captured by pirates, the event has occurred and is an accident; yet not of itself but by reason of something else. For the storm is the cause of his coming to the place to which he was not sailing, and this was Aegina. And in another sense accident means whatever belongs to each thing of itself but not in its substance; for example, it is an accident of a triangle to have its angles equal to two right angles. And these same accidents may be eternal, but none of the others can be. But an account of this has been given elsewhere.[3]

[1] Plato, *Hippias Minor*, 365-76.
[2] Reading *hic* (with Parma and the Greek text) for *hoc*.
[3] *Analytica Posteriora*, I, 6 (75a 18, 39-41).

COMMENTARY

1119. Here he gives his views about a particular kind of whole, namely, a genus. First (524:C 1119), he gives the different senses in which the term *genus* is used; and second (525:C 1124), he treats the different senses in which things are said to be *diverse* (or *other*) in *genus* ("Things are said").

He accordingly says, first (524), that the term genus is used in four senses. First, it means the continuous generation of things that have the same species; for example, it is said, "as long as 'the genus of man' will exist," i.e., "while the continuous generation of men will last." This is the first sense of genus given in Porphyry,[1] i.e., a multitude of things having a relation to each other and to one principle.

1120. In a second sense genus (race) means that from which "things are first brought into being," i.e., some things proceed from a begetter. For example, some men are called Hellenes by race because they are descendants of a man called Hellen; and some are called Ionians by race because they are descendants of a certain Ion as their first begetter. Now people are more commonly named from their father, who is their begetter, than from their mother, who produces the matter of generation, although some derive the name of their race from the mother; for example, some are named from a certain woman called Pleia. This is the second sense of genus given in Porphyry.[2]

1121. The term genus is used in a third sense when surface or the plane is called the genus of plane figures,

"and the solid," or body, is called the genus of solid figures, or bodies. This sense of genus is not the one that signifies the essence of a species, as animal is the genus of man, but the one that is the proper subject in the species of different accidents. For surface is the subject of all plane figures. And it bears some likeness to a genus, because the proper subject is given in the definition of an accident just as a genus is given in the definition of a species. Hence the proper subject of an accident is predicated like a genus. "For each of the figures," i.e., plane figures, is such and such a surface. "And this," i.e., a solid figure, is such and such a solid, as though the figure were a difference qualifying surface or solid. For surface is related to plane (surface) figures, and solid to solid figures, as a genus, which is the subject of contraries; and difference is predicated in the sense of quality. And for this reason, just as when we say rational animal, such and such an animal is signified, so too when we say square surface, such and such a surface is signified.

1122. In a fourth sense genus means the primary element given in a definition, which is predicated quidditatively, and differences are its qualities. For example, in the definition of man, animal is given first and then two-footed or rational, which is a certain substantial quality of man.

1123. It is evident, then, that the term genus is used in so many different senses: in one sense as the continuous generation of the same species, and this pertains to the first sense; in an-

[1] *Isagoge*, Chap. "Genus" (CG IV, 1, 18-23).
[2] *Ibid*. (1, 23-2, 10).

other as the first moving principle, and this pertains to the second sense; and in another as matter, and this pertains to the third and fourth senses. For a genus is related to a difference in the same way as a subject is to a quality. Hence it is evident that genus as a predicable and genus as a subject are included in a way under one meaning, and that each has the character of matter. For even though genus as a predicable is not matter, still it is taken from matter as difference is taken from form. For a thing is called an animal because it has a sentient nature; and it is called rational because it has a rational nature, which is related to sentient nature as form is to matter.

1124. **Things are said** (525).

Here he explains the different senses in which things are said to be *diverse* (or *other*) *in genus;* and he gives two senses of this corresponding to the last two senses of genus. For the first two senses are of little importance for the study of philosophy.

In the first sense, then, some things are said to be diverse in genus because their first subject is diverse; for example, the first subject of color is surface, and the first subject of flavors is something moist. Hence, with regard to their subject-genus, flavor and color are diverse in genus.

1125. Further, the two different subjects must be such that one of them is not reducible to the other. Now a solid is in a sense reducible to surfaces, and therefore solid figures and plane figures do not belong to diverse genera. Again, they must not be reducible to the same thing. For example, form and matter are diverse in genus if they are considered according to their own essence, because there is nothing common to both. And in a similar way the celestial bodies and lower bodies are diverse in genus inasmuch as they do not have a common matter.

1126. In another sense those things are said to be diverse in genus which are predicated "according to a different figure of the category of being," i.e., of the predication of being. For some things signify quiddity, some quality, and some signify in other ways, which are given in the division made above where he dealt with being (437:C 889-94). For these categories are not reducible one to the other, because one is not included under the other. Nor are they reducible to some one thing, because there is not some one common genus for all the categories.

1127. Now it is clear, from what has been said, that some things are contained under one category and are in one genus in this second sense, although they are diverse in genus in the first sense. Examples of this are the celestial bodies and elemental bodies, and colors and flavors. The first way in which things are diverse in genus is considered rather by the natural scientist and also by the philosopher, because it is more real. But the second way in which things are diverse in genus is considered by the logician, because it is conceptual.

1128. **"False" means** (526).

Here he gives the various senses of the terms which signify a lack of being or incomplete being. First (526:C 1128), he gives the senses in which the term *false* is used. Second (531:C 1139), he deals with the various senses of *accident*.

In regard to the first he does three things. First, he shows how the term false is used of real things; and second (527:C 1130), how it is used of definitions ("A *false notion*"); and third (528:C 1135), how men are said to be false ("A *false man*").

He accordingly says, first (526), that the term false is applied in one sense to real things inasmuch as a statement signifying a reality is not properly composed. And there are two ways in which this can come about: In one way by forming a proposition which should not be formed; and this is what happens, for instance, in the case of false contingent propositions. In another way by forming a proposition about something impossible; and this is what happens in the case of false impossible propositions. For if we say that the diagonal of a square is commensurable with one of its sides, it is a false impossible proposition; for it is impossible to combine "commensurable" and "diagonal." And if someone says that you are sitting while you are standing, it is a false contingent proposition; for the predicate does not attach to the subject, although it is not impossible for it to do so. Hence one of these—the impossible—is always false; but the other—the contingent—is not always so. Therefore those things are said to be false which are non-beings in their entirety; for a statement is said to be false when what is signified by the statement is non-existent.

1129. The term false is applied to real things in a second way inasmuch as some things, though beings in themselves, are fitted by nature to appear either to be other than they are or as things that do not exist, as "a shadow-graph," i.e., a delineation in shadow. For sometimes shadows appear to be the things of which they are the shadows, as the shadow of a man appears to be a man. The same applies to dreams, which seem to be real things yet are only the likenesses of things. And one speaks in the same way of false gold, because it bears a resemblance to real gold. Now this sense differs from the first, because in the first sense things were said to be false because they did not exist, but here things are said to be false because, while being something in themselves, they are not the things "of which they cause an image," i.e., which they re-

semble. It is clear, then, that things are said to be false either because they do not exist or because there arises from them the appearance of what does not exist.

1130. A "false notion" (527).

He indicates how the term false applies to definitions. He says that "a notion," i.e., a definition, inasmuch as it is false, is the notion of something non-existent. Now he says "inasmuch as it is false" because a definition is said to be false in two ways. It is either a false definition in itself, and then it is not the definition of anything but has to do entirely with the non-existent; or it is a true definition in itself but false inasmuch as it is attributed to something other than the one properly defined; and then it is said to be false inasmuch as it does not apply to the thing defined.

1131. It is clear, then, that every definition which is a true definition of one thing is a false definition of something else; for example, the definition which is true of a circle is false when applied to a triangle. Now for one thing there is, in one sense, only one definition signifying its quiddity; and in another sense there are many definitions for one thing. For in one sense the subject taken in itself and "the thing with a modification," i.e., taken in conjunction with a modification, are the same, as Socrates and musical Socrates. But in another sense they are not, for it is the same thing accidentally but not in itself. And it is clear that they have different definitions. For the definition of Socrates and that of musical Socrates are different, although in a sense both are definitions of the same thing.

1132. But a definition which is false in itself cannot be a definition of anything. And a definition is said to be false in itself, or unqualifiedly false, by reason of the fact that one part of it cannot stand with the other; and such a definition would be had, for example, if one were to say "inanimate living thing."

1133. Again, it is clear from this that Antisthenes' opinion was foolish. For, since words are the signs of things, he maintained that, just as a thing does not have any essence other than its own, so too in a proposition nothing can be predicated of a subject but its own definition, so that only one predicate absolutely or always may be used of one subject. And from this position it follows that there is no such thing as a contradiction; because if animal, which is included in his notion, is predicated of man, non-animal cannot be predicated of him, and thus a negative proposition cannot be formed. And from this position it also follows that one cannot speak falsely, because the proper definition of a thing is truly predicated of it. Hence, if only a thing's own definition can be predicated of it, no proposition can be false.

1134. But his opinion is false, because of each thing we can predicate not only its own definition but also the definition of something else. And when this occurs in a universal or general way, the predication is false. Yet in a way there can be a true predication; for example, eight is said to be double inasmuch as it has the character of duality, because the character of duality is to be related as two is to one. But inasmuch as it is double, eight is in a sense two, because it is divided into two equal quantities. These things, then, are said to be false in the foregoing way.

1135. A "false man" (528).

Then he shows how the term false may be predicated of a man; and in regard to this he does two things. First, he gives two ways in which a man is said to be false. In one way a man is said to be false if he is ready to think, or takes pleasure in thinking, thoughts of this kind, i.e., false ones, and chooses such thoughts not for any other reason but for themselves. For anyone who has a habit finds the operation relating to that habit to be pleasurable and readily performed; and thus one who has a habit acts in accordance with that habit and not for the sake of anything extrinsic. For example, a debauched person commits fornication because of the pleasure resulting from coition; but if he commits fornication for some other end, for instance, that he may steal, he is more of a thief than a lecher. And similarly one who chooses to speak falsely for the sake of money is more avaricious than false.

1136. In a second way a man is said to be false if he causes false notions in others, in much the same way as we said above that things are false which cause a false image or impression. For it is clear from what has been said that the false has to do with the non-existent. Hence a man is said to be false inasmuch as he makes false statements, and a notion is said to be false inasmuch as it is about something non-existent.

1137. Hence, the speech (529).

Second, he excludes two false opinions from what has been laid down above. He draws the first of these from the points made above. He says that, since a false man is one who chooses and creates false opinions, one may logically refute or reject a statement made in the *Hippias,* i.e., one of Plato's works, which said that the same notion is both true and false. For this opinion considered that man to be false who is able to deceive, so that, being able both to deceive and to speak the truth, the same man is both true and false. And similarly the same statement will be both true and false, because the same statement is able to be both true and false; for example, the statement "Socrates sits" is true when he is seated, but is false when he is not seated. Now it is evident that this is taken unwarrantedly, because even a man who is prudent and knowing is able to deceive; yet he is not false, because he does not cause or choose false notions or opinions, and this is the reason why a man is said to be false, as has been stated (528:C 1135).

1138. **And further** (530).

Then he rejects the second false opinion. This opinion maintained that a man who does base things and wills evil is better than one who does not. But this is false. For anyone is defined as being evil on the grounds that he is ready to do or to choose evil things. Yet this opinion wishes to accept this sense of false on the basis of a sort of induction from a similar case. For one who voluntarily limps is better and nobler than one who limps involuntarily. Hence he says that to do evil is like limping inasmuch as the same notion applies to both. And in a sense this is true; for one who limps voluntarily is worse as regards his moral character, although he is more perfect as regards his power of walking. And similarly one who voluntarily does evil is worse as regards his moral character, although perhaps he is not worse as regards some other power. For example, even though that man is more evil, morally speaking, who voluntarily says what is false, still he is more intelligent than one who believes that he speaks the truth when he in fact speaks falsely, though not wilfully.

1139. **An "accident"** (531).

Here, finally, he gives the different senses in which the term *accident* is used; and there are two of these. First, an accident means anything that attaches to a thing and is truly affirmed of it, although not necessarily or "for the most part," i.e., in the majority of cases, but in a minority; for example, if one were to find a treasure while digging a hole to set out a plant. Hence, finding a treasure while digging a hole is an accident. For the one is not neces-

sarily the cause of the other so that the one necessarily comes from the other. Neither do they necessarily accompany each other so that the latter comes after the former as day follows night, even though the one is not the cause of the other. Neither does it happen for the most part, or in the majority of cases, that this should occur, i.e., that one who sets out a plant finds a treasure. And similarly a musician is said to be white, although this is not necessarily so nor does it happen for the most part. Hence our statement is accidental. But this example differs from the first; for in the first example the term accident is taken in reference to becoming, and in the second example it is taken in reference to being.

1140. Now just as something belongs to some definite subject, so too it is considered "to belong somewhere," i.e., in some definite place, "and at some time," i.e., at some definite time. And therefore it happens to belong to all of these accidentally if it does not belong to them by reason of their own nature; for example, when white is predicated of a musician, this is accidental, because white does not belong to a musician as such. And similarly if there is an abundance of rain in summer, this is accidental, because it does not happen in summer inasmuch as it is summer. And again if what is heavy is high up, this is accidental, for it is not in such a place inasmuch as the place is such, but because of some external cause.

1141. And it should be borne in mind that there is no determinate cause of the kind of accident here mentioned, "but only a contingent cause," i.e., whatever one there happens to be, or "a chance cause," i.e., a fortuitous one, which is an indeterminate cause. For example, it was an accident that someone "came to Aegina," i.e., to that city, if he did not come there "in order to get there," i.e., if he began to head for that city not in order that he might reach it but because he was forced there by some external cause; for example, because he was driven there by the winter wind which caused a tempest at sea, or even because he was captured by pirates and was brought there against his will. It is clear, then, that this is accidental, and that it can be brought about by different causes. Yet the fact that in sailing he reaches this place occurs "not of itself," i.e., inasmuch as he was sailing (since he intended to sail to another place), but "by reason of something else," i.e., another external cause. For a storm is the cause of his coming to the place "to which he was not sailing," i.e., Aegina; or pirates; or something else of this kind.

1142. In a second sense accident means whatever belongs to each thing of itself but is not in its substance. This is the second mode of essential predication, as was noted above (C 1055); for the first mode exists when some-

thing is predicated essentially of something which is given in its definition, as animal is predicated of man, which is not an accident in any way. Now it belongs essentially to a triangle to have two right angles, but this does not belong to its substance. Hence it is an accident.

1143. This sense of accident differs from the first, because accidents in this second sense can be eternal. For a triangle always has three angles equal to two right angles. But none of those things which are accidents in the first sense can be eternal, because they are always such as occur in the minority of cases. The discussion of this kind of accident is undertaken in another place, for example in Book VI of this work (544:C 1172), and in Book II of the *Physics*.[3] Accident in the first sense, then, is opposed to what exists in itself; but accident in the second sense is opposed to what is substantial. This completes Book V.

[3] *Physica*, II, 5 (196b 10).

LIST OF WORKS CITED *

ARISTOTLE: *Aristotelis Opera,* edidit Academia regia Borussica (Berlin, 1831-1870), vols. I-II, *Aristoteles Graece* ex recogn. I. Bekker (1831):
Categoriae
De Interpretatione (De Int.)
Analytica Priora (Anal. Pr.)
Analytica Posteriora (Anal. Post.)
Topica
Sophistici Elenchi
Physica
De Coelo
De Generatione et Corruptione (De Gen. et Cor.)
Meteorologica (Meteor.)
De Anima (De An.)
De Sensu et Sensato (De Sen. et Sen.)
De Generatione Animalium (De Gen. An.)
De Motu Animalium (De Motu An.)
De Partibus Animalium (De Part. An.)
Metaphysica (Met.)
Ethica Nicomachea (Eth. Nic.)
Politica
AUGUSTINE, St. Aurelius: *Opera Omnia,* Patrologiae cursus completus, series latina, ed. J. P. Migne, 221 vols., Paris 1844-1864. *(PL)*:
De Civitate Dei, vol. 41.
AVERROES: *Aristotelis Stagyritae omnia que extant opera . . . Averroes cordubensis in ea opera omnes . . . commentarii,* Venice: Iunta, 1550-1552:
In libros de Generatione Animalium (In de Gen. An.)
In libros Physicorum (In Phys.)
In libros Metaphysicorum (In Metaph.)
AVICENNA: *Avicenne perhypatetici philosophi ac medicorum facile primi opera in lucem redacta,* Venice, 1508:
De Animalibus
Sufficientia
Metaphysica
BOETHIUS, Manlius Severinus: *Opera Omnia* in Migne, *PL.*
Commentaria in Categorias Aristotelis, PL 64, cols. 159-392.
De Hebdomadibus, PL 64, cols. 1311-1314.
De Persona et Duabus Naturis, PL 64, cols. 1337-1354.
In Isagogen Porphyrii commenta, editio secunda, ed. Samuel Brandt, Vienna (F. Tempsky) and Leipsig: G. Freitag, 1906 (CSEL, vol. 48).
BURNET, John: *Early Greek Philosophy,* 4th edition, 1930, London: A. & C. Black.

* This list contains the editions of works of authors cited in the Commentary and in the version of Aristotle, and also of certain works referred to in the footnotes. The abbreviations for works cited are indicated in parentheses after the work in question. When the same edition contains the works of more than one author, it is described in full the first time given, and thereafter designated by its proper abbreviation.

CICERO, Marcus Tullius: *Scripta Quae Manserunt Omnia:*
  Fasc. 2: *Rhetorici Libri Duo* (De Inventione), ed. E. Stroebel, Leipsig: B. G. Teubner, 1923.
  Fasc. 45: *De Natura Deorum,* ed. W. Ax, Leipsig: B. G. Teubner, 1933.
DIELS, Herman: *Die Fragmente der Vorsokratiker, Griechisch und Deutsch,* 5th ed. Walter Kranz, 3 vols., Berlin: Weidmann, 1934-1937. (Diels)
DUCOIN, G.: "Saint Thomas commentateur d'Aristote," *Archives de Philosophie,* XX (1957), 78-117, 240-271, 392-445.
EUCLID: *The Elements (The Thirteen Books of Euclid's Elements,* English trans. from the edition of Heiberg, 1883-1888, by Sir Thomas L. Heath, Cambridge Univ. Press, 1926.)
HESIOD: *Works and Days* & *Theogony,* translated from the Greek by Richard Lattimore, Ann Harbor: Univ. of Michigan Press, 1959.
HILLER, Eduardus: *Anthologia Lyrica, sive Lyricorum Graecorum praeter Pindarum Reliquiae Potiores,* Leipsig: B. G. Teubner, 1897.
HOMER: *Homeri Opera,* recognoverunt brevique adnotatione critica instruxerunt David B. Munro . . . et Thomas Allen, Oxford, Clarendon Press, 1902-1912:
  Iliad, vol. I.
  Odyssey, vols. III & IV.
PLATO: *Platonis opera quae extant omnia,* ed. H. Stephanus & J. Serranus, Paris: 1578 (Eng. transl.—*The Dialogues of Plato*—by B. Jowett, 2 vols. Random House, 1937):
  Hippias
  Laws
  Theaetetus
  Cratylus
  Gorgias
  Phaedo
  Sophist
PORPHYRY: *Isagoge* (Introduction to the Categories of Aristotle) ed. A. Busse, in *Commentaria in Aristotelem Graeca,* Berlin:
  Prussian Academy, IV (1887) (*CG*).
  Also in Boethius, *PL* 64, cols. 77-158.
PTOLEMY, Claudius: *Syntaxis* (Almagest) (English trans. by R. Catesby Taliaferro in *Great Books of the Western World,* Encyclopædia Britannica Inc., Chicago, London & New York, 1950). *Liber Ptholemai quatuor tractatuum (Quadripartitum)* cum centiloquio, Venice: 1484.
RITTER, H. & PRELLER, L.: *Historia Philosophiae Graecae,* 8th ed. by G. Wellman, Gotha: 1898.
SIMPLICIUS: Writings edited in *CG.*
  Commentaria in Categorias, ed. C. Kalbfleisch (1907), *CG* v. VIII.
  Commentaria in de Coelo, ed. I. L. Heiberg (1894), *CG,* v. VII.
THOMAS, St. (Aquinas): *De Ente et Essentia,* ed. Marie-Dominique Roland Gosselin, Kain (Belgique): Le Saulchoir, 1926.
XENOPHON: *Opera omnia,* ed. E. C. Marchant, 5 vols. Oxford, Clarendon Press, n.d.

INDEX OF NAMES

(Numbers refer to sections of Commentary)

INDEX OF SUBJECTS

(Numbers refer to sections of *Commentary*)

Abstraction:
    kinds of, *Prologue,* 158, 405, 1683, 2426
    Platonic treatment of, 158, 251, 404-5,
        1683, 2426
    relation to speculative sciences, 2259-64
Accidental being:
    basis of, 1182-83, 1210-12, 1243, 2280
    definition of, 1177-79, 1184-89, 2270-73,
        2276
    distinction from accident, 1139-43, 2270
    no generation of, 1179
    no proper cause of, 1141, 2280-82
    no science of, 531, 1172-76, 1189-90,
        1242, 2269-79, 2280-83
    opposed to necessary, 1182, 2280
    outside art, 1174, 1185-86
    refutation of position abolishing, 1191-
        1214
    relation to:
        providence, 1215-22
        sophistry, 1178-79, 2275
    senses of, 883, 886, 1185, 2270
Accidents:
    change in (*see* Alteration; Change; Mo-
        tion)
    definition of, 894, 1139, 1251-54, 1331-
        38, 1346, 1351-55, 1768, 2270, 2420
    distinction from substance, 558, 1331-35,
        1352
    of artifacts, 529-31
    of higher and lower natures, 531
    predication of, 887
    priority of substance to, 1257-59
    proper or essential (*see also* Properties):
        cause of, 1219, 1284
        treated by science, 395, 397, 400, 402
    subject of, 629-35, 1005
    taken abstractly and concretely, 1253-54,
        1353
    types of:
        permanent and transient, 847
        proper and common, 531
        simple and composite, 1343-46

According to which, senses of, 1050-53
Accoutrement (*see* Having; Possession;
    To have)
Act or actuality:
    a universal principle, *Prologue,* 2482
    compared with potentiality in good and
        evil things, 1883-84
    definition of, 1805, 1823-37
    derived from action and applied to
        form, 1805, 1861, 2480
    different for different things, 1828-31,
        2478, 2481
    how prior to potentiality, 1278, 1815,
        1844-82, 2506-7
    how subsequent to potentiality, 188,
        1278, 1815, 2506
    in movable and immovable things, 1823-
        24
    knowledge of, 1827-28
    pure (*see* God; Mover, first)
    relation to:
        motion, 1860, 2295-97, 2304-7, 2313
            (*see also* Change; Motion)
        truth and falsity, 1888-94
Act of being:
    basis of term being, 553, 558
    proper cause of (*see* God)
    relation to essence, 556-58 (*see also* Es-
        sence, of sensible substances; God,
        identity of essence)
Action or activity:
    as an end, 1861-65
    distinction from:
        affection, 2313, 2386 (*see also* Affec-
            tion)
        making, 1152, 1788, 2253 (*see also*
            Production)
    for a good, 781
    good and bad:
        power of, 1794
        relation to choice, 1000
    in singulars, 21
    no motion of, 2386

427

438

Life (*see also* Living things):
  difference between animal and human, 14-16
  God's (*see* God, life of)
  intellectual activity a form of, 2544
  twofold meaning of, 14
Like, meanings of, 907, 918-20, 2006-12 (*see also* One)
Limit:
  compared with principle, 1049
  meanings of, 1044-48 (*see also* Contradictories; Contraries; Opposites)
Limited and unlimited, 148, 162
Line:
  circular, 871
  curved, 858
  definition of, 874, 978, 980
  motion of, 1923
  prior to surface, 949
  straight, 857
Living things (*see also* Life):
  act for an end, 1000
  definition of, 1442e
  generation of (*see* Generation, natural)
  parts of, 1634
Location (*see* Place)
Logic (*see* Dialectics)
Logician (*see* Dialectician)
Love, 100-2
Luck (*see also* Chance; Fortune):
  good and bad, 2287
  meaning of, 2284-86, 2445
  not first cause, 2285
  relation to inexperience, 18

Magnitude (*see* Quantity, continuous)
Making (*see* Production)
Male, 167, 2134
Man:
  as considered by logic, 1536
  causes of, 2481
  definition of, 1463
  free, 58
  held measure of truth, 1959, 2224
  knowledge (*see* Knowledge, human; Science)
  no separate universal, 1427-28, 1570
  of experience, 20
  single substantial form in, 321
  "third" (Plato), 213, 216, 1586-87
Manual laborers, role of, 25-28, 41

Many:
  basis of diverse, unequal and unlike, 2013-16
  distinction from much, 2079
  genus of number, 2090-92
  meanings of, 881-84, 978, 2079-83, 2091
  opposed to one, 881, 1982-98, 2075-95
  relation to:
    being, 2091
    few, 2096
Master planners, 26-28
Material cause (*see also* First matter; Matter; Subject):
  definition of, 763
  early opinions of, 73-92, 112-13, 181-200
  no infinite regress in, 305-12
  not proper concern of first philosopher, 384
  relation to other causes, 775, 782, 2474 (*see also* Agent; Efficient cause; Final cause; Mover)
Mathematics:
  abstraction in, 989, 1760, 2202
  attributes studied by, 1145, 2202, 2208
  definitions in (*see* Definition, in mathematics)
  distinction from other speculative sciences, 1152-65, 2256-58 (*see also* First philosophy; Philosophy of nature)
  intelligible matter, 1496
  no demonstration by final cause, 375, 2156 (*see also* Final cause)
  objects of:
    knowledge of, 1305
    multiplied by matter, 1494-96, 1507-8, 1520-22, 1760
    not intermediate substances, 158, 410-22, 2160-62
    Platonic view of, 157, 1689
    separable only in definition, 2160-62
  place of origin, 33
Matter:
  as substance, 1281, 1388, 1687 (*see also* Substance)
  common, 1468, 1473, 1491
  conditions of, 74
  differs for different substances, 1690, 1740-42, 2436
  early views of, 73-74, 1284, 2439
  extended sense of, 1839-43

Index of Subjects

Perfect, senses of, 1034-44, 2028
Perfection:
 of first mover (*see* God; Mover, first)
 of intellect in knowing, 1239
 of things, 1230
Perspective, 412
Philosopher:
 first (*see* Wise man)
 compared to poet, 55
 meaning of, 1330
Philosophy:
 first (*see* First philosophy: Wisdom)
 natural (*see* Philosophy of nature)
 origin of term, 56
 relation of parts of substance to parts
  of, 563
Philosophy of nature:
 distinction from:
  first philosophy, 1156-59, 2260 (*see
   also* First philosophy)
  mathematics, 1160-65, 2256-58 (*see
   also* Mathematics)
  practical sciences, 47, 398, 1145-46,
   1155, 1170, 2209, 2252-55, 2267 (*see
   also* Practical science)
 excludes study of separated soul, 1159
 how confused with first philosophy,
  398, 1170, 2267
 method of defining in, 1157-59, 1163,
  2256-57 (*see also* Definition)
 subject matter of, 47, 593, 1155, 1158,
  2165, 2209, 2255, 2427
Place:
 as a measure, 986, 2313
 change in (*see* Motion, local)
 kinds of, 2352
 natural, 2340-44
 no infinite, 2345, 2349, 2353
 relation to:
  quantity, 986, 2313
  where, 892, 1005, 2431
Planets:
 effects of, 2560-62
 motions of (*see* Celestial motion)
 movers of, 2556-57, 2564 (*see also* Separate substances)
 spheres of (*see* Spheres)
Pleasure, of intellect and sense, 2537-38
Plurality (*see* Many)
Poets:
 distinguished from philosopher, 55

Poets (Cont.):
 theological, 83-84, 186, 2508, 2652
Point:
 definition of, 47, 874
 Platonists' view of, 2415
 relation to line, 507
Position:
 held to be basic difference (Democritus), 116, 1692-93
 meaning of, 892, 1005, 2377
 no motion of, 2377
 relation to disposition, 1061
Possession (*see also* Having; To have):
 divine science not a human, 60
 relation to privation (*see* Contrariety;
  Contraries)
Possible:
 considered dialectically, 973, 1775, 1808-
  14
 meanings of, 961, 972-73, 1811-12 (*see
  also* Capable; Potency)
 not everything, 1807-9
 opposed to impossible (*see* Impossible)
 relation to powers, 1817 (*see also* Potency; Power)
Posture (*see* Position)
Potency or potentiality:
 active:
  acquired and natural, 960, 1786, 1815
  as force, 1395
  end of, 1850, 1862-65
  meaning of, 955, 961
  of doing and doing well, 1794-80
  of seed, 145
 analogical and equivocal senses of, 1773-
  80
 compared with actuality in evil things,
  1885
 conditions for actuation of, 1816-22,
  1832-34
 distinction:
  active and passive, 955, 1781-82, 1786
  rational and irrational, 1786, 1789-90,
   1793, 1819-20, 1881
 meanings of, 1804
 passive:
  definition of, 1782
  how prior to actuality, 188, 1278,
   1816-22, 2506
  how subsequent to actuality, 1278,
   1815, 1844-82, 2506-7

444

Potency or potentiality, passive (Cont.):
  reduction to active potency, 1777-79,
    1781
  relation to motion, 2294-97, 2304-5
    (*see also* Motion)
  senses of, 955-56
Power:
  active (*see* Potency, active)
  cogitative, 15-16
  intellective (*see* Intellect)
  metaphorical sense of, 974, 1774
  passive (*see* Potency, passive)
  rational (*see also* Intellect):
    actuation of, 1820-22
    contrasted with sense, 947
    distinguished from irrational (*see* Po-
      tency, distinction, rational)
    relation active and passive, 1023-25,
      1862-65
  sensory (*see* Imagination; Memory;
    Senses)
Practical science:
  distinguished from speculative (*see*
    Speculative science)
  kinds of, 1155, 2253
  principle of motion in, 2254
  uncertainty of, 47
Predicates (*see also* Predication):
  accidental:
    kinds of, 630, 845, 866, 903
    no infinite regress in, 631-35
    relation to singulars, 845, 910
  distinction of essential and accidental,
    628
  relation to subject, 891-93
Predication:
  accidental (*see* Predicates, accidental)
  denominative, 196, 1288-89, 1414-16,
    1841-43
  distinction:
    analogous, equivocal and univocal,
      535-36, 2197
    essential and accidental, 1308-14, 1326,
      1377
  essential:
    meaning of, 1325-26, 1362
    types of, 1054-57
  figures of (*see* Categories)
  of being, 889-94 (*see* Being; Categories)
  of unity (*see* Unity)

Principles:
  contraries as, 2639-63
  definition of, 761
  distinguished from:
    causes, 750-51, 760 (*see also* Causes)
    elements, 795-801 (*see also* Elements)
  early opinions about material, 73-74,
    90-91, 138, 148, 201-3, 2507
  extrinsic and intrinsic, 754-55, 762, 2469
  genera as, 355-56, 427-28
  numbers held to be, 201-7
  of change (*see* Change; Generation;
    Motion)
  of demonstration (*see* Demonstration,
    principles of)
  of moral science, 1146
  of sensible substances (*see* Sensible sub-
    stances)
  of separate substances (*see* Separate sub-
    stances)
  science of (*see* First philosophy)
  various senses of, 750-60
Prior and subsequent:
  definition of, 936, 945, 953
  in:
    being, 950-53, 1580, 1990
    generation, 1500
    knowledge, 946-49, 1900
    motion and quantity, 751, 938-44
    order, 944-45
    subject, 188
    time, 751, 940-41
  relation to perfect and imperfect, 188
Privation:
  knowledge of, 566, 1791
  meanings of, 566, 964, 1070-73, 1754,
    1785, 2043, 2051
  reciprocal change and, 2052-53
  relation to:
    change (*see* Change; Motion)
    contradiction, 2040-48 (*see also* Con-
      tradiction; Contradictories)
    contrariety, 1791, 2037-38, 2049-58
      (*see also* Contraries; Contrariety)
    incapacity, 967
    negation, 1074-79
    possession (*see* Contrariety; Having;
      To have)
  unity as, 565-66
Problem, 339

445

Sadness, 63

Same:

accidentally, 908-10, 1360-61

essentially, 911-12, 2002-5

relation to one, 1999

Science:

cause of, 291, 395-96 (*see also* Demonstration; Syllogism)

certainty of, *Prologue,* 47

consideration of difficulties by, 339

difference between practical and speculative (*see* Practical science; Speculative science)

different views of method in, 343-44

distinction from other intellectual habits, 34

diversity of (Plato), 1177

divine (*see* First philosophy; Wisdom)

excludes accidental being (*see* Accidental being)

first (*see* First philosophy)

growth of, 54-66

held to be a mean, 1765

hierarchy in, 2267

identified with thing known, 1790, 2620

logical (*see* Dialectics)

mathematical (*see* Mathematics)

natural (*see* Philosophy of nature)

object of, *Prologue,* 529, 531, 533, 1145, 2247

of the universal, 323, 1323

proceeds from better known, 1301-5

questions asked by, 1651-71

role of definition in (*see* Definition, role in demonstration; Term, middle)

speculative (*see* Speculative science)

subject of, *Prologue,* 390

Second substance (*see also* Essence; Species):

essence, nature and quiddity as, 902, 1270, 1606, 1648-49, 1684, 1979

genus and species as, 902, 1272, 1275, 1581

proper object of definition, 1325, 1331

Seed:

active power of, 1456

generation from, 1399-1400 (*see also* Generation, natural)

Sensation (*see* Cognition, sensory; Senses)

Senses:

apprehend singulars, 30, 45, 947

Senses (Cont.):

basis of knowledge, 5, 45, 1302

cognition of (*see* Cognition, sensory)

distinction from intellect, 30 (*see also* Intellect, human)

exclude knowledge of:

cause and effect, 1146

truth, 1235

impediments to, 283-84

internal (*see* Imagination; Memory; Power, cogitative)

judgment of (*see* Judgment)

organs of, change in, 6

primary senses (*see* Hearing; Sight; Touch)

Sensible substances:

common examples of, 898-902, 1263, 1683

definition of, 1705-11

dialectically considered, 1308-9

different matters for, 1690, 1740-42, 2436

held to be numbers, 156, 163

Heraclitus' view of, 152, 684

kinds of, 2424-27

parts of, 1631-36

potentially intelligible, 2541

principles of, 447-48, 1442a, 1686-90, 2441, 2465 (*see also* First matter; Form, substantial)

relation to separate Forms (*see* Separate Forms)

Separate Forms (Platonic):

characteristics of, 1704, 1715

distinction from divine ideas, 233

how united to matter, 360 (*see also* Participation)

inconsistencies in theory of, 210-24, 1642-47

nature of, 153, 169, 1362, 1469, 1619, 1719, 2190

reason for positing, 360, 1381, 2449

rejected as:

causes of generation, 225, 1381, 1427-35, 1455

cause of knowledge, 268-72, 1368-69

essences of things, 1369-70, 1470, 1592-1602, 2143-44

excluding artificial forms, 1719, 2190

exemplars, 231-35, 1432-35, 2554

formal causes of things, 236-38

Untraversable (*see* Infinite)

Vain or in vain, 286
Violence (*see* Force)
Vision (*see* Sight)
Virtue:
  defined, 999
  intellectual, 34
Void (*see* Atomists; Full and empty)

Water, 77-85
Whatness (*see* Essence)
When (*see* Time)
Where (*see* Place)
Whether, senses of, 2060-61
Whole:
  "all" in reference to, 1105-8
  artificial and natural, 1104
  concrete (*see* Concrete whole)
  defined, 1098
  integral and universal, 1099, 1101
  relation to parts, 605, 1102-3, 1105-8
  simultaneous, 360, 447 (*see also* Concrete whole)
Will:
  in separate substances, 385

Will (Cont.):
  object of, 385, 2522
  relation to intellect, 2522
Wisdom (*see also* First philosophy):
  characteristics of, 40-50, 53-68, 289-90, 378
  common opinions of, 36-43
  defined, 51
  distinction from art and science, 34-35
  end of other sciences, 59
  identified with first philosophy, metaphysics, theology, *Prologue,* 56
  originates in wonder, 66
  ruler of other sciences, *Prologue*
  treats first causes and principles, 36-51
Wise man:
  common opinions of, 36-42
  defined, *Prologue,* 43
  origin of term, 56
Wonder, 67
Words:
  elements of, 424, 799
  nature of, 1224, 1233, 1253
World (*see* Universe)

Zodiac, 2481, 2511, 2575